HARVARD STUDIES IN BUSINESS HISTORY
VII

EDITED BY N. S. B. GRAS

STRAUS PROFESSOR OF BUSINESS HISTORY
GRADUATE SCHOOL OF BUSINESS ADMINISTRATION
GEORGE F. BAKER FOUNDATION
HARVARD UNIVERSITY

MODERN MACY'S
Looking east from Seventh Avenue

HISTORY OF MACY'S OF NEW YORK
1858–1919

Chapters in the Evolution of the Department Store

BY

RALPH M. HOWER

CAMBRIDGE, MASSACHUSETTS
HARVARD UNIVERSITY PRESS

COPYRIGHT, 1943
BY THE PRESIDENT AND FELLOWS OF HARVARD COLLEGE
DISTRIBUTED IN GREAT BRITAIN BY OXFORD UNIVERSITY PRESS, LONDON

Third Printing 1967

PRINTED IN THE UNITED STATES OF AMERICA

To
N. S. B. GRAS
*An original and indefatigable scholar,
a stimulating teacher, and a valued friend*

CONTENTS

ILLUSTRATIONS	xiii
TABLES	xvii
EDITOR'S INTRODUCTION	xix
AUTHOR'S PREFACE	xxiii

PART I

ROWLAND MACY'S PREPARATION, 1822–1858

I. NANTUCKET TO POINTS WEST	3
Family Background	5
Four Years in Pursuit of the Whale	7
First Experiences in Retailing	11
To California with the 'Forty-niners	12
II. A COCK CROWS IN HAVERHILL	16
Establishment of the Haverhill Store	16
Early Macy Policies	20
Methods of Operation	21
Macy Advertising	24
Competitive Tactics	27
Queequeg Dies Game!	29
Westward Again	31

PART II

THE FOUNDING OF MACY'S, 1858–1887

III. SUCCESS IN FEATHERS AND LACE	37
The Setting	38
The Start	42
Macy's Business Policies	48

	Early Macy Advertising	54
	First Woman Executive	65
IV.	An Interlude on the Evolution of Retailing	67
	Definition of the Department Store	67
	European Antecedents of the Department Store	70
	Major Movements in Retailing	73
	Early Retail Trade in America	77
	Increasing Specialization after 1800	82
	Retail Policies in Europe before 1860	88
	The Rise of Progressive Retail Policies in America	92
V.	Hitch Your Shopping to a Star	98
	Increasing Variety of Goods Sold	98
	Growth and Integration, 1858–1877	107
	Store Organization	114
	Personal Leadership	116
	Promotional Developments	118
	Fragments of a Portrait	121
	The First Partner	123
	The Partnership Enlarged	128
	A Glimpse of Early Macy Operating Figures	128
VI.	The Emergence of Department Stores	141
	New Tendencies in European Retailing	141
	Parallel Tendencies in American Retailing	143
	Reasons for the Rise of the Department Store	145
	Opposition to the Department Store	156
VII.	From Progress to Doldrums	157
	Changes in Ownership	157
	Further Diversification and Integration	160
	Sales Promotion Turns to Convenience and Comfort	164
	Complacent Conservatism	170
	Analysis of Operating Data, 1877 and 1887	172
	Comparison of Owned and Leased Departments, 1876–1887	183

VIII. SWEAT FOR DUTY ... FOR PROMOTION	191
Size of the Staff	191
Employment of Women	193
The Working Hierarchy and Employee Compensation	194
Hours and Vacations	200
Working Conditions	202

PART III

THE FIRST GENERATION OF STRAUS MANAGEMENT
1888–1902

IX. BLOOD TRANSFUSION	211
Admission of the Strauses to Partnership	211
Straus Background	214
The Education of Isidor Straus	215
The Founding of L. Straus & Sons	218
Straus Departments in Macy's, 1874–1888	220
Early Straus Influence on Macy Management	224
The Strauses Acquire Complete Ownership	226
X. MATURITY OF THE FIRM AND THE INDUSTRY	231
Growth of Sales and Earnings, 1888–1902	232
Expansion of Merchandise Lines	234
Sources of Goods Sold	237
Manufacturing Activities	244
Private Brands	251
Operating Data, 1888–1902	253
XI. HEYDAY OF FOURTEENTH STREET	264
Extent of the Advertising Effort	265
Macy Advertising Copy, 1888–1902	269
Display and Publicity	275
New Store Services	279
Improved Store Facilities	283
Price Policies	287
Competitive Tactics	291

Management, 1888–1902	294
Staff and Working Conditions	303

PART IV

THE SECOND GENERATION TAKES COMMAND
1902–1919

XII.	A Plateau in Macy Development	311
	Sons Learn the Business	311
	Northward the Course of Retailing	314
	Transactions in Real Estate	318
	Construction Work	322
	The Course of Sales, 1902–1913	327
	Changes in Departments	330
	Developments in Store Services	333
	Delivery Facilities	338
	Deposit Account Department	341
	Old Partnerships and New	345
XIII.	Problems of Price and War	349
	The Rising Threat of Resale Price Maintenance	349
	Fighting for the Right to Sell Cheaply	353
	Difficulties in Buying Price-Fixed Merchandise	357
	The Growing Problem of Administration	360
	Steps Toward Better Administration, 1900–1919	362
	The Impact of the First World War	374
	Grading Up	381
	Staff and Working Conditions, 1900–1919	382
	Operating Data, 1902–1919	389

Epilogue	398
Appendix A. Some Notes on the Rise of Department Stores in Paris	411
Appendix B. Early Macy Accounting	417
Notes and References	423
Index	483

ILLUSTRATIONS

Modern Macy's. Photograph, looking eastward from Seventh Avenue, taken in 1939. In the Macy Archives . . . *frontispiece*

Model of the whaleship *Emily Morgan*, Rowland Macy's home during a whaling voyage to the South Pacific, 1837–1841. Photograph of an exact-scale model owned by R. H. Macy & Co., Inc., and built from specifications contained in registry papers on file in the New Bedford Custom House, supplemented by details from the sister ship *Charles W. Morgan*, which is still in existence. The *Emily Morgan* was built in Portland, Maine, 1833, and was lost in the Arctic Ocean north of the Bering Strait in 1871. Macy Archives 10

The end of a western adventure. Announcement of the dissolution of Macy & Co. Reproduced from the Marysville (California) *Herald*, September 24, 1850 11

Cash policy in 1852. Example of Macy's advertising in Haverhill. Haverhill (Massachusetts) *Gazette*, April 3, 1852 20

Macy's Haverhill store, 1852. The "New Granite Store," which is still in existence. Haverhill *Gazette*, December 25, 1852 . . 21

Margaret Getchell La Forge (1841–1880), Macy's first woman executive. From an enlarged photograph in the Macy Archives. Probably taken about 1871, when the subject was 30 . . . 64

Sales promotion in 1859. Typical early Macy advertisements. New York *Herald*, January 18, February 10, March 12, and June 29, 1859 65

Rowland Hussey Macy (1822–1877), founder of Macy's, when he was about 50 years old. From an enlarged, retouched photograph in the Macy Archives. Date unknown, but probably about 1872 100

Macy's star in 1872. Early version of the famous trademark, illustrating also contemporary custom of seeking emphasis by repetition. New York *Times*, September 22, 1872 101

Abiel T. La Forge (1842–1878), partner in R. H. Macy & Co., 1871–1878. From an enlarged, retouched photograph (date unknown) in the Macy Archives 124

ILLUSTRATIONS

Balance sheet, January 15, 1872. Financial condition when La Forge acquired an interest in Macy's. From La Forge's Ledger. Macy Archives 125

Macy's in the late 1860's. The original store, at 204–206 Sixth Avenue, is just behind the telegraph pole in this picture. From a photograph in the Macy Archives, taken between 1868 and 1871 . . 128

Robert Macy Valentine, partner in R. H. Macy & Co., from 1875 until his death in 1879. From an enlarged, retouched photograph (date unknown) in the Macy Archives 129

Charles B. Webster, partner in R. H. Macy & Co., 1879–1896. From an enlarged photograph (date unknown) in the Macy Archives . . 158

Jerome B. Wheeler, partner in R. H. Macy & Co., 1879–1887. From an enlarged photograph (date unknown) in the Macy Archives . . 159

Main floor of Macy's, 1882. View from 14th Street staircase through to 13th Street. Reproduced from a woodcut advertisement first used in 1882. Macy Archives 164

Macy's in 1885. Draped in black for Grant's funeral. From a sketch in *Leslie's Illustrated Weekly Newspaper*, August 15, 1885 . . 165

Macy's lunchroom, 1882. Located on the second floor. From a woodcut advertisement first used in 1882. Macy Archives . . 168

Retail selling in the 1880's. Ladies' and Children's Shoe Department. From a woodcut advertisement first used in 1882. Macy Archives 169

Isidor Straus (1845–1912), partner, 1888–1912. From a photograph taken shortly before his death. Macy Archives 216

Nathan Straus (1848–1931), partner, 1888–1914. From a photograph in the Macy Archives 217

Macy's in 1902. The new building in Herald Square reproduced from an architect's drawing in *The American Architect*, May 10, 1902 322

Change-making in the good old days. Macy's tuberoom in the 14th Street store. Macy Archives 323

Jesse Isidor Straus (1872–1936), partner, 1912–1919; president, 1919–1933; ambassador to France, 1933–1936. Photograph taken between 1930 and 1933. Macy Archives 334

Typical Macy advertising layout, 1906. Portion of a full-page newspaper advertisement. New York *Herald*, October 21, 1906 . . 335

ILLUSTRATIONS

Percy Selden Straus, partner, 1912–1919; vice-president, 1919–1933; president, 1933–1940; chairman of the board of directors, 1940– . From a photograph taken about 1930. Macy Archives . . . 366

Departmental advertisement, 1918. One of a new series introducing a lighter touch in Macy copy. New York *Times*, May 30, 1918 367

Herbert N. Straus (1881–1933), partner, 1912–1919; secretary and treasurer, 1919–1929; treasurer, 1929–1933; vice-president, 1922–1933 382

When Macy's began to emphasize style, 1919. Newspaper advertisement showing improved copy and layout used by Macy's in this period. New York *Tribune*, April 13, 1919 383

Departmental operating statement, 1872, showing method of calculating profit and loss. From La Forge's Ledger 418

Operating statement, January 12, 1874, showing combination of balance sheet and profit and loss statement. This form was used for many years 419

TABLES

1. Analysis of Annual Sales by Owned and Leased Departments, 1870–1877 109
2. Operating Results, 1872–1876 130
3. Miscellaneous Operating Data, 1872–1876 133
4. Operating Results by Departments, August 7, 1876–January 6, 1877 136
5. Operating Results, August 7, 1876–January 6, 1877 . . . 139
6. Analysis of Annual Sales by Owned and Leased Departments, 1877–1888 171
7. Operating Results by Departments, Six Months Ending December 31, 1887 174
8. Analysis of Operating Results, Six Months Ending December 31, 1887 176
9. Comparison of Principal Operating Data, Fall Seasons of 1876, 1877, and 1887 180
10. Analysis of Contribution of Leased Departments, 1876, 1877, and 1887 184
11. Analysis of Stock Turnover, Six Months Ending December 31, 1887 186
12. Original Rates and Benefits of Macy Mutual Aid Association, 1885 207
13. Sales in Straus Departments in Macy's, 1874–1888 . . . 222
14. Balance Sheet, R. H. Macy & Co., December 31, 1887 . . 224
15. Sales and Earnings, 1888–1902 233
16. Merchandise Departments, Fall, 1902 238
17. Manufacturing Volume and Profits, 1888–1902 245
18. Analysis of Sales, 1888–1902 254
19. Analysis of Revenue, 1888–1902 256
20. Analysis of Selected Expenses, 1888–1902 258
21. Miscellaneous Operating Data, 1888–1902 261
22. Analysis of Sales, 1902–1914 328

TABLES

23. Analysis of Deposit Account Transactions, 1902–1919 . . 343
24. Operating Indices Showing Effect of First World War, 1913–1920 376
25. Analysis of Revenue, 1902–1919 390
26. Operating Expenses, 1902–1919 394
27. Operating and Financial Data, 1902–1919 396
28. Departmental Ratings, 1872, 1877, 1888 421

CHARTS

I. Average monthly sales, five-year periods, 1870–1929, showing seasonal pattern of sales. Source: Macy accounting records 278
II. Organization chart, 1922. The organization was substantially the same in 1919. Redrawn from a chart in the files of the Macy Planning Department 371

EDITOR'S INTRODUCTION

THE present volume is meant to be the first of two dealing with the history of R. H. Macy and Company. Stopping at incorporation in 1919, instead of 1942, is much to be regretted, but compensation lies in the possibility of getting fuller treatment at a later period — when the war is over and the author returns to the pursuits of peace. Moreover, developments now under way but not yet clear cut will by that time be more open to definitive treatment.

In business history we may emphasize the firm or its function. Although Dr. Hower has dealt with almost every activity of Macy's, he has chosen to emphasize the principal function of retailing. To him it has seemed that a store is what a store does; a great store is what a great store does. True, Macy's has been an integral part of New York City: indeed, it has been an *institution* in the minds and experience of millions; but beyond this, Macy's is essentially a system of buying and selling goods. Since these functions have been performed successfully, finance has not been a major problem. Throughout this book, Dr. Hower has been most interested in sales, somewhat less in finance, and least in merchandise procurement. This emphasis has been due in part to the availability of materials.

Executives and what they have stood for have been most closely examined because their policy and their management and control have made the store what it is. At first, there was a strong personal element in the store's administration, but in recent years there has been a continuing effort to institutionalize jobs, duties, and functions. All this looks toward smooth operation and continuity of policy and effort, but, of course, always with the danger of growing rigidity and formalism.

Employees have come in for less attention than executives, but they have not been neglected. In view of their great number, employees must be considered, in any general history such as this, as a part of the whole mechanism rather than as individuals. There was a time when individuals worked in Macy's, but the store is now too large to allow for much that is personal. Dr. Hower has not stopped to analyze the customers at great length, but he knows that they have cut through the social classes from upper middle to lower middle class to lower working class. It has been an achievement for any store to cater to such diversity of needs with such success. The city, State, and nation, in which the store has operated, have been given least attention because these may be for the most part assumed; and the author has been forced at many points to assume a good deal so as to find space for what must be explicitly set forth.

The history of Macy's is a chapter in the development of industrial capitalism within the field of retailing. Industrial capitalists have stood for large-scale operation within a special line of business: though Macy's has spread over from the function of retailing into wholesaling, importing, and even manufacturing, these related activities have always been in subordination to retailing. Industrial capitalists have been lusty competitors one with another, and Macy's has rather had the last word in intensifying and regularizing competition. Its price policy — such as underselling competitors by 6 per cent — is the very epitome of industrial capitalism. The nineteenth century saw thousands of overcompeting firms go onto the financial rocks. Macy's, however, has been successful in this competitive strife. The firm has never had to seek favors from financial capitalists at the price of sharing control with outsiders. For this reason, Macy's may be regarded as belonging to that group of the élite, the financial industrialists, made distinctive by such exemplars as Cornelius Vanderbilt I, J. J. Hill, Henry Ford, Swift and Company, and the Standard Oil concerns. In dwelling upon Macy's independence of financial capitalists, I do not mean to condemn financial capitalism, for that system has been and may again become a beacon and a refuge to many a large and useful industrial capitalist.

In the history of Macy's we observe the firm take its start in the efforts of the petty capitalist R. H. Macy. In his hands, and especially in the hands of the Strauses, we see the firm reach industrial capitalism. Beyond this, the alternatives seem to be financial capitalism and national capitalism. As we have seen, the firm has escaped financial capitalism up to date; but, like other large business units, it seems now to be faced with the issues of national capitalism. This new régime involves control of policies, with reference to such matters as prices and wages, advertising, and standards of merchandise, by politicians and political administrators in accordance with ideals not closely hitched to profits. It seems generally to involve the sharing of management not only with the government but with trade unions as well. Whether mere shifts will be all that are required or whether fundamental changes must in the end be adopted remains to be seen. Clearly, we can already discern dilemmas which the politicians must meet, such as the interest of the consumer in conflict with that of the worker. If the New Deal continues to run true to pattern, it may decide against the consumer and for the worker. This might involve the abandonment of the underselling policy that has characterized Macy's for so long a period. And so there remain many matters of high import for treatment at a later date.

The present work, which reveals the past rather than anticipates the future, is the first history of an American retail firm that goes into detail and that deals critically with the function of retailing. Because of the fact that retailing is presented against the background of an actual institution having its own peculiarity of organization and personality and located in a definite center, the reader is given a high degree of concreteness and reality.

There are indeed two kinds of histories of retailing. In one, we find the general story of sales policies, styles, grades, costs of operation, and so on, studied from advertisements, retail journals, and association reports. This is a valuable type and is the only history of retailing now in existence. In the other type, yet to be developed, the general story will be compiled chiefly from the histories of individual stores, carefully worked out. Dr. Hower has laid sure foundations for this second type of history of retailing. I do not know what all the logical results of efforts to write this second type of retail history will prove to be, but one seems to stand out with certainty, namely, that the various administrative policies and managerial methods adopted will be related to a multiplicity of actual situations. This is the only way to make business history scientific. In other words, this type of history will be less a matter of principles of retailing and more a matter of case studies with an emphasis on alternatives of policy and the implications involved in each alternative.

This present history has been written in coöperation with the firm. No other method is satisfactory, for outside judgments are always partly wrong and outside knowledge largely inaccurate. Of course, I do not imply that inside opinion is itself always correct or acceptable. At any rate, in this instance, the firm has given all the information available — in the form of both documents and oral statements. The executives have given the author their confidence and expected only fairness and candor in return. They have allowed him to dig out evidence wherever he could find it. They have been helpful in criticizing and revaluing his conclusions and judgments. They have given no financial aid in doing the research, but before the work was begun they agreed to help finance the publication of the book so that it might be sold at a reasonable price.

In the gradual growth of a scientific approach to the study of business, college-trained men are playing an important part. In the first World War, chemists, employed by sundry firms, hitherto jealous of their secrets, developed the invaluable habit of exchanging views and opinions. The Macy firm, long in the possession of executives who have been trained in the detached position of the scholar, has exhibited candor in self-appraisal, generosity in giving information, and willingness to coöperate with outsiders who had really scientific interests.

Dr. Hower has made a diligent search for facts within the archives of the firm and on the outside. He has used the correspondence, advertisements, minutes, and accounts of the store. He has supplemented these by conversation and observation. He has striven for impartiality of judgment, which I have had occasion to applaud. He has had a constant problem of selection in view of the fact that the materials, especially for sales policy and sales management, have been so extensive.

N. S. B. GRAS

AUTHOR'S PREFACE

LIKE most people in this age of haste, I disapprove of long books. When the task of preparing this study came into my hands, I felt sure that Macy's history could be set forth adequately within the limits of about 350 printed pages — certainly not over 400 — and I vowed not to allow the book to exceed that estimate. Perhaps I should have known better. The manuscript, like the fabulous firm which is its subject, persisted in growing. From time to time new materials unexpectedly turned up, and many events which at first had seemed to be unimportant later proved to be of fundamental significance in explaining the firm's development and consequently required more than cursory attention.

Even the table of contents does not reveal the full extent of the error in my initial estimate. In order to keep the history within practical limits I have had to excise words, delete sentences, boil down paragraphs, and condense chapters, far beyond the revision which is inherent in historical writing, and I have been compelled by space limitations to omit a number of topics which had been originally planned for inclusion. The inevitable result is that I have set before the reader a large repast which is mostly meat, with few trimmings and practically no dessert. In an effort to spare the general reader statistical indigestion, however, I have assembled most of the operating figures at the ends of the chapters to which they apply, thus facilitating judicious skipping. To many students and professional retailers, of course, those figures will be the most interesting part of the history.

Throughout this study I have tried to keep in mind two objectives: (1) to trace and explain all the significant developments connected with the origin and growth of R. H. Macy & Co., Inc.; and (2) to show the relation of the firm to its economic and social environment. Accordingly, the store's early history and general developments in retailing before 1870 have been set forth in considerable detail. It was not feasible to sustain the same scale of treatment throughout the study. For the period of expansion and maturity, from 1870 to 1902, I found it increasingly difficult to include more than a passing reference to external events. All the available space was needed for Macy's itself. For the period after 1902 it proved impossible even to continue the practice of analyzing in great detail the developments within the store itself, and I had to be content with more summary treatment of some phases. If, as a result, the history appears to focus rather narrowly upon Macy's and to telescope or ignore certain aspects of development, let the reader bear in mind that to remedy the defect would require a great many more pages.

The start of this book really goes back to 1928–29 when Jesse I. Straus was strong and active both in Macy's and in the Harvard Graduate School of Business Administration. At that time the late Dr. Mildred L. Hartsough made a substantial beginning with the collection of material for a documentary history of Macy's. When, in 1938, I undertook the preparation of a narrative history, we had hoped that the collected documents would supply the main body of source material. Actually it was necessary to go far beyond them to obtain anything like an adequate picture of the firm's development. As a result of Dr. Hartsough's efforts, however, valuable material was saved which would otherwise have been destroyed, and her collection provided me with an excellent starting point.

Macy's own archives have supplied most of the information used in this volume. Essentially, therefore, it is a history written by an outsider from inside the firm. In no sense, however, is it an "official" history. While I have received the fullest possible coöperation from members of the Macy organization, I alone am responsible for its final form and content. I have invited and received criticism of my manuscript, but there has been no censorship of materials or statements. Although the firm's executives have disagreed with my interpretations and conclusions at a number of points, they have upheld my right to independent judgment.

Original records relating to Rowland Macy and the early years of the Macy firm are almost non-existent, and for the period before

1870 I have been compelled to rely mainly upon outside sources, principally newspaper advertisements. Mr. Alfred W. Swinyard gave me effective assistance in the laborious and dusty work of examining newspaper files in Boston and New York. For assistance in tracing Rowland Macy's experience as a whaleman, 'forty-niner, and speculator in Wisconsin land, I am indebted to Mr. William H. Tripp of New Bedford, Mass., Mr. Earl Ramey of Marysville, Calif., Mrs. Dolores W. Bryant of San Francisco, the public libraries of New Bedford and Haverhill, Mass., Marysville, Calif., and Superior, Wis., officials of the National Archives, and, above all, Mr. Edouard A. Stackpole of Nantucket Island.

Thanks to the kindness of Dr. Laurence La Forge and Mrs. Rose La Forge Maxson (son and daughter of Abiel T. La Forge and Margaret Getchell, Rowland Macy's first partner and first woman executive, respectively), I am able to include some exceedingly valuable operating data for the early 1870's. Miss Dorothy M. La Forge was kind enough to lend me legal documents relating to agreements between her grandparents and Rowland Macy, thus clearing up a number of points concerning the firm's ownership, financing, and accounting in the 1870's. Dr. La Forge, Mrs. Maxson, and Mrs. Lily La Forge Prentice have supplied me with much useful information about their parents.

The principal Macy accounting records now extant date from the fall of 1887. This fact has enabled me to present a continuous series of retail operating data from 1888 to 1919, inclusive. Mrs. Rose Kneznek (of the Harvard Bureau of Business Research) deserves special commendation for the skill with which she executed the exceedingly difficult job of analyzing and grouping the Macy figures so as to make them comparable from year to year. I cannot emphasize too strongly the importance of this long series of data relating to a retail store. It provides exceedingly valuable quantitative information in an area where we formerly had nothing but conjecture, and students of marketing owe Macy's a special debt of gratitude for making the records available.

I am indebted to a great many people in the Macy organization for help in the preparation of this history, so many that only a few can be cited individually. Mr. Percy S. Straus, in addition to making the firm's records available for research, gave me the benefit of his long experience in the store. His memory is prodigious, and the patience and objectivity with which he responded to many hours of questioning have won my undying admiration. Not the least of his services to me was the careful reading of the entire manuscript, as a result of which I received many valuable corrections and suggestions.

Mr. Delos Walker, vice-president of Macy's, has likewise read the whole manuscript, and I am indebted to him for much wise counsel. Mr. Ernest Katz, Macy's Controller, read many sections of the manuscript and in the course of many conversations made available to me his long and intimate knowledge of the business. Mr. Paul Hollister, formerly executive vice-president of Macy's and now vice-president of Columbia Broadcasting Co., was exceedingly kind and helpful in getting me off to a good start within the Macy organization. Of the many past and present employees of the store who have helped me, I am particularly indebted to Miss Agnes Finegan and Mr. Charles O. Winship for information about working conditions in the 1880's and 1890's. To the many other employees and ex-employees who have helped I extend my sincere thanks.

Such unpredictable factors as advancement and marriage on the part of my assistants are responsible for my having had a succession of helpers during the course of preparing the manuscript. In addition to Mrs. Kneznek (mentioned above), the principal persons who have helped with the research and secretarial work are Mrs. Dorothy Pratt Jaquith, Mrs. Faith Crossman Welpton, Miss Josepha M. Perry, and Mrs. Frances Carpenter Holbrook. Mrs. Elsie Hight Bishop has succeeded in performing the delicate task of editing the manuscript without doing violence to either the author's text or his feelings. To her experienced hands, in addition, has fallen the responsibility for reading proof and preparing the index — tedious but essential work which, fortunately, she enjoys and does with distinction.

A grant from the Harvard Committee on Research in the Social

Sciences covered a substantial part of the expense of research assistance, travel, microphotography, and secretarial service.

My colleagues at the Harvard Business School have helped me generously. Professor Wallace B. Donham, formerly dean of the School, enabled me to devote most of my time to research and writing, and Professor John C. Baker conducted the negotiations between Harvard and Macy's that were necessary to place the project upon a proper academic basis. Dean Donald K. David made it possible for me, in spite of war work, to complete the last portion of the study.

Professor Malcolm P. McNair, notwithstanding eye trouble and a heavy load of administrative and academic duties, found time to give the entire manuscript his painstaking attention, and there is hardly a section of the book which has not been improved as a result. Professor Edmund P. Learned read the first two-thirds of my manuscript and gave me the benefit of his wise counsel until special work for the War Department made it impossible for him to continue his assistance.

I owe a special debt of gratitude to Professor N. S. B. Gras. He read not only the final draft of the manuscript but also earlier versions, and he has a positive genius for giving expert guidance without encroaching upon an author's independence. Both Associate Professor Henrietta M. Larson and Dr. J. Owen Stalson repeatedly helped me with knotty problems of research and composition, and Professor Gras and Dr. Larson have assumed responsibility for supervising publication. Mr. Richmond F. Bingham prepared the drawings for Charts I and II. Lastly, I want to acknowledge the valuable editorial assistance and moral support given throughout the project by my wife.

RALPH M. HOWER

October 30, 1942

PART I
ROWLAND MACY'S PREPARATION
1822–1858

CHAPTER I

NANTUCKET TO POINTS WEST

TODAY's department store is an institution of vast economic and social importance, far greater indeed than most of us would ever realize unless we were deprived of its services. Its very size gives it significance — the large building required for its operations, the army of people employed to conduct its business, the crowds of customers who throng its aisles, and the enormous quantity of merchandise that it sells.

The department store gains additional importance from the fact that it occupies a place of great influence in its community. Every business enterprise, from the lowly pedlar to the enormous and complicated industrial plant, has social implications, and this is particularly true of the department store. Like the mediaeval fair and the oriental bazaar, it forms a market place, a convenient point at which people meet to exchange goods and services. It brings to one place a truly amazing assortment of merchandise from all parts of the world and thus influences our mode of living and our standards of taste.

Like the fair and the bazaar, the department store is composed of a number of stores gathered in one place. But, in contrast with those amorphous antecedents, the department store is not a haphazard agglomeration of independent enterprises. It is a formally created and managed organization, with a hierarchy of control culminating in one man or, at most, a mere handful of executives. It has an intricate and responsive central nervous system and an alert brain, so that it can adjust quickly to new situations and ideas. It anticipates public demand and tries to direct it into certain channels. While the fair and the bazaar formed lively market places, they were essentially passive retailing institutions, depending on the active participation of the consumer to determine what goods should be offered and the prices at which they should be sold. The modern department store is far from passive. By means of skillful advertising, special exhibitions, and tempting bargains, it actively attempts to influence our daily behavior. Its function is not so much to sell what the manufacturer produces as to obtain from the manufacturer what the public wants to buy or, in its judgment, what the public should want to buy. Child of urban development, the department store helps to make urban life possible by offering economy and the convenience of buying a variety of goods under one roof.

The historical evolution of the department store has hitherto received little attention. It is, however, an important subject, and considerable light will be thrown on it by an examination of the history of R. H. Macy & Co., of New York. For many years this firm has been the largest single retail store in the world, both in volume of sales and in amount of floor space. It grew out of an apparently insignificant retail effort begun in the middle of the nineteenth century. Most, if not all, of the forces leading to the emergence of the modern department store can be discerned in its history. In short, the story of Macy's is, to a large extent, the story of the American department store and one of the main chapters in the history of American retailing.

When did Macy's begin? The store was opened in 1858, to be sure, but when did the fundamental concept of the store take form? To ask such a question is a little like asking when life itself began. In one sense its origin goes back to the beginning of business, to the first occasion on which man began to exchange goods in the hope of obtaining a profit. In another sense it goes back to the mediaeval fair and the bazaar, for those institutions, as already suggested, had much in common with the department store. But there is no direct generic connection between these historical developments and the foundation of Macy's

Perhaps the best point at which to begin the story of Macy's is the career of its founder, Rowland H. Macy. It was he who established the fundamental Macy policies of buying for cash, selling for cash, and underselling competitors. There is considerable support for the view that the store which he founded was the first one in the United States, if not in the world, to develop into a full-fledged department store. Certainly his store was among the earliest to do so, and it completed most of the steps in that evolution under Macy's personal direction.

Only a few insignificant fragments of Macy's own personal papers have survived the ravages of time, housecleaning, and careless handling. In spite of this initial difficulty, however, it is possible, by diligent use of various published materials and official records, to reconstruct the outline of his life with considerable accuracy and fair completeness.

Family Background

Rowland Hussey Macy was born on Nantucket Island, Massachusetts, on August 30, 1822. He came of good, fearless, Quaker stock. Indeed, he was descended (by four different lines) directly from that Thomas Macy who was the first white man to settle on Nantucket (sometime between 1659 and 1661), after the stern Baptists of Salisbury, Massachusetts, had made it advisable for him to seek voluntary exile. Thomas Macy was an Englishman by birth, and his fault was not that he lacked religious fervor but rather that he dared to show tolerance toward Quakers and their beliefs. He had, in fact, gone so far as to give temporary shelter to four Quakers for three-quarters of an hour during a rainstorm! As a result of this flagrant act he was fined thirty shillings and solemnly admonished by the governor of the colony. Thomas Macy thereupon decided, for the sake of an independent conscience, to risk the unknown hazards of life among the Nantucket Indians. The natives proved to be friendly, other liberal-minded settlers from Salisbury soon joined the Macy family, and a flourishing colony came to be established, most of the members of which eventually adopted the faith of the Society of Friends.

Those events of the seventeenth century seem to have little bearing upon the great store at Broadway and 34th Street, and yet that busy institution owes its start to the bold, unhesitating spirit of enterprise which Thomas Macy evidently passed on to his children of the seventh generation. Moreover, at its very beginning, when haggling over price was the accepted practice in retail trade, that store adhered to a one-price policy, which may well have originated in the Quaker principle that there could be only one true price for an article, just as there was only one standard of truth generally, and that to depart from it in dealing with a customer was to be guilty of a form of dishonesty, to say nothing of the waste of time involved.[1]

Rowland Macy's father, John Macy, had been captain of a merchant ship, after which, for a year or two at least, he operated a small retail store at No. 2 Fair Street, Nantucket, devoted mainly to books and magazines. The boy's grandfather, Sylvanus Macy, had been in the coasting trade for many years, following which he seems to have engaged in whaling, the manufacture of sperm candles, and shoemaking. The important point for us at the moment, perhaps, is the fact that the family had had first-hand experience with retail business, as well as with seafaring. In view of Rowland's subsequent whaling experience, it is tempting to think that he might have been given his middle name for that Christopher Hussey who caught a sperm whale after being blown out to sea and so led the men of Nantucket to abandon "boat whaling" (i.e., off the shore) for the more profitable chase on the high seas; but it is much more likely that he was named after Rowland Hussey, who married his father's sister Rachael.

Rowland was the fourth of six children, having three older brothers and two younger sisters. Since we shall encounter the brothers later, it may be well to note their names: Charles B., born in 1812; Andrew M., born in 1814; and Robert B., born in 1820.

No records survive to tell us the kind of education which Rowland Macy received, but we can be sure that it was a rudimentary one. In violation of Massachusetts law, Nantucket managed to avoid having any elementary public schools at all until 1818, and there were no private schools of note on the Island at the time. Those which were in operation by the time Macy was of school age could scarcely have been very effective, particularly when elementary schools on the mainland were at best none too good. The prevailing practice certainly was to provide schooling only up to about the age of twelve. In any case, Macy could not have received any formal education after he was fifteen, for at that point he went to sea, and thereafter his training consisted solely of the things that he learned in a hard but interesting world. In view of the important book department which Macy eventually developed in his New York store, we should not overlook the fact that his father ran a bookstore when the boy was at the impressionable age of ten.

Considering the family's background, it is plain that Rowland Macy, at an early age, was familiar with ships and the sea and that as a boy he had a taste of hard work and hardship. Life on Nantucket had never been easy, and it was many years before the Island recovered from the economic distress that it suffered as a result of the War of 1812.

We may surmise, too, that the boy had to a considerable degree the qualities engendered by a niggardly soil and the admixture of Puritan and Quaker philosophies: stouthearted courage, persevering enterprise, thrift, ingenuity, a taste for shrewd bargains, remarkable self-reliance, contempt for luxuries, and an independent spirit which nothing could daunt. Certainly these qualities were displayed in his subsequent career.[2]

Four Years in Pursuit of the Whale

Rowland Macy sailed from New Bedford on December 11, 1837, as a member of the crew of the whaling ship *Emily Morgan* (owned by Charles W. Morgan of New Bedford) bound for Cape Horn and the Pacific. We can only guess at the motives that led to this step, although probably there never was a healthy boy who did not at some time or other want to go to sea. Certainly no Nantucket youth of the 1830's escaped the longing, for whaling was at the very heart of Nantucket life, and it provided the traditional start for the self-respecting Island boy. Moreover, any lad who, in 1837, looked to a business career on the mainland must have had his hopes dashed by the severe financial crash which occurred in the spring of that year and by the subsequent depression which touched every branch of American life.

Rowland Macy was not among complete strangers in the *Emily Morgan*, for the captain, Shubael Clark, and the mate, Prince W. Ewer, were from Nantucket, and so were six others of the 31 men in the ship. Also, there were other boys aboard, two of them aged 15 like himself, and one who was only 13. It was a crew of youngsters anyway, for more than half of them had not yet passed 22, and only one had reached 30. "Thus have these naked Nantucketers, these sea hermits, issuing from their ant-hill in the sea, overrun and conquered the watery world like so many Alexanders."[3]

We may easily imagine Macy's feelings as, according to the custom with "green hands," he was sent aloft into the swaying rigging immediately after the ship had sailed, in order to get his sea legs. He was leaving home for the first time, launched on a voyage which was certain to last several years, certain to involve hardship and danger, and from which there could be no turning back. His home was to be a 368-ton, three-masted ship, only 27 feet wide and 111 feet long, its two decks crammed with all sorts of gear and supplies to last a journey of unknown length.

The story of that voyage is of importance here only because of the part it played in forming Macy's character. While the log of the *Emily Morgan* for that voyage has disappeared, it is possible to reconstruct the main outlines from other sources of information. From numerous authentic accounts of whaling expeditions we know the type of experiences that Rowland Macy underwent. He had to go aloft to handle sails in all sorts of weather; he must repeatedly have felt the menace of the hissing line as the harpooned whale plunged into the depths; and he took more than one thrilling "Nantucket sleigh-ride" through Pacific waters, towed by a pain-maddened sperm. If he escaped the experience of a "stove" boat, he was luckier than most members of whaling expeditions. Certainly there was no possibility of avoiding long stretches of hard work, "cutting in" whales, boiling down blubber, and cleaning up the resulting mess. For an unusually vivid account of normal whaling experience, one should read the expository chapters of *Moby Dick*, which recount to a large extent the experience of Herman Melville on a whaling voyage begun in January, 1841, while Macy was still at sea.

The *Emily Morgan* touched at Pernambuco, Brazil, 37 days out, rounded Cape Horn, and then spent three years cruising in the Pacific. All the evidence indicates that she spent most of the time among the islands to the south and west, especially the Tonga or Friendly Islands, Samoa, and the Kingsmills (Gilbert Islands). The first year's efforts yielded practically no oil, but in 1838 and 1839 better luck prevailed; when she "spoke" the *Daniel Webster* off Ocean Island, in January, 1841, she had nearly a full cargo of sperm oil.

During the course of the cruising the *Emily Morgan* stopped at the Island of Ascension (now under Japanese control and known as Ponapi) to discharge Orin Blanchard, who was too sick to continue the voyage, and somewhere along the way Lewis Cheshire died and was buried at sea. Meanwhile she restored the size of the crew by taking on two "foreigners," probably South Sea Islanders. Since the *Emily Morgan* undoubtedly put in for water and fresh supplies a number of times, Rowland Macy must have had a close view of the South Sea Islands at their best and their worst. Whether he drank deeply of the vaunted pleasures of shore leave we cannot know, but at any rate he was not demoralized by the temptations offered. Unlike most whaling ships of the period, the *Emily Morgan* had no trouble with deserters. The food and discipline on board were evidently acceptable to the men. By April, 1841, the ship was full of oil and put in at Bay of Islands, New Zealand. There she loaded supplies for the homeward journey, and took on as passengers for New England "Mr. Robert George & Lady," departing on May 17, 1841.

On Sunday, September 26, 1841, the *Emily Morgan* dropped anchor at New Bedford, having been gone nearly four years, and that night her owner made the following entry in his diary:

A strong S. West wind & fine weather. Two good sermons from Mr. Osgood. Towards evening the Emily Morgan made her appearance, all full and all well, a capital voyage & capitally conducted. She has also more [than] 250 lbs Ambergris taken from the stomach of one whale — a prize indeed if it proves pure. The E.M. has been absent 45½ mos. & has 3100 bbls. oil.

The inventory of the *Emily Morgan's* cargo reveals that, in addition to the cask of ambergris, the ship had on board 2,879 barrels of sperm oil, 108 barrels of whale oil, and 1,000 pounds of whale bone as the fruits of the long voyage. Her cargo was valued for customs purposes at $85,000 and at current prices must have been worth nearly $90,000. As a "green hand" Rowland Macy's share probably was 1/175 of this amount, or about $500, as his compensation (beyond food and shelter) for nearly four years' work.[4]

When Rowland Macy first went to sea, he was a boy of 15 years; when he returned he was only 19, but he was a man. He had been toughened by strenuous physical exertion and dangerous adventure. He had been matured by close association with men from many walks of life, who differed widely in character and ability; and he had been broadened by extensive travel, contacts with foreigners, and glimpses of unfamiliar cultures. The whaling cruise gave him no direct training for retail trade, but by teaching him the habits of hard work and self-discipline and the art of getting along with people it laid a valuable foundation for his future career.

Although he might have continued as a whaleman, he decided to abandon the sea. Possibly he saw the limitations of whaling as a vocation. Probably he had had his fill of seafaring life and wanted to try his fortunes on land. Like many other Americans of the period, he turned his back upon the sea of his fathers and looked toward the development of a vast new continent. Although in later life he was often called Captain Macy, he never sailed the sea after 1841 except as a passenger.

In view of his subsequent career, it is evident that Macy had no clear idea in 1841 as to what his life work should be. Four years of adventure had left him ambitious but restless, confident of his ability to get along in the world but uncertain as to the work he should pursue. There was reason for uncertainty, too, quite apart from any wanderlust that a whaling cruise might have planted in a young man's heart. On the one hand, it was an era of tremendous change: the steam engine which had already transformed industry was beginning to revolutionize transportation on land and sea; new machines and techniques were changing distribution as profoundly as production; and men were swarming recklessly into the West. Amidst this confusion of novelty and expansion, the pattern of action

MODEL OF THE WHALESHIP *EMILY MORGAN*
Rowland Macy's home, 1837–1841

We beg leave to recommend PHILIP W. KEYSER, to the citizens of this District as a fit Candidate for the office of District Attorney.
au27tf   MANY FRIENDS.

We are authorized to present the name of H. W. CARPENTIER, Esq., of San Francisco, as a Candidate at the coming election, for the office of Superintendant of Public Instruction.
sept13tf

Dissolution of Copartnership.

THE firm of MACY & Co., heretofore doing business in this place, is this day dissolved by mutual consent.
ROWLAND H. MACY,
CHARLES B. MITCHELL,
CHARLES B. MACY,
EDWARD R. ANTHONY.
Marysville, Sept. 23d, 1850.   sept.24,3t.

E. W. Tracy,
Successor to MACY & Co.,

WOULD respectfully inform the inhabitants of Marysville and vicinity, that he is prepared to furnish them with any kind of Merchandise they may wish, CHEAP FOR CASH.
Marysville, Sept. 23, 1850.   sept,24,tf

To Let,

A SPLENDID STORE, 20x50 feet, situated in a business part of the town, on Second street, next door to Beauleau & Co. This store has been made so as to prevent merchandize from getting wet from the heavy rains, during the winter season. Inquire of Gabellot, Hotel de France.   sep24.2t*

Notice.

ALL PERSONS who have not paid their Taxes and License, are hereby notified to call at the Treasurer's Office, and settle the same and thereby save costs.
LEVI W. TAYLOR,
County Treasurer.
Marysville, Sept. 23, 1850.   sep24tf

Edward W. Tracy,
Agent for Hawley & Co's Express,

CORNER of second street and Maiden-Lane, Marysville.
Letters and packages forwarded to Sacramento City, San Francisco, and through to the States, by Adams & Co's Express.
Sept. 23, 1850.   sep24tf

established by previous generations gave little guidance to a hesitating lad. On the other hand, it was a period of severe depression: the closing of Biddle's Pennsylvania Bank of the United States in the spring of '41 had precipitated a new series of business failures, and there seemed to be no prospect of relief from the long period of economic difficulties which, with a few bright interludes, had persisted ever since the inflationary peak of 1815. In such bewildering circumstances what should a young man do?

First Experiences in Retailing

For several years after his return from whaling, Macy's trail is lost. He went to Boston and tried different kinds of employment, and it is said that he entered a printing office to learn the printer's trade but gave it up after six months' trial. If this story is true, it reveals where Macy picked up the foundation of the advertising skill which he later displayed.[5]

Within a year or two he became acquainted with George W. Houghton, a dry goods retailer in Boston, and in August, 1844, he married Houghton's sister, Louisa. It is said that Houghton set up Macy in a small thread and needle store in Boston. At any rate, we find him in the Boston directories for 1844 with a dry goods store at 78½ Hanover Street. What became of this business no one knows. The disappearance of Macy's name from the directories suggests that his first attempt at retailing came to an untimely end, the outcome of inexperience and hard times. In 1846, however, he was again established in a retail dry goods store, this time at 357 Washington Street, Boston. If he publicized his business, the advertisements have escaped diligent search, with the exception of a small notice in the Boston *Daily Mail* (June 2, 1846) in which Macy featured "DRY GOODS From Cash Auctions Every Day." It is evident from this that most of the merchandise that Macy sold was obtained from the public auctions, where large quantities of European merchandise were dumped on the market for what they would fetch. Such procedure, if managed by a clever buyer, would yield attractive bargains, but it required skillful trading and a shrewd knowledge of values.

Macy's second effort seems to have lasted through at least the first half of 1847, possibly longer; but in 1848 he was evidently employed by his brother-in-law, Samuel S. Houghton (who later founded the old Boston department store, Houghton & Dutton), in a store specializing in laces and embroideries, at 175 Tremont Street. The fact that Macy's and Houghton's addresses were identical suggests that the two families had pooled resources in an effort to economize. There was need for economy, too, for Rowland Macy, Jr., had been born in 1847.[6]

It is a fair conclusion that during these first efforts at retailing Rowland Macy had experienced indifferent success, if not actual failure. On the other hand, he had acquired first-hand knowledge of the dry goods trade and knew some of the mistakes to be avoided in the future. Possibly it was in Boston that he learned the dangers of doing business on credit and first perceived the possibilities of aggressive advertising in the management of a retail store.

To California with the 'Forty-Niners

When the news of the discovery of gold in California reached New England, Rowland Macy decided (with scores of other Nantucketers) that it was time to try a new venture. Leaving his family behind, he and his brother Charles B. Macy sailed in March, 1849, on the brig *Dr. Hitchcock* for Panama. Four and one-half months later the two men reached San Francisco, after having made the hazardous journey across the Isthmus of Panama and taken the steamer *Sylph* up the western coast.

What the two brothers did immediately after reaching San Francisco cannot be determined, but in July of the following year we find them in what is now the city of Marysville, California, forty miles north of Sacramento, at the junction of the Feather and Yuba rivers. They may have tried their hands at gold mining and decided that trade offered a better path to riches. At any rate, by July, 1850, they had formed a partnership with Charles B. Mitchell and Edward R. Anthony, doing business under the name of Macy & Co. In the advertisements which appeared in the early issues of the Marysville *Herald* the firm announced themselves as "General Dealers in Provisions, Dry Goods, Clothing &c. &c. Also Agents for Hawley Co's Express. Letters, Packages and Gold Dust Forwarded to all parts of the world, through Adams & Co."[7] Another advertisement stated that Macy & Co.[8]

Have just received a large addition to their present stock of goods, and are prepared to furnish about everything necessary for the use of Miners. They have on hand now a stock amounting to eighty thousand dollars, and the bulk of it was received during the higher stages of the water, when freights were less than half what they are at present. Country Merchants, Packers, City Traders, MINERS &c., will do well to give us a call before purchasing elsewhere.

The reference to the high stages of the water was made because most of the supplies to Marysville had to be brought up from San Francisco by steamboat via the Sacramento and Feather rivers, and during the summer of 1850 the water had dropped so low that it was impossible to transport by boat; freights jumped to extravagant figures as a result. The advertisement implied that Macy prices were lower than those of competitors, but it may be significant that nothing was said about underselling or selling for cash.

On September 23, 1850, Macy & Co. was dissolved and succeeded by E. W. Tracy. Since Tracy, unlike Macy & Co., stressed in his advertising the phrase "CHEAP FOR CASH," it is possible that Macy & Co. came to grief because of an overuse of credit, although the same phrase was frequently advertised in the East. It is clear, in any event, that the partners had attempted to do business under unusual circumstances, in a boom town which consisted mainly of tents and shacks and the chief commerce of which was the business of handling supplies for the miners. There is no evidence to indicate whether the business was exclusively wholesale or combined retailing and wholesaling. The following comment from the chief historian of Marysville about Macy's and other early Marysville stores is pertinent:[9]

Of course, it was no counter trade; the bulk of supplies went to the mines in large lots. Some of these firms were called wholesale, and all might well have been so called. . . . There probably were few really fixed current prices, because all stores, excepting the larger and more dignified ones, disposed of a great amount of goods at auction. One suspects that this manner of bartering and purchasing appealed to the miners and storekeepers from the diggings and satisfied their desire to gamble. The town probably had more of the character of a combined carnival and European public market than of our modern conception of a busy trading center.

No evidence has survived to indicate what Rowland Macy did immediately after the dissolution of the partnership. His brother Charles remained in Marysville as agent for the Adams Express Co. until his death in 1856, and another brother, Andrew, who had gone to California at an unknown date, died in San Francisco in 1853; but when we next find Rowland Macy he is again in Massachusetts.[10]

In the absence of definite information about this episode in Macy's life, a number of tentative conclusions suggest themselves. The Macy firm was probably forced out by the severe competition which had sprung up in Marysville during the first feverish attempt to capture the business created by the gold rush. Toward the end of 1850 there were in this small mushroom town at least thirty general stores like the one in which Rowland Macy was a partner. Apparently at least a hundred individual business men were interested in these enterprises, and yet only a handful were able to survive for any length of time.[11] Even if Macy & Co. had a large sum of money to divide after selling out (a doubtful assumption), it seems unlikely that any one of the four partners obtained a considerable amount.

The official records of Yuba County show that Rowland Macy and Thomas R. Anthony purchased for $1,200 a small piece of land in Marysville on August 20, 1850, and sold it to E. W. Tracy on September 14, less than a month later, for $3,000. Since the $1,800 profit resulting had to be split two ways, this venture, although obviously successful, certainly did not line Macy's pockets heavily. The irony of the transaction is that Tracy sold the same lot only three months later for $7,000, more than doubling his money.[12]

The only account of his life which touches on this episode states that Rowland Macy returned from California with between three and four thousand dollars.[13] After making a discount for the exaggerations which were characteristic of nineteenth-century biographies, it is evident that Macy's California venture yielded no great riches and may even have been a financial failure. It is possible, of course, that he returned to the East simply because he had decided that the gold-mad frontier environment was not a suitable place to which to bring his family. This explanation, however, is weakened by the fact that his brother Charles, who was married, chose to remain in Marysville and that his brother Andrew, who had a wife and two daughters, settled in San Francisco.[14] Had Rowland considered the Marysville venture a conspicuous success, it seems probable that he would have settled in the region.

On the other hand, we must not overlook certain gains which must have come from this second journey to the Pacific. Macy, whose previous retailing experience had been confined to small, urban retail stores specializing in dry goods (indeed, that rather limited line known as fancy dry goods), now possessed first-hand knowledge of a general store handling a variety of merchandise under primitive conditions and evidently doing more business at wholesale than at retail. Moreover, he had had the benefit of numerous contacts with men from all parts of the world. The gold rush had brought an extraordinary mixture of men to Marysville, not only from the eastern part of the United States but also from foreign countries — from France, Germany, England, Scotland, Switzerland, and even South America. While some of them were obviously floating riffraff, others were respectable men of good education, genuine ability and integrity, and considerable enterprise.[15] Rubbing elbows with them for a year probably taught Macy many a lesson about business and people and must have modified his original insularity.

One should recognize, too, the possible psychological influence of operating in an atmosphere of inflated prices, grandiose schemes, and (for Rowland Macy at least) operations on a relatively large scale. Somewhere the young man from Nantucket picked up some big ideas about business. Is it too much to suggest that he got them in the California gold rush?

CHAPTER II

A COCK CROWS IN HAVERHILL

BACK from the California gold rush without much gold, Rowland Macy decided to have another try at the retail dry goods business, this time in Haverhill, Massachusetts. The reasons for choosing that particular location are not known. Haverhill, near the mouth of the Merrimack River and a short distance above Newburyport, was already gaining fame for its shoe manufacturing, but it was relatively small (population 5,877 in 1850). Even if one included as a part of the community the village of Bradford just across the river, it was still smaller than the fast-growing neighboring town of Lawrence, and many a Massachusetts town was more important in wealth, industrial or commercial importance, or size. Probably Macy's choice, like so many important business decisions, was not based on logic at all.

By the most conservative estimates the Haverhill store was Macy's fourth venture into retail trade (three times as a proprietor or partner and once as an employee). For us its chief interest lies in the fact that the details of operation reveal for the first time the basic retailing policies which later became famous in New York City. As will be explained in a subsequent chapter, not one of these policies, strictly speaking, was originated by Macy, but the particular combination which he tried, and the extent to which he gave it aggressive promotion, made him stand out as an innovator and pioneer. One is likely to conclude that the Haverhill undertaking paved the way for Macy's success in New York.[1]

ESTABLISHMENT OF THE HAVERHILL STORE

The Haverhill store was first opened in April, 1851, under the name of Rowland's brother, R. B. Macy, and it was not until 1852 that Rowland's own name was publicly connected with it. From the existing evidence, however, it is practically certain that Rowland Macy was in charge of operations from the very start. Why the subterfuge? Possibly Rowland Macy's previous experience in Boston had injured his credit, so that he was able to start again only by using his brother's name. Another likely possibility is that R. B. Macy supplied much of the capital involved or arranged to have the initial stock of goods supplied on credit by the Boston firm with which he had been connected. Certainly, as we shall see presently, the difficulties encountered by the new firm at the end of the first year indicate credit problems of some sort.

Robert B. Macy had gone from Nantucket to Boston and entered the dry goods business without any preliminary seafaring experience. He had been employed for a time as a clerk in the firm of F. A. Jones & Co., who were importers and wholesalers as well as retailers of dry goods, and he may have served his apprenticeship with them. In 1850 he had established himself as a dry goods retailer on School Street, Boston, and, since he was still in business in Boston in 1851 and 1852, it is obvious that he must have depended upon somebody else to manage the Haverhill store. His previous experience, his former employment with a prominent dry goods house, and his own going concern in Boston would all have been definite assets in the new enterprise.

The first advertisement, dated April 5, 1851, announced that R. B. Macy had taken a store at No. 5 Kittredge's block (Nos. 94–106) on Merrimack Street, "for the purpose of transacting business in the Fancy and Domestic DRY GOODS LINE" in what was referred to as the "Haverhill Cheap Store." There was also a plain statement of the Macy cash policy: "His Goods are all bought for Cash, and will be sold for the same, at a small advance." The merchandise advertised included prints, cotton goods, ginghams, muslins, cambrics, laces, ribbons, and delaines. Subsequent advertisements mentioned, in addition, sheetings, linens, hosiery, gloves, thread, trimmings, and general notions.[2]

In short, the Macy store handled a rather full line of dry goods and nothing else. In this respect it differed little from the many other specialized dry goods stores which operated in the eastern part of the

United States. One feature which was certainly far from typical was the assertion that "NEW GOODS will be received from Boston and New York every week," for the prevailing practice was to add new goods mainly in the spring and fall.[3] The announced cash policy, although not really an innovation, was another departure from prevailing practice in retail trade.

A few weeks later Macy announced another part of his general policy:[4]

> It is . . . his intention to give this Store such a reputation for *NOVELTY AND LOW PRICES* as shall make it a *marked and distinct feature* in the Dry Goods trade of Haverhill. At this store may be found at all times the best stock of FANCY DRY GOODS in town, at prices which defy competition. Most of the time he has a good stock of heavy DRY GOODS and DOMESTICS, but never, unless bought in such a way as to be sold at LESS THAN THE REGULAR PRICES. . . .
>
> We do not profess to keep a large Stock of Goods, but we *do* keep a FAST one. . . .

Novelty, selling for cash, very low prices, and rapid turnover of the stock — here is the preliminary sketch of the Macy success formula.

At first the venture was evidently a tentative one, for in his second advertisement Macy thanked the inhabitants of the district for their patronage and stated that he was "satisfied with the result of his experiment, viz: the introduction of a Cheap Dry Goods Store into the town of Haverhill."[5] Competitors promptly used against him the argument that he did not intend to stay in Haverhill, and Macy was then obliged to protest that he had intended from the very outset to establish a permanent business.

In spite of Macy's avowed contentment with patronage, there was trouble before the end of 1851. For reasons about which we can only guess, the store was closed during the four weeks immediately preceding Christmas. This led to the announcement of Macy's first sale under the bold headline: "PEREMPTORY SALE OF THE WHOLE Stock at Cost and Less than Cost For 20 Days commencing CHRISTMAS DAY." The following cryptic explanation of the sale was given:[6]

We have not the least article of faith in the annual and semi-annual Dry Goods sales of the day at cost &c. &c., as we always manage to sell our Goods low enough to close them off in the season. But when, as in this case, by circumstances over which we had no control, our store is closed and stock locked up for four of the best weeks in the season in consequence of other parties, it becomes necessary to close off the Goods and we proceed to do it.

It is not, neither has it been our intention to leave this town, and notwithstanding all the opposition which the *Original Haverhill Cheap Store* has received from certain competitors, facts have transpired connected with the transactions of the past four weeks which, had we been intending to leave, would have decided us to stop here permanently.

The announcement of the sale was signed "Rowland H. Macy, Agent," and from this time onward the name of R. B. Macy was absent from the store's advertising. It is impossible to determine for whom Rowland Macy was supposed to be acting, but it was probably for creditors. Whatever the explanation, the term "Agent" was dropped before the end of 1852.

The underlying hint that financial difficulties had led to the temporary closing finds confirmation in the public notice which appeared in January, 1852. Referring to the twenty-day sale, Macy stated:[7]

We have been enabled by this sale to carry out all our calculations, and now find ourselves in a position to go into the market with the money as usual, and it will be our endeavor to place before our customers a constant successions [*sic*] of bargains from this time onward, and when the Spring Trade opens we SHALL HAVE the EARLIEST STYLES at the LOWEST Cash Prices.

It having been suggested by some that our Store was only temporary, we would call *Particular Attention* to this: That we now proceed to lay out our business for a period of TEN YEARS, and if FAIR TRADING and LOW PRICES will sustain us, we have no fears for the result. We believe emphatically in Large Sales and Small Profits.

Thus, like certain modern governments, Macy had a Ten-Year Plan. But the best-laid plans of mice and men sometimes went agley in the 1850's as they did in Robert Burns' time and do today.

Early Macy Policies

The advertisement reproduced here, published exactly a year after the store's opening, contains an extremely interesting and explicit statement of the policies to which Macy claimed to adhere during the entire period of his experience in Haverhill.[8]

In view of the fact that Macy's Haverhill store eventually failed, owing substantial sums of money, it is probable that he did not apply up to the hilt his policy of buying for cash. It is possible, of course, that he borrowed money with which to make purchases on a cash basis. However that may be, all the evidence indicates that he followed strictly his announced policy of *selling* for cash, and it is perhaps significant that a number of other stores in Haverhill adopted the same policy within a year or two after the opening of Macy's "Original Cheap Store."

There is reason to believe that Macy carried out to the letter his avowed one-price-to-all policy. It was a policy which, as shown later in detail, was not new, either in the United States or in Europe, but it had not received widespread attention, nor was it featured so prominently by the few other merchants of the period who asserted that they followed it. The reference to shopping by a child comes, directly or indirectly, from a statement in George Fox's *Journal*[9] and is strong evidence of the influence of Macy's Quaker background upon his price policy.

The last paragraph of the advertisement shown here adumbrates the future Macy policy of underselling. Later it was amplified. Thus, in November, 1852, Macy copy asserted: "We are not to be undersold at any rate, Boston not excepted. The very smallest profit will be asked on each article, and the lowest price always named first."[10] A fuller discussion of this point in 1853 threatened that Macy would not only match the lowest prices but might cut under them:[11]

Particular Notice

One or two Dry Goods merchants in this town are in the habit of taking advantage of my one price system in this manner: — Knowing that I have but one price, and finding that customers are determined to *come here*, they, as a last resort, tell them to get our lowest price (which they

MACY!!!
Haverhill CHEAP STORE!
Ever Onward!! Ever Upward!!!

English, French and American

DRY GOODS.

1. We buy exclusively *FOR CASH!!!*

2. We sell exclusively *FOR CASH.*

3. We have but one price, and that is named first! No deviation except for imperfection!

THESE are the three great principles upon which we base our business. Buying *exclusively* for cash, we keep our stock in constant motion and are having new goods from New York, Philadelphia and Boston *every day.* It also enables us to procure many of our goods under the market price, and our customers have the advantage of these bargains for this reason, viz:—selling exclusively for cash, we have no bad debts on our books, consequently our good customers do not have to pay them in the shape of extra profits.

By adopting one price and never deviating, a child can trade with us as cheap as the shrewdest buyer in the county. Following out these three great principles as we do, to the letter, we return the public many thanks for the generous manner in which they have sustained us, and it shall be our endeavor, as it ever has been, to merit your most liberal patronage.

Taking "*Onward and Upward*" for our motto, we challenge any competition —confident that we cannot be undersold—and with a larger and better stock (bought exclusively for cash) and with a constantly increasing patronage, we govern ourselves accordingly.

Particulars next Week.

CASH POLICY IN 1852
Example of Macy's advertising in Haverhill

MACY'S NEW GRANITE STORE.

AS SEEN FROM THE HAVERHILL POST OFFICE.

THE largest and most extensive Dry Goods Store in Haverhill. The original Haverhill Cheap Store, where goods are sold entirely for cash—always at a small profit and invariably at one price!!!
We removed into our *new store* Nov. 16th, and have received this week,
  100 Pieces best Hamilton and Manchester De Laines, 12½ and 14 cts a yard.
  100 pieces Dark Prints 10 cts a yard.
  100 do Fast colored dark prints, 6¼ cts a yard.
  20 Bales sheeting 6¼, 6¼, 6 3-4, 7 and 8 cts a yard.
  A fine assortment of Alpaccas, Lyonese cloths, Thibets &c selling very low.
  A good assortment of Shawls very cheap.
  100 wrought collars at 4 and 6¼ cents each.
  300 Linen Hdkfs from 5 cts and up!!
  Cloak goods and Dress silks very low.

d25   R. H. MACY.

Christmas and New Years.!!!

AT MACY'S New Granite store you will find a good assortment of Toys all prices.
If you wish to present a friend with a nice Collar, under Hdkf, Embroidered Hdkf, or anything in that line, there is where you will find them right. d25

MACY'S HAVERHILL STORE, 1852

The "New Granite Store," which is still in existence

can easily do as we have but one,) and they will sell them less. This would do very well if we were in the habit, as they are, of extorting from one customer what we lose on another, and we should have nothing to say. I wish customers to distinctly understand from this time forward that when such inducements are held out and I am convinced of it, I will sell the *article in question* so low as to put all competition on that article at rest at once!! I sell *all* my goods at a small profit and serve all customers alike — sell all the goods I can, and do not mean that any one shall take advantage of my method of trading, which I consider the only honorable way in which the retail business can be done.

R. H. MACY

June 4, 1853

Here, indeed, is a foretaste of the policy which was to lead Macy's New York store into some bitter price wars. The militant spirit of competition which this advertisement reflects has been an outstanding characteristic of the New York store during at least the past two generations, although no one in the present Macy organization ever saw that "Particular Notice."

Methods of Operation

Instead of purchasing his merchandise from jobbers and wholesalers, Macy claimed to buy directly from importers and manufacturers, thereby eliminating one series of middlemen and adding to the savings which he claimed to achieve by purchasing for cash. The sign which was painted on the side of Macy's store proclaimed the fact that he sold at wholesale as well as at retail, and this tends to support his assertion that he was eliminating the wholesaler by buying directly from the manufacturers and importers. However, Macy's volume was too small to justify much direct buying, and a place like Haverhill could hardly support much wholesale trade.[12] All the other evidence indicates that he concentrated on the retail end of the business. Everything considered, the wholesale end of the business must have consisted mainly of big talk.

Macy repeatedly asserted that he personally bought goods in the Boston and New York markets. Indeed, he stated on several occasions that he spent about half of his time in picking up bargains.

The advertisements indicate, too, that many of his goods were acquired at dry goods auctions and at sales of bankrupt stocks. Buying of this sort would certainly demand personal attention and skill. Far from trying to hide the fact that he was handling bargain lots of merchandise, Macy boasted of it. To a considerable extent he seems to have carried the kind of stock that is now frequently sold in bargain basements, appealing very definitely to the customers who sought low prices.

While the practice of guaranteeing a customer satisfaction or refunding money for returned merchandise was not developed to any extent at that time, it is interesting in the light of recent developments in testing merchandise that Macy made the following claim at the end of 1854: "A print or gingham is never warranted from this establishment unless it has been thoroughly tried, the colors found to be perfectly fast." At the same time he also asserted: "Anything that I sell for a Linen Hdk'f I will warrant all linen." [13]

A clue to Macy's method of stock control is to be found in a descriptive booklet which he put out at the end of 1854: [14]

My store is conducted systematically throughout. There is but one mark on the Goods, and that is the selling mark, and no clerk in my store knows any other mark but that.

The whole stock is examined thoroughly every few days, and new prices put upon whatever is not selling satisfactorily. By this means the whole stock is kept thoroughly clean, and no old goods allowed to accumulate.

It is obvious, however, that goods did accumulate, for Macy had periodic "closing out" sales. The expression "closing out," incidentally, did not then have its modern connotation but referred simply to what we should call today a clearance sale, designed to move out old stocks of merchandise.

The business seems to have expanded rapidly after the temporary closing in 1851. In November, 1852, new and larger quarters were occupied at 68–74 Merrimack Street, only a few doors from the original location (see illustration opposite page 21), and there were repeated references to the growing size of the business. In August, 1854, the store quarters were enlarged. The advertising clearly indicates that Macy increased the variety of goods handled, adding shawls, bonnets, a limited line of underwear for women and children, fancy soaps, perfumes and toilet water, fans, fancy baskets, toys at Christmas time, and even parasols. Discernible in this list is a definite tendency to go beyond mere textile lines during the course of four years, but the volume of business done was apparently too small to justify a clear-cut departmental organization. There was nothing new about the sale of "fancy goods" and "notions" in a dry goods store, and, if the concept of a department store was taking shape in Macy's mind, its realization was still long years ahead.

The following quotation from an advertising pamphlet gives a brief insight into the system of handling sales transactions: "All money taken in this establishment goes through the Cashier's hands by tickets, and any mistakes are almost impossible." [15] In other words, the store was beyond the simple stage in which the proprietor merely put receipts into a money drawer and noted transactions in his daybook or blotter. Employees were waiting on customers, and, to check mistakes or dishonesty, they had to write out a memorandum of the sale. The printed sales check had not yet been invented, but the inevitable red-tape of modern business was already showing its exasperating head.

How Macy managed to supervise operations is not clear. He himself apparently did most of the buying and was consequently out of town a great deal. There is reason to believe, moreover, that he personally wrote the store's advertisements. Evidently he had an assistant who could superintend the business in his absence, but we know nothing of the store's organization except that he had a number of employees, including one "Sales-Woman" and a boy.[16]

Those who think of the American decimal system of coinage as having supplanted the inherited English system shortly after the American Revolution may be surprised to learn that many of Macy's prices reflected the entrenched custom of thinking in terms of foreign coins. Thus, prices were sometimes quoted in shillings (computed in New England at six to the dollar or 16⅔ cents each), and frequently items were advertised at 6¼ cents and 12½ cents per unit. In part the explanation lies in the persistence of established custom, but there was also a more practical reason. American silver coins were undervalued at the time and tending to pass out of circulation. The local circulation requirements were met by Spanish fractional silver — the quarter (25 cents), the eighth, called ninepence (12½ cents), and the sixteenth, called fourpence ha'penny (6¼ cents). Apart from a few "pistareens" (17 cents), no coin existed for the New England shilling, but prices were often quoted in shillings and pence until the Civil War brought an ample supply of fractional paper notes to fill the need for small decimal currency.[17]

MACY ADVERTISING

One of the notable features of Macy's store was extensive use of newspaper advertising. When other stores were devoting a column inch or two of space to their announcements, Macy employed a half column and even a full column, and scattered smaller advertisements in other parts of the paper. Many merchants of the period were content to use newspaper advertising for a limited period only at the beginning of each season and even then to allow the copy to appear unchanged week after week. Macy advertised the entire year round with hardly a break and often ran his advertisements in both the Essex *Banner* and the Haverhill *Gazette* instead of employing only one medium. After the first year he made frequent changes in copy, giving his advertisements a note of freshness which was woefully lacking in most of the advertising of his competitors. During the year 1854 he inaugurated a series of advertisements which were changed each week and headed "Macy's Weekly Dispatch." These weekly announcements mentioned tempting new arrivals of merchandise and featured particular lots of goods which offered attractive values or which were being closed out at greatly reduced prices. This step seems to have been a distinctly original idea, and it indicates that Macy keenly sensed the news value of fresh merchandise.

A distinctive characteristic of Macy advertising after June, 1851, was the use of a trade-mark, a drawing of a cock or rooster. From its beak flew a ribbon which bore the legend "THE ORIGINAL." There is nothing to indicate the exact significance of the emblem.

The cock was classically dedicated to Mercury because it summoned men to business by its crowing. Possibly it was meant to suggest that Macy intended to be the cock of the walk in Haverhill. Certainly there was plenty of crowing in the text of his advertisements.[18]

Whatever the meaning of the trade-mark, it unquestionably made Macy advertisements stand out in a striking manner. This feature was a distinct advantage in a period in which newspaper advertising rarely contained any illustrations at all and when publishers habitually massed most of the advertisements on one page, so that all looked very much alike.

One appearance of the Macy rooster smacks of modern publicity methods. In the issue of the Haverhill *Gazette* of November 19, 1853, the familiar Macy symbol appeared at the head of a jubilant editorial on the victory of the Whig party at the preceding Monday's election. No explanation of the arrangement was forthcoming and no mention was made of the name Macy, but placed squarely on the opposite page was the same rooster topping a Macy advertisement which bore the headline "STOCK MARKED DOWN!! A Regular Clear Out!" Was it an innocent printer's mistake or a sly dodge to gain attention?

To make his advertisements more conspicuous, Macy employed large block headlines and subheads in a manner which other merchants rarely used. The modern observer is bound to be struck by the contrast between the typical Macy advertisement of this period and the announcements of competitors. Macy's copy was lively, interesting, and informal. It reflected a talent for modern methods of publicity which was apparently unique at the time and which we find again in the early years of the New York store. There is little doubt that the man who wrote the copy was Rowland Macy himself.

It would be a pity to drop the subject of Macy's advertising without quoting, as an example of the personal element which was usually present, the following barbed paragraph which Macy flung at a competitor in 1854:[19]

N. B. Am glad to notice that one of my neighbors has concluded to use no deception in his business, and *give good measure*. Room for more improvements yet!! For instance, instead of copying my advertisements, get up one of your own!!

The inclusion of personal opinion in the copy may not have added to sales volume, but it certainly gave spice to Macy advertisements. It would be unfortunate, too, to close the subject without giving a longer example of Macy copy:[20]

Macy's Weekly Dispatch

R e c e i v e d   t h i s   W e e k .

WEDNESDAY MORNING, Oct. 11, 1854

Great Bargains at Macy's this week!

Although we are proverbially modest, we cannot but feel flattered when we look back upon our four years' experience in the Dry Goods business in this town, and notice how closely our every act and motion has been followed by others in the trade. When we came here four years ago, the Dry Goods business was done under what is called the "old fogy" system. Dealers bought their Goods of regular Jobbers in Boston, at a profit of from 25 to 50 per cent and sold them to their customers in this vicinity at enormous profits taking pay in due bills, orders, &c. &c. There was no regular price for anything, and the most ignorant were the most imposed upon. We claim to have broken down this *cut throat* business, and by *selling goods at one price — selling them cheap* — serving all alike, buying where we could buy cheapest (being perfectly independent in that respect) we claim to have made the business here *respectable*. Then there was a monopoly in the business. It was in the hands of two or three parties, who took the ground that interlopers were not wanted, and had no right here. We think we have been instrumental in proving to these gentlemen that "some things can be done as well as others," and we think we are willing this day that in *this*, as in every other improvement of the age, it is an inevitable law that the whole community must share its blessings.

We have received many new goods this week — New Thibets, Lyonese, Low Priced Prints, Plaids, Black Silks &c., which we are selling very cheap — Do not fail to look in at MACY'S this week, for we have some GREAT BARGAINS, and no mistake.

Lowest Prices always named First.

R. H. MACY

Competitive Tactics

It is already evident from the quoted excerpts of his advertising that Macy encountered stiff opposition from competitors in Haverhill. Naturally they resented the intrusion of another dry goods firm in a market which apparently was already adequately supplied, and they were especially antagonistic to a newcomer who employed aggressive tactics and almost unprecedented policies in his efforts to establish a store.

One fairly reliable indication of the impact of Macy's methods upon Haverhill business is the large extent to which they were imitated. Macy set a fast pace which would be difficult to match, but his rivals lost little time in responding to the challenge. Thus, Thomas H. Merritt, Jr., who had opened a small dry goods store early in 1851, began to refer to it as a "Cheap Cash Store" only a few weeks after the first Macy advertisements appeared. Soon Abel Page, Ebenezer Porter, and James E. Ames (successor to Ezra C. Ames) all began to claim the lowest prices in town. Of course, it is impossible to determine now which of the many advertised claims and counterclaims were well founded and which ones were simply hot air aimed at a supposedly gullible public. Macy unquestionably placed more emphasis upon low prices than his competitors did.

Within twelve months Merritt dropped out of the running, but the other competitors continued the race, gradually increasing both the quantity of their advertising and the magnitude of their claims. There was more imitation, too. When Macy vacated his original location for larger quarters, S. P. Bradley promptly moved in with a "Cheap Cash Store," advertising that he had one price only, bought his goods mostly in New York at low prices, and would sell them "as cheap as the cheapest."[21] Abel Page likewise moved his store close to Macy's and announced (June, 1853) that his mottoes were "To keep the Best Assortment, and Never to be Undersold," while Ames attempted to outdo the rest by proclaiming that his was "a truly 'Cheap Cash Store.'"

Macy eventually met such imitative tactics by claiming to sell goods at prices a definite percentage lower than those of his rivals.

Thus in January, 1854, he characterized certain of his prices as "20 per ct less than the market price." [22] And as if that phrase left some doubt as to what he meant by market price, Macy subsequently clarified his intentions: "I pledge myself to sell the same [articles] 20 per ct. cheaper than they can be bought at any other store in this town." [23] On another lot of goods he claimed to be fully 25 per cent under the market price. Usually such declarations applied to a special lot of goods for a limited time, but later he announced that he intended "to be full 10 per cent under the market price on all domestic goods throughout the season." [24]

It must be said in support of Macy's claims that his advertisements from the beginning listed definite prices as evidence of the bargains he was offering. This in itself was unusual at the time, and it is probably significant that the other Haverhill merchants rarely quoted a price, contenting themselves with such vague claims as "best bargains in town," "as cheap as the cheapest," and "prices which can't be beat." Those who did not adhere to the one-price policy were thus free to make the price fit the customer. If Macy's prices had not really been low, he would not have dared to publish marks for his competitors to shoot at. He himself intimated more than once that competing firms could not match his prices because they were not free agents, being obliged to take orders from wholesalers to whom they were heavily indebted or who owned them outright; thus: [25]

> Not being situated as some Dry Goods dealers are in town, I am pleased to say that I can act perfectly independent. Those of our dealers who are kept going out here in the "rural districts" for the special benefit of certain Importers and Jobbers in Boston and other localities, cannot do so, but have to take their cue from others. I buy my goods where I can buy best, especially at Auction, at the present time, when our largest importers are putting their best goods in at auction to be sold to the highest bidder for Cash.

None of Macy's rivals ever published a denial of such charges, but one of them did attempt to retaliate by insinuating that Macy's merchandise was of poor quality. In advertising a stock of goods A. Page & Co. asserted that it was "not composed of refuse and almost worthless AUCTION GOODS" — a direct slam at Macy.[26]

Page, indeed, was the only Haverhill merchant of the period who came near matching Macy in originality. In July, 1853, he announced a policy which departed radically from prevailing retail practice: "Ladies may be assured of finding good bargains and all goods as represented or the money refunded." [27] This constitutes one of the first money-back guarantees on record in America, and the fact that it was not repeated or imitated suggests that it was too startling an innovation to catch hold. Apart from this single instance, Macy's rivals were content to follow routine methods and to copy only in part the progressive measures that Rowland Macy introduced in Haverhill.

Queequeg Dies Game!

One gathers from the frantic closing-out sales which were advertised at the end of 1854 that all the dry goods stores in the Haverhill area were finding the competitive pace difficult. In part this was caused by the general financial stringency and depressed trade which had developed in the country at large after four rather prosperous years. Macy ran a full-column advertisement in the Haverhill *Gazette* with large block-letter headings announcing a bona fide closing-out sale at cost prices, offering the following explanation: [28]

Owing to the lateness of the season, the present stringency of the money market, and the desire to close out my stock of Goods which is about $18,000, I have fully determined to reduce it to one quarter of that amount, and shall commence this Monday Morning to close every article in my store at the actual cost. . . .

During this whole sale, only ONE PRICE will be named on any article, and that shall be the actual cost from the Invoice Book, as every article in the store is numbered and invoiced.

In an advertising booklet which he published at this time Rowland Macy looked bravely to the future:

Having built up my business in Haverhill by doing it strictly on the *One Price* system, and *exclusively for cash* — buying for *cash* and *selling cheap* — I intend to lead on; and altho' I take to myself the credit of battering down and exploding the old system in this town, yet there is room for many improvements, and they will be adopted by me from time to time, as required; and nothing will be left undone in the future to keep my store where it is *now*, at the head of the Dry Goods business in Haverhill.

It was a stalwart attempt to whistle in the dark, for we know from what followed that failure was staring Macy in the face. He kept up a brave pretense of doing business as usual during the early part of 1855, but in July the following advertisement appeared:[29]

> Having made arrangements to add some other departments to my business the coming fall, it becoming absolutely necessary that I should get my stock reduced to the lowest possible point before that time, I shall commence to sell, on Thursday, July 5, every article in my store at the actual cost, except styles of goods that I do not wish to keep even until another season, and they will be closed out at 10 per cent less than cost.
>
> N.B. As a further inducement to our customers to increase their goods now, an additional discount of 5 cents on the dollar will be made in every trade amounting to over $5, during this sale.

The explanation of the sale was, of course, a blind. Under date of July 30 Macy announced that he had sold the store to E. F. Cushman, and thereafter it was conducted by Cushman under the name of "R. H. Macy's Old Stand," with the Macy rooster prominently displayed in the advertising. There was no help to be had from Rowland's brother, for Robert had given up his own store in Boston in 1853 and gone back to F. A. Jones & Co. as a clerk, probably because his own venture had not succeeded.

Rowland Macy's Haverhill venture was unquestionably a failure. When he opened his New York store three years later, a credit report stated that the bankrupt merchant had offered, in the settlement of the Haverhill store's affairs, to compromise with creditors for 50 cents on the dollar and finally settled for 20 to 25 cents. Out of the wreckage Macy somehow managed to rescue two or three thousand dollars, a fact which simplified his problem of getting a livelihood in the immediate future but stood as a blot on his credit record for more than ten years.[30] This time there is no question about the outcome of Macy's venture: it was an unmistakable failure.

The trouble, apparently, was not that Macy's ideas were inherently faulty but rather that they were being applied in the wrong place at the wrong time. The combined population of Haverhill and Bradford in 1855 was only slightly more than 9,000 inhabitants.[31] Granted that considerable trade was to be derived from the surrounding territory, it seems obvious that there was not sufficient business in the community for five or six prosperous dry goods stores, especially when there was considerable competition from firms in Newburyport, Lawrence, and Boston. In view of the restricted market in which he was operating, the aggressive advertising Macy employed could hardly yield sufficient returns to pay for itself. Possibly both the cash and one-price policies were too advanced for Haverhill, for neither was well suited to a Yankee community which was still agricultural in outlook. Applied in a large city like New York, Macy's methods probably would have succeeded — in fact, they did succeed there only a few years later — but it is significant that the kind of advertising which he used and the scale on which he used it were not to be common even in New York until the 1860's and 1870's.

Macy had failed, but he was not daunted. In *Moby Dick* there is a remarkable description of the scene in the *Pequod's* forecastle as the South Sea Islander, Queequeg, lies dying of fever. Since the book had appeared in 1851 and dealt with whaling, Macy may well have read it. Poor Pip supplied a weird commentary: "Oh for a game cock now to sit upon his head and crow! Queequeg dies game! — mind ye that; Queequeg dies game!" Like Queequeg, Macy was as game as the cock chosen to symbolize his business. Like Queequeg, he was down but not out. He had met adversity before and knew that he would meet it again. Like his contemporaries in American business, he was full of courage, energy, and resource. A failure simply meant that one began anew.

Westward Again

For a while Rowland Macy was at a loose end. He continued to live in Haverhill until the close of 1856, but he soon attempted to establish himself as a "stock and exchange broker" at 18 Congress Street, Boston. We have no evidence to indicate what particular kind of brokerage business he was doing or how the venture turned out.[32] Late in 1856 or early in 1857,[33] however, Macy went to the booming town of Superior City at the head of Lake Superior and established himself as a money and real estate broker. The Soo Locks had just been opened, and he apparently was one of those who hoped to profit from the growth of a new city, the geographical location of which promised to make it a second Chicago at the western terminus of lake navigation. Until a few years ago, there was a house in Superior which was supposed to have been built by Rowland Macy. Possibly he intended to settle in the town. Whatever his intentions, the financial panic of 1857 put an end to profitable real estate speculation. Once again, Rowland Macy turned his back on the West.[34]

While Macy may have managed to acquire some capital during the Wisconsin venture, it seems highly improbable that he did so. He apparently reached Superior early in the spring of 1857, and by August the crash of '57 had started, hitting land values as it hit everything else. Since Macy was back in the East by the fall of 1858, if not earlier, there was no chance for prices to make any substantial recovery before he left Superior. With good luck and some exceptionally rapid moves Macy might have escaped serious loss, but if he succeeded in making any money in Wisconsin, why did he leave it so soon?

How unpromising Macy's prospects must have appeared in 1858! He was thirty-six years of age. Behind him lay a career checkered by many changes, indifferent success, and even actual failure. It was not an unusual pattern for the times. Bankruptcy was a common experience, and the fundamental business changes of the period inevitably led men to shift from one enterprise to another and to try out new locations. Even so, the most successful men of the time usually pursued a single goal. Vanderbilt spent his whole life in transportation. A. T. Stewart and Eben Jordan specialized in the dry goods trade. McCormick's activities always centered in the mechanical reaper. Jay Cooke never left the field of finance. Behind Macy's chopping and changing there seemed to be little reason beyond the desire to try something new.

Looking at Macy's early career, a contemporary would probably have considered him restless and incompetent, a man who had shown himself incapable of settling down to one job and working at it effectively. He had made at least four different beginnings in the dry goods business in the East without success. Three times he had yielded to the lure of adventure and the West: first, as a whaleman to the Pacific; secondly, as a 'forty-niner to California; and lastly, as a land speculator in Wisconsin. Now he was again in the East looking for a new start.

It was not Macy's destiny to be a pioneer after the typical American pattern of the time. His pioneering was to be in the field of business. Instead of exploiting natural resources at the frontier, he was to exploit markets in the New World's most highly developed city by applying new methods to retailing and by creating a new institution. Into that enterprise he was to put the lessons he had learned in twenty-one years of hard knocks. He had gained wide experience in dealing with men. He had learned at first-hand the art of buying and selling dry goods and had developed a rare talent for advertising. At a time when money was scarce and business depressed he had also demonstrated a remarkable ability in acquiring capital for his successive business ventures. A variety of experience had given him resource and imagination, and he had developed a set of forward-looking policies which, in spite of his failure, offered a sound basis of operation. With all this and with his indomitable perseverance, Macy was headed for success once he reached **New York.**

PART II

THE FOUNDING OF MACY'S
1858–1887

CHAPTER III

SUCCESS IN FEATHERS AND LACE

IN 1858 Rowland Macy opened a small fancy dry goods store in New York City and so launched the venture which brought him wealth and fame. Since none of his own records for this period have survived, one can only guess at the problems he encountered and the reasons for his various decisions. Many facts can, however, be unearthed from other sources, and, while some of the details are lacking, we can recover at least the main outline of the founding years. It is amazing — to modest persons sometimes disconcerting — to realize what a plain trail even an unimportant man or firm leaves in the corridors of time.

Although Macy had carried a complete line of dry goods in Haverhill, he began operations in New York by concentrating on a relatively narrow portion of the dry goods trade. Thus he conformed at the outset to the pattern of intense specialization which was characteristic of contemporary business organization. On the other hand, he applied in New York the same business policies that he had established in Haverhill, policies which, as we have seen, differed materially from the ones pursued by most contemporary retailers.

According to one school of historical thought, a man or firm is usually the pawn of circumstance, a product of the times. Success therefore becomes a matter of favorable circumstances and luck. One may, without denying the importance of environment, question this view. It is possible, of course, that fortune, which had shown Macy little favor in the past, now gave him better support; but, unless Macy's highly individual response to circumstances can be dismissed as entirely behavioristic or accidental, the man himself must be given considerable credit for the results. As the story unfolds, the reader is likely to conclude that Macy succeeded in New York not because he was lucky but rather because he consciously adopted a course of action which was especially appropriate to the situation in which he found himself.

THE SETTING

No business, of course, exists in isolation. Each firm operates in a community of people engaged in many activities and influenced in incalculable ways by ideas and events. No historian dares to ignore that environment. But the business historian, because he has to concentrate upon developments inside a firm, is obliged by the limitations of time and space to take most of the external situation for granted and to assume that the reader will provide his own supplement to the story. In the preparation of this book that general assumption has been made, but here are a few reminders intended to help the reader to get his bearings with particular reference to the founding of Macy's store.[1]

As the scene of his new undertaking Macy had chosen by far the largest city in America. New York in 1858 had a population of approximately 750,000 inhabitants, while across the river in Brooklyn lived an additional 200,000 who formed an integral part of the rapidly developing metropolitan city. Nearly two-thirds of the goods imported into the entire Union entered through the port of New York, while a third of the exports left by the same gate. Fully 90 per cent of the dry goods imported into the United States landed there, and, since foreign textiles were still overwhelmingly important in the trade, New York dominated the dry goods wholesale market. It had long been the country's banking and financial center, and its manufactures were steadily increasing, particularly in the production of ready-made clothes.

Fast growth, bewildering opportunities, continuous change — these elements in Macy's new environment stood out. New York was rapidly losing the landmarks and memories of its Dutch and British colonial days as shipload after shipload of Irish, German, and other immigrants joined its native residents. Its aristocracy was swamped by the onrush of an enterprising middle class, and in every phase of its life the city was experiencing a continuous transition. Differing greatly in atmosphere and tempo from the stiff-necked

Boston in which Macy had first engaged in retailing, it presented even stronger contrast with the other places in which he had conducted business ventures: Marysville, Haverhill, and Superior. To be sure, agriculture still continued to thrive on the northern half of Manhattan Island, and the city, because of its feverish growth and activity and because of the number of new arrivals who settled in its midst, possessed much of the flavor of a frontier community. But New York was an aggressive commercial city of tremendous importance in which old firms and new struggled for survival and growth, a metropolis in the full sense of the word and unlike any other city in the world.

The distinctive characteristics which mark it today were already in evidence: the baffling mixture of crudity and sophistication, of callow youth and mellowed age; the intermingling of honest toil and genuine achievement with charlatanism and parasitic life; the bewildering complexity of races, nationalities, religions, and accents; the existence side by side of vast wealth and extreme poverty, of decadence and enterprise; the unexpected blend of crass, self-seeking materialism with sentimentality and lofty ideals; and widespread superficiality, prejudice, and pride all but concealing a developing culture of a high order. In short, New York was then, as now, a perplexing place. To the man who could penetrate the confusion and master its intricacies, and to a few others who were lucky, it offered rich rewards. Towards the rest it was ruthless and mean.

There were certain definite obstacles to the orderly conduct of business in New York. The city's growth was so rapid that it constantly outstripped the development of effective government and checked the emergence of those intangible but powerful stabilizing influences which arise in settled community life. Because of this there was more than an ordinary degree of political corruption, administrative incompetence, and graft. Crime and vice flourished, gangs of hoodlums terrorized certain neighborhoods, and periodic riots broke out in which the lives and property of decent people were seriously jeopardized. Because the municipal government persisted in depending mainly upon volunteer firemen, the city suffered unusual losses from fire. Because of a combination of ignorance and official neglect, it had to endure epidemics of yellow fever and cholera, during which business firms as well as private citizens suffered loss.

One of the worst manifestations of rotten government was the condition of the streets, a matter of real concern to the merchant who wanted women to visit his store. By modern standards it was almost unspeakably bad; even by contemporary standards — there had been little education in personal or public hygiene — it was well-nigh intolerable. Householders and merchants alike complained of the filth — not merely of dust in dry weather and mud in wet, but of the accumulation of rubbish, ashes, garbage, and excrement which obstructed traffic, menaced clothing and health, offended the eye, and gave forth a nauseating stench. In the better residential sections conditions were tolerable because of private effort, but in the lower part of the island, in streets often adjacent to business premises, the municipal street-cleaners made little effort to cope with the problem. Citizens wrote letters, editors fumed, and merchants made voluntary contributions to have the main streets, particularly Broadway, kept reasonably clean.

On the other hand, a vast network of public conveyance was gradually coming into being to meet the mounting transportation problem. Railroads and a number of sailing vessels and steamship lines connected New York with distant points, while ferries connected it with the surrounding communities. Within the city there were horse-drawn streetcars operating on Second, Third, Sixth, Eighth, and Ninth avenues; in addition there were more than four hundred omnibuses plying regular routes, one of which ran along 14th Street and another along Sixth Avenue. As a result Macy in particular benefited by having at his very entrance two systems of transportation to carry people to and from his store. In his first winter in New York he tried to capitalize on this by advertising, "Ladies, if walking is too bad, just take the cars."[2]

The times in which Macy began were in many respects favorable. Business in the United States, after a long secular swing downward from the inflationary peak of 1815, had scraped bottom in the 1840's and was working up to more prosperous times.[3] The panic of 1857 had interrupted that upward movement with a sharp, severe depression, but American optimism and energy were undaunted, and the summer of 1858 saw prices, volume, and profits again moving upward. Factories were rehiring workers, and the construction of railway and telegraph lines was resumed as men renewed their efforts to bind the Union together with iron. Thus Macy opened his New York store at the very time when confidence was returning and the outlook good.

Yet there were clouds on the horizon. As a few perspicacious men realized, perhaps intuitively, the intense specialization in business which marked the period was leading to excessive competition and a woeful lack of coördination between production and distribution. In addition there were doubts about the financial system, especially with regard to the banking situation.

There was political trouble in the air, too. The Dred Scott decision of the previous year had aggravated the dispute between slaveholders and abolitionists. In the summer of 1858 Abraham Lincoln had made his famous "house divided" speech, and later Seward had frankly spoken of "an irrepressible conflict." Northerners with business interests directly or indirectly connected with the South were worried, and all who considered the future of the Union hardly dared to visualize the outcome.

The rank and file of people, however, could not devote all their attention to vague specters of the future. Usually they were thinking about news of a more immediate and topical kind. New Yorkers talked of the Central Park project, the construction of which was just well under way, and of St. Patrick's Cathedral, the cornerstone of which had just been laid at 51st Street, many blocks beyond the uppermost mansion on Fifth Avenue. In August the transatlantic cable had sputtered a few messages from England and then, unmindful of the delirious celebrations over the completion of this link across the sea, had fallen inexplicably silent, justifying all the skeptics. Crystal Palace, the immense exhibition building in what is now Bryant Park, had, early in October, burned to the ground in a magnificent conflagration. And everyone was vehemently taking sides over the "Quarantine Rebellion" on Staten Island where long-suffering citizens had finally wrenched matters out of the hands of scheming officialdom by burning unwanted pesthouses to the ground. Then, on the very day Macy opened, there was a championship prize fight between Heenan and Morrissey in Buffalo, and on West 13th Street a particularly horrible murder had taken place, to which the leading newspapers devoted entire pages of fine print, serving up the gore in a manner which puts modern tabloids to shame. On the same day the *St. Louis* unloaded a million and a half dollars in gold from California, one installment of the stream of yellow metal which, in wind-driven ships, had flowed into New York from the West ever since 1849, whetting the exploitative instincts of men.

Events farther afield likewise caught the New Yorker's interest. The Overland Express had just reduced the time between St. Louis and San Francisco to 25 days, and it brought more news of the "Indian War" in Oregon, additional tales of "Mormon outrages" in Utah. Out in Kansas Territory the settlers had rejected a proslavery constitution, while men along the Atlantic seaboard pondered the possibilities of the American trade treaties just concluded with China and newly opened Japan.

In a world in which so many exciting events were going on, how could the opening of a small fancy goods store on Sixth Avenue attract any notice!

The Start

Macy first opened his doors to New York shoppers on Thursday, October 28, 1858, presumably after several weeks of preparation. It is true that the present firm has for many years celebrated its birthday in February, but that is a matter of business expedience rather than historical accuracy: February is a dull month when sales need the stimulus of what the trade calls a "special event." This slight tampering with the seasonal clock-hands does no serious violence to historical truth. The new enterprise began humbly on the street floor of an unpretentious, four-story, brick building on the east side of Sixth Avenue, one door below 14th Street, at Nos. 204 and 206, with a corner drugstore on one side and a stove dealer on the other.[4]

I use the word "humbly" because Macy's store was small and crude in comparison with many of the large, well-furnished, and well-stocked establishments of the city. It was only 20 feet wide and 60 feet long. Counters extended the length of the store on both sides, and one ran down the center, leaving two narrow aisles. At the rear was a round counter at which kid gloves were sold. Also to the rear were the cashier's desk and an office occupied by Macy and a bookkeeper. Arriving shipments of merchandise were slid down a chute from the front sidewalk to the marking room in the basement. If there were any heating facilities beyond the stove in Macy's office, the memory of old employees failed to record the fact: they recalled only that cash girls, in cold weather, were occasionally allowed to warm their hands at the office stove.[5]

The new enterprise was situated a considerable distance from the customary principal retail market. Fourteenth Street was then nearly as far above the main shopping center of Manhattan as it is below it today. Jostling one another along downtown streets, the city's leading dry goods stores were concentrated in the vicinity of the City Hall, mainly on Broadway between Park Row and Grand Street. A. T. Stewart's "marble palace," for example, was on Broadway at Chambers Street; Lord & Taylor was just completing a "new and elegant marble structure" at Grand Street; Bowen, McNamee & Co. occupied "one of the most costly and extensive edifices of its class in New York" at Pearl Street; while Arnold, Constable & Co. had a large store at Canal and Mercer, only one block from Broadway. Of course, these examples were among the leading dry goods firms in the city, but many others of less importance vied with them along the same thoroughfare, often literally side by side.[6]

Was there any conscious logic behind this concentration of the retail dry goods trade into a small area? To milady in search of a particular ribbon or piece of lace it was, of course, convenient, but had the storekeepers originally had that in mind? Probably it came about with little thought of customers' wishes. Newcomers in the trade doubtless crowded alongside an eminently successful firm, such as Stewart's, expecting to pick up crumbs of trade, hoping by some means to lure an occasional patron away from the rival store.

Macy had chosen a location farther uptown, some distance from Broadway and, if not actually in the residential section, at least on the outer edge of the business district. Both the residential and the business communities of Manhattan had, to be sure, shown a definite tendency to move northward, and it took no great foresight in 1858 to predict that an eventual shift of the shopping area would bring trade to Macy's very door. The fact remains, however, that fully two-thirds of New York's teeming population lived below 14th Street;[7] and, while no figures on trade are available, all the evidence indicates that a much greater proportion of the city's retail trading took place there. Had Macy deliberately chosen his site uptown and away from the established center in the hope of profiting from the movement northward? Did he believe that his location would be more convenient for uptown residents? Or was his choice determined simply by an opportunity to obtain space at a low rental? Whatever the explanation, his location for some years gave him no great advantage and, despite horsecar and omnibus service, probably put him under a definite handicap.

On the financial side, too, Macy seems to have labored under difficulties. His assets were mainly intangible: a varied business experience and some unusual ideas about the way a store should be run. Good petty capitalist that he was, he had managed to scrape together the money needed to put his ideas into effect. Just how he financed the new venture is not clear. He told an inquirer that he had made some money out of his land speculations in Wisconsin, that he had $8,000 in cash and $2,000 in maturing notes due from real estate transactions to put into the business, and that he expected to keep a stock worth about $20,000, to be bought for cash and short-term credit.[8] Naturally he endeavored to present a favorable picture of his resources, but at best it was none too good.

While it may be that the Wisconsin episode had yielded a profit in spite of the panic of 1857, I have already suggested reasons for thinking otherwise. Another and in some respects a more credible source of capital was a loan which Caleb Dustin Hunking of Haverhill is supposed to have made to enable Macy to get started in New York, but nothing definite is known about it.[9] It has also been suggested that Macy's brother-in-law, Samuel S. Houghton, was a partner in the venture.[10] All the available evidence indicates, however, that

Houghton was a clerk in the store rather than part-owner. It is not even clear that he could have lent money to Macy. While he had operated a lace and embroidery store in Boston for a number of years before 1858, his removal to New York in that year suggests the possibility at least that his Boston store had failed as a result of the panic of '57. Certainly if Houghton possessed any substantial sum of money while in New York, the credit sources failed to find it out.[11]

Undoubtedly Macy was financed in part by jobbers and wholesalers from whom he bought his original stock. The dry goods trade was notorious for the amount of business done on long credits — not simply 60 or 90 days but 6, 8, 10, and even 12 months without interest, and frequently a subsequent renewal if interest was promised. Such a credit policy, of course, involved expense and risk, and periodically an event like the panic of 1857 would bring the whole structure tumbling to the ground. Contemporaries noted the dangers in the system, and there were occasional efforts to restrict sales to a cash or short-term credit basis. But, in the wholesale trade then as in retailing now, firms were so hot in pursuit of orders that they grew reckless: easy credit was one of the devices by which they sought to win patronage from a competitor.[12] This situation gave men like Rowland Macy a chance which they seldom hesitated to exploit.

We have direct testimony on this point by one of the men who helped Macy at the outset, J. Maidhof, of Meeker & Maidhof, Importers and Manufacturers of Ladies' Dress Trimmings:[13]

In the Fall of 1858 . . . a short robust but pleasant looking gentleman . . . came to my store . . . , introducing himself as R. H. Macy. . . . I gave him a line of credit of Eight Hundred ($800) Dollars, on Four Months time. I then took him over to see Edward Lambert & Co., a silk and ribbon house [wholesale as well as retail], . . . and they also gave him a fair line of credit on six months. Then I introduced him to the large Ribbon and Feather Firm of G. Rosenblatt & Bro., who also opened an account with him. Then we went to the old firm of Calhoun, Robbins, & Co., the largest house in what is called Yankee Notions, who gave him a liberal credit on three months. After seeing a few more leading houses in the class of goods he proposed to keep, all granted him a liberal credit. With all these houses, I had business relations for years, and it was on my recommendation that they opened accounts with Mr. Macy.

The credit sources, knowing about his failure in Haverhill, hinted in their reports that firms dealing with Macy would do well to observe all precautions. Such reports, however, did not appear until after the opening of the store, when goods bought on time were already on its shelves. It is evident that, unless Macy could convert his merchandise into cash at an early date, he would soon end in another financial jam. As we shall presently see, this fact doubtless had a bearing upon his policy of selling for cash. Certainly it is significant that subsequent purchases were mainly for cash and short-term credit.[14]

The merchandise in which Macy first specialized was known as "fancy dry goods." This term was used mainly to differentiate from staple dry goods the various materials used in finishing dresses and millinery, sometimes called "findings." The scope of the line was apparently indeterminate, even to contemporaries, but it is somewhat clarified by examination of the specific items which Macy initially handled: ribbons, laces and embroideries (including "collar and sleeve sets"), artificial flowers, feathers, handkerchiefs, cambric flouncings, hosiery, and gloves. It could be, and was, extended to include many other items, but for years Macy carried no staple dry goods worth mentioning.[15] In a later chapter we shall see the successive steps by which he gradually diversified the merchandise he sold; for the moment the important point is the narrow range to which he initially confined his efforts. In Haverhill he had maintained a stock worth approximately $20,000, running (though scantily) the entire gamut of dry goods; in New York he expended about the same amount upon a very small section of the same field. The explanation of the change in policy probably lies in his location in an enormous market which permitted specialization and also in the wide selection which relatively sophisticated customers would expect. To provide adequate choice in all branches of dry goods within one store would require a tremendous inventory which very few merchants could afford.

The frequency with which Macy announced "goods from auction" indicates that he acquired a substantial portion of his stock in bargain lots, as he had done for his Haverhill store, at the numerous public auction sales where imported goods were sold for what they would fetch, often well below prices at which an American importer could land them in New York.[16] At the same time he was known to be buying goods from importers and wholesalers. Observers noted that he made most of such purchases from one house, the accepted explanation being that his brother was an employee of that firm. Thus Robert B. Macy, who was connected in an obscure way with the founding of the Haverhill store, also played a part in the early history of the one in New York. The firm with which he was connected there until 1861 seems to have been Rushmore, Cone & Co., dry goods jobbers, 12 Warren Street, after which he was for seven years a partner in Seeligman & Macy, 300 Broadway.[17]

We have very little knowledge of the actual operation of the store during the first few years. Macy reported that his sales for the 13 months ending December 1, 1859, totaled $90,000, revealing an annual rate at the start of about $85,000. Judging from the sales per employee at a later date when we have definite information on the point, the Macy organization must have included about fifteen people. Rent was $1,600 a year. Macy claimed that he paid out $2,800 for advertising during that first accounting period. If correct, this was 3 per cent of sales, undoubtedly a high figure for the time, but probably to be expected during the critical founding year.[18]

Less than three weeks after its opening, the store "was burglariously entered and robbed" of over a thousand dollars' worth of goods, a discouraging blow to one who could ill afford a loss of any sort.[19] At the very end of the first year's operations, moreover, the gas light in a window started a fire which caused a loss of two thousand dollars, fortunately covered by insurance.[20] Notwithstanding these setbacks and in spite of the fact that his prices were considered by rival storekeepers to be too low to permit a profit, Macy considered that he had increased his net worth by $3,000 by December 1, 1859.

He valued his stock of that date at $34,000.[21] The strict accuracy of these figures may be open to some question. Even after discounting Macy's natural desire to make a favorable impression, however, one is likely to conclude that the first year of operations in New York was a successful one. At the same time Macy was not yet on easy street if living arrangements are any criterion. The Macy and Houghton families had combined into one household on coming to New York, as they had done once before in Boston, doubtless for the sake of economy, and until 1862 they continued to live at the same address, 332 Sixth Avenue. Macy at this time had a daughter as well as a son, and if Houghton had any children the household must have been a crowded one.[22]

The important thing for Macy was that the enterprise was going ahead in spite of gathering war clouds, in the face of distrustful credit reports, and contrary to the expectations of rivals who, while admitting that he did a large volume of trade, continued to assert for five years that Macy could not be making much at the low prices at which he sold.[23] The boom which eventually developed during the Civil War seems to have helped Macy, it is true, but such evidence as we have indicates that he was gaining strength in 1859 and 1860 when the widening breach between North and South seriously depressed the New York dry goods trade and brought about a financial crisis in May, 1861. Had Macy's business not attained considerable success at the start, it could not have survived until wartime prosperity brought relief. Surely part of the outcome must be attributed to Macy policies, which were now being applied at the right time and in the right place.

Macy's Business Policies

From the very beginning Rowland Macy pursued certain rather definite patterns of action or business policies which have come down to the present with little modification and which are of basic importance. The major policies are four: dealing for cash only; selling at one price to all customers alike, regardless of bargaining ability; selling at very low prices (in today's terminology, underselling competitors); and aggressive advertising. Even before these four were put into effect another decision of paramount importance had been made, namely, to specialize intensively in the retailing of fancy dry goods. That policy, however, was gradually given up, and the story of its abandonment is so important as to require treatment in a separate chapter.

First as to the cash policy. So far as advertising goes, Macy did not feature selling for cash until he had been in business for two months, but for several reasons it is fairly certain that he started with a definite rule in the very beginning. He had sold only for cash in Haverhill; his financial position practically prohibited the extension of credit to customers; and, when he did mention the policy in his advertisements, he referred to it not as something new but as an established rule of his store. According to his daughter, even members of the family were required to pay cash for purchases; there simply was no mechanism for handling charge accounts.[24]

As we have already seen, however, Macy did not apply his cash policy to buying when he first opened his store. A part of his original stock was bought on time, apparently because he lacked sufficient capital to pay for everything. He was evidently successful in converting his original merchandise into cash at a very rapid rate. Later credit reports, at least, reveal that he made all purchases for cash or very short-term settlements, and buying on credit seems to have been confined to the dry goods firm with which his brother was connected. In part this rapid shift to a cash basis may have been at the insistence of the jobbers, who feared a repetition of the Haverhill failure, but Macy's credit period decreased rapidly as his fortunes advanced. Thus in 1864 the term was 30 to 60 days, and Macy paid up promptly when bills fell due. By 1866 he regularly bought on 10 to 15 days' time.

Of course, even when a firm buys for cash, a few days regularly elapse between the selection of merchandise and the settlement of bills, but after 1866, if not earlier, Macy seems to have made a special point of being entirely free of debt when accounts were closed in January and July.[25] In 1869 the credit sources were compelled, somewhat grudgingly, to admit that he was in good standing with the entire trade and had overcome the early impressions resulting from his experience in Haverhill.[26] On the whole, it is a safe conclusion that from a very early date he carefully observed the rule of buying only for cash. A few other stores in the 1850's and 1860's advertised sales for cash only, but I have found none that emphasized, as Macy did, the connection between cash purchases and low prices. At the same time, he himself never emphasized this relationship nearly so much as his successors have done.[27]

While the first mention of Macy's one-price policy was in an advertisement published nearly two months after the opening, it was undoubtedly applied at the very start.[28] The fact that Macy took the trouble to mention it suggests that it was not universal practice and that it was supposed to benefit the customer. On the other hand, the fact that he could refer to it by name without further explanation indicates that the public was not a complete stranger to the idea, and one can be reasonably certain that many stores applied the policy without publicizing it. The difficulty is that we have no way of knowing the extent to which it was enforced. Many who claimed adherence to the one-price system occasionally evaded it by giving special discounts to particular classes of customers, such as the clergy, milliners, and particular friends. Later on, Macy made no secret of the fact that he allowed special discounts to Sunday schools and church fairs when they bought goods for resale.[29] This, of course, is hardly the same as making special concessions to individual custmers, and was regarded as a charitable move regularly made at Christmas-time. In view of his repeated insistence upon the one-price policy, Macy probably gave it regular enforcement. This conclusion is supported by operating requirements: the one-price policy was virtually a necessity in any store which employed more than one or two sales people, because the general run of employees could not be depended upon to bargain successfully. Whatever the reasons for its adoption, Macy and other merchants harped upon its fairness and upon the injustice of shading prices to a favored few.

Without knowing more about the way in which his rivals operated, it is difficult to be sure that Macy was consciously underselling his competitors. Certainly he was not alone in advertising goods at low prices. Arnold, Constable & Co., for example, used the expressions "much under cost," "at very low prices," and "50 per cent under price." Chas. Heard & Co. claimed prices "full 40 per cent below cost," and Lord & Taylor did not hesitate to proclaim goods "to 50 per cent below regular prices," or "much below usual prices," while Strang, Adriance & Co. advertised goods "greatly under their actual value." The Cash Ribbon House topped all claims with an assertion that its merchandise was being offered at "60 per cent less than the usual prices." In the early years, so far as I know, Macy made no general claim to the lowest prices in town, but he consistently stressed low prices and used such phrases as "half Broadway prices," "25 per cent under market," "half the cost of importation," "less than the cost of manufacture," and "50 per cent under price." [30]

Such claims are meaningless without a basis for definite comparison. No such basis now exists, of course, but it is surely significant that Macy regularly quoted many definite prices in his advertisements, while most of the other stores avoided (with equal consistency) giving specific figures. Unless Macy's prices had really been low, he would hardly have dared to lay himself thus open to attack. There is, furthermore, no question but that Macy's contemporaries considered his prices low. Repeatedly they assured the credit sources that he could not be making much more than expenses, if as much, the implication being that they didn't like his competition.[31]

Before proceeding to a consideration of Macy's advertising policy we may note several other points which, if not matters of fundamental policy, have a bearing on it. First, the continuous succession of special bargains offered by the store indicates that for many years it was concerned chiefly with picking up odd lots of merchandise which could be sold at spectacularly low prices. Far from attempting to conceal this fact, Macy, as in Haverhill, publicized it as a reason for low prices. One advertisement (1860) went into considerable detail:[32]

We go to the package auction houses and purchase [job lots]. . . . R. H. MACY pays cash for all his JOBS in ten days. We endeavor to SELL all

our jobs in ten days! And what is MORE we CAN, we WILL and we DO Sell our JOBS in ten days.
Ladies,
    you
        now see
            how
                we can sell you the
Very
    best
        goods
            the market affords
At such
    very, very
        reasonable, reasonable
            prices as we do. . . .

We shall see later that Macy buyers became so imbued with the special bargain idea that the management had great difficulty in getting them to carry proper stocks of staple merchandise.

Secondly, Macy claimed that he periodically cleared all his stock so as to avoid accumulations of unsalable goods and keep only fresh merchandise on hand. Thus, at the close of his first season he advertised that he had marked all his goods "much below our usual figures . . . , and many articles below cost, to make a regular closing out of them this month." [33] Such sales were featured at fairly regular intervals, sometimes with the notation that the particular class of dry goods (e. g., mantillas) was being closed out for the season, and they may well have contributed to Macy's success by speeding the turnover of his stock, thereby enabling him to offer a constant succession of new goods.

Thirdly, Macy's method of quoting prices deserves a note. A legend of long standing insists that Macy originated the practice of quoting prices ending in odd cents ($.97, $1.34, and so on) and that he did so in order to check dishonesty among sales people. Since customers usually tendered even amounts of currency in payment, the odd price would oblige the clerk to make change at the cashier's desk, thus reducing the opportunity of pocketing receipts.[34] There may be some slight truth to the legend, but another factor unquestionably played a greater part in bringing odd prices into existence. Owing to custom and the shortage of fractional American currency before the Civil War, it was common in New York, as in other parts of the country, to quote prices in shillings and pence. Before 1865, Macy frequently listed prices both in dollars and cents and in shillings and pence in the same advertisement, and in at least one long advertisement prices were quoted exclusively in shillings and pence.[35] In New York the shilling was one-eighth of a dollar or 12½ cents, the coin for sixpence was worth 6¼ cents. Thus the following typical prices, 1/, 1/6d., 2/, 2/6d., 3/, 3/4d., 4/, 4/6d., 5/, 6/, 8/4d., became in dollars and cents, 12½¢, 19¢, 25¢, 31¢, 37¢, 42¢, 50¢, 56¢, 63¢, 75¢, and $1.04, and we find Macy quoting such prices regularly. In other words, prices which appear at first glance to be odd were really even by popular custom and in terms of the coinage used. This conclusion is supported by the fact that Macy regularly advertised in even figures items costing over a dollar both before and after the Civil War. Obviously it is in the higher price brackets that the temptation to dishonesty would be most serious, and any system of odd prices designed to force change-making would, therefore, be applied particularly in the upper ranges. That is contrary to what we find in Macy's until a later period.

Lastly, there is in Macy advertising a suggestion of a money-back guarantee on the goods sold. If such a policy was actually applied, it would constitute an important innovation, although earlier instances in retailing history are to be found. The difficulty is that Macy's statements on the point are not clear-cut, consisting rather of such phrases as "warranted pure linen," "guaranteed a prime article," and "every pair [of gloves] warranted or no sale."[36] These may not mean much. Certainly it is difficult to find examples of explicit guarantees of satisfaction among any of the New York dry goods advertisements of the period before the late 1860's. We have a full and unmistakable declaration of Macy policy in 1875:[37]

> Every article sold in this establishment
> is guaranteed to be what it is represented.

> Any article sold from this establishment
> not suiting, or not being what it is guaranteed,
> will be exchanged or the money refunded
> (as the customer may elect),
> within one week after the purchase.

No customer could fairly ask for more, and it is likely that the policy had been in operation for some years before this advertisement appeared.

One cannot single out any one policy, either in 1858 or today, as the basis of Macy's success. Nor, since there is little magic in systems, can one say that any particular combination of policies led directly to growth and profits. Personalities, favorable circumstances, and luck unquestionably have played a part. But the early Macy policies — particularly one-price, cash, and underselling — dovetailed neatly together and formed a particularly effective basis for aggressive selling. Indeed, Macy had no other basis; he could not possibly offer a better quality or selection of merchandise than his well-established rivals, nor could he match them in convenient location or attractive store equipment. Only through his cash and price policies could he hope to compete. For the store they meant profits; for the public they meant service that was appreciated. Without them the store's history would have been different in fundamental ways.

Early Macy Advertising

The main point of difference, at the outset, between Macy and his competitors lay unquestionably in his use of advertising. Because of the expense involved and his own limited means, Macy could not hope to surpass the amount of advertising done by such large and well-established firms as Lord & Taylor and Arnold, Constable & Co. He could, however, strive to excel his rivals in the methods used to publicize his store. In point of fact, he employed about as much newspaper space as did any of the competing stores. This means that in proportion to the size of his business he was spending at least four or five times as much money as the others — nearly 3 per cent of sales, as we have seen, when the leading stores must have been spending less than one per cent.

While Macy's advertising was impressive in quantity, the feature which made it remarkable was not volume but quality. Macy advertisements had a distinctive character which made them stand out from the surrounding mass of print. It is of at least equal importance that they were usually interesting to read, which was very seldom true of the other dry goods announcements adjoining them. Giving small advertisements high visibility and avoiding dry, stereotyped messages called for perseverance, ingenuity, and skill. Considering the circumstances, the success of Macy advertising amounted to a personal triumph. For it is plain that the man who wrote the copy for the Original Haverhill Cheap Store also composed the early advertisements for the store at Sixth Avenue and 14th Street, and that man must have been Macy himself.[38]

The initial Macy advertising was evidently confined to the sign over the door and some sort of display of goods in the windows, for the first newspaper advertisement which can now be found appeared on November 25, 1858, a full month after the opening. One section of it featured linen cambric handkerchiefs; another was headed, "CHEAP RIBBONS!!! You want them, of course. Go to MACY'S." The third section began, "FRENCH EMBROIDERIES from AUCTION!," while the fourth and most prominent part bore the heading, "FRENCH FLOWERS, FEATHERS, and IMPORTED HEADDRESSES, AT ONE HALF THE COST OF IMPORTATION!!!" After this first Macy advertisement came a steady stream, first in the *Daily Tribune* and subsequently spreading to other dailies.[39]

One gets the impression that Macy saw in newspaper advertising the solution to his initial problem. Without customers his store would soon have to close. It was off the beaten path; it was small and unimpressive in appearance; and only those who actually passed along Sixth Avenue would notice its sign or its window display. There was no way in which Macy could materially improve the location or appearance of his store; nor could he wait until the news of his bargains spread by word of mouth. By resorting to aggressive advertising he could make his store known to thousands of New Yorkers. Some of them could be persuaded to come and inspect his goods. If that did not bring success, nothing would. It would take money, but the alternative was certain loss. It would take time and effort, but until the customers came in streams Macy would have time on his hands.

Conditioned as we are to seeing our newspapers filled with page after page of large dry goods and department store advertisements, we find it difficult to visualize any other state of affairs. Only within the past two generations, however, has such advertising formed a prominent part of the daily paper. In the 1850's and 1860's a New York newspaper might have as much as three or four pages of advertising of all kinds combined, but they consisted entirely of classified advertising; brief, single-column announcements in small, closely packed type — the kind that we see in legal notices and want-ad columns today. Dry goods advertisements made up only a small portion of the total. At the height of the spring and fall seasons a single issue might contain as much as two or three columns of them. Occasionally a Sunday paper would devote nearly a whole page to dry goods. As a general rule, however, the announcements of Macy and all his competitors seldom totaled as much as a single column. In the summer months, indeed, they sometimes disappeared altogether. Extremely rare was any advertisement longer than one or two inches, and not one of them stretched across two columns. Typically they began "At Retail," "A Card," or "Messrs. Blank & Co. announce the opening of a fresh lot of family dry goods," or something equally formal, prosaic, and dull.

To some extent this drab uniformity may have been the result of long-established custom and a widespread lack of imagination with regard to the technique of advertising. More important, however, was the widely observed publisher's rule, said to have originated with James Gordon Bennett, which flatly prohibited breaking a column, using illustrations, and even having large or bold-faced type beyond a two-line initial capital letter at the beginning of the advertisement. The theory behind this leveling restriction was that no one should be allowed to gain any advantage over other advertisers beyond what he could achieve by the use of longer space, more interesting text, or more striking arrangement of agate type.[40] Thus bound in a typographical strait jacket, most advertisers responded by cramming a small space with all the words it would hold. To modern eyes the result is esthetically repelling, difficult to read, and exceedingly tiring in any quantity.

Despite the agate-only handicap, Macy managed to make his advertisements stand out from the gray mass of closely packed newsprint. He did so by employing unusual arrangements of type and white space to attract notice and by devising interesting copy to hold attention and make an impression. It would be an exaggeration to proclaim Macy as the father of modern advertising technique, for there was apparently little continuity between his work and that of later men, but he certainly anticipated most of the uses of the printed word which are cardinal practice today. And we may safely give him credit for smashing the agate shackles which held copywriters in check.[41]

Macy employed a variety of devices in order to attract attention to his advertising. He repeated words and phrases over and over again, thus giving them at least part of the increased visibility that larger type would have yielded. Instead of filling the allotted space entirely full of type, he arranged the text so as to leave areas of white space and make zigzag patterns or narrow columns which would catch the eye.[42] He increased the likelihood that his advertisement would be seen by having it substantially longer than the others or, alternatively, by breaking it up into a series of small, boxed advertisements, now gaining a cumulative effect by placing them in unbroken succession, now scattering them piecemeal among the other dry goods advertisements on the page, so that the reader who skipped half the column would still encounter the name Macy. He advertised oftener than most of his competitors, and he employed three, four, and even five different newspapers when competitors were usually content with fewer. Also he generally avoided dates on which the papers would be relatively crowded with dry goods advertising. Thus he rarely advertised in Sunday papers, he usually waited until the first big rush of spring and fall seasonal announcements had passed before he began his own, and he used newspapers in June and July when most competitors had dropped out of them entirely.[43]

The following excerpt is a fairly typical example of the way Macy often used reiteration:[44]

> ALL ARTICLES MARKED, WAY DOWN
> AT MACY'S.
> WOOLLEN SACKS, marked way down.
> WOOLLEN HOODS, marked way down.
> WOOLLEN GLOVES, marked way down.
> WOOLLEN HOSIERY, marked way down.
> WOOLLEN SOCKS, marked way down.
> WINTER RIBBONS, marked way down.
> WINTER HEADDRESSES, marked way down, . . .

Another interesting example illustrates both the reiteration and the unusual arrangement of type which Macy employed. It might serve as a parody on Gertrude Stein — except that it makes sense:[45]

> OUR
> MOTTO
> FOR
> JULY AND AUGUST
> IS
> MARK WAY
> IS MARK WAY
> DOWN,
> is mark way down, to make a full and regular closing out of our whole stock, if possible, during
> July and August,
> as we wish to commence the fall trade with an entire new
> STOCK OF GOODS.
> COME, COME, TIME, TIME,
> COME, COME, TIME, TIME,
> THE TIME HAS COME.
> WHAT IS TO BE DONE? IS THE QUESTION
> WHAT IS TO BE DONE? IS THE QUESTION
> WHAT SHALL BE DONE?
> WHAT SHALL BE DONE?

MARK EVERY ARTICLE
MARK EVERY ARTICLE
        WAY
WAY
        WAY DOWN
WAY DOWN
TO SOME PRICE WHICH WILL MAKE IT
TO SOME PRICE WHICH WILL MAKE IT
     SELL AND GO QUICK.
     SELL AND GO QUICK.
     SELL AND GO QUICK.
  LADIES,
Ladies, all this has been [done] in a most thorough manner.
OUR GOODS SHALL BE SOLD CHEAP!
OUR GOODS SHALL BE SOLD CHEAP!!
    IN THIS GREAT SELL OUT.
    IN THIS GREAT SELL OUT.

Of course, it was not sufficient merely to catch the reader's eye. Macy had to arouse interest and hold it until he could present his message. So far as one can judge today, it was in this particular phase of copywriting that Macy excelled. Other stores occasionally resorted to repeated phrases and typographical devices to attract notice (though rarely with the particular skill that Macy displayed), but one may search column after column, day after day, without finding anything to compare with the lively spirit and fresh variety of Macy's early advertisements. By modern standards the ideas may sometimes seem crude, the expressions clumsy, the humor introduced with a heavy hand, but it is historically inaccurate to use a modern yardstick. In the light of contemporary practice Macy copy stood far ahead of the rest. Rivals clung to formal announcements which did little more than give the store's name and a list of its merchandise. Macy introduced an informal, personal note, and he occasionally condescended to tell the public something about his store and its policies. It would never have occurred to him to exploit his own views and achievements as John Wanamaker was to do twenty years later, but he understood the need for making copy interesting.

Simply by changing advertisements regularly Macy gained an advantage over rivals who typically used the same copy over and over again, but he went far beyond constant change. He would introduce a humorous touch, or make a reference to the day's news, or resort to a pun or a colossal exaggeration of the kind that nineteenth-century Americans thought funny, and occasionally he even broke out into rhyme. Here, for example, is an early verse, with meter so bad that it is almost good:[46]

HOUSEKEEPING GOODS, EMBROIDERIES, RIBBONS and more
Than I can recount, may be bought in the store
of MACY, of whom, if you'll take my advice,
You'll patronize, seeing he has but *one price*!
In Sixth-avenue, 204 and 206 is his stand
And everything there you look for is at hand.

A longer effort at versification ran in part:[47]

"Westward the Star of Empire takes its way!"
    So does the Star of Fashion and of graces,
Judging, at least, by the vast crowds each day
    Rushing to MACY'S.

Broadway no longer tempts with costly glare,
    With fancy shop fronts and still fancier prices,
Cheapness — if good and tasteful for the fair —
    Is what entices. . . .

"Westward the Star of Fashion takes its way!"
    That it should poise o'er MACY'S is not funny;
'Tis that he SELLS GOODS EQUAL TO BROADWAY
    FOR MUCH LESS MONEY.

No one at the time had heard the term institutional advertising, but advertisements like the ones just quoted show that Macy had a feeling for the concept. Could anything be more modern and institutional than the following?[48]

THERE is an ART or SCIENCE
In spending money, and few know how to spend to the best advantage. Buy the best the market affords. Buy for cash. Buy cheap, and you are wise.
Nos. 204 and 206 6th-av.
Is the place to lay out money judiciously for HOUSE-KEEPING GOODS.
For RIBBONS, TRIMMINGS and FLOWERS,
For the nicest kind of THREAD EDGINGS.
For the nicest kind of LACE GOODS.
. . .
For the nicest kind of LADIES' STORE is at
R. H. MACY'S

A month later appeared another of the same excellence:[49]

C.	O.	D.
	and	
P.	O.	D.
On Which		
	The Principle	
	We Do	
		Business Is
	P.O.D.	
	and	
	C.O.D.	

Which literally means PAY ON DELIVERY and COLLECT ON DELIVERY. By this style of doing business we can sell every article in our store at its proper value, and many articles much less.

During the past two decades Macy's has employed copywriters of great skill and experience to drive the same point home, but all they have managed to do — indeed, all that can be done — is to write subtle and elaborate variations on the same theme. Rowland Macy could not coin such a neat slogan as "It's Smart to be Thrifty," but he could do the equivalent for his own times.

Another advertisement illustrates Macy's use of the pun, the exaggeration, the zigzag layout, and the constant repetition of an important phrase:[50]

SIXTY-THREE CENT SATION!
204 and 206 SIXTH AVENUE,
CORNER OF FOURTEENTH STREET.
63,000 LADIES WITHIN 6,300
MILES HAVE PURCHASED
63 CENT KID GLOVES
AT MACY'S,
WITHIN THE LAST 63 DAYS.
THE DEMAND FOR THEM
INCREASES ABOUT 63 PER CENT
EVERY 63 DAYS.
WE KEEP ONLY ONE STYLE.
WE SELL THEM FOR 63 CENTS.
THEY ARE MANUFACTURED
EXCLUSIVELY FOR US IN PARIS.
WE CONTROL THE STYLE AT 63 CENTS;
WE SELL THEM FOR 63 CENTS.
THEY ARE WORTH A DOLLAR.
WE PREFER TO SELL THEM AT 63 CENTS
THEY CANNOT BE EQUALLED IN NEW YORK
FOR 63 CENTS.
ONLY ONE STYLE   ONLY ONE PRICE

Competing dry goods firms chose to ignore current happenings, so far as their advertising copy was concerned, but not Macy. Late in 1860, for example, he began an advertisement, "ANNEXATION INSTEAD OF SECESSION. We have annexed Maiden Lane [center of the wholesale fancy goods trade] and shall open 14 wagon loads of French and German fancy goods."[51] As the breach between North and South widened, he headed the announcement of a sale:[52]

COINCIDENCES!!
  MONDAY, FEB. 4th, WILL BE A DAY LONG TO BE
       REMEMBERED IN HISTORY!!
At 9 a.m. R. H. MACY
commences his first great sale for February, 1861.

> At 10 a.m. the COTTON CONGRESS meet at MONTGOMERY, ALABAMA.
> At 11 a.m. the DELEGATES meet at WASHINGTON, D.C.
> The two last Conventions to discuss abstract questions. The first deals solely in facts which we now offer for your DIGESTION!!!
> We shall open at 9 a.m. on that eventful day. . . .

When the threat of war depressed the market and caught him with a large stock of toys, Macy managed to rise above his own predicament and the general pessimism with a cheerful piece of copy:[53]

> TREMENDOUS EXCITEMENT!
>
> THE IRREPRESSIBLE CONFLICT!
>
> R. H. MACY,
> Nos. 204 and 206 6th–av.,
> HAVING GONE IN, WAY UP TO HIS NECK, TO WAX DOLLS, CRYING BABIES,
> BABIES THAT CAN'T AND WON'T CRY,
> BABIES THAT CAN AND BABIES THAT CAN'T OPEN THEIR EYES OR SHUT 'EM,
> RUBBER DOLL HEADS (preferable to dough-heads), SWISS COTTAGES,
> FANCY BOXES,
> CHINA FIGURES and 10,000 OTHER THINGS IN THE SAME LINE, including NOAH'S ARK,
> HAS NOW DETERMINED TO GET OUT!
> Not by backing out himself, but by scattering these opposing forces among his customers, not by cannon or sword.
> R. H. MACY relies upon ENORMOUS REDUCTION from the usual prices as the
> GENTLE PERSUADER
> which will not only relieve him, but carry peace and happiness to EVERY HEARTH STONE,
> and LIFT the CLOUD OF GLOOM
> which has hung like a pall over the EMPIRE CITY,
> during the last sixty days.

The very qualities which made Macy advertisements interesting helped to make them convincing. It is unlikely that Macy's superlatives, taken by themselves, carried much weight with readers, for such assertions as "the lowest market prices," "best quality in town," and "largest selection to be found anywhere," were as commonplace and unimpressive in the 1850's as today. What did impress readers, apparently, was Macy's readiness to support his claims by detailed price quotations, an unusual practice which gave readers an idea of the sort of bargains they might expect to find. The steady succession of attractive offerings would inevitably arouse curiosity about Macy's store, curiosity which would be whetted into action by some particularly telling appeal. Unlike his competitors, Macy did not take everything for granted, and when he advertised corsets, for example, he probably dispelled many a doubt by adding "experienced sales women to show and fit them." [54] And few women, after perusing a mass of trite, uninteresting announcements, could fail to respond to such a frank, sprightly appeal as the following: [55]

> Ladies, Ladies,
> We Want Your Money!
> You Want Our Goods!
> We Keep the Very Best!
> We Do Our Very Prettiest
> To Buy Low and Sell Cheap. . . .

In the first few weeks of his advertising effort Macy must have had many qualms, and there may be a hint of desperation in such a plea as "Ladies and gentlemen, please give us a call; our goods are all new. We sell you them at low figures." [56] But, as the insistent repetition of announcements, claims, and merchandise began to have its effect, the first Christmas trade began to roll in. There is no mistaking a Nantucketer's exultation in Macy's salute to the New Year of 1859: [57]

> Trade is good at MACY'S, and they
> are as happy as clams at high water
> at MACY'S. Go, all hands; go in
> together, and be happy at MACY'S.

MARGARET GETCHELL LA FORGE
Macy's first woman executive

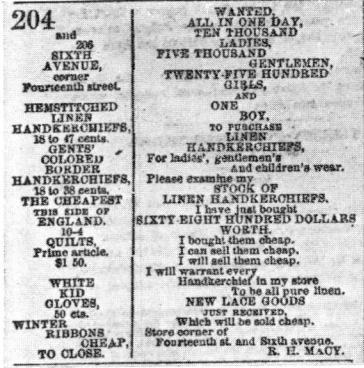
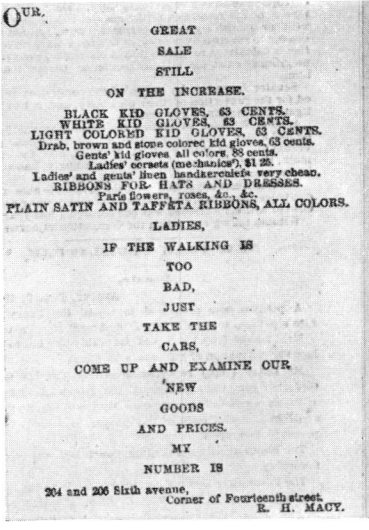
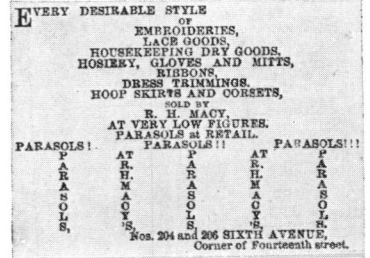
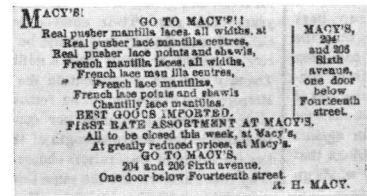

SALES PROMOTION IN 1859
Typical early Macy advertisements

As the business progressed, Macy himself seems to have become preoccupied with other activities and to have left the advertising in less enterprising hands. There is less originality in the copy after 1863, less variation in the attack. The same advertisement sometimes appeared for weeks in succession without change. The war may have been a factor in this, for it drove dry goods prices to fantastic heights and gave storekeepers unexpected profits. After the first months of depression, moreover, the deceptive flush of war prosperity whipped New York trade into lively activity as public spending became prodigal.[58] Thus the stern necessity which first drove the old whaleman to aggressive advertising was no longer present. Macy's central problem was changing and evolving as business problems always do. His store was known, its policies were accepted, and a stream of regular patrons flocked its narrow aisles. The main question was no longer how to draw people into the store but rather how to manage efficiently the growing business. It is a proof of business genius that Macy was able to delegate advertising to other hands and tackle effectively that problem of giving his growing organization the managerial supervision it required.

First Woman Executive

Macy always attributed a large part of his success in New York to one of his employees, a remarkable woman named Margaret Getchell, possibly the first of her sex to attain an executive position in American business. Like Macy, Margaret Getchell was a native of Nantucket Island, and was in fact distantly related to her employer. Born in 1841, she had completed her formal education at the age of 16 and taught school on Nantucket Island for a year following her graduation, after which she taught in Lansingburgh, New York, during the winter of 1858–59, and in the Lawrenceville Female Seminary, of Lawrenceville, New Jersey, during the winter of 1859–60. How she happened to go to work in Macy's is not known. She had lost the sight of one eye as a result of a childhood accident and, as a result, may have felt handicapped in teaching. At best, of course, teaching offered meager compensation and left her idle during a good part of the year. She had already gained a reputation for having a quick mind, and Macy was a Nantucketer and a relative who undoubtedly took seriously the responsibilities which these ties imposed. Whatever the explanation, she seems to have obtained employment in the store late in 1860 or early in 1861.

She began to work in the store as a cashier. A natural aptitude for mathematics gave her an unusual grasp of the intricacies of accounting, and Macy soon promoted her to the bookkeeper's position. Apparently he depended upon her for an understanding of his ledgers for many years thereafter. Finding that she was too valuable a person to be left long in a bookkeeping job, Macy soon made her superintendent of the store, a position in which there was ample scope for her fine personality, unusual intelligence, and obvious talent for administrative work. As superintendent Margaret Getchell supervised routine store operations with the stern vigilance and exactitude of the traditional schoolmistress. However, she managed to do so in a tactful manner which, together with her unfailing fairness and charm, won her the respect and affection of the entire staff. Those who knew her still speak of her remarkable executive ability and attractive personality. Her importance in the history of the store transcends routine supervision. She apparently influenced Macy's policy on many occasions, and we shall see that she initiated several new lines of merchandise in the store.[59]

CHAPTER IV

AN INTERLUDE ON THE EVOLUTION OF RETAILING

It is advisable to turn aside at this point in order to examine briefly the general developments in retailing and related marketing activities in both Europe and America up to the time Macy founded his New York store. Only by keeping the broader picture in view can we realize the extent to which Macy merely followed established precedent and the extent to which he made innovations in business procedure. Every business firm inherits well-established policies and practices, and its contribution is usually in the nature of an alteration in pattern rather than a genuine innovation.

To a large extent our problem is to trace the gradual emergence of the department store during the nineteenth century, but some of the roots lie deep in the past. Throughout the survey we must focus attention upon the developments which have a bearing on retailing today: antiquarian details are interesting, to be sure, but historical effort is justified only if it helps us to understand the present. The real object of this book is to contribute to that understanding. Unfortunately, since most historians have written as if retailing had no place in daily life or even in commerce, we have little precise knowledge about the changes which have occurred in the history of retail trade; we also lack a careful analysis of the forces at work.[1] Some points are reasonably clear, however, and others will emerge from the present discussion. All of them will receive fuller treatment when the Macy story is resumed in the chapters which follow the present search for perspective.

DEFINITION OF THE DEPARTMENT STORE

Since our present object is to distinguish the emerging development of the department store, it is necessary to have a clear conception of the main features by which it is identified. What is a department store? While no two of them are exactly alike and a precise definition is consequently difficult to formulate, there is general agreement about the essential characteristics.

As the name implies, the department store is a retail institution which is organized by merchandise departments; that is, with administrative subdivisions corresponding to physical segregations of merchandise, each one having its own manager and salesforce, with a central accounting system which keeps a record of the income and expense attributable to that particular division of the store. This gives the effect (though not the actuality) of an aggregation of separate stores under one roof, owned and operated by one firm. While buying and selling are done within the individual merchandise departments, certain activities, such as bookkeeping, receiving, delivery, advertising, and so on, are centralized in functional divisions, each of which performs its particular function for *all* departments.

But the department store has no monopoly on the departmental plan of organization. Other types of retail stores are sometimes arranged in the same manner. Large grocery stores, women's ready-to-wear shops, and other specialized retail units are often divided into departments. Hence we must look for other distinguishing features.

An important characteristic, obviously, is that the department store carries many kinds of merchandise. The same, of course, is largely true of the variety store, particularly the ones which have extended their lines of merchandise to include a good many items of wearing apparel, food products, and hardware. But the typical variety store is not technically organized by departments (even though its wares are physically separated into groups) nor does it sell certain types of merchandise that we expect to find in a department store. The latter invariably carries a complete line of ready-to-wear garments and accessories for women and children, dry goods, toilet articles, and a wide assortment of home furnishings (kitchen ware, china and glass, draperies, linens, and the like). It usually carries, in addition, clothing for men and boys, furniture, floor coverings, jewelry, drugs, and often groceries. Certain large department stores, like Macy's, Marshall Field's, and Wanamaker's in the United States and Harrod's in England, can supply almost every material want the average family might have — or could have done so, at least, before the outbreak of the present war.

One may, at this point, recall the perennial general store of the country crossroads or certain suburban supermarkets which stock a wide assortment of merchandise. But the general store's volume of business is too small to make departmentalization feasible; while the supermarket, although it may qualify on the score of the merchandise handled, falls down in that it is mainly an agglomeration of leased departments — independently owned shops gathered under one roof with very little managerial connection — closely akin to the mediaeval fair or market and the oriental bazaar.[2] Moreover, it does not provide the liberal services offered by the typical department store, such as free delivery, charge accounts, generous return privileges, restrooms, information bureaus, and the like. (These services are said to be "free" in that their use ordinarily involves no extra charge to the customer. Of course, their cost is included in the retail price.)

Thus it is difficult to find any one criterion which sets the department store apart from neighboring retail institutions. It is to be identified rather by a *combination* of features, as follows:[3]

1. A large volume of business; the Bureau of the Census includes in the classification only those stores whose annual sales total $100,000 or more.
2. Organization by merchandise departments with some centralization of such operating functions as accounting and delivery.
3. A wide range of merchandise, including ready-to-wear, dry goods, and home furnishings.
4. Catering primarily to women.
5. Location in an urban shopping area.
6. Many "free" services made available.

In addition, since the department store usually buys directly from manufacturers in large quantities, it performs many functions which would otherwise be done by wholesalers and importers. Many large stores even manufacture some of the goods they sell. Thus it is both an integrated and a diversified institution.

There is clear evidence that this combination of features did not appear in either Europe or America until about 1860. The developments after 1860 will be apparent in the rest of the Macy story. The beginnings, of course, are to be found much earlier, so that we must get our bearings by means of a quick survey of retail developments before 1860.

European Antecedents of the Department Store

While American retailing has been shaped largely by American conditions, like all our business institutions it stems from European origins. It is necessary, accordingly, to obtain a brief historical perspective of retail trade in Europe in order to distinguish those features of department store evolution which are of native inception. We want to discover, in short, how much the character of the Macy store originated from within and how much was adopted from other firms.

As intimated in Chapter 1, one apparent antecedent of the modern department store is the mediaeval fair. Merchants gathered periodically at places like St. Denis and Troyes on the Continent and Stourbridge and Winchester (St. Giles's Fair) in England to buy and sell wares of all sorts. But such merchants were entirely independent of one another, lacking even the tenuous bond which connects leased departments in modern stores. The fairs, moreover, were of temporary character, and the trade conducted in them was primarily at the wholesale level.[4]

The pedlar or petty chapman might also be regarded as another antecedent. In the pack which he transported on a horse or on his own back he brought ribbons, laces, caps, needles, purses, gloves, furs, spices, and a general miscellany of small wares to the village housewife. Occasionally he settled down to operate a permanent store, and once in a while he rose, like St. Godric, to be a great merchant, although typically his character was more like that of Shakespeare's Autolycus than saintly. There is no questioning his importance, for, apart from the local market or fair, he was the chief supplier of numerous small communities down through much of the nineteenth century.[5] But he comes closer to being the genetic ancestor of Woolworth's than of Macy's, quite apart from the one-man organization and the peripatetic nature of his business. Even so we shall find him turning up in Macy history later on.

Then there were certain general stores in mediaeval Europe, from the twelfth century onwards, which ought to be considered here. In places like Paris and London the mercers, haberdashers, and drapers were explicitly permitted to trade in all kinds of merchandise, whereas most shopkeepers, because they were engaged principally in manufacturing the articles they sold, were narrowly restricted by gild regulations. Many of the general stores combined wholesaling and retailing operations. The variety of goods they sold was even more extensive than that of the pedlar, and the mercers' bazaars in Paris were called the *paradis des femmes* as early as 1300. Again the resemblance to the department store is mainly superficial: these bazaars carried merchandise which really went little beyond dry and fancy goods, their annual sales were small, the internal organization was so simple as to make the term almost inapplicable, and they offered little of the modern store's service.[6]

The aggregation of retail shops in large buildings, like the Royal Exchange in London or the Paris Halles Centrales, has likewise been suggested as the prototype of the department store because of their resemblance to leased departments.[7] Of course there is no real similarity, any more than there is between the department store and an arcade or the ground floor of the R.C.A. building at Rockefeller Center or any city block of retail stores. The departments of a store like Macy's are linked together by a definite over-all plan, central management, and uniform policies.

In short, nothing bearing more than a superficial resemblance to the department store existed in Europe until the nineteenth century was well advanced. Retailing in large cities like London and Paris took place either in relatively small general stores or in specialized shops such as those of tobacconists, goldsmiths, drapers, hatters, clockmakers, stationers, and bakers. Most of the specialization found in retailing was closely connected with the extreme specialization among handicraft workers which had developed in the mediaeval town: they were often simply workshops. In eighteenth-century

London, however, there were many specialty storekeepers, such as glovers, hosiers, grocers, and chinamen, who manufactured nothing and bought everything they sold. That is to say, they were specialized not only in the commodity handled but also in the retailing function alone, although there were also dealers specialized as to commodity who combined or integrated the retailing, wholesaling, and even importing and manufacturing functions. Of course this particular development was related directly to the extent of the market. Some idea of the degree of specialization by commodities may be obtained from the fact that 492 different trades and kinds of shops were listed in a London directory of 1791.[8] But in England and on the Continent the general store was much more common at the time,[9] and the largest London store in 1800 was that of a haberdasher who had only sixteen employees.[10]

The earliest approach to the department store that I have been able to discover in nineteenth-century Europe is the London firm of W. Hitchcock & Co., who called themselves "warehousemen." By 1839 this concern was organized into twelve separate departments. The merchandise in stock comprised a complete line of staple and fancy dry goods, but in addition one department was devoted to hosiery, gloves, and what we should now call notions (needles, thread, buttons, and the like), while there was also an "horlogerie" department, selling imported clocks and fancy vases. Here, certainly, was a dry goods store exhibiting a definite tendency to go into non-dry goods lines, organized by departments (though we do not know the degree of segregation), and possessing other features that we associate with department stores.[11] Whiteley's, however, was the first London concern to become a full-fledged department store (in the early 1870's), and William Whiteley did not even open his doors until 1863.[12]

Crossing the Channel to Paris, we find nothing before 1860 closer to the department store than *magasins de nouveautés* tending, after about 1830, to grow substantially larger and to branch out into an unusually comprehensive assortment of dry goods and "novelties." Thus the Bon Marché, long reputed to be the world's first department store, was nothing more than a dry goods store of ordinary size in 1838, and it did not come under the presiding genius of Aristide Boucicaut until 1852, when its sales were less than $100,000 per year.[13] In 1844 the Ville de Paris, another famous store of the period, was a giant in comparison, having about 150 employees and annual sales of about $2,000,000. It was evidently organized by departments, but its claim to distinction lay simply in its size, its progressive policies in dealing with customers, and the fact that it sold in one store a variety of dry goods which the public previously had been able to obtain only by going to a number of specialized stores.[14]

Major Movements in Retailing

Before we go on with the background material, it may be helpful to note one point about the way in which business generally seems to have developed. Throughout the history of retail trade (as, indeed, in all business evolution) there appears to be an alternating movement in the dominant manner of conducting operations. One swing is toward the specialization of the functions performed or of the merchandise handled by individual firms. The other is away from such specialization toward the integration of related activities under one management or the diversification of products handled by a single firm.

Specialization has taken two forms — one as to the economic function performed and the other as to the particular merchandise handled. Thus, in late eighteenth-century England many firms which had combined the importation, wholesaling, and retailing of woolen cloth found that the retail end of the business offered more profitable opportunities than the other operations, or that they could purchase from rival firms more economically than they themselves could import, with the result that they decided to abandon importing and wholesaling and concentrate upon the retail function. Similarly, firms which had been handling a general assortment of merchandise, such as silk, woolen, and cotton textiles, dry groceries, and chinaware, decided to restrict activities to one of these lines or even to a part of one of them, such as woolens.

In some instances merchants found it advisable to adopt both forms of specialization, restricting activities as to function as well as to type of merchandise. As we have seen, Rowland Macy began his retail experience in New York with a store which sold only at retail and handled nothing but fancy dry goods, exhibiting a high degree of specialization. There have been periods in history in which the most successful business men turned to specialized activities in a way that amounted to a general movement, not merely in retailing but in all branches of the business world. Some such tendency may be gaining strength today.[15]

The reverse tendency, the swing toward nonspecialization, likewise manifests itself in either or both of two ways: integration of functions or diversification of merchandise within a single firm. Colonial America provides us with a good illustration. Thomas Hancock (who made the fortune which his famous nephew, John, wasted) started out with a retail bookstore in Boston. He specialized both as to the marketing function performed (retailing) and the merchandise handled (books). As soon as his means permitted, however, he rapidly took up the importation and wholesaling of books. That is to say, he ceased to specialize in the retail function, choosing instead to integrate the successive marketing operations.[16] The leading merchants of the seventeenth and eighteenth centuries tended to integrate not only the importing, wholesaling, and retailing functions, but also manufacturing, banking, shipping, exporting, and insurance. In the latter part of the nineteenth century a tendency of this sort was again in evidence as the development of corporate enterprise and holding companies facilitated the integration and coördinating of many activities in such industries as iron and steel, meat-packing, and oil. Later we shall see that the rise of the department store was a manifestation of this tendency.[17]

Diversification, the other type of nonspecialization, is often found at work beside integration. Thomas Hancock, for example, extended his dealings beyond books to include sugar, flour, tea, dry goods, hardware, rum, and many other items, during the same time that he was integrating many functions.[18] And we shall see that Rowland Macy, while integrating importing and wholesaling operations with his retailing, diversified his line to include a wide variety of merchandise besides fancy dry goods. A firm may integrate functions while confining itself to one line of goods, or it may diversify at the retail or wholesale level, that is, without integrating. Where both tendencies merge in the same firm, we have the combination of many activities and a wide variety of goods within a single business enterprise. The modern department store is the product of such a joint movement.[19]

The tendency towards specialization, of course, is opposed to these latter movements, pulling apart into separate firms the activities of integrated and diversified enterprises. Toward the end of the nineteenth century another main tendency became apparent in the movement towards the combination of many similar units under one management, often referred to as horizontal combination. But that is mainly a very modern phenomenon and need not concern us here.

Plainly evident in mediaeval trade, these dominant forces have by no means ceased to operate in modern times. In recent years we have seen, for example, the emergence of such specialized outlets as phonograph record and maternity dress shops; a few exist which sell nothing but neckties, and one is said to specialize in white shirts selling for one dollar. On the other hand, we have the extension of the scope of drug and cigar stores during the past two decades to include hardware, books, and even clothing. At the same time we have seen the retail chain organizations absorb wholesaling, importing, and oftentimes manufacturing functions.

Such shifts in the organization of retail trade are of more than mere academic interest. The rise of a new form of retailing institution like the chain store results in very decided changes in the consumer's shopping habits. It also means profits for the successful innovators, headaches for the competing retailers, and basic readjustments in the operating arrangements of wholesalers and manufacturers. Frequently there are serious implications for the surrounding business district and even adjoining residential property values. New managerial policies and techniques emerge, capital investments shift, workers lose or gain employment, and subtle repercussions spread throughout the community.

In short, the innovation is constructive and progressive in one direction, destructive in another. While we praise successful entrepreneurs like Macy for their contribution to economic progress, we should never forget that their innovations spell ruin for many competing firms. It is unscientific and inaccurate to consider either the destructive or the constructive elements alone, and, apart from selfish private interests, nothing is gained by such a one-sided approach.

There appears to be a regular alternation in the strength of these opposing major tendencies. For a generation or more the prevailing movement is towards specialization, with one firm after another splitting off an activity or commodity upon which to concentrate efforts. Then the tide reverses, and a swing towards integration and diversification takes place. Neither tendency is so overwhelming at any time that instances of movements in the opposite direction do not occur. Nor, as these alternating currents bring forth new forms of retail organization, do they wipe out entirely the older forms. To some extent the new form is an adaptation to new circumstances found only in restricted areas. Then, too, the older units sometimes succeed in modifying themselves to meet the situation. Thus the old and new will be found existing side by side, and while the old may appear to be more numerous, the new institution occupies a strategic position and wields the dominant influence. The pattern of business history is a complicated one, but if we trace the two main threads — specialization (by function and merchandise), and nonspecialization (integration and diversification) — the over-all tendencies which are discernible in the history of retailing both here and abroad will become fairly intelligible.

The developments sketched in the preceding section reveal a very definite tendency toward diversification in certain enterprising retail establishments in both London and Paris as the nineteenth century advanced. This was a kind of unconscious reaction to the amount of specialization which had developed by 1800: enterprising men discerned weakness in narrow concentration or, to put it another way, competitive advantage in broadening the line of goods carried. It reflected, too, the increasing concentration of people and trade in urban centers, the growing availability of capital for retail trade, and the developing skill of business men in managing large-scale undertakings. The specialized shopkeepers suffered from the new form of competition, and in 1843 the *Journal des Economistes* published a petition which denounced as a "horrible" thing the fact that one could, in certain establishments, purchase at the same time stockings, handkerchiefs, chemises, shawls, and silk and woolen piece goods. A prolonged struggle then ensued to restrain the new competition by means of special taxes and legislative restrictions.[20] There was an integrating tendency present, too, for these larger stores were buying more and more of their stocks directly from manufacturers instead of from wholesalers. Probably it was this, more than the diversification, which was crushing the small shopkeepers, because it meant buying on better terms, but it was the diversification which attracted most attention at first, possibly because it was physically apparent. These tendencies toward integration and diversification, too strong to be checked by verbal protests or legislative action, were leading directly to the emergence of department stores (see below, Chapter vi).

Early Retail Trade in America

The evolution of retailing in America forms a pattern which, apart from strict chronology, bears a definite resemblance to that of Europe. Before 1800 there was little specialization in the retail function or in particular lines of merchandise (certain exceptions to this are noted below). Subsequently the pendulum swung fast in the direction of a high degree of specialization in function performed and goods handled by any single firm. Macy's first attempts at retailing took place during this period, and in his narrow specialization he followed the established trend. The movement began to reverse itself about the middle of the nineteenth century when tendencies towards integration and diversification developed, only a few years later than the movement in Europe. Apart from the general store, nothing very much like the department store appeared on the scene before 1860, but in America as in Europe both the policies and organization of retail enterprise plainly moved toward such an institution. Rowland Macy came along at a time when retailing was on the verge of far-reaching change.

The undifferentiated nature of trade in this country before 1800 was especially evident in the settled but sparsely populated country districts and at the frontier, a fact which continued to hold true as the frontier moved westward during the course of the nineteenth century. Whether one was trading with Indians or meeting the needs of outlying agricultural communities, circumstances made it necessary to handle a variety of staple goods such as cotton and woolen cloth, gunpowder, kitchenware, sugar, rum, axes, drugs, and trinkets. Generically there is little difference between the trading-post, the general store, and the pedlar so far as merchandise sold is concerned. Further, the same merchant commonly conducted wholesale as well as retail operations in the same store if any wholesale trade existed in the region.[21] And yet we cannot speak of his operations as diversified or integrated; they were simply unspecialized. Macy's store in Marysville was of this character and accordingly was the proper type for a community at the frontier.

One gets a fascinating picture of the early American store from early newspaper advertisements. The famous piece of copy attributed to Samuel Temple, of Dorchester, Massachusetts, was certainly a parody, published (in 1805) to amuse his readers, but it differed from genuine advertisements of the day in no important respect beyond its superior humor and literary style. This is plainly evident in the following authentic advertisement, published in the *Norfolk Repository* (of Dedham, Massachusetts) at frequent intervals during 1806, which clearly reveals the enormous variety of merchandise stocked: [22]

WHEATON and DIXON

Opposite the Post-Office, in Dedham,
RESPECTFULLY inform their Customers and the Public,
that they keep all kinds of Drugs and Medicines

An Assortment of Paints, such as

White Lead,	High Wines,
Red Lead,	Spirits of Turpentine,
Spanish Brown,	Liquid Blue,
Yellow Oker,	Virdigrise,
Whiting,	Umber,
Spruce Yellow,	Madder,

Pumice Stone,
Black Lead,
King's Yellow,
Prussian Blue,
White Vitriol,
Vermillion,
Rotten Stone,
Indigo,
Aqua Fortis,

Autor,
Copperas,
Allum,
Glue,
Sponge,
Linseed Oil,
Spermaceti Oil,
Paint Brushes.

*An Assortment of Hard Wares
among which are*
a great variety of Lamps,
and all kinds of Nails and Bradds.

An Assortment of Groceries, such as

Brandy,
Gin,
West-India Rum,
New-England Rum,
Molasses,
Salt Fish,
Aniseed,
Stoughton's Elixir,
Raisins,
Figgs,
Chocolate,
Shells,
Molasses,
Pepper,
Allspice,
Cinnamon,
Ginger,
Nutmegs,
Mace,
Essence Spruce,

Lisbon Wine,
Sherry Wine,
Port Wine,
Loaf Sugar,
Brown Sugar,
Hyson,
Hyson Skin,
Souchong,
Bohea Tea,
Coffee,
Flour,
Rice,
Sweet Oil,
Salt Petre,
Coarse and fine Salt,
Pearlash,
Mustard,
Starch,
Windsor Soap.

*An Assortment of Crockery and
Glass Ware.
A large assortment of European goods*

*particularly for the Spring and Summer,
among which are*

Silk and Muslin Shawls,	Dimities,
all kinds of Muslins,	Ribbons,
Blue and Yellow Nankins,	Colonade and Picket Muslins,
Modes and Lutestrings,	Linins, from 2s3 to 5s6,
Patent Cords,	Silk and Cotton Stockings,
Cotton Checks,	Cambric Dimoties,
India Cottons,	Cambricks,
Brace, Coat and Vest Buttons,	Yellow Bandannahs, Fashionable Calicoes,
Tapes, Bobbins,	Silk and Leather Gloves,
Sewing Silk, Twist,	Kid and Morocco Shoes.

*An assortment of Jewelry,
among which are*

Lockets,	and Seals,
Ear-rings,	Handkerchief Pins,
Neck-laces,	Paste Combs.
Scissors' Chains,	
Watch chains,	

A large assortment of Cotton Yarn for Stocking & Weaving.

*The above goods will be retailed as low as at any Store, either in town or Country, for cash down, but no credit.
Dedham, May 6, 1806.*

In populous centers of trade like Boston, Philadelphia, and New York before the nineteenth century there was the same prevalence of nonspecialization as in the back country. To be sure, as the volume of trade increased, there was some division of labor among firms, as a result of which we do find a few men who were retailers and nothing else and others who clearly concentrated on importing and wholesale trade. Likewise a certain amount of specialization developed according to the type of merchandise sold, but this latter tendency was connected primarily with the arrival of craftsmen who specialized bcause the technical processes of manufacture compelled them to do so.[23] The majority of business men — certainly the dominant ones of the period — engaged in an astonishing variety of activities; and nearly all the stores (as distinct from shops where goods were manufactured) handled a general assortment of merchandise, usually mingling wholesale with retail transactions. Moreover, when one does come across an eighteenth-century retailer who seems to have specialized, e. g., the bookseller, further investigation frequently reveals that he also dealt in such commodities as tea, drugs, clothing, and scientific instruments.[24]

To a large extent this spreading of effort, this general unwillingness to focus effort on a small segment of trade, arises from the primitive character of American business before 1800. The market, just beginning to develop, was small in extent, and specialization is impossible unless there is a large market in which to operate. Both on the seaboard and inland, moreover, men were adapting themselves to a new land and rapidly changing conditions. Commerce had not yet had an opportunity to carve out the channels of well-ordered trade, and merchants tried everything that promised a profit or was necessary to the conduct of money-making enterprise.

Another factor was the shortage of specie, which compelled men to conduct a great proportion of their business transactions by means of money-barter (that is, exchanging goods for goods but using money as a standard of value). Anyone intending to deal with a man whose purse, so to speak, contained only a bundle of furs or a barrel of pork, obviously had to maintain a stock of flour, cloth, whisky, hardware, and other daily necessities. And the retailer, in turn, had to use much the same currency when he bought a fresh stock of goods for his store. Of course, accounts were kept in terms of money, and various types of credit instruments were widely used, but final settlement was usually worked out through an exchange, often three- or four-cornered, of goods or services.[25] The frontier retailer, like the pioneer settler, had to be a resourceful jack-of-all-trades.

But there is more to the story than primitive circumstances. Specialization could take place only if trade was concentrated at particular points in large volume, so that a man might carve off as his own field a small slice which would keep him reasonably well occupied throughout the four seasons and provide him with a livelihood. Moreover, it was more likely to arise if the nature of the trade or the goods themselves raised important technical or financial problems which could best be solved by concentrated effort. There is also a close connection between specialization and pioneering with new markets or new merchandise. To make a change requires concentrated effort and attention; once success has been achieved and methods routinized, the need for specialization tends to diminish.

As matters stood in early nineteenth-century America, the relatively sparse population was scattered over a large area; transportation was difficult, expensive, and slow; and marketing as yet involved no novel technical difficulties. In the circumstances, trade tended to remain decentralized and unspecialized. The only way in which a merchant could advance his fortunes was to fit together a variety of functions and commodities, usually dovetailing activities which were related, according to the opportunities he could discern and the capital he could raise.[26] Usually "one thing led to another" in a natural, even inevitable, way. We seldom realize the extent to which individual business firms rely upon the existence of an elaborate external business organization. In an immature economy a merchant has to provide for himself (and often inefficiently) services which can be readily hired in a more advanced stage, such as transporting, banking, wholesaling, and even manufacturing.

Increasing Specialization after 1800

Between 1800 and 1860 America saw the rapid development of intense specialization in all lines of business (by both function and merchandise), and retailing took on differentiation with a vengeance. Naturally the pattern of events was determined by local conditions, so that the general merchant survived in the back country and at the frontier (witness Macy's commercial venture in California in 1851), while he practically disappeared from American cities. This was true not only of those on the eastern seaboard like Boston, New York, and Philadelphia, but also in such rapidly growing western centers as Pittsburgh, Cincinnati, St. Louis, and New Orleans.

It is practically impossible to find a specialized retail store in

America around 1800 (apart from those involving a great deal of technical knowledge or skill, such as a drug or jewelry store), but by 1850 the cities were full of them. Trade at first tended to split into four general lines: groceries, dry goods, hardware, and house furnishings. But these were, in turn, rapidly divided into narrower classifications, with the result that you find in the city of 1850 many separate lines, such as books; boots and shoes; carpetings; china and glassware; cloaks and mantillas; combs and fancy goods; cutlery and hardware; fancy dry goods; feathers and mattresses; furniture; men's furnishings; groceries; hats, caps, and furs; hosiery and gloves; india rubber goods; laces and embroideries; millinery; saddles, trunks, and harness; silks and ribbons; tea and coffee; tobacco and snuff; upholstery; umbrellas and parasols; butter and cheese; and ready-to-wear clothing for men.[27]

We are so familiar with specialized retail stores today that this list has little significance until one realizes that it was an entirely new development in America, one which had appeared in European centers only a generation or so earlier.[28] The dividing lines between the different types, moreover, were quite sharply drawn. A drugstore in those days sold drugs and little else. Sometimes it also carried flavoring extracts and toilet goods, and in St. Louis and certain other western cities it frequently stocked varnish, paint brushes, and window glass. But it did not sell ice-cream sodas, books, toys, kitchenware, magazines, groceries, and articles of clothing, as many a corner drugstore does today. Nor did tobacconists sell razors, candy, watches, or books. Local conditions occasionally led to a combination of two or three lines, such as dry goods and groceries or dry goods and crockery, and dry goods stores sometimes combined carpets and "floorcloths" with regular textile stocks. The strong tendency, however, was unmistakably towards specialization in particular lines of merchandise.

This movement progressed so rapidly along the eastern seaboard that in 1855 a Philadelphia publication described a general store for the benefit of its readers much as if it was presenting a dodo resurrected from a forgotten past. And the same article confidently declared:[29]

Division of trade into distinct branches appears to be in the natural order of things. Even where two or more branches are yet united in the same establishment, there is an avoidance of incongruity — as when fur robes are kept for sale in a hat store. . . . The tendency, in all great commercial marts, is to simplification, and in many cases only a single class of articles is kept by the merchant — as in cotton goods, woolen goods, silk goods.

By 1853 specialization had already gone to such lengths that one New York observer felt called upon to sound a half-serious note of alarm:[30]

The tendency is to a still more minute division, and thus we have a dealer in hosiery, a dealer in lace, a dealer in perfumery, a dealer in pocket handkerchiefs, a dealer in shawls, and a house is just starting to keep nothing but suspenders! We suppose in ten years more there will be an establishment for spool cotton, and another for corset-laces, if such instruments of torture shall then be in vogue.

That this summary statement was no great exaggeration of the tendency is strongly indicated by the testimony of another contemporary observer, a professional historian and a man less likely than a commercial reporter to note gradual changes in the organization of trade. Describing the increased specialization of trade about 1850, Lossing wrote:[31]

One house was engaged in trade in woollens exclusively, another in cottons, another in silks, and another in fancy goods. There speedily appeared another subdivision of the dry-goods business. For example, one merchant dealing in woollens kept only tailors' goods, another goods for women's wear; in cotton, one confined himself to prints, another to white goods; and in silks, one dealt in piece goods, and another in ribbons and smaller articles. Then came a more minute subdivision — a dealer in hosiery, a dealer in lace, in pocket handkerchiefs, and shawls.

Macy's fancy goods business, of course, was an example of this subdivision.

We find, moreover, a decided tendency in urban firms of the period towards specialization in marketing functions as well as in goods handled. Before 1800, as already indicated, it was not uncommon to find one firm performing the whole gamut of distributive functions, but after 1800 there was a noticeable separation. By 1838 the division was so well established that a popular merchant's manual could assert: "The mercantile community is divided into two leading classes — wholesale and retail dealers. . . . Had the wholesale dealers attempted also to retail their goods, they could not have given that undivided attention to any part of their business so necessary to insure its success." [32] The flow of goods in the dry goods trade was likely to be from manufacturer or importer to commission house to wholesaler to retailer, and this was true of many other lines. Indeed the number of middlemen was sometimes even larger, although a merchant like A. T. Stewart could eliminate them all.

The forces behind this broad movement from nonspecialized to specialized business in America have never been carefully investigated.[33] At present one can only point to the most obvious and likely explanations. However tentative and incomplete such speculation may be, it throws considerable light upon the subsequent rise of the department store.

The main influence at work was certainly the Industrial Revolution, which began to exert its full impact upon America after 1815. Machines began to pour forth a swelling stream of goods, resulting not only in an increased quantity of the wares that men had used in the past but also in a greatly expanded variety. Trade grew in volume and complexity, raising problems in distribution which were about as difficult to solve as those in the field of production. For example, the man who wanted to maintain a reasonably complete assortment of dry goods in his store in 1860 had to invest a great deal more capital in inventory than would have been necessary fifty years earlier when a few staples would have sufficed.[34] Naturally this made correspondingly more difficult the decisions as to what to buy and how much, to say nothing of the increased risks involved. It would be an exaggeration to say that the business problem shifted from one of producing the goods that people wanted to that of distributing goods which factories produced, but the change was fundamentally of that nature. Of course, the transfer of a substantial amount of production out of the household into the factory necessarily added to the quantity of goods which had to pass through the retailer's hands.[35]

Another direct consequence of the Industrial Revolution was the unprecedented growth of transportation facilities — improved roads, new canals and railways, and such advances in ocean transport as the inauguration of fast, regular packet service between New York and Liverpool in 1817. Large territories were opened for settlement and exploitation, and immigration from Europe received added impetus. Population began to concentrate in towns and cities as trade and manufacturing gained in relative importance. As a result of increased productivity, too, there was a marked improvement in the standard of living, a phenomenon closely connected with the growing importance of the middle class.

For business men all this meant a vast increase in the quantity of merchandise handled and a rapid expansion of markets in terms of population, geographical extent, and per capita consumption. While increased volume alone would have induced a certain amount of specialization, there were other forces driving men in the same direction. Each branch of business required increasing amounts of capital which were not easy to raise. Each branch presented new problems and a growing complexity which demanded concentrated attention. At the same time the expansion and elaboration of the general business structure made it possible for the individual firm to rely on others for services (such as importing, or wholesaling, or retailing, or banking) which it had formerly been obliged to provide for itself.

The result was that, while some men devoted all their energy and capital to mastering the task of production by power-driven machinery, others gave up importing to concentrate on wholesaling or abandoned wholesaling activities to expand the retail end of their business. Few, if any, of them saw the situation so clearly as we can see it now with benefit of historical perspective. What evidently became apparent was that most of those who continued the time-honored way of nonspecialization had increasing difficulty, while those who confined their efforts more narrowly found it easier to make profits. To take a specific example from retailing, Macy's lace and ribbon store undoubtedly could offer a more attractive selection of finery to the ladies of the community than the general store which stocked a few yards of ribbons and lace along with groceries, hardware, and china. Such a specialized store, furthermore, would be likely to obtain substantial advantages in buying because of the quantities purchased, and this in turn would enable it to quote lower prices to customers.

Underlying all, of course, was the never-ending struggle for survival and profits. And not the least of the forces leading towards specialization was the fact that profits became harder to make after 1815. In that year prices began a long slide downwards which continued with few interruptions until the middle 'forties, bringing losses and ruin to all who failed to move quickly. Just as in the early 1930's firms dropped one expensive service after another and combed their records in order to discover and eliminate unprofitable activities, so business men after 1815 scrutinized their operations and found salvation in reducing the lines handled and the functions performed.

Macy's various efforts in retailing reflect not only this tendency towards specialization but also the influence of circumstances upon the degree to which it develops. Thus in the primitive environment of Marysville his business was not specialized as to either goods or marketing function. In Boston and Haverhill, both of which offered substantial markets, he specialized in dry goods. As we have seen, when he finally opened a store in the enormous market of New York City, he began by concentrating in that relatively narrow subdivision of the dry goods business known as fancy dry goods.

General movements, like this drive towards specialization after 1800, tend to go to the extreme, and even before they have gone too far an opposing reaction sets in. Thus in the 1840's and 1850's we find in America, as in Europe, a tendency on the part of certain specialized firms to branch out into new activities, to integrate retailing and wholesaling or manufacturing and wholesaling operations. Thus A. T. Stewart, who operated an unusually successful dry goods store in New York, began to do his own importing from Europe and to buy directly from manufacturers instead of dealing with importers and jobbers. Similarly, the firm of Hovey, Williams & Co., of Boston (now C. F. Hovey Co.), who had been importing foreign dry goods and selling to jobbers, decided about 1846 to eliminate middlemen by opening a retail dry goods store.[36] Both apparently increased the variety of dry goods handled, exhibiting a tendency towards diversification which was later to lead them beyond textile lines.

Other firms evidently were starting to integrate in the same fashion, for in 1848 Hunt's *Merchants' Magazine* issued a general admonition against the movement:[37]

> We have seen the retailer striving hard to connect jobbing with his retailing; and the jobber, in his turn, grown envious of the importer, seek to range out of his appropriate sphere, and in *nine* cases in *ten* these departures from legitimate trade have been *failures* in their results. . . .
>
> Our advice is, to the retailer, do not attempt to job; to the jobber, leave importing alone; and to the importer, allow not the offer of an extra price induce you to break a package, for it is as completely unjust for you to rob the jobber of his legitimate profit as it would be for the jobber to retail goods . . . stick to your regular business.

This new tendency, just appearing on the business horizon, was a movement of far-reaching significance in American life, and no such injunction could stop it. In two generations it was to bring forth not only department stores like Macy's but also retail chains and vast, integrated industrial giants. With integration and diversification was to develop a movement towards horizontal combination on a national scale. But by 1860 these forces had made only a small beginning on the eastern seaboard. Inland the drive towards specialization was still in full swing, and this continent, like Europe, had yet to see its first real department store.

Retail Policies in Europe before 1860

In addition to noting secular changes in retail organization, we need to glance briefly at the origins of modern retail practices which we associate with the department store. While neither London nor Paris possessed a department store by 1860, storekeepers in both cities had already introduced many of the retail policies and services that are common among modern American department stores: the one-price system, the privilege of taking goods out on approval and returning anything not wanted, free delivery, attractive displays, and low prices.

One of the oldest of these is the so-called one-price policy under which the retailer marked the selling price on his wares and refused to deviate from it: the same price was charged to all customers regardless of gullibility or bargaining skill. The more widespread procedure was to mark the cost price (in symbols, of course) and ask the highest price above cost that the customer appeared likely to pay, abating it if necessary to complete the sale. George Fox, the famous Quaker leader, protested against this practice as early as 1653, arguing that it was both deceitful and time-wasting. At first the refusal to bargain aroused suspicion among customers and resulted in lost business, but Fox insisted that his followers obey his injunction, and eventually people came to realize that "they might sende any childe & be as well used as y^{m}selves att any of these [Quaker] shopps." [38]

It has been said that the founder of the Mitsui business was the first to proclaim a one-price policy, in 1673.[39] But Dr. Shigeto Tsuru, a careful student of Japanese history, has assured me that a more exact translation of the Japanese phrase used would be "no bargaining," since Hachirobei continued the established custom of varying the price according to the social status of the customer. In any case, the Quakers had definitely adopted the policy at least twenty years earlier.

Defoe asserted in his *Complete English Tradesman* that Quakers had been compelled "by the necessities of trade" to deviate from a strict one-price policy,[40] but a Frenchman who visited England about the same time was deeply impressed by the Quakers' refusal to ask more for goods "than their worth," [41] so that at least some tradesmen were continuing the policy. This is borne out by the fact that, although later in the century Josiah Wedgwood (who was not a Quaker) adhered to the one-price system in his London showrooms, he made no claim to an innovation in this respect.[42]

French tradesmen, too, made an early start with fixed prices. The date of their beginning is not known, but the one-price policy is said to have contributed to the success of the Ville de Paris, Pygmalion, Pauvre Diable, and other *magasins de nouveautés* established after Waterloo. Certainly the Bon Marché claimed adherence to the policy in 1838, and by 1844 it was so widely observed that a writer in *L'Illustration* could assert without reservation that the system had become an established custom (*"est maintenant passé dans nos moeurs"*) among all but the petty shopkeepers.[43]

Closely related to the fixed or one-price policy is the one which is best described by the phrase "satisfaction guaranteed or your money back." John Wanamaker has been credited with originating it,[44] but other American merchants had adopted it before he even entered business. While it was relatively late to appear in America, there is definite evidence of its existence in Europe before 1800. Probably many storekeepers practised it, at least with regular customers, years before we have any record of its use. At any rate, as early as 1771 Wedgwood urged customers to order his china freely with the understanding that they could return any pieces "if they do not find them agreeable to their wishes." He was confident that such a policy would greatly increase sales and profits.[45] Other London merchants doubtless employed the same device to stimulate trade. Similarly we find the Ville de Paris offering in 1844 to exchange goods or refund the price of any purchase which the customer decided not to keep.[46] The Bon Marché probably meant to imply as much even earlier when it proclaimed itself a *maison de confiance à prix fixe*, and in 1854 its sales invoices bore the explicit statement: *"tout achat qui laisserait quelque regret sera échangé, ou le montant remboursé si on le désire."* [47]

The origin of the practice of delivering purchases free of charge in the immediate neighborhood of a shop is probably lost in the beginnings of commerce, but Wedgwood offered to deliver goods anywhere with carriage "paid so far as the first carrier takes them;" moreover, he replaced or refunded the price of any goods damaged in transit.[48] It would be surprising if at least a few other English merchants failed to follow his example, but I have not come across any instances of their doing so. In 1839 W. Hitchcock & Co., of London, advertised two deliveries a day within five miles of the store.[49] Evidence of Continental practice before 1850 is lacking, but it was probably much the same.

Whatever English tradesmen may have done about pricing their merchandise, at least one Paris storekeeper adopted, as early as 1840, the policy of taking only a small profit on each item in the expectation that the resulting low prices would induce large sales and greater total profits. The Coin de Rue followed in 1843. Others, including the Bon Marché, were using the same tactics in the 1850's if not before, and the Belle Jardinière may have instituted the policy as early as 1827.[50]

The practice of tempting buyers by attractive display of goods is doubtless as old as trade, but not so the investment in window and store fixtures designed to enhance the attractiveness of the store. Defoe was shocked at the "modern custom" (i. e., about 1726) of contemporary tradesmen who laid out two-thirds of their capital "in painting and gilding, in fine shelves, shutters, boxes, glass-doors, sashes and the like."[51] Later in the eighteenth century Wedgwood found it advisable to establish spacious and attractive display rooms in London to accommodate the crowds who came to buy his china.[52] Whatever the state of affairs before the restoration of the French monarchy, it is obvious from the articles and illustrations in *L'Illustration* that Paris stores were already gaining a reputation for their magnificent galleries and displays in the 1840's.

Eighteenth-century Europe was no stranger to the cash policy which Macy's has so long emphasized. Defoe warned that one of the chief reasons for mercantile failures was the practice of buying and selling on credit to an unwise degree. At the same time, however, he pointed out that those who attempted to sell for cash lost business, and he therefore dismissed as "a presumption in trade" the idea of refusing to grant credit to retail customers.[53] Not a great deal is known about the actual conditions of granting credit in Europe in the eighteenth century, but the issue of cash versus credit was a familiar one and merchants recognized the effect of liberal credits on sales volume.

While some of these features of European retail trade may, at first glance, appear to be of minor importance, we must not lose sight of the total effect. Retailing was receiving a strong emphasis which had previously been unknown. Instead of waiting for customers from the neighborhood to come in to make purchases, retailers were reaching out to draw patronage from a whole city. Demand was no longer taken for granted: people were being tempted to spend money, and shopping was being transformed into as pleasant, convenient, and attractive an occupation as ingenuity and enterprise could contrive. Innovations were being tried out in retail methods as well as in manufacturing techniques. The spirit of the modern department store was certainly born, and its form was beginning to emerge.

THE RISE OF PROGRESSIVE RETAIL POLICIES IN AMERICA

In 1860 American retailing generally lagged behind developments in Europe, but it was fast catching up, and many of the features and policies which were later to be incorporated in the department store had already made their first appearance. Indeed a few of the very firms whose names are prominent in the department store world today were already in existence: Jordan Marsh & Co. were dry goods wholesalers in Boston; Gimbel Brothers ran a general store in Vincennes, Indiana; while Arnold, Constable & Co., Lord & Taylor, and James McCreery were well established in the retail dry goods business in New York.

The most famous store at the time was that of A. T. Stewart. Founded in 1823, it had grown rapidly in the 1830's and 1840's. By 1846 it had integrated back towards the manufacturer by establishing a wholesale business. While it probably had a departmental organization, it continued to handle dry goods lines alone and, like certain large stores in London and Paris, fell considerably short of being a department store.[54]

In Philadelphia there was a retail establishment which, according to a contemporary description, had much of the organization and system of the modern department store as early as 1847:[55]

> The amount of sales made at this store, is about $300,000 annually; each department in the store is alphabetically designated. The shelves and rows of goods in each department are numbered, and upon the tag attached to the goods, is marked the letter of the department, the number of the shelf and row on that shelf to which such piece of goods belongs. The cashier receives a certain sum extra per week, and he is responsible for all worthless money received. Books are kept, in which

the sales of each clerk are entered for the day, and the salary of the clerk cast, as a per centage on each day, week and year, and, at the foot of the page, the aggregate of the sales appear, and the per centage that it has cost to effect these sales, is easily calculated for each day, month or year. . . .

. . . .

. . . . The proprietor's desk stands at the farther end of the store, raised on a platform facing the front, from which he can see all the operations in each section of the retail department. From this desk run tubes, connecting with each department of the store, from the garret to the cellar, so that if a person in any department, either porter, retail or wholesale clerk, wishes to communicate with the employer, he can do so without leaving his station. Pages are kept in each department to take the bill of parcels, together with the money paid; and return the bill receipted, and change, if any, to the customer. So that the salesman is never obliged to leave the counter; he is at all times ready either to introduce a new article, or watch that no goods are taken from his counter, excepting those accounted for.

His peculiar method of casting the per centage of a clerk's salary on his sales, enables him at all times, (coupling it with the clerk's general conduct, and the style of goods he is selling,) to form a just estimate of the relative value of the services of each, in proportion to his salary. By the alphabetic arrangement of departments, numbering of shelves, and form of the tools, any clerk, no matter if he has not been in the store more than an hour, can arrange every article in its proper place, and at any time, if inquired of respecting, or referred to by any clerk, the proprietor is able to speak understandingly of the capabilities and business qualities of any of his employees. He has brought up some of the best merchants at present engaged in the trade, who do honor to the profession as well as their tutor.

The context clearly indicates that it was nothing more than a dry goods store. Of course, the high degree of departmental organization and close control over operations represented a great advance over contemporary practice. We shall meet the same system of using "pages" or cash girls in Macy's New York store.

While America lagged behind Europe in applying progressive retail policies, the main ones had been introduced here at least on a small scale. The one-price policy, for example, while traditionally supposed to have been introduced by A. T. Stewart,[56] was adopted at an early date by a number of stores. Arthur Tappan certainly adhered to it in the 1820's,[57] and Lord & Taylor advertised "no deviation from first prices" as early as 1838,[58] while in Boston at least two firms had adopted the policy before 1850.[59] Macy had adopted it in 1851. Of course, there were real difficulties about strict adherence to this policy in a market which was keenly competitive, especially among people to whom bargaining was a natural, indeed pleasurable, accompaniment of everyday shopping.

Specific evidence is lacking on the early application of a money-back guarantee, but an advertisement of J. Sullivan Foster, of Manchester, New Hampshire, indicates that in 1843 something of the sort was customary in the district.[60] Stewart's basic policy of strict honesty between buyer and seller may have included a guarantee. Much more specific is the guarantee advertised by Smith & Strong, a men's clothing store in Oswego, New York, which appeared in 1855 and may have been instituted earlier:[61]

> Persons who are still unacquainted with our principles of business are respectfully informed that we guarantee every article sold to be what it is represented, and that we cheerfully return the money when any dissatisfaction exists.

Similarly, Bowen, McNamee & Co., of New York, advertised in 1859: "All goods shall be precisely what they are represented to be, or they may be returned by the buyer at our expense."[62] While such explicit statements of policy are rare in the mid-nineteenth century, and while we can be certain that no American retailer of the period would think of extending the generous return privileges which stores allow today, it is likely that most reputable merchants would take back purchases when the customer had a really legitimate reason for being dissatisfied apart from a capricious change of mind. At the same time, one must recognize that anyone who publicly offered to return money for goods which were not satisfactory was opening the way for the abuse of honest policy and was practically asking for trouble. Not many were willing to take the step until competition forced it upon them, and contemporary evidence indicates that not many stores were willing to practice any sort of guarantee of satisfaction, to say nothing of giving it wide publicity.

Again, numerous stores claimed to employ "the Cash System." Stewart is supposed to have sold only for cash at the beginning (1823).[63] It is not always easy to determine whether the oft-repeated phrase "lowest prices for cash" meant simply a reduction in price for cash transactions or sales exclusively for cash. However, the advertisement for Wheaton & Dixon, quoted above, page 78, explicitly barred credit transactions as early as 1806, and in 1843 a store in Lockport, New York, claimed strict adherence to a cash system,[64] while in 1848 Michael Uhler, operating a general store near Peekskill, New York, likewise asserted that he bought and sold for cash.[65] By the end of the 1850's a number of stores in New York City sold only for cash.[66]

If, however, any man really adhered to a cash policy, it is plain that he was decidedly in a minority group. The retailer in nearly all lines of business was accustomed to giving long credits to his customers. Annual settlements for family bills were not at all unusual, especially in rural communities where farmers sold much of their produce to the local store, and early account books supply many instances of even longer periods of waiting for payment. The wholesaler, in turn, bought and sold on long-term credit, usually being glad to give at least 5 per cent discount for cash. While the wary merchant frequently attempted to safeguard final settlement by taking notes instead of extending open-book credit, this merely changed the form of the transaction, and the fact remains that retailers rarely bought or sold on a cash basis. In part this was the result of the general shortage of currency and extensive use of money-barter to which reference has already been made. In part it was a matter of long-standing practice aimed at both the convenience of the customer and the ultimate profit of the merchant, who knew that most people would buy larger amounts on credit than for cash. Of course there were losses from bad debts, and when any stringency arose in the money market a series of failures was likely to ensue.

Hence the merchant who could succeed with a cash policy stood to reap definite gains.[67]

By 1860 American retailers were just beginning to make more than superficial use of newspaper advertising. The modern reader of their advertisements, once he has become accustomed to the crude copywriting and quaint typography, is likely to be struck by the absence of any emphasis upon the quality of merchandise offered. The main stress is upon low prices, and it is evident that many a nineteenth-century American merchant paid lip service to the theory of low unit profit and large volume of sales. They called it "pursuing a nimble sixpence before a slow shilling."[68]

These relatively modern policies, however, were the exception rather than the rule. Rowland Macy was to be in business a long time before they gained wide acceptance, and it is evident from the emphasis which a few daring retailers placed upon the one-price, satisfaction-or-money-back, and cash policies that they were radical departures from normal practice. In the circumstances it took courage and vision to maintain them, and most retailers took the easier course.

With fixtures as with policies, most retail stores of the period before 1860 seem to have taken the easiest course — they were small, dingy, and unattractive, even in large eastern cities. At the same time it is true that A. T. Stewart had erected a spacious, marble-fronted building in New York in 1842, and by 1850 one commentator asserted that extravagance in fitting up stores was depleting working capital and causing business stringency.[69]

The state of retailing in 1858, when Rowland Macy again entered the field, must have presented a confusing picture. It was bad enough to have to decide whether to go into trade, or try one's hand at factory production which was springing up everywhere, or rejoin the stream of men moving into the interior. Having decided to remain in the East and cast his lot with retailing, Macy still had to decide what to sell and how to conduct his business at a time when the pattern was beginning to change. To us today the trend of developments is fairly clear, and it seems perfectly logical that Macy should have chosen a big city for his start rather than a town of less size, that he should have begun by specializing narrowly, and that he should have adopted the cash and one-price policies without any doubts as to their success. American retail developments, while lagging a decade or more behind those of Europe, were moving in the same direction, and the man who adapted his business to the new trend was likely to reap rich rewards. But no man in 1858 or 1860 could see what we see as we look back. He could only try a course of action that looked promising and then hope for the best.

CHAPTER V

HITCH YOUR SHOPPING TO A STAR

AT some point between 1858 and 1877, the year of Rowland Macy's death, the little fancy dry goods store on Sixth Avenue became a department store — and a big one, too — according to the definition set forth in the preceding chapter. As Macy achieved success he extended the lines of merchandise handled to include all sorts of nontextile goods, until the variety that his store sold was practically without precedent. To accommodate the additional sales he was obliged to expand his premises. As his volume of business increased, Macy began also to eliminate middlemen, by importing goods directly from Europe, by purchasing directly from manufacturers instead of wholesalers, and even by taking over certain manufacturing processes. The new pattern developed slowly, possibly because Macy was feeling his way towards a goal which at first he could not clearly see, possibly because it took time and thought and hard work to build the organization of employees and managers needed to run the store. We do not have all the details of the story that we should like, but the rise of Macy's as a great retail institution is plain enough.

INCREASING VARIETY OF GOODS SOLD

Macy shifted from specialized to diversified merchandise so gradually that the whole process of increasing the variety must be regarded as one of slow growth rather than distinct innovation. The final outcome was of revolutionary significance, to be sure, but it came as the result of a series of small changes, most of which taken separately seem to have no particular importance and to emerge quite logically and naturally from what went before. One might almost say that the fancy dry goods store, if it expanded at all, would inevitably become a department store, just as a tree grows from a seed. And yet we know that many department stores started from other origins — some from general dry goods, some from men's furnishings, other from general stores, and at least one from groceries.[1] Moreover, the existence today of long-established specialty stores proves that survival did not always depend upon diversification. There was nothing inevitable about the way in which Macy's matured.

During the first two years of operation Macy continued to emphasize the flowers and feathers, ribbons, embroideries, and lace goods with which he had started. Almost from the very outset, however, he began to add new items to his stock, never departing from the field of fancy dry goods, but well nigh exhausting the possibilities of that very elastic category. Thus, in December, 1858, he started to sell gloves and hosiery for men as well as for women and children. This step provided the basis for the subsequent expansion into a complete line of men's furnishings. In the same month he put in a small stock of housekeeping goods (towels, sheets, quilts, linens, and the like), together with a few items of ready-to-wear clothing, including women's underwear, skirts, cloaks and raglans, "mechanical" corsets, muslin dresses for women and infants, and such men's furnishings as neckties, shirts, underwear, and linen bosoms.[2] In the spring of 1859 Macy supplemented existing lines by the addition of blankets, lace curtains, shawls, and mantillas, and a noticeably larger selection in all departments. In addition, he instituted a parasol department which, because of the seasonal demand for parasols and umbrellas, regularly dwindled into insignificance during the winter months.[3]

Macy himself was not certain about the precise combination of goods to be carried. In the spring of 1859 he advertised that he was closing his corset department in order to provide for the increasing trade in his lace department, and a year later he announced the closing of the housekeeping department because he intended "to relinquish that part of my business." In both instances, however, he soon revived the departments with a wider assortment than he had carried in the first place.[4]

Up to this point there was nothing unusual about Macy's store. There were scores of similar ones in the city, struggling to survive.

Macy was filling out his stock of fancy dry goods, but there was no departure from well-established precedent. In the fall of 1860, however, came a step which opened the way to fundamental changes. Macy installed a distinctly new department devoted to "French and German fancy goods," which he had not previously sold in New York. His new merchandise included such items as pocketbooks and handbags, tea sets and certain other chinaware, ash trays, photograph frames, and an extensive assortment of games, dolls, and toys of all kinds, as well as many things which would ordinarily be included under the heading of Yankee notions.[5] Thus, in a single move the store went heavily into nontextile lines. Even in this apparently radical step Macy, strictly speaking, achieved no marked innovation. Contemporaries made little distinction between fancy goods and fancy dry goods, and Macy himself, as we have seen, had stocked with his dry goods in Haverhill many of the fancy goods that he now introduced into his New York establishment. The only thing novel in his action was the extent to which he began to feature the new fancy goods as well as the unusually large assortment that he carried.[6]

If it is possible to assign any single date in answer to the question, "When did Macy's *start* to become a department store?", the answer probably is the fall season of 1860. At that time, by opening a fancy goods department, he launched his store on the course which eventually led to separate departments completely stocked with drugs and toilet goods, china and glassware, silver, house furnishings (kitchenware, etc.), sporting goods, luggage, toys, musical instruments, and even books. And we may date from December, 1860, the annual display of dolls and toys which has so long been a notable feature of Macy publicity as well as of its merchandise.

One suspects that Macy had been casting about for a profitable combination of goods to handle, seeking by means of diversification to cut down expenses, to supplement the profits from dry goods which competition tended to wipe out, and to iron out the marked seasonal demand for dry goods. While Macy's reasons are unrecorded, the last of these objectives is reflected in the manner in which, after 1860, the parasol department regularly closed and made way for

ROWLAND HUSSEY MACY, FOUNDER
When he was about 50 years old

DRY GOODS.

GRAND CENTRAL
OPENING EXHIBITION!

```
                o
              ooo
             oooo
            ooooo
           oooooo
          oooo oooo
         ooooooooo
        oooooooooo
oooooooooooooooooo  oooooooooooooooooo
   ooooooooooo        ooooooooooo
    ooooo ooo   GRAND   ooo ooooo
    oo ooo              oo ooo
     oo o    OPENING    oo o
      oo                  oo
       o   R. H. MACY & CO.  o
      oo ooo              ooo oo
      ooooooooo        ooooooooo
     ooooooooooooooo  ooooooooooooooo
     oooooooo oooo      oooooo ooooo
      ooooooooo          ooooooooo
        oooooo            oooooo
          oo                 oo
```

	R. H. MACY & CO.	
	Have devoted	
MACY.	the last three months	GRAND
MACY.	to	CENTRAL.
	ENLARGING, DECORATING	
MACY.	AND REFURNISHING	GRAND
MACY.	their establishment;	CENTRAL.
	and having now completed	
MACY.	their extensive improvements,	GRAND
MACY.	they can justly claim	CENTRAL.
	to be the	
MACY.	LARGEST FANCY GOODS	GRAND
MACY.	STORE IN AMERICA.	CENTRAL.
	They cordially invite the public	
MACY.	to attend	GRAND
MACY.	A GRAND OPENING	CENTRAL.
	EXHIBITION,	
MACY.	to be held on	GRAND
MACY.	WEDNESDAY, Sept. 25,	CENTRAL,
	and	
MACY.	THURSDAY, Sept. 26,	GRAND
MACY.	BOTH DAY AND EVENING.	CENTRAL.
	Many of the goods to be displayed	
MACY.	have been imported by them	GRAND
MACY.	especially for the occasion.	CENTRAL.
	On both	
MACY.	Wednesday and Thursday	MACY.
	the establishment will remain open	
MACY.	until	MACY.
	half-past 9 in the evening.	
MACY.	R. H. MACY & CO.,	MACY.
	Fourteenth-street and Sixth-avenue.	
MACY.	GRAND CENTRAL	MACY.
	FANCY GOODS ESTABLISHMENT.	

MACY'S STAR IN 1872

Early version of the famous trademark, illustrating also contemporary custom of seeking emphasis by repetition a fur department each fall, opening again in the spring.[7] Whatever the explanation, it is plain that during the first two years Macy emphasized complete stocks only in ribbons, laces, embroideries, feathers, and flowers, and was content to handle odd lots of other items, as if experimenting to see whether he could sell them at a profit. This was the slow way but a sure one.

For some years after 1860 Macy made no moves comparable to the introduction of the French and German fancy goods. He did, however, amplify existing lines, so as to provide a better assortment for his customers. Thus we find him increasing his stock of ready-to-wear goods by the addition of nightdresses, sacks, zouave jackets, capes, infants' cloaks and dresses, and a larger stock of skirts. The housekeeping department was improved by the addition of a larger variety of table linen, curtains, and white goods; the kinds of gloves and hosiery stocked were substantially extended; and the selection of ribbons, feathers, and flowers was enlarged. The addition of fancy soaps, perfumes, and toilet extracts in October, 1861, opened the way for the modern drug and toilet goods departments, but it still left the store safely within the fancy goods category. And when, in the same month, Macy announced a new department containing trimmed and untrimmed hats, he was merely enlarging the trade in millinery goods with which he had opened his store.[8]

The stock of fancy goods was enlarged in 1864 to include bracelets, earrings, fancy pins, and other items of costume jewelry, and there was a substantial addition of ornaments made of bronze, ivory, china, wood, and other materials. Both, however, were again merely extensions of existing lines, leading the firm farther and farther away from the dry goods field but not constituting any abrupt departure. Increasingly the emphasis was upon such furnishings as gloves and hosiery and upon the growing assortment of fancy goods. By 1867 Macy advertising asserted, "We have the largest fancy goods store in New York. The largest stock, the greatest variety and the best assortment of desirable goods," but the store still carried very few dress materials.[9]

By 1868 Macy (probably with some encouragement from Margaret Getchell) apparently had begun to visualize something like the modern department store, for the additions began to come thick and fast, carrying the store well beyond the established precedents of the dry goods trade. In the fall of that year the assortment of fancy goods was extended to include clocks, silver-plated ware, and Gorham's solid silver.[10] In April, 1869, came a new department devoted to a wide selection of house furnishings: kitchen utensils, woodenware, baskets, bird cages, brushes, dusters, baby carriages, and a larger stock of plated ware.[11] We cannot possibly comprehend today the horror with which Macy's rivals must have regarded this new step — the complacent ones because of the ridiculous folly of any attempt to combine such dissimilar merchandise in one store, the smarter merchants because they sensed the competitive threat which was involved in Macy's policy of diversification. If a man could sell dry goods, silverware, and house furnishings to the customer who had formerly bought only dry goods in his store, his expenses would be reduced. The variety displayed might itself attract patronage, and lower expenses would lead to lower prices and even greater patronage; competitors would face ruin.

Macy ignored any dissenting views that may have been advanced. If one wants to sell gifts for children, why not books as well as toys and dolls? If books for children, why not for adults? And why not candy for both? These steps were taken in December, 1869.[12] At first the adult literature was confined to prayer books and bibles, but within a month Macy opened a separate department which stocked "all the popular books of the day," as well as stationery and a large selection of magazines.[13]

No evidence has survived for the period before the fall of 1869 that would enable one to decide conclusively whether the successive additions of merchandise were amplifying the stock of existing departments or bringing new departments into existence. Beginning in September, 1869, however, we have original firm records which show the way in which the store was subdivided. The departments then in operation were as follows:[14]

1. White goods, linens, curtains.
2. Laces, embroideries, underclothing.

3. Notions and trimmings.
4. Flowers and feathers.
5. Ribbons.
6. Hosiery and furnishings.
7. Ladies' ties.
8. Furs (parasols in spring and summer).
9. Fancy goods, jewelry, toiletries.
10. Straw and felt hats.
11. House furnishings.
12. Toys and dolls.

The book and candy departments were opened early in 1870. As each line proved itself successful Macy added to it in order to make his assortment more attractive, scouring the American and European markets for an ever increasing variety. Instead of bringing out dolls, toys, and candies for the Christmas season, Macy stocked them the year around and for good measure added (1870) one of the new-fangled soda fountains as another means of inducing people to enter his store.[15] Once they were in, tempting prices and attractive merchandise would loosen their purse-strings.

Bohemian glassware and ice skates (the entering wedge for a sporting goods department) were among the additions in 1872, and in the following spring the store began to offer rocking chairs, folding chairs, ottomans, commodes, and rugs, thereby paving the way for a complete line of furniture. At the same time Macy announced velocipedes, barometers, gardening sets, bathing suits and beach equipment, and, of all unheard-of things, a new picnic department which sold crackers, jams, preserves, potted meats, and other fancy groceries.[16] This latest innovation, we know, was introduced by Margaret Getchell, who also experimented for a short period with the sale of fresh flowers and potted plants. For the first time, too, we have direct testimony on the reasons for the new departments: the management was trying to discover new sources of revenue to offset the effects of some exceptionally bad weather and adverse business conditions (the panic of 1873 was already in the making). Macy had left Miss Getchell in sole charge of the store while he and her husband (of whom more later) went abroad to buy new merchandise. One of her husband's letters from Europe, after commenting favorably on the first results of the grocery department, indicated that further experiments were under consideration: [17]

Perhaps in these bad times it would be well to add a shoe store and barber shop. What do you think? We bought some ladies' and gents' slippers to come out this spring . . . ; if they succeed, there is no telling what it may lead to.

The experiment with flowers and plants showed a small loss at the close of the first season and was promptly discontinued. From the very start, the picnic department developed fair volume and a satisfactory gross profit margin, but in 1875 results became unsatisfactory, and it was discontinued after approximately two years of operation. The suggestion has been made that the employees ate up the profits: Macy is said to have once encountered a cash girl in tears after a floorwalker had reprimanded her for eating in the department; learning that her family was too poor to provide adequate food, he is supposed to have ruled that the girl could help herself because children should not be allowed to go hungry. Obviously such a decision could not have been applied on a large scale. Probably the principal reason for closing it was that it failed to grow to the extent that Macy thought desirable.[18]

Another move of more lasting character and greater significance took place in March, 1874, when Macy installed a complete assortment of china, glassware, and silver — not as subdivisions of the fancy goods business but as separate departments carrying a variety of patterns and qualities intended to rival the offering of any specialized store in New York. (A few months after its opening Macy advertising proclaimed it to be "the most extensive assortment of china, glassware, majolica, and parian ever displayed in America.") [19] The new departments were in the basement of the store; this location was apparently so unprecedented that Macy advertisements carefully refrained from mentioning it. The firm also avoided revealing that the new departments were stocked by L. Straus & Sons, wholesale dealers in china and glass, about whom we shall learn more in later chapters. While the exact details are not known, the arrangement was much like that of leased departments which exist in many stores today. The idea of having the Strauses install the new departments did not originate with Macy himself, but he recognized its merit, and in adopting it he took a major step in the process by which his business became a full-fledged department store.[20]

Steadily the additions continued — now a new item or two, now a whole new department. Sewing machines appeared shortly after the new china department. Early in 1875 came a larger assortment of chairs, mats, and rugs, followed by additional hardware, a small selection of paintings and other art goods, a wide assortment of fishing tackle, luggage, and archery equipment, and live canaries.[21] These were expansions of the nontextile side of the business, but clothing and dry goods were not neglected. In May, 1875, the store opened a shoe department for women and children (see illustration opposite page 169). This, like the china and silverware departments, was leased to an outsider, but it was an integral part of the store.[22] Early in 1876, following the abandonment of the picnic department, a boys' clothing department was introduced, and later in the same year appeared a suit and cloak department, evidently representing an enlargement of the store's trade in women's ready-to-wear clothing. This move was accompanied by the establishment of a department selling black dress goods (woolens) and black dress silks, neither of which had been stocked in any quantity before so far as one can tell from the advertisements.[23]

No further lines of merchandise were introduced into the store before Macy's death. It is impossible to indicate, short of a catalog, the immense assortment of items offered within the various lines by that time, but a list of the store's departments as they stood in the spring of 1877 gives some idea of the extent to which diversification had taken place:[24]

1. White goods, linens, curtains.
2. Laces and embroideries, corsets.
2$\frac{1}{2}$. Ladies' underclothing.
3. Small wares and notions.
4. Ribbons.
5. Silverware.

6. Hosiery and furnishings.
7. Ladies' ties.
8. Furs.
8½. Parasols and umbrellas.
9. Fancy goods, jewelry, toiletries.
10. Boys' and youths' clothing.
11. House furnishings.
12. Toys and dolls.
13. Books, stationery, albums, etc.
14. Worsteds and worsted embroidery.
15. China, glass, and crockery.
16. Soda fountain and candy.
17. Kid gloves.
18. Millinery.
19. Flowers and feathers.
20. Ladies' and children's shoes.
21. Cloaks and suits.
22. Black dress goods and silks.

Here was a store selling such an extensive variety of merchandise that there was no name for it. Even Macy himself seems to have been at a loss for a descriptive phrase which might, in his advertisements, convey some notion of his business. He tried calling it "Macy's Grand Central Fancy Goods Establishment," which didn't fit as well as the even more cumbersome title, "Macy's Grand Central Fancy and Dry Goods Establishment," that he sometimes used. In one period, when he was trying to connect the store with his general trade-mark (the red star), Macy referred to his business as "The Grand Central Star Establishment." Another variant was "Grand Central Mercantile Establishment." Often he tried to make his point clear by asserting that his store was "unlike any other in the country" because of the enormous assortment it contained.[25] Today we should, without any difficulty, recognize the institution as a department store, but in the 1870's such a name would have been utterly without sense. It takes time for the public to fit a word to a new kind of institution. Not until the 'nineties did the term department store come into current use.

Growth and Integration, 1858–1877

To a considerable extent because of the great variety it sold, Macy's store grew so rapidly that within a period of fifteen years it rivaled the largest retail establishments in New York which had been in business for fifty years. Most of the competing houses were content to expand by capturing such trade as they could within the single field of dry goods proper. Macy, on the other hand, sought to grow in two ways: (1) within each given line that he carried, and (2) by adding new lines of merchandise. It was as though he had added a new store from time to time, each of which immediately began to increase its sales.

In point of fact the store expanded physically in precisely this manner. Thus, in 1866, Macy added to his establishment a store at 66 West 14th which joined the rear of the original premises facing Sixth Avenue to form an L-shaped structure. (The Macy staff celebrated by having a party in the vacant building just before it was occupied. Although the "orchestra" consisted merely of a violin and a harp and the refreshments were meagre, it was 3 A.M. before the merry dancers could bring themselves to go home.) Two years later he acquired a similar extension at 67 West 13th, by which time he was also using the corner building, as well as 204 and 206 on Sixth Avenue. Towards the end of 1871 another store on 14th Street was connected with the group, and in April, 1872, Macy finally added still another on Sixth, thus making four on the Avenue, two facing 14th Street, and one opening on 13th.[26]

This piecemeal addition went on until the Macy business occupied the ground space of eleven stores, giving rise to the claim that the firm had more floor space than any other firm in New York except A. T. Stewart. Naturally the union of somewhat dissimilar buildings (some of them had originally been built as residences) did not result in a particularly handsome or imposing place of business, certainly nothing to compare with the impressive mercantile places in which Macy's leading competitors were doing business. Macy was more interested in sales and profits than in appearances, and, while substantial alterations were made in 1872 and in 1874 to enlarge

Macy's quarters and give some semblance of unity to the conglomeration of stores, the firm avoided sinking a great deal of money into premises. Indeed, before 1870 at least, the leases which it held were regarded by outsiders as exceptionally favorable to Macy. Most of the selling departments were on the street floor, but china and house furnishings occupied a part of the basement, and several ready-to-wear departments were on the second floor. The rest of the building was devoted to receiving-rooms, stockrooms, cloakrooms, and a certain amount of manufacturing. By 1871 Macy also had a stable for delivery horses on West 15th Street; in 1875 the stable was moved to West 19th.[27]

Such physical growth was, of course, a reflection of the increasing volume of business. While we lack definite figures for the first decade of the store's existence, by 1870 sales were running slightly over a million dollars a year, representing a more than tenfold increase over the first year's results. Table 1 shows the actual net sales for the years between 1870 and Macy's death. Revealed in this set of figures are two facts of particular significance: in the first place, sales were at a standstill between 1870 and 1873; indeed, they showed a slight tendency to decline. Of course, American prices were falling at this time, and it is probable that the physical volume of goods sold by Macy was actually increasing in spite of the slight decrease in the dollar volume of sales. Whatever the explanation, this situation would give Macy cause for concern and encourage him to try new ideas for improving results. Secondly, there is a substantial and steady increase in sales beginning in 1874. The new leased departments account for a considerable part of the increase but not all of it. Clearly the rest of the store began to forge ahead at the same time that the new leased departments were introduced. Considering that the panic of 1873 started prices on a new downward slide, this growth is especially noteworthy, and it suggests that Macy's increasing diversification was drawing additional patronage to the store. It is evident that Macy's store was a large one for the period; even by modern standards its sales amply met the size test for the department store classification.

While we have no detailed information about Macy profits until

1872, the firm undoubtedly made money. Macy paid a federal income tax on $7,677 in 1863; this was presumably the most conservative calculation of the year's earnings that he could make, and, while some of it may have been derived from outside investments, the store's profits unquestionably contributed most of the sum.[28] Credit

TABLE 1

ANALYSIS OF ANNUAL SALES BY OWNED AND LEASED DEPARTMENTS
1870–1877

Year	Total Sales[a]	Ratio to Previous Year's Sales	Sales in Owned Depts.	Ratio to Previous Year's Sales	Sales in Leased Depts.[b]	Percentage of Leased to Total Sales
1870	$1,024,621	...	$1,024,621	...	...	...
1871	1,023,034	99.9	1,023,034	99.9	...	...
1872	1,002,528	98.0	1,002,528	98.0	...	...
1873	1,022,255	102.0	1,022,255	102.0	...	...
1874	1,197,867	117.2	1,090,095	106.6	$107,772	8.9
1875	1,366,889	114.1	1,184,818	108.6	182,071	13.3
1876	1,612,788	117.9	1,401,221	118.2	211,567	13.1
1877	1,873,205	116.1	1,639,259	116.9	233,946	12.5

[a] These figures include the sales in leased departments which began in Mar., 1874. For the years 1872–77, at least, they are net sales. The data for 1870 and 1871, coming from a different source, may not be strictly comparable, but it is unlikely that there is any serious discrepancy.

[b] It must be remembered that the sales for 1874 represent less than a full year's results, since the new departments did not open until the middle of March.

SOURCE: A. T. La Forge's Private Ledger, 1871–77; "Black Book," 1870–88.

reports indicated that Macy himself was worth $25,000 at the end of 1863, representing an increase of $15,000 in four years. Towards the end of 1868 estimates of his personal wealth ran from $50,000 to $75,000, and in 1869 they rose to $100,000. Rumors of financial trouble circulated in 1870, but Macy denied that there was any foundation for them, pointing to the fact that he had no charge accounts and paid cash for purchases. The credit sources were satisfied that Macy was "prompt, doing well and in snug shape. His business is certainly very prosperous." [29]

By 1870 the doubts about Macy's financial stability and integrity, arising out of his failure in Haverhill, seem finally to have disappeared.[30] A credit report in 1873 went so far as to declare that Macy was "doing the most extensive retail business on the avenues." This was undoubtedly an exaggeration, but the operating figures available for the years 1872–76 (see Table 2, page 130) confirm the indirect evidence of the earlier years about the earning power of the store. Unlike many of his contemporaries, Macy did not plow all his profits back into the business or put them into speculative ventures. Perhaps he had learned his lesson. In 1875 he had $35,000 in his private bank account, and he was able to produce a list of "good dividend paying stocks" totaling $170,000, besides which he had just bought a residence on 49th Street costing $49,000. It is said that during the eight years before his death Macy withdrew from the business approximately $40,000 annually, most of which he invested in securities. As a result, at the time of his death the value of his estate was variously estimated at from $300,000 to $500,000. Compared to the millions accumulated by A. T. Stewart, who had died in 1876, it was a modest sum — in 1863 Stewart had topped the earnings of the wealthiest men in New York, paying income tax on $1,843,637.[31] For Rowland Macy, who had started on a shoestring less than nineteen years before, it was a genuine fortune.

The remarkable thing about this financial success is that most of it came after 1864, when the fall in prices began to play havoc with all branches of trade. For firms in the dry goods business the situation was particularly difficult because a substantial portion of their merchandise had to be imported from Europe and paid for in gold at a time when gold prices in terms of greenbacks were fluctuating constantly, sometimes over a very wide range. Thus, late in 1864 a panic in the gold market led to drastic cuts in dry goods prices: Macy announced an over-all 50 per cent reduction. Two weeks later the price of gold went up again, but Macy promptly declared that he would keep his prices at the level to which they had been reduced. Further price declines came after peace in 1865, and the slide continued with little interruption down to 1879. When the panic of 1873 made necessary a sudden reduction in prices, Macy not only cut sharply on individual items but also offered an extra discount of 10 per cent on every purchase of 50 cents or more, a step which helps to account for the relatively poor earnings made in that year.[32] If he benefited by the rise in prices before 1865, the prolonged downward swing which subsequently ensued must have more than wiped out all such gains, especially when one considers the relatively small size of the business in the first period and its great increase in the second. That he was able to make substantial profits in both circumstances is evidence of unusual managerial ability.

During the time that Macy's store was undergoing diversification of lines and expansion of sales and profits, it was experiencing another fundamental change in the direction of integration: instead of concentrating on the retail end of marketing, Macy was branching out into other functions. Thus, a few months after the opening of his store, he announced that he was making men's shirts and women's and children's underwear to order. Once he had started to make some of the goods he sold, Macy promptly expanded such operations, adding cloaks, skirts, and dresses in 1859 and continuing such manufacturing in subsequent years. Until the 1870's the manufacturing was apparently done off the premises, possibly by an independent contractor. (Lord & Taylor were doing much the same thing in 1866, if not earlier, and other stores were doubtless moving in the same direction.) In 1873 a hat-trimming and millinery-manufacturing division was instituted in Macy's, and in the following year when the china and glassware department was opened, the firm maintained glass-cutters and china-decorators on the premises to execute monograms and special designs. By 1877 the firm claimed that it employed 200 girls in the manufacture of ladies' underclothing and infants' wear alone.[33]

The manufacturing done by Macy in this period was of course relatively less important than the marketing functions undertaken. During the first year of operation he claimed that the kid gloves sold in his store were his own importation. This does not mean that he went to Europe to make the purchases; probably he handled the transactions through some sort of agent. Almost at the outset he had given particular emphasis to glove sales, and the volume in that line doubtless soon grew to the point at which direct purchases became advantageous, reaching it sooner than other lines of Macy merchandise. Of course, few manufacturers would have permitted direct transactions on a small scale: small orders were usually handled through wholesale dealers. In any case it would not ordinarily have been profitable, because of the expense involved, for Macy to buy directly until he had attained considerable volume in the item concerned. During the course of the 1860's there were increasing references to "own importations" and direct purchases in several lines of merchandise, suggesting that Macy was eliminating importers and wholesalers as rapidly as increasing sales enabled him to do so.[34]

In 1870 Macy made a trip to Europe, apparently his first, for the purpose of buying merchandise for his store. He spent six months abroad, and the store advertisements subsequently featured goods which had been personally selected by Macy himself from London, Paris, Berlin, Rome, Naples, and Switzerland.[35] From this time on, Macy or his subordinates seem to have made regular buying trips abroad, not only for the purpose of getting lower prices, but also in order to obtain a better selection than would be possible in dealing with importers in New York.[36]

In going directly to manufacturers in America and in handling his own importations from Europe, Macy was, of course, performing for himself some of the services which wholesalers and importers (or the manufacturers in their stead) would otherwise have had to do. For a while (beginning in 1865) Macy even went further than this and sold goods at wholesale to other dealers. It is natural that he should have made some effort to branch out into wholesaling, for rival merchants like A. T. Stewart did more wholesaling than retailing. The extent of Macy's wholesale business is not known, but the records which have survived indicate that it was a very unimportant part of the total volume, conducted intermittently as a sideline.[37]

Closely connected with this matter of integration is the use of a trade-mark to identify Macy merchandise. The first instance of this occurred in 1860, when Macy sold hoopskirts made to his order and bearing his name stamped by the maker.[38] In 1862 or 1863, if not earlier, he began to use the five-pointed red star which is the general trade-mark that the firm has used ever since, but the extent of its use at that time on particular articles is not known.[39] For the first appearance of the Macy star in newspaper advertising see the illustration opposite page 101.

A legend of long standing attributes Macy's adoption of the red star to an experience which he had at sea. According to this story, he was trying to make port through fog on a dark night and had no bearings by which to steer until he discovered a single star shining through a rift in the clouds. With this as a guide he made port safely, and he later took the red star as a symbol which would guide him to business success. Since Macy was never in command of a ship, the story is doubtless apocryphal; certainly it will not bear close scrutiny from the point of view of navigation. Possibly the idea came to him when he composed the advertising verse quoted in Chapter III, in which the Star of Empire and the Star of Fashion are mentioned. Another suggestion is that he simply took as his trade-mark the red star which had, in whaling days, been tattooed on his arm.[40]

Whatever the origin of the trade-mark, its use meant that Macy, rather than the manufacturer, assumed responsibility for the merchandise on which the star appeared, and its adoption at so early a stage of the store's development is additional evidence of Macy's business genius. Many of the steps which have been taken by the firm since the 1860's mark a growing realization of the responsibilities which such private branding entails.

As a result of this diversification and integration, R. H. Macy's firm was safely launched on the course which enabled it to offer goods in astounding variety at low prices. Just as the growth of the city contributed to the firm's success, so the firm was helping to solve the shopping problems of urban life. Macy's was definitely headed for the day when many families of metropolitan New York would obtain from it practically everything they required, from sheets and canned soup to pianos, toothpaste, and even automobiles. Whatever the red star may have done for Macy in his seafaring days, it was beginning to guide New Yorkers to a good port of supply.

Store Organization

To handle the expanding operations and apply Macy's ideas there had, of course, to be a corps of workers fitted into a plan of coöperation which grew more complex as the range of store activities increased. The limited amount of evidence available reveals the emergence of a definite departmental framework within the store at an early stage. Thus a description of the store's organization in 1862 reveals that managerial responsibility was allocated by merchandise lines, even though a formal departmental structure may not have existed. A man was in charge of hosiery with a girl clerk to assist him; the woman who "had the lace counter" and the man in charge of white goods likewise had one clerk apiece. Corsets, flowers and feathers, notions, and ribbons were headed by women, each of them assisted by two clerks, while one woman alone was in charge of the glove counter. In addition to these eight selling divisions, the store had a delivery force consisting of a man and a boy who made their rounds with packages strapped on their backs. There were also a bookkeeper, a cashier, two cash girls, a marking clerk, and a man who combined the duties of superintendent, floorwalker, and timekeeper. This made a total of 27 employees, most of them women, although the size of the staff undoubtedly varied to some extent with the volume of business.[41]

Originally the supervision of all operations had received Macy's personal attention, and it is probable that he himself continued to do much of the important buying for many years. As the store grew, of course, he had to delegate part of his work to other people. Some of this delegation is apparent in the description of the organization in 1862; by the 1870's the process had gone further, and the whole organizational structure had begun to crystallize along modern lines. In keeping accounts, for example, sales and purchases were definitely allocated to individual departments by 1869, if not earlier, for the purpose of analyzing the results achieved: later certain expenses were similarly allocated. At the head of each department was a "buyer" who bore the main responsibility for the selection of goods offered, the amount of merchandise stocked at any time, and general operations within the division. One buyer usually superintended two or even three departments, but in all instances he was largely responsible for results. Some of the proprietor's duties were shared by floorwalkers (nowadays often called service managers) who directed customers and saw that clerks did their work properly. Although, as the title implies, buyers were concerned primarily with merchandise, they generally arrogated to themselves complete command within their own bailiwicks and acknowledged no authority except the proprietor's.[42]

The store superintendent served as Macy's assistant and substitute in the direction of operations, handling customers' complaints, hiring employees, maintaining store discipline, and the like. The first person to serve in this capacity was a man named Smith, but he was little more than a glorified floorwalker and shortly after 1866 he was succeeded by Margaret Getchell, the Nantucket lass to whom reference has already been made. While it was not at all unusual at this time to employ women in retail stores, to give one of them an executive position of such importance seems to have marked a radical departure from normal practice.

Besides the store superintendent, buyers, and floorwalkers there were, by 1870, several subordinate categories within the Macy organization. Thus there were clerks, who sold the merchandise; cash girls, who carried the merchandise, the money, and the salesbook to the cashier's desk for the purpose of making change and having the parcel wrapped; the cashiers, who did the actual change-making; and the parcel clerks or checkers, who wrapped up the goods. Then there were receiving-room clerks, who checked invoices and marked the incoming merchandise; an "exchanger" or "corrector," who made exchanges and refunds; boys and men to handle deliveries (the store owned 6 horses and 6 wagons in 1873); several porters to move heavy merchandise around the store; milliners and seamstresses engaged in manufacturing operations; a night watchman; a carpenter; an artist; several bookkeepers; and two scrubwomen. The number of employees in 1873 (our only payroll for the period terminates in February, 1874) ranged from 188 in the dull season to 387 at the peak just before Christmas, representing an increase of more than 50 per cent over the corresponding figures for 1869.[43]

In other words, by the early 1870's Macy's had already become a complicated organization, composed of various grades of specialized workers whose activities had to be planned, directed, and coördinated by the management in order that the store might perform its manifold duties.

Personal Leadership

The driving force and leadership in the Macy organization came from the founder himself. When the store was small, he himself had a part in every phase of its work. He bought goods, waited on trade, hired employees, wrote advertisements, and gave a hand personally wherever it was needed. Eventually many of his duties had to be delegated to others, but he continued to give close supervision. To the employees it seemed as if his stocky figure and flowing beard were omnipresent as he examined the merchandise in stock, checked the appearance of the store, maintained an eagle eye on expenses, and saw that every person was on the job. In the one surviving record of actual operations for his time there are many notations in Macy's handwriting to prove that he also spent much time in his office, going over the accounts and studying the operating figures.[44]

The growth of his business naturally made it impossible for Macy actually to oversee with his own eyes all activities within the store, but he continued, by means of the hierarchy of clerks, buyers, floorwalkers, cashiers, and superintendent, plus the multiplication of accounting records, to maintain intimate contact with every phase of operations. It became his practice, early on Monday mornings, to stand outside his office at the head of a short series of steps and announce impressively the name of the person who had made the largest amount of sales during the preceding week. And he himself seems to have established the time-honored Macy custom of having each buyer confer once a week with a member of the firm, going over the totals of sales and purchases for the preceding week, discussing plans for the future, and determining the amount of money to be spent on purchases for the department during the next six days. By such means Macy supplied, personally and directly, the supervision and stimulus which kept the organization going in the right way.[45]

At this point it may be appropriate to point out that certain managerial functions in Macy's were centralized at an early date, possibly from the very beginning. Activities like hiring and discharging employees, receiving and marking merchandise, advertising, and delivery arise in varying degrees in all merchandise divisions. Conceivably they could be almost entirely decentralized so that each department would handle all such operations for itself, making it largely a self-contained, autonomous unit, a member of a federation of stores within a single firm and only partially controlled by the top management. (In point of fact some decentralization existed in fairly large department stores until recently and possibly may still survive here and there.) There are, however, advantages in having the central management handle the main operating functions so as to permit the departmental heads (buyers) to concentrate upon buying and selling their goods. Some authorities regard functional centralization of this sort as one of the essential characteristics of the department store. By 1873, if not earlier, as the preceding section indicates, a number of functional activities were handled by separate divisions, controlled by Macy and the superintendent, rather than the merchandise departments: employment, receiving and marking, accounting, delivery, returns and adjustments, and, to a considerable extent at least, advertising.[46]

It is worth noting, too, that Macy expansion seems always to have been achieved by placing at the head of each new merchandise department a buyer charged with responsibility for both buying and selling. In recent years there has been much debate on the question of having these two activities separated for the sake of greater efficiency; but no one in early Macy history seems to have considered making additions by having an expert buyer take over the selection and purchase of merchandise for the new department while assigning the selling to someone who had shown particular ability for that side of the work. It evidently seemed both natural and wise to put a single person in charge.[47]

Promotional Developments

The most significant aspect of Macy's career from a historical point of view is the firm fabric of business policies which he developed and applied in his business. For the most part these have already been set forth in Chapter III, but certain additions must be considered.

Macy continued his one-price and cash policies without modification, and it is noteworthy that his ample cash resources, when the panic of 1873 brought paralysis or ruin to many merchants who operated on a credit basis, enabled him to step into the market and pick up especially good bargains by offering cash on delivery instead of payment in ten days. "We are," he advertised, "buying . . . goods for cash *for a Mere Song*. It will pay you to go to Macy & Co. *Every Day — Twice a Day — Three Times a Day*." [48]

As this excerpt indicates, he continued to advertise aggressively. His copy was somewhat less interesting and original after the first few years, but the use of large, boldface type (1865), the five-pointed star as a display piece (1872), and two- and three-column spreads (1874) made Macy advertisements stand out more than ever. Moreover, he advertised widely in newspapers, magazines, and by means of chromolithographed cards, as well as (after 1874) by catalogs.[49]

There is evidence, too, that the store was beginning to develop an appreciation of the promotional value of special exhibitions, the sort of affairs that we now regard as publicity devices. Thus, for the Christmas season of 1874 Macy's arranged a large window display of dolls in the form of a series of tableaux. While it may not have been the first effort of the sort (Macy had long featured his Christmas showing of dolls, but 1874 seems to mark the first featured window exhibition arranged in a coherent pattern), it marks the beginning of an annual Macy event to which New Yorkers look forward. It attracted much attention at the time, and the exhibit of the following year evoked special comment and a picture in Leslie's *Illustrated Newspaper*.[50] Similarly, in connection with the celebration of Washington's birthday the store announced a special exhibition of "the Martha Washington dinner service, a facsimile of the set given to Washington by the French Officers during the American Revolution."[51] On another occasion Macy's aided local charities by a popularity contest in which store customers were invited to cast their votes for one of three orphanage asylums (Protestant, Catholic, and Jewish) with pennies as ballots.[52] The modern retail store, of course, makes frequent use of such means to keep its name and merchandise constantly before the public.

Macy began to use the annual clearance sale as a promotional device in 1863.[53] (We have already observed his use of occasional sales at an earlier date.) Another means employed to stimulate sales was the solicitation of mail orders. The absence of anything like parcel post facilities made it impossible to do this on a large scale, but Macy as early as 1861 advertised gloves to be delivered by mail (63 cents a pair, 69 cents by mail). In 1874, after the establishment of Montgomery Ward Co. but before the general mail-order business had developed to any extent, Macy began to solicit mail orders for anything in stock which would go through the post, and he established a special mail-order department to handle transactions.[54] Without much doubt, he delivered purchases free of charge within the city from the very beginning, and by 1875, if not earlier, Macy advertising reminded the public that the store's free delivery service extended "to any part of New York City, Brooklyn, Williamsburg, Jersey City or Hoboken."[55]

Before Macy's death the store's low-price policy had crystallized into something very like that prevailing until the early 1930's. As we have seen, the original emphasis was on low prices, which were asserted to be substantially under those charged by Broadway stores. Gradually there emerged a definite policy of attempting to undersell all competitors, no matter where their stores were located. At first this was simply expressed in an occasional general claim that Macy goods were "cheaper than any other house in the city," but the more usual manifestation was the assertion that the price of some particular item featured was lower than in other stores, or (when gold prices were soaring) that Macy goods were being sold at less than the importing price in gold.[56] While we know that competitors thought Macy prices were too low to yield much profit, his early claims do not reveal a consistent underselling policy, even though on one occasion Macy guaranteed "our retail prices to be lower than wholesale prices in this city at present."[57] The modern Macy formula appears more clearly, however, in a statement issued in 1870:[58]

> Always buying everything for cash direct from the manufacturers in the European as well as the American markets, we are enabled to place all our goods before the public at 25 to 50% below the usual prices, saving our customers all the charges between the manufacturer and our own small profit.

In 1873 the modern theme was unmistakably sounded in advertisements of goods "sold at such low prices as cannot be met by any other house." One piece of Macy copy went on to explain: "Owing to the fact of our importing direct and in such large quantities, we are enabled to make and sustain low prices against any competition."[59] In 1874 the firm boasted that it sold silverware at prices well under the manufacturers' list quotations. By 1875 Macy advertisements declared, "We will not be undersold."[60] This defiance of all competition was not always in evidence, but the essence of the modern Macy policy of underselling rival stores was unmistakably developed in the early years of the store's history by a Yankee of Quaker descent, long before the Straus family had any connection with the firm.

Just before Macy's death another modern Macy practice put in its first appearance — the use of odd prices instead of quoting in even dollars or in even fractions of a dollar. As indicated above, the odd endings to early Macy prices may safely be attributed to the lingering practice of thinking in terms of shillings and pence, plus the peculiar fractional currency in existence at the time. The first unmistakable use of odd prices was in 1875, when Macy quotations on chinaware included the following: $4.33, $24.47, and $596.66. The last two prices are of particular interest because previous Macy practice would unquestionably have been to quote $25 and $600. Again, we find shoes being offered at $3.89, $4.84, and $4.99, revealing even more clearly the use of odd prices to give the appearance of a bargain. (We shall see later that the uneven endings may also have come about by the routine application of fixed percentages to cost in determining the retail prices.) Macy himself cannot be credited with originating the device, for it was first employed in the china and shoe departments, departments which were leased by outsiders, and was not applied in other Macy departments until some time later. In point of fact, the idea of pricing so as to suggest bargains seems to have been introduced by the Bon Marché in Paris and subsequently imported into American retail practice.[61]

Fragments of a Portrait

The picture of Macy that emerges from documentary fragments and the recollections of old employees is that of a man who worked indefatigably and expected employees to do the same, who had struggled long and hard to attain a comfortable living and had no intention of sharing with his staff any more of his income than circumstances absolutely required. On the other hand, he could be kind and generous to individual persons, and more than one of his employees attributed advancement to the frequent encouragement received. Certainly Macy employees were as well treated as those in other large stores in New York; those who criticize wages and working conditions in a particular department store are seldom aware of the condition of the industry generally. A. T. Stewart, who could afford to be generous if anyone could at the time, was notorious for the low wages he paid, and he maintained a system of harsh, disciplinary rules which was considered extreme even at the time; yet those who were in a position to know admitted that conditions were substantially worse in many other stores, particularly the smaller ones. We shall have a chance to examine this whole subject of working conditions in detail in Chapter VIII.

Macy had a quick temper and (until he got religion at a Moody and Sankey revival) he was noted for outbursts of particularly choice profanity, a relic of days before the mast and evidence that he had strayed from the Quaker principles of his parents. His temper sometimes undid some of his strenuous efforts at economy. He refused, it is said, to have any shades on the gas lights in the store on the theory that he had paid for all the light and did not intend to have any of it curtailed. On one occasion he returned from Europe to find one of the gas jets bearing a large glass globe. Without a word, Macy seized a hammer from a workman who was making repairs nearby, smashed the offending glass to bits, and strode into his office without further comment. On another occasion, having received complaints from customers that the handles on some of his umbrellas were too weak to be serviceable, he went to the department, broke the umbrellas over his knee, and walked away, leaving a pile of wreckage in the aisle.[62]

It is clear that Macy was much more of a human being than cold, calculating A. T. Stewart, less narrowly righteous than John Wanamaker. He liked to drop into Delmonico's for a sociable luncheon, and in the evening he enjoyed smoking a cigar while listening to his daughter play the piano, or else he went out for a round of billiards with a friend. On buying trips to Europe he was not above flirting with the girls, and on a few occasions he even got pleasantly drunk — though not until business transactions had been completed.[63]

We know too little about Macy personally to form an adequate judgment of him as a man, but we know much about his business record, which speaks for itself. A failure at 36, he had overcome obstacles, withstood the competition of older and wealthier firms, and established his store on a prosperous footing. He managed its operations during years of rapid change in business, national political strife, and world-wide economic difficulties (in England the period from 1873 to 1896 is still known as "the Great Depression"), contriving not only to adapt his enterprise to new circumstances but also to maintain profits during the process. He left behind him a modern department store, equipped with operating policies which were unusual for the times and which, continued down to the present, have played an important part in the enduring success of the store which bears his name.

To many thoughtful observers it is socially desirable, by introducing new forms of organization and new operating methods, to make shopping convenient, to cut down expenses, and to offer merchandise to the public at reduced prices. Progress along such lines is admittedly materialistic, but it is of major importance to society and unquestionably forms the basis for cultural advance. Considering his work in this light, Rowland Macy performed a great public service: the modest profits that he gained in the process were amply deserved, and modern New Yorkers are still in his debt.

During the early 'seventies Macy began to suffer from poor health, and in the spring of 1877 he went abroad to see if rest and medical treatment would bring relief. The fact that he made his will before leaving indicates that he knew his condition was dangerous. He became seriously ill in Paris and died there on March 29, 1877, when he was nearly 55 years of age.[64]

THE FIRST PARTNER

Some years before his death Macy had taken steps to share with others the ownership and management of his business. Probably he would have preferred to see members of his own immediate family relieve him of sole responsibility and prepare to succeed him in control, but fate determined otherwise. At the very beginning, he had employed his brother-in-law in the store's operations, but for reasons which are not known the two men quarreled; and, after an abortive attempt to establish a rival store in New York, Houghton returned to Boston.[65] Macy might also have been expected to bring his brother Robert into the enterprise, but Robert seems to have lacked the requisite energy and ability; upon the dissolution (in 1868) of the jobbing firm of Seeligman & Macy with which he had been connected, Rowland placed him in charge of the receiving and marking department of the store, a position which he held until the time of his death.[66] An even more likely candidate for succession to ownership was Macy's own son, Rowland, Jr. The reason why he did not inherit the store is set forth in a poignant paragraph in R. H. Macy's will:[67]

> I am grieved to say . . . that I cannot entrust him with the care or management of any property. . . . Although I have done everything in my power to aid him in establishing habits of temperance and sobriety, yet I am compelled to acknowledge the failure of every effort made by me and others to that end. His passion for strong drink has not hitherto been controlled by him.

Curiously enough, Abiel T. La Forge, the man who actually was selected by Macy for admission to partnership, owed his initial employment in the store to the delinquencies of the son. It is worth while to relate La Forge's story in some detail because he is the only important person connected with the store about whom we have much first-hand information, besides which his career, though short, illustrates the way in which the men of his generation, blessed with ability and a little luck, could rapidly achieve positions of responsibility and wealth.

La Forge was born near Fishkill, New York, in May, 1842. Not much is known about his youth except that he received very little formal schooling and went to work in his early 'teens. In October, 1861, he enlisted in Company C of the 85th New York Volunteers and soon saw active service. Incapacitated by dysentery, he served as a hospital orderly while recuperating and then went back to the front, being promoted to first lieutenant in 1864 and advanced to captaincy in February, 1865. He participated in the hard fighting in Virginia in the spring of 1865 which led to Lee's surrender, and later he was appointed brevet major "for gallant and meritorious services before Petersburg, Virginia." [68]

Shortly after La Forge became captain of Company I, 106th New York Volunteers, Macy's son, Rowland, Jr., was assigned to his company; possibly because La Forge was a member of the divisional court martial. Late in 1864 young Macy had been given a heavy sentence for an offense (exact nature not known) which included being absent three days without leave. The lad's postwar conduct suggests that he had probably been drunk and insubordinate. La Forge took a personal interest in young Macy, made him company clerk, and later, at the elder Macy's request, successfully interceded to have the remaining penalties removed. Naturally the father was grateful and invited La Forge to visit him. Once out of the army, La Forge joined the throng of men who sought civilian employment in New York. He soon found that "seeking employment in a great city is no very easy matter. One should be very meek and not show the spirit of a man no matter how large his bump of independence may be." [69]

ABIEL T. LA FORGE
Partner, 1871–1878

1872. 3

Statement of the Business of R. H. Macy & Co. Jan 15th

Assets

Stock No. 1		6636.51
2		26147.76
3		11434.15
4		5951.35
5		18833.37
6		15426.64
7		913.20
8		No Stock.
9		32145.27
10		497.56
11		8106.46
12		18862.23
13		4524.74
14		8211.15
Total Stock		157712.10
Store and Stable Fixt.		10807.20
Miscell. debts.		95.94
Manhattan Gas Co.	4346.15	60.00
Cash in Hand,		
Am't paid La F.	2153.54	1711.18
		170386.42

Liabilities
(On Stock acc't) 10473.48
Eliza Macy 1700.00
R. H. Macy 35212.94

45386.42

Balance left by R. H. Macy 123000.00
Cash put in by A. T. La Forge 2000.00
Total Capital 125000.00

BALANCE SHEET, 1872
Financial condition when La Forge acquired an interest in Macy's

Macy offered him a job in the store but suggested that he would have a better chance of permanent success in a wholesale firm. Macy personally introduced him at Stewart's, Claflin's, and Jaffrey's, and was instrumental in getting him finally placed in the new dry goods firm of Mills & Gibb, initial salary to be $500 a year. The Macys frequently invited La Forge to see them, partly because they liked him personally and partly because he seemed to have a good influence on young "Roly," whose conduct continued to give his parents much anxiety. He restricted his visits because he feared that the Macys might think he was "presuming on the position of confidant which I hold in the family," but he spent many an evening in the Macy home, and he was also a frequent caller at the store — "sold my first goods to a Mr. Mount for Mr. Macy on the 17th [January, 1866]. I hope it will not be my last." [70] It was in this way that he met Margaret Getchell. She had seen him in the store and had instantly fallen in love with him, a fact which soon came to Macy's knowledge. A plot was hatched, as La Forge's diary recorded: "I was again around to Mr. Macy's Tuesday evening. Miss Getchell — his cashier — was there also; spent the evening very pleasantly, saw Miss G. on the car when she left for home." The young lady also saw to it that the captain was invited to the employees' dance referred to above. She got her man. When Macy invited La Forge to see the crowd of shoppers which thronged the store on Christmas Eve, 1867, the diary reports: "Such a crowd as I never before saw in a store. Could not help a bounding of the heart when I saw Margie. I spoke with her and the rich melody of her voice thrilled me as of old. Macy kept the store open until mid-night, taking over $6,000 in the one day, which was the best day during his business life." [71]

Meanwhile, Macy had offered La Forge a position as lace buyer at $1,000 a year. Still fearing to presume upon Macy's gratitude, he turned it down, only to find that Mills & Gibb proposed to pay him only $700 for his second year. Macy repeated his offer, Mills & Gibb increased their rate to $850 with traveling privileges, and later Macy made a new proposal which La Forge finally decided to accept, early in 1869: [72]

How Mills & Gibb did take on when I told them that I was going to leave! They just discovered that I was a much more valuable man than they had previously supposed and offered me an extra inducement to stay of course, and of course I did not accept it. So here I am Macy's buyer of Laces Embroideries, Hdks, Trimmings &c. My branch of the store will sell about $200,000 a year. . . .

I am better pleased with the situation which I occupy now. . . . I am in a position to learn what I can in time apply to business for myself. The wholesale trade requires such a large capital to start with that I could hardly hope without aid to ever get into business for myself. Now in retail it is different, after one is master of his trade he can swim without further aid.

The strongest reason for the change, however, as La Forge plainly hinted in a letter to his sister, was that he had become engaged to Margaret Getchell and naturally wanted to work in the same store. They were married in June, 1869, and took rooms over the store.[73] Many members of the Macy staff have married fellow employees in the course of 84 years, but the union of Margaret Getchell and A. T. La Forge surely deserves recognition as *the* romance of the great store.

La Forge proudly reported to his sister that Margaret was to continue her work in Macy's. "She is the Superintendent, having full charge of the entire business; as we sell a million dollars worth of goods a year and have nearly two hundred employees, her position is a very responsible one. . . . Just think, nearly two hundred employees in one store!"[74]

Macy soon began to depend upon La Forge for assistance in merchandising, just as he depended upon Margaret Getchell to keep the organization and store systems running smoothly. When La Forge was offered $5,000 a year to go with a Boston publishing firm, Macy made him (January 1, 1871) a "trial partner" — he had no interest in the capital but received $1,500 annual salary and 5 per cent of the net profits of the business after allowing $10,000 salary to Macy.[75] In 1872 La Forge became an open partner, contributing $2,000 out of a total capital of $125,000. He was to receive a salary of $3,500 per year, 7 per cent interest on his investment, plus a share of the profits (initially 10 per cent), with the understanding that he should let them accumulate in the business until he owned at least a third of the capital. The agreement contemplated that Macy would gradually withdraw capital until his share was 55 per cent of the total. La Forge was to devote his entire attention to assisting Macy in the management of the store.[76]

The La Forges continued to live over the store until 1875, and they often worked nights long after the employees had gone home, marking special lots of merchandise or figuring inventories and profits for the season. After the arrival of her first child, Margaret had to give up regular employment, but she continued to lend a hand in the busy seasons and at inventory time, and, as said before, she took complete charge of operations for three months in the spring of 1873 while her husband and Macy were buying in Europe, despite the fact that she was carrying her third son at the time.[77]

The young couple got along beautifully with the staff, but it was not always easy to maintain amicable relations with the head of the firm. Physically sick and mentally disturbed about the behavior of his wayward son, Macy was often irascible, and on several occasions relations between the partners were strained almost to the breaking point, although the rows were always of short duration. One source of irritation was the fact that Macy drew the profits out of the business as fast as they were made. He was entitled to do so under the partnership agreement, but the store was kept short of cash as a result, and when La Forge needed cash beyond his salary allowance, he had to borrow from Macy at 7 per cent interest, giving as security a lien (amounting to 120 per cent of the value of the loan) against his interest in the business. Another source of annoyance was the fact that Macy thought small gifts were sufficient compensation when Margaret La Forge helped in the store — even when she was in complete charge for three months! On the whole, however, the La Forges were prospering financially, probably beyond their youthful dreams, and relations between them and the Macys were generally marked with real affection.[78]

The Partnership Enlarged

In January, 1875, a third partner was admitted to the firm, Robert Macy Valentine. Not much is known about the new member except that he was the son of Macy's youngest sister, enjoyed close friendship with the La Forges, and had worked in the store for at least four years, having succeeded La Forge in 1872 as buyer of laces and books. Under the new agreement the capital of the firm was increased to $150,000, distributed as follows: Macy, $121,500; La Forge, $19,500; and Valentine, $9,000. Macy unquestionably was admitting others to partnership in order to transfer to them the burdens of ownership and management rather than to increase the capital of the enterprise. Valentine's original share was small even at face value, but actually he brought much less than that amount into the business. By the terms of the agreement Macy was to lend La Forge $382 and Valentine $5,000, to be contributed by them as cash capital, so that Valentine's net original contribution was really only $4,000. The partnership agreement explicitly states, moreover, that Macy desired to reduce his investment in the business and to permit the younger men to increase their share out of earnings.[79]

Whether La Forge or Valentine had any influence upon store policy before Macy's death cannot be determined. Certainly the partnership agreements explicitly provided for a continuation of the established policy of buying and selling for cash. As already indicated, of course, there is some evidence for the view that Margaret La Forge, with her husband's approval, encouraged the Macy policy of diversifying the merchandise departments of the store. For the present our interest in the two partners lies chiefly in the fact that Macy had begun, six years before his death, to transfer ownership to younger men. As a result, his passing occasioned no complete break in the continuity of the enterprise.

A Glimpse of Early Macy Operating Figures

If we are to obtain anything like a realistic view of Macy's business, we must go beyond a description of merchandise, policies, activities, and men; a great deal of such a description is bound to be abstract

MACY'S IN THE LATE 1860'S
The store behind the telegraph pole is the original one

ROBERT MACY VALENTINE
Partner, 1875–1879

EARLY OPERATING FIGURES

and general, lacking tangible dimensions, couched in terms which, no matter how carefully chosen, hamper nice comparisons with other stores, whether in the 1870's or today. Admittedly no yardstick exists by which accurate comparisons can be made possible, but the accounting records provide dollar-and-cents measurements by means of which we can give our picture greater depth. Dollar values fluctuate, to be sure, and operating figures invariably involve arbitrary judgments at certain points (such as inventory valuation and allocation of overhead expense) and so fall short of the absolute precision which they seem to have. Even so, they help to answer concretely such questions as how productive, how expensive, how profitable, how big — some of the most fundamental questions one can raise.

It is unfortunate that we do not have a complete account of operating results during Macy's lifetime. However, a few surviving fragments yield valuable information. In 1870, for example, Macy's stock of merchandise was estimated to be worth $130,000 at cost, when sales were approximately $1,000,000 per year.[80] Assuming that the store's gross margin (the difference between the net invoice cost and the selling price of merchandise, or the sum out of which the expenses of running the business are paid and the profits, if anything remains, are derived) was about the same in 1870 as in 1872, these figures for 1870 indicate that Macy must have been turning his stock about six times during the year. This is a substantially faster rate than modern dry goods and department stores ordinarily achieve.[81]

We have in Table 2 a summary of the only detailed operating figures extant for the business during Macy's lifetime, figures relating to the years 1872 to 1876 inclusive. The importance of this series must not be overlooked. So far as can now be discovered no similar data concerning retail operations — one might almost say no factual data of any kind — have ever been published for the period before 1900. This series accordingly yields precise, concrete information in an area in which we have hitherto been compelled to rely upon guesses, some of them very wild.

Perhaps the most significant fact which emerges is the size of the gross margin, which ranged from a low of 18.89 per cent of sales in the adverse year of 1873 to 22.88 in 1874. It is quite possible that

TABLE 2
OPERATING RESULTS
1872–1876

Year	Net Sales[a]	Discounts Received[b] %	Jobbing Income[c] %	Gross Margin[d] %	Total %	Expense[e] $	Net Gain[f] %
			(*Percentage of Net Sales*)				
1872	$1,002,528	3.43	1.73	20.96	16.82	$168,643	4.14
1873	1,022,255	3.34	1.63	18.89	17.34	177,319	1.55
1874	1,197,867	3.80	.92	22.88	17.53	209,951	5.35
1875	1,366,889	3.21	.79	20.47	15.37	210,132	5.10
1876	1,612,788	3.11	.65	20.66	14.33	231,165	6.32

[a] Includes sales in leased departments after Mar., 1874.

[b] These figures refer to allowances made by vendors for cash payments. They were treated by the management as other income.

[c] The jobbing department handled the importing activities of the firm, and the revenue shown represents the difference between the projected cost of importations, as originally charged to retail departments, and the actual cost calculated after receiving a complete account of the expenses incurred. The estimate was evidently maintained well above the actual expense in order to cover the risk of loss from foreign exchange transactions, etc.

[d] These figures represent the difference between the amount received for sales and the net cost of the goods, after the deduction of all discounts and before deduction of any of the store's operating expenses. Presumably inward freight and trucking expense was included in the net cost.

[e] The total expenses apparently include a charge for interest on partners' capital. Therefore, in order to make these figures comparable with later data from which such interest charges have been eliminated, it is probably necessary to deduct the following amounts from the figures given for the respective years: .87%, .86%, .73%, .77%, .65%. Shortages have been treated as a deduction from gross margin rather than expense.

[f] The figures in this column represent the profits as calculated for the purpose of dividing earnings among the partners. No deduction was made for salary to R. H. Macy, but La Forge received a salary of $3,500 annually for the years 1872–74 which has been included under expense. Expenses for 1875 and 1876 include $3,500 a year to La Forge and $3,000 to Valentine. Moreover, the expenses probably included a charge of 7% interest on capital invested. Therefore, to calculate the total earnings of the partners one should add to these percentages the amounts set forth in note e above.

SOURCE: La Forge's Ledger, 1871–77.

the difference between 1873 and 1874 resulted from some error or change in the accounting system, for the two years taken together show a gross margin closely comparable to those before and afterwards. The typical figure, at any rate, was a little over 20.5 per cent. These facts should put an end to the widely held belief that dry goods store margins used to be as low as 15 per cent of sales. In this connection one should remember that Macy's, then as now, stressed low prices and small profits. The gross margin of many contemporary rivals was probably somewhat higher than 20.5 per cent.[82]

Note, however, that the store gross margin was made up of three components: discounts received (concessions in price because of cash payments), jobbing income (gains derived from importing merchandise and selling it to the retail departments at a price designed to cover importing expenses and a little more for contingencies), and "margin" or "rating" (it might be called the selling department's margin because it represents the difference between cost and selling price *before* allowing for discounts and jobbing income). The most widely accepted practice in retailing today is to calculate gross margin by starting with the net cost of merchandise delivered at the store, after all deductions for cash and the like. This is the figure to which reference is made in current discussions about the cost of distribution. It has increased since the 1870's, but not so much as many people have assumed.

Another significant piece of information which is derived from these early Macy figures is the fact that the store's expenses ranged from a low of 14.33 to a high of 17.53 per cent of sales, the lower figures in the series reflecting the sharp increase in volume in 1875 and 1876. Expenses tend to lag behind rises in sales because of the influence of such fixed charges as rent; spreading the overhead expenses over a larger sales volume brings about a lower expense ratio. There is good reason to believe that the expense total for the 'seventies included a charge of 7 per cent interest on invested capital, because of which the net gain accruing to the partners probably should be stated as 5.01, 2.41, 6.08, 5.87, and 6.97 per cent of sales. In other words, despite the severe depression which prevailed during most of the 1870's, the Macy business was usually producing income for the partners at the rate of about 6 per cent of net sales. The sharp drop in 1873 was caused by a net loss in the spring season and relatively poor profits in the fall, resulting from greatly decreased "margins" obtained on sales. This confirms the notations in letters and diaries that weather conditions were unusually bad and consumer demand poor at all times, and it suggests that the dry goods trade was hard hit even before the severe financial panic of September actually broke loose.[83]

Table 3 presents a number of revealing ratios for the period. Advertising expense, not calculated separately until 1874, shows an increase in 1875 followed by a sharp drop in 1876. Incomplete figures for 1877 indicate that expenditures for advertising declined still further — both actually and in relation to sales — during 1877. At the high point (1.4 per cent of sales) the advertising ratio was well below modern figures.

Delivery expense — apparently consisting of stable expense — rose in 1874, followed by a decreasing ratio. This fluctuation is probably to be accounted for by the fact that the delivery department, having been enlarged in 1874, was able to handle the increased volume of business during the next two years without any material advance in costs.

It is unfortunate that we have no adequate data for a further analysis of expenses. According to such information as is available for 1876 and 1877, the total payroll expense was approximately 8 per cent of sales, while rent was about 2 per cent of sales. Payroll data indicate an increase of at least 1 per cent in the ratio of salaries and wages between 1870 and 1877. The reason for this is not altogether clear, but some light is shed by another set of statistics. During 1870 the Macy sales averaged $5,150 per employee; in 1871 this average was $5,090; in 1872 it declined to $4,660; and in 1873 it dropped still further to $3,980.[84]

This decline in the average production per employee would, if not accompanied by decreases in wages, bring about an increasing expense ratio. Several forces were probably at work. The persistent decline in prices after 1865, aggravated by the sudden drop accompanying the panic of 1873, brought sales practically to a standstill un-

TABLE 3
MISCELLANEOUS OPERATING DATA
1872–1876

Year	Advertising Expense[a] (% of Net Sales)	Delivery Expense[b] (% of Net Sales)	Total Assets to Net Sales[e] %	Inventory to Total Assets[e] %	Fixed Assets to Total Assets[e] %	Net Gain to Total Assets[d] %	AVERAGE STOCK-TURN[e] Owned Depts.	AVERAGE STOCK-TURN[e] Leased Depts.	AVERAGE STOCK-TURN[e] All Depts.
1872	..	..	20.7	91.9	7.6	19.9	4.6	..	4.6
1873	..	.43	17.0	81.8	10.3	9.1	5.3	..	5.3
1874	1.04	.79	16.7	71.5	12.2	32.0	5.6	2.2	5.4
1875	1.40	.61	15.0	66.5	11.6	33.9	6.8	2.4	5.7
1876	.69	.60	15.5	61.4	9.5	40.8	8.1	2.6	6.5

[a] This item refers mainly to newspaper and magazine space; it apparently includes no salaries.
[b] Apparently includes direct stable expense but no salaries.
[c] The ratio for 1872 refers to assets on the books in Jan, 1873, at the close of the fiscal year, and so on for the succeeding years. This ratio does not allow for the fact that the partners probably received interest on their capital; nor does it take into account the salaries paid to La Forge and Valentine.
[d] In calculating this ratio sales at cost have been divided by the average of the cost of merchandise on hand at the beginning, middle, and end of the fiscal year. The leased departments were silver, china and glassware, and women's and children's shoes.

SOURCE: La Forge's Ledger, 1871–77.

til 1875 (as already shown in Table 1), when measured in dollars. In physical volume, and doubtless in number of transactions, there was unquestionably an increase during these years, and the store had to expand its staff in order to handle the additional work. It also is possible that the store had been understaffed in 1870 and that Macy was adding employees to improve service within the store; certainly the number did increase.[85] To some extent the same forces were undoubtedly at work between 1874 and 1877, and it is also possible that some wage increases were granted as the worst effects of 1873 wore off, thereby swelling the ratio.

The asset ratios in the third, fourth, and fifth columns show to what a large extent Macy's was a merchandising organization. Sales were accomplished with a relatively small amount of assets, and those assets consisted mainly of stock-in-trade, with very little money tied up in fixed equipment. The steady decline in the ratio of inventory to total assets reflects the fact that the firm was improving its cash position, acquiring additional fixtures, and adjusting stocks more closely to sales.

The last three columns of Table 3 show the rapidity with which Macy departments turned their inventories each year. Owned departments achieved an average annual stock-turn of 4.6 in 1872 (which would be good by modern standards) and subsequently improved results until in 1876 they had reached the exceedingly high rate of 8 times. Leased departments (silver, china, and glass after 1874, with the addition of women's and children's shoes in 1875) showed a lower stock-turn, a little over two times a year. This low rate may be explained chiefly by the kind of merchandise involved, for all three departments typically had to maintain relatively large assortments in order to do business (this is true of such departments generally today). In addition, the fact that all three departments had just been installed would account in part for the slower turnover, and we find that the rate improved substantially in the course of three years.

In Table 4 we have an analysis of operating results by individual departments for the fall season of 1876. The period covered is only five months because the management apparently did not insist upon having stock taken punctually every half-year. Those five months, however, thanks to the stimulating effect of the Christmas season, accounted for more than half (53.3 per cent) of the store's sales volume for 1876 and nearly two-thirds (62.8 per cent) of the Macy earnings for that year. The leased departments contributed 13.5 per cent of the volume. Because of the seasonal nature of the demand in certain lines and the newness of several departments, it is impossible to estimate accurately from this limited period what their normal contributions would be for the year, but the importance of nontextile lines is obvious. Sales in the china, house furnishings, and fancy goods departments each far exceeded those in most of the departments handling conventional dry goods, and the combined volume in nontextile departments actually amounted to more than 45 per cent of the total business done.

The margins obtained by the various departments show some interesting variations. Among the owned departments the highest was for toys, doubtless because the rate of stock-turn in that line was naturally very low as a result of its extreme seasonal demand and also because there was probably a large amount of damage to stock from handling. Breakage was certainly a factor in the margin of the china department (40.88 per cent before dividing with the lessees), although here, as in ribbons and silverware, the semi-luxurious nature of the commodity entered into the margin obtained. One must bear in mind, moreover, that Macy's imported directly from European manufacturers a large portion of the ribbons, fancy goods, toys, flowers, and feathers sold, while the silverware and china were put into the store at the net delivered cost to the lessee from the manufacturers. Consequently, the respective figures in these lines really constitute the retail and wholesale margins combined. In certain other lines this is less likely to be true, the wholesaler's margin usually being hidden in the cost to Macy. This point is important in any general discussion of costs of distribution because conclusions based on retail percentages, without regard to the functions performed, can so easily be wrong, as the following illustration shows:

Assume that a manufacturer sells an item to a wholesaler for $1.00, which the wholesaler in turn sells to the retailer for $1.25 and the retailer

TABLE 4
OPERATING RESULTS BY DEPARTMENTS
August 7, 1876–January 6, 1877

Department	Net Sales	Percentage of Dept. Sales to Store Total	Margin before Adjustments[a]	Percentage of Margin to Sales
1. White goods	$36,891.90	4.2	$ 4,227.52	11.45
2. Laces and embroideries	86,964.59	9.9	13,098.97	15.06
2½. Ladies' underclothing	16,995.71	1.9	2,492.41	14.66
3. Smallwares and notions	32,975.99	3.8	7,269.05	22.04
4. Ribbons, etc.	51,081.51	5.8	10,391.89	20.34
6. Hosiery and men's furnishings	62,328.73	7.1	9,053.57	14.52
7. Ladies' ties	11,027.89	1.3	1,497.52	13.57
8. Furs[b]	13,371.24	1.5	859.49	6.42
9. Fancy goods	72,776.91	8.3	13,987.69	19.21
10. Boys' clothing[c]	13,009.52	1.5	824.92	6.34
11. House furnishings	79,922.81	9.1	17,351.17	21.71
12. Toys and dolls	55,381.89	6.3	15,504.68	27.99
13. Books and stationery	68,962.64	7.9	11,017.62	15.97
14. Trimmings and worsteds	37,342.06	4.3	6,190.32	16.57
16. Candy and soda water	16,971.91	1.9	4,052.65	23.87
17. Kid gloves	22,565.50	2.6	4,360.31	19.32
18. Millinery	21,778.33	2.5	4,428.28	20.33
19. Flowers and feathers	17,427.29	2.0	4,345.04	24.93
21. Suits and cloaks	27,578.85	3.2	4,852.13	17.59
22. Dress silks[d]	12,223.64	1.4	284.77	2.33
Total Owned	$757,578.91	86.5	$136,090.00	17.96

TABLE 4 (*continued*)

Department	Net Sales	Percentage of Dept. Sales to Store Total	Margin before Adjustments[a]	Percentage of Margin to Sales
Leased:[c]				
5. Silver	$ 13,388.20	1.5	$ 2,508.85(½)	18.73(37.46)
15. China and glass	83,398.30	9.5	17,053.31(½)	20.44(40.88)
20. Shoes	22,201.45	2.5	1,155.31(½)	5.2 (10.4)
Total Leased	$118,987.95	13.5	$20,717.47	17.41
Total Store	$876,566.86	100.0	$156,807.47(½)	17.88(35.76)
Derivation of Gross Margin:				
Total sales		$876,566.86		100.00
Total margin before adjustments		$156,807.47		17.90
Discounts earned[f]		26,908.96		3.07
Jobbing department[g]		6,356.00		.73
Gross margin			190,072.43	21.70
Cost of goods sold			$686,494.43	78.30

[a] These figures represent the difference between the sales price received for the goods and their original cost. They do not represent gross margin as defined by the Harvard Bureau of Business Research because earned discounts were treated as income and not deducted from the cost of goods sold; moreover, no allowance was made for the favorable balance achieved by the jobbing department which handled importations for the store. Adjustments for these two items are shown below for total operations, but they cannot be made for individual departments without more information than we possess.

[b] Sales and profits are small for the period because the department was a seasonal one and opened in the middle of Sept.

[c] This department was opened the preceding Feb. and had not yet attained its normal operating level.

[d] This department was first opened in Oct., and its sales represent only three months' operations.

[e] Macy's received half the margin, the other half going to the lessees; hence the total percentage of margin is indicated in parentheses.

[f] Discounts earned were treated by the management as other income.

[g] The jobbing department handled the importing activities of the firm, and the revenue shown is apparently an estimate of the difference between the projected cost of importations, as originally charged to departments, and the actual cost calculated after receiving a complete account of the expenses incurred. The estimate was evidently well above the actual expense in order to cover the risk of loss from foreign exchange transactions, etc.

SOURCE: La Forge's Ledger, 1876–77.

sells to the public at $1.75. The retailer's margin is 50 cents, or 28.6 per cent of the selling price. If the retailer should buy the article directly from the manufacturer at $1.00 and sell it for $1.65, his gross margin would be 65 cents, or 39.3 per cent. The customer would actually receive a reduction in price of 10 cents. Yet, looking solely at the percentages, one would say that the cost of distribution had risen sharply as a result of the change.

In examining Macy figures for later years, the reader must guard against false conclusions of this kind, which are unfortunately all too frequent in current economic debates.

One other item in Table 4 calls for comment, namely the income from the jobbing department. This revenue, obviously an estimate, arose from the firm's importing activities and represents the difference between the cost estimated at the time the merchandise was charged to retail departments and the actual cost as subsequently determined. Some of the difference arose from the fluctuating price of gold in terms of American dollars (the United States had not yet resumed specie payments). It is evident that the management, in order to be sure that all the expenses involved in importing would be fully covered, was conservative in arriving at the estimated cost.

In Table 5 we have the Macy figures for the fall of 1876 in summary form. They relate only to the last five months of the fiscal year and include the Christmas season when retail trade (as today) was usually much heavier and more profitable than during the spring and summer. Allowing for this distortion, they help to round out the quantitative analysis of the Macy business during a normal period of operations.

The item "shortages" arose in part from accounting errors, explained in Appendix B. In part this entry resulted from the fact that, in the 1870's as now, goods were damaged, lost, or stolen. Indeed, the store's difficulties with shoplifters and suits for false arrest began as early as 1867, and at the close of a busy Christmas season the kindly disposed La Forge was impelled to note in his diary, "still a heavy trade and no doubt much stealing." [86]

The gross margin and profit ratios in Table 5 are larger than the annual figure shown in Table 2. This is largely the consequence of

TABLE 5
Operating Results
August 7, 1876–January 6, 1877

			Percentage of Net Sales	
Net sales, owned departments	$757,578.91		86.42	
Net sales, leased departments[a]	118,987.95		13.58	
Total net sales		$876,566.86		100.00
Cost of goods sold	$675,296.10		77.03	
Shortages	11,198.33		1.27	
Total cost of goods sold		686,494.43		78.30
Gross Margin		$190,072.43		21.70
Operating Expenses[b]				
General expense	$44,668.02		5.10	
Delivery	5,198.03		.59	
Advertising	8,387.06		.96	
Insurance	1,230.05		.14	
Total payroll[c]	64,323.24		7.34	
Total operating expenses		123,806.40		14.13
Net operating profit		$66,266.03		7.57
Interest on capital		4,375.00		.50
Total net gain		$70,641.03		8.07

[a] The leased departments (china, silver, and shoes) were stocked by outside concerns and operated jointly by R. H. Macy & Co. and the lessees. The exact manner in which the expenses were divided is not known, but the "rating" (gross margin before any adjustment for earned discounts) was divided equally.

[b] Nothing is known about the exact classification of expenses. A charge for interest on capital invested at 7% per annum was apparently included in "General expense."

[c] The payroll charges included salaries for La Forge and Valentine at the annual rate of $3,500 and $3,000, respectively. No salary was paid to Macy.

SOURCE: La Forge's Ledger, 1876–77.

the profitable holiday shopping, but it may possibly reflect some improvement in general business conditions.

A brief statement of the accounting methods used by the Macy firm in the 1870's and '80's is presented in Appendix B for the benefit of readers who wish to see how the operating results were calculated.

CHAPTER VI

THE EMERGENCE OF DEPARTMENT STORES

Now that we have a detailed picture of Macy evolution, it is feasible to consider the store's relation to general developments in contemporary retailing. By 1877 Macy's was a full-fledged department store. Among the largest retail firms in New York City in size and sales volume, it was organized by departments, with many functional activities centralized, it carried a well-diversified line of merchandise, and it catered primarily to women. It was also an urban institution and it offered (apart from its cash policy) the basic free services in accordance with the standards of the period.

And what about other retail stores? Were they moving in the same direction? If so, was Macy imitating others or did he lead the way? At this stage of our knowledge it is impossible to give a definite answer to such questions, but available evidence suggests some tentative conclusions. Incidentally, here is a rich field for further investigation which should keep more than one student occupied.

New Tendencies in European Retailing

The dominant business tendency, both in Europe and in America, in the 1860's and '70's was away from the intense specialization of the earlier part of the century, moving towards integration of functions and diversification of merchandise. As a result, on both sides of the Atlantic we find many retail stores at that time tending to grow into department stores. It has long been assumed that the department store appeared in Europe earlier than in America, and that the American department store arose because men like A. T. Stewart and John Wanamaker decided to imitate the developments which they found abroad, particularly in Paris. There is, however, ample proof that the department store was emerging in both America and Europe at approximately the same time. The existing evidence indicates, too, that the American department store was essentially a product of its own native environment rather than an importation from Europe.[1]

Whether the Bon Marché was really the first in the world to become a department store depends upon the precise definition used, but such information as I can find does not fully support the longstanding assumption. Unquestionably it was doing a large volume of business (about $1,400,000 in 1863), it was an urban institution catering primarily to women, it was organized by merchandise departments, and it offered many free services to customers. (There was apparently some centralization of managerial functions, but the evidence on this is not clear.) During the 1850's and '60's, moreover, it moved unmistakably towards diversification of lines, adding to its wide assortment of dry goods such merchandise as furs, oriental rugs, some of the fancy goods which Macy carried, a complete line of bedding, and even iron beds. But, apart from the beds, it seems to have gone no further in that direction by 1865 than several American firms, including Arnold, Constable & Co., Lord & Taylor, and A. T. Stewart; and I find no conclusive evidence that it was handling a much wider variety in 1872 than in 1865. It seems to me highly significant that all the advertisements of the Bon Marché and all the descriptive articles that one is able to find about it up to 1872 in contemporary sources, such as *L'Illustration,* deal at length with its wealth of dry goods, ready-to-wear clothing, and such luxury items as fancy vases, oriental rugs, perfumes, ornaments, and the like, but never mention books, shoes, or everyday household furnishings like kitchenware, table silver, and ordinary china and glass. Later on, the Bon Marché and other Parisian stores expanded to include common necessities of this sort.

Like the Bon Marché, such famous establishments as the Magasins du Printemps, Louvre, Magasins du Coin de Rue, Pygmalion, and Tapis Rouge were extending their business beyond the traditional dry goods lines during the 1860's. In the early 1870's, however, they were still placing the main emphasis upon dry goods, devoting the remainder to expensive fancy goods rather than a wide assortment of merchandise suitable for ordinary family requirements. What Americans seem to have brought back from them is not so much their diversification of merchandise as certain physical features which appealed to the patrons' desire for comfort and elegance — typically French contributions to life on the higher plane, but not the essence of the department store.

If the French *grands magasins de nouveautés* had really been greatly in advance of American developments (so far as diversification is concerned), it is extremely difficult to understand a comment published in *L'Illustration* as late as September, 1872. An article which described new arrangements in the Tapis Rouge goes on to assert that the Tapis Rouge, as a result of these changes and the great variety of its departments, was going to be like the most advanced of the great American stores (*va devenir, par le fait de sa nouvelle installation et l'immense variété de ses comptoirs de vente, le type le plus accompli des grandes maisons américaines*).[2] In other words, to a contemporary French observer a leading Paris store was revamping itself upon the latest American lines!

Across the Channel in London there were fewer signs of innovation in retail trade. William Whiteley, however, had founded a fancy dry goods store in 1863 which, like Macy's, began to expand and diversify rapidly towards the end of the decade. But Whiteley's diversification came principally after 1875, when he seems to have decided to sell every kind of merchandise that a customer might want, from meat and coal to houses and theatre tickets. If extreme diversification is the criterion of a department store, the "Universal Provider" probably wins the priority award by a small margin. English retail stores, however, were generally lagging behind those on the Continent, although the leaders were definitely moving towards integration and diversification.[3]

Parallel Tendencies in American Retailing

The same movement away from specialization was plainly evident in America among many stores besides the one which Macy owned. Here again the question as to which firm led the way is difficult to answer because we lack conclusive evidence. Of the department stores now in active operation the one which has been in business the longest is probably the Hager Store of Lancaster, Pennsylvania, established in 1821 as a general store; but it was not until the 1880's that Hager's conformed, either in organization or in merchandise handled, to our definition of a department store.[4] Doubtless there are many other firms now in the department store category whose origins are to be found early in the nineteenth century, but the only definite information available indicates that none of them emerged from the general or specialized store phase of development until the last quarter of the century.

We may without much difficulty eliminate some of the leading candidates for the title to chronological priority. In New York A. T. Stewart and Arnold, Constable & Co. each had a very large retail trade (how large we cannot say because much of their business was wholesale), and there is little doubt that they were organized systematically by departments in the 1860's, if not earlier. Both were, however, selling only the traditional dry goods lines as late as 1875; to be sure, they handled furs, many types of fancy goods, and rugs and carpets, but the combination was a common one in the 1850's and does not constitute the kind of diversification which marks the department store.[5] While John Wanamaker seems to hold undisputed claim to the first department store in Philadelphia, his "new kind of store" did not come into existence until 1877 and did not start to branch out beyond dry goods and clothing until 1878.[6] Another firm to be reckoned with is the Jordan Marsh Co., of Boston, which shifted from the wholesale to the retail dry goods business in 1861. It was content, however, to stock only the conventional dry goods assortment until the 1880's.[7] The firm of Field, Leiter & Co. (later Marshall Field) was one of the nation's leading stores by the 1870's, but it, too, clung to the usual dry goods departments until the 1880's;[8] and the first Chicago firm to qualify as a department store is probably The Fair, which was founded in 1875 and expanded rapidly in size and variety of merchandise within the next decade.[9]

Two firms, both in New York City, apparently tied in the international race to become department stores: Lord & Taylor and R. H. Macy & Co. While some store now long out of business may have preceded them in completing the metamorphosis, it is highly unlikely that it could have done so without leaving fairly conspicuous evidence behind. Present knowledge, therefore, favors the two firms named. Of the two Macy was the first to establish book, house furnishings, china, and silverware departments. On the other hand, Lord & Taylor broke precedent in 1874 when they opened a furniture department in which they sold products of their own manufacture. It must be said, at the same time, that Macy's had started to carry certain items of furniture, such as chairs, several years earlier. Lord & Taylor unquestionably anticipated the Macy shoe department by a whole year, although, as we have seen, Macy's sold some shoes as early as 1873. Both firms had a large variety of fancy goods, and if Macy went further in house furnishings, Lord & Taylor until after 1880 regularly stocked a much wider line of dry goods.[10]

All things considered, it is safe to say that Macy's was among the two or three stores in both Europe and America which first completed the transition from specialized stores to modern department stores. It is pertinent to note that John Wanamaker, before he became "historically minded" and began to award to himself credit for all innovations, publicly testified that Macy was the earliest to have a department store.[11]

Reasons for the Rise of the Department Store

In the Macy store's metamorphosis, then, we have a concrete instance of a business development which was manifesting itself widely at the time. There is, accordingly, justification for an attempt to arrive at some generalizations, based upon Macy history, to explain the evolutionary process which was taking place. We must, of course, recognize that there were forces at work which, for one reason or another, are not clearly reflected in Macy experience; and it is advisable to examine them for the light they throw upon changes in Macy's business. To put the matter another way, we find in the Macy story evidence which points to tentative generalizations about the rise of the department store. On the other hand, we can formulate, from outside evidence and logical deduction, theories which help to explain some phases of Macy evolution. Let the reader keep the two types of generalization separate, for the first has a solid basis of fact, while the second is entirely hypothetical — it aids our understanding, but it stands wholly in need of verification.

General developments, like the rise of the department store, result from a complicated tangle of causes and circumstances. While no complete explanation is yet available, a number of influences undoubtedly played a part. Some of them relate to the changes in the social and cultural environment, while others are matters of internal and external business developments. In singling out for attention the changes in the retail trade at that time, one should bear in mind that American business as a whole was going through a process of integration and diversification.[12]

First of all, the many economic changes which we habitually sum up as the Industrial Revolution were reaching flood stage by the middle of the century. Both the factory system and steam transportation encouraged the rapid growth of cities, and all three developments favored large-scale operations in both production and distribution. At the same time there was a steady transfer of production from the household to the factory: to an increasing extent, families which had formerly made most of their own clothing and processed the bulk of their own foodstuffs now bought necessities from retail stores thereby swelling the volume of goods which had to be handled through commercial channels.

The speed of urbanization is evident in the growing number of Americans living in cities. The proportion inhabiting cities of 8,000 or more jumped from 8.5 per cent in 1840 to 16.1 in 1860 and on to 22.5 per cent in 1880. New York, itself, fast tightening its hold upon the commercial and financial hegemony of the nation and one of the world's busiest ports, was growing by leaps and bounds and overflowing from Manhattan to the adjacent shores. Improvements in streets and urban transportation facilities, partly the result and partly the cause of the concentration of life within cities, gave men unprecedented mobility and so encouraged the growth of large-scale retail operations by pushing out the boundaries of the market area within which the average family found it convenient to shop: the omnibus and the horsecar provided rapid transit only in a relative sense, but they accomplished for the 1860's and early '70's what the elevated railway, the electric streetcar, the subway, and the motorbus were to do in the succeeding years.[13]

Similarly, the development of newspaper advertising and of store delivery systems enabled enterprising merchants to extend appreciably the area from which they could attract patronage. Public water and sewage systems, gas lighting, improved sanitation, and many other devices which facilitate life in the city all combined to attract more dwellers; and the swelling population, in turn, encouraged or necessitated additional improvements. The circle was vicious in more ways than one. Our present concern, however, is not to obtain a qualitative appraisal of the over-all result but rather to grasp the central fact that the trading area of the individual retail store had increased and was continuing to expand.

Not all lines of merchandise were affected to the same extent. Housewives found little advantage and much inconvenience in going far afield to purchase daily necessities like meat and groceries, particularly in an age when refrigerating facilities were poor and canned or packaged foods were expensive novelties. As Macy's experience with the picnic department indicates, the department store offered no threat to the neighborhood grocer. But people were willing to shop at a distance for items which were important because of appearance, durability, or the amount of money involved. In buying a dress, for example, or a wedding gift, or a piece of kitchen equipment, it was important to make a careful comparison of the prices and styles available, and consumers preferred a wider market because of its greatly increased range of choice.

Of course the expansion of the retail market, taken alone, tended to promote specialization and integration rather than diversification. The increased volume of business available, as we have already seen, made it possible for a man to concentrate upon the retailing of fancy dry goods; and the expansion of sales in that narrow field would induce him to integrate marketing functions by eliminating the wholesaler and importer and might even encourage him to manufacture some of the goods sold, but it would not necessarily lead to any diversification. Certain other environmental forces, however, undoubtedly encouraged firms to increase the variety of lines they sold.

It was more convenient and less time-consuming for customers in a large city to make their purchases under a single roof than to visit one specialized store after another, scattered among various crowded and dirty streets. In consequence, the stores which offered an attractive variety of merchandise were likely to gain in sales and profits. A number of recent technical developments were beginning to contribute to the same end by making it possible to construct tall, spacious buildings containing many floors, by contributing improved central heating plants which would make such huge structures comfortable in cold weather, and by providing mechanical elevators which helped to overcome the reluctance of customers to penetrate above the street floor.

These general economic and social influences undoubtedly made themselves felt in Macy development, but it is difficult to find definite supporting evidence in the store's history so far as we can reconstruct it. One important exception to this statement is the course of annual sales volume after 1870. There is good reason to believe that the increasing variety of merchandise offered was bolstering sales in all parts of the store. General price declines would have caused a noticeable reduction but for the presence of a counteracting force. It is particularly important to note the rise after 1873, which is accounted for only in part by the new leased departments, as shown in Table 1, page 109. While factors other than variety might have caused the increase, a careful investigation fails to bring to light anything in the form of more aggressive management or greater amounts of advertising. It is significant, however, that we find at this time a new emphasis upon mail-order business and also an extension of free delivery service to points beyond the confines of Manhattan.

Probably business factors had more to do with the emergence of the department store than any general social or cultural influences. Many of the basic marketing problems which had forced firms to specialize earlier in the century had by 1860 been solved and reduced more or less to routine. This permitted store owners to devote attention to other projects, to uncover new opportunities for profitable activity, to experiment with ideas, and to satisfy personal ambition for expansion and power. It also permitted industrial firms to relax their intense concentration on production and to take over some of the selling activities which had formerly been handled by outside middlemen. That is to say, they were more able and willing to sell directly to retailers.[14] On this point Macy evidence is of little assistance. We see the integration and diversification but not the reasons why.

Again, business men were gradually mastering the subtle problems connected with the welding of many employees into an effective organization; the employees, on the other hand, were learning to accept the discipline involved in a large-scale enterprise and to collaborate readily in a manner which would have been impossible among the restless, intensely individualistic, American workmen of half a century before. We forget that the transition from a business enterprise comprising a few people to one involving a hundred or more employees — in Macy's from an informal group consisting of Macy himself, a bookkeeper, ten or twelve clerks, and a delivery boy to an organization of over two hundred people, comprising partners, buyers, clerks, cashiers, cash girls, floorwalkers, and other specialized employees — calls for new attitudes and habits of collaboration on the part of the workers, new duties and techniques on the part of management. That American business achieved so much of this early in the nineteenth century, with relatively little confusion and friction, is something like a miracle.

Probably the task of buying wisely and economically a variety of merchandise was easier in the 1860's than it had been earlier: a modicum of standardization in qualities inevitably came about as manufacturers mastered the problem of turning out uniform products; a growing familiarity with the boundless variety of merchandise which the Industrial Revolution loosed upon the country doubtless made the business of selection seem less bewildering; and, possibly most important of all, the delegation of buying to specialized employees opened the way to unprecedented combinations of merchandise within a single firm. This delegation of authority and responsibility, of course, involved a slow, difficult learning and adjustment process for everyone concerned; the division of managerial tasks was probably not well done even among the leading firms until sometime after 1850. To this generalization the Macy records give only mute assent.

There are, theoretically, obvious economies to be derived from large-scale operations in retailing — in buying, finance, advertising, delivery, and other functions — as soon as large retail units become feasible from the consumer's point of view and from that of business organization and management. The savings come in part from using the same buildings and equipment, approximately the same amount of advertising, the same or only slightly augmented staff, and so on, to handle larger volume, thereby spreading expenses over more sales dollars. In part the savings arise from the ability to intensify the division of labor, so that each task is done by experts and therefore presumably with greater efficiency. And, once volume is sufficient to permit direct buying and importing, it is often possible to obtain goods at lower cost or at least to obtain a better selection of merchandise. Diversification of lines makes possible large additions to the volume of business which a given store can attract, thereby making it possible to take full advantage of the savings inherent in large volume.

Whether he actually got them or not, Macy certainly claimed such advantages. Again, by handling a diversified stock of merchandise a firm spreads the risks resulting from sudden changes in price or demand — risks which can quickly put out of business the specialist dependent on a narrow line of goods. Similarly, diversification enables a firm to experiment with new ideas, new departments (as Macy did with fancy groceries) without jeopardizing its continuous existence. If the innovation does not pan out, the other departments bear the loss; if it is a success, the store's profits grow.

Of course, to have a number of well-stocked departments requires a substantial amount of capital. It is no accident that diversification and integration began to spread just when the supply of business capital in America was increasing, thus making it easier for a single firm to meet the enormous financial resources which the department store required. Macy's store was able to expand into many lines because its owner was willing to plow back a good portion of the profits.

The situation was not ideal, of course. There are disadvantages in large-scale operations, advantages in business units of moderate size, though few people seem to have considered them at the time. A large organization is inevitably complicated, cumbersome, and expensive. It demands energy and ability of a rare sort on the part of management, and the elaborate systems of information and control which have to be developed to replace the proprietor's direct personal supervision not only tend to lag behind current needs but also engender miles of red tape. Some of the disadvantages of the department store idea did not become fully apparent until sometime later. In the latter half of the nineteenth century many men thought that there was something like magic in large size, and the department store appeared to be a marvelous device for combining the advantages of specialization (through the departmental form of organization) with the advantages of the large volume resulting from the combination of many kinds of merchandise under one ownership and management.[15]

The force which seems to have driven retailers towards integration and diversification, whether they liked it or not, was the competitive situation. As we have seen, during the first half of the century the specialist had enjoyed advantages over the nonspecialized operator. When specialization became widespread, however, it was one specialist against another. This restored competition to an even plane and so wiped out easy profits. So long as Macy sold only fancy dry goods, he had no particular advantage over other fancy dry goods stores; when he sold not only a great variety of dry goods but also millinery, house furnishings, chinaware, and shoes, his store was inherently more attractive to shoppers and (to the extent that his operating economies were genuine) he could offer greater bargains. Probably no contemporary storekeeper could see the ultimate answer clearly, but the situation called for a new pattern of business organization which would create the kind of advantage over the specialized store that the latter had formerly enjoyed over the early nonspecialized firm.

The downward secular trend after 1865 greatly aggravated the struggle for survival by subjecting all lines of business to repeated declines in prices, thus undermining profits and even creating heavy inventory losses. As one department store owner subsequently summed up the difficulty:[16]

> So many men in business . . . had nothing to do in the early sixties but to go to their places of business in the morning and mark up the prices of their goods. When the great change came in the end of the sixties they did not know how to do business on a falling market; that is, as we say, they were not quick sellers enough.

In other words, men of superior business ability saw in the diversification of merchandise sold a means of cutting overhead costs by spreading them over a larger volume of business. Consciously or unconsciously, Macy was responding correctly to the needs of the situation. Diversification had the added merit of drawing more customers into the store than any single line could do. Evidently the storekeepers were not thinking primarily of the convenience of customers: until the department store had reached a mature stage of development, none of them thought of mentioning in their advertisements the saving in customers' time and carfare which they made possible.[17] To put the matter another way, when profits dwindled, the proprietor had to combine several stores into one in order to make the living a single line of goods had previously yielded. I think it is highly significant that most of Macy's diversification came in the downward trend of prices after 1868 and received new impetus in 1873. La Forge's letter to his wife (quoted above, page 104) is clear and direct evidence on this point.

The business situation, too, encouraged the tendency towards integration. The downward trend of prices cut sharply into profits and even created losses; consequently, the firm, or series of firms, which could reduce the time period between finishing goods in the factory and selling them to consumers was in the best position to win out in the desperate struggle for survival. Here the advantage tended to lie with the retailer who bought directly from the manufacturer. Just consider Macy's position as compared with that of a competitor who bought from a wholesaler, both ordering on the same day a lot of staple merchandise: Macy could obtain goods sold by the manufacturer at prices prevailing at the time of purchase; his competitor obtained goods sold by the manufacturer to the wholesaler weeks and even months before, which, on a falling market, meant that the price started from a higher point. If the wholesaler took the markdown, he lost; if he managed to obtain his usual margin, the competing retailer had to take the cut or see the goods remain unsold on his shelves. The prolongation of this process would seriously weaken both the wholesaler and the small retailer to the advantage of the direct buyer. (Later on, rapidly changing styles began to have the same effect, but there is not much evidence of the style factor in the 1870's.)

The retailer who eliminated the middleman, moreover, was usually able to obtain his merchandise at somewhat lower prices than wholesalers could offer. (One must guard against a common misconception on this point. Eliminating middlemen never completely cuts out the middleman's margin.) The retailer had to perform for himself the selection, transportation, storage, financing, assumption of risks, and similar functions which middlemen had formerly handled; and the manufacturer was obliged similarly to undertake the various activities involved in selling to retailers. To some extent there was simply a transfer of functions from one type of business to another, accompanied by a shift in the incidence of unavoidable expenses. The readjustment of margins between manufacturer and retailer depended upon the circumstances, but whatever the retailer gained in lower prices was offset at least partially by additional costs.[18] It has often been true that actual economies were achieved in the process. In such instances, when the retailer could retain the resulting extra margin, his profits benefited. If competition from other retailers forced him to pass the savings on to his customers, he at least gained from the fact that lower prices usually made it easier to sell his merchandise. The fact that Macy steadily increased the amount of direct buying for his store, together with the fact that L. Straus & Sons, importers and wholesalers of china and glassware, found it profitable to enter into a leased-department arrangement with Macy, suggests that the traditional manufacturer-wholesaler-retailer sequence was outmoded and in need of revision.

Still another advantage of direct buying was the fact that a retailer such as Macy, who had immediate contact with the public, could respond immediately to changes in taste or style and instruct the manufacturer to produce the type of merchandise currently in demand. The wholesaler, lacking this direct contact with the ultimate market for manufactured goods, obtained such information only indirectly and usually after he had already acquired stocks for sale; as a result, he was likely to accumulate unsalable merchandise or sell at unfavorable prices. In short, the integrated firm was in a better position than the specialized wholesaler to coördinate the manufacturer's production with actual consumption.

It is possible that all the foregoing considerations, in combinations of varying pattern and intensity according to the local circumstances, led to the emergence of department stores in America. While the facts unearthed about Macy history do not give explicit support to this explanation at all points, it is likewise true that none of the Macy experience goes against it, and we can at least conclude — until further evidence is available — that the hypothesis advanced to explain the decline of extreme specialization among business firms *seems* to fit.

Whatever the precise explanation, Macy and many other store owners found salvation in diversification and integration — that is to say, in developing the modern department store. This was in harmony with the general business tendency of the times (and we should note in passing that the new preference for nonspecialization differed from that existing before 1800 in that it placed the main emphasis upon retailing rather than upon wholesaling and foreign trade). Not all those who adopted the new policy were consciously aware of the problem they were solving. Some of them seem to have hit upon the department store more or less by accident, others by imitating the firms which were succeeding with the new pattern. Macy was in the vanguard and had little opportunity to imitate, but he may not have been conscious of the full significance of his actions.

Of course, not every store owner could avail himself of the new device. There is a definite limit to the number of department stores which any community can support. Not every storekeeper had the managerial ability which the department store demanded, and few of them could raise the enormous capital it required, even if they resorted to the increasingly popular corporate form of ownership. Many local situations continued to favor the specialized store, particularly the one operated by a man who could adapt his methods and organization to the new competition. However, the department store attained a position of leadership and influence in the retail field which it was destined to retain for many years.

What frequently happened was that one little specialized store after another was put out of business — transferred, in effect, from an independent unit to a subdivision within a department store. In the 1870's this submergence of petty capitalists was not readily apparent. We shall see later that the men who were hurt by the department store's competition tried to strike back by political and legislative means.[19] Just as diversification hit specialized retailers, so integration wiped out many importers and wholesale firms; the effects were often not so immediate because the wholesaler frequently managed to readapt his methods and sell to the smaller department stores.

It is a fair conclusion that the American department store, in its essentials at least, grew out of American conditions. There was no need to copy French institutions; moreover, we lack evidence that there was any imitation involved in the core of the American development. Such information as we do have indicates that after 1860, if not before, the evolution here was abreast of that in Europe, possibly a little in advance. To the extent that American retailers brought back from Paris any features of the *grands magasins*, their importations consisted of grandiose store architecture, elaborate interior decorations and fittings, and the provision of such conveniences as luxurious writing and restrooms, store restaurants, art galleries, and sending merchandise out on approval — superficial adornments rather than fundamental structure. It is a matter of opinion whether the artistic contribution was worth the cost. Certainly it led to some of the additions to retail expense which burden department store operations today.[20]

This conclusion does not mean that the department store's emergence was inevitable. The aggressive enterprise of able business men is evident throughout its evolution. Now adjusting their firms to changing environment, now bringing about in that environment important change, men like Samuel Lord, Rowland Macy, and Marshall Field shaped the institution; and the differences today in the stores which bear their names reflect the individual personalities of the founders. Nor does this conclusion mean that every man who converted his business into a department store thereby guaranteed his success. Here, as elsewhere in business history, failures litter the way, mocking those who speak of "the profit system" as if there were no red ink on the record.[21]

Opposition to the Department Store

As always happens when a new institution threatens the existence of an old one, the specialized retail stores fought back against the department store with all the means at their disposal. When economic measures proved of no avail, they sought political (i.e., legislative) remedies, fostering bills which would impose special taxes on department stores or restrict the lines of merchandise which they could handle. In Europe some of these efforts succeeded but in the United States they invariably failed, although not without causing department stores' owners some concern.

In the Macy records we find only one echo of this struggle for survival, an echo relating not to the Macy firm itself but to Abraham & Straus, the Brooklyn store in which the owners of Macy's had acquired an interest in 1893. When Abraham & Straus opened its grocery department, late in 1894, the competing retail grocers held a mass meeting in protest. The only result, as one of the Macy owners pointed out, was that the new department received some excellent free advertising which helped to insure its initial success.[22] Of course, the rise of the chain store soon caused the small retailer to turn his protests in another direction, and the department store was allowed to continue its natural growth.[23]

CHAPTER VII

FROM PROGRESS TO DOLDRUMS

FOLLOWING the death of Rowland Macy there came a series of changes in the ownership of the store, culminating in 1888 with the admission of Isidor and Nathan Straus as partners in the firm. The entrance of the Straus brothers into Macy's is important because it marks the beginning of the store's present-day ownership and management. Before they acquired an interest, however, the firm went through a critical decade in which the absence of the founder's guiding hand became plainly evident. Although the store continued to grow in both sales volume and scope of activities, the rate of progress definitely slowed down, precisely as if the enterprise, having received a vigorous shove, was coasting to a stop. General business conditions and growing competition go far to explain this unsatisfactory condition, but internal evidence indicates that the firm's management was also at fault. This chapter deals with the history of Macy's from 1877 through 1887.

CHANGES IN OWNERSHIP

The surviving members of the Macy firm — La Forge and Valentine — purchased Macy's share of the business from the heirs and immediately formed a new partnership. At the inventory preceding his death Macy's capital in the business amounted to $77,724. The partnership agreement had provided that, in case of dissolution, the value of a partner's share should be discounted 15 per cent. La Forge and Valentine were consequently able to settle with the Macy estate for $66,065, paying in serial notes of $3,000 maturing at one-month intervals. Profits earned by July 1, 1877, enabled the new firm to reduce the indebtedness to $39,000 by discounting some of the notes.[1]

The new partnership agreement continued the capital at $150,000, with La Forge's share standing at $82,500 (55 per cent) and Valentine's at $67,500 (45 per cent). This capitalization seems to have been fairly conservative: La Forge asserted on several occasions that the firm's assets were worth about $200,000; and in terms of earning power the value was even greater, considering that the annual earnings must have been nearly $100,000. Apparently the two men placed no great value upon the original firm name, for the agreement provided that it was to continue as R. H. Macy & Co. only until January 1, 1879, after which it was to become La Forge & Valentine. (Fate intervened to prevent this change.) The partners were to devote their entire time to Macy affairs (with La Forge having final decision in case of disagreement), were to share profits in proportion to capital invested, and had the privilege of drawing up to $10,000 per year in anticipation of profits.[2]

This partnership was of brief duration, for La Forge died in the following year. His Civil War experiences had aggravated a tendency to tuberculosis, and, although his doctors apparently insisted that his lungs were not affected, he had suffered lung hemorrhages as early as 1871. The fact that he habitually overworked, of course, made matters worse, and by 1876 the attacks became so severe that he could no longer endure northern winters. Death came in Florida, in February, 1878. The entire Macy staff grieved with the devoted Margaret, for La Forge's innate gentleness and his unfailing sympathy and friendliness had won them all. His heart-broken widow died only two years later.[3]

Valentine purchased La Forge's share in the business at face value ($82,500) in accordance with the articles of partnership, no allowance being made for goodwill.[4] It seems unlikely that Valentine had completed payment for the portion of the business which he bought at Macy's death, but he agreed to settle with Margaret La Forge at the rate of $5,000 per month for the additional share. Valentine promptly announced his intention "to continue under the old style" of R. H. Macy & Co.[5]

A few weeks later Valentine admitted to partnership Charles B. Webster. A distant cousin of both Macy and Valentine, Webster had entered the store's employ in 1876 as a floorwalker at $10 per week.

CHARLES B. WEBSTER
Partner, 1879–1896

JEROME B. WHEELER
Partner, 1879–1887

eventually to his father's store in Providence, Rhode Island. He soon decided upon a career in the 14th Street store, however, and La Forge's death gave him an unexpected opportunity for advancement. He invested little, if any, capital upon admission to the firm, and the terms of partnership are not known except that Valentine undoubtedly held the controlling interest. The new partners promptly announced that the store would continue to operate on a cash basis, and subsequent reports indicated that they were able to do so without difficulty.[6]

Barely a year after La Forge's passing, death struck for the third time in quick succession, removing Valentine and leaving the business in the relatively inexperienced hands of Webster. To assist with the task Webster called in Valentine's brother-in-law, Jerome B. Wheeler, a flour merchant and man of considerable business experience whose presence in the firm strengthened it in the opinion of outside observers. Neither Webster nor Wheeler had much capital, but they were coexecutors of Valentine's estate and therefore in a good position to arrange to have the heirs leave their money in the business until the partners could finish paying for it.[7] Webster clinched matters by marrying Mrs. Valentine within a year of her husband's death, a hasty action which alienated the rest of the Valentine family. Some observers felt that Webster's motives were mercenary, but Mrs. Webster's subsequent conduct, according to a number of persons who knew her, strongly indicated that she was not one to be willingly deprived of male companionship, and the initiative in the union may well have been hers.[8]

From May, 1879, to the end of 1887 Macy's was owned by Webster and Wheeler, with Webster holding the controlling interest of 55 per cent. Webster was a tall, dignified man whose taciturnity and sober mien gave the impression that he had no sense of humor. In reality he was a kindly person, but he seldom spoke to employees, and they hesitated to approach him unless circumstances made it necessary. He was conservative, particularly in the matter of remuneration, and apparently kept a close watch on the firm's finances. Wheeler, in sharp contrast, had a nod and a smile for everyone and was very popular with the staff. By disposition he was optimistic and venturesome (in keeping with his red hair and equally red beard), ready to try any new idea which might be profitable. This trait led him to speculation in western lands and mining ventures and eventually put a strain on his relations with Webster. Taken together, the two men evidently made an excellent team but one which would probably have separated sooner than it did if both the partners had not been connected with the Macy family (Wheeler had married Macy's niece and Webster was a cousin).[9]

Further Diversification and Integration

Under the young partners the Macy business grew appreciably in every respect — types of merchandise handled, services offered, volume of sales, and physical size. To some extent the growth took the form of additional departments, most of which were offshoots of existing lines. Thus, in November, 1877, the assortment of black dress goods was expanded and the old department then split into two new departments — one devoted to black dress silks and the other containing alpacas, cashmeres, Henriettas, and other black dress goods. This step, the store announced, made its shopping facilities complete, enabling it to "supply every want of ladies and children excepting colored dress goods," a deficiency which was remedied a year later.[10] At the beginning of 1878 a new department was created out of department 14, the old one confining its attention to worsteds and worsted embroideries and the new one handling buttons, fringes, and dress trimmings.[11] Such changes, of course, were the outcome of increased sales volume and elaboration of offerings within existing lines, as a result of which departmental specialization became desirable.

A more significant addition was the installation of a ladies' lunchroom, or restaurant, in May, 1878, only a month before the Sixth Avenue Elevated inaugurated its rapid transit service and began to bring more people to 14th Street with unprecedented noise and speed. Since store restaurants had appeared in Paris some years earlier, the idea was not entirely original; but the Macy lunchroom (see illustration, opposite page 168) was apparently the first one on this side of the Atlantic. It was located on the second floor of the store and was operated by one Davidson on the same basis as the china, silverware, and shoe departments, the gross margin being divided equally between the lessee and the store.[12] For many years the menu was limited to cold food, which was prepared off the premises, and supplemented by hot tea, coffee, and chocolate [13] — a cheerless offering by modern standards, perhaps, but a boon to the tired shopper of the 1870's and '80's whom progress had not yet supplied with convenient and inexpensive restaurants like Childs' and Schrafft's.

In January, 1879, a new department was created to handle colored dress silks, which Macy's had not carried in any quantity until the preceding fall. At the same time a separate department was organized to sell men's furnishings, which had previously been grouped with furnishings for women and children. Similarly a new department was established in July, 1879, for bustles and corsets, divorcing them from laces and embroideries. Six months later the fancy goods department gave birth to a new division handling toilet goods, perfumes, and drugs (chiefly patent medicines); and in July, 1880, the now famous Macy book department attained independence when a separate department was set up to sell stationery and visiting cards. Already Macy's had an enormous selection of books in stock and was prepared to obtain any other title a customer might want.[14]

The roll of new departments at this time may be completed as follows: upholstery goods out of the white goods department, July, 1880; handkerchiefs, collars, and cuffs out of laces and embroideries, January, 1881; knitted worsteds out of worsteds and embroideries, January, 1882; untrimmed hats out of the millinery department, July, 1882; and the establishment of separate departments for suits and cloaks in January, 1883. No further changes in departments took place until 1888, and therefore the list of Macy departments in December, 1887, was as follows: [15]

1. White goods, linens, and blankets
2. Laces and embroideries
2½. Ladies' and children's muslin underwear
3. Notions, sewing supplies, and other smallwares
4. Ribbons
4½. Colored silks

5. Silverware
6. Hosiery
6½. Men's furnishings
7. Merino underwear
8½. Umbrellas, parasols, and canes
9. Fancy goods, jewelry, and leather goods
9½. Toilet articles, perfumery, and patent medicines
10. Boys' clothing
11. House furnishing goods
12. Dolls and toys
13. Books, picture frames, and albums
14. Worsteds, worsted fringe, canvas, and felt
15. China and glassware
16. Candy
17. Gloves
18. Ladies' untrimmed hats
18½. Ladies' trimmed hats
19. Flowers and feathers
20. Ladies' and children's shoes
21. Ladies' and children's suits
21½. Ladies' and children's cloaks
22. Black silks
23. Black and colored cashmeres and dress goods
24. Silk fringe, dress buttons, and trimmings
25. Restaurant
26. Corsets and bustles
27. Stationery and visiting cards
28. Upholstery goods, lace curtains, and portieres
29. Handkerchiefs, collars, and cuffs
30. Knitted worsted goods

The selection of merchandise in the store was even wider than this impressive list suggests, for as early as 1879 the toy department offered a wide selection of sporting goods, including archery and tennis equipment; department No. 2½ carried a complete stock of infants' wear; the notions department sold opera glasses and spectacles; the china department included a large assortment of lamps and statuary; and in the house furnishings department was to be found an amazing variety of items which extended to trunks and luggage, mirrors, rugs and small pieces of furniture, hardware, pictures (engravings, photographs, and lithographs), and seeds and garden tools.[16]

By 1882 all these lines had been expanded and certain new ones added: dog collars and leashes, hunting coats and other sports clothing, and clocks.[17] At some time between 1882 and 1885 the store began to carry a large assortment of artists' supplies, to stock a full line of telescopes and field glasses, and, more important still, to make suits and coats for men. In 1885 it featured statuette reproductions of the Goddess of Liberty for the benefit of the fund devoted to erecting a pedestal for the statue which France had just presented to the United States.[18] Rubber footwear (Goodyear) for women and children appeared on the counters in the fall of 1887.[19]

Meanwhile the store was placing increasing emphasis upon custom dressmaking and ready-to-wear clothing for women, and after 1880 formal openings became the regular means of introducing new models in the spring and fall. By 1882, if not before, these exhibits included cloaks and costumes imported from Paris, but the announced policy of the firm was "to offer a class of goods which will meet a popular demand rather than to represent extreme styles." [20]

One notable aspect of the merchandise sold at this time was the growing extent to which it was manufactured by the firm itself. As we have seen, a large organization had been set up even before Rowland Macy's death to make underclothing for women and children. In 1879 another workshop was opened for the manufacture of men's shirts, and before 1885 an office was opened in Belfast, Ireland, to take charge of the production of linen articles manufactured in neighboring households on Macy's order. By 1885 the store manufactured the following articles: ladies' and children's underwear, men's shirts, linen collars and cuffs for both men and women, women's dresses, bustles ("wire and others"), lace fichus, velvet wraps, and linen handkerchiefs. The avowed purpose of this manufacturing was to enable the firm to sell quality merchandise at low prices, but the accounts from 1887 onwards show that a satisfactory profit was achieved in the manufacturing departments.[21]

In addition to selling goods of its own manufacture, the store offered an increasing array of merchandise made by others but bearing Macy brands, such as La Forge kid gloves (1877), Red Star silk (1878), and Red Star velveteen (1886). By 1884 the store also had the exclusive agency for Foster kid gloves in New York City, stocking the three different grades which the line included.[22]

Considering the scope of goods covered, it is hardly any wonder that an article in the New York *World* estimated that a brief description of the different articles sold in Macy's, written out on ordinary commercial paper, "would reach to Central Park!" The same article went on to assert that the store had "spread itself out along Fourteenth Street and Sixth Avenue until one is at a loss to tell where it begins or where it ends. It is a bazaar, a museum, a hotel, and a great fancy store all combined." [23]

Sales Promotion Turns to Convenience and Comfort

The Macy firm continued to promote sales by means of advertising. Most of the effort was devoted to newspapers, but advertisements were occasionally placed in magazines — a series of nine full-page institutional advertisements in the *Century Magazine* between June, 1882, and January, 1883, probably marks the first Macy advertising on a national scale. Catalogs were issued twice yearly after 1879 to solicit mail-order business, and at least one large outdoor sign (at Park Place) was used in 1886. Much of the newspaper copy had a strong institutional turn, calling attention to the store's determination not to be undersold, reiterating its endeavor to reduce prices by eliminating middlemen, and urging the convenience of its central location and the many departments under one roof. A few quotations may convey the general flavor: [24]

Purchasers to the amount of $25 may come by car or boat fifty miles and save money. Even a $10 purchase will pay for twenty-five miles. [1877]

A week's shopping can be accomplished in one day. [1878]

The public may rest assured that *we will not be undersold* on a single article in any one of our 26 departments. [1878]

The completion of the elevated Railroad, bringing shoppers from New Jersey, Long Island, and New York suburbs directly to our doors at

MAIN FLOOR OF MACY'S, 1882
View from 14th Street staircase through to 13th Street

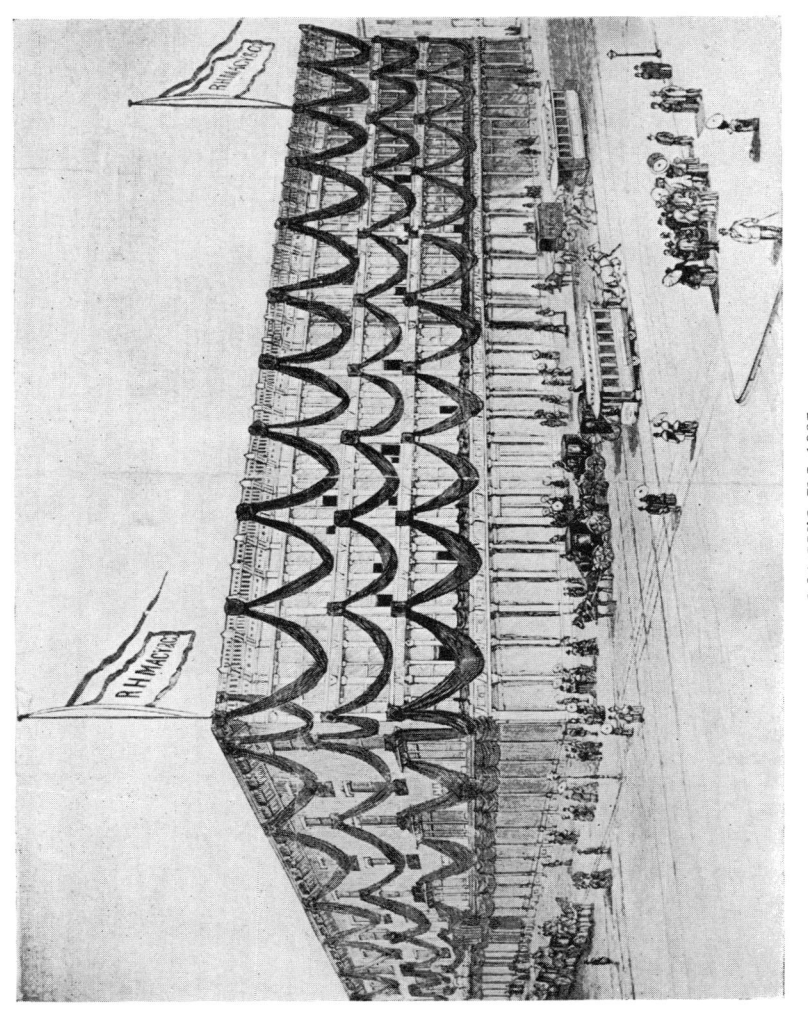

MACY'S IN 1885
Draped in black for Grant's funeral

the station, corner 14th st. and 6th av., renders this strictly the Grand Central Establishment of the City, — Spend the morning in our store and be home in time for lunch, or have it in our lunch department.
[1878]

You are saved the trouble of going to twenty or more stores to find articles that you can obtain from us. [1879]

Ceramics for the Million. Ceramics for the Millionaire. [1884]

Goods suitable for the millionaire at prices in reach of the millions.
[1887]

Low prices, to be sure, continued to receive considerable emphasis in Macy advertising. One piece of copy asserted that the store's prices were "absolutely unapproachable," adding by way of explanation a brief statement of its policy of cash dealings and low profits:[25]

> We are enabled to do this simply because
> we buy and sell for cash.
> Buying for cash both in this market and Europe
> we are enabled to save all trade discounts,
> which are invariably given to our customers.
>
> We have a method of doing business peculiarly our own.
> We do not sell one article for less than cost
> and atone for it by selling many at an advance of from
> 50 to 100 per cent,
> but are satisfied with a moderate profit,
> and all our patrons may confidently rely upon having saved from
> 10 to 25 per cent
> on every bill of goods purchased from us.

There was, however, a new element in the institutional appeals which contrasted strongly with earlier insistence upon economy. This new content was an emphasis upon the comforts and conveniences of the store — not merely the convenience of its location and enormous variety of offerings, but the amenities and free services which customers would find there. Apparently the management felt that it was obliged to offer something more than low prices to attract patronage. Thus, an advertisement in 1878 asserted that Macy's had "the best lighted store in the city," and another pointed out that the management had, to facilitate Christmas shopping, doubled its force of cash girls, cashiers, parcel clerks, and wrapping desks.[26] Still another boasted (1881) of the immense crowds which came to Macy's:[27]

> The question is often asked by strangers
> why so many people patronize us.
> The answer is simple and easy.
> First, because goods can always be purchased
> at minimum prices;
> and second, because the well lighted
> and admirably ventilated buildings,
> with their many conveniences,
> always give people a sense of comfort,
> safety and security
> that continually grows upon them
> as their visits are repeated.

The nature of these added attractions becomes clearer when we read the announcement (1878) that "ladies will find near superintendent's office conveniences for writing, also the leading daily papers."[28] Other evidence reveals the fact that the firm's display windows were (1879) "brilliantly illuminated with electric lights until 10 o'clock," and that by 1880 it had installed, for the convenience of its customers, a branch office of Western Union and also a Bell telephone. As early as November, 1877, it had contracted for "5 Telephones and 5 Bell Calls to be used in connection with a Telegraph Line in our Store," and, while these were obviously for internal communication, an outside connection may well have been made as soon as the first commercial exchange in the city was put into service.[29]

During the summer of 1880, partly to attract customers by means of more attractive quarters and partly to accommodate increased business, the Macy management had had the premises facing Sixth Avenue enlarged and rebuilt, with a new iron face. By this time the store extended along the entire end of the block between 13th and 14th streets. (Some of the reconstruction continued into 1882, because of the necessity for altering small sections at a time.) At the same time ventilating apparatus was installed to supply 1,500,000 cubic feet of fresh air every hour, relieving an atmospheric condition which few moderns can appreciate because now we take fresh air in large stores for granted and assume that summer air conditioning is all that is done to keep the air from being oppressive. The installation was probably occasioned by four weeks of abnormally hot weather in the preceding autumn. Another improvement which the firm made at this time was the introduction of electric illumination within the store. Here we have an example of management being too hasty in adopting new inventions, for the sputtering arc lights used were so undependable that gas jets had to be retained and frequently called into service. A year's delay would certainly have led to the installation of Edison's new incandescent lamps, which were much superior. The result of all this modernization, in the firm's own opinion, made the store "the largest, best lighted and most comfortable shopping resort in the city." [30]

Another feature intended to please Macy customers was a "Mail and Found Office:" [31]

Here postage stamps of all denominations are kept on sale for the convenience of our patrons. To this desk is [sic] also brought all articles that are found in the store. A careful record is kept of them, even if not claimed for months after they are found. This desk is also used for checking all articles that customers may wish to leave for safe-keeping. All pocketbooks are taken to the head cashier's office on the second floor of the 13th Street side.

The Macy management was, in other words, conforming to the tendency of stores in both the United States and Europe to spend increasing amounts of money to win customers, resorting to impressive fittings and new comforts and conveniences in order to gain the individual distinction which price and merchandise had once given. When competitors match the leader's bargains, his quality and assortment, and even his advertising, the store premises and routine retail services themselves become an instrument of sales promotion, thus tending to injure profits and even "bidding up" operating expenses to the point where prices have to be increased.[32] So long as the amounts spent in this direction were small and sales volume continued to expand appreciably, the expense ratio would not suffer; but the process could not be prolonged indefinitely.

One of the forces which were inducing the Macy management to modify its founder's policy of avoiding elaborate quarters and fixtures and eliminating all possible expenses was the rising American standard of living; the improvements in services and equipment in retail stores matched the improvements in domestic life, and the general advance in real income took some of the edge off the Macy appeal to economy. A force of greater immediate importance, however, was increasing competition from other stores, as the preceding paragraph suggests. Possibly spurred on by the successful example of John Wanamaker in Philadelphia, the New York stores seem to have been offering additional free services and pleasanter surroundings, and the public was probably responding by giving increased patronage.[33]

One must bear in mind that by the 1880's the Macy store was no longer a unique institution; other firms had adopted the department-store form of retailing, and some of them were putting new touches to the idea. Ridley's in Grand Street had come forward rapidly in the 1880's, Denning (successor to A. T. Stewart's business) was making a valiant effort at 9th and Broadway, two blocks farther up James McCreery was gaining increased prominence, and James A. Hearn & Son had carried the battle to R. H. Macy & Co.'s very doorstep by moving alongside on 14th Street and launching a vigorous competition which included price wars.[34]

To complicate matters, the principal shopping district of New York City continued its northward movement; and Macy's, which had been on the northern edge of the area in 1858, now found itself south of the center. Thus, Arnold, Constable had moved along Broadway up to 19th Street by 1870, Lord & Taylor advanced to 20th shortly afterwards, and there was a large cluster of stores on both Broadway and Sixth Avenue near 23d Street, including B. Altman, Le Boutellier Brothers, H. O'Neill, Stern Brothers, and Simpson, Crawford & Simpson; while still another group was on Eighth Avenue near the old Manhattan Opera House. Thus there were

MACY'S LUNCHROOM, 1882
Located on the second floor

RETAIL SELLING IN THE 1880'S
Ladies' and Children's Shoe Department

competitors on all sides of Macy's geographically, and this was probably true also in the realm of price and quality of merchandise stocked. Little information on this point is available, and doubtless there was no uniformity in the matter; but Macy's apparently concentrated on medium-priced merchandise, thus laying itself open to attacks from stores like Hearn's and Ridley's in the bracket below and Altman's and Lord & Taylor above.

That the Macy management recognized the significance of the movement uptown is evident from a letter written to John Jacob Astor II in 1879, in anticipation of the expiration of the firm's leases in 1883, in which the proposal was made that Astor erect a building for the store on the southeast corner of Broadway and 34th Street, (diagonally opposite the site of Macy's today).[35] Nothing came of the suggestion, however; and the old leases were renewed, postponing to another generation the problem of proper quarters for the Macy business. In point of fact the matter of location can hardly have been a serious factor at the time, for, as the Macy advertisements increasingly pointed out, the store enjoyed unrivaled transportation facilities — the Sixth Avenue Elevated and surface lines were at its very door, and two horsecar lines served it on the 14th Street side. These facilities connected with every car and stage line in the city, and after the opening of Brooklyn Bridge in May, 1883, they brought new crowds of shoppers to the store.

On the whole, Webster and Wheeler did little after 1880 to improve premises or services, being content to promote business mainly along the lines established by Rowland Macy. They continued to hold clearance, pre-inventory, and post-inventory sales at frequent intervals, to feature a special sale of valentines in February, and to emphasize the Christmas season by special advertisements and elaborate window displays. (In 1883, apparently for the first time, the annual exhibition of toys and dolls contained moving figures, operated mechanically by steam power.)[36] They also held formal openings in the spring and fall to display the latest styles, and occasionally they staged publicity stunts, such as a special exhibition of ceramic reproductions or an archery contest held in the store (the china displays probably originated with the Strauses). But promotional devices of this kind were no longer unusual, leading competitors having likewise adopted them in one form or another. About the only claim to distinction that can be advanced in favor of the Macy management of this period is that its spring advertising pioneered (1878) in the now traditional emphasis of retailers upon the Easter season. To judge by the advertisements, at any rate, hardly another store in New York saw the commercial opportunities of Easter until 1881 and even later.[37]

Complacent Conservatism

In general there was a noticeable relaxation of Macy promotional effort after the first part of the 1880's. By 1885 competing firms were regularly devoting considerably more space to newspaper advertising than Macy's used, and Macy copy plainly lacked its former distinction and vigor.[38] This fact, together with the general absence of real innovations in equipment, service, or merchandise after 1885, suggests that the firm had lost its original momentum and was coasting into complacent mediocrity.

The sales figures tend to support this conclusion. As Table 6 plainly proves, the annual volume increased by substantial amounts each year between 1877 and 1883, after which the gains declined to relatively insignificant sums. To some extent these results reflect contemporary circumstances, for business operations in the United States began to improve late in 1878, after five years of severe depression, and a fair degree of prosperity ensued until 1882, towards the end of which the long, post-Civil War downward slide was resumed, gradually developing a panicky situation in 1884. A new period of recovery started as 1885 drew to a close, but lasted only two years.[39] Macy sales figures matched these general fluctuations closely, and one might therefore assume that the firm's management was achieveing reasonably satisfactory results.

Contrast the store's performance in the 1880's, however, with its record in the previous decade. Under Rowland Macy the sales had advanced in spite of the severe depression after 1873 — had advanced because action was taken to bring more business into the store. Consider also the remarkable progress which John Wanamaker was making in Philadelphia during the 1880's. While we lack definite figures,

TABLE 6

ANALYSIS OF ANNUAL SALES BY OWNED AND LEASED DEPARTMENTS
1877–1888

Year	Total Sales[a]	Ratio to Previous Year %	Sales in Owned Depts.	Ratio to Previous Year %	Sales in Leased Depts.[b]	Ratio to Previous Year %	Percentage of Leased to Total Sales %
1877	$1,875,241	114.9	$1,641,893	115.9	$233,348	108.4	12.44
1878	2,228,863	118.9	1,917,792	116.8	311,071	133.3	13.96
1879	2,924,132	131.2	2,447,300	127.6	476,832	153.3	16.31
1880	3,498,415	119.6	2,910,734	118.9	587,681	123.3	16.80
1881[c]	4,015,485	114.8	3,236,671	111.2	778,814	132.5	19.39
1882	4,485,443	111.7	3,638,794	112.4	846,649	108.7	18.87
1883	4,831,158	107.7	3,909,392	107.4	921,766	108.9	19.08
1884	4,971,573	102.9	4,031,999	103.1	939,574	101.9	18.90
1885	5,026,955	101.1	4,106,669	101.9	920,286	97.9	18.31
1886[d]	5,051,745	100.5	...	...	...	...	...
1887[e]	5,142,083	101.8	...	...	...	...	...
1888	5,049,241	98.2	4,261,303	...	787,938	...	15.61
		(Last Half-Year Only)					
1887	2,650,722	...	2,144,837	...	505,885	...	19.08
1888	2,635,405	99.4	2,222,428	103.6	412,977	81.6	15.67

[a] These figures include sales in leased departments and apparently relate to the calendar year.
[b] Leased departments include silver (No. 5), china and glassware (No. 15) throughout, women's shoes (No. 20) from 1877 until Feb. 1888, and restaurant (No. 25) from May, 1878, onwards.
[c] Sales in leased departments for this year cover 53 weeks of operation instead of 52.
[d] No details available beyond total sales.
[e] No details available beyond total sales until the second half of the year. To facilitate comparison the analysis of the second half is given below, together with the corresponding figures for 1888. The data for the second half of 1887 and later years come from a new series of records and may not be precisely comparable with the earlier figures.

SOURCE: Total sales, 1877 to 1887, inclusive, from the Black Book; they are for the calendar year and probably include a small amount of merchandise subsequently returned. Sales in leased departments are from weekly sales and purchases records and cover the annual period to the week ending nearest to Dec. 31, resulting in 53 weeks for 1881. Sales in owned departments are derived by subtracting leased departments from the total.

there can be little doubt about the rapid expansion of his business. Between 1882 and 1887 his staff increased nearly 50 per cent in numbers,[40] and this fact certainly reflects substantial growth in sales in precisely the period during which Macy's volume was coming to a standstill.

Moreover, the record of the leased departments in Macy's, as shown in Table 6, is considerably better than that of owned departments, at least until 1882. The lack of detailed figures for 1886 and 1887 hampers comparisons, and the data for later years indicate that the performance of leased departments slumped at the end of the period under review; but during the decade, it is clear, the proportion of total business contributed by leased departments rose materially. While sales in owned departments increased two and one-half times, those in leased departments multiplied nearly fourfold. This contrast supports the suggestion that the owners of Macy's were relaxing their efforts.

In short, we should note with due appreciation the fact that Macy sales more than doubled under Webster and Wheeler, but we should also not fail to observe the leveling-off after 1884. In reality this was a failure to move forward strongly when general business conditions began to improve. When one considers the sales data along with the lack of improvements in premises after 1880, the failure to introduce any new departments after 1883, and the general slackening of the firm's promotional activities, one is driven to the conclusion that the store was suffering from some sort of managerial weakness.

Analysis of Operating Data, 1877 and 1887

With adequate accounting records it would be possible to check more definitely my suggestion that Macy management under Webster and Wheeler was losing its drive. Unfortunately most of the records have been destroyed or lost, and, apart from the annual sales and a truncated series of figures on weekly sales and purchases, the extant data on operations at this time are limited to an incomplete statement for the latter part of 1877 and a detailed account covering the second half of 1887. These fragments, however, can be made to yield a surprising number of significant facts about the store.

The statement for 1887 makes possible a detailed analysis of Macy operations for the period just before the partnership of Webster and Wheeler came to an end. Sales by departments are presented in Table 7, accompanied by ratios which show both the relative importance of each department and the unadjusted margin it yielded. As explained earlier, this margin is not the gross margin figure that we usually talk about today. According to the definitions used in this book, the cost of goods sold is the net figure *after* deduction of cash discounts. Since the store's practice was to treat discounts as income, the column headed "Margin before Adjustments" represents the departmental margin *before* taking out the discounts.

Table 7 should be compared with the corresponding figures for 1876 (Table 4, p. 136) to see the changes which took place during the eleven years. The subdivision of departments which occurred between 1876 and 1887 makes it difficult in some instances to determine whether all lines of merchandise kept pace during the period in which sales for the store as a whole grew nearly threefold. It is plain, however, that the leased departments gained on the rest of the store: leaving the restaurant out of consideration because it did not exist in 1876, the increase was from 13.5 per cent of total sales in 1876 to 17.0 per cent in 1887. Laces dropped in importance, although part of the decrease is accounted for by the separation of the corset and handkerchief departments. Underwear doubled its relative sales, while millinery dropped. Cloaks and suits made poor progress, toys and dolls declined somewhat, books and stationery tended to lag behind, along with fancy goods and toiletries, worsteds, and gloves. White goods advanced slightly, and house furnishings remained almost exactly the same.[41]

In general, the changes in the contribution of individual departments to total store sales are of limited significance, because the splitting of some departments and the addition of new lines distort the percentage relationships. It is important to note, however, that the nontextile departments in 1887 contributed approximately half the total volume of sales, continuing the advance noted in 1876.

In Table 8 we have a detailed analysis of the Macy income and

TABLE 7
OPERATING RESULTS BY DEPARTMENTS
Six Months Ending December 31, 1887

Departments	Sales	Percentage of Total Sales	Margin Before Adjustments[a]	Percentage of Margin to Sales %
(Owned)				
1. White goods	$135,876.07	5.1	$16,189.63	11.91
2. Laces and embroideries	65,333.38	2.5	9,075.64	13.89
2½. Underwear and infants' wear	130,490.88	4.9	17,842.89	13.67
3. Notions and smallwares	77,185.88	2.9	16,562.57	21.46
4. Ribbons	38,248.79	1.4	4,573.81	11.96
4½. Colored silks	117,116.02	4.4	15,651.57	13.36
6. Hosiery	65,968.28	2.5	8,367.79	12.68
6½. Men's furnishings	116,387.68	4.4	14,155.91	12.16
8½. Umbrellas	21,358.90	0.8	1,343.91	6.29
9. Fancy goods	83,914.14	3.2	15,255.55	18.18
9½. Drugs and toiletries	81,028.79	3.1	14,039.18	17.33
10. Boys' clothing	44,734.85	1.7	5,967.44	13.34
11. House furnishings	243,744.48	9.2	50,396.84	20.68
12. Dolls and toys	115,778.50	4.4	30,599.72	26.43
13. Books	88,097.88	3.3	12,666.72	14.38
14. Worsted embroideries	52,121.46	2.0	8,230.48	15.79
16. Candy	56,310.40	2.1	12,737.99	22.62
17. Gloves	40,055.52	1.5	6,734.08	16.81
18. Untrimmed hats	21,196.76	0.8	2,821.39	13.31
18½. Trimmed hats	20,080.53	0.8	1,402.70	6.99
19. Flowers and feathers	10,968.26	0.4	1,906.21	17.38
21. Cloaks	19,422.52	0.7	2,714.65	13.98
21½. Suits	23,896.87	0.9	3,224.81	13.49

TABLE 7 (continued)

	Departments	Sales	Percentage of Total Sales	Margin Before Adjustments[a]	Percentage of Margin to Sales %
	(Owned)				
22.	Black silks	122,597.93	4.6	12,496.46	10.19
23.	Dress goods	140,043.21	5.3	13,214.85	9.44
24.	Trimmings	36,151.42	1.4	6,594.15	18.24
26.	Corsets and bustles	31,985.16	1.2	4,973.89	15.55
27.	Stationery and engraving	37,056.08	1.4	7,627.45	20.58
28.	Upholstery goods	32,410.13	1.2	4,471.01	13.80
29.	Handkerchiefs	66,293.41	2.5	8,734.04	13.17
30.	Knitted worsteds	8,982.39	0.3	1,466.82	16.33
	Sales in owned departments	$2,144,836.57	80.9	$332,040.15	15.48
	(Leased)				
5.	Silverware, bronzes, and clocks	74,481.62	2.8	10,851.58($\frac{1}{2}$)	14.57 (29.14)
15.	China and glass	284,147.44	10.7	55,014.48($\frac{1}{2}$)	19.36 (38.72)
20.	Women's and children's shoes	92,701.03	3.5	9,934.40($\frac{1}{2}$)	10.71 (21.43)
25.	Restaurant	54,555.02	2.1	11,910.64($\frac{1}{2}$)	21.83 (43.66)
	Sales in leased departments	$505,885.11	19.1	$ 87,711.10($\frac{1}{2}$)	17.34 (34.68)
	Total sales	$2,650,721.68	100.0	$419,751.25	15.84
	Manufacturing for own departments (included above)[b]	$185,705.02			
	Ratio of own manufactures to cost of goods sold (before deduction of discounts)	10.24%			

[a] These figures represent the difference between the prices received and the cost of goods sold before the deduction of discounts.
[b] Goods manufactured by the firm were charged to selling departments at prices which slightly exceeded the cost of manufacture.
SOURCE: Semiannual balances, 1887–1903.

TABLE 8
Analysis of Operating Results
Six Months Ending December 31, 1887

					Percentage of Sales
Total net sales				$2,650,721.68	100.00
Cost of goods sold:					
Owned departments					
Sales at cost	$1,801,085.82				
Shortages	11,710.60				
Cost of goods sold		$1,812,796.42			
(ratio of cost to sales — 84.52%)					
Leased departments					
Sales at cost	$ 328,454.08				
Shortages	2,008.83				
Total cost of goods sold[a]		330,462.91			
(ratio of cost to sales — 65.32%)					
Total cost of goods sold				2,143,259.33	80.86
Margin before adjustments and deductions				$ 507,462.35	19.14
(ratio of margin to sales, owned departments — 15.48%)					
(ratio of margin to sales, leased departments — 34.68%)					

[a] It is impossible to determine whether or not this amount includes inward freight. If it does not, the cost of goods sold is slightly understated and the gross margin correspondingly increased. At the same time, the freight and trucking charges would presumably be included in general expense, thereby making the operating expense slightly larger than it would be if entries were properly classified. The difference, in any case, would probably not be large.

TABLE 8 (continued)

			Percentage of Sales
Less one-half margin in leased departments		87,711.10	3.31
Margin before adjustments		$ 419,751.25	15.83
Discounts earned		70,801.49	2.67
Gross margin received by Macy's		$ 490,552.74	18.50
(ratio of margin received from leased departments to Macy's gross margin — 17.88%)			
Operating expenses:[b]			
Rent and gas		42,912.55	1.62
Electric light		2,432.10	.09
Insurance		9,047.89	.34
Pneumatic tubes		774.19	.03
Fixtures depreciation, etc.			
Fixtures account	$ 3,884.82		(.15)
Repairs	3,988.42		(.15)
Decrease in fixtures	6,345.73		(.24)
Total fixtures expense		14,218.97	.54
Delivery		18,221.83	.69
Packing		13,624.70	.51
Advertising		32,495.58	1.22
Payroll[c]		182,860.38	6.90
Interest[d]		10,836.84	.41
Mail-order department		6,256.25	.24

[b] Nothing is known about the classification of expenses. Wages and salaries in functional departments, such as advertising and delivery, are almost certainly charged to payroll; but the leased department expense entries may include some wages.

[c] Payroll includes salaries of executives as well as wages of the rank and file, but it does not include any payments to partners.

[d] Most of the interest charged was undoubtedly interest on capital invested ($300,000) computed at 7% per annum. A credit for $10,500 has accordingly been shown below under other income.

TABLE 8 (continued)

				Percentage of Sales
Miscellaneous expense				
Charity	$	1,084.91		(.04)
Stationery		5,079.64		(.19)
General expense		11,385.99		(.43)
Legal expenses		170.75		(.01)
Total miscellaneous expense			17,721.29	.67
Leased department expense				
5 & 15 (Straus)	$	17,299.31		(.65)
20 (women's shoes)		4,424.98		(.16)
25 (restaurant)		4,695.62		(.18)
Total leased department expense			26,419.91	.99
Total operating expense			377,822.48	14.25
Net operating profit			$112,730.26	4.25
Other net income:				
Jobbing department [e]			15,572.71	
Manufacturing department [f]			6,107.12	
Laundry [g]			625.42	
Interest on capital at 7%			10,500.00	
Total other income			32,805.25	1.24
Total net gain			$145,535.51	5.49

[e] This item seems to have represented profit on importing operations, i.e., the difference between the amounts charged to retail departments for goods imported by the store's own organization and the total cost of such merchandise after inclusion of expenses incurred in buying, shipping, customs charges, etc.

[f] This amount represents the difference between the sum charged to retail departments for goods made in the firm's workroom and the cost of manufacturing such merchandise.

[g] This entry apparently represented the profit calculated on the laundry operations performed by the store for various departments, such as restaurant, shirt manufacturing, and the like.

expense figures for the latter half of 1887. These reveal some highly important data, but their full significance does not emerge until comparisons are made with other periods of operation. For that reason it is advisable to consider them in relation to earlier figures in order to determine the changes which took place in the interval. The earliest data available for the decade 1877–87 relate to store operations from July 1 to December 1, 1877. This five-month period cannot be considered wholly typical because the time span includes the very dull months of July and August and omits December — invariably the very busiest month of the year. There is also some doubt as to whether the 1877 figures are complete in all respects, for they contain no reference to shortages or jobbing income. However, they compare rather closely with the data for the fall of 1876 (presented above in Tables 4 and 5, pp. 136 and 139), and they have been summarized in Table 9. Comparison of the fall seasons for the three years 1876, 1877, and 1887 reveals some rather significant developments, and so for the reader's convenience the principal ratios for 1876 and 1877 have been recapitulated in Table 9 for examination along with the figures for 1887.

One noteworthy change which is evident in Table 9 is a decline in the margin before adjustments, from 17.90 per cent of total net sales in 1876 to 15.83 in 1887. There is a corresponding shift in the gross margin received by Macy's, from 21.70 per cent in 1876 to 19.09 per cent in 1887. This is materially below the average gross margin received in the period 1872–76 (about 20.5 per cent), suggesting that some fundamental change had taken place.

There are at least three explanations possible which, individually or in combination, might account for the drop in the gross margin ratio. One is that the downward price movement had caused a general shift in New York retail margins. It is certainly true that the level of prices, after a brief recovery in 1879–81, had resumed the long slide downhill, continuing it through 1886. Theoretically a movement of this sort would tend to depress margins and complicate the problem of management. A second explanation is that, for a time at least, department stores were really reducing the cost of living through their competition with the specialized stores. The

TABLE 9

Comparison of Principal Operating Data
Fall Seasons of 1876, 1877, and 1887

	Fall, 1876	Fall, 1877	Fall, 1887
	(Percentage of Total Net Sales)		
Margin before adjustments	17.90	17.71	15.83
Discounts earned	3.07	3.30	2.67
Jobbing income	.73	..	.59
Gross margin received	21.70	21.01	19.09
Operating expenses:			
Rent	..	3.01	1.62
Delivery	.59	.32	.69
Advertising	.96	.53	1.22
Payroll	7.34	6.95	6.90
General expense	5.10	2.60	3.48
Other	.14	.09	.34
Total expense	14.13	13.50	14.25
Total operating profit	7.57	7.51	4.84
Leased department sales (% of total net sales)	13.57	12.82	19.08
Ratio of margin from leased departments to total gross margin	10.90	13.15	17.88
Margin before adjustment in owned departments	17.96	17.64	15.48
Margin received by Macy's in leased departments	17.41	18.16	17.34

NOTE: This table summarizes information which appears in detail, accompanied by explanations and source citations, in Tables 4, 5, and 8, for 1876 and 1887. Data for 1877 have been taken from a fragmentary operating statement relating to the five-month period, July 1–Dec. 1, 1877. The time spans are not strictly comparable, and the accounting classifications may not be, but the ratios for 1876 and 1887 can be taken as reasonably accurate and comparable. Those for 1877 are, without much doubt, approximately comparable. For purposes of comparison, jobbing income has been included here as a part of gross margin, although it was treated as other income in Table 8.

third possibility is that the Macy management, through complacency or incompetence, had allowed margins to decline.

It is impossible to prove or disprove the first suggestion beyond pointing out that prices leveled off at the close of 1886 so that by the fall season of 1887 conditions were again fairly stable — in fact, more stable than during the years 1874–76 when the Macy gross margin remained comfortably above 20 per cent. Against the second explanation is the fact that operating expenses actually increased slightly from 14.13 per cent in 1876 and 13.50 in 1877 to 14.25 in 1887. This rise is too small to prove much, and, in any case, the tendency of stores to compete in services would inevitably produce an increase in the expense ratio. Of course, the substantial growth in sales between 1877 and 1887 should have had a counteracting tendency to reduce the expense ratio, so far as fixed expenses are concerned, but this tendency would be offset by the expenses involved in the store's constant endeavor to integrate importing and wholesaling with retailing. (That extension of Macy activities would also, as explained on page 153, tend to increase the gross margin, and the fact that we find a *decrease* in margins suggests that the degree of integration was exaggerated.)

An examination of the items of expense does not disclose any particularly significant changes. The fact that the payroll ratio was 7.34 per cent in 1876 and only 6.90 in 1887 is fully accounted for by the fact that the figures for 1876 include salaries to La Forge and Valentine, while those for 1877 and 1887 do not involve any compensation to partners. The drop in rent between 1877 and 1887 may not mean much, for little is known about the expense classifications for either period. In any case, if the leases had been renewed for substantially the same rentals as in the 1870's, the subsequent increase in sales volume would certainly have produced a decrease in the percentage ratio. However, Macy experience after 1887 suggests that the store was crowded for space and should have been enlarged by Webster and Wheeler.

Advertising increased from .96 to 1.22 per cent of sales. At first glance this looks as if the firm had made proportionately greater promotional efforts in 1887 than before, but, if so, they were not effective, for the Macy newspaper advertisements of 1887 do not stand out. In part, this is a matter of relativity, other stores having increased their newspaper advertising and hence reduced the visibility of Macy expenditures. In part, however, it seems to have been a matter of scattering the effort: the store inserted small advertisements in many papers, whereas competitors tended to concentrate on large space in fewer issues. There is something to be said for both lines of attack, but the fact remains that Macy sales in 1887 showed no particular response. It is possible, too, that the cost of catalogs has been included in advertising expense and that the amount spent on newspaper space did not really increase.

The delivery expense ratio increased from .32 to .69, but the figure for 1877 was probably abnormally low, and the .69 should perhaps be compared with the ratio of .59 for 1876. Of course, the steady widening of the Macy market area would inevitably increase the cost of delivery, and it is also likely that a larger proportion of customers' purchases were being delivered as the store increased the amount of bulky merchandise offered for sale.

On the whole, neither the margin nor expense ratios really enable us to reach any dependable conclusions about the effect of external conditions upon Macy's. Turning to the last of the three possible explanations advanced above — the suggestion that the Webster-Wheeler management may have been at fault — we find a number of bits of evidence which appear to confirm it. The fact that earned discounts, which had been running well over 3 per cent in the 1870's, dropped to 2.67 per cent in 1887 cannot be explained by external conditions and indicates that the firm was not sufficiently careful about paying its bills promptly or else failed to insist upon recognition of cash payments. The record of operations after 1887, as we shall see, gives full support to this surmise. It is important to note, further, that the decline in Macy margins was far greater for sales in owned departments than those in leased departments. That is to say, the margins in owned departments (before adjustment) declined from 17.96 in 1876 to 15.48 in 1887. The margin received from leased departments in the same period rose slightly in 1877 and then decreased to 17.34 per cent — very little below the 17.41 recorded for

1876. This suggests that there was a difference in the way in which the owned and leased divisions of the store were managed.

The decline in gross margin, together with the increase in the operating expense ratio, led to a decrease in the operating profit from 7.57 per cent in 1876 to 4.84 in 1887. (The expense ratios for 1876, 1887, and probably 1877 included a charge for interest on capital, as a result of which the total return to the partners was larger than the ratios shown.) To the extent that this lower rate of profit was caused by price or competitive conditions, it is no reflection upon managerial performance, but it should be kept in mind in appraising the Webster-Wheeler régime. Although to the layman the differences in ratios which have been noted may appear to be too small to have much significance, it is just such apparently minute differences which produce profits in retailing. Continued over a period of years, they can make or break an enterprise. While one cannot be sure that an alert and aggressive management could have achieved better results, these data, taken with various bits of qualitative evidence, support the view that the Macy management between 1877 and 1887 was somewhat less effective than it had been during the previous decade.

Comparison of Owned and Leased Departments, 1876-1887

Before reaching a final conclusion, two other tests of performance can be made. One of these is set forth in Table 10, analyzing the contribution of leased departments to the store's total results for the fall seasons of 1876, 1877, and 1887. It is necessary to bear in mind that the figures for 1877 do not include December; since they omit the Christmas trade they are not strictly comparable. Of course, much of the merchandise of the Straus departments, silverware and china and glassware, was sold for gift purposes. (To facilitate later discussion, separate figures are presented for the two departments operated by L. Straus & Sons.) It is evident, as already indicated, that the leased departments had expanded their volume more rapidly than the rest of the store, until their sales constituted nearly one-fifth of the total. In one respect they showed up less favorably in 1887 than in 1877: their very substantial contribution to the store's

TABLE 10

ANALYSIS OF CONTRIBUTION OF LEASED DEPARTMENTS
1876, 1877, and 1887

	Fall, 1876[a]		Fall, 1877[b]		Fall, 1887[c]	
	Amount	% of Store Total[d]	Amount	% of Store Total[d]	Amount	% of Store Total[d]
Sales in Straus departments [e]	$ 96,786.50	11.04	$70,264.37	9.67	$358,629.06	13.53
Margin contributed by Straus departments	19,562.16	10.29	14,656.70	11.39	65,866.06	13.43
Sales in all leased departments	118,987.95	13.57	93,099.36	12.82	505,885.11	19.08
Margin contributed by all leased departments	20,717.47	10.90	16,903.19	13.15	87,711.10	17.88

[a] Period covered is five months from Aug. 7, 1876, to Jan. 6, 1877.
[b] Period covered is five months from July 1 to Dec. 1, 1877. Since this does not include the Christmas season, a matter of particular importance to the Straus departments, the figures are not strictly comparable to those for 1876 and 1887.
[c] Period covered is six months ending Dec. 31, 1887.
[d] That is, departmental sales are compared with the totals for the store including leased departments; departmental margins are compared with the total gross margin received by the store, including discounts earned.
[e] The Straus departments were silver (No. 5) and china and glassware (No. 15). The other leased departments were women's shoes (No. 20) and the restaurant (No. 25).

SOURCE: La Forge's Ledger, 1876–77; fragmentary operating statement for 1877; semiannual balance for 1887.

gross margin (after deducting the 50 per cent of departmental margin which went to the owners) was slightly less than their share of the total sales, 17.88 per cent of the store's total gross margin against 19.08 per cent of its total sales. In 1877 the performance of the leased departments had been better, for they had contributed relatively more margin than sales. However, because the 1877 figures do not include the December business, the seasons' results are not strictly comparable, and it is more accurate to compare the data for 1876 with those for 1887. They show an improvement in the relative contribution of the leased departments during the decade, in both sales and margin. One must remember that the owners of the leased departments had to bear the cost involved in the ownership and obsolescence of merchandise inventories — matters of no small importance in silver, china and glassware, and shoe departments. Consequently the store itself was relieved of these expenses and had to pay out relatively less of the gross margin received from leased departments than it did in owned departments, and it should therefore have obtained proportionately more margin from its own departments if the *net* operating profit was to be comparable to that earned in leased departments. The fact that the store's share of the margin received in leased departments corresponded so nearly to the sales volume that they contributed is an indication that the leased departments were really more profitable than the owned. This suggests a difference in the quality of management. One cannot fail to note that the Straus departments contributed nearly all the sales and margins which Macy derived from the leased divisions.

In Table 11 appears an analysis of stock turnover which affords us a somewhat more tangible clue to managerial performance than we have thus far had. Comparing sales at cost with average inventory (that is, an average of the stocks on hand at the beginning and at the end of the period), we find that the average stock of merchandise in owned departments was turned (bought and sold) slightly more than 6 times during the half-year, indicating a rate of stock-turn for the year of about 12. Since this is more than double the average figure for department stores today (higher even than the prevailing rate for grocery and variety chains), and since a high rate of stock-turn is usually regarded as a favorable index of efficiency, one is tempted to conclude that in one important respect Webster and Wheeler turned in an excellent score, especially as compared with the stock-turn of 1.67 times for leased departments dur-

TABLE 11

ANALYSIS OF STOCK TURNOVER

Six Months Ending December 31, 1887

Owned departments:	
Sales at cost	$1,801,086
Average of beginning and ending inventories at cost	298,301
Rate of stock-turn for the six-month period (sales divided by average inventory)	6.04 times
Leased departments:	
5 (silverware)	
Sales at cost	$ 53,453
Average inventory at cost	29,258
Rate of stock-turn	1.83 times
15 (china and glass)	
Sales at cost	$ 168,991
Average inventory at cost	85,434
Rate of stock-turn	1.98 times
20 (women's shoes)	
Sales at cost	$ 71,993
Average inventory at cost	81,447
Rate of stock-turn	0.88 times
All leased departments, including restaurant	
Sales at cost	$ 328,454
Average inventory at cost	196,257
Rate of stock-turn	1.67 times
All selling departments:	
Total sales at cost	$2,129,540
Total average inventory at cost	494,558
Rate of stock-turn	4.31 times
All departments, including manufacturing	
Total sales at cost	$2,129,540
Total average inventory at cost	511,540
Rate of stock-turn	4.16 times

SOURCE: Semiannual balance, 1887.

ing the half-year (indicating an annual rate of only a little more than 3 times).

The problem which immediately arises is to explain how the owned departments could attain such a high rate of stock-turn and still not make a very distinguished profit record; and how, conversely, the leased departments did so well in producing margin while their average stock-turn was very low and therefore apparently unsatisfactory. The explanation of this paradox seems to me to reveal clearly the difference between the retailing ideas applied by Webster and Wheeler, on the one hand, and, on the other, those held by the principal lessees, Isidor and Nathan Straus of L. Straus & Sons, who — to anticipate Chapter ix — were to set the pattern of operations in Macy's from 1888 down to the present day.

In part, of course, the difference in rates of stock-turn arose from differences in the kind of merchandise handled. Experience has demonstrated that china, glass, and silverware move slowly, even under favorable conditions, and that dry goods, clothing, and accessories sell rapidly by comparison. Thus, in modern department stores, the stock-turn in china and glass departments is not likely to rise much above two times a year, and the rate for silver departments averages little better than three, while for the remaining departments the average annual stock turnover usually ranges around four or five times.[42]

Returning to the Macy figures for 1887 with these differences in mind, we find that the two Straus departments attained a stock-turn rate of nearly four times per year, which compares favorably with modern figures. The stock-turn for the women's shoe department was less than one for the six-month period, substantially below the average rate for a corresponding department today. We shall see that a change was made in this department in 1888, because its performance was regarded as unsatisfactory by contemporary standards. There is no point to considering the stock-turn in the restaurant, for its stock was bought and sold almost daily and its rate would not be comparable. As for the owned departments, while space limitations prevent a detailed analysis, inspection of the original data reveals that the rate of turnover was, with hardly an exception, higher than modern figures in all departments, as is suggested by the stock-turn for all owned departments in 1887 shown in Table 11. The Macy rate of 4.31 times for the six months in all selling departments was, in fact, roughly twice the average stock-turn for stores of comparable volume today.

It is impossible, however, to explain the difference between the stock-turns achieved by the departments owned by L. Straus & Sons and those for the owned portion of the business as being simply the consequence of the types of merchandise involved. I suggest that it is the result of deliberate managerial policy. Considering the variety of goods handled, the extraordinarily high rate in the owned departments could be achieved only by limiting stocks to fast-moving items and by quickly reducing the price of any item which lingered on the shelves. Frequent and drastic mark-downs, of course, reduced the gross margin obtained and so yielded low profits. Limiting stocks meant either restricting the selection carried to the most popular types and sizes or else handling a large number of bargain lots and making little pretense of maintaining regular assortments of merchandise.

Interviews with old employees indicate that Macy's did both in the 1880's. As a result, customers could not depend upon satisfying their needs in Macy's owned departments. ("Sorry, madam, we haven't that in stock at present. . . . No, I don't know when we will have it again.") Again, the assortment which the public found displayed in the store was unlikely to tempt it to make purchases not originally contemplated. In both situations the store lost sales, and the customer, if not actually annoyed, was definitely not favorably impressed. Webster and Wheeler obtained the benefits of rapid turnover only by sacrificing business and profits. To be sure, they were wise in attempting to be conservative, but it is highly probable that they carried the policy too far.

Conditions in the Straus departments stood in marked contrast. The Strauses made a point of keeping an unusually large assortment of merchandise on hand, so that there was hardly anything in the line that a customer might ask for that could not immediately be shown. Goods were purposely displayed in great quantities and attractive exhibits in order to invite the attention of any person who passed by, and many a shopper ordered a purchase sent home who had not originally intended to buy any china or glassware. Moreover, a customer who was trying to find the solution to a gift problem was not likely to visit a Straus department in vain.[43]

This policy involved risk: it increased the possibility of physical depreciation, style obsolescence, and loss from price declines; and it required investing more capital in stock, fixtures, and floor space than would otherwise be needed. On the other hand, it made sales, it impressed customers, and it yielded margins which produced good operating profits. Carried to extreme, it would be dangerous, but the Strauses obviously were avoiding that danger.

If my suggestion is correct, a number of points are cleared up. The steady advance of the Straus departments and the profits they earned actually and in relation to the rest of the store are easily understood. The high stock-turn and relatively low margin and profit percentages in owned departments can now be reconciled and likewise that of comparatively low stock-turn and large profits in Straus departments.

It is unfortunate that we have no other retail operating data for the period with which to compare Macy figures, in order that we might see whether Macy margins and expenses were above or below those of competing firms. Small differences in ratios may be of little significance, but they often make noticeable differences in the retail prices which the public has to pay, differences of a few cents which make him decide to buy in one store rather than another.

My final appraisal of the store's management in the decade following the death of Rowland Macy is that it was earnest, careful, and, at the outset, enterprising, but that it gradually slipped into a rut. Past success apparently bred complacency, and the fact that operating results were less favorable than in previous years was apparently attributed to external circumstances. And yet the hard times did not prevent the emergence of rival department stores which could successfully challenge Macy's entrenched position. The situation called for progressive policies and energetic management which the firm could not or would not produce. Webster's conservatism was strangling profits.

In 1887 Macy's was still a profitable concern, with widespread patronage, policies of tested value, and a well-established reputation for variety and low prices. Its future, however, was endangered by slow stagnation. Although no one criterion taken singly can be advanced to prove this thesis, every piece of available evidence seems to me to point in the same direction. Whatever the explanation, the firm unquestionably was yielding leadership to others. It was going ahead, but competitors were advancing faster.

CHAPTER VIII

SWEAT FOR DUTY . . . FOR PROMOTION

Thus far in our account of Macy history the chief emphasis has been upon the topmost management and its policies. Behind the counters, of course, and also in places where customers never saw them, the rank and file of the Macy staff toiled at the endless round of activities involved in retailing merchandise. Although individual employees were seldom of any great consequence, their combined efforts were of prime importance in the operation of the store, and it is well to turn aside at this juncture to examine their lot.

Our evidence is fragmentary and woefully inadequate, and it is impossible to attach precise dates to many of the known facts, but it is possible, by means of a few quantitative measurements and several illuminating glimpses into the daily work, to convey some notion of what it meant to work in Macy's in the 1870's and '80's, up to the end of the Webster and Wheeler partnership.

Size of the Staff

The Macy staff has long comprised a widely miscellaneous assortment of people — young, middle-aged, and old, a variety of nationalities, some with little schooling and others with college degrees, all differing greatly in talents, experience, responsibilities, type of work, and remuneration. Its size has varied with the amount of business handled by the firm, the number of workers expanding and contracting according to the seasons as well as with the fluctuations in annual volume.

In the 1870's, as today, the peak of employment came in December, after which numbers dropped off sharply during January and February, rose for the spurt of spring trade in April and May, declined again to the low point during dog days, and then gained steadily through the autumn months to the year's maximum in the week before Christmas. Then, as now, the number of employees at the high point was approximately double the minimum for the year, with the average figure falling a little below the midpoint between the extremes. Thus, in 1870, the largest number employed was 270 in the week ending December 24, the low point was 154 in the week ending September 3 (later than usual), and the average number for the year (total of the weekly figures divided by 52) was 198. The corresponding data for the three following years were as follows: 1871 — 304, 164 (week ending August 12), and 200; 1872 — 396, 136 (week ending August 10), and 216; 1873 — 387, 188 (week ending July 26), and 255.[1]

One striking fact emerges from an examination of the payrolls at this time. Careful checks at different dates between 1871 and 1874 prove that the number of Macy employees who were engaged in nonselling activities (delivery, bookkeeping, buying, etc.) varied between 55 and 60 per cent of the total. In other words, those who actually sold to the public constituted less than half of the working force. In recent years there has been much criticism of department stores because such a large proportion of their staffs consisted of nonselling employees, and the general assumption has been that in the nineteenth century the proportion was substantially smaller. If the Macy figures are at all typical, this assumption needs revision. One must remember, of course, that Macy's and other stores used to employ large numbers of cash girls and errand boys, thereby increasing the nonselling ratio.

No detailed information is available for the years after 1874, but we shall not be far from the true facts if we estimate the average number of employees for each year by assuming that the annual sales per employee averaged $5,000. (For 1870 and 1871 the average sales were slightly in excess of this amount, but in 1872 and 1873 the sales per employee dropped to $4,660 and $3,983, so that the assumption is clearly on the conservative side.) In 1875, therefore, when sales were $1,331,670, the average number of people employed by the store was at least 266. In 1880 the retail staff must have numbered about 700, and by 1884 the average was probably over 1,000, with the maximum running at least 1,500 in late December. In addition there was a substantial number of employees engaged in manufacturing operations about whom little information exists.

Obviously the Macy organization was a large one by contemporary standards, but it was not the largest in New York so long as Stewart's great emporium continued to prosper. In 1870 it took approximately 2,200 people to run the Stewart store during the busy season. More than half of these were engaged in manufacturing operations, and it is possible that the figure comprehended the wholesale end of the business; even so, the fact that 200 cash boys were used indicates that Stewart's retail activities employed a veritable army of workers.[2] Doubtless certain other competing stores had organizations about as large as Macy's.

Employment of Women

The Macy payrolls contained a surprisingly large proportion of women and girls. To some extent this was the result of using cash girls to carry money and packages back and forth on the selling floor, but most of the clerks (saleswomen) and cashiers were female, too. Men and boys were, consequently, in a decided minority, ranging from 9 to 17 per cent of the total during the period from August, 1869, to February, 1874, with the typical figure close to 12 per cent.

While Macy's was by no means the first or only store to employ members of the fair sex, such scraps of evidence as have survived suggest that the female predominance was somewhat unusual in New York. A. T. Stewart, for example, used very few women to wait on customers, preferring to employ male attendants. It was said that he hired the handsomest men he could obtain as clerks because he had noticed that ladies who shopped in his store liked to gossip and even to flirt with them. "Stewart's nice young men" were so popular that other stores used the same tactics.[3]

This explanation may be the fabrication of a journalist, but the fact remains that, in contrast with Philadelphia where saleswomen were common and "he-biddies" scarce, male clerks predominated in New York in the 1850's and apparently for many years afterwards. Hunt's *Merchants' Magazine*, at any rate, felt called upon in 1855 to advocate the use of women for retail selling, so as to release men "to more athletic and useful employments." The Civil War probably marked the general turning point, but Stewart continued to favor men as late as 1870.[4]

Macy, on the other hand, had employed women in his Haverhill store and apparently from the very beginning in New York.[5] He had, moreover, given them positions of responsibility: in addition to making Margaret Getchell superintendent of the store, he had hired Belle Cushman as buyer for the fancy goods department, and, after promoting Marie Bowyer from clerk to floorwalker, he had appointed her to succeed Miss Getchell as superintendent. Miss Bowyer held this position from about 1872 to her death in 1886. Cora Crossman was advanced from floorwalker to assistant superintendent, and then placed in charge of the mail-order department. And there was Martha Toye, another floorwalker, who was later to take the top position after Miss Bowyer's death, at least for a short time. We shall hear more about her later. Rowland Macy was one man who did not think that every woman's place was in the home — so much so that he even urged his own daughter to come into the business rather than get married.[6]

The Working Hierarchy and Employee Compensation

Next in importance to the superintendent in the Macy hierarchy were the buyers, of whom there were 5 in 1870 and 16 in 1887. Each had at least one department (in 1888 two had four, one had five, and another six) over which he presided with a power and independence which is rare in large stores today. He decided what and how much to buy (within the maximum set by the firm) and from whom it was to be bought, in addition to which he directed all selling operations in his departments. While the employees who worked under him were supposed to be hired and fired by the superintendent and kept in order by the floorwalker, the buyer's voice was usually the deciding one. In certain lines his duties included an arduous, if exciting, annual trip to European markets and factories. For his responsibilities and pains he received only a modest salary by modern standards: in 1871 three male buyers received $28.85 per week; Redford Mount, who had somewhat less experience, was paid $26.92;

while Belle Cushman, doubtless because she was merely a woman, had to be content with $25.00 ($5.00 more than she had received in 1869 in the same position).[7] They may also have received a commission on the sales in their departments. We know, at any rate, that in 1889 one buyer was paid $35.00 a week and half of one per cent of sales, with a minimum total of $4,000 a year guaranteed.[8]

Since the tendency of both prices and the cost of living was more or less continuously downward during the period from 1865 to 1896, these compensation figures and those which follow may need to be adjusted slightly downward to be accurate for the late '70's and the 1880's. Certainly it is highly improbable that the scale of wages rose during that period, although individual persons might receive increases as they gained experience or promotion.

There was approximately the same number of floorwalkers as buyers, but they were not so important as the latter. Known in many stores today as section or service managers, the floorwalkers kept the clerks and cash girls in order and checked them in and out of the store by means of time books, saw that customers received proper attention, handled complaints and approved refunds or exchanges, and generally supervised the service within the departments to which they were assigned, always taking care not to displease the all-powerful and often crotchety buyers. For many years Macy floorwalkers seem to have been mainly if not exclusively women, and their weekly salary seems to have ranged from $10 to $16, the typical figure being near the upper limit.

Clerks constituted by far the largest classification of Macy employees, amounting to approximately 45 per cent of the total staff. On them fell the important task of waiting on trade, showing merchandise, trying to persuade the customer to buy, and folding or rearranging and placing unwanted goods back upon the shelves. They were (and are) the chief point of contact between the store and the public, and much of the store's reputation has always depended upon the manner in which they performed their work. Inexperienced clerks in the early '70's started at $3.00 or $4.00 a week (these seem really to have been stock girls, helping to keep merchandise in order and serving customers only in rush periods). A great many received $5.00 and $6.00, and a few got as much as $9.00 or $10, but only rarely was a clerk given more than $10, and no commissions were paid on sales.

These wage rates may seem to be low by modern standards, but they conformed to contemporary practice in large stores. In small establishments both wages and working conditions were often even less attractive. It would have been difficult for any employer to pay much more than the current market rate, had he been so eccentric as to want to do so, because he could ill afford any additional expense. Wages, low as they were, formed the principal item in his cost of doing business, and they could not be bettered without a corresponding increase in prices which no single store could possibly bring about. Moreover, the local labor supply was so great that applicants were willing and eager to take the jobs at the prevailing rates — some resigned to their fate, others hopeful of advancement.[9]

That this condition was not entirely new is evident from the following comment, published in 1849:[10]

> Most clerks . . . content themselves with their situations only because they suppose that in a few years they will be able to get into business for themselves, and become rich, and be in a measure, compensated for their past services. . . . With the exception of the retail dry goods business, there is not one that holds out less encouragement to clerks than the jobbing business. The young man who goes into a dry goods store with any other view of making money than that of saving it from his salary, makes a mistake that will cost him the best part of a lifetime to get over.

Doubtless a similar statement could have been made about women clerks in the 1870's. Of course a job at low salary was better than none, and to many an Irish immigrant family it was a boon, giving the numerous offspring a chance to get started and eking out the family income in a substantial way.

Next to the clerks, the cash girls formed the largest group of Macy employees, amounting to approximately a third of the store payroll. These were innocent victims of a public which believed in compulsory education only up to a point. Starting at twelve or fourteen years of age, sometimes even younger, they scurried back and forth between sales counter, cashier, and parcel desk, carrying a basket containing salesbook, money, and purchases.[11] Each had a number embroidered in red on her ecru uniform and was assigned to a particular department. Each had to respond to insistent cries of "Cash! Cash!" all day long; any girl caught loitering was sure to draw the floorwalker's ire. At the close of a long day the cash girls swept the floors and dusted counters, for porters were used at that time solely to handle heavy cases and baskets of merchandise; the housekeeping, apart from scrubbing, was done by the girls after store hours. And, at least while Martha Toye was superintendent, each girl, on leaving the store, had to submit to an intimate search by probing fingers which had no respect for female delicacy, lest money or small items of merchandise be stolen. For all this Maggie Bridgeman, Katie Burke, Annie O'Sullivan, and the rest of the cash girls received $1.50 a week (a very few were paid $2.00) and looked forward to being made stock girls or even clerks. Each one received, in addition, a silver dollar and a box of candy at Christmas. Another perquisite was the summer outing to which the firm treated the "cashes," conveying them by boat to Staten Island where the girls had a bountiful picnic luncheon and played games in which the winners received prizes.[12]

By 1873 a large, new category had been created, the parcel clerks who wrapped up purchases while the cashier made change. Most of them seem to have been just one step up from the bottom of the Macy ladder, for they were paid $2.00 a week, 50 cents more than cash girls. The heavier and more complicated task of packing "send" merchandise was done in the delivery department.

Another numerous group was to be found in the delivery department. In 1870 the drivers, wagon boys, and helpers formed only 8 per cent of the working force, but by 1872 they had increased to more than 13 per cent; in 1873 the proportion was even slightly greater. This, of course, reflects the gradual extension of the store's trade to areas far beyond the immediate environs of 14th Street. Duties and responsibilities in the delivery department seem to have varied widely, and it is impossible now to get a clear picture of the precise arrangements. There were from five to ten drivers in 1873, for whom the standard weekly wage was $12. Wagon boys received $2.00 or $3.00, and Jimmie Woods, who supplemented the horse-drawn wagons by pushing a handcart around in the vicinity of the store, started at $2.50. Boys who ran errands or carried messages (remember that there were no telephones before 1877) usually earned $3.00. Helpers and others attached to the delivery department were paid from $5.00 to $10, and William McCracken, a tall, thin Dubliner who managed the delivery department and found time to study medicine on the side, topped the list with the colossal salary of $25 a week.[13]

One entry may conceal several persons who were indirectly employed by the Macy delivery department. The payroll lists "David Haskins, Express" as receiving $60 a week, obviously too high a figure for a mere employee. The explanation is that Haskins ran an express service and handled Macy deliveries in an area not reached by the store's own system. The money he received paid for at least one driver and a helper, in addition to a wagon and team, and more may well have been included.[14]

Cashiers (Nellie Connel, for example), usually earned $8.00 weekly for the exacting duty of making correct change and keeping track of the money received. In the 1880's they were also given an exciting sleigh ride each winter. Girls who worked at the "Desk" — presumably clerical help — might receive as much as $18 (at least Annie Knight did in 1869), but they were more likely to get from $6.00 to $8.00. Florence French, who was variously described as "corrector" or "exchanger" and was responsible for straightening out wrong orders, was paid $10. Thomas Hodges, "artist," received $17, probably for painting signs, decorating windows, and similar services.

From five to seven persons were usually employed in the receiving department in the basement, checking invoices against merchandise received and marking prices on the merchandise before it was sent to the selling floor. (Marking was centralized before 1870.) The girls who did the routine work received from $3.00 to $5.00, while the woman in charge got $12, and another employee, next in importance, was paid $10.

A number of the people employed had no direct connection with selling operations. There was Sammy Burtis, a negro "engineer," who took care of the heating equipment and was sufficiently well paid to be listed in the special salary ledger, which is now lost. In October, 1872, a full-time carpenter was added to the staff at $23.04 ($1,200 a year) to make repairs and alterations of the sort that a busy store always requires. Hannah Miller, one of the two scrubwomen employed in 1873, received $9.00 a week, while Charles Smith, the night watchman, was paid $20 (a second watchman was added in 1872). The store began to employ a detective as early as 1867 but no information exists as to his pay. Of course, there were no telephone operators, elevator boys, or electricians, and probably no typists.[15]

It would be interesting to know something definite about the origins of this heterogeneous crowd of people, but little information is available on that point. We know that practically everyone in the store, from Rowland Macy down to cash girls, brought in relatives or friends who wanted work; and it is highly probable that most of the people hired were taken on the personal recommendation of someone already in the Macy organization. Both payrolls and interviews indicate that the racial stock was almost exclusively Nordic, with a strong sprinkling of New England Yankees, English, and Scotch, and a great preponderance of Irish, most of whom were born overseas. Judging by names, there was not a single Jew or Italian on the payroll in 1874.

A very substantial portion of the staff seems to have come to the store without any previous retail experience. There were always some, however, who belonged to the growing army of veteran sales people which New York was accumulating as a result of the relatively high labor turnover that apparently was already characteristic of the dry goods and department store trade. The limited evidence available gives support to the statement made by a close observer in the 1890's that few stores reared their own executives, preferring to draw them from other establishments or wholesale houses (the wholesale trade at this time seems to have attracted better talent than retailing, which was not highly regarded as a life work).[16]

There is evidence, too, that many buyers, floorwalkers, and other minor executives were poorly educated and hardened by failure or adversity — capable up to a point, never wholly reliable, constantly shifting from one store to another in search of a "real opportunity" which could never materialize for them, they often sought consolation in the bottle. Indeed, one of management's problems in this period was the buyer or floorwalker who went out to lunch and failed to return or came back too drunk to be tolerated on the selling floor. At least one young clerk won promotion through his ability to act as substitute on such occasions.[17]

Hours and Vacations

The Macy day was a long one. While the store officially remained open from 8:00 A.M. to 6:00 P.M., employees were expected to report for duty at 7:45, and at the close of the day stocks had to be straightened up and the selling departments tidied, so that it was sometimes past seven o'clock before employees left the premises, particularly after a busy sale had left merchandise in chaotic disarray. Even so their hours were shorter than those of the higher executives. La Forge often worked until midnight and later — doing so for 12 days in succession, including a Sunday, on one occasion.[18] Clerks were entitled to an hour off for lunch, but cash girls, most of whom brought their lunches, seem to have had only half an hour or even less at noon. Most of the employees brought their lunches. In fact only those of executive rank were allowed to leave the store at noon. Cora Crossman remembered that one of her greatest satisfactions on being promoted to assistant superintendent was the accompanying privilege of going out to lunch.[19] By 1872 a room on the third floor had been furnished with some rough tables and chairs and reserved as a place in which employees could eat food brought from home. One employee recalled that she had been compelled to protest against the shortness of the time allowed:[20]

Mr. Valentine . . . was preparing to go to Europe and sent a letter around the store which was read to the employees by the floorwalkers. It was to the effect that if all the employees worked well and obeyed all the rules of the house while he was away, it would be a great source of enjoyment and comfort to him. When my floorwalker read the paper, I spoke up and said I could promise all but the lunch time which was only twenty minutes and, considering the distance I had to go, down from the second floor and across the main floor to the Thirteenth Street side of the building and then up to the third floor, stopping the while to answer questions, I would not be able to keep the lunch rule. The floorwalker thereupon allowed me an extra five minutes on account of the distance I had to go.

For some ten days or two weeks before Christmas the store was kept open until ten or eleven o'clock, while on Christmas Eve it was usually close to midnight before the flickering gas jets and sputtering arc lights were finally turned down. Many a clerk had to work into the early morning hours during the hectic holiday rush, and some of the men finished the rest of the night sleeping on the counters with bolts of cloth for pillows. Delivery men quit when the day's assignment was completed, commonly at seven or eight o'clock in the evening. During the worst pressure of the Christmas trade they had to abandon all hope of sleeping in a proper bed and snatched brief moments of rest at the stables. Supper money was provided when the store remained open in the evenings, and one of the earliest recollections of an old employee was the sight of Abiel La Forge, with obvious enjoyment, shepherding an animated crowd of cash girls to a neighboring restaurant as was his custom during the holiday season.[21]

The slackening of trade during the summer months made it possible to ease the pressure on the staff. Regular employees received a week's vacation with pay, and in 1871 the firm began the practice of closing the store on Saturday afternoons during July and August, a concession to summer heat which most stores in New York and Philadelphia refused to make until more than ten years later. Macy's may not have originated this idea, for in 1871 Lord & Taylor were closing at three o'clock on Saturday afternoons during the hot months, but the Macy store seems to have been the first in New York to advance the closing hour to noon and, at least among local retail stores, was for ten years virtually alone in the practice. In 1882 the firm made another generous move in granting a long week-end holiday when the Fourth of July came on Tuesday; it closed the store on Saturday noon and did not reopen until the following Wednesday. Fairly common in recent years, this procedure was distinctly unusual before 1900.[22]

Apart from the Fourth of July, Thanksgiving, and Christmas Day, the Macy store (like the rest) seems to have observed very few of the public holidays which we cherish today for the respite they give from work. New Year's Day, for example, was apparently not celebrated by closing until 1882; a half-holiday on Washington's birthday was given for the first time in the same year, as was a full holiday on May 30. Just why the sudden addition of two and one-half holidays was made in 1882 is not known. On the other hand, the store did no business on several occasions for which we do not ordinarily stop work now. Thus, it closed at 10 A.M. on September 8, 1881, when public prayers were offered for the recovery of President Garfield, and it was closed all day for the funerals of both Garfield and Grant.[23]

Although Macy employees put in a great many more hours of work during the 1870's and '80's than most retail workers do now, their lot was no worse, and in many respects was definitely better, than that of contemporaries in other stores. Only fragmentary information is available for a comparison, but a number of smaller stores in New York seem to have remained open evenings regularly; the large competitors kept open evenings for the Christmas trade just as Macy's did; and, as we have seen, Macy's shortened the workweek in the summer months long before most of its rivals chose to do so. A. T. Stewart's store was open from 7:00 A.M. to 7:00 P.M. in 1870, and, while half the staff was alternately released at 6:00 P.M., only a half-hour was allowed for lunch. It is clear that the hours were longer in similar stores in Chicago and London, and there is reason to believe that they were somewhat longer in both Boston and Philadelphia.[24]

Working Conditions

Long hours and low pay were not the only aspects of the employees' life which seem unpleasant by modern standards. No locker-rooms were provided for clothing and personal possessions. Part of the staff used packing cases in the basement and the rest several ex-bedrooms on the fourth floor, but there were never enough nails to give everyone a separate place. Washroom facilities were primitive, inadequate, and smelly. Store rules forbade unnecessary conversations between employees during business hours, an offense for which the usual punishment was immediate dismissal; and no one on the selling floor was allowed to sit down while on duty. Employees were permitted to shop in the store for their own requirements only on Friday mornings between eight and nine o'clock, and they received no discounts on their purchases.[25]

These circumstances, of course, were typical of the times, and employees seem to have accepted them as inevitable. Indeed, it is plainly evident from conversations with old employees that they thoroughly enjoyed the early days at 14th Street in spite of the conditions which we should regard as definite hardships. Some of them have set down recollections which give a vivid picture. Recalling the various men who succeeded to partnership, one devoted employee recorded that "they treated us lovely."[26] Jimmie Woods, another old-timer, recalled exciting episodes connected with the delivery department when he first began to work in it (1873) as a mere boy:[27]

Delivery had frequently to be helped out by the use of its original equipment, a pushcart, which I took great pleasure in operating much to the discomfort of pedestrians. Its use was finally abolished after I had run into and almost killed a fat man on Fourteenth Street near Eighth Avenue. . . .

Occasionally it was necessary to hire a horse to help out, and whenever this need arose we got the horse from a stable in Mercer Street, near Bleeker. It was my duty to return the horse to his stable at night, and many's the wild ride I've had down Fifth Avenue, past Washington Square. I recall one in particular. I was given a big, rangy animal and while tearing down Fifth Avenue, he stumbled and went down on his knees. He stopped, of course, but I did not. . . . This experience stopped my fast riding.

I had learned the streets and avenues very thoroughly by this time and was much in demand as a sorter in the delivery department. Here I met Mr. C. B. Webster, who was going through the different departments learning the business. Many thought C. B. W. was devoid of any sense of humor, but he was not. Many's the time he and I had a battle royal hurling packages at one another.

Jimmie Woods testified that Valentine was democratic and well loved by the staff during his short term as partner. The fact that Valentine had the grace to give advance warning to employees by snapping his fingers as he descended to the basement, thereby enabling them to cease unofficial conversation and get busy before he could see them, is certainly a clear indication of a wise and considerate employer. Woods remembered the egregious Miss Toye as "a large fine looking woman . . . and, because of her arrogant manner, cordially detested by almost everyone." Like Miss Prunty and others, however, he found that she could be kind and generous, at least to a favored few, and he was grateful for the warm gloves, earlaps, and mufflers which she bestowed upon a small boy when cold weather came.[28]

Miss Prunty, too, left some interesting impressions of her superiors:[29]

Our superintendent in 1877 was Miss Bowyer, generally referred to by the employees as M. J. B. If I could, I would place her on a pedestal so all could see and learn from her example. She was the embodiment of dignity, courtesy, and patience, and justice. The few years I served under her supervision I always look back to as a pleasure. She held no malice and was just to all, the cash girl, the buyer, the firm itself. We lost Miss Bowyer through death [in 1886]. She was succeeded as superintendent by Miss Toye, who had been a floorwalker in the lace department. She was a tall, majestic woman with a coldly handsome face and stern manner, and the employees all feared her. I had occasion to speak to her many times and found her to be only a sweet woman and not the stern creature she looked.

Charles Winship, who began to work in Macy's in 1885, remembers an episode which proves that Miss Toye's stern manner was not entirely a matter of external appearance:[30]

For some days after I became a bill clerk I was detailed to push a truck load of returned and ordered-back house furnishing goods into the house furnishings department and deliver it to the head of stock. Now this head of stock did not appear to like this part of his job and kept me waiting. All unknown to me there was a rule that the truck of returned goods must be off the floor by 10 o'clock. On about the third morning that I had been bringing the truck in, and while I was standing waiting for the head of stock to do something besides talk, I noticed a large, stern-looking woman approaching me. She seemed rather to glide than walk. Straight at me she came, and when she got up to me she reached out a large white hand, took me by the ear, walked me to the door leading into the delivery part of the basement, and, as she shoved me through this door, she gave me the boot. . . ! I fully expected to be fired bag and baggage, but I never heard from the incident, nor can I recall ever having to push goods into the house furnishings department again.

Winship's account of his first day in the store is worth quoting at some length because it gives a remarkably intimate picture of life behind the scenes in Macy's more than fifty years ago:[31]

My uncle, Mr. Amos McDonald, who was at that time [March, 1885] a buyer for the firm, took me to Mr. Joe Webster [C. B. Webster's brother and assistant] who engaged me and sent me with a cash girl to the bill desk in the basement. I shall never forget the first impression of that basement — a low, ill-smelling place, crowded with rows of packing tables, made from rough pine boards, with men and girls standing on either side of them packing goods. . . .

The cash girl took me to a dwarfish man with a tremendous head and a big, blond beard. He stood on a box in order to reach up to a rough, one-man desk, separated by a narrow aisle from the general desk. At first — I suppose in order to properly impress me with the importance of his position as head bill clerk — he did not deign to notice me. After a time, however, he turned to me and in a pompous manner questioned me as to my experience, etc., agreeing to pay me the magnificent sum of eight dollars per week, and prophesying that without experience I could not get along. He had an impediment in his speech and was continuously picking his teeth with his lead pencil. He told me that my hours, if I managed to remain, would be from 8 o'clock in the morning until the work was finished, regardless of the time.

He called one of the bill clerks and instructed him to take me to the clothing room and find a box where I might keep my coat. My guide led me along the main thoroughfare of the delivery department where I had to step aside pretty lively two or three times in order to avoid being knocked down by huge basket trucks being rammed along by human speed demons. Finally we came to a half door between two whitewashed brick columns. This door was opened by my companion, revealing within what looked like an indoor graveyard. It was full of second-hand dry goods boxes standing on end, with their covers fastened on with leather hinges, which had evidently been cut from old shoes, and fastened with a strap hooked over a nail on the side of the case. I hung my overcoat in one of these, and walked back to the bill desk. . . .

At 11 o'clock my dwarfish superior waddled over to me and told me it was my lunch hour, that I had one hour for lunch, but to be back in half an hour as there was so much to do. . . . I was a good penman and soon got the knack of doing my work speedily which I found was all that was wanted. . . .

There were many odd characters in this basement, chief among whom was one Hugh Doon, the head packer, who collected and sold the waste paper as part remuneration of his services. He also sold tea, sugar, coffee, and canned goods to the packers, keeping his stock under one of the tables. On pay days the salaries for his department were sent to him to give out, and he would open the envelopes of those who owed him money and take out the amount before paying them. It was said of him that he sold five and ten cent novels and loaned money, charging usurious interest.

In the daily life of the store there were, of course, many incidents which made deep impressions on the memories of employees — some of them tragic, others humorous, but mostly of no great consequence and rarely recorded. One incident which did get preserved in the recollections of Miss Prunty may be told here, not because it has special significance, but simply because it reveals in the store's round of activities one of the lighter moments which relieved the tedium of endless work: [32]

The departments owned by L. Straus & Sons were under the management of Mr. William Burdett. He was a very bright man but one who occasionally imbibed too freely and was credited with being very erratic while in his cups. I recall that just prior to one of our millinery openings the store decorators had a large number of jardinieres filled with artificial flowers sitting in the marking room waiting to be put up that night. Mr. Burdett came into the room, and, being struck by their natural appearance, caught up a sprinkling pot which the porter had filled to use in sweeping the floor, and before anyone realized what he was doing, began to water the artificial flowers.

There is no record of any effort among the Macy employees to form any sort of labor union in the early days, but a group did start the Macy Mutual Aid Association, a store organization to provide health and life benefits to employees at moderate cost, which has grown enormously in size and scope of activities in the past twenty-five years. Founded on April 22, 1885, Macy Mutual Aid limited its membership to persons who had been employed in Macy's for at least three months, and no one could receive benefits until he had been a member of the organization for an additional three months. Four grades of membership were provided, but the basis for classification is not clear. The original dues and benefits are set forth in Table 12.

Since membership was optional and every cent counted among people whose wages averaged very little more than $5.00 a week, only a small part of the staff took advantage of the scheme. The

TABLE 12

Original Rates and Benefits of Macy Mutual Aid Association 1885

Grade[a]	Initiation Fees	Weekly Dues	Weekly Benefits[b]	Death Benefits[c]
1st	$1.00	$0.10	$10.00	$50.00
2nd	0.75	0.07	7.00	40.00
3rd	0.50	0.05	5.00	30.00
4th	0.25	0.02	2.00	20.00

[a] The grade was eventually determined by the amount of salary received, but no information is available as to the original method of classification.

[b] Benefits were not paid for less than one week, or more than eight weeks during a period of twelve months from the time of the last benefit.

[c] If the organization did not have a surplus of $200, the death benefit was to be raised by a pro rata assessment.

Source: Pamphlet containing constitution, bylaws, and reports for year ending Apr. 6, 1887.

report issued in April, 1887, showed a total membership of 329, which must have been less than a third of the eligible employees at the time. The same report shows that sick benefits paid out during the year amounted to $1,429.00, physicians' fees for 166 calls came to $84.50, and one death benefit of $50.00 was paid. The fees for the period were insufficient to cover the disbursements, by over $250, which may throw some light on the failure of the organization to achieve much importance for many years. Its significance lay chiefly in what it was to become after 1900. Incidentally, the physician selected was William McCracken, who had formerly headed the Macy delivery department while studying medicine.[33]

It is, of course, impossible to obtain anything like a complete and detailed picture of the Macy working force at this time or the conditions in which it had to work. The subject is too complex, too elusive, ever in process of change. The Macy family was a cross section of New York; its environment, activities and state of mind were inseparably linked with the times in which it lived. Like the city of which it was an organic part, the Macy staff was growing in size, changing in composition, becoming more heterogeneous physically and mentally day by day. Just as we can obtain glimpses of this facet or that of contemporary New York but never recover a well-rounded view of the whole, so we have to be content with an incomplete set of verbal snapshots, many of them mutilated, of Macy's staff before 1888. Perhaps the significant point to be grasped is that, given proper leadership, this amorphous group of people was able to create wealth for itself and the store's owners and render essential service to a vast community.

PART III

THE FIRST GENERATION OF STRAUS
MANAGEMENT

1888–1902

CHAPTER IX

BLOOD TRANSFUSION

IN DECEMBER, 1887, reports began to circulate that a change impended in the ownership of R. H. Macy & Co. Wheeler, cornered by questioners, denied that anyone had authority to confirm the rumors but confessed that the first of January might "see some new blood taken in." Ten days later newspaper advertisements announced that Isidor and Nathan Straus had been admitted to the Macy firm as partners.[1] The two brothers were not strangers to the business by any means, for the introduction of the china and silverware departments had brought them, after 1874, into continuous contact with Macy and his associates. We shall see that their influence on Macy operations, evident long before 1888, rapidly became dominant after they achieved the status of partners. This chapter deals with the Straus background and describes the transition period in Macy history during which the Yankee institution received an invigorating injection of fine Jewish blood.

ADMISSION OF THE STRAUSES TO PARTNERSHIP

In January, 1888, Isidor Straus wrote to a London firm with which he had had dealings, to announce with obvious pride that he and Nathan had acquired a share in the Macy business:[2]

The firm of R. H. Macy & Co. [he explained] is one of the largest and oldest establishments in this country. We have been in very close relationship with them for many years past, when the original founder of the house was yet active in the business.

Through a misunderstanding which arose between the retiring partner and the senior, the latter bought out the interest of the former, and a few weeks after the consummation of the transaction Mr. Webster approached my brother and myself and urged us to join him, saying that unless we did he would never take another partner. Nothing was further from our minds than to embark in any new enterprise, but the offer was so flattering personally, and the temptation, owing to the remarkably flourishing condition and remunerative nature of the business, so irresistible that we accepted the proposition under the condition that my brother and myself are to devote between us so much time to this business as is equivalent to one man's services.

I shall probably devote the greater portion of my time for the next year or two to the new enterprise. . . .

I know of but one business in London which is typical of the business of R. H. Macy & Co. That is Whiteley's, but I do not know whether the latter conducts its affairs like the former, namely, all goods are sold for cash strictly. Such a thing as a book a/c is unknown to its organization from its inception. It certainly is the only house in the country where this rule has no exceptions.

Behind the break in the Webster-Wheeler partnership to which the above letter alludes lies an interesting story. It has a legitimate place here, not because of its spicy flavor but because it explains a fact of the utmost importance in the store's development: how the Straus brothers came to own Macy's. In a large measure their admission to the firm was the direct consequence of irregular conduct on the part of several people — a curious irony of fate — just as the misbehavior of Rowland Macy's son had led to the admission of Abiel La Forge as the first junior partner a number of years earlier.

In the Webster-Wheeler partnership it is clear that Webster held the controlling interest and was the one who would naturally be most concerned about the store's future ownership. Suffering from ill health as the 1880's drew to a close, he felt the need of admitting one or two younger executives to the firm in order to provide for a succession of experienced and responsible men in the management. He chose two men for the honor, a buyer named Chase and the head bookkeeper, Terry. Unfortunately, he had no sooner made the decision than it was discovered that Terry had embezzled a substantial sum of money. Webster was so shocked at this example of misplaced confidence that he completely abandoned the idea of promoting anyone from his staff to partnership.[3]

Meanwhile, relations between Webster and Wheeler had been subjected to increasing tension, and the breaking point came in 1887 shortly after the discovery of Terry's defalcation. There were two main sources of disagreement. In the first place, as soon as he could accumulate some spare capital out of the store profits, Wheeler had begun to make substantial investments in Colorado, including mining properties, a smelting company, and a bank. Webster objected to the time which Wheeler spent on these outside interests and probably regarded them as dangerous speculations which, if anything went seriously wrong, might conceivably cause trouble for the store. As the western ventures prospered, Wheeler devoted an increasing amount of time and money to them, and Webster's protest was both well founded and wise.[4] Had this matter been the only point of disagreement, the two men might have parted on friendly terms, but Webster's feelings became anything but amicable.

The explanation of his bitterness lay in the second source of friction. At an early stage in the partnership Webster had become interested in a strikingly handsome woman who was employed in the store as floorwalker. (Her name was Toye, which, in the circumstances, was rather appropriate.) He chose to reward her services by making her superintendent of the store, a position for which Wheeler felt, with considerable justification, she was unsuited. In the course of time Webster went on a buying trip to Europe; Wheeler, left in command, found occasion to discharge the favorite and appointed a man in her place. Whatever the merits of the case, Webster was understandably furious and, since his majority interest gave him the upper hand, promptly dissolved the partnership.[5]

Feeling the need for partners and having just decided against advancing any of his own employees to ownership, Webster turned to two men whom, in the course of nearly twelve years of association, he had learned to trust — Isidor and Nathan Straus. It was a happy solution: while they were outsiders, they knew the Macy business intimately through having owned the china and glassware departments for so many years, they had both ability and capital, and Webster knew from experience that he could work well with them. With their acceptance of his invitation to join the partnership a new era in Macy history opened.

Straus Background

For information about the new partners in the Macy firm we must digress for a few pages, going back several decades to the 1840's and across the Atlantic to Otterberg, in the Bavarian Palatinate, where Lazarus Straus was born and raised and where he married his first cousin, Sara Straus. From this union came a daughter and three remarkable sons — Isidor and Nathan, destined to become famous for their business success and their philanthropies, and Oscar, who was headed for a distinguished career in diplomacy and government service.[6]

Lazarus Straus was an able, cultured, and respected Jew who owned farmlands and traded in the grain which he and his neighbors raised. A liberal by temperament, he gave substantial aid to Carl Schurz and other protagonists in that unsuccessful struggle for political reform in Germany in 1848 which did so much to enrich America's citizenry. Although he escaped compulsory exile after the failure of the movement, Lazarus was no longer content to live in Germany, and as soon as he could conveniently arrange to do so he sailed for America (in 1852), leaving his family behind until a home in the New World should be ready.

German friends in Philadelphia advised him to seek his fortune in the South; and in Oglethorpe, Georgia, he formed a connection with the brothers Kaufman, who operated a number of pedlars' wagons in the region. Thus it was that Lazarus Straus began a new career by engaging in the earliest form of commerce. His peddling experience was brief: reaching the town of Talbotton in western Georgia, he found trim houses, neat gardens, and relatively civilized inhabitants, in marked contrast with the crude, slovenly, frontier settlements among which he had been traveling. He thought longingly of the family which needed a home and noted that there were good schools. Trade looked promising, too, for he had arrived during "court week," and Talbotton was unusually festive and busy. The half-formed decision to settle there was clinched when he learned that the license which he would need as a pedlar was so expensive that it would be cheaper to rent space and sell as a resident. Within a few weeks Lazarus was well established in a general store in partnership with one of the Kaufmans, and in September, 1854, he went to New York to welcome his wife and four children (Isidor, the eldest, was only nine).

From a strictly business point of view the choice of Talbotton left something to be desired, for it was seven miles from the nearest railroad and so situated that it could never attain even regional importance; Columbus, some thirty miles to the southwest, already overshadowed it. On the other hand, in a small town in the deep South the Straus family was probably better able to maintain its cultural standards and make the difficult transition to American life than it would have been in a crowded eastern city. Perhaps Lazarus had some hope of reëstablishing the comfortable rural position which he had occupied in Otterberg.

In solving the religious problem which faced him in Talbotton (where no Jewish synagogue existed), Lazarus demonstrated both his political acumen and his liberalism. Finding the town divided, geographically as well as in numbers, almost exactly between Methodists and Baptists, he chose a house near the middle and sent his two elder children to the Methodist Sunday school, the other two to the Baptist! His affability and his broad European background quickly won for him and his family an honored place in a community which regarded ability to discuss political, historical, and religious questions as proof of culture and good breeding.

The Education of Isidor Straus

Isidor Straus entered Collingsworth Institute, the best school that the locality had to offer, and there received all the formal education he was to have, for the Civil War blasted plans for college study. At best his schooling undoubtedly had limitations, but between it and his parents, Isidor received an education in fundamentals which may well have surpassed anything he could have obtained in contemporary universities: he developed an analytical mind and acquired an insatiable hunger for knowledge; he learned to appreciate more keenly than most men that education is a continuous process which formal schooling can only begin.

From his father the boy got urbanity, a love of learning, and a grasp of the rudiments of business. His father was a successful storekeeper, and the lessons that Isidor learned from him in a time of rapidly changing conditions must have been of the utmost value. And yet there came to be a dynamic quality in the son's business activities which the father never showed. Lazarus was easygoing, fond of books and lively conversation, and more interested in giving to visiting clergymen the benefit of his knowledge of Hebrew than in a relentless drive toward material success.

All evidence indicates that it was from the dark-eyed Sara that Isidor acquired the traits which made him an outstanding business man — infinite patience, ability to manage many activities well, and, above all, a remarkable financial sense. For it was the mother who, despite having been permanently crippled by a paralytic stroke before leaving Germany, ran the large household frugally on a small monthly allowance and systematically saved money out of it in order to provide such "extravagances" as a piano for her daughter and extra books for her sons. As Isidor admiringly recorded in his autobiography, she was "able to manage her affairs like a financier, and . . . no matter how small such an allowance might have been, she would manage to save something out of it."[7] This was no mean achievement in a community which had little cash. In terms of physical needs the family was comfortably situated, but it required foresight and the strictest economy to put aside hard money for future needs, and it took tact and wisdom to succeed in this task while instilling into the children a strong sense of social responsibility and spontaneous generosity toward people in need.

At the outbreak of the Civil War Isidor, barely sixteen, left school to assist in the store, for his father's partner had immediately enlisted in the Confederate Army. In 1863 came a splendid opportunity to obtain broader experience: a group of local men organized a private venture to acquire a fast steamer in England for the purpose of running the Union blockade, carrying much-needed supplies to the South and cotton back to England; Lloyd C. Bowers of Columbus, Georgia, went to London to complete the arrangements, taking Isidor Straus as his secretary and assistant. The venture was

ISIDOR STRAUS
Partner, 1888–1912

NATHAN STRAUS
Partner, 1888–1914

shortly abandoned, and Isidor found himself alone in London, with his entire savings of $1,200 in gold sewn into his underclothing and some $1,500 in bills of exchange belonging to his father's firm.

The boy's adventures during the next two years (which included frequent business trips to Amsterdam, Cologne, and other Continental cities and two voyages back to America) have no direct connection with Macy history, but two experiences at this time illuminate his subsequent management of the store. First of all, he worked in a Liverpool office for six months, during which he struck up a close friendship with the head clerk, from whom he acquired, in his own words, "a very practical insight into double entry bookkeeping." [8] We shall see later that he obtained not merely the technique of keeping books but also a thorough grasp of the significance of accounting as a means of directing a business effectively.

His second noteworthy experience taught him an important financial lesson. In 1864 he had joined an uncle in London and developed a thriving trade in Southern securities, buying and selling them mainly in London and Amsterdam at substantial profit. To comply with the request of his former employer, he made a hurried trip to Nova Scotia concerning the disposition of several blockade-runners, their use having become too dangerous; during his absence a block of bonds which he had failed to sell dropped in value and wiped out most of his earnings. After returning and recouping his losses, he took the advice of a Dutch banker and invested a large sum in the shares of a leading Amsterdam business concern. According to his friend, the shares were certain to appreciate as soon as the firm's income statement was made public. The banker friend was honest, but an official of the company was not, and Isidor's savings immediately took another heavy blow. The boy of twenty gained wisdom: "The two losses I sustained . . . proved a blessing in disguise for me; they cured me of all speculative tendency and I profited thereby afterwards. During the subsequent course of my career I was many times approached with 'sure propositions,' none of which had any charms for me. . . . I learned to say 'No' on the spot." [9]

The Founding of L. Straus & Sons

Shortly after peace had been restored, Isidor returned to New York and there learned that his family, with whom he had lost touch as a result of interrupted mail services, had left Georgia and were temporarily living in Philadelphia. The father had quickly recognized the futility of trying to continue business in the South and, after investing all his remaining capital in raw cotton, had brought his family northward to make another start in life.

Isidor abandoned other plans at once and decided to assist his father. He immediately showed his mature business judgment by persuading his father not to settle in Philadelphia, arguing that if they were to establish themselves, "it would be better to start in the chief market rather than a secondary one." [10] The new home was to be in New York, where the Strauses had first set foot upon American soil, in a house to be paid for out of the $10,000 which Isidor had brought back from Europe.

As soon as Lazarus was able to get his cotton shipped to market and sold, he went around to various firms with which he had formerly dealt in order to pay them the money he had owed at the outbreak of hostilities. To merchants who had entirely written off Southern accounts (one of them had quite forgotten the Straus debt and experienced difficulty in digging up the bill) the mere discussion of payment was a welcome surprise; and the arrival of a man who was prepared to settle in full, even if it took his last dollar, was almost beyond belief. One of the creditors, George Bliss of the well-known dry goods wholesale house which bore his name, was particularly impressed, and insisted that Lazarus pay only a third of the amount due, keeping the rest for several years as working capital to be used in getting established. We shall see later that Bliss also made a mental note about the high integrity of the Straus family.[11] Lazarus Straus paid out to creditors the best part of $25,000, and the profound impression which he created in doing so formed another lesson which Isidor never forgot.

In May, 1866, the firm of L. Straus & Sons was founded, a wholesale business in crockery, china, and glassware which possessed only

$6,000 in capital but managed to sell ten times that amount of merchandise in the first year of operation. Lazarus Straus seems to have played a rather passive part in the enterprise, leaving most of the work to his two elder sons (Oscar was still in school). Isidor kept the books, bought the merchandise, saw that orders were filled and delivered promptly, and looked after the general management of the firm, while Nathan (admitted to partnership in 1873) devoted most of his time and energy to selling china and glass to the trade. Isidor, looking back upon the first years, described them thus: [12]

It was a great struggle, which kept me awake many nights planning and calculating. . . . But our mother provided us with a comfortable home and managed with such frugal and circumspect economy, [and we were all] working together in such complete harmony, that each year we added, without a single exception, something to our capital, so that encouragement prodded us on to ever renewed efforts.

Working capital was pitifully small, and many times there arose a temptation to sell the house which Isidor had bought, but this solution was always rejected in favor of the slower process of growth from accumulated profits.

Diligence and careful management made the little business prosper and expand, and yet the greatest step forward for both the firm and family came when Nathan sought a means of avoiding unpleasant work. He was highly successful at selling and had steadily extended the Straus market until a large part of the firm's business came from the Middle West. Nevertheless, he disliked the salesman's life, saw no promising future in it for himself, and grew tired of the traveling that it entailed. Simply to give up the sales activities was out of the question, for most of the firm's business would fall off as soon as selling effort stopped, and with it would go the family income. Given the intense feeling which all the Strauses had of family loyalty and responsibility, Nathan's only course was to continue as traveling salesman or find some other means of obtaining business. It occurred to him that a possible solution might be to establish china departments in a few large stores, with L. Straus & Sons supplying the stock of merchandise and leaving the rest of the retailing operations to the store's own organization. Such an arrangement would create lasting connections which should result in a considerable amount of continuing business for the Straus firm.[13]

At this point the Straus and Macy business histories came together, and we may resume the main narrative.

Straus Departments in Macy's, 1874–1888

Nathan Straus had made the acquaintance of Rowland Macy through selling small amounts of china for the store's fancy goods department, and he went to Macy with his new idea. After the details had been worked out, Macy agreed to give the proposal a trial, and before arrangements were completed, L. Straus & Sons undertook also to stock a silverware department as well as one for china and glass. As we have already seen, the new departments were opened in March, 1874, and quickly became an important part of the Macy business.

While the precise details of the agreement between the Strauses and Macy have been lost, the general arrangement is clear enough. L. Straus & Sons supplied the stock in the two departments and kept it up to date, retaining ownership of the goods and so relieving Macy of the risk of losses which arise from the accumulation of unsalable merchandise. All stock was charged at the net cost to the Strauses (that is, after deducting all discounts and adding the transportation expenses);[14] Macy supplied the floor space (originally 25 by 100 feet in the basement) and equipment needed; and the store received, marked, advertised, sold, packed, and delivered the Straus merchandise and took inventories, just as it handled the regular Macy merchandise. In brief, the Strauses furnished buying facilities, expert skill in purchasing, and inventory capital; Macy provided space, store facilities, and retail selling service.

The two firms settled accounts periodically, dividing the gross margin received (the difference between the charged cost and the sales price) equally between them. Out of his share Macy had to pay the various expenses involved in retailing, including shortages and breakage. Out of their half the Strauses had to pay the expenses involved in buying and maintaining the stock, the risk of obsolescence, and a certain amount of supervision. It looks as if the Straus firm got the better part of this bargain, and the arrangement was, in fact, repeatedly revised in subsequent years in order to shift a greater share of the expenses to L. Straus & Sons.

The china and silverware departments in Macy's were Straus departments in the sense that the Strauses selected and owned the merchandise and presumably determined the selling prices. Strictly speaking, however, they were not leased departments, for Macy retained full control over all retail operations. The arrangement was technically a rather unusual type of consignment selling,[15] and the term "leased department" is used in this book to describe it simply as a matter of convenience.

The Strauses apparently found the plan a desirable one, for they subsequently concluded similar agreements with John Wanamaker in Philadelphia, R. H. White in Boston, Woodward & Lothrop in Washington, D. C., Wechsler & Abraham (later Abraham & Straus) in Brooklyn, and J. H. Walker in Chicago. A substantial investment was involved, and, particularly in the stores outside the New York area, the Straus firm incurred a considerable amount of risk: leaving control in the hands of the retailer meant that the Strauses had to rely upon the integrity of the store management for honest and efficient conduct. It is a striking commentary upon the principals involved that the only serious disagreement which L. Straus & Sons encountered was with John Wanamaker, who, after 15 years of amicable dealings, chose to reinterpret the agreement to his own pecuniary advantage, forcing the Strauses to carry action to the State supreme court before they could obtain full settlement.[16]

It is worth noting, in this connection, that the departments which L. Straus & Sons had in Macy's were substantially larger in sales volume than the corresponding departments they maintained in Wanamaker's (Philadelphia) during the years for which comparative figures are available, namely, 1885 and 1887, despite the fact that Wanamaker had by that time attained national fame as an enterprising retailer.[17] Was Macy's a more favorable location for the particular departments, or does the explanation lie in the fact that the

Strauses lived in New York and were able to give better supervision there than in Philadelphia?

As the figures in Table 13 show, the Straus departments in Macy's forged steadily ahead from the very start, both in dollar volume and in relation to the sales of the store as a whole. Thus, apart from a slight dip in the ratio in 1877 and 1878, the Straus departments contributed over 10 per cent of the annual sales of the store as a whole; and in the 1880's the ratio climbed steadily until it was nearly 13 per cent at the time the Strauses became partners.[18] Indeed, the china

TABLE 13

SALES IN STRAUS DEPARTMENTS IN MACY'S, 1874-1888

Year	Sales	Ratio to Previous Year's Sales	Ratio to Total Store Sales[a]
1874	$102,430	...	8.55
1875 (53 weeks)	147,635	144.1	10.80
1876	163,674	110.9	10.15
1877	174,535	106.6	9.31
1878	212,893	122.0	9.55
1879	314,272	147.6	10.75
1880	382,604	121.7	10.94
1881 (53 weeks)	494,039	129.1	12.30
1882	524,145	106.1	11.69
1883	575,113	109.7	11.90
1884	593,532	103.2	11.94
1885	602,956	101.6	11.99
1886[b]	...	...	...
1887 (last half)[c]	358,629	...	13.53
1888 (last half)	360,994	100.7	13.70
1888 (total)	650,614	...	12.89

[a] Total store sales here include both the sales in owned departments and those in leased or consignment departments. A slight discrepancy in the data arises from the fact that until 1887 total sales are for the fiscal year, while Straus sales have been calculated to the Saturday nearest Dec. 31.

[b] No data available.

[c] No data available for spring season. To facilitate comparison, figures have been included for both the fall season and the entire year of 1888.

SOURCE: Straus department sales, 1874-85, from Sales and Purchases record, 1869-85; for 1887-88, from semiannual balances in private ledgers, 1880-1900. Total sales taken from Black Book.

department quickly grew into the largest one in the store in terms of sales, and by 1884 its merchandise was being displayed not only in the basement but also on the street and second floors.[19]

In view of the obvious importance of the Straus departments in Macy operations it is easy to understand Webster's high regard for the Strauses and his desire to have them become members of the firm. It is equally clear why the Strauses welcomed the chance to acquire part ownership in Macy's. Their departments in the store constituted the greatest single source of revenue for L. Straus & Sons, and consequently they had a vital interest in the continuation of Macy's as a successful enterprise. Possibly they saw opportunities for making it even more successful. Certainly its current earnings made it an exceedingly attractive investment, for its net gain at the time was running better than $270,000 annually, and at this rate the money which the Strauses put into it would be repaid within four years. (When we come to a detailed analysis of the operating figures after 1888, we shall see that the Strauses got their money back in three years with a tidy sum to spare.) Moreover, the assets of the firm were highly liquid, nearly nine-tenths consisting of cash and merchandise, as Table 14 shows.

The capital of the firm at the close of 1887 was $300,000. The Strauses purchased 45 per cent of this (the portion which Wheeler had owned), which gave them an interest amounting to $135,000. Since they paid a premium of $310,000 on this, their total original investment was $445,000 and the goodwill of the business was valued at approximately $689,000, or more than twice its stated capital.[20]

To finance their purchase, Isidor and Nathan Straus paid Webster $235,000 in cash, plus three notes of $70,000 each, due at 12-month intervals at 6 per cent interest. (Webster had paid Wheeler partly in promissory notes in the same manner.[21]) They obtained the cash by borrowing it from L. Straus & Sons, which in addition to being a thriving wholesale china and glass business was, to an increasing extent, a kind of private bank or family treasury into which all members of the Straus family paid their surplus cash and from which they drew money to meet business or personal requirements. Just how the details were handled is not now clear and need not concern us here beyond noting that the two brothers paid 6 per cent interest on the money borrowed until it was repaid; for many years they assigned, in addition, one-third of their share in Macy profits to L. Straus & Sons. The existence of the family jackpot meant that

TABLE 14
BALANCE SHEET
R. H. MACY & CO.
December 31, 1887

Assets	
Cash	$130,556.36
Foreign Debits	5,729.37
Inventory (excluding leased departments) at cost	309,605.01
Miscellaneous Accounts Receivable	2,912.26
Bills Receivable	2,500.00
Fixtures	42,860.10
Total	$494,163.10

Liabilities	
Miscellaneous Accounts Payable	$ 43,258.85
Accrued Rent	11,868.74
Bills Payable	4,000.00
Capital	300,000.00
Profit for Season	135,035.51[a]
Total	$494,163.10

[a] This profit figure takes no account of interest on capital at 7%, which was charged among the expenses and paid to partners. The business really earned $135,035.51 plus $10,500 interest, or $145,535.51 for the half-year.

SOURCE: Semiannual balances in private ledgers, 1888–1900.

after 1888 there was, beyond the assets which appeared on the Macy balance sheet, a financial reservoir of unknown but certainly impressive dimensions if ever a pinch should come.[22]

EARLY STRAUS INFLUENCE ON MACY MANAGEMENT

Even before the Straus brothers became members of the Macy firm, they seem to have had some influence upon the store's management. It is impossible to gauge the extent of that influence, owing to the absence of definite records, but certain points may be noted. In the first place, it is certain that the china department regularly quoted odd prices (e.g., $4.33 instead of $4.50 or $5.00 even) for three years before they appeared in any other part of the store, and the subsequent extension of this idea to other departments may be regarded as a Straus contribution.[23]

Again, the first mention of a bargain counter in the store (1878) appears in connection with the china department,[24] and by the middle of the 1880's the store was apparently referring to the Straus buying office in Paris as "our Paris house." [25] It is hardly a matter of chance that the most aggressive Macy advertisements in the 1880's featured Straus departments, and one is struck by the fact that the china department was the only one (with the exception of the elaborate toy displays at Christmas) to feature special exhibitions of merchandise and to stress underselling at this time.

To be sure, the Straus departments were manned by Macy employees, and Webster and Wheeler had control over all their operations beyond the selection of merchandise, but it is obvious that Isidor and Nathan Straus (especially the latter) actually had a hand in promotional activities by direct participation in the leased departments, by example and subtle suggestion in the rest of the store. One gets the definite impression, which later store history tends to confirm, that the china department was the driving center of R. H. Macy & Co. in the 1880's and that the two Straus departments, more than the others, were carrying on the original policies of the firm.[26] It was as if the Strauses, and not the existing store owners, had donned the mantle which Rowland Macy left.

Influence, however, is very different from control. Outside their own departments the Straus brothers could affect the course of managerial policy before 1888 only by example and suggestion. The position of importance which they quickly attained in the store could not alter the fact that they were not members of the firm and hence were in no position to give Macy's the kind of shake-up that it needed. The admission of Isidor and Nathan Straus to a share in the ownership altered the situation materially. It gave the firm a strong infusion of new blood, restored its vigor and enterprise, and equipped it to meet the hard times which lay ahead.

THE STRAUSES ACQUIRE COMPLETE OWNERSHIP

Once Webster had brought in his new partners, he immediately began to turn over to them the administration of the business, and within a comparatively short time he likewise conveyed to them a larger share in its ownership. Webster, although not yet an old man, was becoming increasingly concerned about his health; there are indications, too, that he was shifting his interest from active business management to the investment of his wealth. Whatever the full explanation, we find him shortly allowing the Strauses to acquire a larger share in the Macy capital and profits. By the terms of a new partnership agreement which went into effect on January 1, 1893, Webster transferred an additional $15,000 of the firm's capital to the Strauses, plus 5 per cent ($55,000) of the undivided profits, which then stood at $1,100,000. This transaction gave the Strauses a 50 per cent interest in the firm. (For reasons not now known, no payment was made for goodwill.)

The profits subsequently earned, however, were to be divided equally among the three men instead of being apportioned, as before, according to capital investment. Thus the Straus brothers, owning half the business, were to receive two-thirds of the profits. This provision was undoubtedly made in recognition of Webster's dwindling participation in the active management of the store.[27]

In 1896 Webster sold the remainder of his interest to the Strauses, having decided to retire completely from the store. The amount involved in the transaction was $1,200,000, calculated as follows:

Webster's 50% of the capital account ($300,000)	$ 150,000.00
Webster's 50% of the old undivided profits account ($1,100,000)	550,000.00
Webster's 33 1/3% of the new profits account ($275,000)	91,666.67
Amount of money left by Webster in the partners' loan account	155,000.00
Webster's third of the estimated profits from January 1 to June 1, 1896	41,333.33
Goodwill	212,000.00
Total paid by Isidor and Nathan Straus	$1,200,000.00

These computations show that the business as a whole was valued at $2,254,000 in 1896, excluding the profits for the five-month period. It is worth noting that the Strauses paid substantially less for goodwill on a half-interest in 1896 than on a 45 per cent interest in 1888 ($212,000 against $310,000). This reduction undoubtedly reflects the adverse trend of the store's profits in the early 'nineties, and the memorandum bearing the calculations by which the profits to June 1 were estimated proves that a further decline was anticipated.[28]

The two brothers paid Webster $500,000 in cash and the remaining $700,000 in seven notes of $100,000 each at 5 per cent, payable serially at intervals of six months. Only the first note was paid at maturity, for on October 26, 1897, Webster exchanged the other six for a new note of $600,000, to run five years *without* interest. The explanation of this change doubtless lies in the fact that the Macy profits dropped sharply in 1896 and 1897, and the three men were on such friendly terms that Webster was willing to ease the financial burdens resting upon his former partners by postponing payment and renouncing interest.[29]

Before leaving this description of proprietary interest, one other event should be noted. Early in 1893 the Strauses were invited to bid for Wechsler's interest in the firm of Wechsler & Abraham, who operated the leading department store in Brooklyn. The property unquestionably was a good bargain, and the brothers wanted it, not only for the potential direct profits but also because they anticipated considerable advantages to be derived from coöperation between the two stores, in both buying and management. They were, however, unwilling to take action unless Webster, who was in Egypt at the time, would agree to join them in the purchase. The letter which Isidor wrote to acknowledge Webster's cabled consent clearly reflects the close friendship which had developed between the partners:[30]

> We wanted it — that is true — but did not want it bad enough, no matter how good a thing it might be, without your being in it with us. Our relationship always has been of such a sincerely harmonious character that we could not think of embarking in any enterprise that under any circumstances could develop or had the remotest possibility of evolving conflicting interests. One of the chief advantages we foresaw was

based on the complete and harmonious combination of certain features that would redound to the benefit of both [stores]. This can only be done if we have a common interest and that we have, but not with you out of it.

In the new venture Webster shared the half-interest equally with the Strauses, the three acting individually rather than as a partnership. Thus the connection between R. H. Macy & Co. and the Brooklyn store, which took the name Abraham & Straus, was indirect rather than direct, but close coöperation between the two institutions began in 1893 and continued until 1919. This coöperation took the form of a certain amount of combined purchasing, joint ownership of facilities for processing drugs, toiletries, and grocery products, cooperation in foreign buying, and a continuous exchange of information by which the two managements pooled invaluable knowledge and experience.[31]

The manner in which the Strauses financed their growing investment in Macy's is not known in detail, but the general procedure is a matter of record. When they first acquired an interest in Macy's, the cash required was borrowed from the family business, L. Straus & Sons, which (as already indicated) amounted to a kind of private bank. Interest was paid on this loan, and, in addition, the two brothers turned over to L. Straus & Sons one-third of the profits which they received from the Macy business, an arrangement presumably based upon a sense of family kinship and responsibility rather than business considerations.

The purchase of the half-interest in the Wechsler & Abraham business, coming just after the Strauses had completed paying for their half of the Macy business, evidently called for more cash than the family jackpot could spare. This is not surprising in view of the fact that a substantial amount of Macy profits had not been divided, owing to the need to keep the money in the store for larger quarters and improved equipment. Isidor Straus arranged, accordingly, to borrow $1,500,000 on the credit of L. Straus & Sons. That he was able to do so at 5 per cent interest without any collateral security during the hard times of 1893, is convincing evidence of the extraordinarily high credit standing enjoyed by the family. This went back, at least in part, to the conscientious manner in which Lazarus Straus had repaid all his northern indebtedness after the Civil War. The United States Trust Co. was asked to take $500,000 of the loan. When the matter went before the board of directors the only question came from George Bliss, who, recalling the unexpected settlement in 1865, wanted to verify the identity of the firm. "Well," he said, upon learning that it was the same family, "if the old man is still with the firm, he is good for anything to which he will put his name." [32]

In Isidor Straus's Autobiography there is a clear statement of the financial policy which the Strauses followed for many years.[33]

.... Through continuing to practice the strictest frugality, our capital grew so that the means for supplying the needs of an enlarging business did not necessitate a greater strain on the credit. That is to say, our credit never showed any evidence of strain. We enjoyed the unbounded confidence of all with whom we dealt. The strain was on our apprehensions — not based upon any lack of self-confidence, but rather of caution, influenced perhaps by an unnecessarily keen nervousness to maintain the unquestioned credit which under all circumstances was ours. In other words, to avoid any possibility of ever arousing the remotest suspicion of overtrading or calling our conservatism into question. To be enterprising and to avoid creating any apprehension as to overstepping the limits of caution, that was the reason that possibly at times I was subjected to an acute sensitiveness and caused, I confess many nervous anxieties. But on the other hand I cannot but feel that it saved us from all setbacks. . . . The growth of the business steadily demanded greater capital or greater borrowing, and while I never hesitated to go into debt, — that is to say, was never deterred from the legitimate enterprises that presented themselves in the line of development of the business from fear of debt, — it was, nevertheless, an ever present desire on my part to strive to get out of debt, and for that reason we avoided outside investments.

The acquisition by the Straus brothers of the entire Macy business did not sever the close relationship between them and Webster, for he retained an office in the store and was a frequent visitor there until his death many years later. Nor did it put an end to the arrangement between L. Straus & Sons and the store by which the china firm leased and operated the Macy china and silver departments. Henceforth, however, the leased departments and the store were under virtually the same ownership, and the arrangement was largely a device by which money was taken out of one Straus pocket and put into another. For us the chief importance of the acquisition of complete ownership by the Strauses is that it placed the managerial control of Macy's entirely in the hands of men who were not afraid to conduct the business along the lines tested by its founder and who were no longer deterred by consideration for an excessively cautious partner.

CHAPTER X

MATURITY OF THE FIRM AND THE INDUSTRY

AFTER the Straus family had acquired a financial interest in the Macy firm, the history of the store's operations began to form a steady stream, flowing onward without pronounced changes in direction or tempo. The enterprise continued to grow in size and complexity, to be sure, and important innovations were achieved within it, but much of the subsequent development came about by an accumulation of relatively inconspicuous alterations. So much progress had been made in the field that there was inevitably less opportunity for pioneering of the spectacular sort.

Developments within Macy's, however, were no less significant because they were often subtle and intangible. In some respects the evolutionary advance of the institution after 1888 is more important than in the earlier stages during which most of the pioneering had been done. In dealing with the later years, however, a problem of presentation arises: it is impossible to deal effectively with the whole flow of developments at once, and there are few well-defined points at which the story may be broken without doing undue violence to the natural continuity of events. The year 1902, however, provides one fairly satisfactory division point, for in that year R. H. Macy & Co. moved twenty blocks northward along Broadway to its present location and occupied for the first time in its history a building especially designed for department store requirements.

This chapter, accordingly, deals with certain phases of Macy evolution in the period from 1888 to 1902. During that time both the individual firm and the department store industry of which it was a member reached a stage of maturity in which progress slowed down, competition became bitter, and profits tended to shrink. To make matters worse, they arrived at that trying stage at the very time when American business, battered and strained by the long, downward trend that accompanied the severe problems of readjustment in the post-Civil War period, was scraping the depths of depression. Hard times in the 1890's were more akin to the threadbare 1930's than most people realize; and Macy management had to contend with extremely unfavorable business conditions as well as intense rivalry and problems of internal consolidation. If that management made few exciting innovations between 1888 and 1902, it triumphed over adversity and advanced steadily toward the great Macy's of our own times. Indeed, resourceful efforts of the kind exhibited here may well have been a major factor in bringing about the end of the downward secular trend and starting the long swing upward which began about 1897.

In the present chapter we shall examine the growth of the business to 1902; the next two will describe some of the means by which that growth was achieved.

Growth of Sales and Earnings, 1888–1902

The data on sales and profits, of course, form one of the most tangible indications of the progress of a business. The Macy figures for the period under discussion have been set forth in Table 15 and show a substantial increase during the fifteen years. In appraising the sales figures several preliminary facts must be taken into account. Because of the practice of ending the accounting period with the Saturday nearest the terminal calendar date, certain years contain results for more than 52 weeks; this necessitates a periodic readjustment. Thus the years 1890, 1896, and 1902 cover an abnormally long period and are not exactly comparable with the years which immediately precede and follow. Allowing for this discrepancy, it is apparent that Macy sales increased every year except for a slight drop in 1893. At times the growth was negligible, but the general effect was an approximate doubling of sales between 1888 and 1902 (the volume for 1902 would be over $10,000,000, even if sales for the extra five weeks were eliminated).

This increase in dollar volume meant an even greater increase in the physical volume of goods sold annually, for the tendency of prices over most of the period was downward, and it was not until

1902 that the general price level recovered to the point at which it had stood in 1888. Thus, if the physical quantity of goods sold in the

TABLE 15

SALES AND EARNINGS

1888–1902

Year[a]	Net Sales[b]		Net Gains[c]	
	Amount	Ratio to Previous Year %	Amount	Percentage of Net Sales
1888	$ 5,049,241	98.2	$319,556	6.33
1889	5,469,078	108.3	361,510	6.61
1890[d]	5,825,614	106.5	390,307	6.70
1891	5,691,399	97.7	342,206	6.01
1892	6,694,965	117.6	417,520	6.24
1893	6,653,748	99.4	407,110	6.12
1894	6,738,009	101.3	382,042	5.67
1895	6,907,144	102.5	379,718	5.50
1896[d]	7,095,729	102.7	252,940	3.56
1897	6,870,054	96.8	285,312	4.15
1898	7,058,955	102.8	368,123	5.21
1899	7,825,141	110.8	439,032	5.61
1900	8,148,254	104.1	510,263	6.26
1901	8,812,171	108.2	547,978	6.22
1902[e]	10,765,066	122.2	548,151	5.09

[a] Until 1902 the accounting year terminated with the Saturday nearest Dec. 31.

[b] Sales of leased departments are included, but not goods which were sold and subsequently returned.

[c] Net gain includes both retail profits and other income after deducting all expenses. In these calculations no deductions have been made for interest on capital invested or compensation to partners.

[d] Accounting period covers 53 weeks.

[e] Includes 57 weeks, ending Jan. 31, 1903, advancing the terminal date of the accounting year from the Saturday nearest Dec. 31 to the one nearest Jan. 31.

SOURCE: Semiannual balances, 1887–1903.

store had remained constant, the sales in dollars would have decreased substantially during the first ten years of the period and would then have recovered only to the original level of 1888. In other words, until 1898, Macy sales in both dollars and physical volume expanded in spite of a persistently unfavorable price situation. Between 1898 and 1902, moreover, the growth in dollar volume was greater than could be accounted for by any improvement in prices.[1] Using sales as a yardstick, then, we may safely conclude that Macy's achieved substantial progress during the entire period.

The record of the firm's earnings during this time is not so consistently favorable as of sales, but in view of the general business difficulties of the 1890's, it reflects considerable credit upon the Macy management. In amount the net profits ranged from a low of $252,940 in 1896 to a high of $548,151 in 1902. Using as our criterion the somewhat more accurate ratio of profits to sales, we find that net gain rose to 6.70 per cent in 1890, declined to 3.56 per cent in the panic year of 1896, and then climbed back to 6.26 per cent of sales in 1900. There will be occasion later on to examine operating results in detail, but for the moment let us note that Macy's earned a substantial sum of money every year in the face of great adversity. Between 1888 and the latter part of 1897 America experienced tight money, falling prices, depressed trade, industrial stagnation, serious strikes and widespread unemployment, thousands of bankruptcies and receiverships, numerous bank failures, radical political agitation, and two violent financial panics — a decade of misery and disaster in which a few brief periods of revival served only to intensify the prevailing gloom.[2] The institution which avoided losses in such circumstances was certainly worthy of Rowland Macy.

EXPANSION OF MERCHANDISE LINES

One of the means by which sales volume was increased was the addition of new items to the selection of merchandise that was offered to customers. To some extent this addition took the form of rounding out lines which had already been introduced. In 1888, for example, the firm claimed to stock a *complete* line of fishing tackle and accessories; it added watercoolers and refrigerators to its household furnishings in the same year; it advertised occasional tables, oriental goods and rugs, and engraved stationery in 1889; and in 1890 it announced the sale of brass beds, writing and music cabinets, made-to-order lampshades and awnings, floor matting, watches, and a wide selection of rowing machines, chest weights, trapeze bars, and other athletic equipment. In 1891 the toy department began to stock bicycles, while the Christmas advertising revealed that other departments stocked a variety of crucifixes, rosary beads, holy-water fonts, and other devotional paraphernalia.

Similarly in 1892 the store, which for some years had made men's suits to order, began to sell ready-made clothing and shoes; and the jewelry department went beyond relatively inexpensive articles of adornment to include diamonds and other precious stones. In much the same category were stringed musical instruments and paintings in oil and water colors (1893); lawnmowers and boys' and men's hats (1894); amateur photographers' supplies (1895); bicycle clothing for men and women (1896); carpenters' tools, firearms, and a greatly expanded line of household stoves (1897); wallpaper (1898); fire extinguishers, fire-escape equipment, a complete line of optical goods, and cocktail shakers and bar spoons (1899); oilcloth and linoleum, infants' haberdashery, and nursery furniture (1902); and the gradual completion of the assortment of dry goods materials during the entire period. Meanwhile the firm had also provided such services as fur storage, watch and jewelry repairing, and picture framing.[3]

More important than these supplementary items, perhaps, were the departments which marked new departures in the merchandise handled in a department store. The first innovation of this sort was the opening of a harness and saddlery department in the fall of 1889. Success in selling riding and driving whips "both plain and silver-mounted" in the previous year may have suggested the step, but it was undoubtedly encouraged by Nathan Straus, who was a devoted lover of horses. The extent to which the new division expanded may be judged by the fact that the store held a special sale of carriages in the fall of 1895 in order to make room for the winter's stock of sleighs.[4]

A new feature which attracted greater attention and possessed greater significance was the introduction of groceries. Starting experimentally in 1892 with certified Tokay wines and a selection of teas, Macy's expanded the new department in January, 1893, putting in a complete line of staple and fancy groceries.[5] Of course, Rowland Macy's brief experiment with a picnic department in the early 'seventies had established a precedent, and Whiteley's Universal Provider had demonstrated the possibilities in London by operating food departments which dated from 1875; but the Macy grocery department seems to have been without parallel in America at the time.[6] Its immediate success, contrasting with the failure of the earlier picnic department, may be attributed in part to better management and in part to the changing habits of New Yorkers, who were becoming accustomed by the 1890's to both packaged foodstuffs and the idea of satisfying in a department store almost any need they might have. Thanks to a growing patronage, Macy's found it advisable to transfer the cigar trade into a new department late in 1894, and in the spring of 1895 a separate wine and liquor department emerged.[7]

The enormous variety of merchandise handled by Macy's today was practically completed (in general scope but not in detail) in September, 1896, by the opening of a large, well-stocked furniture department. As we have seen, the store had begun to carry a few scattered items of furniture in the 'seventies, gradually amplifying the selection; but it made no pretense of offering a complete line until 1896, when the stock of furniture was suddenly enlarged to such an extent that it covered three entire floors of a large building.[8]

In 1898 Macy's launched another ambitious departure from tradition when the firm announced the opening of a piano store, apparently aimed at the thriving but highly competitive market for musical instruments. John Wanamaker imitated this move in 1899, but, unlike Wanamaker, Macy's abandoned the idea within a short time. Probably the heavy investment required, combined with the slow stock-turn and the obvious difficulty of selling such an expensive item for cash in any large numbers, made the piano department an unnecessary burden to the store. On the other hand, Macy's did continue to handle talking machines, which the firm had begun to sell in the fall of 1898.[9]

By 1902 the human wants were few indeed that the Macy store could not meet. Furnishings for the home, clothing for the entire family, food and drink for the table, tools for the handyman, drugs for the sick, harness for the prevailing mode of transport, and, as a contribution to life's fuller enjoyment, a growing assortment of jewelry, candy, cosmetics, sports equipment, smokers' supplies, music, pictures, devotional goods, and books — so ran the formidable array of merchandise that was assembled from the four corners of the earth and sold under the aegis of the Red Star. As the variety expanded and the volume of trade in particular lines increased, old departments had to be divided or rearranged and new ones created. The list of Macy retail departments, shown in Table 16, may convey some notion of the extraordinary range of coverage which the store had achieved by 1902.

Having built up an institution designed to meet so many human needs, the firm inevitably received numerous proposals that it should establish a dental department, a beauty parlor, and even a funeral-directing department. It drew the line at such services, just as it refused to follow the example of Whiteley's and certain other London stores which even undertook the construction or decoration of houses, sale of railway tickets and coal, and catering service that once led Whiteley to go so far as to supply a live elephant! While Macy management avoided such fantastic extremes, the fact that customers could buy at its counters such odd items as left-handed scissors helped to popularize the idea of going to Macy's for practically every kind of merchandise. The beneficial effect upon sales is obvious.[10]

Sources of Goods Sold

Of course, before the enormous stock of merchandise could be made available to customers, a great many preliminary operations had to take place. The general public seldom realizes the extraordinary extent to which a large store devotes its staff and resources to buying rather than selling. Someone has to be familiar with the various dealers and manufacturers from whom goods can be obtained. Someone has to decide what to buy, how much of it to order, and where to obtain it — always bearing in mind current prices, stocks on hand, and the estimated state of consumer demand. Someone has to examine merchandise and negotiate with vendors, even to the point of going to obscure villages in foreign lands. Then the goods selected have to be transported to the store, checked for damage or shortages, priced, marked, stored until needed, and finally placed on the selling floors. It is unfortunate that little direct evi-

TABLE 16
MERCHANDISE DEPARTMENTS
Fall, 1902

No.	Merchandise	Date Created		Origin
1.	Linens	Before 1888		...
2.	Laces and Hamburg embroideries	"	"	...
3.	Notions	"	"	...
4.	Ribbons	"	"	...
5.	Silverware, bronzes, and clocks	"	"	...
6.	Hosiery	"	"	...
7.	Merino underwear	"	"	...
9.	Jewelry	"	"	...
10.	Men's clothing	"	"	...
11.	Housefurnishing goods	"	"	...
12.	Dolls and toys	"	"	...
13.	Books, artists' materials, sheet music	"	"	...
14.	Art embroideries and machine worsteds	"	"	...
15.	China and glassware	"	"	...
16.	Candy and favors	"	"	...
17.	Gloves	"	"	...
18.	Ladies' untrimmed hats	"	"	...
19.	Feathers and artificial flowers	"	"	...
20.	Ladies' and children's shoes	"	"	...
21.	Ladies' and children's suits	"	"	...
22.	Black silks	"	"	...
23.	Black and colored dress goods	"	"	...
24.	Dress trimmings	"	"	...
25.	Restaurant	"	"	...
26.	Corsets	"	"	...
27.	Stationery	"	"	...
28.	Upholstery, curtains, etc.	"	"	...
29.	Handkerchiefs	"	"	...
30.	Colored silks	"	"	old 4½
31.	Men's furnishings	"	"	old 6½
32.	Harness and saddlery	Fall, '89		new

dence has survived concerning the details of these operations during the 1890's, but the main part of the story is clear enough.[11]

New York was, even more than today, the main trading center of the great dry goods business of the country. It also formed the

TABLE 16 (*continued*)

No.	Merchandise	Date Created	Origin
33.	Groceries	Spring, '92	new
34.	Sewing machines	Fall, '92	11
35.	Furs	Fall, '94	old 21½
36.	Cigars and tobacco	" "	mainly new
37.	Wines and liquors	Spring, '95	33
38.	Sporting goods	Spring, '96	12
39.	Boys' and men's hats	Fall, '96	mainly new
40.	Umbrellas and canes	Before 1888	old 8½
41.	Furniture	Fall, '96	mainly new
42.	Drugs and toiletries	Before 1888	old 9½
43.	Soda fountain	Spring, '88	16
44.	Trimmed millinery	Before 1888	old 18½
45.	Women's and children's cloaks	" "	old 21½
46.	Men's shoes	" "	new
47.	Card-engraving	Spring, '89	27
48.	Rugs	Spring, '92	new
49.	Pictures	Fall, '96	11
52.	Fancy metal goods	Spring, '97	9
53.	Wallpaper	Spring, '98	new
54.	Ladies' neckwear	Spring, '99	29
56.	Optical goods and photo supplies	Fall, '99	3
57.	Carpets	Spring, 1900	48
58.	Boys' clothing and furnishings	Spring, '01	10
59.	Blankets and sheetings	" "	1
60.	Linings	" "	"
61.	White goods and flannels	" "	"
62.	Muslin underwear and misses' skirts	Spring, '02	old 2½
63.	Waists and blouses	" "	"
64.	Wrappers, silk petticoats, bathing suits	" "	"
65.	Infants' wear and haberdashery	" "	"

SOURCE: This list has been compiled from semiannual reports, supplemented by miscellaneous memoranda, catalogs, advertisements, interviews, and various other means of identifying numbered departments. Fifteen manufacturing departments have not been included.

chief wholesale market for many of the other lines of merchandise handled by department stores. In consequence, Macy buyers were able to deal directly with wholesalers, manufacturers' representatives, and even manufacturers themselves, and so bought a large part of the goods required without going outside the city. It is not possible to determine now the proportion which the store acquired from middlemen, but in a great many instances merchandise was bought directly from manufacturers without the interposition of middlemen of any kind. (As indicated in Chapter vi, this procedure did not eliminate all the services performed by middlemen, but simply transferred some of them back to the manufacturer and others forward to the retail institution, in the hope of improved service or lower expenses and prices.)

The enormous volume of goods sold by the store, which usually meant large purchases from merchandise vendors (producers, importers, commission houses, or wholesalers), facilitated buying directly from manufacturers. In 1892, for example, a Macy advertisement asserted that the store had bought the entire season's production of a necktie manufacturer as the basis for a special sale of men's ties. On another occasion the store took the whole stock of a silk textile factory.[12] It is possible, of course, that the producers involved were not large, but the fact that the store could absorb a large part of the output of even a small factory improved its bargaining position as compared to that of a small retail concern. One must remember, on the other hand, that not all lines of merchandise in the department store necessarily involve large sales or purchases. In certain departments, such as notions, sporting goods, house furnishings, and the like, the volume of trade in any single item may be small — possibly even less than the volume developed in a competing specialty store. It is quite possible, therefore, that the Macy rug department (to take a possible instance) sold fewer rugs in 1895 than a specialized firm like W. & J. Sloane and bought on less favorable terms.[13] In situations of this sort the Macy buyers may well have found advantages in buying from wholesale houses rather than from producers. The rule then, as now, was to buy from the source which, service and quality taken into account, proved to be the most economical one.

In general, the store claimed at the time that it bought directly from manufacturers, and old employees believe that the claim was substantially correct.[14]

In some instances Macy's negotiated special arrangements with manufacturers, obtaining special prices, advertising allowances, or exclusive selling rights in exchange for the substantial volume and prominent display which the store could offer. For many years Macy's had an exclusive agency for Foster kid gloves (Foster, Paul & Co.) as a result of which the store maintained special Foster displays, refrained from handling competing button gloves, obtained a rebate on annual purchases, and received, in 1892 and 1893 at least, a yearly newspaper advertising allowance of $2,500.[15] Similarly Macy's undertook to sell Menier chocolate, and Chocolat Menier agreed not to sell to any other dry or fancy goods house in the city.[16] As a result of other agreements Macy's had exclusive arrangements to sell Royal Bavarian and certified Tokay wines; the firm also held the sole agency in the United States for the wines of Renard Frères of Rheims, thus entering into the importing and wholesaling business to a limited extent.[17]

A Macy advertisement in 1894 asserted, "We never deal in old or bankrupt stocks. We sell new and desirable goods only." This does not mean that the firm ceased its practice of picking up bargains wherever it could find them. When a manufacturer found himself overloaded with merchandise or short of cash, he was sure to obtain a sympathetic hearing from Macy buyers if his prices were low. One of the first large sales held by the grocery department was based on a purchase from the receiver of C. Burkhalter & Co., a well-known wholesale grocery firm which had gone bankrupt. A special sale of underwear in 1896 avowedly included garments with slight imperfections; this probably represented the complete stock of some manufacturer who preferred to sell the lot at a low price rather than sort out the seconds. Similarly the furniture department bought up the entire inventory of T. L. Sloan, Deverey & Co., a Chicago furniture house which succumbed to the panic of 1896. In addition the firm bought goods at auction when suitable opportunities arose.[18]

If buying such bargain lots violated usual Macy policy, it created at the same time some fine opportunities for store customers, helped to relieve bad market situations, and swelled the volume of Macy sales when competition for business was keen. Indeed, the fact that competitors were running sales of bankrupt stocks may well have induced Macy management to pursue the same course. It is clear that there was no deception involved, for Macy advertisements explained the situations which made bargain prices possible. It is also plain that the firm kept an eye on quality. When competition in smoked hams, for example, made it advisable for Macy's to try to add a slightly lower-priced line to its grocery department (which was already selling Armour's top grade), Isidor Straus' main inquiry was whether the line under consideration was of dependable quality "such as a first class retail house can afford to place on sale ... sufficiently reliable that we can afford to offer it to our general trade." [19]

It is worth recording that even in this early period the store occasionally encountered difficulty in obtaining merchandise from manufacturers who refused to sell because they disliked the Macy policy of underselling competitors. If circumstances made it necessary to continue to handle the line, the store enlisted the coöperation of other retailers. Thus we find Isidor Straus buying Keystone eggbeaters and Bromley curtains through John Wanamaker, while on one occasion he was obtaining Sapolio from faraway Savannah, Georgia, through a relative.[20] We shall see that the firm was compelled to resort to similar tactics later on, combing the entire country for books which publishers refused to supply to Macy's because of the firm's insistence on the right to sell them below list prices.

In addition to domestic buying, the Macy organization did a considerable amount of importing. Buyers regularly went to Europe every year, particularly those who bought toys, millinery, linens, women's wear, and fancy goods. In 1893 Macy's opened a buying office on the avenue de l'Opéra, Paris — partly because the growing volume of foreign purchases necessitated improved facilities and partly because the firm believed that a European office would have advertising and prestige value — and seriously considered having another one in Berlin.[21] Within three years, however, this step was regarded as a mistake, and the firm reverted to its former procedure of having its buyers handle their foreign purchases through *commissionnaires*. Experience proved that it was still necessary to have certain buyers go abroad "to become conversant with what the coming styles and colors will be," [22] and that the Paris office, which was expensive to maintain, was of little value "without having a buyer on the spot whose practical knowledge of both markets enables him to cultivate and increase the business profitably by his own efforts, instead of being dependent entirely upon the initiative from this side." [23] Those who have had experience with department store management will at once recognize a familiar problem in this situation.

Unable to obtain the required combination of experience and ability, the firm reduced the Paris office to a single employee to handle routine matters and appointed an import manager who was to divide his time between Europe and America, maintaining contacts in principal cities by means of foreign representatives. These agents, who gave their attention to Macy work only when needed, assisted buyers in locating merchandise and handled the details of purchasing, shipping, customs clearance, and payment. They were located in London, Berlin, Vienna, Chemnitz, and even in Constantinople after Macy's had begun to sell large quantities of oriental rugs. Macy buyers also received a certain amount of assistance from relatives of the Straus family who were connected with the European factories which L. Straus & Sons owned. Indeed, while the Paris office was in existence, the expense of maintaining it was shared by L. Straus & Sons and Abraham & Straus, a Brooklyn department store in which, as we have seen, the members of the Macy firm acquired an interest in 1893.[24]

Before leaving the discussion of Macy buying, it may be well to point out that the firm continued the founder's policy of paying cash for all the merchandise acquired. Ability to do so was an advantage at all times, but it was especially useful during periods of depression when valuable goods could be picked up at bargain prices by any concern which could use large lots and pay for them at once. While it is impossible to estimate the extent of the savings achieved by this means, comment by a contemporary trade paper (even after being treated to a large dose of salt) provides impressive evidence that the Macy cash policy yielded considerable benefits for both store and customer: [25]

What ready cash will do with manufacturers nowadays is demonstrated in the furniture department of R. H. Macy & Co. It is said that they secured most of their goods at nearly 50 cents on the dollar. Taking, for instance, a sideboard which was purchased from a firm in Grand Rapids, Mich. It is offered by a Twenty-third street dealer for $120. R. H. Macy & Co., who, it is stated purchased goods from the same firm, offer the identical sideboard for $59.66.

This may well have been an exceptional instance, but Macy's unquestionably offered numerous bargains which cash buying helped to make possible.

Manufacturing Activities

A substantial proportion of the merchandise which the store sold during this period was manufactured within the Macy organization. There was, in fact, a fairly sizable increase in the quantity and variety of such goods down to 1900. When measured as a percentage of the total sales, however, Macy manufactures showed no very noticeable gain, because the absolute increase was offset by a corresponding growth in sales. Data on the volume of manufactures within the firm are set forth in Table 17, together with figures showing the profits attributed to manufacturing activities. Goods were manufactured only for sale in Macy's retail departments and for Abraham & Straus.

As we have seen, the firm had been engaged in manufacturing women's and children's underwear and millinery on the premises for many years before 1888. It had also acquired a factory at Poughkeepsie for the manufacture of men's shirts, and it maintained a factory or production office in Belfast, Ireland, by means of which the firm directed and controlled the manufacture of handkerchiefs and other linen goods by Irish peasant women. Additional facilities were added after the entrance of the Strauses into the partnership.

In the first place, the Macy store advertised as its own the factories which L. Straus & Sons operated in Europe. This claim was, of course, an exaggeration, but the fact that Isidor and Nathan Straus were the principal owners of the china and glass business gave a fundamental veracity to the advertisement. Certainly the arrangement gave Macy's many of the advantages of actually owning the

TABLE 17

MANUFACTURING VOLUME AND PROFITS, 1888–1902[a]
(Sales of manufacturing departments to retail departments)

Year	Amount Sold to Retail Departments $	Ratio to Net Retail Sales (At cost) %	MANUFACTURING PROFIT	
			Ratio to Amount Sold %	Ratio to Total Net Gain %
1888	$346,189	8.77	1.82	1.98
1889	331,546	7.77	3.01	2.76
1890[b]	327,577	7.20	5.96	4.99
1891	307,928	6.93	2.96	2.66
1892	317,597	6.12	2.27	1.73
1893	330,998	6.47	3.31	2.70
1894	373,689	7.18	3.68	3.60
1895	374,922	7.00	7.11	7.02
1896[b]	391,009	7.02	3.50	5.41
1897	447,309	8.37	3.79	5.94
1898	518,393	9.58	4.96	7.00
1899	556,445	9.28	2.55	3.22
1900	547,946	8.91	2.25	2.42
1901	535,600	8.02	1.56	1.53
1902[c]	613,242	7.53	.14[d]	.16[d]

[a] Profits in this table refer to the difference between the amounts charged to retail departments for goods manufactured for them and the calculated cost of such merchandise. The accuracy of the cost calculations cannot now be determined, but there was apparently no important change in accounting procedure during the period. Manufacturing costs appear to have included interest on the value of the equipment used. The figures given do not include the goods manufactured by L. Straus & Sons for Macy's.
[b] Fifty-three weeks.
[c] Fifty-seven weeks.
[d] Loss.
SOURCE: Semiannual statements, 1888–1903.

factories, which were located as follows: Limoges, France (china); Rudolstadt, Thuringia (ivory and bisque novelties); Steinschönau, Bohemia (glassware); and Carlsbad, Bohemia (china).[26] During the course of 1888 the Macy firm transferred at least part of the underwear manufacturing from 14th Street to a factory in Wallingford, Connecticut, and in the following spring it opened another factory devoted to the same line in New Haven. The management was moving all manufacturing departments out of the main store building at this time,[27] probably because the space was urgently needed for sales purposes, but this fact did not mean that there was to be any reduction in such activities. On the contrary, a succession of new manufacturing ventures was undertaken: in the spring of 1889 the store established a shop to handle the orders for engraved cards and invitations which its stationery department obtained. Later in the same year it began to manufacture harness and saddlery, and by 1890 it was also making women's corsets — not in the harness factory, to be sure, but in one of the underwear factories. By this time, too, the store had acquired facilities for upholstering furniture and making slip covers, curtains, draperies, and so on. In 1891, the store was inviting the public to visit its glass-cutting department on one of the upper floors, in which forty highly skilled workmen were producing cut glassware for stock and special orders.[28]

Other, and possibly more significant, developments in production came during the course of the 1890's. Early in 1893 Macy's acquired a silk skirt and blouse factory (it was at 97 Bank Street, not far from the store, and it was probably a small one); by this date the store had also begun to make and remodel fur garments. Later in the same year it began the manufacture of perfumes, drugs, and toiletries, a productive activity which has continued to be an important part of the Macy business ever since. In 1894 the store added men's neckwear, silk lampshades, cigars, and toilet soaps to the list of its own manufactures. It began to roast coffee and package a number of grocery products about the same time. Then, responding to the growing fad for bicycles (and also to the financial difficulties of a small manufacturer), the Macy management leased a bicycle factory in Paterson, New Jersey, in August, 1895, with a capacity of 30 vehicles a week. A picture-framing department and a candy factory were added during 1897, by which time the store was making its own mattresses. Meanwhile the line of Macy-made women's wear had expanded to include skirts, waists, petticoats, and wrappers,[29] and the manufacturing facilities for these were increased by the opening of two additional factories, one in Chester, Pennsylvania, and the other in Rutherford, New Jersey.[30] The firm also boasted of its own baking powder factory in 1902.[31]

This list of the items manufactured by the Macy firm is in some respects more impressive in appearance than in fact. The largest amount manufactured in any one year of this period (apart from the abnormally long period of 1902) was $556,000 in 1899. This figure did not include goods manufactured by L. Straus & Sons, and it may have left out the products of the bicycle factory, which seems to have been operated as a separate undertaking under the name of Webster & Straus. Even so, the total is not large in proportion to the total Macy business. The highest ratio to the store's total sales, in fact, was not quite 10 per cent, and the typical relationship was somewhat less, proving that the Macy firm was still devoting by far the greater part of its attention to retail trade.

Rowland Macy himself, of course, had established the precedent for manufacturing activities, but it is evident that the Strauses carried matters much further, making a definite policy out of what may have been a little-considered experiment. Why? Two reasons seem to have encouraged them to integrate manufacturing with the retailing function. In the first place, they believed that they could make a profit on manufacturing operations and still retail the goods at prices which would be less than those generally prevailing. Indeed, if the assertions made in the advertisements are any guide, the management believed that such integration would yield Macy customers a saving of 20 to $33\frac{1}{3}$ per cent. That this belief was sincere and based upon factual estimates is proved by correspondence between partners. In 1894 Isidor wrote to his brother, "We are making silk waists for them [Abraham & Straus] and as soon as we get the factory more thoroughly organized will also make silk and cloth outside skirts, which we have just begun making ourselves at a saving of one-third of what we paid in the market for the same goods." [32] In a letter to Webster he estimated the gross margin on the bicycles manufactured to be so large that "our entire fixed expense for a year will be covered by the difference between what the wheels cost and what we have been paying for them in one month's production." [33]

The second incentive to extend manufacturing activities was the Strauses' desire to be certain of the quality of the goods which the store sold. During the course of the 'nineties there was growing public agitation for legislation to insure the sale of pure foods and drugs. Nathan Straus, who took a sincere interest in such matters and, at the same time, was quick to see in them new opportunities for favorable publicity, is credited with urging the manufacture of drugs and candies so that the store could be positive that it handled no inferior or impure products, and he may have brought about the decision to make mattresses in order to be able to advertise strictly sanitary bedding.[34] On the other hand, much of the clothing which the firm made was in the lower grades, where quality was not a prime consideration.

In general the manufacturing activities of R. H. Macy & Co. at this time may be regarded as another manifestation of the contemporary tendency in retailing toward the integration and diversification of operations. It was inevitable, of course, that the firm's management should be somewhat influenced by current ideas in business, and the theory seems to have been widely prevalent in the 'eighties and 'nineties that there was magic in large-scale operations and in the elimination of middlemen between the manufacturer and the consumer. With trusts, merges, and vertical integration appearing in so many important industries, it may well have appeared that a retail store would have to enter into manufacturing or else be crushed by manufacturers who were reaching forward into retailing. It is clear, at any rate, that the Strauses did not venture into manufacturing by accident or as a temporary expedient; they sought to obtain factory space through leases running from five to ten years or through outright purchase.[35]

That the tendency of retailers to engage in manufacturing activities was widespread at this time is evident from the fact that the Bon Marché in Paris manufactured many items as early as 1872 and that Lord & Taylor in New York made furniture in 1874, while Whiteley's in London even manufactured pianos. A. T. Stewart operated a number of factories in connection with his mercantile business, but these may have owed their existence more to his wholesaling activities than his retailing. Certainly wholesale dry goods firms like the H. B. Claflin Co. engaged extensively in manufacturing activities in this period.[36]

The store's experience soon proved, however, that the extension of manufacturing activities was not an unmixed blessing. As Table 17 shows, profits from this source, which had never been large, dropped off sharply after 1898 as one manufacturing division after another began to turn in losses. In a few instances, such as the harness and bicycle factories, these unfavorable results came about from a change in demand as well as from competitive conditions arising in the industry from improved methods of production (a factory turning out 30 bicycles a week, for example, would encounter great difficulty in competing, so far as costs were concerned, with a factory which had an output several times larger). For the Macy clothing divisions, a number of reasons were advanced at the time to explain the unfavorable showing: the expected volume of demand failed to materialize; large manufacturers were putting goods on the market at low prices which Macy's could not match; the division of production among a number of widely separated branches (made to ensure an ample supply of labor) interfered with efficient operations; and it was almost impossible to obtain capable managers.[37]

Examined in perspective, however, all the evidence suggests that Macy's had been participating in an integrating movement which was going too far, just as an excess of specialization had taken place earlier in the century. With few exceptions, retail store management could seldom cope effectively with manufacturing problems, just as few industrial concerns could successfully enter the retail trade; and business men found that the advantages to be obtained from integration and large-scale operations were not a matter of magic or of automatic consequences, but could be won only by managerial skill and organizational genius of a rare type, capable of solving problems which were then unprecedented. If there was a theoretical need for complete integration in the department store field, business management had not yet learned how to provide it successfully except in limited areas — in operations like fur-remodeling and upholstery work, for example, which were very intimately connected with the proper provision of full retail service, and in which success did not depend upon applying mass production methods; or else in blending and packaging operations, such as roasting coffee or preparing the simpler types of drugs and cosmetics, which involved no very complicated technical equipment and could be done effectively in limited volume.

Thus Macy's reached a high point in manufacturing activities in this period and then began to retreat. The firm has never entirely ceased production, and in certain lines (particularly drugs and toilet preparations) it has actually increased the output substantially, but the general policy since the late 1890's has been to leave production mainly to independent manufacturers. The Macy firm was not alone in this retreat. By 1900 John Wanamaker, too, had had a fling at manufacturing, just as A. T. Stewart before him, and he had learned that [38]

manufacturing is quite another business, and a man had better attend to the business he knows. . . . You get a better assortment of things. If you have a factory you must keep it going all the time; and you must keep the people employed; you must keep your machinery going. If you have to sell at less than cost, you are losing your own money. A great part of the stuffs that we sell are sold for less than cost, but it is [no longer] our loss.

And Marshall Field & Co., who, because of an extensive wholesale trade, was to carry integration far beyond any point reached by Stewart, or Wanamaker, or Macy's, eventually found it advisable to make substantial changes which amounted to at least a partial reversal of policy.[39]

In considering this tendency toward integration and then away from it, one should bear in mind that the volume of Macy business in the 'nineties was only a fraction of the figure reached in the 1920's: the amount of manufacturing in certain lines must have been too small to permit optimum efficiency from the point of view of costs. One must also remember that great advances have been made during the past generation in the art of business organization and administration, as a result of which it is now feasible to operate subsidiary enterprises with an efficiency that could not have been imagined before 1900. Lastly, it is highly probable that the manufacturing activities of retail institutions like Macy's could be justified on the ground that they educated independent manufacturers, compelling them to improve methods and products and to reduce their selling prices to retailers. If one accepts this view, Macy's manufacturing activities eventually became unprofitable because of their very success: independent producers were obliged to find ways of offering qualities and prices to Macy buyers which the store's manufacturing departments (required by firm policy to transfer merchandise at market prices) could not match and still break even on expenses. Corrective influences of this kind may have played an important part in the general economic recovery after 1897.

Private Brands

Private branding, an activity which is closely related to manufacturing, showed a distinct increase in Macy's during the 1890's. This reflects an increasing desire to identify merchandise with the firm's name and to transfer from manufacturer to retailer the responsibilities involved in trade-marks. Many of the private brands used, of course, were applied to items which the store manufactured; it is probable, however, that the greater portion of goods so branded were of independent manufacture. The word "Macy" seems to have been applied to many items, particularly of clothing, and the Red Star brand was also widely used. That the management definitely decided to feature the Red Star brand is suggested by the fact that the firm filed six different applications with the United States Patent Office late in 1893 in order to register the use of this trade-mark after May, 1892, on a wide variety of perfumes, extracts, and toilet preparations; on certain tonics and remedies (including witch hazel, cod liver oil, and Jamaica ginger), ammonia, benzine, turpentine, and similar household preparations, after 1892; on wrapping paper and stationery, since 1862; on tea and coffee and on kitchen and laundry soaps, after 1892.[40] An incomplete list of items bearing Macy names, together with dates on which they were apparently first advertised, is a further indication of the adoption of a definite and consistent policy with regard to private brands:[41] "Our Own" soap, 1890; "Star" sewing machines and "Red Star" tea, 1892; "Macy's Star" novels, 1893; "Macy" ties and shoes, and "Red Star" bicycles, baking powder, and flavoring extracts, 1894; "Straus" cut glass, "Webster" bicycles, "Lily White" canned goods, and "Red Star" California wines, 1896; "Straus" bicycles and "Macy" candy, 1897; "Straus" pianos and "Red Star" ham and boneless bacon, 1898 (previously the store had featured Armour "Star" hams, which fitted fairly well into its scheme of brands); "Webster" collars for men and "Macy-made" mattresses, 1901; "La Forge" and "Valentine" watches, 1902. The existence of two private brands of bicycles and two of watches shows that the store was beginning to handle more than one price range under its own name.

One should not overlook the broader significance of the manufacturing and private branding which the Macy firm did at this time: the retail firm was no longer selling whatever the manufacturers chose to produce; the store itself was determining the goods that were to be made. The Macy management explicitly recognized this in an advertisement published as early as 1889:[42]

We are prompt to introduce novelties and quick to discern new currents of public demand. In most cases the manufacturer takes his initiative from us, not we from the manufacturer. Standing, as we do, in close and constant contact with all classes of purchasers, and controlling, as we do, a vast organization of productive forces, the fault must be ours if we fail to satisfy every taste, minister to every want, and meet every necessity within the limits of our business.

This statement may exaggerate the extent to which Macy's influenced manufacturers at the time, but the very fact that the firm's management was articulately conscious of a new responsibility is in itself highly significant, foreshadowing the day when the department store would act, at least to a limited degree, as the purchasing agent of the public. Certainly it is impossible to find a better or more challenging contemporary expression of the direction in which retailing was to move during the next two generations.

On the whole, the diversification and integration within Macy's during this period were but the culmination of policies adopted before 1888, and there was evidently a tendency for evolutionary developments to slow down: by 1896 the emergence of the modern department store was substantially complete. While the Macy firm continued to make progress in both retail ideas and sales volume, there was no spectacular innovation or growth. In a large measure this leveling-off tendency was inherent in the contemporary situation. The firm and the department store industry alike had passed through a period of rapid progress and were reaching that stage of maturity in which there is necessarily less scope for originality. Moreover, a long period of unfavorable business conditions handicapped all efforts to improve the volume of transactions. In consequence, as we shall see in the following chapter, competition between units began to manifest itself in extreme forms of rivalry.

Before passing on to a discussion of competitive efforts, however, it will be helpful to examine operating statistics so as to see in a quantitative way what was happening to the firm.

Operating Data, 1888–1902

For this period we have a fairly complete set of accounting data by means of which it is possible, for the first time, to reach definite conclusions about store operations. Information of this sort has never been available for any department store for the period before about 1912, and its importance can scarcely be overemphasized. In the absence of comparable data from other stores, it is impossible to tell whether Macy figures were typical of New York firms, but the tendencies which are apparent in the continuous series of Macy figures throw significant light on general marketing developments and the rising cost of distribution.

In Table 18 we have an analysis of Macy's sales for the period.

TABLE 18
ANALYSIS OF SALES
1888–1902

Year[a]	Total Net Sales[b] Amount	Total Net Sales[b] Ratio to Previous Year %	Sales in Straus Departments Amount	Sales in Straus Departments Ratio to Previous Year %	Sales in Other Leased Departments[c] Amount	Total Leased Sales Amount	Total Leased Sales Ratio to Total Net Sales %
1888	$5,049,241	98.2	$650,614	...	$137,325	$787,939	15.6
1889	5,469,078	108.3	689,126	105.9	101,271	790,397	14.5
1890[d]	5,825,614	106.5	703,552	102.1	101,961	805,513	13.8
1891	5,691,399	97.7	715,008	101.6	93,050	808,058	14.2
1892	6,694,965	117.6	771,610	107.9	...	771,610	11.5
1893	6,653,748	99.4	742,186	96.2	...	742,186	11.2
1894	6,738,009	101.3	695,772	93.8	...	695,772	10.3
1895	6,907,144	102.5	639,413	91.9	...	639,413	9.3
1896[d]	7,095,729	102.7	613,148	95.9	...	613,148	8.6
1897	6,870,054	96.8	553,886	90.3	...	553,886	8.1
1898	7,058,955	102.8	532,660	96.2	...	532,660	7.6
1899	7,825,141	110.8	600,200	112.7	...	600,200	7.7
1900	8,148,254	104.1	605,784	100.9	...	605,784	7.4
1901	8,812,171	108.2	619,822	102.3	...	619,822	7.0
1902[e]	10,765,066	122.2	746,517	120.4	...	746,517	6.9

[a] Until 1902 the accounting year terminated with the Saturday nearest Dec. 31.
[b] Sales in leased departments are included, but not goods which were sold and subsequently returned to the store.
[c] The shoe department was taken over by Macy's early in 1888. Apart from shoe sales of $34,737 in 1888 the figures are for the restaurant, which ceased to be a leased department at the close of 1891.
[d] Accounting period covers 53 weeks.
[e] Includes 57 weeks ending Jan. 31, 1903, owing to advancement of the accounting year from the Saturday nearest Dec. 31 to the one nearest Jan. 31.

As already pointed out, the slow rate of increase before 1898 reflects the depressed times and the growing competition for business. The figures for the Straus departments are of interest because, in contrast with results in the preceding period, they show a decline in relation to the total business of the store. The explanation seems to be that the Straus brothers, being now responsible for all divisions of the Macy business, were unable to give the china and silver departments the concentrated attention which they had formerly received. Thus the store as a whole benefited from Straus management at the expense of the Straus leased departments. By 1898 this situation was apparently recognized and remedied. The sharp drop in the ratio of sales in leased departments to sales for the store as a whole, apparent in 1889 and 1892, came about primarily because the store took over the shoe department and restaurant, which had formerly been conducted on a leased basis.

Table 19 analyzes the principal sources of revenue. It is worth noting that discounts received, which had previously declined, experienced a fairly steady increase after the Strauses entered the firm. This was undoubtedly the result of closer attention to buying terms on the part of the management, with Isidor Straus supplying the main inspiration.

The steady rise in the gross margin percentage figure is especially significant. To some extent it represents a transfer of margin which formerly went to importers and jobbers, for Macy's undoubtedly bought the greater portion of merchandise directly from manufacturers at this time. It also shows that the store was able to pass on to the consumer some of the increased expense resulting from improvements in service and equipment. The fluctuations in "Net Other Income" arise chiefly from changes in the profits derived from importing and manufacturing operations, the latter tending to decrease noticeably toward the close of the period.

The net gain figures prove that the store was relatively profitable in spite of adverse conditions, about six cents going to the owners of the business out of every dollar paid by customers. Certain fluctuations in the earnings figures, together with expense figures given in Table 20, reveal a fairly consistent influence of volume on profits.

TABLE 19

ANALYSIS OF REVENUE
1888–1902

Year[a]	Total Net Sales[b]	Discounts Received	Gross Margin[c]	Operating Profit[d]	Net Other Income[e]	Total Net Gain Amount	Total Net Gain % of Sales
			(Percentage of net sales)				
1888	$5,049,241	3.03	19.08	5.43	.90	$319,556	6.33
1889	5,469,078	3.20	19.50	5.38	1.23	361,510	6.61
1890[c]	5,825,614	3.21	19.70	5.63	1.07	390,307	6.70
1891	5,691,399	3.30	19.53	5.13	.88	342,206	6.01
1892	6,694,965	3.49	20.52	5.42	.82	417,520	6.24
1893	6,653,748	3.42	20.68	5.28	.84	407,110	6.12
1894	6,738,009	3.34	21.07	5.17	.50	382,042	5.67
1895	6,907,144	3.37	20.85	4.94	.56	379,718	5.50
1896[f]	7,095,729	3.32	20.16	3.24	.32	252,940	3.56
1897	6,870,054	3.32	21.22	3.56	.59	285,312	4.15
1898	7,058,955	3.32	22.16	4.61	.60	368,123	5.21
1899	7,825,141	3.53	22.45	5.22	.39	439,032	5.61
1900	8,148,254	3.39	23.19	5.83	.43	510,263	6.26
1901	8,812,171	3.55	23.20	5.77	.45	547,978	6.22
1902[g]	10,765,066	3.95	23.17	4.11	.98	548,151	5.09

[a] Until 1902 the accounting year terminated with the Saturday nearest Dec. 31.
[b] Sales of leased departments are included, but not goods which were sold and subsequently returned.
[c] Gross margin includes cash discounts earned and is the difference between the price received and the net cost of goods sold after deducting all discounts received. The margin contributed by leased departments has also been included.
[d] These figures refer to the profits from retail sales after deducting from the gross margin figure all expenses pertaining to retailing operations (interest on capital has not been included as an expense).
[e] The principal items of other income were profits from importing operations, manufacturing, store laundry, and found money.
[f] Accounting period covered 53 weeks.
[g] Included 57 weeks, ending Jan. 31, 1903, advancing the terminal date of the accounting year from the Saturday nearest Dec. 31 to the one nearest Jan. 31.

Any substantial increase in sales volume usually raised the percentage of operating profit, but even a small drop in sales was likely to bring about an appreciable decline in the profit ratio. The explanation seems to be that increased volume can be handled without a proportionate addition to the plant and operating force, but, once the staff has been built up to a certain level of operations and new space acquired, it is practically impossible to retrench sufficiently to compensate for any decline in business. The sharp drop in 1896 and 1897, however, must be attributed to the pronounced intensification of competition which took place when the Siegel-Cooper and Wanamaker stores opened, together with the increased rental following the opening of the annex. The decline in net income in 1902, marking a clear exception to the above generalization, seems to have resulted from heavy expenses incidental to moving the store to 34th Street.

In many respects the analysis of expenses (Table 20) contains the most significant series of data in this book. It reveals a steady rise in the cost of doing business (relative to sales volume as well as in absolute dollars) during the whole of the period 1888–1902 in the principal categories of expense. The accounting classifications behind these figures are not fully known, and there seems to be some mixing of accounts which prevents positive conclusions about the individual items which make up the total. We know, for example, that the "Salaries" column does not include all money paid out for wages, for the compensation of certain employees has been included in the figures headed "Packing," "Delivery," and "Leased Department Expense." However, there is every indication that the principles and procedures used were uniform throughout the entire period, so that the tendencies revealed may safely be regarded as valid, and the accuracy of the total expense figures can be accepted without any hesitation at all. The rise in the total cost of doing business, from 13.65 per cent of sales in 1888 to 19.06 per cent in 1902, proves that the increasing cost of distribution, which many writers have regarded as essentially attributable to conditions since 1914, was already making substantial progress in the 1890's.

TABLE 20
ANALYSIS OF SELECTED EXPENSES
1888–1902

Year[a]	Total Net Sales[b]	Salaries[c]	Rent[d]	Advertising[e]	Packing[f]	Delivery[g]	Prepaid Freight[h]	Leased Department Expense[i]	Total Expense[j]
				(Percentage of total net sales)					
1888	$5,049,241	7.15	1.59	1.16	.41	.61	.12	.76	13.65
1889	5,469,078	6.99	1.50	1.32	.52	.56	.18	.66	14.12
1890	5,825,614	7.12	1.46	1.23	.52	.73	.22	.69	14.07
1891	5,691,399	7.37	1.52	1.22	.51	.77	.20	.71	14.40
1892	6,694,965	7.31	1.34	1.68	.63	.89	.21	.65	15.10
1893	6,653,748	7.86	1.34	1.57	.56	.88	.23	.63	15.40
1894	6,738,009	7.72	1.36	1.92	.51	1.10	.27	.62	15.90
1895	6,907,144	7.77	1.42	1.48	.47	1.27	.26	.61	15.91
1896	7,095,729	8.38	1.56	1.60	.45	1.44	.23	.62	16.92
1897	6,870,054	8.98	2.13	1.53	.35	1.44	.25	.60	17.66
1898	7,058,955	8.85	2.05	1.87	.34	1.46	.25	.60	17.55
1899	7,825,141	8.55	1.96	1.59	.40	1.55	.23	.56	17.23
1900	8,148,254	8.68	1.81	1.78	.50	1.49	.22	.57	17.36
1901	8,812,171	8.83	1.77	1.67	.48	1.55	.21	.53	17.43
1902	10,765,066	9.51	2.11	2.11	.51	1.65	.19	.53	19.06

TABLE 20 (continued)

[a] Until 1902 the regular accounting year was the 52-week period ending on the Saturday nearest Dec. 31.

[b] Sales in leased departments have been included.

[c] These figures do not include any compensation to the partners. It is possible that a few charges for salary or wages are concealed in other expense figures, but the proportion is certainly not large and is probably about the same year after year.

[d] Includes gas but not electricity or heating expense.

[e] This heading refers mainly to charges incurred for newspaper and magazine space; mail-order catalogs and window display were separately itemized.

[f] Precise charges under this heading are not known, but it apparently refers to materials used in preparing merchandise for delivery or shipment.

[g] Includes stable expense and possibly some salaries.

[h] This column refers to expense incurred as a result of the decision made in April, 1888, to prepay freight on paid purchases of $5.00 or more sent to addresses beyond the store's delivery system but within a radius of 100 miles of New York.

[i] The account from which these figures are derived represented an attempt to segregate certain expenses incurred specifically in leased departments that were not borne by the lessees. Judging from practice in 1910, they were mainly direct payroll expense which would ordinarily be charged as salaries.

[j] In computing total expense the interest charges recorded on the operating statements have been eliminated because it is known that they consisted mainly, if not entirely, of 6% interest imputed on invested capital and money left in the business by partners as a "loan" (no interest was allowed on undivided profits). In making this correction it is possible that we have cut out a few actual disbursements for interest, but the expense so eliminated is unquestionably of negligible amounts. On the whole, this series of expense data is as complete, accurate, and homogeneous as one is ever likely to obtain.

SOURCE: Semiannual statements, 1888–1902.

This increase in the cost of doing business may correctly be attributed to a variety of causes rather than to any single influence. It does not mean that the middleman was getting more profit (his ratio of gain was actually tending to decrease) or that the consumer got less for every dollar spent. One factor involved was the declining tendency of the general price level during much of this period. (If the unit cost of merchandise and the retailing expense remained constant in terms of dollars and cents, the *percentage* ratio of expense would automatically rise simply because of the mathematical relationships involved.) At the same time a part of the increased cost of distribution undoubtedly resulted from additional services which the customers wanted, such as more liberal return privileges, more clerks to wait on trade, delivery service to points in suburban areas, restrooms, elevator service, more attractive buildings, and the like. Approximately half the increase went to the store's employees, apparently in the form of both higher rates of pay and more employees in proportion to sales and customers.

To measure the cost of improved delivery service the figures for delivery and prepaid freight should be combined, for both were involved and there was a certain amount of shifting of expenditure from one category to the other. Thus, the decline in prepaid freight after 1898 simply means that the Macy delivery system had been expanded, with the result that many purchases which would previously have been shipped by freight were thenceforth delivered in Macy wagons.

Certain miscellaneous ratios are presented in Table 21. The first column shows the amount of purchases returned to the store for one reason or another. In the course of ten years the ratio more than doubled, and in 1902, out of every $100 worth of merchandise sold, more than $2.00 worth came back. Compared with modern figures, this rate is very low, but the fact that it increased steadily after 1891 is no less significant.

The data on stock-turns show a decline from 7.90 times in 1888 to 4.64 in 1898, after which there was some improvement. Such a change is sometimes evidence of inefficiency, but it is not necessarily so, and other factors seem to have influenced the Macy rate. The

Straus policy was definitely to increase the available selection of merchandise so that customers would have a better chance of finding what they wanted. This increased the inventory on hand and reduced the rate of stock-turn, but it probably improved sales and

TABLE 21

MISCELLANEOUS OPERATING DATA

1888–1902

Year	Ratio of Returns to Net Sales[a] %	Annual Stock-Turn[b] (Times)	Ratio of Inventory to Total Assets %	Ratio of Fixed Assets to Total Assets %	Ratio of Total Assets To Net Sales %	Ratio of Net Gain to Total Assets %
1888	...	7.90	64.51	5.46	16.37	38.65
1889	...	7.46	69.74	23.40	16.87	39.18
1890	...	7.15	58.66	21.04	19.87	33.72
1891	0.82	6.68	51.86	16.70	24.82	24.22
1892	0.99	6.90	43.89	44.26	27.56	22.63
1893	1.03	6.26	38.90	39.70	33.58	18.22
1894	1.02	6.16	40.88	46.29	33.61	16.87
1895	0.88	5.90	44.76	46.59	33.33	16.49
1896	0.98	5.80	48.24	47.29	32.38	11.01
1897	1.35	4.82	50.19	45.55	36.34	11.43
1898	1.52	4.64	47.17	42.25	38.84	13.42
1899	1.65	4.86	49.90	40.09	36.41	15.41
1900	1.76	4.77	49.31	37.93	36.18	17.30
1901	1.95	4.85	51.78	35.61	35.28	17.63
1902	2.29	5.12	56.77	30.01	35.19	14.47

[a] No data have survived on merchandise returned during the first three years.

[b] Computed by dividing sales at cost by the average inventory at cost, the latter being the average of stocks on hand at the beginning, middle, and end of the 12-month period.

SOURCE: Semiannual statements, 1888–1903.

profits. Another factor was the introduction of lines of slow-moving merchandise, such as rugs and furniture, where sales are invariably low in relation to the amount of stock carried. This undoubtedly accounts for the drop in the rate between 1896 and 1897 (the furniture department was not opened until the middle of September, 1896). The addition of groceries, on the other hand, must have tended to improve the stock-turn rate, although the bulk of the stock consisted of fancy groceries which would not move so fast as staple items. On the whole, the tendency was unquestionably to round out the merchandise carried with items which were not in great demand but which were needed to complete the assortment.

Table 21 also shows the marked effect of the expenditures made after 1888 for buildings and equipment. The proportion of the firm's capital which was invested in fixed assets (land, building, machinery, and fixtures) rose sharply in spite of several substantial write-offs on account of depreciation. In part this simply means that the firm owned assets which it had previously rented, while in part it is the outcome of increased manufacturing activities. At the same time it is a reflection of the growing amount of plant and fixtures — such as an electric light plant, elevators, improved heating equipment, restrooms — required to conduct retail trade. The over-all result may be expressed in another way, as shown in the last two columns. The ratio of total assets to sales more than doubled, while the ratio of net gain to total assets dropped to less than half the rate in 1888.

This last ratio must be interpreted with care, but it unquestionably reveals a decrease in the average productivity of capital invested in the business. At least three factors may be advanced to explain the decline. One is the familiar principle of diminishing returns: it paid the firm to install pneumatic tubes, more elaborate fixtures, and so on, but refinements of this kind did not yield so great a return as the investments in the bare essentials of equipment without which no business could be done. Obviously there was a limit to the amount of money which could be profitably spent on fittings.

The second factor reflected in the decline in productivity was contemporary business conditions. Interest rates had moved steadily downward, and earnings in many industries showed a similar tendency. These indices reflected the difficulty which American business as a whole encountered in making profits at the time. According to one theory, business was under the influence of a downward secular trend which began about 1864 and continued without real abatement until 1897. New industries, not yet subject to intense competition, were not greatly affected, but those which were maturely developed could do little beyond trying to ride out the storms. According to this view, Macy's enjoyed prosperity in the 1870's despite adverse conditions because it was well in the vanguard with the department store concept and its competition consisted largely of small, specialized stores. In the 1880's and '90's, however, competition between department stores had emerged, and Macy's began to conform to the trend.[43]

Whether one accepts the theory of the secular trend or not, contemporary conditions must be kept in mind. They undoubtedly hampered the progress of Macy's during both the 'eighties and the 'nineties. I am inclined, however, to regard conditions between 1890 and 1897 as more unfavorable than those in the 1880's; for this reason it seems to me that the managerial performance of the Strauses was superior to that of their immediate predecessors, even though the results in terms of sales volume and profits showed no remarkable improvement. This judgment is supported by the analysis of promotional efforts set forth in the following chapter.

The third factor involved in the decrease in the productivity of Macy capital was the maturing of the department store trade in New York City. With the rise of competition from other full-fledged department stores — strong rivals who possessed the same advantages of organization, size, and managerial techniques — the Macy store no longer enjoyed a privileged position. It had to fight hard to maintain its business, resorting to forms of competition which involved new capital outlays and cut into profits.

In other words, the increase in assets employed in the business between 1888 and 1902 is, among various things, another manifestation that competition was shifting to some extent from price and wide selection of merchandise to equipment and services. Such a shift is by no means to the discredit of the firm or the public. People had a choice between buying in department stores and trading in the small, specialized stores. They exercised that choice by favoring the department stores. No one — unless he proclaims an arbitrary standard of value or efficiency — can say that they were wrong in doing so. They simply voted for Progress.

CHAPTER XI

HEYDAY OF 14TH STREET

To move the enormous quantities of merchandise which Macy's stocked, it was necessary, of course, to attract customers to the store. If the firm was to survive and grow, people had to be encouraged to want more goods than they would ordinarily consume without urging, and they had to be induced to buy at Macy's rather than at rival stores. In short, the Macy firm had a continuing problem of sales promotion. Rowland Macy had handled it superbly; Webster and Wheeler had met it rather ineffectively. Under Straus management the work of sales promotion was once again attacked with spirit and resource.

Throughout the period from 1888 to 1902, as before, newspaper advertising was the chief means of stimulating Macy trade, but a number of other devices were also employed, including special sales, publicity efforts, unusual store exhibitions, window displays, and an elaboration of facilities designed to attract customers by making the task of shopping easier and more pleasant.

The problem of sales promotion after 1888 was aggravated by a number of difficulties which Rowland Macy had not had to face — at least, not to the same degree. One of them was the need to overcome the inertia which the store had developed during a régime of complacent, overcautious management. Another was the competition of powerful and competent rivals. The third was the necessity of working against depressed business conditions of unusual severity. The Straus brothers surmounted these obstacles and made the business grow. During the early 'nineties, 14th Street was the Mecca of New York shoppers, and Sixth Avenue was the liveliest part of it. This state of affairs — a happy one for the Macy firm — was not wholly the result of Straus policy or action, but the new management was an important factor in the store's ability to advance in the face of bitter competition. No summary account can convey a detailed picture of the various promotional activities of Macy's at this time — they changed from day to day and ought to be studied in relation to competitors' efforts — but it is possible to outline the principal policies which seem to be revealed.

Lastly, having traced the growth of the store between 1888 and 1902 and examined some of the principal factors in its expansion, we shall be in a position to analyze and appraise its management.

Extent of the Advertising Effort

As shown by the operating figures presented in the preceding chapter, the amount of money spent on Macy advertising increased substantially during this period, with only occasional minor setbacks. It rose from $58,500 in 1888 to $72,000 in 1889, jumped to $112,000 in 1892, on up to $129,000 in 1894, and then, after hesitating for several years, it advanced to $145,000 in 1900 and leaped beyond the $200,000 mark in 1902. The growing efforts to win business were reflected not only in the actual sums spent each year, but also in the ratio of such expenditures to business done: by 1902 the ratio of advertising expense to sales was nearly twice that of 1888. Often during the 1890's, as Isidor Straus explained to his brother, sales had to be maintained "by artificial stimulants . . . at the expense of profit," although he recognized limitations on such procedure.[1]

A clue to at least part of the increased expenditures is contained in a letter from Isidor Straus to Webster:[2]

You will observe that I have deducted $15,000 from the net result and placed it to the credit of a new a/c called "Advertising Reserve." I did this at the urgent request of Nathan as a nest egg for an ammunition bag with which to fight our Chicago friends [Siegel-Cooper] when they open. Nathan claims that when they open, profits will fly in every direction and he desires therefore to accumulate a fund which can be used, and thereby save handicapping a lean season with extraordinary drafts for advertising.

The opening of the Siegel-Cooper store in 1896 did start a heavy barrage of advertising, and the battle was intensified when John

Wanamaker, whose propensity for publicizing his business is now legendary, acquired the bankrupt remnants of A. T. Stewart's once flourishing business and forthwith attempted to attain in New York the dominant position that he had won in Philadelphia. More than Nathan's original "nest egg" was needed to keep profits from flying, for, in the midst of the growing flood of advertising, ever increasing quantities of space and constantly improving skill were required to make a showing.

In the early part of the period, Macy's followed the general practice of the leading New York stores by concentrating advertisements in the Sunday papers, usually employing for this purpose from one to five columns in the *Herald, Sun,* and *Tribune.* Occasional pieces of copy appeared on one or two weekdays in the *Commercial Advertiser, Evening Post, Evening Telegram,* or *World,* ordinarily occupying from two to five column inches only. Full-page advertisements were rare, but Macy's began to use them now and then after late 1891. Between 1889 and 1893 the store sought to obtain special advantage by avoiding the pages on which competitors' advertisements, by long tradition, were gathered together: Macy copy appeared regularly as the only advertisement on a page of reading matter, and it was usually placed opposite articles of special interest to women. (While this is familiar practice today, it was not so in the 'nineties.) The store's advertisements, as a result of such tactics, must have attracted more than the usual number of readers.[3]

During most of 1893 and 1894, Macy's used five (out of six) columns on the front page of the Sunday *Herald,* but repeated increases in front-page space rates led Isidor Straus to return to inside pages. He was pleased to observe that no competitor rushed to seize the preferred position thus released. "I guess," he wrote to Nathan, "Mr. Bennett will find that there is a limit even to dry goods extravagance."[4] However, if Bennett was overeager in 1894, he was correct in judging the trend: Sunday papers expanded rapidly, and by 1898 the front page of each section typically bore the advertisement of one of the city's leading department stores.

Until 1896 the Macy management was content to do noticeably less advertising than such competitors as Ehrich Brothers, Hearn's, and Denning's. Isidor suspected that the difference in amount spent was so much gain for Macy's, evidently judging that any additional expenditures during depressed years would not bring increased volume.[5] By 1898, however, the quantity of Macy newspaper advertising had increased relatively to the others until, as far as one can judge from appearances, it was a close match for the efforts of the principal rivals — Simpson Crawford, Wanamaker's, Ehrich Brothers, Bloomingdale's, Adams Co., and Siegel-Cooper.

At the close of the decade, the store relied chiefly upon space in the *Herald, Journal, Sun,* and *Commercial Advertiser,* with occasional advertisements appearing in the *Mail & Express, Times, Telegram,* and New York *Staats Zeitung.* It had ceased to use the *Evening Post* and the *Tribune* and was in the process of dropping the *World*.[6] While the reason for changes in media is not altogether clear, the Macy management abandoned the *Post,* as John Wanamaker did, because of its editorial policy:[7]

This firm has, for a long time, paid for space in the *Evening Post,* wherein to set forth to its readers that R. H. Macy & Co. sold goods to its customers at the lowest possible price consistent with the best quality, and when that paper editorially told its readers that these statements were falsehoods, which is the only possible deduction from its articles attempting to show that goods can be purchased cheaper abroad, with duty added (ergo, N. Y. merchants charge more than a legitimate profit), that paper ceased to have any value as an advertising medium to us.

Typical Macy practice by 1898 (and this is true of many of the other stores, too) was to insert a five- or six-column advertisement on Sundays in the papers principally employed, using at least one single-column advertisement in them daily during the week. This program was supplemented from time to time by small advertisements in the other papers named. Thus, despite the growing volume of retail advertising, the city's vast army of newspaper readers could hardly escape seeing a Macy announcement at least once a day.

The store also employed a few magazines as advertising media. At the beginning of the period both the English and German editions of *Puck* were used, together with *Leslie's Illustrated Weekly* and *The Youth's Companion*, and possibly one or two more. Magazine advertising was not well suited to the store's needs because too much time ordinarily elapsed between the placing of copy and its appearance before readers. "The nature of our business is such," Isidor Straus wrote to one publisher, "that goods will in most instances be closed out before we are able to announce through you that we have them for sale." Despite this difficulty, Macy advertisements were occasionally inserted in *Munsey's*, *Ladies' Home Journal*, *Delineator*, *Trotter and Pacer*, and *Field, Turf and Farm* — the last two probably because of Nathan Straus's personal hobby rather than strictly business considerations.[8]

Until about 1900 the store gave away fans of the type that used to be commonly seen in churches, in homes, and at Chautauqua meetings a generation ago — a piece of cardboard on a stick, bearing a picture on one side and an advertisement on the other. And, in the early 'nineties at least, it also passed out chromolithographed trade cards, advertising booklets, and other souvenirs, such as the picture of General Grant handed out to store visitors in 1897. By 1902, however, the management had taken a definite stand against the once popular but usually unprofitable practice of inserting advertisements in programs of charitable or social organizations, preferring not to confuse business objectives with donations to community enterprises.[9]

The fact that a sewing-machine manufacturer allowed Macy's $100 a month for streetcar advertising during 1893 suggests that car cards formed still another medium which the store employed. In addition, a number of painted outdoor signs were maintained in positions calculated to catch the eyes of "el" passengers.[10]

Two other types of printed advertising used by the store require brief mention. One is a store magazine, called the *Macy Journal*, which was published, apparently bimonthly, during 1893 and the early part of 1894. It was sold at two cents a copy and evidently contained fashion notes and other material of special interest to women, probably similar to a publication which Ridley's of Grand Street had issued for many years. The *Macy Journal* ceased before it was two years old, having cost the firm over $10,000.[11]

The other promotional device referred to above is the store catalog, which appeared annually during this period. Few copies survive today, but that of 1891 was a substantial volume of 307 pages, containing an enormous list of merchandise and numerous illustrations. It was intended for mail-order customers mainly, and the frequent mention of mail orders in the store's advertising indicates that a vigorous effort was being made to develop the kind of business which Montgomery Ward had brought into prominence. Only 5,000 copies were printed in 1888 and 15,000 in 1889, but the succeeding editions, judging by the cost of publication and mailing, must have been very large. To defray the expense of this medium, the firm sold a certain number of pages of advertising in it to manufacturers and dealers whose merchandise was stocked by the store. In 1889, for example, it was estimated that the advertising revenue would exceed the direct printing costs. Of course other expenses more than absorbed the difference. The store issued a special catalog of perfumes and toilet requisites in 1894, and by 1898, if not earlier, a grocery and liquor catalog began to appear several times each year.[12]

Macy Advertising Copy, 1888–1902

Apart from the increased use of space, there was little about the department store advertising of the 1890's to impress the modern student. Magazine copy at this time was beginning to reflect technical progress in the art of commercial propaganda, but newspaper advertisements for various reasons clung to obsolete tradition. Layouts were unattractive: prevailing practice, even after newspapers had relaxed the restrictions against display type and broken columns, was to place the copy within the conventional columns, breaking them only to spread a heading across the advertisement. Within the columns the items of merchandise to be offered were listed in close-set type, giving prices but practically no description. There was seldom any message beyond the list of goods and prices; if one was included, the text was, by modern standards at least, prosaic and dull. The deadly effect of a five- or six-column advertisement arranged in this fashion can easily be imagined. When any store attempted to depart from the prevailing practice, the results were usually forced and inept. For the most part, rival firms contested with one another by means of screaming headlines, large amounts of space, and (allegedly) unprecedented price bargains — like warriors using bludgeons instead of rapiers.

This general comment applied, without many qualifications, to Macy advertisements of the period. They were definitely above the average in appearance and general interest, and they were among the very few to show any improvement during the period under observation. They exhibited, however, little of the spontaneous originality and sparkling variety which had put the early Macy advertising into a class by itself. As an instance of the stereotyped character which was too often evident at the time, there is the phrase, which the store publicized in 1890 and even later, "every variety of holiday goods to suit the purses of the million as well as the millionaire." This not especially brilliant idea, with very slight alteration, had been repeated periodically by Macy's since 1884. Again, a piece of institutional copy (reproduced on page 271), which had first appeared early in 1889, was repeated almost verbatim in the catalog for 1891; and parts of it were used in daily newspaper advertisements over several years. It was above average in quality, to be sure, but certainly not beyond improvement.[13]

To the rash of slogans which broke out in contemporary advertising, apparently the best response Macy copywriters could make was the uninspired phrase, "The attraction of our stores is their very low prices." Similarly, an effort to achieve a striking headline by means of alliteration fell flat with "A Rousing Riddance Rug Sale — Rattled Prices!" or "Macy's Methods Mark Macy's Name for Fame." An attempt to avoid the commonplace was likely to involve such ponderous verbiage as "The irresistible fascination of unwearying energy is the potential influence that is widening, brightening, and heightening the destiny of our enterprise."[14] Florid effusions of this kind, it may be well to remind the reader, were a perfect counterpart of the over-elaborate styles prevailing in women's clothing and the extraordinary gingerbread trimmings that men were putting on contemporary architecture. Everyday America was striving for aesthetic effect at a time when taste, both here and in Europe, was mostly bad. We must not condemn Macy copywriters for failing to rise above their cultural environment.

Definite improvement in Macy advertising copy is discernible over a period of years. The real test of advertising is, of course, the effect on sales. Macy's volume increased, but it is impossible to say how much of that increase was attributable to the current advertising. (To be sure, it is still not possible to assemble conclusive evidence on such matters, although substantial progress has been made in analyzing the effects of advertising.) From time to time the store published institutional advertisements which stressed Macy bargains, facilities, and policy. Some of these stand out as superior to anything that I have been able to discover in contemporary retail promotion (John Wanamaker's not excepted), and the following copy, which appeared in 1889, is a fair sample:[15]

THESE ARE SEVEN LAMPS OF ARCHITECTURE OF OUR BUSINESS

RECIPROCITY

For every cent expended in our store we return full value, because we give no credit, and, therefore, incur no losses. The cash buyer is not taxed to pay for uncollectible accounts. There is no discrimination made at our counters between the small person and the great, the rich and the poor, the experienced and the inexperienced. All have the same advantages, and no one is given any special concession, discount, or commission.

ENTERPRISE

We are the only retail house having offices and running factories in all parts of the world. To enumerate a few of these, we make Handkerchiefs and Linen Goods in Belfast, Ireland; Fine China in Limoges, France; Underwear in New Haven, Conn.; Hamburg Embroideries at St. Gall, Switzerland; Ornamental Glassware in Steinschönau, Bohemia; Shirts in Poughkeepsie, N. Y.; Ivory and Bisque in Rudolstadt, Thuringia; China at Carlsbad, Bohemia, with foreign offices in Belfast, Ireland, and Paris, France. We have the greater portion of our stock at first hand, and require no middle-men between us and the makers of the goods. We thus bring producer and consumer into the closest possible relations, to the advantage of both.

UNIFORMITY

We have but one price, and hold out no alluring bargains in one department to facilitate selling goods at high price in another. Every article in our store is a BARGAIN. We have no "leaders," and therefore no lame and halting array of superannuated articles. Plus a fraction of profit on distribution, all our prices are manufacturers' prices, and every department is conducted in the interest of the purchasing public.

ADAPTIVENESS

We carry no dead stock, and we allow no department to get into a rut. We are prompt to introduce novelties and quick to discern new currents of public demand. In most cases the manufacturer takes his initiative from us, not we from the manufacturer. Standing, as we do, in close and constant contact with all classes of purchasers, and controlling, as we do, a vast organization of productive forces, the fault must be ours if we fail to satisfy every taste, minister to every want, and meet every necessity within the limits of our business.

ECONOMY

The cash system is the cheapest, alike for buyer and seller. It relieves the seller of all expense save that of handling the goods. There is no costly system of bookkeeping, and no needless locking up of capital. Credit is a convenience for which some one must pay; the ability to buy for cash is equivalent to a command of cash, from which its possessor ought to profit. The cash system makes cautious and critical purchasers, and the business that attains vast proportions under it is necessarily conducted on a sound basis. The crowds that daily throng our store bear eloquent testimony to its merits.

INTEGRITY

We never offer more of a given article at a given price than we have to sell. If the amount in stock is limited, it is so declared, and neither exaggerated nor understated. Absolute accuracy is the uniform characteristic of every claim made in our advertisements, and no employee is permitted to make representations about goods which cannot be sustained. We tolerate no conventional weights or measures. A pound never means 14 ounces; a dozen yards always means 12 times 36 inches. There is nothing so lasting in business as the simple truth, and nothing that will stand the test of time like scrupulous honesty.

MODERATION

We have everything to gain by trading on a narrow margin of profit. We could not fill our shelves with goods at the lowest prices known in the market if we did not produce them or buy them on a large scale, and we could not sell on a large scale unless we gave the public the benefit of our close buying and cheap production. Huge as is the volume of our business, it keeps steadily growing, because the cost of conducting it is a hardly perceptible element in the price of any article, and because the smallest percentage of profit suffices for an adequate return on the whole.

Another ran, in part: [16]

UNDER THE RED STAR

I suppose that in this city there are thousands upon thousands of people who know not one star in the heavens from another, who are yet thoroughly familiar with the red star. . . .

And truly it is a star which has brought comfort and consolation to . . . people . . . trying to find out what to get and where. . . .

Better still was a third example: [17]

Follow the crowd and it will always take
you to
R. H. MACY & CO.
What better evidence do you wish that ours is
The All Around Store
of New York City? Ride our bicycles,
read our books, cook in our saucepans,
dine off our china, wear our silks,
get under our blankets, smoke our cigars,
drink our wines
— Shop At Macy's —
and life will
Cost You Less and Yield You More
Than You Dreamed Possible.

. . . .

Toward the close of the 'nineties a number of improvements began to appear gradually in Macy advertising. There was less crowding, better arrangement of headings and subdivisions, larger type, and more white space, with the result that the advertisements were more distinctive in appearance and much easier to read. The incessant emphasis on mere price was lessened, and an attempt was made to describe the merchandise briefly and attractively — so that occasionally the copy had a modern ring: "Golf Capes — The Scotchiest garments you ever saw — the canniest colors and the bonniest plaids." While not exactly factual, descriptions of this sort were a vast improvement over lists which gave nothing but the name of the item and a price, and they must have aroused considerable interest in the store's offerings. Sales appeals were beginning to replace mere announcements as rival stores, in ever intensifying competition for volume and profits, sought (perhaps unwittingly) to induce customers to vie with one another in consumption.

There were faint signs, too, of an awareness that retail advertising in New York could stand some restraint in the interest of greater veracity. "We'd welcome legislative enactment restraining the present freedom of the advertising pen. Our own advertisements are limited to exact facts. We do not allow even the slenderest margin for flubdub. Every word is weighed, every claim verified before given to the types." [18] One must not take such a statement too seriously. Macy copy had contained obvious exaggerations in the past and was to involve some in the future. The assertion just quoted was itself overstepping the bounds of truth. But henceforth there seemed to be a realization that claims ought to be kept somewhere near the bounds of possibility.[19] It is not surprising, therefore, to find some genuine candor in an announcement of a sale of silks: "Among the latter are several patterns that are a bit passé, but they are all right in respect to quality and the effects will please many whose tastes are not controlled by the novelties of the period." [20]

Unlike Wanamaker, Siegel-Cooper, and a number of other large stores, Macy's apparently did not employ any of the well-known copywriters. Nathan Straus was in charge of all publicity, and, while he undoubtedly hired specialists to handle the work of the advertising office, he seems not to have been interested in buying superlative talent. One of the store's advertisements suggests why:[21]

> Macy advertising ... contains news of goods and facts concerning prices that claim the thoughtful attention of the conservative and the thrifty. We do not write for literary stylists and critics. ... Our English may not be classic, but the motives, principles, and theories it advocates are sound and honest.

If there is a faint odor of sour grapes about this statement, there is also embedded in it a large kernel of sound policy: fine words do not necessarily make good bargains and they may cost a great deal of money. In the period under observation no one could really assert that the Macy management erred on the side of having too clever advertising copy.

Display and Publicity

Window displays formed still another means of promoting sales, but no information has survived about this aspect of the Macy business, apart from the special Christmas windows, annual events to which New Yorkers, young and old, looked forward. These exhibitions, involving hundreds of mechanical figures, lasted a full month and were costly to stage, even if one does not accept at face value the assertion that a single season's display cost $10,000. It is, of course, impossible to calculate the patronage and goodwill that they created, but the yield was undoubtedly large.[22] Apart from this yearly event, the firm seems to have frowned upon lavish window decoration. "Elaborate scenic store displays are costly," ran one Macy advertisement. "They add to the expenses of merchandising and are paid for by customers. Our ingenuity and industry are devoted to securing values for patrons. Money saving is the Macy ideal of proper service."[23] A skeptical person might connect this attitude with the fact that certain rival stores possessed new buildings and could easily arrange windows which would outshine those of Macy's.

As in earlier years, the store periodically arranged special events or stunts which would attract attention. In 1891 and for a number of years afterward, the store saluted spring with a series of coaching expeditions. Passengers paid $2.50 for the privilege of riding in "the elegant four-in-hand 'The Lakewood'" from the store to High Bridge and back.[24] Thus Nathan Straus pursued his favorite hobby, while many people had fun, and the store reaped a certain amount of publicity.

In 1895 Macy's imported two horseless carriages from France (made by Roger and powered by Benz motors). Since they were the first to be brought from Europe, they attracted a great deal of attention, standing in front of the store and later running about the city. They were used to a limited extent for deliveries, but Isidor Straus explained privately that they were "more for advertising purposes than for practical use." One of them was entered in the famous *Times-Herald* race which took place on Thanksgiving day from Jackson Park, Illinois, to Evanston and back. On account of bad roads, plans to drive to Chicago had to be abandoned after the car reached Schenectady, but it participated in the race and was one of the three to finish, the prize going to the American-made Duryea.[25]

When the bicycle craze was at its height, Macy's constructed a track on the third floor of the store and staged hourly exhibitions of trick riding. The Spanish-American War provided another opportunity for publicity: Macy's stretched an enormous American flag across 14th Street, "the largest United States' flag in the world."[26]

Of more direct relation to retailing were the special promotions which Macy's arranged from time to time to stimulate the sale of merchandise. The spring and fall seasons were opened with special exhibitions of imported Parisian models. (The opening in 1888 had to be postponed a week because the famous March blizzard struck New York on the very day originally scheduled.) Twice a year there were pre-inventory sales to reduce stocks and post-inventory sales to clear old merchandise, and in 1890 Macy's tied Wanamaker's in Philadelphia for the honor of starting the now universal August sales, designed to stimulate trade during the dull season. The explanation given for the August sale in later years was a desire "to keep our factories and workrooms busy."[27] Similarly, the store began to feature sales of school outfits as early as 1888, and February furniture sales in 1898. In addition to this type of seasonal promotion, destined to become regular events in department-store life, there were occasional sales intended to accomplish some special objective. Thus, we find Macy's staging a practical demonstration of Keystone eggbeaters and Good Morning coffeepots, an 1889 version of the kind of introductory promotional work which now goes on in some section of the vast Macy basement every day. Then there was the one-day sale of Foster's Hook Gloves, reduced from $2.00 to 99 cents to induce customers to try them — "not over three pairs to be sold to a customer." When trade lagged in 1898, a "great May sale" was held "to beat '97 at any price." And for a while in 1901 the store featured "Macyettes," special bargains scattered throughout all departments to tempt patrons to explore the store. With rare exceptions, the Macy sales lasted from several days to several weeks, a practice which contrasted with the one-day events conducted by certain rivals.[28]

Lastly, efforts were occasionally made to feature merchandise which would tie in with prominent happenings of the day. As the Columbian Centennial approached, the store brought out a large selection of Italian filigree silver, including a Columbus souvenir spoon, "all made doubly interesting as mementos . . . from the fact that they were made in Genoa, Italy, the birthplace of the great navigator." After the sinking of the *Maine*, to give another instance, the store promptly offered plates and cups and saucers bearing pictures of the ill-fated battleship, and Admiral Dewey's return in the following year led to a special sale of flags and another flood of china souvenirs.[29]

To a public which is so prodded by an endless series of special promotions that it sometimes seems to have become benumbed and indifferent, these efforts may appear to be much ado about nothing — feverish attempts which accomplish little beyond cramming into a few hectic days the shopping that customers would otherwise do at a slower pace. The Macy sales figures (see Chart 1) indicate, however, that the firm altered its seasonal pattern materially by such means, bringing up the low months of January, July, and August, and leveling off to some extent the peaks formerly hit in May, No-

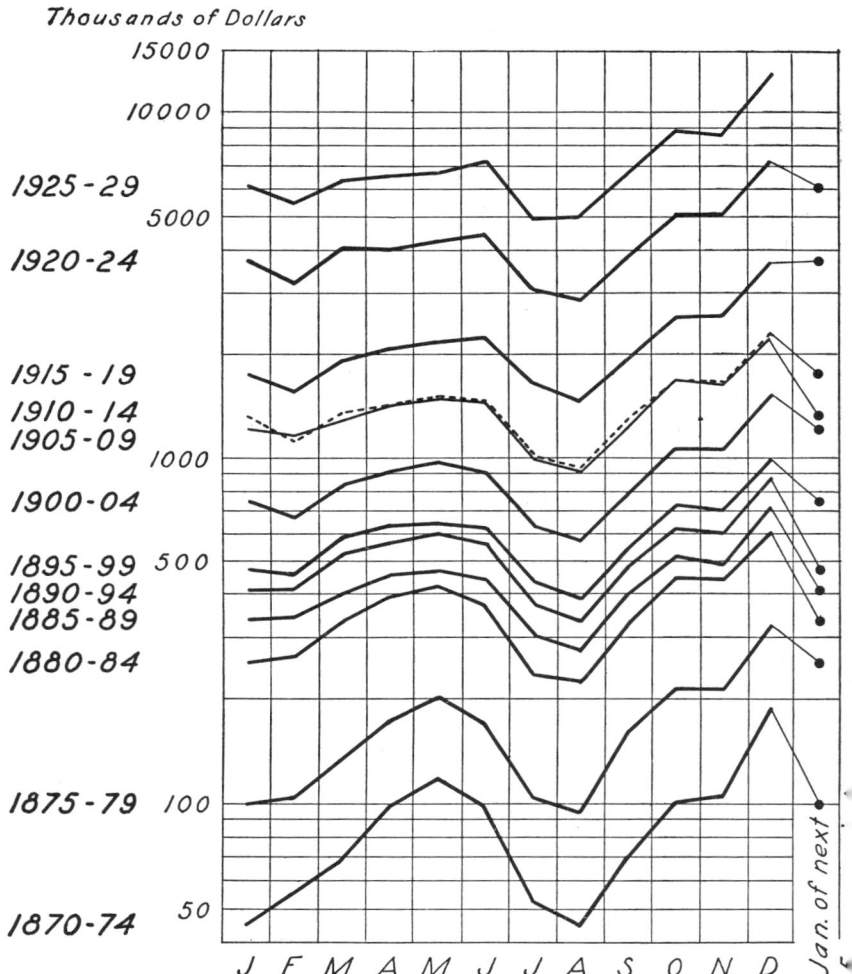

CHART I. AVERAGE MONTHLY SALES, FIVE-YEAR PERIODS, 1870–1929 SHOWING SEASONAL PATTERN OF SALES

vember, and December. Of course, one must recognize that some of this result may be attributed to the increasing variety of goods stocked, but the lines of merchandise added in the 'nineties suggest that most of them must have tended to intensify the existing seasonal pattern rather than correct it. In any case, it is evident that the combined promotional activities played an essential part in the growth of Macy's during this period.

New Store Services

During the period under survey, Macy's expanded the various services which patrons might have without extra charge. Indeed, it was at this time that American department stores generally taught the public to expect a great deal from the retailer beyond mere merchandise. Like the increase of advertising efforts which accompanied it, this growth in store services was a reflection of the intensifying competition of the era. Granted that the merchandise was of acceptable quality, people tended to patronize the stores which gave them the most attractive surroundings, the most convenient delivery, and the most satisfactory all-around treatment. Once the store owners discovered that price was not the sole means of attracting customers, they promptly began to exploit services and equipment. Another factor in the change was the continued urbanization of the community, for matters like expeditious delivery and the right to return unwanted goods attain primary importance to people who, coming long distances to shop, are prevented by circumstances from trading on the personal basis that prevails in small towns. At the same time, the accumulation of wealth in the city inevitably develops standards of luxury and elegance to which even poor immigrants are bound to respond.

The most noticeable innovation in Macy service at this time was the extension of free delivery to a greatly enlarged geographical area. On April 15, 1888, the store advertised that "From this date we prepay freight to all towns within a radius of 100 miles on paid purchases of $5 and over." Previously the store had provided free delivery only within the limits reached by its own delivery system, which at the time included Manhattan Island, Jersey City, and

Brooklyn. It must be said at once that Macy's did not start the innovation of prepaid freight. Just which firm pioneered in this marked extension of free delivery in New York is a matter of doubt, but the initiative seems to have been taken by a few stores of minor importance. During 1887, if not earlier, J. Lichtenstein & Sons, Grand Street, had advertised an offer similar to that which Macy's made in 1888, while Callahan & Morrissey, only a few doors from Macy's, had offered free freight within 50 miles, and H. O'Neill & Co. had set the limit at 75 miles. Among the better-known stores, however, Macy's seems to have taken the lead, and its announcement touched off a series of similar offers by Denning's, Ridley's, Daniell's, Ehrich's, and other competing firms. Ehrich's raised the ante by paying half the freight within 200 miles, and one-third within 300 miles, but the standard practice soon settled down to prepayment within a radius of 100 miles, with a minimum requirement of a $5.00 prepaid purchase.[30]

Macy's own delivery system likewise gradually increased its coverage: routes were established in Newark, Orange, and Bayonne, New Jersey, in 1891; Bloomfield, Montclair, and Elizabeth, New Jersey, in 1893; Long Island City, Bay Ridge, Bath Beach, and Flatbush, on Long Island, in 1894; Guttenberg and Rutherford, New Jersey, in 1895; Paterson and Englewood, New Jersey, in 1896; and by 1900 Macy wagons were regularly serving such distant points in New Jersey as Plainfield and Morristown. Meanwhile, the store had established special summer routes in order to bring Macy merchandise within easy reach of customers who spent the hot months along the Jersey coast and the southern shore of Long Island. By 1896 these summer deliveries reached as far south as Asbury Park and Bradley Beach, New Jersey, and as far east as Far Rockaway and Cedarhurst on Long Island.[31]

A few surviving statistics reveal that in 1896-97 Macy's delivered packages at the rate of over 2,500,000 a year. About three-fourths of these were delivered by Macy's own delivery department, and the rest, going mainly to distant suburbs, were carried by delivery facilities hired under contract. According to a delivery department memo for 1897, the cost of delivery averaged about 8.75 cents per package when delivered by hired carriers and 7.85 when handled by Macy's own system.

Improvements in Macy delivery included special service at Christmas. As early as 1888 the store began to guarantee that purchases made on December 24 would be delivered to addresses within the city on the same day or, if desired, on Christmas day. The number of packages delivered during December, 1889, was 162,624 — only a big day's work in recent years, but a heavy month for the horse-and-buggy era. To accomplish this feat, the store had to hire extra men and wagons, plus more than a hundred messenger boys, and the whole delivery staff was obliged to work interminable hours overtime.[32]

In expanding its delivery service, as in putting forth greater promotional efforts, Macy's was, of course, reaching out for more business, encouraging customers from suburban towns to shop at 14th Street for all their wants. It could not have done so successfully had not the streetcars, the elevated railways, and the various other commuting services continually increased the mobility of the inhabitants of greater New York. (The Sixth Avenue Elevated even ran special trains from 14th Street during the late afternoon rush hours.) But this obvious response to better transportation had to be translated into horses, wagons, stables, men and boys, and a complicated system for directing the flow of merchandise and controlling the efforts of an army of workers. To make good the store's promises, there were times when even a partner's son had to work all night, trying to bring order out of chaos. While there had been a faint hope that the horseless carriages of 1895 — faster than horses and not requiring rest — would ease the delivery problem, they had proved impractical. In 1902 the firm acquired a motor truck as another experiment, using it to convey goods from freight depots to the store, but satisfactory motor transportation was still a thing of the future. For a time the answer continued to be more men and wagons, larger stables at 19th Street, a delivery branch and stables at 148th Street (acquired in 1896), and the employment of delivery contractors in suburban areas.[33]

Macy's cash policy automatically eliminated one of the services which most stores offered, that of allowing customers to buy on credit. In this matter the management sternly refused to budge an inch, for cash was the keystone of the major policy of keeping prices down. Occasionally, to oblige some customer, one of the partners would pay for the merchandise selected and personally extend credit, but the store itself brooked no exceptions to the rule. On at least one occasion the firm sincerely regretted that no discretion was allowed. Mrs. Hobson, mother of the famous naval hero, sent for a pair of slippers for her son and failed to enclose payment. When the slippers were not immediately forthcoming, she complained of discourtesy, and the management, with the memories of the Santiago Bay episode still fresh, sent a letter of apology and explanation: [34]

> When your order was received, the clerk . . . treated it in accordance with our strict rules. . . . We feel distressed that the matter was not placed before one of the firm, who would more than welcome the opportunity of being of even the slightest service to your illustrious son by paying for the slippers, facilitating the delivery, and afterwards sending you the bill.

Mrs. Hobson was not the only person who received a polite explanation of the firm's cash policy, but neither fame nor fortune would induce the store to make an exception.

There is some evidence that Macy's began to be more generous in allowing customers to return purchases. Macy had long guaranteed satisfaction, offering to exchange goods or refund money if the customer found fault with the merchandise. Nothing is known about the early administration of this policy, but correspondence which has survived proves that it was no empty promise after 1887. When a customer complained, the store promptly sent for the goods and made an adjustment. Since the public had not yet become completely spoiled, the store examined the grounds for complaint before making a settlement, thus protecting itself to some extent against unscrupulous shoppers, but it is clear that legitimate claims were given prompt and reasonable adjustment. The percentage of returns, though smaller than today, more than doubled between 1891 and 1902, indicating a more liberal treatment of customers. In matters of weight and measurement, where the shopper might not readily detect shortages, the store management specified that any margin of error should be in the customer's favor even if stock shortages should result.[35]

The store introduced a new service in 1895 by giving free lessons in the art of riding a bicycle to all purchasers of the "Webster" wheel. To this end it established a "bicycle academy," first in the old Scotch Presbyterian Church on 14th Street, across from the store, and later in the former Hotel de Logerot Garden on 18th, near Fifth Avenue. The expense of maintaining this instruction was more than $3,000 a year.[36]

Late in the 'nineties came more services of the kind that we take for granted now. Within the limits of the area covered by Macy's delivery system the store's employees would set up, without extra cost, stoves or ranges bought in the store. In 1895 Macy's offered to store free of charge until November 15 goods purchased in September, and customers who bought furniture were given 60 days of free storage after the new department was opened. Another device which the firm subsequently introduced to facilitate shopping was that of sending a man to estimate the cost of furnishing a house or any part of it, and the grocery department at the same time began to publicize expert service in packing and shipping supplies for yacht cruises, camping trips, and the like.[37]

Improved Store Facilities

Among the inducements which Macy's offered to customers were such comforts as improved elevator service, larger floor space to relieve crowding, and attractive restrooms. Incandescent electric lighting began to replace the sputtering uncertainty of gas mantles throughout the store in 1888.[38] In the following year the firm opened salesrooms on the third floor and provided three passenger elevators to overcome the average customer's reluctance to go so far above the street floor:[39]

The comfort of our patrons is greatly improved by this change, and, as we will, if desired, deliver goods sold now at any designated day, the SAVING OF AT LEAST 25 PER CENT. IN PURCHASING OF US becomes an object even to those whom the crush and crowd of former years precluded from availing themselves thereof.

To provide still more space for the ever increasing crowds the Macy firm again began to add to its premises by buying land adjacent to the store and remodeling or constructing additional buildings. The property at 56 West 14th was added to the store early in 1890.[40] During 1891 Macy's put up a six-story addition extending eastward from the existing quarters on 13th Street through Nos. 59 to 63, completing the process of occupation during the first part of 1892. Incorporated in it was a new ladies' waiting-room:[41]

> It is the most luxurious and beautiful department
> devoted to the comfort of ladies to be found
> in a mercantile establishment in the city.
> The style of decoration is Louis XV,
> and no expense has been spared
> in the adornment and furnishing of this room.
> On the way to it you will pass through
> our new art room, containing a most complete
> and carefully selected line of
> onyx, bronze, . . .

As a part of the attraction of the new artroom the firm hung a collection of oil paintings which represented an investment of $11,200. Firms like Macy's in New York, Wanamaker's in Philadelphia, and Marshall Field's in Chicago thought they saw profits in bringing art to the public.[42]

The new building on 13th Street had increased the store's floor space by 75,000 square feet, but new departments, additional sales promotion, and the city's rapid growth in population kept the store continually crowded. There must have been complaints, for the management felt obliged to urge that customers avoid the two entrances on 14th Street, which were usually jammed, and come in by one of the three entrances on Sixth Avenue or the two on 13th Street. "We would especially recommend the 13th Street entrance to carriage shoppers who come after 10 o'clock." Some relief was afforded in 1893 by the incorporation of another building on 13th,

Nos. 55 and 57, which provided an additional 25,000 feet of space and three more elevators.[43]

Although the panic of '93, meanwhile, had caused a short halt in plans for further expansion, 1894 saw the management again trying to obtain more space. It proved impossible to acquire any additional land to the east, and the owners of the land at the corner of 14th and Sixth Avenue refused to put up a new and taller building to meet the need, except on terms which the Strauses regarded as wholly unreasonable. As a temporary expedient the firm moved its cigar and liquor departments across the street in 1895 to 59 West 14th, and arranged to have a syndicate of Boston capitalists put up a six-story annex on the north side of 14th Street, Nos. 53–57, directly opposite the store's main entrance and running through to 15th, Nos. 54 and 56. Opening in the depths of the 1896 depression, the new annex was devoted principally to merchandise of special interest to men and boys; clothing, furnishings, and shoes were sold on the first floor; harness and "horse goods," sporting goods, and bicycles, on the second. In the annex, the store provided a "desk for the receipt of 'want' and other advertisements for the newspapers," a service that can hardly have been much used, but one which indicates the prevailing tendency to introduce almost anything that might draw people to the store. Another new feature was a smoking-room on the second floor:

> . . . where men can meet and enjoy the same comfort as is afforded to the ladies by our famous Ladies' Parlor.

This attempt to make Macy's as popular with men as it had been with women was doomed to failure, but the men's departments continued to forge ahead. The third, fourth, and fifth floors of the annex housed the new furniture and rug departments, while Macy mattresses were made on the sixth.[44]

In the meantime Macy's had sought to enhance its prestige by opening (1893) a "luxurious Reading Room and Parlor" in Paris, on the avenue de l'Opéra:

> All of the New York daily papers
> and the principal American periodicals
> are to be found on the tables,
> and stationery is provided
> for the free use of our guests.
> Information about the railroads,
> locations of theaters, stores
> and points of interest in Paris
> is cheerfully furnished by the person in charge.
> We hope travelling Americans will use our Paris
> reading room with the same feeling they would have
> in the parlors and reading room of a hotel
> whose guests they may be.
> Letters may be addressed in our care.

Of course, this idea, which might have been appropriate in the 1920's, was futile in the 'nineties and was abandoned early in 1896.[45]

The annex seems to have relieved most of the congestion in Macy's, and the only noteworthy innovation in the next few years was the installation of electric fans for summer use. "Come stroll through the broad aisles," ran an advertisement, reflecting both the ample space and the new style in copy. "Electric fans supply artificial breezes. They're as pleasant and inspiring as the winds that blow from wooded hill tops."[46] But the day had arrived when neither new services nor additional facilities quite met the Macy problem. Up the Avenue between 18th and 19th, Siegel-Cooper had built a huge, modern, and well-appointed store which emphasized more than ever the rather makeshift agglomeration of buildings under the Red Star, and B. Altman, Simpson Crawford, and others were quick to follow the leadership of the "Big Store" from Chicago. Manhattan trade was relentlessly moving northward. John Wanamaker's pretentious establishment at 9th Street might act as a deterrent, and crowds of shoppers still thronged 14th Street, but the best people were patronizing stores farther uptown. Fourteenth Street was losing caste in a way that impaired volume and profit, and the new swarms of immigrants who replaced its middle-class trade did not fully compensate for the loss. Fortunately, as we shall presently see, Macy management was neither asleep nor hidebound.

Price Policies

In no aspect of retail trade was the growing competition more apparent than in price policies. All through Macy history, to be sure, low prices had been stressed, and the 'nineties saw rivalry expressing itself in services and quality as well as in cheapness, but conditions compelled the Macy management to strive harder than ever to undersell the competing stores. Regularly the firm's advertising claimed that Macy prices were below the rest by 20, 30, and even 50 per cent, depending upon the line of merchandise. From time to time (especially between 1894 and 1898) the firm even went so far as to assert, "We sell goods cheaper than any house in the world."

Extreme statements of this kind were not unique in Macy history, but there is reason to believe that there was less exaggeration in them during the 'nineties than in the previous years. Thus, explaining plans for a sale of china and glassware, Isidor Straus wrote Webster: [47]

You very well know that when we mark goods down ever so low, our neighbors feel that they have to meet us, but when we can advertise a stock bought 50 cts. on the dollar and to be sold at that rate, you know no one attempts to follow it. . . . The department will get the benefit of a boom, increasing sales all over the house in consequence thereto, and all at very fair profit in doing it.

On another occasion he described to Nathan how prices had to be slashed: [48]

In many lines prices are simply demoralized: as an instance, dress goods with which we opened the season at $2.98, we had to mark down yesterday to $.89. In the cloak and suit department . . . we are, in many instances, selling goods at less than one-quarter of the price which the same goods commanded early in the season. Even cotton dress goods prices have been cut to a third less than when the season opened, and that on low grade goods costing 15 cts.

The store management seems to have determined that its price claims should be maintained at all costs, and any rival who attempted to undersell Macy's usually found himself engaged in a price war that hurt. "Ninety-nine times out of a hundred our regular prices are lower than other people's special prices, but if in a moment of desperation any competitor cuts our price, we in turn cut again and are still the lowest."[49] At first comparisons were made informally. A buyer or partner would send a clerk around (sometimes every hour or two) to ascertain the current quotations of competitors who attempted to match Macy prices. By 1900, however, the store was regularly employing a number of "competent, confidential shoppers who have no motive beyond ascertaining the truth," in order to keep buyers informed on the activities of rivals: "The market is watched with tireless vigilance and whenever we find that a house, for mere sensational effect, has paralleled a price established by us, we cut under."[50]

Evidently Macy's had not yet evolved a determined, consistent policy of underselling, taking no special action against the firm which met Macy prices, but cutting ruthlessly under the prices of any rival who dared to undersell. New Yorkers are familiar with the price wars which occasionally break out between Macy's and other stores today, but none of these modern affairs go to the lengths reached forty years ago. Here is a contemporary account of one in 1902:[51]

In Monday evening's papers R. H. Macy & Co. advertised a big purchase of Jap wash silks made at a price enabling them to be retailed at 41 cents a yard, though worth more at wholesale. Hearn & Son, their neighbors and close rivals, happened to be in possession of the identical goods, and at once put them on sale at 39 cents. Macy then cut to 37 cents, Hearn to 35 cents, Macy to 33 cents, Hearn to 31 cents, and so the battle raged all day until the curtain rang down upon the scene of carnage at 6 o'clock, with the erstwhile 41-cent silks going at a cent a yard. . . . But the suspense was of short duration. When [the next day] the "one-cent-a-yard" ticket was taken down, it was replaced by one reading "2 yards for 1 cent," then "3 yards for 1 cent," then "4 yards for 1 cent," then 5, and 6, and 7, until at 6 o'clock when the bell rang, the quotation was "11 yards for 1 cent," amid scenes of the wildest excitement ever witnessed in a retail store.

While this was not an isolated instance, wars of this sort were fairly rare. There were not many firms that had the nerve or the financial resources needed to stand up under such onslaughts. The Macy management was determined to uphold store policy at all costs (even to the point of threatened commercial anarchy), and that policy was gradually shaping into one of consistently underselling competitors.[52] As early as 1899 the firm had begun to publish comparative prices, listing numerous items followed by a column of figures headed "Others Charge" and a second one, "Our Price." The rate of differential was by no means uniform. Some items would be as close as 45 cents against 39, others as far apart as $15 against $9.99.[53]

Such comparisons may, of course, be deceptive, particularly in view of the wide variations in the grades of merchandise sold in any market, but the Macy management seems to have been sincere in trying to undersell when identical goods were involved. Thus, when a customer alleged that Wanamaker's was selling a certain book below the price he had paid in Macy's, the firm asked him to buy a copy from Wanamaker's and bring it to Macy's with the bill. "We will not only refund you the amount you paid for the book and make you a present of the book itself, but will in addition take back the copy you purchased from us and refund you the amount paid us for it."[54] Since Macy's was becoming involved in a fight against book publishers at this time, there may have been special reasons for making so generous an offer. It is clear, however, that the store was beginning to make adjustments whenever a customer complained of paying more in Macy's than another store was charging at the time.

The attitude of certain vendors supplies additional evidence that the Macy prices were really low. Retailers were agitating for protection against severe competition, and certain manufacturers, in response, attempted to fix retail prices. Macy's met this challenge defiantly in one instance by announcing a special sale of a particular manufacturer's product "at prices lower than the manufacturer permits retailers to sell them at, under penalty of refusing their orders. . . . We submit to no dictation. . . . Our customers are the friends we aim to protect."[55] A later advertisement suggests that Macy's occasionally agreed to maintain prices on certain items, but, when book publishers united in an effort to compel the store to adhere to their prices, the Macy management decided to take a stand:[56]

> We not only sell books cheaper than other stores, but everything else, except a few proprietary articles that we are not at liberty to cut. We are compelled to charge regular rates for them because we agreed to do so. But we do not care to make any more trade contracts of that sort.

This announcement was followed by a bold challenge:[57]

> The American Publishers Association refused to let us have their books because we make the prices to you so low. . . . We consider this action an unlawful combination in restraint of trade which should be investigated. . . .
> We mean to continue to have [the books] at from 10 to 25% less than any other house, no matter what we have to pay to secure them.

The firm vindicated its position, too, but the story belongs to a later chapter. For the present the point is that by 1902 R. H. Macy & Co. had brought the price policies of its founder into sharp focus. The store would seek profits by taking the customer's side in the battle against high prices. It would make the firm name synonymous with economical shopping, to the point that the public would readily understand the meaning of a headline like "Macy's Undersells Macy's During This Carpet Sale."[58]

One of the reasons which Macy's gave for its low prices was its firm refusal to give discounts or special price concessions to favored customers. These discriminations, according to Macy reasoning, could be made only if something was added to the prices charged to the general public; as soon as a store could afford to make reductions to anyone, all customers should benefit alike. There seems to have been an outbreak of special discounts in the 'nineties (somewhat analogous to the discounts and "wholesale" prices which reappeared in the 1930's among many firms), for Macy's published a number of advertisements against them. The management refused to permit discrimination of any kind, even to ministers, benefit fairs, Y.M.C.A. organizations, or Sunday schools, and boasted that dressmakers, coachmen, and shopping agents were advising people not to buy at Macy's because the store declined to allow a commission to such intermediaries.[59] Quantity discounts were barred, too:[60]

> We have one price only and no discount whatever is made to anyone, no matter what quantity of goods may be purchased. Even a member of this firm in purchasing here must pay the price marked on the goods, and must pay cash or have goods sent C. O. D. . . . Our regular prices are always lower than those obtainable elsewhere, with all discounts deducted.

Competitive Tactics

In general, Macy's maintained a fast competitive pace, but certain rival stores refused to yield any ground, answering sale with sale, matching Macy services, and often exceeding the Macy volume of advertising. Sometimes the tactics used violated prevailing business ethics, which were not on a very high plane at best. Hearn's, who grappled with the Macy firm more than once, launched one prolonged attack which deserves brief mention because it reveals a belligerency which, now generally barred by general consent, was only too common in contemporary advertising; even more important, it shows the deep antagonism which the medium-sized dry goods stores felt towards the large department stores.

The row started because Macy's published a somewhat backhanded condemnation (without mentioning any names) of the one-day bargain sales which Hearn's regularly staged on Fridays:[61]

> Selling goods at exorbitant prices five days in the week and pretending to sell bargains on one particular day is not and never has been our practice. We have six bargain days every week as we always aim to give greater value than any other house.

For reasons which are not altogether clear, Hearn's took this statement as a direct attack which had to be answered at length. Evidently the Hearn management had been nursing a grudge and seized this opportunity to give vent to indignation. Every day or two for a period of six full weeks, large Hearn advertisements poured forth ecstatic wrath, interrupting lists of goods and prices every few inches to heap scorn and abuse upon the big store a few doors to the west. The stream of turgid prose, doggerel verse, Latin quotations, and strained proverbs ran the gamut of sarcasm, puns, broad insinuations, direct accusations, and cheap jests. Many a reader must have been completely baffled to know the meaning of it. One burden of the argument was that Hearn had lower prices than its neighborhood rival, a store which, Hearn alleged, had been going downhill for ten years (the period of Webster and Wheeler management). Another complaint was that Webster and the Strauses continued "to peddle kettles in a dead man's name," using the old firm name instead of their own: [62]

Some who shall be nameless (who long will nameless be through merits of their own), trading as a firm, from which the life, alas! has some time since departed, would, envious, disparage the values others give. 'Twould be better far to give attractions than to try to reap great profits on the former reputation of a name.

A third grievance, possibly the main cause of the episode, was the Macy policy of handling nontextile lines along with dry goods: [63]

> Black pots and tin pans, new kettles and drums,
> Candy and hash, fishing tackle and brooms,
> Are all very useful things in their way,
> And, with soda water, can be made to pay.
> But they are not dry goods as the jealous MAY SEE
> (Who should stick to his pots and let dry goods be),
> Will shortly find out to the loss of his profit,
> And with ninety-nine cents be a cent out of pocket.
>
> . . . .
>
> Some who deal in fishing tackle
>   Night school should attend,
> And study up the dry goods trade,
>   In hopes their ways to mend.
> Elements of success they'll find
>   Are, first, in keeping quiet
> (Unless they can the truth proclaim) —
>   Falsehoods may cause a riot.

> And next avoid a bigger job
> Than can be managed right;
> And not to hit too big a man,
> Lest possibly he'll fight.

In reply to such nonsense the Macy management did nothing except to reprint, once a week, the advertisement which set off the tirade. This procedure led Hearn to assert that his rival would not fight because it cost money or because the Macy skin was too thick to feel a kick; he was also inspired to publish such odd punning as the following: [64]

> The blind may see and better see than any one may see
> Who, while he sees, sees not.
> If he can see, how can he see? He cannot see —
> all but the name's forgot.
>
> If this short enigma's hazy,
> It's because the subject's crazy —
> Just as crazy as one may see.

When Macy advertising continued to ignore the clamor, new efforts included attempts to belittle the Straus partners. One verse, for example, ended with a feeble pun and metaphor: [65]

> For STRAWS are oft by whirlwinds blown,
> Lost to sight and quite unknown,
> Impossible to find.

Another piece of copy made a more direct personal attack: [66]

SOME FOLKS

are so wrapped up in their own conceit that they think the world is made for them and them only. They want the earth and all of it. In this free country there is room enough for all who do not want all of this free country. We were born here and expect to stay if some who are in the crockery business have no objections, even if the china man must go.

Perhaps the publisher eventually intervened — certainly no reputable newspaper would print such stuff today. Perhaps Hearn's copywriter had exhausted his ideas and had grown tired of repeating himself (certain phrases and verses were republished many times).

Probably spite had to yield to Christmas promotional activities. At all events, Hearn's suddenly dropped the matter.[67] One immediate result of it was that Macy's moderated its underselling claims for several years, after which, as noted above, they became more sweeping than ever. As to the long-run effect of the campaign, time and the public have awarded an unqualified verdict.

Other Macy competitors refused to waste money on printed attacks, but it is worth noting that some of them confused and intensified the bitter rivalry of the period by making gifts to patrons. Ehrich Brothers, for example, at one time gave away a spool of thread or a paper of pins to each person who made a purchase at the notion counter, while Adams Co. gave away theater tickets to customers.[68] This was an expensive and ineffective way to buy patronage which Macy's refused to imitate. However, whether competition took the form of gifts to customers, additional services, more advertising, or price wars, the tendency was to increase retail costs. To be sure, there were other factors involved in the rising cost of distribution, but competition for business was an important element. And the general public, by patronizing those stores which made the increased expenditures, thereby voted in favor of more expensive retailing. Those who want "progress" and "efficiency" have to pay for it.

Management, 1888–1902

Thanks to the survival of letterpress copies of a considerable amount of Isidor Straus' correspondence, we have a revealing picture of the management of the Macy business during the years 1888 to 1896. According to the plan adopted at the beginning of the new partnership, Webster and Isidor Straus were to bear the main burden of management, while Nathan was to continue to direct most of his attention "downtown" (at the headquarters of L. Straus & Sons on Warren Street).[69] Initially, the partners seem to have regarded their responsibilities as being rather light, and Isidor assured his youngest brother that there was no danger of overwork:[70]

I am spending my time entirely uptown so as to familiarize myself with the workings of everything. It is an exceedingly pleasant task as all the surroundings are happy in the extreme & Charley [Webster] takes special delight to render everything rather a pleasurable pastime and not an earnest task. . . . We seem by instinct determined that we shall get a lot of fun & agreeable episodes out of each day's hours. To prevent drudgery of every kind, too long or too close application to work, each forms a watcher over the other to warn him — if need be, drive him into more reasonable and less wearing habits.

Another letter gives a fuller picture of the concept of the managerial function which prevailed — probably in most rival stores as well as in Macy's — at the beginning of the partnership: [71]

We [Webster and Isidor] take two solid hours in the middle of the day. We go to lunch to Delmonico's, walking both ways when weather permits. . . . Once in a while we go up to the Manhattan Club for a change . . . ; when doing so, we invariably walk up Sixth Ave. to 23rd St., then down to Fifth Ave. and along Fifth to 15th St., so that we get our full quota of exercise and fresh air. . . . My office is quiet and away from the turmoil & dust; when I close my desk, my mind feels as fresh as before I began. The work is disconnected from all worry and care, as the petty annoyances which are constantly coming up are settled without ever reaching any of the firm; and aside from all that I have arrived at that philosophic age when any little matter that might heretofore have disturbed me does not bother me. . . .

Downtown bothers me very little. I have a telephone in my office with a private wire running to Warren St. The work down there is thoroughly organized and well divided.

As the weeks went on, however, Isidor found that he had a great deal more to do than he had contemplated. Webster went to Europe, and as Isidor gained insight into the business, he found that efficient conduct of the business demanded far more than Webster seemed to realize. It was necessary to keep subordinates up to the mark, there was need to maintain a closer watch over inventories and expenditures — a surveillance which necessitated some refinements in accounting methods — and the combination of hard times and growing competition meant that Macy management had to be alert, trying to anticipate trouble and exploring ideas for improvement. In the circumstances, to leave the details of management to subordinates was to invite disaster. Isidor lacked any intimate knowledge of the merchandise handled by Macy's outside the Straus departments (and contemporary practice in department stores left most questions connected with merchandising in the hands of the departmental buyers), but he had had ample experience with accounting and finance which he could now apply with immediate benefit. A little investigation, for example, soon disclosed that the shoe department, long operated on a leased basis, was yielding exceptionally poor returns and that the man in charge was not living up to his agreement. Isidor promptly terminated the arrangement and incorporated the shoe department into the Macy organization.[72]

By 1893 the management of the store was almost entirely in the hands of Isidor and Nathan Straus, and the depressed conditions were giving them much concern:[73]

> While up to a week ago some people thought the panic was not so severe as it was in '73, there is but one opinion that this country has never seen anything like it before, and there is no use in fooling ourselves with the belief that this slaughter of values will not take a long time for the country to recoup from. . . .
>
> The strain has lasted so long now, that it has permeated in every direction — mills and factories are shutting down, and of course that carries with it a tremendous suffering of laboring people that are out of employment.

Isidor found that the telegraphic code which the partners used in communicating with one another contained no word to indicate that sales were running behind, and the ones he added to fill the gap had to be used again and again.[74]

It was cold comfort that other houses seemed to be even harder hit and that Macy sales responded fairly well to the strenuous efforts made to maintain volume at former levels.[75] Nor was the managerial task lightened when the Siegel-Cooper store opened in New York and touched off a new battle for trade. Macy's was successful in preventing rivals from cutting down its volume, but increases were difficult to achieve, and the severe competition is clearly reflected in the sharp drop in Macy profits for 1896 and 1897. No longer could the store coast, as it had done in the preceding decade, on the advantages which it derived from being one of the first to apply the department store idea. Others had caught up, and the times were bad. Small wonder, then, that Webster was ready and even eager to let the Strauses take over his responsibilities in Macy's.

Of the two Straus brothers, the one better known to the public was Nathan. Having taken charge of Macy advertising, Nathan handled all contacts with the press. When any news about the store developed, therefore, it was Nathan who was ordinarily interviewed, and he was usually quoted as if he alone managed the business. Moreover, Nathan's large-scale gifts of food, coal, and clothing to the poor of New York, together with his campaign for pure milk and the establishment of milk depots in the slums, made him something of a national figure. Unquestionably there was an element of vanity in the man's character, which manifested itself not only in public benefactions but also in personal attire and behavior. Contemporaries describe him as a "natty dresser," with a tendency to indulge in flashy patterns and rather extreme styles. As he wandered about the store, Nathan usually whistled. The tune was almost invariably "There'll Be a Hot Time in the Old Town Tonight," which he interrupted to cry greetings to a friend, crack a joke with an employee, or reprimand a careless worker. His brother, Isidor, never conspicuous in conduct or dress, always preferred to remain quietly in the background.

In most respects, indeed, the two brothers presented a study in contrasts. Isidor, the elder, was serious, diligent, and methodical in his work, while Nathan did everything by impulse, avoided details, and never applied himself to anything for long. Isidor was reserved, even-tempered, and full of dignity. Nathan made friends with everyone, was never formal except by special effort, and possessed a mercurial temperament which made him gay and jaunty at one moment, moody and depressed at another, equally capable of flying into a sudden rage at some slight annoyance or giving the overcoat from his own back to a shivering workman. Isidor was scholarly, analytical, of a conservative disposition, and circumspect in his judgment; he never made a decision without giving careful thought to every aspect, whether cost, available means, results, or long-run implications. Nathan possessed a quick mind and a lively imagination which, though lacking discipline, exhibited flashes of brilliance; he generated ideas by the score but did not appraise them with critical judgment.

Even in their recreation the two men were different. Nathan was fond of gaiety and pleasure, and raced trotting horses as a hobby. Isidor had little taste for play, but devoted his spare moments to the study of currency, banking, and tariff problems. An articulate "Gold Democrat," he generally is credited with persuading Cleveland to call Congress into special session in 1893 in order to repeal the Sherman Silver Purchase Act. He modestly disclaimed credit — "I don't deserve it, but I presume that it was the last straw," [76] but he was undoubtedly a friend and adviser whom Cleveland valued.

Both brothers were actively interested in politics, but Nathan confined his interests mainly to local government, achieving the rather difficult feat of being a member of Tammany and yet retaining the respect of the better elements in the city. In fact, when the disclosures of the Lexow Committee (1894) made it imperative for Tammany to show some sign of internal reform, Nathan Straus was offered the Democratic nomination for mayor. He refused the bid, but he did serve one term as park commissioner and one as president of the board of health. Isidor focused attention mainly on national politics and took an active part because he was sincerely concerned about the need for tariff and monetary reforms. An ardent opponent of protection, he campaigned on the issue of the Wilson Tariff and was elected to Congress in 1894 to fill an unexpired term. He refused to seek reëlection: the store could ill spare his services, the outlook for reform bills was distinctly unfavorable, and the victory of the Free Silver faction dampened his enthusiasm for the Democratic Party.

In many respects the two brothers formed an ideal team from which the Macy business derived great benefit. Nathan poured forth a constant stream of suggestions about running the store — some of them picked up from friends, some from casual acquaintances, some his own. Isidor patiently listened, ignored or discarded the extravagant proposals, tactfully yielded on those which were of doubtful value but not expensive to try, and skillfully converted the best ideas into effective action. Nathan had hunches, some of which unquestionably helped to keep the firm in the van of retailing. Indeed, it was one of these hunches that brought the Strauses (through their leased departments) into Macy's in the first place.

It was Nathan who insisted that the store windows be kept well filled with merchandise, arranged most of the exhibitions and publicity stunts, and maintained the barrage of advertising which helped to keep Macy's before the public. It is probable that he was chiefly responsible for the introduction of many of the new departments and customer services which aided in the battle for patronage. Isidor found the money needed to pay for them. Nathan captured the loyalty of the working force by his informality, his good nature, and the sincere personal interest which he took in them. A man with a sick wife received free medical assistance and groceries; an ailing clerk was sent to a rest home, expenses and salary paid, with instructions not to come back until completely well; a messenger boy who was given a twenty-dollar bill to make a small purchase would be told to keep the change; and so on. They all knew his faults, but they liked him, and they worked all the harder for Macy's because of his presence.

Isidor's contribution was less spectacular but, in the opinion of most observers, more important. It was he who financed any acceptable proposal for improvement which Nathan made. It was he who converted ideas into plans and made them work, who patiently and systematically followed every detail of the business, budgeting expenditures, guarding against accumulations of unwanted merchandise, working out efficient methods for handling goods and cash, and generally introducing order where there had formerly been a great deal of complacency and waste. For example, in tracing the cause of persistent shortages in the lace department, Isidor discovered that the usual store practice was to accept the invoice statement of quantities sent by the vendor and to place new shipments in stock without making a tally of the quantity actually received. He immediately instituted a routine system by which lace was measured upon its arrival, and an important source of loss was at once stopped.[77]

Nathan, on the other hand, had no stomach for financial analysis. He could usually be depended upon to drive a hard bargain when it came to business negotiations, and he took obvious pleasure in obtaining a rebate which some buyer, through ignorance or incompetence, had failed to collect;[78] but such activities meant dealing with people, and Nathan liked that — all the more so if a lively scrap was involved. The fact that he asked Isidor to set up a reserve for advertising in anticipation of trouble is an indication of his grasp of competitive situations and his determination to fight. At times he appears to have been interested in advertising and publicity for its own sake, giving little consideration to costs and results. This, to be sure, is a common failing among business men, but it is one more indication of the contrast between the two brothers. Against the better judgment of his partners, Nathan arranged the establishment of a Paris office on the theory that it would be a useful advertisement for the store. Macy's, however, catered to the lower and middle classes, and the number of New Yorkers who would use the Paris office or be impressed by its existence was obviously small. Experience soon proved, as Isidor had anticipated, that the Paris office had little advertising value. Fortunately Isidor had been successful in opposing Nathan's desire to establish similar offices in Berlin and Chemnitz.[79]

Impatient of detail, Nathan was quite content to leave to others the somewhat tedious but highly important task of managerial control. He disliked office work so heartily that he could hardly bring himself even to sign a letter, to say nothing of writing one, and he made little attempt to delegate details to subordinates. Thus, while Isidor was in attendance at the store (that is, most of the time) the letterbooks show a regular flow of correspondence, often in longhand. Whenever Isidor left the city and Nathan was in charge, the flow dropped sharply to a trickle of brief notes, usually handled by a secretary. Isidor kept a careful, day-to-day account of the store's sales, constantly comparing them with past performances and jotting down notes about the weather — for sky and temperature conditions have such a marked effect on retail shopping that the department store manager is necessarily as weather-minded as a farmer. In Isidor's absence that daily record was kept by a clerk who simply entered the daily sales. Every surviving Macy record mutely testifies that Isidor kept close watch on operations, that Nathan avoided paper work like poison. Nathan, like the late Edward A. Filene in Boston's famous store, was mainly content with being an idea man.

Nathan's shortcomings as a manager must not be allowed to obscure his very valuable contribution to Macy development. The entire organization caught something of his ambitious and dynamic character, and the application of his better ideas unquestionably helped the store to forge ahead. Without Isidor's excellent management those ideas would have come to naught, but without Nathan's aggressive and original policies the firm would probably have lagged behind. The two made an excellent combination.

The main burden of managing the store fell upon Isidor Straus and, to a lesser extent, upon C. B. Webster. Nathan and Webster spent a great deal of time away from the business, traveling in Europe or visiting health resorts. Isidor remained on the job most of the time, keeping close touch by means of frequent journeys between New York and Washington even while serving in Congress. His long letters to his partners clearly reveal their interests. To Nathan he wrote mostly about family matters and business affairs in general. To Webster he sent long, detailed reports, telling how this department was expanding, that one was suffering from an excess of old stock, this buyer was incompetent and too often smelling of whiskey, that assistant was doing a good job and worthy of advancement, and so on. From Isidor came the steady drive, constant supervision, and broad perspective without which the firm would unquestionably have met the fate which befell so many of its rivals.

Although Isidor concentrated his attention upon Macy's, he occasionally took a hand in the management of Abraham & Straus. One letter written by him about affairs in the Brooklyn store affords a good illustration of his attention to detail and his tact in conveying suggestions to his associates.[80]

Dear Mr. Abraham:

I have just received a comparative statement of stock and sales covering the period from August 1st to October 31st and I find some stocks so exorbitantly out of proportion to the amount of business they have done that I deem it my duty to call your attention thereto. I know you will not take it amiss that I should criticise freely the defects that occur to me, although I give the business over there no attention, and I know further you will not misconstrue the motives. It is an old saying that the looker-on can see many a move that the chess player himself overlooks, and that I presume also holds true in looking at cold statistics without being influenced by sympathy with the department that is born of personal contact. First and foremost, I must take Department M, upholstery. This fastidious stock, so sensitive to the freaks of fashion, I find carrying $66,000 stock where the sales for three months foot up $35,000. I do not think I am exaggerating when I say for the amount of business done in that department the stock is almost double what it should be. It is utterly impossible for you to make any money in that department under such conditions. It is radically wrong and drastic remedies should be applied. I venture the assertion, if an unbiased hand would overhaul that stock, there will be enough depreciation found by reducing the accumulated old stock to its proper basis that will more than wipe out all the gross profits that have been made on the three months sales, to say nothing of the expense it cost to run the department.

Department N, boys clothing. The same criticism applies to the stock in this department, as it is double the sales for three months. There is no justification for carrying a larger amount than the three months' sales; hence this stock is too large.

I am sorry to observe that Department E, respecting which I have on former occasions written you, makes a most unsatisfactory showing. $111,000 stock with $50,000 sales for three months requires no comments.

I started off with my criticism respecting Department M because that cropped out before my eyes as the most conspicuously mismanaged department, but since writing and casting my eyes over the sheet again I find Department G, laces, makes a far far poorer showing. $63,000 stock on hand equivalent to 9 months sales is all but criminal. This seems to be the most incorrigible stock in your store. I find that it was just as large last year, but when I take into consideration that your total stock is over $200,000 less than it was last year, it goes to show the gross mismanagement that must dominate there. There is but one conclusion that

I can come to and that is this stock must be rampant with unsalable, undesirables and superannuated stock. You should take it personally in hand and stick the pruning knife to the hilt in paring it down by one process or another. You are surely fooling yourself to carry a stock so disproportionately to the needs of the business it does.

Department P is another department where the stock on hand is two and a third times as large as the three months sales.

Is there not a mistake in Department Art Embroidery? The stock on hand last year was $18,880, and stock on hand this year is $71,756. The last figures can not be right. Please let me hear from you.

I guess I have done enough scolding for one letter.

Sincerely yours,
Isidor Straus.

Isidor Straus had to keep an eye out for L. Straus & Sons, too, repeatedly urging Nathan to keep stocks within bounds and to curtail production when times looked bad. So far as the staff was concerned, he kept Nathan's quixotic generosity within reasonable bounds. A firm disciplinarian, he constantly exhibited a kindly sympathy and strong sense of justice which won him the respect of the entire organization. Old employees often disagree in their opinions about conditions and personalities in Macy's, but on one point there is universal agreement: in ability, in character, and in personality, Isidor Straus was the finest man they have ever known. To him without question must go the main credit for bringing the store successfully through the 'nineties.[81]

Staff and Working Conditions

To complete the picture of Macy management at this time it is necessary to present some concrete details about the organization below the level of the partners. The superintendent, as before, was in charge of personnel, delivery service, maintenance, and general store operations. For the first time in the store's history, however, this position was held by a man, William Pitt having succeeded Martha Toye. Apart from a growing amount of specialization among the employees, there was no significant change in the organization under his control.

The merchandise departments were managed by buyers as in earlier days. Each buyer conferred with a member of the firm once a week, going over the figures of sales and stocks on hand and considering the purchases to be made during the next week. This control was aimed at financial soundness rather than wise selection of merchandise. So long as dead stocks did not accumulate, the buyer had substantially a free hand in deciding what to buy. He was not even shown the figures as to the margins earned in his department, and such data were apparently not given much consideration by the firm in appraising his performance. He was expected to show increased sales; the firm fixed the "ratings" or profit margins and assumed responsibility for producing profits. The typical buyer received an annual salary of about four thousand dollars, and sometimes a bonus or commission if his department did well. If sales fell below expected performance without good reason, if "hard stock" (merchandise difficult to sell) accumulated in his division, or if there were substantial shortages which could not be satisfactorily explained, he would be given a month's salary and replaced by a new buyer. Then, as in recent times, there was a tendency to blame the buyer if the departmental operations were considered unsatisfactory, even if the trouble was actually beyond his control. Accordingly, the first remedy considered was likely to be replacing the buyer.[82]

One innovation affecting the sales clerks was the introduction in 1896 of bonus payments on any sales over individual quotas. The accounts show, however, that the average commissions earned in this way were never very large.[83] No data have survived on the average wages of Macy employees for this period, but the steady rise in the payroll expense for the period (Table 20, p. 258) confirms the impression of old employees that the rates of pay were tending to increase. Some of the improvement was doubtless the result of a general rise in the wages of retail employees, reflecting, in turn, both rising standards of living and increased cost of living in New York. The general testimony of old employees, however, is that the Strauses were more liberal in their treatment of employees — in remuneration as well as in welfare benefits conferred — than Webster had been.

There is clear evidence that a number of gains in working conditions date from the beginning of Straus management. In 1888, for example, regular provision was made for the first time to provide payment of doctors' bills, funeral expenses, or pensions for employees who had grown old or become incapacitated in the store's service. Decision as to whether a person should receive such benefits was left to the discretion of the members of the firm rather than being placed on any standard, automatic basis, but payments for clerks' relief show a steady increase. Although the firm itself did not provide sick benefits, most of the employees belonged to the Macy Mutual Aid Association, through which, in case of illness, they received from five to seven dollars a week, together with free medical attention. This program was not self-supporting, and the firm took care of its annual deficit.[84]

The firm also instituted "gratuity lunches" in 1888, supplying milk, tea, or coffee free of charge to cash girls, parcel wrappers, and stock girls. Anyone occupying a higher position paid one cent for such beverages. Soup, sandwiches, pie, cake, and other refreshments were furnished to all employees at nominal prices ranging from one to four cents per serving, well below actual cost.[85]

The staff had become so large by the 1890's that the management could no longer have much personal knowledge of individual employees — in 1898 there were approximately 3,000 in the organization. Nonetheless, Isidor Straus found time to give aid in many cases of need, just as his brother did, and the firm provided such social affairs as an annual sleigh ride for the cashiers, a summer picnic for the entire store (at which special precautions had to be taken against drunkenness and brawling, though never with complete success). Isidor gave the cash girls a week's vacation in the country, sending each one to a home of her religious faith. In 1888 the Strauses likewise began the practice, still observed, of giving a Thanksgiving turkey to every married employee in the organization.[86]

During the 'nineties the store began to provide uniforms for an increasing number of its employees. Cash girls had been provided with a covering garment as early as the 1870's, but other employees had been expected to provide their own clothing and, contrary to modern practice, were not allowed any discounts on clothes purchased in the store (the management thought at the time that such discounts would violate its one-price policy). In 1896, however, the promotion of a woman to the position of buyer for books and stationery resulted in her being placed in charge of the printing and engraving shop maintained by the store. Disliking dirty and disreputable garments, which seemed to be the standard costume of the men in the shop, she got Isidor Straus's authority to provide uniforms and have them washed twice a week. To men who disliked the idea of being supervised by a woman anyway, this was a bitter pill to swallow, but they yielded to her insistence and soon came to like the idea. Within a few months the firm was likewise supplying caps and uniforms to its deliverymen.[87]

Apparently there was no agitation among the main body of employees for unionization at this time — only in the years since 1932 have retail employees made appreciable efforts in that direction. Certain skilled operators on the Macy staff, however, did manage to organize. The Macy cigar-makers, for example, staged a successful strike for higher wages in 1895, and operations in the upholstery workrooms were interrupted by a strike in the fall of 1902. A list of "union approved" stores, published in 1899 by the typographical union, contained the name of R. H. Macy & Co., indicating that its printshop was fully organized on a union basis.[88]

The regular working hours within the store remained from 8:00 to 6:00 during this period, with Saturday afternoons off during July and August. To get stocks in order it was always necessary to work beyond the closing hour, and a considerable amount of overtime was not unusual. In 1901, however, Macy's for the first time omitted the time-honored practice of keeping the store open during the evenings for ten days before Christmas, with such favorable results that it definitely abandoned the old custom and published its reasons for the change:[89]

> The custom was started when New York was much smaller than at present — when clerks and patrons were not scattered throughout such wide-lying distances. At that period Macy's was a "neighborhood" store.

WORKING CONDITIONS

> The majority of the clerks lived hard by,
> and they were not subjected to personal inconveniences
> and long delays in reaching their homes after leaving the store.
> We held on to the holiday night work habit,
> in common with others, until last year,
> at which time we announced its discontinuance.
> Various reasons were attributed to our action.
> The public, generally, hit upon the true one: —
> Consideration for the Health of our Employes.
> Many of them now live miles from the store.
> Night schedules are slow — especially the ferryboats.
> Were they to work until 10 o'clock
> many would not arrive home till midnight or later.
> By [our] closing at 6 o'clock, they are enabled to retire
> at a reasonable hour, enjoy needed rest
> and appear at the store in the morning refreshed
> — bright and alert mentally and physically.
> Statistics from the Macy Employes' Mutual Aid Association
> show that the last year we kept open at night
> there were three times more people on the sick list
> at the expiration of the holidays than there were
> the first year we kept closed during the corresponding period,
> in spite of a large increase in the membership roll for the latter year.

Meanwhile two annual holidays had been added to the list, Labor Day (1894) and Washington's Birthday (1900), thereby giving a few more breathing spells to a large number of hard-working, city-bound employees.[90] It is difficult now to judge the relative situation of Macy workers in the 'nineties, but they appear to have been fully as well off as any department store employees in the city so far as working conditions and pay are concerned. The existence of good morale and a definite *esprit de corps* in the staff can hardly be questioned. In such a large organization occasional grievances and injustices are inevitable, but the run of employees seem to have liked their work and to have been proud of being members of the Macy staff. Certainly they played their part in the store's success.

PART IV

THE SECOND GENERATION TAKES COMMAND
1902–1919

CHAPTER XII

A PLATEAU IN MACY DEVELOPMENT

AFTER 1902 there is no breaking point in the history of Macy's until the end of 1913, when the three sons of Isidor Straus acquired the complete ownership of the firm. About halfway between those dates, operations leveled off in a manner which suggested that the store had about attained the limits of growth. In the first years after moving to 34th Street both sales and profits increased substantially, but after 1907 they seem to have reached a ceiling and, in spite of diligent efforts on the part of management to keep the business moving ahead, there was little progress for the next six years. From developments which matured after 1914 it is plain that the enterprise was experiencing some fundamental transitions. Once the store had moved into new quarters, nothing of dramatic interest seemed to happen, but changes were going on beneath the surface, particularly on the administrative side, which eventually enabled Macy's to rise to new heights beyond the plateau which it had reached. This chapter deals mainly with the developments between 1902 and 1914 which the public could see. The next chapter will analyze the underlying situations.

SONS LEARN THE BUSINESS

Like their father before them, Isidor and Nathan Straus each had three sons who reached maturity, and the general assumption was that they would all find a place in the Macy business. Unfortunately Nathan's eldest boy was fatally stricken with illness just after being admitted to Cornell University. The two surviving brothers, Nathan, Jr. (born in 1889) and Hugh Grant (born in 1890), were considerably younger than their cousins, and thus it came about that two of Isidor's sons (Jesse Isidor and Percy Selden) entered the business in the 1890's, while Nathan's did not begin until 1910. This fact was to have an important bearing on the later history of the store.[1]

Jesse Isidor Straus was the eldest son of an eldest son — which was also true of his father and grandfather. Born in 1872, he was graduated from Harvard in 1893 and promptly entered business. There had never been any question about his being intended for the store, but since his father thought it best for him to gain some financial experience first, Jesse began his career as a clerk in the Central Hanover Bank. After a few months, however, the transaction (mentioned in Chapter IX) took place which converted Wechsler & Abraham into Abraham & Straus, and Jesse entered the Brooklyn store to learn retailing. (In the smaller store he could get a better comprehensive grasp of operations, he could keep a close watch on his father's interest in the firm, and — possibly this was the main consideration — his rapid advancement would not create any of the embarrassment which might arise in Macy's, where C. B. Webster's younger brother was already established as a junior executive.) It was a proud day for Isidor when, after the Websters had withdrawn from the store, he was able to note in his Black Book under the date of September 3, 1896, "Jesse came to Macy's."[2] It was also a fortunate day for the store, as Jesse's subsequent record of leadership abundantly proved.

Percy Selden Straus, born in 1876, entered Macy's in September, 1897, a few months after receiving his bachelor's degree from Harvard. Just as Jesse had acquired his father's superb financial acumen, so Percy had inherited Isidor's scholarly tendencies and analytical ability. He had thoroughly enjoyed his academic experience and would have liked to make teaching his career. But his father had made definite plans for having him in the business, and into Macy's he went, accepting the situation with good grace and throwing his full energy and ability into store activities.[3] Undoubtedly that decision cost America an outstanding educator but gave it a business executive of rare capacity.

Both boys began their retailing careers by working in the receiving department, where incoming merchandise was unpacked, invoiced, and marked with prices. There, as Isidor had often pointed out, was where the store made its money. From the receiving department the boys moved to other divisions of the business until they were familiar with all the principal operations. Then they were given buyers' positions in selling departments, and their experience as executives began. From the outset they were trained as a team: Jesse learned "soft goods" — principally clothing and dry goods — while Percy familiarized himself with furniture, house furnishings, groceries, and the like. Jesse prepared himself to handle the financial and sales promotional aspects of store administration, and Percy specialized in store systems and management, including personnel, maintenance, and delivery. Both boys were industrious, able, and enthusiastic about their work. By 1900 they had pretty well mastered the intricate details of Macy administration and were beginning to render valuable assistance to the senior partners. Neither was given a share in the partnership, but in 1898 Jesse began to receive 5 per cent of the net profits, and Percy received a similar allocation in 1903 and later years.

Herbert, Isidor's third son, did not enter the business until after his graduation from Harvard in 1903. By that time Jesse and Percy had gained such a head start in experience and prestige that Herbert could never quite catch up with them. On the other hand, possibly because of his youth and sympathetic nature, he quickly won a place in the affections of the rank and file of the Macy staff which his brothers never really enjoyed. The employees respected and admired Jesse and Percy but regarded them with awe; they liked Herbert. Something of the same difference was apparent in the relations between the three brothers and the public. Besides taking over administrative duties in the absence of either of his brothers, Herbert acted as a kind of unofficial ambassador for the firm. It is no discredit to his brothers to state that he had wider interests outside the store than they and that he was more tactful and friendly in his relationships. He also developed better artistic taste, as a result of which his judgment was invaluable when it came to grading up the store's offering of style goods. Herbert's contribution to the firm's management, if at times somewhat intangible, was no less valuable and real.[4]

Northward the Course of Retailing

Late in April, 1901, the New York real estate market and department store circles alike were electrified by the news that R. H. Macy & Co. was to move to new quarters on the west side of Broadway at Herald Square, occupying the entire Broadway front and approximately half the block between Broadway and 7th Avenue. The importance of this decision, both for the firm and for the community, can scarcely be exaggerated. One of the oldest and largest retail houses in the city had decided to abandon the site that it had occupied for 43 years; it planned to leave the shopping district which had become almost synonymous with the name Macy's and move its vast, complicated organization and its enormous collection of merchandise a full mile to the north. Such a move meant that the firm was to attempt to transfer its long-established patronage — not to the popular shopping area between 18th and 23d Streets, but to a point eleven blocks beyond the uppermost department store of any consequence then operating in New York. (Bloomingdale's at 59th and Third Avenue belonged to an entirely different retail district, although the growth of the city and improvements in transportation had begun to make it a competitor of some importance.) To all observers it was evident that Gotham's retail traffic and land values were about to undergo some extensive changes.[5]

The move uptown involved considerable risk and a heavy capital investment, for the Macy firm had decided to construct its own quarters, a building of vast proportions. Naturally such a far-reaching decision had not been made hastily. For some years, in fact, the Strauses had found their 14th Street store unsatisfactory in several respects. The old premises, owing to the manner in which the business had expanded, consisted of a conglomeration of old stores, old dwellings, and several new additions. To be sure, the firm had adapted the various parts to its requirements and thrown them together by cutting through the partitions, but the arrangement was a makeshift at best. Parts of the store were old to the point of dilapidation; the main building, for example, badly needed an entire new roof, while the plumbing and heating facilities and other mechanical equipment were almost hopelessly obsolete.[6] Although the new façade on the Sixth Avenue front had, from one point of view, given a semblance of unity to the store and bettered its outward appearance, like any face-lifting operation it could not improve the whole or work any fundamental rejuvenation.

Apart from their age and obsolescence, the Macy premises lacked unity. They consisted of a main store, with the 13th and 14th Street Annexes (so-called) adjoining to the east, and the New Annex across 14th Street to the north. The successive additions had not only caused complications from the managerial point of view but also had confused the public. Indeed, an unscrupulous retailer whose store stood next to Macy's 14th Street Annex had been able, by the simple expedient of concealing his name, to delude many customers into thinking that they were in another Macy annex when they were in fact making purchases in the establishment of R. Smith & Co.[7]

The actions of rival firms had accentuated the problem which confronted the Macy management. Over a period of years a number of such well-known stores as Lord & Taylor, B. Altman, James McCreery & Co., Ehrich Brothers, Stern Brothers, Arnold, Constable & Co., and Simpson Crawford had been moving uptown beyond 14th Street, following the general tendency of Manhattan's trade and residential sections to expand northward. In 1896 the Siegel-Cooper firm had dealt a severe blow to 14th Street by opening a huge modern department store on Sixth Avenue between 18th and 19th Streets. To be sure, Ridley's remained in Grand Street and Wanamaker's and John Daniell & Sons continued to do business below 10th, but the uptown drift of retailing was unmistakable. Most of Macy's rivals occupied large modern buildings, and most of them were situated between 18th and 23d Streets. Thus, in addition to being outmoded, Macy's was being left on the retrogressing edge of the principal department store district.[8]

The problem, to be sure, was a familiar one in the annals of New York business, for the principal shopping area had been moving northward during almost the entire history of the city. But the solution of the problem was not to be easy. Would the northward tendency continue indefinitely? Since there was obviously a serious risk involved in moving uptown as well as in remaining at 14th, which course was the safer one? If the firm decided to move, how far uptown should the new location be? And when should the move take place — should the firm wait until sales began to taper off, or should it anticipate events?

By 1900 the question of proper timing was not wholly a theoretical one for the Macy management. The principal leases involved in the 14th Street location were to expire in 1903, and a decision would have to be reached well in advance of that date. The senior partners would have been willing to remain at the old location had it been possible to obtain a new building there on satisfactory terms. To this end, in fact, Isidor negotiated with the various landlords concerned during the better part of two years. However, several of the property owners thought they were in a position to dictate terms and refused to sell or rent at figures which the Strauses could regard as reasonable in view of the fact that 14th Street had deteriorated.[9]

In the end, Isidor decided to accept the judgment of his sons. They had urged the necessity of moving uptown, arguing that a new building would not offset the disadvantage of a location which, from the point of view of the kind of people who frequented the district, seemed to be going downhill. Macy's had always been a "popular" store in the sense of catering to the middle class, and they believed that it should so continue, but the lower classes were beginning to predominate in 14th Street traffic. The baby-carriage trade was driving out the carriage trade, and Macy's would have to grade downwards or move north as its regular patrons were tending to do.

The result was that, toward the end of 1900, Jesse and Percy were given permission to choose another site for Macy's. The two brothers painstakingly examined locations on both sides of Fifth Avenue as far northward as 45th Street. They soon came to the conclusion that Herald Square offered the greatest advantages to the firm. Although relatively far uptown for the site of a large store, it was directly on the line along which the retail area had advanced in the past. From the point of view of traffic it was, indeed, promising. Like the original Macy location, it combined the busy, main artery of Sixth Avenue with a wide, cross-town street of unusual width, and in addition there was Manhattan's main thoroughfare, Broadway, intersecting the other two at a sharp angle and, like them, double-tracked for street cars. Thus, at Herald Square there were four north-south surface lines crossing two east-west lines, in addition to the Elevated Railway, which would serve the store at 34th Street as it had done at 14th. To be sure, the steam engines which drove the "El" trains poured forth noise and sooty smoke, but a store on the west side of the "Square" (really an acute triangle formed where Broadway crosses Sixth Avenue) would be far enough away to escape the worst of the nuisance, and anyway the process of electrifying the "El" had already begun. Some observers might have wondered at the choice of the West Side of the city when on the East Side the long-promised subway was already under construction, extending northward from the City Hall along Fourth Avenue, and there were definite plans to extend the line southwards and under the East River, thus promising rapid transit between Brooklyn and the East Side of Manhattan. Still, the public had long favored the West Side, the subway in 1900 remained little more than a promising experiment, and a successful tunnel under the East River would certainly lead to the completion of the partially constructed Hudson River tubes and so provide rapid transit between the West Side and the populous Jersey shore. When the two brothers reported their decision, the senior partners immediately approved the choice and steps were taken to acquire the necessary land.[10]

The wisdom of the Herald Square location was shortly confirmed by the announcement that the Pennsylvania Railroad was to construct an enormous passenger station between 31st and 33d Streets and Seventh and Ninth Avenues. The company's main lines from the west would be brought under the North River and its Long Island lines under the East River by means of tunnels. In other words, as soon as this mammoth construction project could be completed (service actually began in the fall of 1910), thousands of suburban and out-of-town passengers would be landed daily within three blocks of the new Macy site. The Strauses had had no inkling of the Pennsylvania's plans, but the announcement undoubtedly helped to assure the success of the store's new location. If any further guarantee was needed, it was certainly forthcoming when, in 1902, the Rapid Transit Commission approved plans for a subway extension from 42d Street down Broadway to 14th Street, with a station at the very door of the new store.[11]

Transactions in Real Estate

The new building which Macy's constructed in 1901-02 still stands and is probably the part of the store best known to the public today because of its commanding position on Herald Square. Within the Macy organization it is known as the East, or Broadway, building because it occupies the eastern half of the store and contains the Broadway entrances to the main selling floor. It covers a large block of land running westward from Broadway approximately 400 feet and extending through from 34th to 35th Street — covers all of it except a small, odd-shaped piece at the corner of 34th and Broadway, as a result of which the building looks like a large cake with a narrow chunk cut out of one corner. A cake is sometimes in that condition because someone has been greedy. The Macy building owes its shape to the same human failing, manifested when the Strauses set about to acquire the site for the new store.

The process of leasing the needed land had begun, of course, long before the public knew anything about the contemplated move. The layman seldom realizes the complexities involved in acquiring a large building site in a place like New York — the leases and subleases which must be unraveled and purchased, the delays and difficulties resulting from the fact that certain plots are held in trust for individuals or joint heirs, and the problems of valuation. Jesse Straus was charged with the responsibility for the real-estate negotiations, but illness sent him to the hospital, and much of the task fell to Percy. To reduce the likelihood of holdup prices, negotiations were conducted through a real-estate operator, Leopold Weil, and the utmost secrecy was maintained. None of the landowners (six different groups of owners were involved) was permitted to know the identity of the persons for whom Weil was acting, though the news did leak out that "a certain dry-goods man" was the principal.[12] Since most of the land concerned was held by trustees for undivided estates, it proved impossible to acquire it by outright purchase, and most of the portions were leased for 21 years with renewal privileges. The piece on the southeast corner of the block was owned by a clergyman named Alfred Duane Pell, who was traveling in Spain at the time negotiations began. By means of letters and cablegrams Weil obtained Pell's agreement to sell the plot for $250,000. Considering that it contained less than 1,100 square feet (the dimensions are 31.1 by 45.7 by 16 by 50.6 feet), this was a high price; but the corner obviously had strategic value, and since the Strauses wanted to complete their frontage along Broadway, they agreed to the amount.[13]

However, Pell was not willing to complete the transaction until his return to this country. While he was still abroad, Macy plans were made public, and apparently a rival merchant saw a chance for a squeeze play. Immediately upon his return to America, Pell was persuaded to sell to R. Smith & Co. Any qualms that the reverend gentleman may have had about the ethics of this deal were soothed by a price of $375,000.[14] Smith, who bought the land, operated a small store on 14th Street and was the same man who, when Macy customers wandered into his door by mistake, encouraged them to think that they were really in one of the Macy buildings.

A difference of opinion exists as to Smith's motives. According to the explanation passed on to his sons, he had decided that his business was to a considerable extent dependent upon proximity to Macy's and would suffer unless it was moved up to 34th Street beside the new Macy store. Another explanation — one which better fits the known facts and has always been accepted by the Strauses — is that Smith was acting as agent for Henry Siegel, president of the Siegel-Cooper Co. The decision to move Macy's to 34th Street was a direct threat to the newly established Siegel-Cooper business, and, in casting about for remedial measures, Siegel had hit upon the idea of taking over the old Macy site. To some extent he would then be able to capitalize upon deep-seated buying habits and obtain patronage from former Macy customers who continued to shop along 14th Street. By this means he might possibly check the upward drift of retailing (a tendency to which he himself had given great impetus in 1896). In a surprise move, therefore, Siegel leased a large part of the ground occupied by the old Macy premises and announced that he would put up a new store as soon as the Macy leases expired.[15]

Siegel then sought to purchase the unexpired part of the Macy leases at 14th Street, hoping to take possession just as soon as Macy's moved out. The Strauses, who had anticipated tactics of this sort, flatly refused, stating that the old buildings were to remain vacant until their leases expired. According to the Straus interpretation of events, Siegel thereupon tried to force the issue by getting hold of the Pell property and offering it to the Strauses on the condition that they relinquish the 14th Street site. Certainly Smith offered the land to the Strauses at the price Pell received for it, on the condition that they sublease some 14th Street property. The Strauses believed that he did so as Siegel's agent. His sons understand that he did so because he had come to the conclusion that the corner piece was too small for his purposes and wanted to enlarge his 14th Street store. Whatever the explanation, the Strauses flatly refused. They declined to consider paying $375,000 for the corner piece, and they did not intend to allow another dry goods or department store to move into the old premises until Macy customers had had ample opportunity to learn the way to the new store. As the plans for the new building progressed, a decision as to whether the corner was to be included had to be made. Since Pell would not conclude the sale, the Strauses withdrew their offer and planned an arcade open to the street around the Pell corner.[16]

Thus the attempt to force matters backfired. Whether Smith was acting for himself or for Siegel, the corner property was unquestionably owned by Siegel within a short time. Because of its small size and isolated position, it could hardly have been a productive investment. Only by erecting a building of many floors could it have been made to yield an adequate rental; but that would have entailed elevator service, and a single elevator shaft would have taken up 10 per cent of the total floor area. To this very day the building on the corner of 34th Street (which Siegel sold back to Smith in 1907) is only three stories high, and it will probably never be any higher until circumstances make it worth while to incorporate it into the adjoining structure. In recent years its primary function has been to support a large Macy sign.

Siegel had other reasons to regret antagonizing the Strauses. A small portion of Macy's 14th Street store stood on land which was leased to the firm until 1913. To get that lease canceled (as of May 1, 1903) Siegel had to pay a bonus of $2,000 a year for ten years, a sum which amounted to half the previous annual rental.[17] When Siegel's agents, hoping to expedite the erection of his new building, requested permission to enter the old premises and make borings two months before the Macy leases finally expired, the Strauses refused. They explained that "for the purpose of separating and disassociating from that location a business of the nature of ours for as long a period as possible, we had arranged to leave the buildings vacant at a loss to us of approximately one hundred thousand dollars," and that Siegel could hardly expect them to hasten matters.[18] Lastly, in constructing the new store at 34th Street, the Strauses had an open passageway or arcade built into the southeast corner of the store at street level, so that people passing between 34th and Broadway could cut off a few steps by walking through the Macy arcade rather than around the building on the Pell site.[19] This action probably impaired the value of the corner property by short-circuiting some of the pedestrian traffic which would normally have gone around it, but the arrangement was not simply a matter of spite. So long as the arcade existed (it was eventually closed to provide more space within the store), it served to give the store many of the advantages that a corner is supposed to yield to a retail business — advantages which, had it not been for Siegel, Macy's would have enjoyed.

Originally the Strauses, having encountered difficulty in obtaining enough land between 34th and 35th Streets, had decided to construct a separate building on the north side of 35th Street to house the heating and power facilities and the delivery department. This was to be connected with the main store by means of a tunnel under the street. Soon after the agreement with Pell to sell the corner plot fell through, the way was cleared for leasing additional land to the west, and plans were revised to house all departments in one building. The additional property acquired was occupied by the Koster

& Bial Music Hall, a theater which had earned a small niche in recorded history when it made the first successful public showing of a motion picture, April 23, 1896, using Thomas Armat's Vitascope projector.[20]

Koster & Bial's was not the only well-known institution included in the real estate purchased at the time. The lots purchased on the north side of 35th Street were occupied by the Pekin and the Tivoli, two of the most notorious resorts in a city which was well supplied with brothels. The fact is that Macy's had dared to invade a section of the city which had an evil reputation, and many of the old brownstone houses to be razed were, in the language of the period, "dens of vice." It took courageous foresight, but the Strauses were confident that their move would transform the neighborhood, and contemporary editorial opinion shared their confidence. The *Mail & Express* boldly predicted that Herald Square would "no longer be the center of the Tenderloin, but the heart of the greatest retail shopping district on the American continent."[21] The oldest of the arts (to revise President Lowell's description of business) was displacing the oldest of the professions.

Construction Work

The Strauses chose as architects the firm of DeLemos & Cordes, who had had considerable experience in designing department stores. Determined to have the very best arrangement and the most efficient equipment possible, they instructed the architects to make a special study of store buildings before drawing any plans. In addition, the Strauses themselves devoted a great deal of attention to the project — inspecting stores in both the United States and Europe, analyzing methods of handling merchandise, studying intrastore communications, examining devices for transporting customers from one floor to another, and so on. The wisdom of the resulting designs is evident from the fact that it has taken relatively little alteration to keep the Broadway building modern in appearance and convenient for use.[22]

The contract for clearing the site and erecting the building went to the George A. Fuller Co., with the provision that the store was

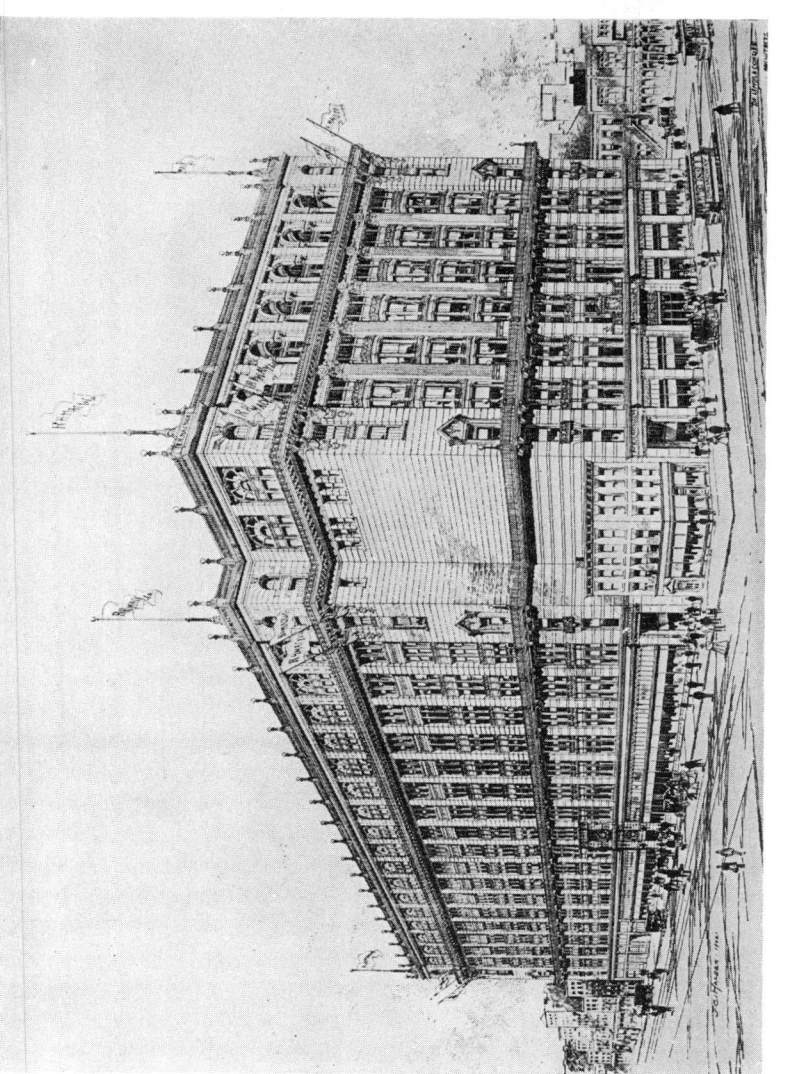

MACY'S IN 1902
The new building in Herald Square

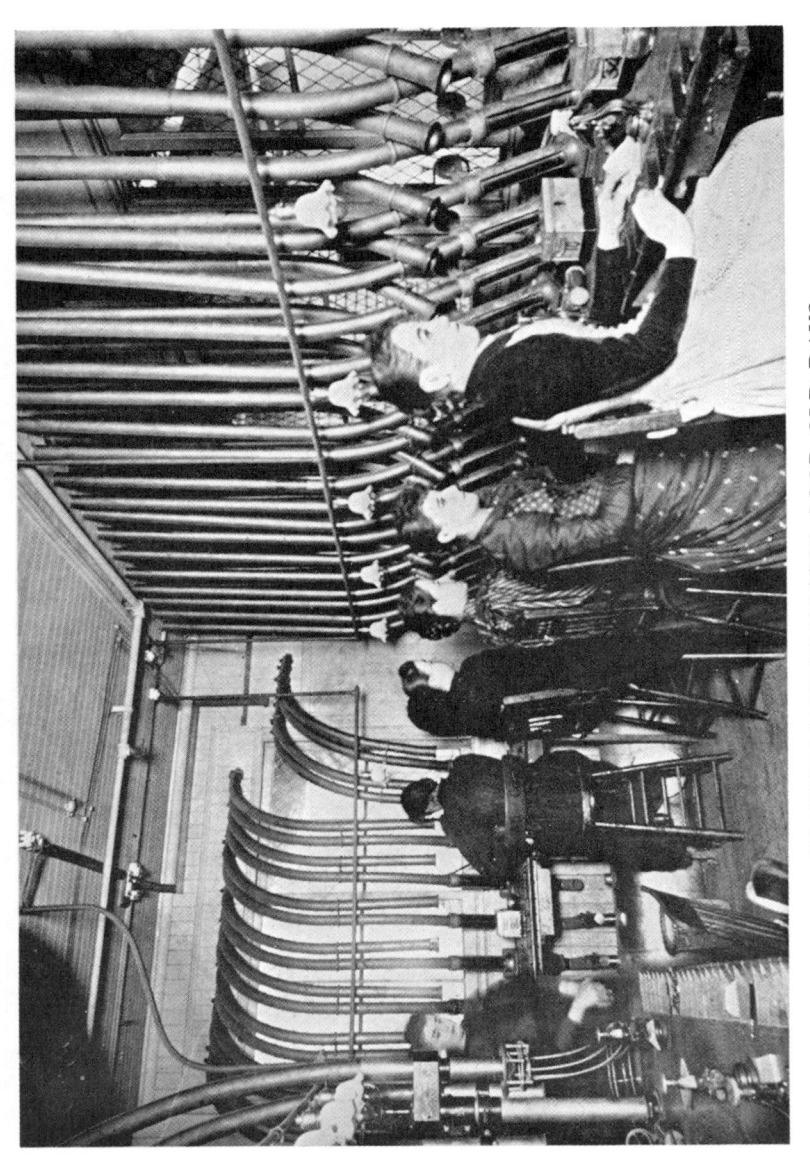

CHANGE-MAKING IN THE GOOD OLD DAYS
Macy's tuberoom in the 14th Street store

to be complete and ready for occupancy by August, 1902. The Fuller Co. had just won public acclaim by putting up the Flatiron Building, famous as a skyscraper at the time but long since dwarfed by higher structures to the north and south. On May 16, 1901, the process of wrecking the old buildings on the site began, and the cornerstone of the new store was laid on April 23 of the following year in the presence of three generations of Strauses.[23]

Today we are so accustomed to large buildings and astronomical figures that it is difficult to appreciate the impression which the new building made upon contemporary New York. It was not particularly tall even for 1902, being only nine stories high, but it occupied a large area. In addition to Koster & Bial's theater, 32 buildings had been razed to make way for it, and the completed structure contained 23½ acres of floor space. To provide both a basement and a sub-basement the contractors had been obliged to remove earth and rock to a depth of 30 feet below street level, and the resulting excavation was the largest in the city. Being executed without benefit of steam shovels or powerful trucks, it was a stupendous task. Digging was done by pick, shovel, and dynamite, with horse-drawn dumpcarts hauling away the earth and blasted stone. Only when the depth made it difficult for teams to haul out the heavy loads did anything like modern technique come into use: spanning the great hole by means of a roadway built on trestlework, the engineers had the empty carts driven out on the resulting bridge and, after detaching the horses, lowered the entire vehicles to the bottom by means of a large steam-powered crane. Once filled, the carts were hoisted back by the same means and then driven away. To newspapermen and "sidewalk superintendents" this version of the horseless carriage was an object of intense interest — as indeed it would undoubtedly be today.[24]

As often happens in the circumstances, some of the buildings to be razed were occupied by tenants who tried to make trouble. One can never be positive about the motives in such cases — whether a sincere desire to defend real or imaginary rights, hope of rich compensation, or simply a desire to make the headlines — but a large firm seems to be widely regarded as fair game for holdups of this kind. A woman, for example, whose basement resturant was included in the new site demanded $25,000 for the cancellation of her lease; it had two years to run and was worth a small fraction of that figure. The courts enjoined the destruction of the basement premises but permitted the demolition of the upper floors. When the contractors began to tear down the house right over her restaurant, she gave up.[25] A barber and a tailor refused to vacate their rooms in a corner building even though they had no leases at all. The contractors dug right up to the walls and then one morning the entire structure was found to have collapsed into the excavation. The irate tenants charged that the contractors' men had jerked out the supports under cover of darkness, but the workmen simply pointed out the possible effects of a localized cyclone or earthquake, and no other witnesses could be found, so nothing came of the matter.[26] Eventually all such difficulties were removed. The building was not finished on schedule, however, for changes in plans combined with other factors to delay completion by three months.

Contemporary newspaper accounts described the new Macy store as the largest and best-equipped department store in the world, and the best information available confirms this view, although Gimbel's in Philadelphia and Marshall Field's in Chicago made similar claims. After the passage of 40 years some of the statistics quoted still make impressive reading. It is easy to forget that a store contains many things besides showcases and merchandise. In the new building were embodied 13,000 tons of structural iron and steel alone, to say nothing of more than 1,000 tons of ornamental iron and bronze. Six "massive iron and marble stairways" led to the upper selling floors and there were 33 hydraulic elevators to transport passengers and freight vertically through the building, besides which there were four Otis escalators to convey customers between the first and fifth floors. The escalators could accommodate 40,000 people an hour and were a means of conveyance so new that the newspapers felt obliged to explain them in some detail. To expedite the rapid handling of packages there were 26 horizontal belt conveyors and 6 vertical conveyors. Cash and sales checks were shot from one part of the store to another by means of an elaborate pneumatic tube system which contained 18 miles of brass tubing, with 130 double and 30 single stations terminating in the basement tuberoom and 90 double and 15 single stations terminating in a second tuberoom on the fourth floor. Four 160-inch fans drove washed air into the store at the rate of 12,000,000 cubic feet an hour, and two exhaust fans removed stale air at the same rate. A vacuum cleaning system (which contemporaries referred to as "suction dusters") was built into the building and, like several other items of equipment, gave rise to many inquiries from other stores.[27]

The main selling floors were lighted mainly by 1,400 Jandus enclosed arc lamps, while 15,000 incandescent lamps and 42 miles of wiring completed the lighting system. The store had its own power plant, the largest private one in the city. It consisted of four 400-kilowatt and two 200-kilowatt generators, driven by six Corliss-type steam engines totaling 3,040 horsepower. In the very first year of operation (1903) this plant produced 3,013,090 kilowatt hours of current. The layman has difficulty in comprehending details of this kind, but here is one figure that nearly everyone can easily grasp: to supply heat and electricity for Macy's in 1903 it took 10,851 tons of coal — enough to heat more than 1,000 homes of the average size for a year. The refrigerating plant produced nearly two tons of ice per day. Within four years the annual production of electric current exceeded 4,000,000 K.W.H., and the rate of coal consumption was over 14,000 tons.[28]

The public restaurant on the eighth floor seated 2,500 people. The building also contained restrooms and a restaurant for the 4,000 employees in the Macy organization. At the top was a huge exhibition hall, the theory being that the automobile shows, poultry shows, and similar exhibitions which were held there would help to instill into New Yorkers the habit of coming to Herald Square.

If any doubts existed about the speed with which other stores would come uptown, they were soon dispelled. Almost before the ink was dry on the Macy deeds and leases came the announcement that Saks & Co. would open a store across the street, running between 33d and 34th Streets on the west side of Broadway. In fact the Saks firm, as the result of having a smaller building to erect, was able to open for business five weeks before Macy's moved into the new quarters.[29] Other concerns rapidly followed suit.

The new building, together with the ground leases involved, cost slightly more than $4,800,000, in addition to which there was a substantial sum invested in fixtures. In point of fact, the whole project was done in the name of L. Straus & Sons, who in turn leased the premises to R. H. Macy & Co. To finance the project Isidor Straus borrowed $4,200,000 from the National City Bank, the Farmers' Loan and Trust Co., and the United States Trust Co.; all of this was obtained at 5 per cent without collateral, an arrangement which gives ample testimony as to the credit standing of the Strauses as well as to contemporary banking opinion of Macy's prospects. All these loans were repaid in full by 1906. The fact that James Stillman of the National City (which had supplied $2,500,000) was also a director of the George A. Fuller Co. seems to have determined the selection of the construction company, for it was at Stillman's recommendation that the Strauses awarded the contract to the Fuller concern.[30]

While the building was in process of completion, the Macy management was busily making plans to move. So far as was feasible, stocks of merchandise were reduced during the summer and fall of 1902 by means of special sales, in order to cut down the bulk which would have to be carried uptown. Then plans were carefully drawn up, showing where every lot of merchandise and every fixture should be placed in the new building, and the Macy Delivery Department, under the direction of James Price, made arrangements to handle all the transportation, hiring 50 wagons in addition to its own 200 wagons and trucks. On Monday, November 3, 1902, the old store closed at the usual time, and for the next four days New Yorkers had to forego the privilege of buying Macy merchandise. On Tuesday the moving started, with a steady procession of wagons leaving the old store, crossing over to Fifth Avenue, then up to 34th Street, and over to the entrances assigned to them. Empty wagons returned down Sixth Avenue and took on new loads. To guard against theft or mishaps, the management posted men along the route to check each vehicle as it passed intersections as well as to record its departure and arrival at the terminals. Extra police protection was also provided. The whole process went on without serious interruption, and on the appointed day, Saturday, November 8, the doors of the new Macy's opened to the public.[31]

The moving of customers naturally could not be controlled so deftly, but there was no great problem. All through the summer and autumn the Macy advertisements referred to the contemplated move, and a barrage of announcements informed the public of the actual date of the opening. In addition, the store arranged with the Mobile Rapid Transit Co. to supply transportation for several months between the old store and the new by means of four "steam wagonettes." In the weeks immediately following the closing at 14th Street the number of passengers conveyed by this means averaged 600 daily. As the sales figures amply show, the general public approved the new location and made large purchases at Herald Square.[32]

The Course of Sales, 1902–1913

Between 1902 and 1907, as Table 22 shows, Macy sales rose rapidly, from 10.76 million dollars to 16.78 million, after which no progress was evident until the outbreak of the first World War. How much of this result may be properly attributed to internal developments and how much to external conditions is beyond precise analysis. Certainly commodity prices and business conditions had considerable influence. While it is impossible to obtain a reliable price index for the merchandise handled by department stores, the substantial rise in the level of prices between 1896 and 1907, together with widespread improvement in business conditions, unquestionably aided the dollar sales volume of Macy's; and the short, sharp panic of 1907, in turn, cut into the store's total sales for 1908 both by lowering prices and by curtailing business generally. On the other hand, before 1908 the Macy sales figures rose much faster than prices, suggesting that forces or conditions within the store were responsible for much of the progress.[33]

After 1908 Macy's annual results were less satisfactory when compared with contemporary conditions. The general price level, though fluctuating, showed a certain amount of improvement, while Macy volume remained at the 16 million level and even showed a slight tendency to decline. To be sure, a business recession and lower prices in 1910 and 1911 combined to keep dollar sales from showing improvement. The level of prices in the textile field particularly —

TABLE 22

ANALYSIS OF SALES

1902–1914

Year	Total Net Sales[a]	Ratio to Previous Year
1902[b]	$10,765,066	122.16
1903	12,203,974	113.37
1904	13,135,446	107.63
1905	15,009,037	114.26
1906[c]	16,723,462	111.42
1907	16,779,425	100.33
1908	16,132,823	96.15
1909	16,580,101	102.77
1910	16,211,296	97.78
1911	16,575,590	102.25
1912[c]	16,234,152	97.94
1913	16,430,818	101.21
1914	17,289,047	105.22

[a] Includes sales in the departments leased by L. Straus & Sons, but not goods sold and subsequently returned.

[b] Accounting period covers 57 weeks ending Jan. 31, 1903. Henceforth the Macy fiscal year ends with the Saturday nearest Jan. 31.

[c] Accounting period covers 53 weeks.

SOURCE: Semiannual balances, 1902–14.

a matter of paramount importance to department stores — stubbornly remained well below the point reached in 1907.[34] In the spring of 1911 Jesse Straus complained to an English friend that political developments were an important factor which seemed to be holding business at a standstill: [35]

There seems to be a spirit of unrest due to the fact that Congress is again at work on tariff legislation, and due further to the general feeling that the large corporations do not know just what attitude the courts are going to take. We have had for over a year a decision pending in our

Supreme Court on the "trust" question, and the longer the decision is delayed, the greater seems the fear that it is going to be adverse to the corporations. As a result, railroads, steel companies, and, in fact, all of our large combinations of capital are hesitating to contract for extensions and new equipment. In addition, we shall have in another year a Presidential Campaign which always causes a certain amount of upset.

Contrary to these expectations, general conditions did improve in 1912, but Macy volume showed a small drop at the end of the year. This unfavorable showing may well have been caused by changes within the management of the store, resulting from the death of Isidor Straus. We shall hear more about that tragic event later in this chapter.

Of course we should be better able to judge Macy results of that period if we knew what was happening to rival department stores. Unfortunately it is impossible to obtain information about the results achieved by other firms or the state of local retail trade in general. However, we do know that competitors were taking steps which made it difficult for Macy's to achieve gains in patronage. Saks & Co., directly across the street, must have diverted a certain amount of business, and John Wanamaker, after opening a fine new store in September, 1907, put forth renewed efforts to increase his share of the city's trade. True, Wanamaker had decided to remain at Astor Place rather than move uptown, but the new fifteen-story building was an *addition* to his premises rather than a replacement of the old Stewart store, and it was filled with attractions unexcelled anywhere in the world.[36] Undoubtedly some of the increased volume which Macy's might otherwise have enjoyed went to Wanamaker. All through this period the Siegel interests were making desperate efforts to capture business for the Siegel-Cooper store and the newer Fourteenth Street Store. In addition, a new and formidable rival joined the fray in 1910, when Gimbel Brothers invaded the Manhattan retail territory by opening a large store just a block south of Macy's. The Gimbels not only captured a substantial amount of business but also took for their new staff a good many executives from Macy's and other retail organizations.[37] All things considered, Macy's probably did well to maintain the gains won before 1907.

Changes in Departments

To some extent the sales figures reflect the fact that after 1902 no important additions were made to the merchandise stocked by Macy's. In earlier years new lines undoubtedly contributed to the growth in volume, but by 1902, as already shown, the store had just about exhausted the possibilities of diversification. Further gains would have to come from an increase in the number of patrons, larger individual purchases, and minor innovations in the merchandise carried; and subsequent progress was accordingly more difficult. Indeed, the only noteworthy additions to merchandise were the reopening of a piano department in 1903, the installation of a delicatessen department in 1904, and the creation in 1911 of a department to handle fresh fruits. In 1909 and several subsequent years Macy's operated a department in which were sold articles made by blind craftsmen; the store provided space, fixtures, and sales clerks without charge, turning over all receipts to an institution for the blind. This undertaking, although it admittedly had some publicity value, was a matter of charity and civic duty rather than a source of additional revenue.[38]

The increased sales in individual departments, on the other hand, together with the need for more exact accounting control, led to the emergence of a large number of new departments in Macy's. For the most part these were offshoots from the formidable array of departments already in existence. They appeared as follows: cotton piece goods, 1903; leather goods, 1903; misses' goods and children's garments, 1903; real laces, 1903; veilings, 1903; girls' coats, 1904; ladies' dresses and gowns, 1904; fur storage, 1905; motorists' clothing and automobile supplies, 1905; clocks and bronzes, 1905; cutlery and belts, 1906; music, 1906; jewelry repairing, 1907; solid gold jewelry, 1907; oriental rugs, 1908; cutlery, 1910; boys' hats, 1910; photographic supplies, 1910; trunks and bags, 1910; silk shirts and bathing suits, 1911; artists' materials, 1913; cakes and pies, 1913; and baby carriages, 1913.[39] Amidst the welter of departments, customers and staff members alike must sometimes have wondered about the advantages of a big store.

And yet Macy's really did draw the line at having *everything* in the store. The management repeatedly rejected proposals to open a manicuring or hair-dressing department, just as it turned down many suggestions that it set up dental service within the store. There was even one proposal to install an astrologer in the store![40] In 1914 the management discontinued the piano department because ten years of experience had proved that the cash policy made it difficult to sell pianos in profitable volume. With this exception there was hardly anything used by the average family that the store could add to its very comprehensive offering, short of venturing into some quite new field such as selling automobiles. In point of fact, Macy's sold a few automobiles in 1903, but it did so only on a commission basis and largely because it was more or less responsible for the management of an automobile show that took place in the ninth-floor exhibition hall.[41] In 1904 John Wanamaker went into selling automobiles on a much wider scale, but the day was far distant when the department store could profitably handle motor cars.

Several new divisions appeared in the Macy organization which, although involving no innovations in merchandise, cut across the existing departmental lines and amounted to a new manner of offering goods. Thus, in 1910 the store opened a "pick-up booth" in the Hudson Terminal Building as soon as the new tubes opened for service. Here commuters on their way to work in the morning could leave orders for merchandise and pick up their purchases on the way home in the afternoon. A second booth of this type was established in the Grand Central Terminal in 1913. Both these extramural divisions developed additional volume by offering extra convenience to busy people, but the expense involved in maintaining them was too great to permit net profits, and they were eventually abandoned.[42] Possibly the commuters were in too much of a hurry to save time by patronizing the booths.

For over a year there was within the store still a third division which sold to the public by drawing on many merchandise departments. It was known as "Old Fashioned Macy's" and appeared early in 1912. Located on the sixth floor, this enterprise assembled low-priced merchandise from all the regular selling departments and was apparently the Macy equivalent of the bargain basement which other department stores (notably Filene's in Boston) were beginning to use as a means of increasing their trade. After a year's experience, however, the management decided that the idea of a store within the store was not feasible, and "Old Fashioned Macy's" gave way to main-floor bargain tables which have been used ever since to sell special lots of low-priced goods.[43]

One other change at this time was a definite attempt to develop a mail-order business, followed by its virtual abandonment. Like the terminal booths and "Old Fashioned Macy's," the mail-order department drew upon the regular merchandise departments for its stock-in-trade. Nathan Straus had favored its expansion because it spread the name of Macy's far afield, and his associates seem to have agreed with him in thinking that it might be made an important part of the firm's business. Unfortunately, while the volume grew, the expense connected with it mounted even faster. No data have survived on the amount of business done by mail, but some idea of the efforts to push it may be gained from the money spent in printing and mailing catalogs, an expenditure which rose steadily from a negligible amount in 1902 to $400,000 in 1911. This expense, which did not cover the entire cost of operating the division, amounted to 2.4 per cent of the total net sales of the whole store for the year and was obviously too high. It was the inevitable result of distributing by the thousands a large catalog (460 pages) filled with illustrations, some of them in color.[44]

On reviewing the situation the management decided that a fundamental conflict in objectives existed and that the mail-order business should be discontinued at once. Success with it depended upon handling the kind of staple merchandise which ordinarily did not change greatly in style or price during the course of a year. Regular department store operations, in marked contrast, called for a rapidly changing assortment of offerings, the very novelty of which would tempt people to buy, with price and style neatly adjusted to the momentary whims of New York's mercurial market. Of course, operating a mail-order business in the heart of New York's retail district involved heavy expense ratios because it used high-rent property and expensive fixtures, relatively well-paid clerks, and so on. In addition, there is some evidence that the combination of mail-order with over-the-counter transactions aggravated for both divisions the physical problem of handling orders expeditiously: conflicts of authority, misunderstandings, and friction were bound to develop. As a matter of convenience to customers, Macy's has, of course, continued to fill mail orders and even to solicit them from time to time on particular lots of goods, but the expensive annual catalogs and efforts to rival Sears, Roebuck & Co. came to an end in 1912.[45]

Developments in Store Services

Although there were no startling innovations in store service after 1902, the tendency to stress extra services to customers continued without abatement in Macy's as well as in rival concerns. As in the preceding period, these extras appeared in a variety of forms — restrooms, more attractive fixtures, store restaurants, improvements in delivery service, and the like. Thus, in 1904, Macy invited tired shoppers to stop in its Japanese tearoom, on the fifth floor adjoining the grocery department, where they could rest, obtain refreshments, and give grocery orders at their leisure.[46] By 1907 the management had not only installed a special force of telephone clerks to receive orders in the grocery department but had also arranged to have them call customers for orders at appointed intervals.[47] (Perhaps this is the forerunner of a kind of retail "service" which some retail firms have made an unmitigated nuisance.) To facilitate the problem of gifts at Christmas time Macy's began, as early as 1906, to feature merchandise bonds, which customers could buy and give to friends; obtainable in amounts from one to five dollars and redeemable in merchandise at Macy's, these bonds enabled the recipients to select their own presents. At the same time the firm had already started to provide fancy boxes and wrappings for the merchandise that it offered for gift purposes.[48]

In many respects, of course, the new building itself must be regarded as a kind of service to customers, since it embodied spacious shopping aisles, quick and easy transportation from floor to floor, a large restaurant (it served a million people in 1908), attractive furnishings and fixtures, and comfortable restrooms, all designed to please the shopper. Within the building the firm not only provided public telephones, a telegraph office, a post office, and an information bureau but also installed a theater-ticket office. It is impossible to trace all the improvements which the management made in the premises from year to year, but it is worth noting that the ninth floor, originally devoted to exhibition purposes, had to be taken over for store purposes within a few years in order to release additional selling space below, and that a tenth floor was added to the building in 1910 in order to allow patrons enough space in which to shop without undue crowding.[49] In 1913, partly to relieve congestion on the first floor and partly in recognition of changes in public demand, Macy's moved dress goods, silks, wash goods, and untrimmed millinery up to the second floor, thereby making possible the installation of new showcases and a better display of main-floor merchandise.[50] Yard goods no longer on the first floor! A new era had arrived in the dry goods trade.

In this connection certain general improvements in the technique of display may be noted. The year 1908, for example, marked an innovation (at least so far as Macy's is concerned) in the spring and fall "style opening," when the firm employed living models to display imported gowns against an elaborately decorated background prepared especially for the occasion. This practice was continued in subsequent years and helped to inform thousands of women about changes in styles, as well as to convey the idea that Macy's offered expensive, fashionable merchandise along with popularly priced staples.[51] In the language of current retailing, Macy's was "trading up."

The same type of improvement was apparent in the show-windows and in the display of regular merchandise within the store. The day had passed when the firm was content to have goods piled up on shelves and counters without much regard to appearances; no longer was it considered wise to fill up an entire window with a single type of merchandise. By 1909 the store was beginning to exhibit related merchandise together (e.g., shoes, stockings, and dresses, or a completely furnished room), so that customers could see total effects rather than isolated parts. We take such techniques for granted

JESSE ISIDOR STRAUS
Partner, 1912–1919; president, 1919–1933; ambassador to France, 1933–1936

TYPICAL MACY ADVERTISING LAYOUT, 1906
Portion of a full-page newspaper advertisement

today, but they have not always been in common use. By such means Macy's helped many persons to buy more intelligently, doubtless with a beneficial effect on sales. Further, both window and interior displays became aesthetically more appealing, presenting an attractive scene as well as focusing attention upon particular items or styles. By 1911 Macy's was winning prizes for window decoration. The limited evidence now available suggests that the store, after having paid only a moderate amount of attention to display, was beginning to catch up with the advances made by its principal competitors.[52]

In so far as advertising may be considered an informational service to the public, it is well to note the broadening of the media used at this time. Macy's depended principally upon newspaper advertising in the New York *American*, *Sun*, *Times*, *Tribune*, and *World*, but by 1913 it was also using a large number of papers in neighboring towns, including the Asbury Park *Evening Press*, New Brunswick *Daily Home News*, Plainfield *Daily Press*, Nyack *Evening Star*, Perth Amboy *Evening News*, Newark *Evening News*, Passaic *Daily Herald*, Paterson *Morning Call*, Elizabeth *Daily Journal*, Ossining *Citizen*, Peekskill *Daily Union*, Orange *Daily Chronicle*, Tarrytown *Daily News*, Mount Vernon *Daily Argus*, White Plains *Daily Record*, Flushing *Evening Journal*, Stamford *Advocate*, Yonkers *Herald*, Montclair *Times*, and New Rochelle *Pioneer*.[53] This wide coverage, of course, reflects not only the store's efforts to extend its market but also a corresponding disposition on the part of the public to go farther afield to satisfy its wants.

In addition to newspaper advertising, Macy's began to distribute attractive leaflets and folders to call attention to particular departments or lines of merchandise within the store. In 1913, for example, one folder described the February furniture sale offerings, another featured the corset department, several leaflets contained instructions for planting shrubs and the care of roses (each spring the firm sold plants, seeds, and bulbs), another booklet explained both imported toiletries and those made in the Macy laboratory, and so on. Beginning in 1912, if not earlier, Macy's sent postcards to customers each spring to remind them of the need for protecting furs and woolens against moths; a stamped return postcard was attached so that they might readily avail themselves of Macy storage facilities.[54] The store, in other words, was beginning to help in the intricate task of household management.

Another service of which Macy customers availed themselves on an increasing scale was the privilege of returning purchases which, for one reason or another, they did not wish to keep. The goods returned in 1902 amounted to 2.29 per cent of sales (see Table 27, p. 396), and this ratio rose steadily until returns amounted to approximately 4 per cent of the store's net sales volume. This meant that for every $100 of final sales the store had to sell $104 worth of merchandise and then receive back $4 of it, often delivering the purchase a considerable distance and then calling again to take it back.[55] The desire to satisfy the customer was natural and commendable, but returned merchandise involved the waste of sales clerks' efforts, delivery equipment, and clerical work, to say nothing of the damage to merchandise which often resulted.

By today's standards the returns ratio for the years 1902–13 was low, but the trend is highly significant. It reveals a more liberal policy on the part of the store and increased use of the return privilege by Macy customers. To some extent the more liberal policy may be the consequence of the increased size of the staff, for mistakes in filling orders seem to occur more frequently as an organization expands. It may also be attributed to the substantial growth in the sale of ready-to-wear clothing. Certainly it is necessary and legitimate to return merchandise which does not fit, is defective, or differs from the goods ordered. To an increasing extent, however, returns were made simply because the customer had changed her mind. There has always been less of this in Macy's than in stores selling on credit because the customer is less likely to take goods out on approval if the transaction involves an actual cash outlay instead of a mere bookkeeping entry on the store's accounts, but the growing tendency in all department stores was to accept returned merchandise without raising much question as to the reasons involved. As one looks back upon the abuse of the return privilege, which has since developed, it is plain that the public was being permitted and even encouraged to behave like spoiled brats so far as department stores were concerned. Here, of course, is one of the sources of the increased cost of distribution about which we now complain.

The reader may wonder at the inclusion of such topics as telephone service, style shows, display, and advertising under the heading of "store services," and it is certainly true that they might also be considered as sales promotional devices. Of course, they belong to both categories; it is simply not possible to draw a sharp line between, on the one hand, measures taken to give customers information, improve their taste, or make shopping more attractive and, on the other, efforts put forth to increase sales and profits. The best kind of promotion does both. One may not fully approve the kind of service that is sometimes included as a part of the selling effort, and some of it admittedly might be better performed by other agencies, but the fact remains that retailing has come to involve, to an increasing degree, a great deal of service besides the mere selling of merchandise. The individual firm has had little choice in the matter. As the Macy management explained in 1913, "the modern shopper has been educated to shop under conditions far different from those which existed fifteen, or even ten years ago." [56]

In this connection the reader may be reminded that retail advertising and window display have unquestionably been a strong influence in shaping the American standards of living, although it is impossible to measure the precise effect. Probably New York department stores should be given credit for a large part in the Americanization of the vast streams of immigrants which flowed through Ellis Island — at least in the period before the rise of motion pictures. The windows of firms like Macy's showed the newly arrived European what the rank and file of Americans wore, something about their character and habits, and how they furnished their homes. The same influence must have stimulated his ambition to work and to save so that he, too, might enjoy the material wealth of the New World. America's culture is predominantly a business culture, and the department store has been one of the chief participants in its propagation.

Delivery Facilities

One of the most important services performed by department stores in connection with their selling, of course, is the delivery of purchases to the customer. Although a distinctly subordinate phase of retailing, this activity is one of the most important to the continued success of a department store. Efficient delivery service may not do much to increase sales, but slow, unreliable, or discourteous delivery service quickly drives patronage away. Accordingly, one of the main concerns of Macy management in the period under discussion was to maintain an effective delivery department. As Macy's continued to grow, its delivery problem increased in scope and complexity. It was not simply a question of hauling more packages to a greater number of customers over approximately the same routes. A great many of the store's customers were moving to the suburbs and adjacent towns, and it was necessary to extend delivery routes in order to retain old customers as well as to obtain new ones.

The geographical territory covered by Macy's own delivery department steadily increased, with the result that the firm had not only to employ more men, wagons, and horses, but was obliged also to establish substations at a distance from the store in order to facilitate reaching the outlying districts. Otherwise the horse-drawn vehicles would spend most of the day in merely traveling to the point where a suburban route began. The store already had one substation at 148th Street in 1902, and in 1906 it established a second at Woodlawn in the Bronx; in the course of the next four years the Woodlawn station gradually absorbed the work of the 148th Street unit. By 1910 the store had depots as far out as Portchester, New York, and Hackensack, New Jersey, besides substations in Newark, Queens, and Staten Island. Each night large vans conveyed loads of merchandise to each of these distributing points, after which the local wagons took over the task of delivering the packages to customers in the surrounding territory.[57]

It is impossible to give an adequate picture of the organization required to handle Macy deliveries, but one gets a rough notion of it from the equipment used. In 1902 the store operated 200 wagons, the motive power being provided by approximately 500 horses. Giving proper care to so many animals was in itself a special problem, and each year the firm had to purchase about 70 horses (mostly imported from the West) as replacements in order to keep the system going. The average cost per horse rose from $193 in 1902 to $225 in 1910. For severe winter conditions a large number of sleighs were kept on hand. It required a veritable army of drivers, helpers, wagon-boys, stablemen, harness-makers, and blacksmiths to complete the array. With an organization involving so much equipment and so many men, the very best management could hardly avoid occasional breakdowns, misunderstandings, and delays, and it is small wonder that occasionally there were complaints from customers about the service.[58]

One solution to the increasing distance which the delivery department had to cover was mechanization. As already mentioned, Macy's experimented with a five-ton gasoline truck in 1902, using it for the heavy hauling between freight depots and the store. In 1903 the management decided to try electrically driven trucks for retail delivery service and purchased 15 at $2,000 each. Some firms used the horseless vehicles primarily for their advertising value, but the Macy management had passed that stage and wanted trucks only when they provided economical transportation. In the congested, horse-drawn traffic near the store the superior speed and endurance of the electrics was of little use, but for the long hauls they were definitely more efficient than horses, and the firm added 14 more of them in 1907. By 1910 Macy's operated 36 one-ton electric trucks, in addition to 8 gasoline trucks of heavier capacity and 140 horse-drawn wagons.[59]

For the intermediate runs the electrics proved to be more satisfactory than the gasoline-powered vehicles, but they were unable to reach the distant points and return without recharging, and so gasoline trucks were used on the long runs from the store to the substations and in transferring heavy loads of merchandise from freight depots to the store. By 1912, however, the efficiency of gasoline engines had improved to such an extent that Macy's found it advisable to add 18 Chase trucks to the fleet, raising the total to 23 gasoline and 35 electric vehicles. At the same time the management found mechanized transport less economical than horses for a considerable part of the delivery work — principally in the central part of Manhattan, where the frequency of delivery stops and the prevalence of horse-drawn traffic made motor delivery slow and expensive, and in certain suburbs where bad road conditions, combined with the tendency of the trucks to break down far from garage facilities, made horses more reliable. In addition to the trucks, therefore, Macy's had 150 wagons and 175 horses. Old Dobbin was to remain an integral part of the store's delivery system for many years to come.[60]

Not all purchases were delivered by the store's own facilities; even with the aid of motor vehicles Macy's could cover only a radius of roughly 50 miles from the store. Beyond the bounds of its own delivery system Macy's sent merchandise by freight, prepaying the charges on purchases amounting to $5.00 or more to stations within 100 miles of New York City. In 1906 the management greatly extended the limits within which it would, according to the amount purchased, pay transportation charges, as follows:[61]

$5. Free delivery to any town in New York, New Jersey, Delaware, Pennsylvania, Connecticut, Massachusetts, Rhode Island, New Hampshire, Vermont, Maryland, and the District of Columbia.
$10. Free delivery to any town in Maine, Illinois, Michigan, Indiana, Ohio, Kentucky, Virginia, and West Virginia.
$25. Free delivery to any town in Florida, Alabama, Georgia, South Carolina, North Carolina, Tennessee, Iowa, and Wisconsin.
$50. Free delivery to any town in Louisiana, Mississippi, Texas, Arkansas, Missouri, Kansas, Oklahoma, Indian Territory, Nebraska, South Dakota, and North Dakota, and Minnesota.
$75. Free delivery to any town from the Atlantic to the Pacific.

Nominally this extended Macy's market to the entire United States; in point of fact, not many people at distant points found it feasible to buy from Macy's, and the extension was therefore chiefly a matter of publicity. The same is true of the step taken by John Wanamaker when he announced (January, 1910) that he would deliver free of charge purchases of $5.00 or more to any part of the world within the international postal limits.⁶² Macy's, however, refused to follow Wanamaker's lead.

Deposit Account Department

Unlike Wanamaker, who abandoned his original cash policy in favor of extending short-term credit to customers, Macy's steadfastly refused to do any charge-account business. In this respect, and in this only, Macy's declined to match the services offered to customers by rival department stores. Not until 1939 did the firm relax its cash policy sufficiently to permit customers to buy merchandise on credit, and then only upon payment of the fee involved in the "cash-time" arrangement. The reasoning behind the management's policy was and still is that it is cheaper to buy and sell for cash, and that those who prefer to buy on credit should bear the extra expense involved. Believing (until recently) that it was not feasible to charge a differential to cover this expense, Macy's chose to sell for cash only so as to keep its prices as low as possible.⁶³

From the customer's point of view, of course, the charge account is a great convenience, and it is an accepted theory, borne out by long experience, that a charge account usually acts as a bond between the customer and the store, so that credit customers tend to provide more "repeat business" than those who pay cash. Recognizing both these factors, the Macy management devised a plan in 1902 to reap the advantages of charge accounts without incurring the expense of bad debts.

Simultaneously with the opening of the new building in November, 1902, the firm announced the establishment of a Department of Deposit for the convenience of Macy customers. Those who desired to have the convenience of charge accounts deposited with the new department a sum of money against which their subsequent purchases would be charged, replenishing the fund whenever desirable. In effect the customers paid in advance, and to encourage them to do so, Macy's paid interest on unspent balances at the rate of 4 per cent a year, compounded quarterly. At the end of each month the "D/A" (deposit account) customers received a statement of items charged against their deposit and the balance on hand. They could not transfer money to third parties by means of a check, but they were free to withdraw it at any time they cared to do so.⁶⁴

To some extent the D/A department merely formalized and extended to all customers an arrangment which the firm had previously permitted on a limited scale to customers who wished to avoid the nuisance of carrying cash for all purchases. It was, moreover, an adaptation of a scheme which William Whiteley had introduced into his famous London store thirty years earlier.⁶⁵ Whiteley, however, had sought deposits because he needed capital for his rapidly expanding business; Macy's had no such motive and definitely wanted to avoid a banking business as such. In fact, for many years the Macy management had to wage a constant campaign to get depositors (some of whom deposited as much as $30,000 and $40,000) to reduce their balances to amounts commensurate with their regular purchases. Particularly after the crash of 1907 had closed many commercial banks, a number of people seemed to think that their money would be safer invested in tangible merchandise than in commercial loans. Isidor Straus was flattered, but he sent back the checks.⁶⁶

In an effort to increase the amount of sales made through the D/A arrangement, Macy's began in 1905 to distribute Christmas bonus checks based upon the total amount of purchases made by each customer against his deposit. For many years this bonus was 2 per cent of the customer's annual purchases. As additional encouragement the store began the practice in 1907 of free delivery of purchases during the summer months to any point east of the Mississippi, regardless of the amount, if they were charged against D/A accounts.⁶⁷

Table 23 presents some statistics on the growth of D/A business. It is evident that the amount, as compared with the total sales volume, was relatively small — less than 9 per cent of the total even after 10 years of development. Perhaps this figure should be compared with the proportion of business done through charge accounts by stores granting credit; judging by recent figures, that proportion must have been about 50 per cent. In other words, the D/A arrangement was not used nearly so extensively as charge accounts probably would have been.⁶⁸ On the other hand, the data reveal a

TABLE 23
Analysis of Deposit Account Transactions
1902–1919

Year	Total Amount on Deposit on Dec. 31	Approx. No. of Accts.	D/A Sales Amount	D/A Sales % of Total Net Sales	D/A Expense % of D/A Sales[a]
1902[b]	$ 7,889	500	$ 26,432	0.25	...
1903	221,571	2,000	174,899	1.43	...
1904	633,053	3,850	287,310	2.19	...
1905	1,342,873	7,000	472,471	3.15	3.14
1906	2,010,878	10,000	674,312	4.03	1.64
1907	1,615,017	13,250	810,675	4.83	1.81
1908	1,552,276	15,500	867,091	5.37	1.71
1909	1,529,199	17,500	1,025,122	6.18	1.67
1910	1,497,497	19,500	1,085,980	6.70	1.82
1911	1,506,896	21,500	1,239,236	7.48	1.72
1912	1,459,691	23,900	1,348,943	8.31	1.73
1913	1,421,327	25,650	1,449,642	8.82	1.70
1914	1,056,475	27,000	1,425,511	8.25	1.77
1915	1,216,029	29,000	1,583,029	8.31	4.37
1916	1,597,056	31,500	1,814,117	8.32	2.80
1917	1,768,957	34,450	1,878,218	8.01	3.24
1918	1,894,920	36,500	1,797,158	6.96	7.19
1919	2,635,671	38,500	2,440,037	6.82	2.12

[a] This column refers to disbursements by the store in the form of dividends to depositors on their purchases, together with payments to R. H. Macy & Co., Private Bankers, in 1915 and subsequent years, to indemnify the bankers for losses on securities held against deposits. Such losses arose because the D/A department was set up as a private bank in 1914 to conform with new requirements of the New York State Banking Department at a time when security prices, as a result of the impact of the War, were depreciating. It is not possible for the period covered by this table to segregate the bookkeeping expense which was involved in the D/A transactions and which was borne by the retail firm.

[b] The D/A department opened for business on Nov. 8, 1902.

Source: Records of R. H. Macy & Co., Private Bankers.

steady growth in the number of D/A accounts and in the sales transacted by means of them, both absolutely and in relation to the store's total sales. It is worth noting that until 1913 the amount on deposit at the close of each year regularly exceeded the total D/A sales for the year, proving that patrons were using Macy's as a savings bank in spite of the management's efforts to eliminate the excess deposits.

No reliable data are available by which one can determine whether or not the D/A business was worth what it cost. Macy's had to pay customers interest on their deposits and, after 1906, paid an annual bonus on D/A sales; in addition, there was undoubtedly a good deal of clerical expense directly attributable to the deposit department. On the other hand, the firm was able to maintain its cash policy while offering patrons the convenience of an open account, it avoided the expense of credit investigations and losses from bad debts, it derived a good deal of useful publicity from the D/A department, and it had the use of a substantial sum of money as an offset to the interest paid. (In 1914, in order to conform to the requirements of the New York State banking laws, Macy's had to set up a separate entity, known as R. H. Macy & Co., Private Bankers, to handle the D/A deposits.[69] Before that date the store's arrangement had not been classified as a bank, and D/A funds were intermingled with the regular assets of the store. The banking firm consisted of Jesse, Percy, and Herbert Straus, and the contract between it and the store provided that the banking firm should receive 8 per cent on its investment and be indemnified by the store against any losses, including those arising from any depreciation of the securities held by the bank as security for deposits.) In 1940 the name of the D/A division was changed to Macy's Bank. Whatever the advantage might have been from a strict accounting basis, it is clear that (1) the management did not know precisely what the costs and revenues of the D/A business were and (2) it was firmly convinced from its actual experience that the D/A business was definitely desirable in terms of store operations as a whole.

Old Partnerships and New

In many ways the period from 1902 to 1914 was one of important but subtle transitions within the Macy firm — a period in which a new generation began to take over the administration of the store, in which the problems of management altered in character and new policies and methods had to be devised to meet them, and in which an entirely new price situation developed. Since most of these transitions reached a climax after 1914 and deserve extended treatment, it is necessary to consider them separately in the following chapter. For the moment the topic on which we must focus attention is the shift in ownership which took place between 1912 and 1914.

Despite the entrance of Isidor's three sons into the business between 1896 and 1903, no change in the legal partnership was made. Isidor and Nathan shared the ownership and profits equally, and Isidor in turn assigned part of his share of the profits to Jesse, Percy, and Herbert. When Nathan's two sons, Nathan, Jr., and Hugh Grant, began to work in the store (1910), that arrangement continued without alteration. Meanwhile, both Isidor and Nathan had experienced occasional periods of poor health, and the active direction of the business was falling more and more upon Isidor's sons. No important decisions were ever made without consulting the older men, but by 1910 the three boys had clearly proved their abilities, had won from the organization full recognition of their authority, and had taken over the main task of store management.[70]

In 1912 Isidor Straus and his wife went to Europe for travel and rest. They decided to return to America on the maiden voyage of the world's largest and finest ship, the supposedly unsinkable *Titanic*. The story of the ensuing tragedy is fairly well known.[71] When the crash of steel and ice roared through that April night, a new-fangled gadget, called "the wireless," crackled a message of distress, and the eastbound *Carpathia*, four hours distant, responded.

Among the *Carpathia's* passengers was John Badenoch, head of the Macy grocery department, on a buying trip to Europe. Knowing that his employer was on board the *Titanic*, Badenoch hurriedly arranged, while the Cunarder raced toward the sinking ship, to turn over his cabin to Mr. and Mrs. Straus. He did so in vain; long before the *Carpathia* could reach her, the *Titanic* went down with a loss of over 1,500 lives. As the lifeboats of the doomed liner were being launched, men urged Isidor Straus to get in with his wife. He quietly declined; there were not enough lifeboats, and there could be no exceptions to the unwritten law of women and children first. With equal firmness Ida Straus decided to remain with her husband, and the fine old couple faced death as they had faced life, with simple dignity, courage, and honor. . . .

Isidor Straus left his share of the Macy business to be divided equally among his three sons, so that after the spring of 1912 the Macy firm consisted of Nathan Straus, who held a half-interest, and Jesse, Percy, and Herbert Straus, each of whom owned one-sixth.

The resulting situation was inevitably difficult. Nathan, as the senior partner and owner of the largest individual share, felt that his decisions should prevail, while the three boys, as the active administrators of the business and owners of an equal interest, were convinced that their combined judgment should dominate. Differences of opinion arose over policies, conflicting orders were issued to employees, and relations between Nathan and his nephews soon became strained to the point where further coöperation became impossible.[72]

To some extent this friction may have originated from the fact that circumstances had placed Nathan's sons in subordinate positions within the store. Having entered in 1910, they had hardly got well started in the process of learning the business when an iceberg, far out in the Atlantic, precipitated a family crisis. They were considerably younger than their cousins, they lacked experience, and they had not yet won a place in that indefinable but important hierarchy of authority which employees carry in their minds. Isidor's sons had acquired an entrenched position within the Macy organization simply by their years of service, quite apart from any question of abilities, and it would have taken many years for Nathan's sons to overcome this long headstart. Essentially they were still in their apprenticeship stage and, in fact, were not directly involved in the growing difference between Nathan and his nephews. Even so, Nathan and his wife could hardly be expected to view the situation without feeling sparks of parental jealousy which differences of opinion would fan into actual resentment. And differences of opinion were bound to emerge, if for no other reason, simply because of the unbridgeable gulf between youth and old age. Nathan tended to cling to the methods of store management which had served Macy's so well in the past. His nephews strongly believed that the Macy organization and methods of doing business required thorough modernization.

Added to these difficulties were the problems created by Nathan's unpredictable individualism. Even Isidor Straus, whose enduring patience was bolstered by deep brotherly affection, had sometimes found Nathan's impulsive nature a sore trial. In fact, Isidor had enclosed with his will a copy of a letter which he had once been impelled to write to Nathan. There was no comment appended to the message, but the three sons understood its import: Isidor had realized that some day the family ties within the business would probably have to break and had chosen this method of indicating the course which he felt that his sons should pursue.

The three brothers made an appraisal of the Macy business and concluded that at a conservative valuation it was worth $15,000,000, including $7,000,000 goodwill. They then proposed that Nathan buy their half-interest, indicating at the same time their willingness to buy his share on the same terms. To this Nathan replied on October 26, 1913, as follows:[73]

Your suggestion as to my purchase of your interest in R. H. Macy & Co. under conditions named by you I do not feel justified in accepting in view of the state of my wife's and my health.

If you would buy me out, however, at the same figure and under practically the same conditions which you put in your tender, I should consider it a very satisfactory consummation of the existing negotiations. Inasmuch as you have first offered the business to me on this basis, I should feel that if you buy it as now proposed I should have no ground for complaint and would feel that you have acted in good faith and without taking any advantage of me. Under those circumstances a sale as now proposed would not cause any rupture in the family relationship heretofore prevailing between us.

Thus it came about that Nathan Straus and his two sons withdrew from Macy's at the close of 1913, with Jesse, Percy, and Herbert Straus sharing equally the full ownership of the business. To meet the purchase price of $7,500,000 the three brothers transferred the shares that they had inherited in Abraham & Straus and L. Straus & Sons and their combined deposits in L. Straus & Sons, these assets totaling $3,773,180. Included in the transaction was the transfer of the store building at 34th Street from L. Straus & Sons to the Macy firm. To settle the balance due, they paid $926,820 in cash and $2,800,000 by means of a certificate of indebtedness to be gradually liquidated out of subsequent profits.[74]

CHAPTER XIII

PROBLEMS OF PRICE AND WAR

AFTER 1913 the sons of Isidor Straus were in complete control of Macy's and entirely free to run the business according to their own ideas. The subsequent history of the store, even after one makes allowance for the inflationary influence of the first World War, amply proves that the second generation of Strauses knew how to make Macy's forge ahead once more, after having paused for at least five years during the period before the change in partnership. It is not mere coincidence that most of the steps taken to modernize the business were made after 1913.

As we have seen, of course, the three brothers had already taken charge of most of the store operations before they acquired complete ownership, and they therefore had a hand in the solution of a number of critical transition problems which confronted Macy's after the move to 34th Street. This chapter deals with the most important of those problems, namely, the clash between the traditional Macy policy of underselling competitors and the efforts of manufacturers to fix retail prices, the general administrative problem which emerged from the growth of the organization, the adjustment to conditions created by the first World War, certain developments in personnel management, and the beginning of a shift in emphasis from price to quality and style. At the end of the chapter is a brief analysis of Macy operating data during the years 1902–19.

The Rising Threat of Resale Price Maintenance

At Herald Square, as at 14th Street, the Macy firm continued to pursue its long-established policy of underselling competitors. After 1902, indeed, this policy, which formerly had not been very clearly defined or consistently applied, began to crystallize into a definite rule which the firm attempted to apply systematically throughout the store. In fact, the persistent effort made by the Straus management to undersell competitors and keep retail prices low may well be regarded as the greatest single service which Macy's has rendered to the public.

As indicated in the preceding chapters the Macy policy of trying to undersell competitors occasionally led to lively battles in which prices were cut well below cost. Such fights broke out because, as Macy's advertisements once explained:[1]

. . . just for the transient glory of underselling Macy's, a competitor now and again reduces his price below ours. As soon as we find it out, we cut still lower — not for the passing victory of beating an isolated competitor, but in order to sustain our fifty-two-year-old policy of selling at the lowest prices. Our "return" cut is based on and justified by an ancient Macy principle, and is not the result of a sporadic rivalry.

These price wars, of course, had a vicious aspect which the Macy management could not deny, but there was more behind them than blind adherence to established policy, desire for publicity, or pigheaded rivalry. Every phase of Macy operations was dominated by the belief that low prices were the store's chief attraction, and that the firm's success depended upon maintaining a favorable difference, by means of lower operating expenses, between Macy prices and those of competitors. Because it sold for cash, the management maintained that its prices to the public could and should be lower than those of stores which extended credit. The actual loss incurred when a price war broke out was doubtless offset by the favorable publicity which resulted, but it also acted as a spur to keep the Macy organization on its toes, a challenge to the management to find new ways of making bargains possible.

After 1900 the Macy management found increasing difficulty in pursuing its underselling tactics. Rival firms, large and small, objected vociferously to what they regarded as unethical competitive practice, and out of the protests came efforts to find legal remedies. Between 1900 and 1914 a number of ingenious attempts were made to establish prices which could not be cut by any retailer without incurring some sort of penalty. In other words, resale price maintenance was viewed with favor by a considerable number of retailers, wholesalers, and manufacturers.

Although this movement probably affected Macy's more than any other single store, it was almost nationwide in scope and directed against price-cutting in general. Its growing strength may be attributed to a number of factors. In the first place, by the turn of the century manufacturers' brands were becoming increasingly important. During the preceding decades consumers had depended largely upon the integrity of the local dealer who sold the merchandise they desired. By 1900, however, manufacturers had acquired considerable control over the marketing of their products, a manifestation of the integrating movement in business to which reference has already been made. Some of them had undertaken their own wholesaling operations, and many had attempted to stimulate and control the consumer demand for their products by establishing trade-marks, supported by national advertising.

It was inevitable that the price wars should focus upon nationally advertised goods. The standardized, branded merchandise enabled the consumer to compare the competing prices for identical qualities, with the result that enterprising dealers offered well-known brands at low prices in order to create a favorable impression upon their customers. Other stores were obliged to follow suit as best they could. Although demand increased for the branded products, the profit from handling them dwindled, and many retailers were reluctant to stock them — or so the argument ran at the time. Large firms with diversified merchandise, such as department stores and mail-order houses, could afford to sell the popular brands at low margin, but small, specialized stores could ill afford to sacrifice any potential revenue and resented any reductions in price.

Another force behind the movement in favor of resale price maintenance was the hostile attitude of numerous wholesalers and small storekeepers toward department stores, mail-order houses, and (especially after about 1910) chain stores in general. These new marketing institutions were putting many retailers and wholesalers out of business, largely because their improved methods of distribution enabled them to place goods in the consumers' hands more cheaply or conveniently than the older system of middlemen. They were large in size, revolutionary in methods, and successful in operation, which was enough to damn them in the eyes of many a petty capitalist storekeeper. Moreover, they employed low prices as a competitive weapon, and the injured rivals frequently attributed their success mainly to this device. In consequence, the small retailers and the wholesalers who served them tended to identify price-cutting with the new competition and sought price maintenance as a means of survival. The fact that the hated "trusts" and combinations had employed cut prices as a means to exterminate local competition seemed to confirm the small retailer in his view that underselling was an instrument of the devil.

Unable to strike back by economic means, the small retailers and the wholesalers encouraged manufacturers to employ legal means to prevent the cutting of retail prices. Agitation of this kind had arisen before 1900, and a few manufacturers had taken action, for they had the legal right at the time to obtain from their dealers agreements to sell at specified prices. For the most part, however, there was a general reluctance, owing to the depressed conditions between 1866 and 1896, to do anything that might interfere with sales. In other words, a buyer's market prevailed, and the sellers in general felt obliged to accept the situation. After 1897, however, as the nation's economic and business conditions showed continued improvement, the general price situation materially changed. The old buyer's market gave way to a seller's market, with prices hardening and the terms of sale becoming more stringent. After Bryan was defeated and the Republicans were once more safely in power, a feeling of optimism spread through the business community. Manufacturers, feeling economically more secure, desiring to extend control over their ultimate markets, and roused by the clamor of disgruntled dealers, began to take measures to prevent price-cutting on their products.

Lastly, it was only natural that there should be a reaction to the chaotic price situation of the 1890's. Depressed business conditions had resulted in cutthroat competition, aggravated by bankruptcies and receiverships. America was in the difficult transition from small-scale to large-scale business enterprise. No one could see the situation clearly, but the fact that many concerns were suffering was obvious, and business firms which had long been content to operate in a free market felt obliged to experiment with restrictive measures in an effort to establish what is euphemistically called "orderly competition." [2]

Fighting for the Right to Sell Cheaply

The change in the general price situation brought Macy's into direct conflict with vendors (both manufacturers and selling agents) as a result of the Macy underselling policy. Proceeding on the belief that patent rights and copyrights gave them the legal power to control retail prices, a number of suppliers began to insist that the Macy firm sell at the prices they named or give up selling the products concerned. As a result Macy's soon encountered serious difficulty in obtaining certain brands of merchandise, and in some instances the firm was compelled to modify its underselling policy by handling such goods at prices set by the vendor. The ultimate result was a series of bitterly contested law suits.

It began with a battle of books. In 1900 the leading book publishers of the country formed the American Publishers' Association, with a view to compelling all retailers to conform to the minimum prices. The membership of the organization included over 90 per cent of the nation's book publishers. Shortly afterwards the American Booksellers' Association was formed, including about 90 per cent of the wholesale and retail booksellers in the country, to coöperate with the Publishers' Association in the maintenance of retail prices and to assist it in preventing books from reaching any dealers who were believed to be underselling. Early in 1901 the Publishers' Association began to ask dealers to sign an agreement to maintain the prices fixed by the individual publishing houses. One of the first firms to be approached was R. H. Macy & Co. The Strauses immediately went into a family consultation, for the matter was obviously important. Was the firm to surrender to the "book trust?" To do so was to abandon the basic Macy policy. To refuse meant trouble, for the Association's representative had asserted that books would be shut off within a month from any retailer who failed to comply. This threat, if executed, might doom the Macy book department, valued not merely for its own sales but also because its bargains drew people into the store and helped other departments. It seemed unthinkable that Macy's, having purchased books outright, should not be able to sell them at any price it chose. Even more inconceivable was the idea that a store should not be allowed to pass on to its customers any savings it achieved by its methods of operation.

Macy's consulted their own legal counsel, Edmond E. Wise, who studied the problem. Judging from past legal decisions the right of individual publishers to demand and enforce contracts to maintain prices seemed to be well founded, but to combine with other publishers and force the maintenance of prices of all books, uncopyrighted as well as copyrighted, appeared to be without precedent and in direct violation of the Sherman Anti-Trust Act. The decision was to fight the Association with every available resource.[3]

One by one the publishers began to refuse to fill orders from Macy's. By placing orders through other firms, the store was able to obtain enough books to supply its needs for a time, but gradually the publishers closed one source after another until it became exceedingly difficult to keep the Macy book department going. In December, 1902, the Strauses filed a suit against the American Publishers' Association as a combination which restrained competition and caused injury and damages to R. H. Macy & Co.

After the Macy firm had won two rounds in the lower courts, the Publishers' Association retaliated by having two of its members file suits to enjoin Macy's from selling certain copyrighted novels at less than the fixed prices. The Bobbs-Merrill Co., for example, tried to prevent Macy's from selling *The Castaway* at less than $1.00 per copy. The publishing house regularly sold this novel to its distributors at a reduction of 40 per cent from the list price, so that it cost the retailer 60 cents a copy. Quantity and cash discounts enabled large firms to buy it at even a lower price. Macy's insisted on selling the novel at 89 cents, at which rate (assuming that the books cost the store 60 cents a copy) the gross profit was 29 cents, or 32.6 per cent of the selling price, which was substantially more than the average gross margin obtained on goods sold by the store. In effect, therefore, the publisher was trying to compel Macy's to take a larger profit than the Strauses thought necessary or desirable. In another instance a book listed by the publisher at $1.50 was sold to retailers with a provision that the price should not be cut below $1.08. Macy's insisted on selling it at 98 cents. Assuming that the store obtained the most favorable trade discounts in buying books of this kind (40 per cent, less an additional 10 per cent for large orders, less 5 per cent for cash), the cost per volume was 77 cents and the gross margin was 21.5 per cent of the Macy selling price. This was slightly below the average Macy gross margin at the time but still above the store's average expense ratio (see Table 26, p. 394).

To summarize very briefly, the Bobbs-Merrill Co. maintained that the Macy firm, by selling their copyrighted book below the fixed price, had injured and tended to destroy the market for their book through lowering the profits of other retailers, causing them to reduce the number of copies purchased from the publisher. This action, according to the publisher's argument, impaired the value of the copyright and constituted infringement. However, the Circuit Court, the Court of Appeals, and the United States Supreme Court all decided in favor of Macy's. They held that, while the copyright statute gave the publishers an exclusive right to multiply copies of a book, it did not give them the right to control the price of the book, once they had sold it "to the trade" in the normal manner.[4]

We need not analyze here the individual law suits against Macy's or examine in detail the various legal points involved. For the purposes of this history it is perhaps enough to say that appealed decisions made it necessary for the Macy firm to defend itself in five court trials before it won final victories in the suits brought by the Bobbs-Merrill Co. and Scribner's. In addition, to win the suit against the Publishers' Association the firm fought a total of nine actions in the State and federal courts. It produced evidence that members of the Association had not only refused to sell their copyrighted books to Macy's but also had attempted, with some success, to cut off all supplies of books, both copyrighted and uncopyrighted, whether published by members of the Association or not. The Association had threatened with coercion any nonmembers who might have been willing to sell to Macy's and had likewise threatened to injure the business of any book dealer who attempted to sell books to Macy's.

By a unanimous decision the Supreme Court held (December, 1913) that the Publishers' Association had formed a combination in restraint of trade which was not justified by the Copyright Act and, in consequence, had violated the Sherman Anti-Trust Act. On a wall in one of the Macy offices today there hangs a small, framed photograph of a check. The amount is $140,000, representing the damages which the American Publishers' Association had to pay to the Macy firm.[5]

The litigation with the publishers was hardly settled before Macy's was involved in another important suit over price maintenance, filed by the Victor Talking Machine Co. The Victor Co., noting the reasoning of the Supreme Court in the decision against the publishers, had attempted in 1914 to regulate the price of its product by attaching a license notice to every machine sold. The notice said, in effect, that the purchaser did not own the machine but had merely acquired the right to use it by paying royalties in a lump sum. On the basis of this device the Victor Co. contended that any dealer who failed to charge the price fixed thereby infringed the manufacturer's patent rights.

Unable to buy machines directly from the Victor Co. or its agents, Macy's bought them indirectly and, in defiance of Victor's warnings, advertised them at reduced prices. Macy's sold for $89 machines which the Victor Co. said should sell for $100. Had the regular trade discounts been allowed, the store would have been able to buy the machines at $54, as a result of which its gross margin would have been $35 or 39.3 per cent. This was well above the average gross margin received by Macy's, and the management asserted its right to sell at that margin rather than the larger one which the Victor Co. insisted that it should obtain.

It took five court trials in the course of three years before the Macy view was vindicated by the Supreme Court, and it took five more trials to determine the extent of the damages. The Supreme Court decision pointed out that the Victor license notice was in reality a subterfuge. The manufacturer's price, called a "royalty," had been paid before the Victor Co. released possession to distributors, and no effort had been made to check on the subsequent use of the machine, as would have been necessary had its use been really licensed. In the opinion of the Court the license notice had the sole function of fixing and maintaining the price of Victor machines to the dealers and to the public. Accordingly, it was a device to restrict the price and came within the principles laid down in the decision of *Bauer* v. *O'Donnell*, 229 U. S. 1 (1913). The total damages paid by Victor to Macy's amounted to $154,628.[6]

Difficulties in Buying Price-Fixed Merchandise

While these various legal battles were being fought through the courts, Macy's encountered considerable difficulty in obtaining supplies of price-fixed merchandise — not only books but also razors, watches, and many other branded items. The management employed every legitimate means at its disposal (and some which cut ethical, if not legal, corners) in order to continue selling price-fixed merchandise at reduced prices. For the most part it was successful, but the effort involved considerable expense and a great deal of ingenuity on the part of many people to get round the restrictions which were imposed. In a few instances Macy's yielded to the extent of refusing to handle certain items, and occasionally it was obliged to modify its underselling policy in order to sell popular merchandise which could not be obtained without an agreement to maintain the prices established by the manufacturers.[7]

When the publishers blacklisted the store, the management established a private checking account for Miss Lillian Kinnear, head of the Macy book department, and authorized her to buy books from out-of-town wholesalers, retailers, buying agents, or any other persons who might be able to supply the needed volumes. The records show that in 1901 a single agent in Chicago supplied books to Macy's at the rate of over $2,000 a month.[8] An agent in New York sold books to the store during 1911 to the amount of $72,554, obtaining them in the names of a number of out-of-town firms that he represented.[9] An attempt was even made to use an agent as far afield as Havana, Cuba, and in one instance the firm asked an author to obtain 250 copies of his book for Macy's without disclosing their destination to his publisher.[10] Whenever it was impossible to get books in any other way, the store dispatched a messenger to the nearest bookseller where he purchased the desired volume at the full retail price. It was then resold at Macy's reduced price. In an effort to discover the loopholes through which Macy's succeeded in obtaining books, the Publishers' Association used detectives and spies, one of whom was employed in the Macy receiving department. The management saw to it that he was able to see only falsified lists of sources.[11]

Macy's persistently tried to avoid concluding any agreements to maintain prices. In a number of instances it flatly refused to handle merchandise unless it was allowed to sell at its own price. Small suppliers frequently gave in rather than antagonize so important a customer, but a number of vendors not only refused to grant Macy's permission to undersell but threatened legal action when the store obtained their wares by indirect means and tried to sell them below the fixed price. Since the firm already had a number of law suits on its hands, threats of this sort usually led Macy's to drop the line or else to maintain the price.[12] In a few instances Macy's signed price agreements and subsequently violated them, pointing out by way of excuse that competing stores were failing to adhere to the manufacturer's price. For example, after agreeing to maintain the price of Ingersoll watches, Macy's obtained through L. Straus & Sons a shipment which had been sold for export only. The Ingersoll Co. promptly compelled Macy's to return the unsold watches.[13] There is some evidence that manufacturers watched Macy's much more closely than its competitors for evidence of cutting fixed prices. At times the store was able to obtain price-fixed merchandise in roundabout ways and so avoid making agreements, but large manufacturers usually succeeded in blocking such moves. Rubber manufacturers, indeed, made it so difficult for Macy's to obtain automobile tires that the firm eventually gave up trying to handle them.[14]

To some extent Macy's avoided the price maintenance issue by bringing out products under its own name to compete with national brands. The items sold in this way were usually of quality identical with that of the national brands or even better. Yet Macy's was able to sell them at 20 to 50 per cent less than the national-branded equivalents and still make a substantial profit.[15]

Although the Macy victories in the Supreme Court proved that the store had the legal right under existing statutes to sell its merchandise at any price it pleased, they did not bring peace in the long struggle over resale price maintenance. The contest was simply transferred from the courts to the legislative halls. It has been there more or less continuously ever since, and the Macy firm has taken a leading part in the opposition to all proposals which might interfere with its right to free and open competition and to price its merchandise to sell basically for cash.

The whole question of resale price maintenance is far too big and complicated to be discussed at length here. As a result of court decisions, legislative hearings, trade association propaganda, and academic studies, the subject has developed an extensive controversial literature of its own. The issues involved are far from simple, for there are excellent arguments to be brought forth on both sides. If it is true that unrestrained price-cutting is contrary to the public interest, it is likewise true that measures which attempt to fix resale prices without allowing for differences in operating efficiency produce serious disadvantages both to the efficient business firms and to the consuming public. There is good reason to believe that price maintenance will not work satisfactorily in a dynamic economy and that it tends to produce static situations by discouraging efforts to lower the cost of distribution.[16]

Professor Taussig concluded in 1915 that resale price maintenance was essentially a device to compel "retail dealings to be conducted in the good old way and at the good old expense," [17] and that was substantially the view of the Macy management. The Macy firm felt that the strongest appeal to its customers was price and that it should have the right to offer lower prices in return for cash payments, just as competing stores offered charge accounts or other free services as a means of winning patronage. It was convinced, with considerable justification, that it was fighting in the consumers' interest — not because of any altruistic motives but simply because there was honest profit in doing so.[18]

One may question whether, from the point of view of long-run self-interest, it was wise for Macy's to fight price maintenance to the extent of claiming a right to price merchandise below invoice cost. Underselling at that extreme breeds commercial anarchy. I suggest the possibility that the store's bitter experiences with price maintenance between 1901 and 1917 made it hypersensitive in this area of competition, with the result that it developed a more extreme attitude of hostility towards price regulation than later circumstances might seem to warrant. On the other hand, there are many independent observers today who hold that the evils involved in resale price maintenance are worse than those which arise from freedom to cut prices. If the tide of legal decisions and legislative enactments in recent years seems to have turned in favor of restrictions against underselling, it should be remembered that the change came largely under the influence of severe depression and unusually well-organized pressure groups. The problem is still being debated, and the public has not yet reached a final conclusion.[19]

The Growing Problem of Administration

The struggle for price freedom which the Macy firm had been waging between 1901 and 1917 possessed dramatic and tangible features which made it easy to grasp both for the management and for others. During the same period, however, the firm was confronted with another problem which, although probably of greater fundamental importance, was yet so subtle and intangible in its nature that the firm had difficulty in perceiving it and even greater difficulty in working out the solution. I refer to the problem of administering effectively a store of the size and complexity that Macy's had attained by 1900.

In the course of 25 years the store's sales had increased eightfold and the number of employees had expanded to about the same extent. Moreover, the organization had grown in complexity as well as size, for by 1900 there were more than 50 different merchandise departments, to say nothing of the great increase in manufacturing activities, the expansion of the store's delivery facilities, and the continual elaboration of specialized jobs within individual departments. As a result the task of coördinating and supervising the operations as a whole had grown to colossal proportions, and yet the firm was still trying to handle that task with substantially the same kind of organization and approximately the same quantity of top administrative personnel that it had had in the 1870's. That is to say, Isidor and Nathan Straus, assisted by Jesse and Percy, were attempting to manage the entire enterprise, just as Macy, La Forge, and Valentine had run it in 1875, directly by personal oversight of operations and indirectly by supervision of departmental heads. Actually the business had become so large and complicated that it had outgrown its administrative organization. The Strauses could meet the situation to some extent by redoubling the intensity of their efforts, but there could be no real solution without revamping the entire administrative system in all its ramifications. Of course, a solution had to be found or the firm would gradually succumb to inefficiency.

To resort to an extreme but perhaps helpful metaphor, Macy's in 1900 was threatened with the fate of the dinosaur: through the course of time and evolution it had acquired great size and brute strength but stood in need of additional brain mechanism in order to survive. Fortunately, being a business organism instead of a biological one, Macy's could consciously strive to readapt itself once the difficulty was recognized. It is hardly too much to say that the principal problem of the Macy firm (and of many other business enterprises) since the turn of the century has been to develop a brain and nervous system commensurate with its large and expanding organization.

Biological analogies may be very misleading unless used with care, but at times they can be extremely illuminating. Julian Huxley has pointed out a number of useful parallels between biological evolution and the evolution of economic and social institutions, by means of which the layman may possibly obtain a better grasp of the Macy administrative problem. Thus, the evolution of the brain "represents the latest phase of a more inclusive trend — the trend towards greater knowledge of the outer world and greater efficiency in adjusting action to it."[20] One can discern this same trend in a number of social organisms and it is evident in the history of R. H. Macy & Co. There were numerous changes and innovations on the managerial side which, taken individually, seem to be of trivial importance, but which, viewed as manifestations of a tendency, acquire real significance. Some of them are clearly receptor mechanisms, analogous to the human sensory nervous system, designed to keep the Macy firm informed about its environment — sources of supply, public demand, competitive activities, staff morale, and the like. Others are mechanisms of coördination and decision (the store's brain) by which the incoming data are correlated, plans worked out, and decisions made; while still others are more like effector mechanisms (muscles) for translating decisions into effective coördinated action by the various specialized departments. We can discern the development of automatic controls, such as the installation of an inventory system which revealed approaching shortages in staple items, comparable to reflex responses and the involuntary actions which take place in the human body without the intervention of conscious will. There is even a process analogous to memory in the collection and analysis of recorded data by means of which the store's management attempts to modify plans and objectives in the light of past experience.

Looking back from today, the Macy administrative problem seems clear enough, for it is similar to situations which emerged in various other enterprises about the same time.[21] It was not obvious in 1900, however, and the achievement of a satisfactory solution was even less apparent than the existence of the problem. Indeed, American business as a whole is still working out the answer to the problem of administering large-scale enterprises. Accordingly, we cannot yet be sure which particular developments are the most significant in terms of the ultimate solution. Even so, the Macy experience — in so far as it can be recovered — reveals some illuminating tendencies.[22]

Steps Toward Better Administration, 1900–1919

When Jesse and Percy Straus began to participate in the management of the store, they soon discovered the pressing need for administrative improvements. Goods were not always bought intelligently, the delivery department was notorious for mistakes and delays in handling orders, the financial records yielded inadequate information about operations, waste and inefficiency were obvious in many areas, and there was need for closer coördination between various divisions. Just what should be done was not altogether clear. The two young brothers tackled one situation after another in a strenuous effort to bring about improvements by directing and supervising the existing organization, but progress was slow and difficult. Being young, enthusiastic, and full of ideas, Jesse and Percy doubtless were occasionally impractical and often impatient, but time has vindicated their general view that fundamental changes would have to be made in the type of personnel employed as well as the way in which it was organized.

A brief analysis of the way in which individual departments were managed illustrates the kind of situation which was encountered throughout the store. Until about 1900 the buyer or manager of a Macy department enjoyed almost complete independence. To be sure, he conferred once a week with a member of the firm, at which time there was a brief review of his previous purchases and sales, current inventory, and financial requirements for the coming week. But the buyer was essentially free to decide for himself what he should buy, when and where he should buy it, and so on. He wrote his own advertisements and he directed the salesforce in his department. Apart from watching the financial aspects of the department, the top management assumed no responsibility for results. If sales dropped off or dead stock accumulated, the assumption was that the buyer was at fault and the usual solution was to replace him. From the records supplied to him the buyer knew how much stock he had on hand, how much his department was selling, and how much the gross margin was, but neither he nor anyone else knew how much it cost to run his individual department and, therefore, no one could be certain whether it was really profitable or not.

In addition to this independence and lack of important information there was a general absence of systematic procedure in buying. Insufficient effort was made to see that a department had an adequate selection of sizes and colors on hand, and there was still a tendency (handed down from the operations of R. H. Macy himself) to look for individual lots of merchandise which could be bought at a special price advantage, rather than to maintain complete assortments. There was not even any system for recording the orders that the buyers placed. Too often the buyer would give a verbal order for goods or hurriedly send off a note without keeping any memorandum of the transaction. Apparently procedures were no better in the 1890's than in the 1870's when a buyer dashed off the following order: [23]

July 8, 1874

Bremer & Higgins
Gents —
    Will please ship us on the spot, a duplicate of our last order on shawl straps

And oblige
J. B. Stearns, Jr.

In short, there were no definite specifications as to price, quantity, quality, style, or terms, and probably no record of having sent the order. In the circumstances a buyer seldom knew precisely what he had bought, misunderstandings with the vendor were frequent, and stocks of merchandise were often depleted just when they were most in demand.

Perhaps even worse than the lack of efficiency and system within the individual departments was the commercial bribery which often developed as a result of the buyer's independence. Many a manufacturer, in order to obtain a favorable hearing, lavished favors and gifts on the individual buyers even to the extent of allowing them a percentage in cash on their departmental purchases. Thus the buyer was tempted to select sources of merchandise according to the perquisites he received instead of the quality and price of the goods. In some instances he may well have received more income from vendors than from his employers.[24]

The situation was not peculiar to Macy's but was common throughout the department store industry. The store owners knew about it but felt powerless to do anything beyond keeping the worst abuses within bounds. It was hard enough to find buyers who possessed executive ability and a sense of merchandise values, without adding strict honesty to the list of qualifications. The assumption was that to dismiss a buyer who accepted bribes meant replacing him with another buyer brought up in the same tradition and therefore subject to the same weakness. Accordingly, when Jesse and Percy Straus complained about the situation, they learned that the senior members of the firm were aware of the problem but convinced that it was a trade custom about which little could be done. However, they did begin to provide order blanks and require duplicates to be kept, and they instituted a rule that any orders for future delivery would not be valid unless signed by the firm. It took at least ten years to make compliance with these regulations a matter of habit with the buyers. As a check against the accumulation of old merchandise, the management began (about 1900) the practice of marking every item with a season letter at the time it was priced, so that one could tell at a glance afterwards how long it had been in stock.[25]

When the firm moved to 34th Street, it immediately became apparent that more drastic changes would have to be made. Transferred to new surroundings and confronted with sudden expansion of trade, the old organization bogged down almost completely, with the result that the firm had to publish advertisements apologizing for unsatisfactory service, and Percy S. Straus, who had just started on his honeymoon, was hastily summoned back to assist in restoring some sort of order.[26] This crisis marked the beginning of systematic efforts to revise Macy management from top to bottom. Baffled by the difficulty of persuading members of the organization to abandon old habits and methods, the boys began to bring in new personnel — men who had received enough formal education and special training to qualify them to serve in executive capacity, men who were sufficiently adaptable to consider new methods and to experiment with various procedures until satisfactory systems could be developed.

One of the men thus hired was John A. Badenoch, employed in 1902 to take over the Macy grocery department. Badenoch and William A. Titon, an assistant whom he trained, were largely responsible for the preëminent position which the Macy grocery department enjoys today. Another person hired at this time was Ernest Katz (now Macy controller), who was engaged in 1905 to devise methods which would yield a more detailed and useful accounting picture of the business, department by department. It was largely because of his efforts that the management was able to start using accounting records as a means of controlling current operations instead of merely as a record of past performance. In other words, after 1905 there was a shift from mere bookkeeping to the systematic accumulation and analysis of operating facts as a basis for intelligent administration. Still another able executive acquired at this time was the late William J. Wells (the Strauses eventually made him president of Bamberger's in Newark), employed in 1906 to assist in improving bookkeeping operations in the D/A department, where errors abounded and statements were four months late in appearing.[27]

In general, Jesse and Percy Straus found themselves engaged in an uphill battle. Many of the departmental heads fought innovations and resented the new personnel. Worst of all, it was difficult to find the kind of employees that the situation required. Retail trade generally had not attracted able and ambitious people. For the most part wages were relatively low, the hours were long, working conditions were far from ideal, and even executive positions in retail stores did not command much respect in society. The two young Strauses concluded that they should make a definite effort to obtain employees who had received a college education, in addition to which it would be necessary to train the entire staff in new methods of operation and to impose systematic control from above, so that all operations would be conducted according to central plans and policies and supervised in execution. There were no sudden changes or major developments but rather a series of small developments — additions to personnel, formulation of standard operating procedures, establishment of coördinating committees, and changes or additions in the use of records of all kinds.

It is impossible to trace in detail all the steps in the evolutionary process by which the management of Macy's was gradually institutionalized, but certain important changes may be noted. In 1908 William Pitt, store superintendent since 1887, was retired and his place taken by Sylvester Byrnes, general manager. The change of

PERCY SELDEN STRAUS
Partner, 1912–1919; vice-president, 1919–1933; president, 1933–1940;
chairman of the board of directors, 1940–

DEPARTMENTAL ADVERTISEMENT, 1918
Introducing a lighter touch in Macy copy

title is significant. Pitt handled routine affairs in the old-fashioned way. Byrnes, well-educated and progressive, understood what the young Strauses were trying to do and was able to give valuable assistance in both the planning and execution of improvements. (It must be remembered that the term "general manager" has a somewhat peculiar application in the department store industry. The general manager controls store operations but normally has very little to do with over-all policies or merchandising activities.) Early in 1908 the buyers, with the encouragement of the firm, founded the Macy Managers' Association. Although this organization was more social than business in function, it served as a useful medium by which points of view were exchanged and managerial ideas worked out.[28] More important still was the formation of the Board of Operations about the same time. The Board consisted of representatives of the firm, the general manager, controller's office, delivery department, bureau of adjustments, and certain other nonselling divisions. It met once a week to plan and coördinate all Macy activities having to do with employment, equipment, store systems (such as prescribing the exact forms to be used and steps to be taken when a customer asked the store to call for furniture to be returned for repairs), delivery service, housekeeping and building maintenance — all those essential matters which department stores include under the term "management." [29]

Another significant step of the same kind was taken early in 1914 when the firm announced the creation of the Advisory Council, consisting of the three partners, the general manager, the controller, the advertising manager, and five managers of merchandise departments. Thus its membership overlapped that of the Board of Operations, but it was aimed at improving the merchandise and publicity functions of the business, leaving details of management to the Board.[30]

One can hardly exaggerate the significance of these two Macy committees. They broadened the base of administration by drawing in new talent and providing for careful consideration of important questions from many points of view. They provided for the systematic analysis of operations and procedures throughout the store, the standardization of policies, methods, and equipment, and the correlation of efforts and activities, so that the various departments moved together with effective unity. They enabled members of the firm to keep close touch with operations and to guide the formation of policies and decisions, without having to bear the entire responsibility for working out details. Henceforth it was easier for the three brothers to visualize the functions of the store as a whole and to concentrate upon main issues, with assurance that minor matters and interdepartmental relations were receiving proper attention.

The administration of Macy's was thus institutionalized so that it could function continuously without depending upon the presence of any one person. The brothers did not relax their efforts by any means, but henceforth they could exert influence upon the organization as a whole instead of upon individual members. How necessary such an arrangement had become may be seen from the fact that by 1918 the time devoted to the regular Monday conference which each buyer had with a member of the firm had to be limited to three minutes in order to enable the brothers to see everyone.[31]

Naturally Macy's did not attain the millennium at this time, but the firm had certainly opened the way for substantial progress. A few illustrations will show how matters were handled. The Board of Operations, as early as 1911, was regularly collecting and analyzing statistics on complaints and returned merchandise; it offered clerks 10 cents for each error they detected in credit slips made out by floorwalkers; it experimented (May, 1912) with having clerks at certain counters wrap their parcels and make change at cash registers instead of the lengthier process of using pneumatic tubes and special parcel-wrappers; it simplified printed forms and clerical routine.[32] Similarly, we find the Advisory Council discussing automatic controls to prevent departments from running out of staple items, voting to liberalize (1914) the store's policy of allowing returns and adjustments, making tests of Macy packing and delivery service in comparison with that of other New York stores, reminding buyers (1916) that they were to conform to the store's underselling policy by pricing merchandise at least 6 per cent and not more than 10 per cent below that of competitors, arranging to increase (1916) the number of Macy private brands and to intensify their promotion, directing buyers to plan their advertising six months in advance, introducing changes in the style of advertising copy, and so on.[33]

Of course, the use of committees entailed a certain amount of delay in obtaining decisions, but that was not necessarily a disadvantage, and there were, in any case, counterbalancing advantages. Working under vigorous leadership, these bodies produced well-considered policies and coördinated decisions, together with more uniformity and continuity than would otherwise have been possible. It is noteworthy, too, that these committees eventually led to a delegation of executive responsibilities which has proved to be particularly useful. Many questions which, in former days, would have been taken up with one of the Strauses were referred increasingly to those buyers who were members of the Advisory Council, with the result that after the War the firm decided to formalize the practice by creating Merchandise Councillors (to be considered later), each of whom was responsible for a definite group of departments.[34]

It is important to note that the Board and the Council, while relieving the partners of much detailed work, did not shut them off from contact with store operations. Actually these devices enabled the Strauses to exert more effective control over merchandising, store service, and advertising than ever before. In earlier years the firm had made general decisions and, for the most part, had been compelled to rely upon subordinates for their execution. To be sure, the results had been checked, but by that time it was often too late to do anything beyond issuing reprimands or dismissals. The creation of the Board of Operations and the Advisory Council meant that the partners acquired a new means of following decisions through. The independence which buyers had formerly enjoyed was gone. Henceforth the top management, through the Council, the Merchandise Councillors, and auxiliary divisions, took part in decisions as to the kind of merchandise to be stocked, and there was a continuous check on the execution of such decisions. The buyer was still of vital importance, but in the future he was to be under control from above; that is another way of saying that the chief executives were beginning to share the responsibility for the performance of the buyer's department.

By 1919 the structure of the Macy organization was approximately the same as that for 1922, as shown on Chart II, the earliest formal organization chart now extant.

Meanwhile there had been considerable improvement in Macy accounting methods, mainly with a view to getting better information. One major advance was made in 1905 when the controller's office began to allocate expenses, both direct and indirect, to individual departments; it was then possible to know more accurately whether a given department was paying its way or not. This did not mean that any department which failed to cover its overhead expenses would be eliminated. Every department store is obliged to engage in certain unprofitable activities, either because the public expects it to provide particular services or because such activities help to attract patronage. After 1905, however, the Macy management was armed with facts and no longer had to guess about the relative advantages and disadvantages.[35] Between 1910 and 1915 the controller's office worked out a number of procedures for merchandise control in order to bring about a closer and more rapid adjustment of inventories to sales. The result was improvement in stockturn and better maintenance of proper assortments. In 1915, after several years of experimentation, the controller's office abandoned the old rating method of calculating margins and book inventories and adopted the so-called "retail method," which has since become the standard procedure throughout the country. Without going into the technical details involved, it can be said that this new method produced important information with greater speed and accuracy than before and it also represented a change in emphasis from the invoice cost of goods to their retail value by the time they were ready to be placed in the customer's hands. In other words, the management was learning to think in terms of goods sold rather than goods bought for stock.[36]

Perhaps the most fundamental accounting change during this period was the rise in the importance of the controller, in Macy's as well as in other stores. Before 1900 bookkeeping had been largely

CHART II. ORGANIZATION CHART, 1922

The organization was substantially the same in 1919

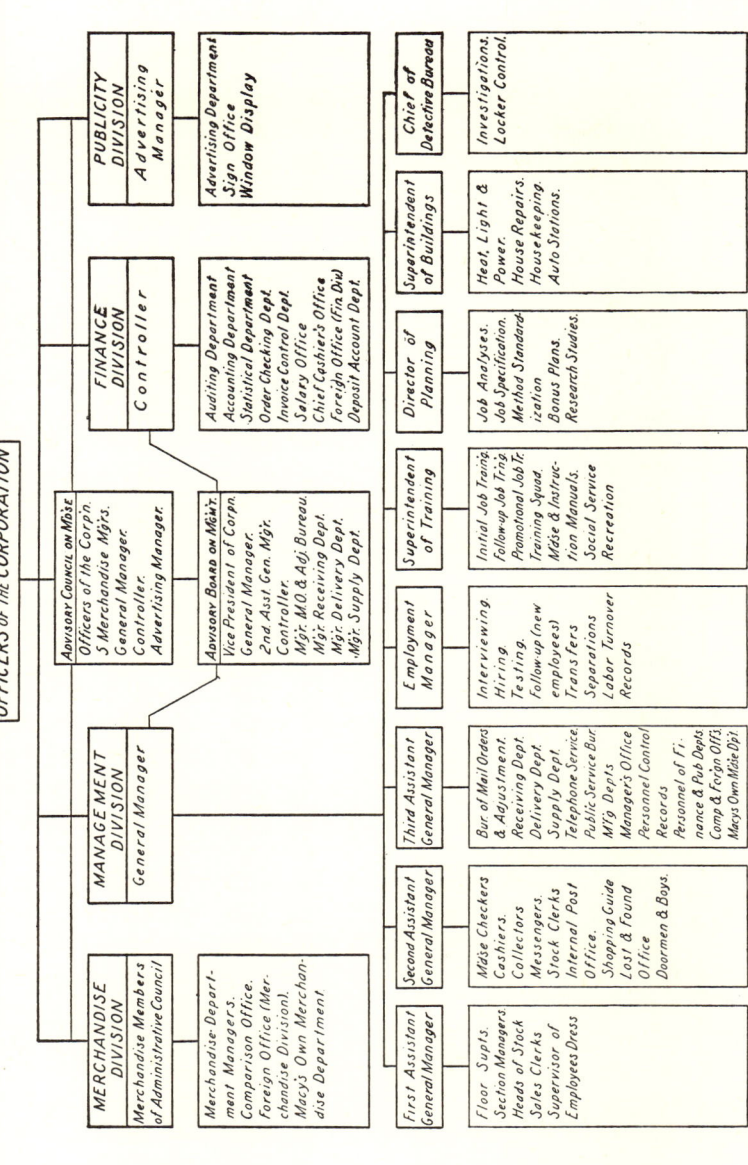

considered a necessary but nonproductive operation — the maintenance of a record of past events. By 1919 it had become accounting and control, a device for analyzing current operations and planning the future — an important adjunct of top management in making the business produce satisfactory results.[37]

To assist the management in handling the growing flood of detail in this period Macy's resorted to a considerable degree of mechanization of routine operations. Thus in 1906 the firm was using both multigraph and billing machines, and by 1910 it had electrically driven devices for opening incoming envelopes and folding outgoing letters. Between 1911 and 1915 it installed electric adding machines, calculating typewriters, stenciling machines, addressographs, and improved cash registers. Then came automatic stamping machines for outgoing mail, payroll machines, measuring machines to facilitate rapid and accurate handling of piece goods, and marking machines to speed up the pricing of new merchandise.[38]

At the same time further improvements were made in the store's delivery service. Seeking to get the best possible advice in handling this ever expanding problem, Macy's employed three engineers from the Massachusetts Institute of Technology in 1914 to study the Macy delivery organization and its work. During the years which followed, the firm gradually applied the recommendations made in the course of the investigation. One result was the increased use of both electric and gasoline trucks, 31 vehicles being added in 1916.[39] This use of outside technical experts established a precedent for calling in consultants on other problems in subsequent years.

Up to 1914 the attention of the Macy firm had focused to a considerable extent upon internal information and methods. About that time, however, the management began to pay systematic attention to the activities of rival stores, apparently with a view to adopting any ideas for improvement which seemed to be feasible. For example, members of the Council were instructed to visit the opening (1914) of Lord & Taylor's new store on Fifth Avenue at 38th Street, to attend special sales at Altman's and Wanamaker's, and even to visit the Strawbridge & Clothier store in Philadelphia. In 1919 the Council arranged to have sales clerks given two hours off each month to enable them to visit Fifth Avenue stores and observe methods, display, and merchandise. Even earlier (beginning in 1912), Macy's had regularly offered monthly prizes to employees for the best suggestions for improvements in the store, and efforts were intensified in this direction in 1918 and 1919.[40]

Another mechanism for standardizing the application of Macy policies and keeping the firm informed about the activities of competitors was the establishment of the comparison department on a formal working basis. Originally the task of checking competitors' prices had been handled by individual merchandise departments without the use of specialized employees. When there was need to compare prices or merchandise, the buyer simply sent one of his clerks out. By 1910, however, steps were being taken to centralize this work, and in 1915 the store's comparison bureau was enlarged and its work intensified. Shoppers were used not only to see that Macy prices were kept below those of rival firms but also to observe operations in Macy's own departments — to see that prompt and courteous service was maintained, to check the assortments of merchandise stocked, and so on. By 1917 the comparison department had the authority to mark down prices in any department as a means of insuring the uniform application of the firm's underselling policy. In addition, whenever there was any question as to the comparative value of merchandise which was to be put on sale in Macy's, buyers were required to have the comparison department shop for similar articles in other stores before they issued any advertisements.[41]

The firm also began to take a greater interest in the opinions of its customers. In 1917, for example, a woman was engaged to devote full time to interviewing customers in an effort to find out what they liked or disliked about Macy's.[42] Surveys of this kind, of course, are a familiar practice today, but the start in 1917 marked a decided advance in retail policies — the beginning of a shift in emphasis from what the management thought the customers ought to have to what the customers really wanted.

In its various efforts to accumulate and use information Macy's did not neglect its sources of supply. Buyers were required to schedule definite times for conferring with vendors, and they were instructed also to make regular visits to the markets in order to develop new sources of supply. Instead of depending upon the memories and records of individual buyers, the firm began to accumulate a central file of information on every manufacturer or jobber who sold merchandise to the store. This file included not only data on the kind of goods handled by the vendor but also his reputation in the trade and Macy's experience in dealing with him.[43]

One must not fall into the error of concluding from the evidence presented that the problem of administration in Macy's was solved by committees, new procedures, or mechanical devices of any sort. The fundamental transition which took place was brought about — if it is possible to single out any one operative force — by the sons of Isidor Straus. It was they who recognized the existence of an administrative problem and took responsibility for working out a solution. It was they who assembled a group of able assistants — men like Katz, Byrnes, Wells, Treu, Chamansky, Badenoch, and Mayer — and organized them into an effective team. The three brothers advanced ideas for consideration and encouraged their subordinates to do the same, but the final decision in all matters was invariably made by the Strauses, not by any of the administrative committees. If, in the course of a discussion, any difference of opinion started to develop among the brothers, all three immediately withdrew to the private office to thresh out the matter. The announcement, "My brothers and I have decided . . . ," gave the final answer and soon became famous throughout the organization. The three men worked themselves unsparingly and drove the rest of the Macy staff with the same vigor. It was their energy and their leadership which made the enterprise go.

The Impact of the First World War

The problems which confronted the Macy firm during this period were, of course, greatly aggravated by the World War. The outbreak of hostilities would have created a great deal of uncertainty in the dry goods trade at any time, and it did so all the more in August, 1914, because New York's department stores had already experienced two severe shocks — one at the close of 1913 when the announcement came of Henry Siegel's failure, and the second in June, 1914, when the great Claflin dry goods empire went into receivership. The Siegel crash involved, in addition to a number of nondepartment store enterprises, both the Fourteenth Street Store (located on the former Macy site) and the Simpson Crawford Co. Siegel's connection with his first New York establishment, the Greenhut-Siegel, Cooper Co., had long been severed, but that fact did not prevent the Greenhut concern from being so affected that it failed in 1915. Among the many retail stores in which the Claflin concern had acquired a heavy interest were Lord & Taylor, James McCreery & Co., and O'Neill-Adams in New York, Hahne & Co. in Newark, and two more department stores in Brooklyn; and it was not immediately clear as to the extent to which these individual units might be affected by the Claflin failure. The outbreak of war and the closing of the New York Stock Exchange, coming immediately after these major commercial catastrophes, intensified the atmosphere of gloom and hesitation in which all New York department stores found themselves.[44]

Macy's sales volume showed some improvement in 1914 in spite of the bad news, and it became clear in the course of 1915 that war in Europe was bringing about a boom in the New York department store business. Macy's volume (see Table 25, page 390) increased from $17,000,000 in 1914 to $19,000,000 in 1915, jumped again to almost $22,000,000 in 1916, and by 1919 had grown to $35,800,000. This rapid expansion came from two sources: the war boom which began to develop in American industry during 1915 led to a great increase in consumer demand; secondly, prices, which had shown a general disposition to sag between 1909 and 1914, began to improve rapidly in 1915 and shot up rapidly thereafter as a result of inflation.[45]

The ratios set forth in Table 24 show very clearly one immediate effect of this price movement upon Macy's. Mark-downs (reductions in retail prices made in order to clear merchandise) declined from 7.63 per cent of sales in 1914 to 6.46 per cent in 1915 and then dropped sharply to 3.38 per cent in 1916, hitting an all-time low of 3.1 per cent in 1918. The sudden jump back to 6.23 per cent in 1920 reflects, of course, the first postwar reaction. It is worth noting too that the average sales transaction rose steadily during this war period

TABLE 24
OPERATING INDICES SHOWING EFFECT OF FIRST WORLD WAR
1913–1920

Year	Mark-downs[a] %	Average Sales Transaction	Returns[a] %	Average Expense per Transaction	Average Annual Salary per Employee[b]	No. of Annual Transactions per Employee	Annual Sales per Employee	No. of Gross Sales Transactions
1913	8.15	$1.42	3.92	$0.34	...	...	...	...
1914	7.63	1.42	3.94	0.33	...	...	...	...
1915	6.46	1.44	4.18	0.31	$ 510	3,154	$4,362	13,774,537
1916	3.38	1.57	4.26	0.33	551	3,185	4,806	14,455,280
1917[c]	3.29	1.80	4.38	0.40	612	2,937	5,054	13,628,779
1918	3.10	2.01	3.29	0.49	737	3,125	6,096	13,239,451
1919	3.23	2.48	3.77	0.57	947	3,276	7,841	14,959,475
1920	6.23	2.67	3.36	0.65	1,185	3,459	8,947	17,190,514

[a] Expressed as a percentage of total net sales.
[b] Part-time employees have been reduced to their equivalent in full-time workers. This column refers only to employees on the weekly payroll and excludes executives.
[c] 53 weeks.

SOURCE: Semiannual statements, 1913–19; auditors' reports, 1919–20; additional data supplied by the controller's office.

from $1.42 in 1914 to $2.67 in 1920. Since this figure was unquestionably influenced by price inflation, it is impossible to say how much of the change may have been the result of an increase in the "real" purchases of Macy customers, but it is significant that the total number of sales transactions declined slightly during 1917 and 1918. Equally significant is the sharp increase in transactions during 1919 and 1920, when a postwar boom took place.

In view of the rapidity with which prices rose after the United States entered the war, it is not surprising that the management found it necessary in 1918 to caution buyers to keep close watch on the advances in order to avoid having Macy prices lag too far behind those of competitors. Of course, the price movement made it extremely difficult for the firm to plan its operations far ahead. The management warned buyers not to speculate in merchandise on the assumption that prices would continue to advance, and yet postponement of buying meant incurring the risk that supplies would cost even more and place Macy's at a competitive disadvantage.[46] In general, Macy's seems to have anticipated by several years the hand-to-mouth buying which became so prevalent in American business after 1920.

Quite apart from the extraordinary rise in prices, it became difficut to obtain adequate supplies of merchandise, and Macy's had to accept inferior quality at times in order to get anything at all. The interruption of the importation of German dyestuffs naturally caused difficulties at the very outset, and complaints about colored goods continued throughout the War. As the replacement of stocks became more difficult, the Advisory Council directed buyers, in arranging sales, to avoid clearing any items which would needlessly break up the usual assortments of sizes and colors. By 1917 it became impossible to get good-quality woolens, and the firm had to modify its all-wool policy. Special labels were prepared to inform customers of the inferior dyes and the mixing of cotton with wool which war conditions made unavoidable. By 1917, too, Macy's had been obliged to withdraw from sale any remaining merchandise which bore German labels. The War had, of course, closed the Berlin buying office which Macy's had established in 1910, and it seriously reduced the importations from other parts of Europe. To some extent this situation was relieved by an expansion of imports from the Far East.[47] On the whole, the interruption of the normal flow of goods between 1914 and 1918, although very troublesome, seems to have been less severe than the difficulties which began to confront department stores after 1939.

One outstanding effect of the War was the curtailment of the store's labor supply. This, together with the steady increase in the cost of living, brought about a substantial increase in the Macy payroll. As shown in Table 24, the average annual earnings per employee rose steadily from $510 in 1915 to $1,185 in 1920. Fortunately for the firm, this great increase in wage expense was accompanied by a similar rise in the productivity of the employees, at least in terms of dollar sales. Thus, the average annual sales per employee rose from $4,362 in 1915 to $8,947 in 1920. In short, although the average wage paid by Macy's more than doubled in the course of five years, the increase in the average sales per employee expanded nearly as rapidly, and the ratio of payroll expense to sales was not seriously affected.

To cope with the problem of maintaining an adequate working force, Macy's resorted to a number of expedients. Women were substituted for men in many positions, and the summer vacations of regular employees were curtailed as far as possible. To curb the loss of employees to other firms the Board of Operations made arrangements to keep strictly up to date on the level of salaries paid in the New York area. It also arranged to review the records of personnel in the lower ranks every month and those of executives every six months, with a view to discovering material for advancement as well as to make sure that rates of pay were maintained at levels which would compare favorably with those of competing firms. The management not only advertised for help — "experience not necessary" — but also urged its employees to recommend friends and acquaintances who might be suitable for the store.[48]

Still another step in the efforts of Macy's to solve the labor problem was the development of formal training as a means of increasing efficiency. In the early years of the store's history new employees had been put to work without any preliminary instructions apart from those given informally by their immediate superiors and fellow employees. Even before the War the inadequacy of this procedure had been recognized, and efforts had been made to have departmental buyers hold weekly staff meetings as a means of giving further instructions. The tendency had been, however, to devote these weekly sessions to matters of store discipline, courtesy to customers, and related topics, rather than to provide information about merchandise or improved sales methods. Macy's worked out a coöperative plan with the municipal board of education in 1914 by means of which the employees who had not yet completed their elementary schooling might obtain additional education in a continuation school. War conditions made it imperative to make a more direct attack on the problem. By 1915 Macy's had organized a separate training department to give employees instruction in store methods and policies. This program was soon broadened to include courses in textiles, leather goods, color and design, and other topics which would make sales clerks more helpful to customers. At the same time the Board of Operations prepared a number of booklets or manuals of instructions in order to standardize rules and procedures and assist the selling force in achieving better results. For example, a booklet entitled *Necessary Information for Selling Jewelry* appeared in 1916, and similar publications soon followed, for sales clerks in general, for stationery, house furnishings, and even for the delivery department and office boys and messengers.[49]

As the need for more highly trained executives became more apparent, the firm instituted (January, 1919) its now famous Executive Training Course by means of which selected employees were given a special course designed to qualify them for executive positions.[50]

As soon as the United States became involved in the War, Macy's began to reduce some of the extra services to customers which had developed in the preceding decades. Restrictions on the return privilege, for example, led to a drop in the returns ratio from 4.38 per cent of net sales in 1917 to 3.29 per cent in 1918 (see Table 24). There was also a reduction in delivery service to one delivery per day beyond 100th Street, in addition to which the store urged customers to carry small packages and refused to accept C. O. D. purchases for less than $1.00. Since Macy's sold only for cash, the proportion of C. O. D. deliveries handled by its delivery department was inevitably much greater than that of stores selling on credit, and one of the resulting Macy problems is reflected in the instructions issued by the Board of Operations at this time, directing drivers to make only two attempts to deliver C. O. D. packages instead of the three which had been customary during peace times. The reduction in delivery expense for 1918 (Table 26, page 394) shows the immediate effect of the curtailment of delivery service.[51]

Naturally the enormous expansion of Macy's sales volume in terms of dollars had a material influence upon operating figures as a whole. To some extent direct expenses kept pace with the increase in revenue, but the gross margin ratio continued its prewar tendency to rise, and such indirect expenses as rent, advertising, and depreciation — being spread over a larger volume of sales — showed declines relative to net sales. As a result, Macy net profits benefited materially, passing the two-million mark for the first time in 1916, and rising to more than three and a half million in 1919.

Of course war-time conditions brought on such annoyances as the fuel shortage in the winter of 1917-18, as a result of which retail stores had to remain closed on Mondays for a short period. Similarly, the influenza epidemic in the fall of 1918 led to a temporary revision of store hours in the interest of public health.[52] But inconveniences of this kind were of little importance as compared with the long-run effects. In general the War may be said to have greatly accelerated movements in Macy's which were already at work before 1914 — the rise in operating expense and gross margin ratios, the increase in annual sales, the improvement in staff training, and the evolution of a new administrative hierarchy. A successful solution of the problem of postwar adjustment was adumbrated by an order of the Advisory Council, immediately after the Armistice, directing buyers to reduce stocks and prepare for trouble.[53]

I cannot leave this topic without recording one minor consequence of the War. As a result of the efforts of the management to coöperate with the government in the economy of clothing, Macy section managers (originally they were called floorwalkers and today they are known as service managers, but the job is essentially the same) were allowed in 1918 to abandon the cutaway coats which had so long been their professional garb. Apparently it never occurred to anyone to resume the old habit after peace was restored. Here, surely, was a change which symbolized the end of an era! [54]

Grading Up

One of the most noteworthy developments in the store during this period was the gradual but persistent effort to add higher grades to the lines of merchandise handled. As already indicated, the emphasis of Macy's in the past had been upon price far more than style or quality. Under Straus management there had been an increasing effort to widen the assortment of goods offered so that the store's customers might expect to satisfy their normal requirements at Macy's at any time, instead of going to the store merely to take advantage of any special bargains that it might have. However, it had been difficult to obtain the full coöperation of the individual departments in this effort, and as late as 1912 Macy's still was buying up special bargain lots of merchandise and bankrupt stocks.[55]

In 1914 and later years, under the supervision of the Advisory Council, systematic efforts were made to improve stocks throughout the store. Buyers were repeatedly directed to clear out old stocks and to see that complete assortments were on hand at all times, particularly in staple lines. The Council began to stress quality and style as well as price, and an entire meeting was devoted to a discussion of methods of bringing about "a reputation for being authentic on style."[56] A resolution of the Council in 1915 clearly reflects the changing attitude of the store:[57]

It was the sense of the Council that all fashion departments should be ready with new goods by August 1st, with great emphasis on taste, quality, and up-to-dateness; that the new merchandise should be shown with descriptive tickets on them, in addition to prices, showing that they are novelties; that we should have a full range, not a jump from low to highest price; that the Advertising Dept. pay particular attention to the new goods as they come in, laying stress on their newness & quality rather than on their price.

Another indication of the increasing stress on style is the fact that the Council arranged at this time to have the magazine *Vogue* sent regularly to 44 buyers as a means of helping them to keep in touch with current fashions.[58] By 1916 the store had set up a style committee to implement the new emphasis. Restrictions were placed upon the sale of "seconds," and buyers were warned against sacrificing quality in an effort to get low prices. At the same time, more attention was devoted to the arrangement of "artistic and harmonious" displays of merchandise in the show windows and within the store. By the end of 1917 the Council discussions were beginning to focus on the relation between style in general and Macy's reputation among customers, and the view was recorded that it was "important to create authoritative style and individuality and thus establish store character." [59]

To a considerable extent this new tendency of Macy's simply reflected the general improvement in the American standard of living which was beginning to be particularly noticeable after 1900. The impact of the first World War on the United States unquestionably gave impetus to the movement. People complained constantly about the high cost of living, but even the masses were beginning to take an interest in style goods and semiluxuries. Workmen spent their increased earnings on silk shirts, their wives began to wear silk stockings, and the demand for richer possessions spread rapidly in all ranks of life as the war boom developed. Hence it is not surprising to find the Macy Advisory Council devoting more consideration to style and quality in 1917 and 1918 than ever before.[60] Most of the Macy efforts to grade up bore fruit in the next decade, but it is plain that the store was aware of a fundamental change in its environment and that it was trying to adapt itself to the new conditions.

Staff and Working Conditions, 1900–1919

What about the Macy staff during the years after 1900? What was happening to the rank and file of the workers whose coöperation

HERBERT N. STRAUS
Partner, 1912–1919; secretary and treasurer, 1919–1929; treasurer, 1929–1933; vice-president, 1922–1933

WHEN MACY'S BEGAN TO EMPHASIZE STYLE, 1919
Newspaper advertisement showing improved copy and layout

was of such vital importance to the success of the business? Although it is impossible to study them in any detail, certain general changes took place in the composition of the working force and in the conditions under which they worked, changes that have an important bearing on the history of the firm and, at the same time, reflect significant developments within the field of retailing.

The staff was, of course, expanding in size as the business grew; the number of employees ranged roughly between 3,500 and 6,000 depending upon the year and the season. In October, 1911, for example, there were 5,207 people on the staff, 61 per cent of whom were women. By that date the store was beginning to use part-time employees for rush periods, so that the organization in terms of full-time workers was somewhat less than the number of individual persons on the payroll at any one time. The average number of employees in Macy's in 1919, adjusted to the equivalent of full-time workers, was 4,566, and the number of persons employed in the Christmas season of that year probably reached 10,000.[61]

It is only natural that the Macy staff should by 1900 begin to reflect the New York racial melting pot. Judging by names, nearly all races and nationalities were represented in the store organization, the Irish giving ground to Italians, Poles, Jews, Russians, Germans, and Scandinavians. Moreover, the Strauses continued their long-standing policy of using Negro elevator operators in spite of occasional objection from race-sensitive Northerners.[62]

Until 1915 no accurate data were available on the compensation of Macy employees but there is some evidence to show that, even before the War brought substantial increases, the average wage rate was somewhat above the level of the 1870's.

In 1914, for example, the minimum rate of pay for selling-employees was $6.00 per week, and the store was in the process of increasing it to $7.00, in addition to which the store had long paid a premium on sales over quotas.[63] In 1915 the average weekly earnings per Macy employee were just under $10, as compared with less than $5.00 in 1870-73. In part this increase came from higher rates of pay, and in part it was the result of a substantial decrease in the number of children employed in the store. The pneumatic tubes had eliminated the cash girls, and increases in the compulsory school age had cut down the number of young people employed to tend stock, carry messages, and so on.[64] As we have already seen, the average wage paid by Macy's more than doubled between 1915 and 1919.

It is difficult to appraise the working conditions of past decades because our standards and points of view have changed so rapidly, but it is clear that by contemporary standards Macy employees were well off after the firm moved into the new building at 34th Street. Investigators of the Employers' Welfare Department of the National Civic Federation found, for example, that Macy working conditions between 1910 and 1912 compared favorably with those of other New York department stores and were considerably above conditions existing in the smaller retail establishments.

The staff worked in clean, well-lighted, and properly ventilated quarters. Each person had a locker for his own individual use, except during the Christmas season when the abnormal expansion of the working force made some doubling-up necessary. The employee cafeteria provided a varied selection of good food at extremely low prices, and the firm served between 1,000 and 1,500 glasses of milk daily to the junior members of the staff free — an act of welfare for which Nathan Straus was unquestionably responsible. Both restrooms and showers were available to employees, although the Federation report noted that the Macy management had been disappointed in the use made of the bathing privilege. Commenting upon the popular complaint of the day that sales girls could not sit down during working hours, the report testified that seats were provided for employees in Macy's — adding that any employee who discharged his or her normal duties properly had little opportunity to use them.[65]

Macy store hours had been changed in 1909 from 8:00–6:00 to 8:30–6:00, but employees were expected to be on the job from 8:20 until work was finished for the day, usually some time after 6:00, with three-quarters of an hour for lunch. Although overtime was occasionally required in order to take inventory or prepare stock for a sale, the store no longer kept open for business in the evenings before Christmas. By 1915 the hour of store opening had been changed to 9 o'clock, and in 1918 the closing hour was changed from 6:00 to 5:30 during the summer months. The reduction in hours, of course, reflected the growth of the commuting habit among the New Yorkers. It is interesting to observe that the management apparently had as much trouble with tardiness after the change had been made as it had experienced when the store opened at 8:00 or 8:30.[66] As in earlier years, Macy's closed on Saturday afternoons during July and August. A number of rival stores had adopted the five-day week for the summer months, but Macy's refused to follow this curtailment of the shopping week until 1919, when the Advisory Council voted to close on Saturdays during July and August as a means of "holding old employees and as an inducement to new ones."[67]

The movement towards organized labor which was going on in many branches of industry after 1900 seems to have had little effect upon Macy employees, with the exception of two strikes which involved certain nonselling employees. During the course of an attempt to organize department store teamsters in 1910 most of the Macy drivers went out on strike, but at the end of a week they returned to work. In the same year 20 carpenters (employed on store alterations and maintenance work) struck for union wage rates. The management took the view that the union rate of $5.00 per day was based upon intermittent and uncertain employment and that the Macy rates ($18.00 per week for the first 6 months, $19.50 for the next 6 months, and thereafter $21.00 per week) were fully adequate for men who were employed throughout the year, fair weather or foul. Moreover, the firm claimed to have no difficulty in getting carpenters to work at these rates. In consequence Macy's used nonunion carpenters and was boycotted by organized labor during the closing months of 1910 and early part of 1911. However, the vast majority of Macy employees at this time were apparently not interested in union activities — at least not to the extent of taking any action. In this they resembled white-collar workers in general.[68]

Thanks to considerable moral and financial support from the Strauses, the Macy Mutual Aid Association, formed in 1885, continued to pay sick and death benefits to its members and to provide them with a considerable amount of medical care. Experience having indicated that those who stood in most need of such help seldom maintained their membership, the Macy management, after 1904, required all employees to belong to the Macy Mutual Aid, and the weekly dues (ranging from 10 to 40 cents a week in 1912) were deducted from weekly pay envelopes. Because membership was compulsory, all employees were required to pass a physical examination before becoming members of the regular staff. The Association had only two nurses and a part-time physician in 1908, but by 1918 its regular medical staff consisted of two physicians, one dentist, one chiropodist, three nurses, and two assistants. Approximately 30,000 treatments were administered during 1917, and the total disbursements for that year were $24,300, to which the firm itself contributed $6,000.[69]

The management used the Mutual Aid Association to handle a considerable amount of welfare work among members of the staff and their families. For example, a fund was set up in 1907 to make small loans to employees, and the Association's visiting nurse was empowered to make gifts of fuel, food, or clothing in cases of urgent need. On the other hand, employees who were incapacitated by health or age received small but regular payments (called clerks' relief) from the firm itself, the recipients and amounts involved being determined by the individual partners without any particular system.[70]

Despite the fact that working conditions were being improved in many respects, however, there was a certain subtle deterioration in the position of the Macy staff after 1900. A situation was emerging which perhaps might be described as the breakdown of the old personal and informal relations between employer and employee, followed by a slow, fumbling process of building up some sort of institutional substitute. As the Macy business expanded, the sheer weight of numbers made it increasingly difficult for the partners to be personally acquainted with individual members of the staff. They knew the employees of long standing, of course, but, as the number of workers grew into the thousands, contact between employer and employee became so tenuous as to be virtually nonexistent. The Strauses were obliged to depend more and more upon departmental heads to handle relations with the rank and file, and these intermediaries, busy with routine operations and inexperienced in personnel management, usually discharged the task badly. It is significant that in 1911 many Macy employees were more afraid of their immediate superiors than of the members of the firm.[71] Morale was inevitably impaired. Employees tended to feel that they were cogs in a machine, and interest in their work declined. The problem was not peculiar to Macy's: it was developing all over America, wherever business enterprises grew large. Labor relations based on paternalism were disappearing. Only in recent years have we really come to grips with the task of developing an institutional substitute.

All this is clear in retrospect, but concrete evidence at the time was scarce, and the firm itself was not conscious of any particular problem until 1914 when a report was prepared by outside investigators on working conditions within the store. Although this report dealt with efficiency, its original objectives had been quite different. For a number of years sensational stories had circulated about immorality among department store employees, supposedly resulting from the low wages received by the sales girls. New York's Committee of Fourteen began to wonder whether there might be any connection between working conditions in department stores and commercialized vice. One of the committee, a minister named John P. Peters, being personally acquainted with Percy Straus, discussed the problem with him, as a result of which the Strauses agreed to give full cooperation in an investigation, as a test case, among Macy employees.

Three young women, selected by the committee, worked as employees in various parts of the store during a period of six months. On the basis of their observations they made detailed reports which the Strauses were allowed to read. The general conclusion of the observers and the committee was that the behavior of the working force, although not always above reproach, was about what could be expected in any large and representative group of people, and that there was no connection between low wages and immoral conduct. What impressed the investigators most was the existence of a surprising degree of inefficiency and a general absence of enthusiasm among the employees for their work.[72]

Deeply impressed by the lack of interest and the inefficiency revealed in the report, the Strauses set about to improve conditions. Almost their first step was to employ one of the investigators, Marjorie Sidney, whose reports had revealed an unusual grasp of the problem, to assist with welfare and educational work. The entire task of recruiting and training employees was centralized (1915) in a separate department, and a systematic effort was made to improve personnel relations. Progress was inevitably slow, for no one really knew what to do. Indeed, Macy's was trying to solve a problem with which American industry as a whole made little progress until the 1930's. Naturally mistakes were made. The basic working assumption was that progress depended upon appeals to economic motives, together with the establishment of efficient procedures. There was a tendency to regard strict discipline as necessary to peak efficiency. Woe unto the clerk who was caught chewing gum, the porter who failed to keep his uniform collar buttoned up, or the driver who was found smoking while on duty! We know today that the emphasis should have been upon means of securing effective collaboration among the workers rather than upon technical methods — morale rather than efficiency — but it has taken many investigators a long time to prove that simple truth.[73] For the moment the important point is that the Macy management became conscious of a problem and quickly set about to find a solution.

The report of the Committee of Fourteen, the World War, and the growing problem of administration all combined to confirm the opinion of the Strauses that the future of Macy's depended upon improving the quality of personnel. The day was past when poorly educated employees could handle the store's work satisfactorily. The vast expansion in the variety of goods handled, the increase in the complexity of records required for efficient operations in a large organization, the growing emphasis upon quality and style, and the need for intelligent initiative and coöperation — such developments made it imperative to obtain employees with a good general education and special training. Retailing, moreover, was beginning to offer a stronger appeal to ambitious young people — partly because firms like Macy's were opening opportunities for important advancement. It was in recognition of all this that the Strauses began, at the close of the War, to seek college graduates as material for the organization that they were building.[74] In the past, Macy's had demanded — and got — hard work and loyalty. In the future it was to demand hard work, loyalty, and brains. It was to get those qualities, too!

Operating Data, 1902-1919

The operating data for the years between 1902 and 1919 are highly significant, reflecting many of the developments within the store and indicating some major trends in American retailing as a whole. Table 25 sets forth the data on Macy revenues for the period. The fact that sales expanded from $10,765,000 in 1902 to $35,803,000 in 1919 must be attributed in part to the drastic price changes which occurred during World War I. However, it is clear from Macy's success in the 1920's that there was more to this increase than mere price inflation. The data on discounts received show that the store was able to maintain at a high level the allowances obtained from vendors because of prompt payment; they also indicate once again the contribution to revenue which resulted from the Macy policy of buying merchandise for cash.

The column headed "Gross Margin" is remarkably revealing. It shows a steady rise in the gross margin — the difference between cost of goods sold and the price received for them — that all-important differential out of which a store pays its operating expense and derives its earnings (if any). It is unfortunate that we do not have any data for other stores with which to compare Macy experience; however, there seems to be little question that department stores in general were experiencing the same upward trend in gross margin received.

The significance of this expanding gross margin is still subject to a good deal of debate. To some extent it was unquestionably influenced by the fact that Macy's and other stores were taking over the wholesale function. That is to say, the volume of business in most Macy departments was sufficiently large by 1902 to enable the buyer

TABLE 25
ANALYSIS OF REVENUE
1902–1919

Year[a]	Total Net Sales[b]	Discounts Received	Gross Margin[c]	Operating Profit[d]	Net Other Income[e]	Total Net Gain	Earnings in Dollars
			(Percentage of net sales)				
1902[f]	$10,765,066	3.95	23.17	4.11	.98	5.09	$ 548,151
1903	12,203,974	3.70	24.58	3.48	.29	3.77	459,682
1904	13,135,446	3.61	25.23	4.34	.06	4.40	577,542
1905	15,009,037	3.63	26.08	6.12	.25	6.37	956,816
1906[g]	16,723,462	3.58	26.94	6.11	.48	6.59	1,102,419
1907	16,779,425	3.46	27.14	4.84	.33	5.17	867,410
1908	16,132,823	3.49	27.35	4.98	.32	5.30	855,116
1909	16,580,101	3.55	28.41	5.39	.43	5.82	963,718
1910	16,211,296	3.46	28.54	4.54	.54	5.08	823,970
1911	16,575,590	3.73	28.91	3.58	.18	3.76	623,871
1912[g]	16,234,152	3.72	29.49	5.43	.38	5.81	942,617
1913	16,430,818	3.68	29.00	4.20	.34	4.54	746,344
1914	17,289,047	3.80	30.06	5.77	1.63	7.40	1,278,523
1915	19,049,905	4.03	30.14	7.47	1.72	9.19	1,751,313
1916	21,811,830	4.17	31.39	9.39	1.88	11.27	2,458,643
1917[g]	23,452,293	4.00	30.60	7.50	.49	7.99	1,874,629
1918	25,827,948	4.00	31.65	6.75	1.70	8.45	2,181,848
1919	35,802,818	3.40	32.74	8.81	1.15	9.96	3,565,758

TABLE 25 (continued)

[a] The Macy fiscal year since 1902 has terminated with the Saturday nearest Jan. 31. Thus the figures for 1902 cover the fiscal period ending Jan. 31, 1902, and so on for the subsequent years.

[b] Including sales in leased departments but not goods sold and later returned for refund or exchange.

[c] Gross margin includes cash discounts earned and is the difference between the price received and the net delivered cost of goods sold after deducting all discounts and allowing for shortages and depreciation. The margin contributed by leased departments has also been included.

[d] These figures refer to profits from retail operations after deducting from the gross margin all expenses pertaining to retailing; interest on capital has not been included as an expense.

[e] The chief items included were profits from importing, manufacturing, store laundry, and found money. After 1913, when the store acquired the 34th Street building, this column includes the *net* revenue resulting from rentals charged to operating expense.

[f] Includes 57 weeks ending Jan. 31, 1903, owing to change in the fiscal year.

[g] Accounting period covers 53 weeks.

SOURCE: Semiannual statements, 1902–19.

to obtain most of his merchandise directly from manufacturers or their agents, rather than from wholesalers and jobbers, and the proportion of goods so bought probably increased as sales expanded. This enabled the store to obtain the trade discounts which had formerly gone to the distributing middlemen. This did not mean that the Macy profits were correspondingly increased; in taking over the wholesale function the store had to incur many expenses which had previously been borne by wholesalers. It is a fair inference that the additional margin obtained by Macy's as a result of direct buying went partly to pay for the resulting rise in operating expenses, partly into lower prices to customers, and partly into the firm's profits.

The increase in gross margin may also reflect decreases in the cost of production generally, as a simple example will show. Assume that existing production methods enable a manufacturer to place an item in a retail store at 80 cents per unit and that it costs 20 cents (including a fair profit) for the store to sell a unit at retail. The customer would pay $1.00 for the article, and the store's gross margin would be 20 per cent of the selling price. If by improving his production methods the manufacturer was able to sell to the store at 50 cents a unit, the cost to the consumer (assuming no change in the store's selling cost per unit) would be 70 cents, but the gross margin ratio would then be 28.6 per cent of the selling price. In other words there would be an *apparent* increase in the cost of distribution here, resulting from the change in the production cost, rather than any increase in the actual expense of retailing. Something of this sort may lie behind the rise in Macy gross margin. It seems likely, however, that a part of the increase originated to some extent in an actual rise in operating expenses, caused by increases in the compensation to employees as well as by improvements and additions to services rendered to customers, such as better delivery, more attractive show cases, improved ventilation, and so on. It is clear that the rise in gross margin percentage did not always add to Macy's operating profits, for there are many years in which earnings declined in the face of increases in the gross margin received.[75]

The operating profits show that Macy's was consistently able to produce earnings in spite of the impact of such unfavorable events as the panic of 1907 and the outbreak of World War I. Of course, after prices began to rise and the war boom gained momentum, there was a noticeable increase in the store's earnings, attributable to the rise in sales volume. The principal change in the column headed "Net Other Income" is explained by the change in ownership in 1914. That transaction, it will be remembered, transferred the building occupied by the store from L. Straus & Sons to Jesse, Percy, and Herbert Straus, i. e., to the Macy firm itself. In order to make the operating data presented here uniform and comparable to those of other department stores, a charge for rent has been included under operating expense, and the net revenue left remaining from the rental, after payment of taxes, insurance, depreciation, and interest on real estate, has been classified as "Other Income." As a result there is a substantial increase in other income beginning in 1914. The noticeable drop in this item in 1917 resulted from payments made by the store to R. H. Macy & Co., Private Bankers, to offset declines in the value of the securities held by the banking division, in accordance with the arrangements made at the time the D/A department was divorced from the retail store. The net earnings of Macy's show clearly the impact of the war boom, but one should not overlook the substantial increase produced in 1914 — before the war boom had started and in the face of a recession caused by the uncertainties following the outbreak of hostilities.

The operating expenses of the business are presented in Table 26. It is at once apparent that one of the major factors in the rising cost of operations was the increase in amounts paid to employees. In other words, a part of the so-called increased cost of distribution originated in the fact that department store employees were receiving a larger share of the money paid by customers for merchandise. Rental expense jumped from 2.11 per cent of sales in 1902 to 3.25 per cent in 1903, primarily because of the move to larger and better quarters at 34th Street. This increase, however, was gradually absorbed by the expansion of sales volume, as a result of which the rent ratio was substantially lower in 1919 than in 1903. It is clear from the data on advertising expense that the store's expenditures for publicity did not add appreciably to the price of the merchandise

TABLE 26
OPERATING EXPENSES
1902–1919

Year[a]	Total Net Sales[b]	Salaries[c]	Rent[d]	Advertising[e]	Delivery[f]	Total Expense[g]
		(*Percentage of net sales*)				
1902[h]	$10,765,066	9.51	2.11	2.11	1.94	19.06
1903	12,203,974	10.07	3.25	1.91	1.67	21.10
1904	13,135,446	9.95	2.95	1.95	1.81	20.89
1905	15,009,037	9.80	2.67	1.57	1.72	19.96
1906[i]	16,723,462	10.24	2.60	1.55	1.93	20.83
1907	16,779,425	10.72	2.60	1.59	2.14	22.30
1908	16,132,823	10.67	2.70	1.58	2.15	22.37
1909	16,580,101	10.55	2.63	1.52	2.15	23.02
1910	16,211,296	11.62	2.69	1.49	1.80	24.00
1911	16,575,590	11.83	2.74	1.73	1.63	25.33
1912[i]	16,234,152	12.35	3.00	2.22	1.84	24.06
1913	16,430,818	12.31	2.94	2.58	1.71	24.80
1914	17,289,047	12.28	3.07	2.50	1.56	24.29
1915	19,049,905	11.69	2.94	2.36	1.44	22.67
1916	21,811,830	11.47	2.58	2.03	1.59	22.00
1917[i]	23,452,293	12.12	2.43	1.92	1.66	23.10
1918	25,827,948	12.09	2.62	2.09	1.47	24.90
1919	35,802,818	12.08	2.40	2.11	1.22	23.93

[a] The fiscal year ends with the Saturday nearest to January 31st. Thus the figures for 1903 are for the 52-week period ending on Jan. 30, 1904, and so on.

[b] Sales in leased departments have been included. The only leased departments involved were those stocked by L. Straus & Sons.

[c] These figures do not include any compensation to the partners. It is possible that a few charges for salary or wages are concealed in other expense figures, but the proportion is certainly not large and is probably about the same year after year.

[d] Until 1914 this includes the amounts paid to L. Straus & Sons for the use of store building. After that date it includes ground rental, real estate taxes, insurance on buildings, and depreciation.

[e] This category refers primarily to charges incurred for newspaper and magazine space.

[f] Includes stable and garage expense and possibly some salaries.

[g] In computing total expense, the interest charges recorded on the operating statements have been eliminated because practically all the amounts so charged consisted of interest to the partners on capital invested. In making this correction a few capital disbursements for interest have doubtless been eliminated, but the amount involved is unquestionably negligible and does not materially affect the accuracy of the ratios.

[h] 57 weeks.

[i] 53 weeks.

SOURCE: Semiannual statements, 1902–19; data supplied by the controller's office.

sold (this expense, of course, was offset by the increased volume of business produced by the advertising). It is a noteworthy fact that the ratio in 1919 was exactly the same as in 1902, indicating that expenditures on advertising space had not increased in relation to dollar sales during the interval. Owing to fluctuations in space rates, it is impossible to say whether the quantity of space per sales dollar had changed. Of course, the enormous sales volume made possible vast advertising expenditures without increasing the advertising expense ratio.

Delivery expense showed a tendency to rise between 1905 and 1909, but subsequently there was a noticeable decline in the ratio. It seems likely that the rise was owing principally to the extension in the territory covered and that, once delivery routes were fairly well stabilized, the increases in volume helped to absorb some of the overhead expense and produce a decline in the ratio. The increased use of mechanical transport may also have contributed to the reduction.

The total expense ratio is probably more significant than its component parts. It is a remarkable fact that the ratio tended to increase between 1902 and 1911 and that thereafter the expense ratio actually showed a tendency to decline, reaching 23.93 per cent in 1919 as compared with 25.33 in 1911. This should go far to explode a widely held notion that the increase in retail expenses and margins came principally as a result of World War I. Doubtless some of the drop in the total expense ratio should be attributed to improvements in expense control within the Macy organization.

A number of miscellaneous operating indices are set forth in Table 27. The returns ratio, for example, shows that customers were returning an increasing proportion of merchandise bought, reflecting a more liberal policy of returns and allowances on the part of the firm. This rise was interrupted by restrictions imposed during the War, but we know from the record after 1920 that customers were to continue the trend which was evident in the prewar period and that other stores experienced the same increase.

The stock-turn figures indicate that for a number of years the Macy management was having difficulty in adjusting stocks of merchandise to the customer demand. As a result there was a rather steady decline in the stock-turn from 5.61 times in 1903 to 3.92 in 1911, after which there was substantial improvement. It will be remembered that the Macy controller's office began to work out improved

TABLE 27

OPERATING AND FINANCIAL DATA

1902–1919

Year	Ratio of Returns to Net Sales %	Annual Stock-Turn[a] (Times)	Ratio of Inventory to Total Assets %	Ratio of Fixed Assets to Total Assets %	Ratio of Total Assets to Net Sales %	Ratio of Net Gain to Total Assets %
1902[b]	2.29	5.12	56.77	30.01	35.19	14.47
1903	2.74	5.61	56.91	38.42	34.30	10.98
1904	2.83	4.51	59.59	15.80	30.18	14.57
1905	3.17	4.79	56.03	13.17	31.27	20.39
1906[c]	3.25	4.54	56.93	12.41	33.02	19.96
1907	3.31	4.20	66.33	14.38	28.72	18.00
1908	3.27	4.14	56.95	12.86	32.01	16.56
1909	3.45	4.28	61.46	14.05	30.48	19.06
1910	3.53	3.97	64.27	12.91	32.54	15.61
1911	4.29	3.92	57.68	12.60	33.06	11.38
1912[c]	3.90	3.93	54.30	13.70	34.96	16.61
1913	3.92	4.25	51.10	13.47	34.14	13.30
1914	3.94	4.37	32.17	55.21	55.14	13.41
1915	4.18	4.69	27.03	48.85	56.43	16.29
1916	4.26	4.90	29.88	44.53	56.89	19.81
1917[c]	4.38	4.47	34.61	41.70	56.49	14.17
1918	3.29	4.29	21.14	28.91	54.84	10.27
1919	3.77	5.28	27.00	26.29	63.06	15.79

[a] Computed by dividing sales at cost by the average inventory at cost, the latter being the average of stocks on hand at the beginning, middle, and end of the 12-month period.
[b] 57 weeks.
[c] 53 weeks.
SOURCE: Semiannual statements, 1902–19.

methods of merchandise control in 1910, and the improvement in the ratio suggests that the controls imposed were increasingly successful. It is important to note that in spite of the temptation to buy large stocks of merchandise in anticipation of further price rises during 1917 and 1918, the rate of stock-turn continued to be fairly high. The jump in the rate in 1919 is probably the result of a hand-to-mouth policy imposed because of the management's feeling that a severe break in prices was likely to take place.[76]

The other ratios in Table 27 are largely quantitative expressions of developments to which reference has already been made. In 1914, for example, when the store acquired ownership of its premises, there was an immediate shift in the ratio of inventory to total assets, fixed assets to total assets, and total assets to net sales. One should not fail to note, however, the effect of the increased earnings after 1914. These were mostly kept in the business, bringing about a rise in current assets and reducing the ratio of inventory to total assets and of fixed assets to total assets. However, this increase in working capital was matched by a corresponding growth in sales volume, as is shown by the ratio of total assets to net sales. The last column, "Ratio of Net Gain to Total Assets," shows rather wide fluctuations, but it is clear that all through this period the capital in the hands of the Straus management was made to produce substantial earnings. The results in any one year are, of course, subject to many vicissitudes, some of which are beyond the power of any individual firm to control, but the record of Macy earnings over such a long period — particularly when one remembers the problems to be solved and the financial difficulties experienced by many rival firms — is convincing evidence of Straus enterprise and ability.

EPILOGUE

IN MANY respects the period of Macy's development which began in 1919 is the most dramatic and significant in the entire history of the firm. Although the firm (and indeed the department store industry) had matured many years before and although from the very beginning Macy's had earned its reputation for leadership in retailing, it was after 1919 that the Macy organization blossomed forth with a brilliant display of growth and achievement which made the store truly world-famous.

For a detailed account of Macy's history since 1919, however, we shall have to wait until the advent of peace. A number of circumstances, not the least of which is the present world conflict, make inevitable this interruption in the story. The delay is for the present unfortunate, but at least we can now see the strong roots which made possible Macy's remarkable record during the past two decades, and the additional passage of time will give much-needed perspective on the dazzling 'twenties and the confusing 'thirties. For the time, then, the reader must be content with a brief preview of the volume which is to come, with a few glimpses of a truly great American firm at the peak of its development.

Shortly after the close of World War I the Macy business was incorporated (May, 1919), with members of the Straus family holding all the outstanding stock. In 1922, after 64 years of growth, Macy's permitted the public to acquire a share in the ownership of the enterprise. Since that time death and the diversification of investments have brought about a gradual decrease in the proportion of ownership held by individual members of the Straus family, until today not one of them possesses a 10 per cent interest in the business, and all the Straus holdings combined constitute somewhat less than 50 per cent of the total stock outstanding. Thus, although the effective control of Macy's remains with the Strauses, it is substantially true to say that the firm which began as a single proprietorship and

EPILOGUE 399

was for half a century a closely held partnership is now a publicly owned corporation.

Meanwhile, death has claimed two of the three brothers who owned the business after 1914. Percy S. Straus, the survivor, still devotes as much time and energy as his health permits to the chairmanship of the board of directors. The president and active head of Macy's, however, is Jack I. Straus, the son of Jesse I. Straus and like him the eldest son of an eldest son, the third generation of the family to be connected with the enterprise. Grouped around him are such able and experienced executives as Edwin I. Marks, Delos Walker, and Beardsley Ruml (author of the pay-as-you-go plan for income taxes), who help to run the vast retailing concern. The Straus influence is still strong — possibly still dominant — but in neither ownership nor management is Macy's a family business today.

The rise of Macy's volume of sales is a good index to the firm's performance in the 1920's. In spite of the sharp business recession in 1920–21 and the precipitous price decline which accompanied it, Macy's sales increased rapidly from $35,800,000 in 1919 to $98,500,000 in 1929 and just under $99,000,000 in 1930. During a single day (December 21, 1929) sales exceeded $900,000 — almost as much as Rowland Macy sold during the entire year of 1870. Price declines and prolonged economic depression made the dollar sales shrink to a low of $76,200,000 in 1933, but subsequently they recovered, until sales for 1942 broke all previous records, being somewhat over $100,000,000. The total sales of certain retail chains exceed this amount, but so far as individual stores are concerned Macy's has for at least 15 years been the largest in the world from the point of view of the amount of business done.

For many years it has also been the largest in the world in terms of physical size. Even before 1919 the growth of sales had crowded the 1902 building, and by 1922 expansion could no longer be postponed. A new 20-story building was erected west of the store and joined to it, the construction being completed by 1924. Two subsequent additions to the west gave Macy's the tallest and largest store premises in the world, covering the entire block from Broadway to

Seventh Avenue and from 34th to 35th Street, except for two small corner pieces, one at Broadway and 34th and the other at Seventh Avenue and 35th. (Macy's was no more willing to pay an excessive price for land in 1929 than in 1901.) Within the store building today there are 45.5 acres of floor space. Moreover, as a result of successive warehouse expansions over on Long Island, the firm has nearly 30 additional acres of floor space for reserve stocks, manufacturing operations, and delivery facilities.

Perhaps the magnitude of the store will be more apparent to the layman from the fact that the Macy power plant (said to be the largest private unit in the world) generates over 20,000,000 kilowatt hours of power a year and consumes approximately 5,000,000 gallons of fuel oil annually — or did before rationing began — in order to supply heat in the winter, coolness in the summer, and power and light throughout the year. About 270 men and women are employed to scrub, dust, and polish every day just to keep the store tidy. To move people from floor to floor there are 29 passenger elevators and 58 escalators, while merchandise is transported within the store by means of 105 conveyor belts, 8 spiral chutes, and 26 freight elevators, several of the latter being sufficiently large and powerful to whisk loaded delivery trucks from one floor to another with perfect ease.

Everything at Macy's is on the same colossal scale. In normal times an average of 137,000 customers shop there daily, and during the busy season before Christmas the patronage increases to some 350,000 persons a day. The number of sales transactions made by Macy's during a peak day has exceeded 390,000, and even before the recent war boom in retail trade the store's total annual transactions had passed the 42,000,000 mark. Some 225 cash registers and 800 pneumatic tube lines (containing 75 *miles* of tubing) are required to record sales, while it takes 180 incoming telephone lines and 100 operators to handle the normal load of telephonic business. During the rush season the store employs twice as many girls to cope with the vocal traffic jam. Before Pearl Harbor the Macy fleet of 410 delivery trucks and furniture vans delivered purchases over a radius of 50 miles at the rate of 1,800,000 packages a year, covering 3,850,000 miles in the process. The last of the store's horse-drawn vehicles was sold in 1926, but the present war may give Old Dobbin another chance at Macy's.

The working force required to handle all the Macy operations varies from 10,000 persons in the dull seasons to 20,000 during the Christmas rush. About 100,000 people normally apply for employment in the store, and 75,000 of them are considered good enough to justify serious interviews. They come because for persons interested in retailing Macy's is a good place to work and because the store gives training and experience which ordinarily command a premium in the labor market.

Indeed, the development of a well-rounded personnel program is one of the most significant features of Macy history since 1919. There were three phases to the program. First, Macy's departed from the long-standing tradition of employing executives whose primary qualification for the job was merchandise experience. Recognizing the implications of the American advance in education and standards of living, Macy's management began to select young men and women mainly on the basis of their formal training and general cultural background. The firm itself accepted the responsibility for giving to desirable recruits the retail knowledge and experience necessary to enable them to handle the management of a department. Thus, the second phase of the personnel program was an expansion of the basic training arrangements and the development of an executive training course for picked workers who showed promise of becoming capable administrators.

Thirdly, Macy's began systematically to build up a well-rounded executive staff, not merely to satisfy immediate needs in manpower but also to anticipate Macy's administrative requirements in years to come. To be sure, every successful firm does this to some extent, but the Macy management began to do so consciously and methodically, whereas the usual practice is too often a matter of intermittent and unsystematic attention, with vague hopes substituting for definite plans and concrete action. As a result, a large proportion of Macy executives today are persons who were selected and trained 15 or 20 years ago for the very positions they now hold. This is one important manifestation of the fact that Macy's is now a continuing social organism.

Although possession of a highly trained staff of workers has played an important rôle in Macy's success during the past two decades, it has not been the only factor. Another important element has been the maintenance — and in some respects the intensification — of the firm's original policy of competing on a price basis. In 1919 Macy's began a comprehensive and systematic attempt to set its prices at a point at least 6 per cent below those of competing stores for comparable merchandise, justifying the policy on the basis of its cash operations and large volume. Over this issue some bitter fights have since taken place between the store and its rivals, two of them terminating in government tribunals, but Macy's still endeavors to maintain a 6 per cent differential, which it refers to as its cash-price policy; others call it an underselling or price-cutting policy.

In a constant effort to keep its price "6 per cent less" the firm has long maintained a Comparison Department. From 80 to 100 comparison shoppers relentlessly scrutinize the offerings of rival stores at the rate of 4,000 comparisons a day. If Macy's prices are found to be less than 6 per cent under, they are promptly revised to conform to the policy. During the past ten years the so-called "fair-trade" laws have interfered with the complete application of this policy, but the store has met this problem by expanding its own privately branded lines. Some 4,500 different articles are sold under the various Macy brands.

A third ingredient in the success of Macy's since 1919 has been the management's increasing emphasis upon style and quality in merchandise. Here, as in its price and personnel policies, the tendency was evident before 1919, but the methodical application of a conscious policy came later. In 1920 Macy's began the systematic development of a trade in well-designed merchandise, so as to cater more effectively to a public which was becoming educated to good taste in color, texture, and line. Before that time style merchandise had meant wearing apparel for the luxury trade. Macy's broadened the idea to include practically everything a customer might want and then arranged to make such merchandise available to the middle- and even the lower-income families.

As a means of improving the technical quality of its offerings the store established (1927) its own Bureau of Standards, probably the first one to appear in a retail store in this country. For many years the Macy Bureau has been testing merchandise at the rate of over 2,000 analyses a month. In addition to helping departmental buyers (and even manufacturers) to improve their wares in the interest of the ultimate consumer, the Bureau has long maintained a close check on Macy advertising copy in order to make it technically accurate. This has meant some headaches for buyers and copywriters but, on the other hand, fewer disappointed customers.

Along with the drive for improved design and quality Macy's has continued and expanded the Straus emphasis upon wide assortments of merchandise. In practically every department the customer may select from a number of different price lines, and within each price line the store offers an extremely wide range of choice. The extent to which this policy has been carried may be judged from the fact that in 1939, before war began to cause shortages, the store stocked over 394,000 different types of merchandise, not counting sizes and colors. The Macy grocery department offered the connoisseur a choice of 186 different kinds of cheese alone, while the store stocked 1,300 different kinds of women's shoes, counting different price lines, styles, and qualities but disregarding sizes and colors. Other departments provided an equally amazing range. It is small wonder that in normal conditions Macy's had about $16,000,000 worth of merchandise on hand, selling it and replacing it at the rate of about $300,000 a day.

That seemingly endless array of merchandise came to Macy's from nearly 20,000 vendors (manufacturers, wholesalers, brokers, or agents) throughout the United States and (before the War) in some 29 foreign countries. Before the War Macy buyers interviewed vendors' representatives within the store itself at the rate of 750 interviews a day. About 320,000 other interviews a year took place in "the market" outside the store, while an additional 20,000 took place annually in foreign countries. The customer seldom gives a thought to such matters, but it takes a vast organization, ceaseless work, and top-notch ability to assemble the fascinating assortment of wares which the modern department store spreads before its patrons.

Macy's expansion during the 1920's was not confined to the sales and plant facilities at Herald Square. Watching the success of retail chain stores in the grocery and drug fields, the Strauses decided that it was desirable to explore the possibility of applying similar methods to department stores. In 1923 Macy's acquired a controlling interest in the Lasalle & Koch Co., the leading department store of Toledo, Ohio, with half a century of success behind it. In 1925 it purchased the control of the Davison-Paxon-Stokes Co. (now Davison-Paxon Co.), of Atlanta, Georgia. Unlike the Toledo acquisition, the Atlanta store was not prospering, and Macy's wanted to see whether improved management could restore it to profitable operations.

In the summer of 1929 came the third extension, when Macy's bought all the common stock of L. Bamberger & Co., of Newark, N. J. Both the Toledo and Atlanta firms purchased by Macy's had been relatively small, with a combined sales volume of less than $14,000,000 a year. In contrast, the Bamberger business was large; indeed, its sales exceeded $37,000,000 in 1929 and were second only to Macy's in the New York area.

Macy's made no further attempts at external expansion until 1940 when it opened an experimental branch store in Syracuse, New York, to test the possibilities of selling selected fast-moving items on a limited service basis. After a year of disappointing results the store was closed and written off as a mistake. The outcome of a second branch undertaking promises to be much happier. In October, 1941, the firm opened "Macy's-Parkchester," a branch store in the new housing development erected by the Metropolitan Life Insurance Co. in the borough of the Bronx. Macy's-Parkchester employs about 350 people, and, in addition to being merchandised by the department managers of the main store, is kept in close touch with the parent organization by means of teletypewriter communication. Consequently, it offers a great many advantages of the Herald Square store. Results for the first year of its operations indicate substantial success.

Perhaps the most startling event in recent Macy history was the inauguration (October, 1939) of the firm's "Cash-Time" plan of extending credit to customers. In one sense this marked a radical departure from the time-honored cash policy that Rowland H. Macy had established. In another sense it was the offer of a new service to customers, supplementing the cash policy and the D/A system, by making purchases possible on credit — at a price. Under the Cash-Time plan customers are allowed to pay for their purchases in installments over a period of time, now from 5 to 12 months (originally up to 24 months), depending upon the kind of merchandise bought. For this privilege the customer pays, in addition to the cash price, a service charge of 6 cents on each credit unit of 94 cents.

Introduction of the Cash-Time plan, by offering the convenience of deferred payment, has permitted Macy's to tap a new segment of the market. At the same time the firm has been able to maintain its original cash-price policy. The customer who buys on credit has to pay an extra charge for the service; thus, Macy's has gained an opportunity to reëmphasize the advantages of cash transactions. The charges for Cash-Time service, though small, are a source of additional net revenue. The plan proved its worth within a few months of operation, and, although recent government credit restrictions designed to curb inflationary tendencies have somewhat curtailed the volume of Cash-Time sales, it is likely that the return of peace will see a substantial increase in the volume of credit business in Macy's.

During the 1920's the Macy business proved to be remarkably profitable. The peak year was 1929, when earnings before income taxes exceeded $10,000,000 — approximately equal to the store's *sales volume* in 1902 and about 6 times the highest annual sales figure reached in Rowland Macy's lifetime. The depression years inevitably brought about a sharp reduction of profits, while rising taxes and wages aggravated the problem of making ends meet. Despite all the difficulties, however, Macy's managed to show substantial earnings during every single year of the depression period. At a time when annual reports were typically spattered with red ink, the Macy star continued to shine in carmine glory against a background of black figures. Considering the economic conditions which prevailed, together with the burdens imposed by the firm's expansion program, this record provides convincing evidence of Macy's enduring strength.

The present world conflict, of course, has had a profound effect upon all branches of business enterprise, and Macy's is no exception. It has become increasingly difficult to obtain supplies of merchandise, while the urgent need to conserve rubber, gasoline, and fuel oil has been forcing a drastic reduction of normal retail services. The armed forces and war industries, moreover, have drawn heavily upon Macy personnel at all levels, and the difficulty of finding replacements combined with the inexperience of the new employees has made it impossible to maintain peak efficiency in operations. Meanwhile the establishment of price ceilings and the extension of rationing to a variety of consumer goods have greatly complicated the normal routine of selling. Indeed, because of the growing number of government regulations which affect retail operations, the store's management has to cope with a stupendous burden of legal and financial detail, one which at times seems almost beyond the capacity of human flesh to bear.

On the other hand, although the problems confronting the store's management today are even more numerous and complex than those which Rowland Macy faced during and after the Civil War, it is likewise true that the modern Macy organization possesses vastly greater resources, in both financial strength and skilled manpower, for meeting them. No one can foresee the eventual outcome of the economic, political, and military turmoil through which we are now passing, but Macy's long record of successful adaptation suggests that the firm will be able to cope with the problems and changes which tomorrow will certainly bring.

When peace returns it will be possible to deal critically and in detail with Macy's history for the period since 1919. We shall then be able to discern more clearly the fundamental transition through which the firm, like all other private enterprise, has been going during the past two decades. At the moment, it is possible only to suggest the probable lines of development by summarizing the dominant phases of evolution through which Macy's has passed.

Founded by a petty capitalist in an era of rampant individualism, Macy's grew and prospered during that phase of economic development which has been called industrial capitalism. For many of America's business enterprises the uncoördinated specialization and fierce competition which were characteristic of industrial capitalism spelled ruin or drastic reorganization under the guidance of financial capitalists (usually investment bankers). Thanks to the administrative genius of the Straus family, Macy's avoided the financial difficulties which typified so many industrial capitalistic firms. It performed for itself the diversification of lines, the integration of economic functions, and, to some extent, the horizontal combination that the financial capitalists imposed upon much of American business in order to adjust various enterprises to changing conditions. In becoming a publicly owned corporation, Macy's relied upon investment bankers to assist in financing its expansion, but in doing so it avoided both bankers' influence and the divorce between ownership and management which have characterized so many large corporations.

During the past decade Macy's has apparently been confronted with another stage in capitalistic evolution — not financial capitalism, which the firm has practically side-stepped, but a new and different phase — one in which the formulation of business policy has been transferred to governmental bodies, leaving only the details and execution to private enterprise. This new stage has been called national capitalism to distinguish it from the industrial and financial capitalism through which we have passed and from the public or communistic capitalism which has emerged in Russia. It is much too soon for us to grasp its inner significance or discern all its possible ramifications. Future historians must do that.

For the present let us be content to note that Macy's is the epitome of a long line of business development which began in thirteenth-century Europe, when the sedentary merchant first rose above the petty capitalist to gear production to market needs and opportunities. It flourished during the era of industrial and financial capitalism, and it embodies all that men have learned about scientific management, business rationalization, and corporate development. Once a small, independent, and socially insignificant store which was owned and managed by one man, it has become a great institution, an enduring organism firmly welded into the economic and social fabric of the community that it serves. Like all human institutions,

Macy's still depends upon the leadership of a single person, but it has long outgrown one-man management. At the top, as throughout the rank and file of the organization, it depends upon the effective collaboration of many workers. It is typical of American private enterprise at maturity.

APPENDICES

APPENDIX A

SOME NOTES ON THE RISE OF DEPARTMENT STORES IN PARIS

As indicated in the text of Chapters IV and VI, we lack detailed knowledge of the history of retailing in Europe, and this gap provides a number of excellent opportunities for ambitious students. It will, of course, be difficult to make much progress until conditions in Europe again permit academic research. Meanwhile it should be possible to glean many pertinent facts from various French publications, including magazines and newspapers, on file in the United States. The following discussion is intended to give to others the benefit of such fragmentary knowledge as I have come across in preparing the Macy history; it is necessarily tentative at many points and incomplete throughout.

Various writers have stated that the department store originated in Europe and antedated American department stores by a number of years.[1] So far as I can learn, none of them has produced specific evidence on the point, having been content to rely mainly upon legends in the trade. One must, of course, recognize that these writers have been interested primarily in current operations, rather than the history of retailing, and have not had the training in historical method that would enable them to deal effectively with developments in the past.

European scholars have likewise been of little assistance in this matter. Historians like Clapham in England and d'Avenel in France possessed too little knowledge of retail trade or business practices to deal with the problem with any understanding.[2] Such information as they have given

---

[1] Herbert Adams Gibbons, *John Wanamaker* (N. Y., 1926), vol. 1, pp. 124–127, 131–132; George B. Hotchkiss, *Milestones in Marketing* (N. Y., 1938), p. 191; Paul H. Nystrom, *Economics of Retailing* (N. Y., 1930), vol. i, pp. 127, 134, 427, 429.

[2] J. H. Clapham, *The Economic Development of France and Germany* (Cambridge, England, 1921), pp. 117–120, 303, 366–371; G. d'Avenel, *Le Mécanisme de la vie moderne* (Paris, 1902), pp. 1–90; Francis Ambière, *La Vie secrète des grands magasins* (Paris, 1938), esp. pp. 28–29.

Probably some German historian has given the matter careful attention, but I have failed to find in the obvious German sources any information beyond that presented by d'Avenel.

us relates chiefly to the size and grandeur of the stores and the huge sums of capital involved. These, though important, are surface aspects. Where such studies have touched on the diversification of merchandise handled, the few examples they have given lie entirely within the field of dry goods, and there is a very annoying paucity of dates in the sketching of main developments. More than any other student, d'Avenel glimpsed the significance of the rise of the *grands magasins*, but in his discussion of their emergence he emphasized such selling policies as fixed prices, low profit margins, and liberal return privileges as the *éléments constitutifs* and practically ignored the tendencies towards integration and diversification.[3]

In consequence, it is necessary to go to such contemporary French sources as one can readily obtain in the United States. Among the most useful are the files of *L'Illustration*, which contain both articles on Paris shops and advertisements of their merchandise and can be made to yield a good deal of information. Thus, in the very first year of its existence (1843), *L'Illustration* printed a brief description of the Ville de Paris, which shows it to be a relatively large store, handling a variety of dry goods which to contemporaries seemed to be unprecedented.[4] An advertisement of the same store a few months later mentioned two important policies: it operated on the fixed price system, with all the goods marked in plain figures; and it encouraged customers to buy goods with the understanding that, if not satisfactory, the purchases could be returned for refund or exchange.[5]

A general article in 1844 dealt with the rise of various large stores, referred to the fixed price system as a widely established practice, and presented a description of the Ville de Paris, estimating the number of its employees at 150 and its annual sales at 10,000,000 to 12,000,000 francs. Doubtless it is not a matter of chance that the store which at first received the most attention in the editorial pages was the one which advertised the most heavily, but at least we are able to conclude that a very large Paris store was already using publicity as a device for promoting sales.[6] Another general article, published a few years later, reveals that the Ville de Paris and several other Parisian stores, formerly called *magasins de nouveautés*, were beginning to be known as *grands magasins*. The author asserted that one could find "everything" in these immense bazaars, and he explained that, while they were crowding out the small,

[3] d'Avenel, *op. cit.*, esp. p. 13.
[4] Nov. 4, 1843, p. 159.
[5] Mar. 30, 1844, p. 79.
[6] May 11, 1844, p. 173.

specialized shops in Paris, their rise was economically desirable. However, it is significant that the examples he cited to illustrate the great variety sold were, without a single exception, chosen from the conventional range of dry goods to be found in French and American stores at the time.[7]

All authorities agree that the famous Bon Marché was of no importance until 1852, when it came under the presiding genius of Aristide Boucicaut, although it had had many years of previous existence. Its sales were small — about 450,000 francs, or $90,000, per year. Under Boucicaut's management the store is supposed to have enjoyed rapid growth, but no one has given us a detailed account of the various steps involved. We know that in 1854 its merchandise was sold at fixed prices, with the figures plainly marked, and that customers could return for exchange or refund purchases which were unsatisfactory for any reason. We also know that the lines handled included the following: dry goods, millinery, furs, ready-to-wear and made-to-order clothing, carpets, linoleum, mourning goods, upholstery materials, mattresses and other bedding, and iron beds.[8] Apart from the beds, there is nothing in the list that was not regularly sold by a number of large stores in both Paris and New York in the 1850's; and all evidence indicates that by 1850 A. T. Stewart's establishment in New York handled a much larger volume of retail trade than any in Paris, and that all the variety was comparable to that in the Bon Marché, with the single (and I think unimportant) exception of the beds. As a result, we lack sufficient ground for awarding to the Bon Marché the decision in the question as to which firm was the first to become a full-fledged department store. Supporting this conclusion is the fact that contemporary French sources stress the years 1868 and 1869 as the period of the Bon Marché's greatest expansion.[9] By that time Macy's and Lord & Taylor were far along the department store road.

[7] Sept. 27, 1850, p. 187. The range given is *depuis la chaussette de fil jusqu'au cachmire de l'Inde.* He also mentions *robes, cravates, gilets de flanelle, bonneterie, fichus, dentelles de Flandre, toile,* and *parapluies.*

[8] Photostat copies of sales invoices, dated 1854 and 1855, which contain a printed list of the goods sold in the Bon Marché at the time. These photostats were supplied by Joseph Mayer, formerly in charge of the Paris offices of R. H. Macy & Co.

[9] *L'Illustration,* Mar. 23 and 30, 1872, and Oct. 10, 1874; d'Avenel, *op. cit.,* p. 15.

There is reason to question the Bon Marché's primacy in Paris itself, at least in the early 1860's. Boucicaut had difficulty in convincing his partner, Vidau, of the wisdom of his progressive ideas; and it was not until 1863 that Vidau withdrew from the firm, at which time the annual sales were only seven million francs, or approximately $1,400,000. An article in *L'Illustration* reveals that the Magasins du Coin de Rue was among the largest stores in the city in 1860; figures showing in detail its sales for 1859 total 7,236,385 francs. Thus sales volume of the Coin de Rue in 1859 was fully as large as that reached by the Bon Marché after three more years of growth. The variety of merchandise sold by the Coin de Rue was wide, consisting mainly of dry goods. How far it went beyond dry goods is difficult to say, for at this point a problem arises as to contemporary usage of words. The whole question turns upon the precise translation of the word *meubles*. Thus, one of the Coin de Rue departments mentioned is that of *meubles de couleur*. At first glance this looks like furniture, in the sense in which we use the term today, but the question at once arises as to why furniture *de couleur* is segregated. The only other mention of the term is in the department of *blanc* (white goods or linens) which also included *meuble brodé*.[10] If we translate the doubtful word as furniture, we have to solve the question as to why, in a period when colored furniture was not in vogue, the store devoted an entire department to it and at the same time had no department for ordinary furniture. Then we must explain why the store sold "embroidered furniture" in its white goods or linen department. Both are obviously very improbable. It is plain that *meubles* can refer to all sorts of household furnishings besides tables and chairs, and I suspect that *meubles* here did not mean wooden furniture at all but referred rather to such household furnishings as tapestries, embroidered doilies and other pieces of table linen, and possibly even small ornaments, such as china figures, vases, and the like — in short, merchandise which Americans included under the term fancy goods.[11] For the present I feel bound to conclude that the Coin de Rue, which was unquestionably one of the largest and most progressive stores in Paris, sold no greater variety than A. T. Stewart in New York and that as late as 1863 it was essentially, like Stewart's store, a dry goods business organized by merchandise departments.

[10] *L'illustration*, Dec. 1, 1860, p. 375.
[11] Native Frenchmen with whom I have discussed the matter have reached the same conclusion.

Subsequent articles and advertisements support the views presented here. None of the advertisements for the Louvre (founded in 1855) or the Printemps (founded in 1865) mention any goods outside the traditional dry goods lines before 1870, and the only apparent exceptions mentioned in the advertisements of Ville de Paris and the Chausée d'Anton are such fancy goods as Chinese screens, leather pocketbooks, postcard albums, and cigar cases, appearing for the first time in 1867.[12] As late as 1872 the advertisements still featured dry goods almost exclusively, and the exceptions to this consist wholly of fancy goods of the type mentioned, although the variety in all lines is noticeably greater. One finds frequent mention of the word *ameublements* in the early 1870's, but this may or may not include household furniture. In the absence of additional information one is warranted, I believe, in translating it "house furnishings" and assuming that it refers to towels, blankets, curtains, and so on — goods that American stores of the period often called housekeeping goods. As indicated in Chapter VI it seems to me highly significant that a description of the Tapis Rouge, after its reorganization and enlargement in 1872, should stress its resemblance to the most advanced type of American retail store, instead of comparing it to the Bon Marché and other *grands magasins* of contemporary Paris.[13]

From many points of view the most illuminating statement of the evolution of the *grands magasins* comes not from a historian but a novelist. In *Au Bonheur des dames*, one of the novels which Emile Zola designed to depict in detail the contemporary life of Paris, we have an extraordinarily complete and intimate description of the internal mechanism and routine activities of the leading store of the 1860's (really a fictional blend of the Bon Marché and the Louvre), together with a penetrating analysis of both the forces which shaped its evolution and the effect of its growth upon the neighboring shops. By way of preparation Zola spent a considerable amount of time in personally observing operations in all departments of the Bon Marché and the Louvre, and he obtained additional information from the managements of the two stores. His notes were subsequently deposited in the Bibliothèque Nationale, and, when the return to peacetime conditions permits, it is to

[12] See especially advts. in *L'Illustration*, Nov. 4, 1865, p. 302, Dec. 21, 1867, p. 399, and Nov. 8, 1869, p. 303.
[13] *Ibid.*, Sept. 21, 1872, p. 189, Oct. 19, 1872, pp. 236, 238, 254, 255, and Dec. 14, 1872, p. 383.

be hoped that someone with the proper training will give them the thorough examination they deserve.[14]

The difficulty with Zola's elaborate picture is that we cannot be sure of the chronology. The main action is dated in 1865–66,[15] but there are indications that Zola projected into the 1860's a number of operating methods and evolutionary developments which took place only shortly before the novel appeared (1883). As a remarkably complete exposition of the operations of the *grands magasins* before 1883, *Au Bonheur des dames* is unquestionably a reliable document. No novelist could have invented the precise and detailed description of operating figures, methods of compensation, managerial hierarchy, and store arrangement which Zola's book contains. On the other hand, because we have no present means of knowing to what extent the author may have departed from strict historical chronology, it is not possible to rely upon *Au Bonheur des dames* as an accurate account of the emergence of the French department store, particularly when developments on both sides of the Atlantic were moving so swiftly in the same direction.

It is clear that the French stores became very large establishments, selling a wide variety of merchandise in immense volume, and that they were organized by merchandise departments and handled their business much in the manner of the American department stores. At the same time, the evidence points overwhelmingly to the fact that they were little more than elaborate dry goods stores with the major emphasis upon textile products and upon the luxury end of the dry goods trade. If size and form of organization are the criteria, A. T. Stewart's business preceded them by at least a decade in becoming a department store. If, in addition to these aspects, we emphasize the handling of non-textile merchandise and we emphasize the satisfying of everyday needs of the ordinary family, the conclusion, until new evidence is forthcoming, seems inevitable that New York stores led the way. Certainly there is no present basis for asserting that American stores were imitating those in France.

---

[14] Details of the method by which Zola obtained his information are to be found in Sydney Barlow Brown, *La Peinture des métiers et des moeurs professionnelles dans les romans de Zola* (Montpélier, 1928); Henri Massis, *Comment Zola écrivait ses romans* (Paris, 1906). The citation for the notes is as follows: *Bibliothèque nationale, XIXe siècle, nouvelles acquisitions françaises*, 10265–10355; those specifically concerned with Zola's novel, *Au Bonheur des dames*, are numbered xi–xiv (10275–10278).

[15] *Au Bonheur des dames*, p. 227.

APPENDIX B

Early Macy Accounting

From the extant records it is possible to reconstruct some of the accounting methods and policies that were used in Macy's in the 1870's. These have an important bearing on the store's system of pricing merchandise as well as the accuracy of the operating data. The firm's books consisted of a general journal, a general ledger, a payroll ledger (after 1871 executives' compensation was recorded in a separate account, possibly in the general ledger), and probably a cash journal and merchandise ledger. In addition, La Forge kept a kind of private ledger in which operating figures were summarized semiannually.[1]

As merchandise arrived in the receiving room, it was unpacked and priced according to a Macy formula which dates from 1872 if not earlier. In brief, the formula (it was formally incorporated in the articles of partnership between La Forge and Valentine) called for fixing a uniform rate of margin, known as the departmental "rating," for each merchandise department. This rating was usually expressed as a fraction of cost — one-ninth, one-fifth, or whatever the decision might be — and retail prices were normally set by adding that rating to the cost of the merchandise. If strictly applied, this procedure would often result in uneven or odd prices: a unit costing 96 cents in a department which had a rating of one-sixth would be priced at 96 cents plus 16 cents, or $1.12. Some old employees believe that the Macy odd prices really originated in this way. All the contemporary information I have been able to assemble indicates, however, that prices were "evened off" until 1874, apart from the odd-cent quotations (noted above, pages 52–53) which resulted from the reference to fractional coins.

Because of custom or market situations, certain items of merchandise might call for special pricing, so as to yield a retail price which was above

[1] This discussion is based upon a painstaking examination of La Forge's Ledger, with entries dating from 1871 to 1877; the payroll ledger, covering 1869–74; three memos of operating results covering short periods in 1874, 1876, and 1877; partnership agreement, June 21, 1877; a memo of departmental ratings for 1887; and the series of account books which began with the fall season of 1887.

or below the one determined by the normal rating. Thus, "mark-ups" and "mark-downs" in the Macy organization meant deviations from the retail price as determined by the regular departmental rating. These deviations could be made by the buyer at the outset or after the goods had been put on sale, provided that the partners approved; or the partners themselves might initiate the change.

In all cases the bookkeeper was supposed to be given a record of the cost, the regular rating, and all mark-ups and mark-downs, so that he could, by keeping track of purchases, sales, and prices, maintain a continuous record of inventory and compute theoretically the value of inventory on hand at cost. For example, if the rating was one-fifth, an item costing $1.00 would be priced at $1.20, and the bookkeeper could always ascertain its cost by deducting one-sixth from the marked retail price (one-sixth, because adding one-fifth to the cost made the retail price six-fifths of the original). To compute inventory for the entire department it was necessary merely to add the retail prices and deduct the rating, making proper adjustments for any deviations from normal rating. By comparing the inventory as recorded on the books (as it theoretically should be) with inventory as revealed by physical tally of the stock on hand, the management hoped to determine the existence of shortages arising from damage or theft. Of course, failure to record price adjustments, together with other accounting errors, made it difficult to interpret the net shortage figure.

This early Macy procedure (retained for over forty years) closely resembles general practice today (the "retail method of calculating inventory," adopted mainly after 1915) with two points of exception, both of considerable importance. The first difference is that modern ratings, usually called mark-ups or mark-downs, are generally expressed in terms of the selling price rather than original cost. Thus a 40 per cent mark-up means today that an article priced at $1.00 has a cost which is the retail price less 40 per cent, or 60 cents. This seems to be simply another way of looking at the same thing, but it really involves a fundamental shift in emphasis from cost to selling. The important matter is not so much what merchandise has cost as the price at which it will sell, and the prudent business man starts his calculations with selling price as a base.[2]

[2] The details of the Macy rating procedure are set forth in the partnership agreement between La Forge and Valentine, dated June 21, 1877; La Forge's Ledger shows that the rating system was being used as early as the fall of 1871.

An early explanation of the modern retail inventory method was prepared

Department No. 9

Rated at one fifth. Deduct one sixth from Sales to get cost.

From Jan'y 15th to Aug. 24th 1872.

Gross am't of Purchases and transfers	52656.79
" " " Sales	65557.06
Actual cash Sales	65937.50

Estimated Profit on Same. 10989.63
Add mk up ___ 1214.42
12204.05
Ded. mk down ___ 1644.47
Net Profit ___ 10559.58

Gross Sales 65557.06
Ded. Prof. 10559.58
56027.48
Ded Purch. 52656.79
Decrease 3370.69

Amount of Stock Jan'y 15th	32145.27
Decrease	3370.69
Stock should be	28774.58
Amount of Stock Aug. 24th	27970.15
Stock is short	804.43

Amount of Stock August 24th 1872.

27970.15

DEPARTMENTAL OPERATING STATEMENT, 1872
Showing method of calculating profit and loss

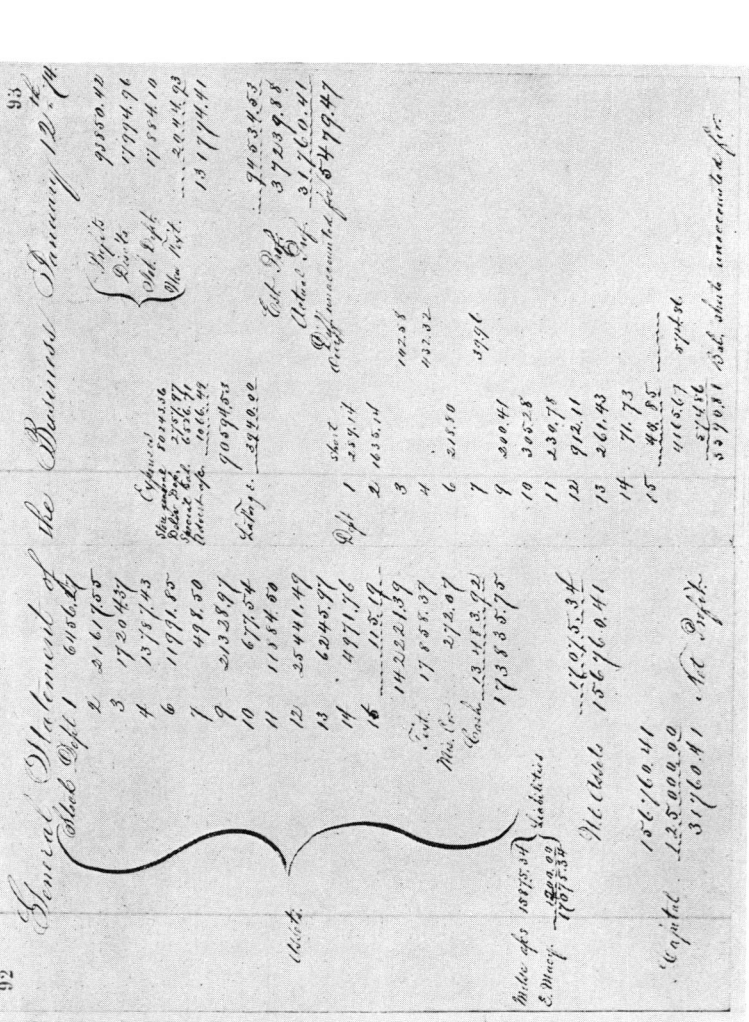

OPERATING STATEMENT, 1874

Showing combination of balance sheet and profit and loss statement

The second difference is related to the first but refers specifically to errors resulting from the use of the formula. Under the old Macy procedure the mark-downs and mark-ups were applied to all the merchandise on hand and so recorded. Actually some of the items would not be sold until a later accounting period, and the effect was that of taking profits and losses on goods which were still on the shelves. As a result, the book inventory and the profit and loss statement were both inaccurate (even assuming absolute accuracy in bookkeeping entries), the size of the error depending upon the net balance of adjustments and the quantity of merchandise carried over to the next season. In point of fact, the final calculation of profits was obtained by taking a physical inventory, but there was always a difference between the physical inventory and the book inventory, a "shortage" in some departments and an "overage" in others. Usually the result for the store as a whole was a shortage (sometimes amounting to several thousand dollars) which the management, not being aware of the mechanical error in the system, usually attributed to theft or destruction.

Quite apart from this false reckoning, the old Macy system differed from the modern because it tried to get back to the *original* cost of merchandise, whereas the modern method automatically adjusts values to the existing market, because the average mark-up rate is deducted from the *current* retail price. If, for example, a unit that was originally priced to sell at $1.00 so as to yield a 40 per cent mark-up should, because of damage or obsolescence or drop in market price, be marked down to 80 cents, it would be valued for inventory at 80 cents less 40 per cent, or 48 cents — 12 cents below its original cost. The modern method is more conservative because it depreciates the value of stock to take account of values at the time of inventory-taking. Of course, the modern method is subject to certain inaccuracies, but they need not be discussed here.[3]

With a fairly rapid turnover of stock, the rating procedure was prob-

---

by A. C. Ernst, of Ernst & Ernst, and published in the *Accounting Bulletin* of the National Retail Dry Goods Association, vol. i, special no. 2 (Jan., 1913). It is apparent that the method was unfamiliar to most retailers at the time. Conversations with Ernest Katz, Controller of R. H. Macy & Co., and others familiar with the subject indicate that the method was beginning to be adopted widely by 1915.

[3] For further discussion of the retail method of inventory see Norris A. Briscoe, *Retailing* (N. Y., 1936), ch. ix.

ably sufficiently accurate for the time. Its chief merit was its simplicity, both for pricing and taking inventories. Table 28 shows the ratings which were regularly applied to the various Macy departments in 1872, 1877, and 1888.

The following procedure was followed in drawing up the semiannual statements. From the records of individual departments (presumably kept in a merchandise ledger) the total amount of cash sales in a given department was obtained. From this figure the regular rating was deducted (that is, if sales were $10,000 and the rating was one-ninth of cost, one-tenth would be subtracted); the resulting figure was then adjusted by adding the mark-ups and subtracting the mark-downs, a process which was supposed to yield the net departmental margin. Next, this net margin was deducted from sales in order to obtain the cost of sales. Sales at cost were then deducted from purchases to determine whether the stock-in-trade had increased or decreased, in order to adjust the beginning inventory and find out what the stock *should* be. This book inventory figure was then compared with the actual stock as determined by physical count, supposedly revealing shorts and overs. In most departments these calculations usually indicated shortages which were at least partially attributable to errors in the system. The net margin figure was then revised by deducting shorts or adding the overs, yielding the estimated margin or rating earned by the department. For an example see the departmental statement shown opposite page 418.

The estimated earnings of the various departments were then added together to obtain the estimated "profit on sales" for the store. To this sum were added the income from jobbing and the discounts earned. The result was what we should today call gross margin, and from it the various expenses were deducted to obtain the *estimated* net profits.

The results for the season were then recalculated by totaling the assets and liabilities as determined by a careful check, including physical inventory, and deducting the partners' capital from the net balance. This figure, based upon a careful appraisal of property, was regarded by the partners as the *actual* profits, and it was probably much more accurate than the estimated profits. In practice the two amounts were sometimes as much as two thousand dollars apart, even after considering the "shortages." The difference, of course, was the consequence of other errors in the accounting system, such as mistakes in taking inventory and arithmetical errors. For an illustration of the semiannual reckoning see the statement shown opposite page 419.

TABLE 28
Departmental Ratings[a]
1872, 1877, 1888

Department	Rating Formula 1872	1877	1888	
1. White goods, linens, and blankets	1/9	1/5	1/5	
2. Laces and embroideries	1/9	1/5	1/5	
2½. Ladies' and children's muslin underwear	b	1/9	1/9	*should be 1/5*[e]
3. Notions, sewing supplies, and other smallwares	1/9	1/6	1/6	
4. Ribbons	1/9	1/9	1/9	*should be 1/6*
4½. Colored silks	b	b	1/9	*should be 1/6*
6. Ladies' and children's hosiery and furnishings	1/9	1/5	1/5	
6½. Men's furnishings	1/9	1/5	1/5	
7. Ladies' ties	1/9	1/5	b	
7. Merino underwear	b	b	1/5	
8. Furs	1/5	1/9	b	
8½. Umbrellas, parasols, and canes	1/9	1/6	1/6	
9. Fancy goods, jewelry, and leather goods	1/5	1/4	1/5	
9½. Toilet articles, perfumery, and patent medicines	b	b	1/5	
10. Boys' clothing	b	1/6	1/6	
11. House furnishing goods	1/4	1/4	1/4	
12. Dolls and toys	1/4	1/3	1/3	
13. Books, picture frames, and albums	1/5	1/5	1/5	
14. Worsteds, worsted fringe, canvas, and felt	1/5	1/5	1/5	
16. Candy	1/4	1/3	1/3	
16½. Soda water	0	0	0	
17. Gloves	b	1/5	1/5	
18. Ladies' untrimmed hats	b	1/9	1/9	*should be 1/5*
18½. Ladies' trimmed hats	b	1/9	1/9	*should be 1/4*
19. Flowers and feathers	b	1/4	1/4	
21. Ladies' and children's suits	b	1/5	1/5	
21½. Ladies' and children's cloaks	b	1/5	1/5	
22. Black silks	b	1/5	1/9	*all specials*
23. Black and colored cashmeres and dress goods	b	b	1/9	
24. Silk fringe, dress buttons, and trimmings	b	b	1/5	
26. Corsets and bustles	b	b	1/5	

TABLE 28 (*continued*)

Department	Rating Formula		
	1872	1877	1888
27. Stationery and visiting cards	b	b	1/5
28. Upholstery goods, lace curtains, and portieres	b	b	1/5
29. Ladies' handkerchiefs, collars, and cuffs	b	b	1/5
30. Knitted worsted goods	b	b	1/5
(Leased)			
5. Silverware	b	1/3	1/4
15. China and glassware	b	1/2	1/2
20. Ladies' and children's shoes	b	1/4	1/4
25. Restaurant	b	b	1/3

[a] The rating was the fraction of cost which was added to arrive at the regular retail price of merchandise in a department. Deviations were often authorized, so that the average rating earned by a department differed somewhat from the formula.

[b] Department not operating at the time.

[c] This and subsequent notations were written in after the original list had been typed. Probably the phrase "should be" was a recommendation that certain ratings be revised for the future.

The notation after black silks seems to mean that black silks were being sold at very low margin as special attractions — price leaders, in modern parlance.

SOURCE: La Forge's Ledger, 1871–77; typed list, undated, but internal evidence proves that it refers to the store as organized after Jan. 1, 1888, and before July 1 of the same year.

In 1872 there was no analysis or breakdown of expenses, all disbursements being summarized in one account, called "store expense." In 1873 the expenditures for executive salaries and delivery were separated as "special salaries" and "stable." Separate entries for advertising, insurance, and ordinary payroll were begun in 1874, while in 1877 separate notations appeared for depreciation ("decrease in fixtures") and rent. It is interesting to note that half the cost of all additions to fixtures and equipment was at once charged against the current expense account and the remainder carried as assets until worn out or sold. In 1876 the partners decided to modify this practice by writing off a portion of the fixtures account each season with a view to wiping it out entirely by 1883 when the partnership agreement and the leases to the store were to terminate.[4]

[4] Fixtures agreement, Nov. 8, 1876; partnership agreement, June 21, 1877.

NOTES AND REFERENCES

CHAPTER I

1. Obed Macy, *History of Nantucket* (Boston, 1835), pp. 4–6, 13–19; Silvanus J. Macy, *Genealogy of the Macy Family* (Albany, 1868), p. 245; James S. Pike, *The New Puritan* (N. Y., 1879), pp. 34–36, 50–55; Alexander Starbuck, *History of Nantucket* (Boston, 1924), pp. 14–22, 653, 787; Carl R. Fish, *The Rise of the Common Man* (N. Y., 1927), pp. 200–205; Isabel Grubb, *Quakerism and Industry Before 1800* (London, 1930), pp. 22, 28, 34–35.

Macy and others had already purchased Nantucket several months before the occurrence of the episode for which he was fined, but this fact does not prove, as recent writers have suggested, that religious views had nothing to do with his removal to the Island. He had, in fact, got into difficulties with the General Court in the preceding year. Macy was a Baptist, but all that we know about his career indicates that he disliked the narrow, far-reaching religious control exercised by the General Court.

2. S. J. Macy, *op. cit.*, pp. 155–156, 245, 372; information supplied through the courtesy of Edouard A. Stackpole of Nantucket Island from old advertisements in the Nantucket *Inquirer*, 1833 and 1837–41; O. Macy, *op. cit.*, p. 30; Starbuck, *op. cit.*, pp. 600–606.

The woeful deficiencies of Nantucket education at the time when Rowland Macy left school are discussed at length in Cyrus Peirce and others, *An Address to the Inhabitants of Nantucket on Education and Free Schools* (Providence, 1838).

3. Herman Melville, *Moby Dick* (Mod. Lib. Ed.), p. 63.

4. Information about Macy's whaling experience has been drawn from the crew list, certificate of registry, and other original documents relating to the *Emily Morgan* for the voyage 1837–41, now on file in the New Bedford Customhouse; from the Consular Return from Bay of Islands, New Zealand, Jan. 1 to June 30, 1841, in the National Archives; together with reports of the *Emily Morgan's* position as noted in the Nantucket *Inquirer*, 1838–41. Information from the *Inquirer* has been supplied mainly through the kindness of Edouard A. Stackpole, whose help in identifying the ship in which Macy sailed made it possible to discover other details of the voyage. The excerpt from C. W. Morgan's diary was supplied to me through the courtesy of William M. Emery of Fairhaven, Mass.

Two detailed studies of the whaling industry give excellent descriptions of the whaleman's daily life: Walter S. Towers, *A History of the American Whale Fishery* (Philadelphia, 1907); and Elmo Paul Hohman, *The American Whaleman* (N. Y., 1928). Of particular interest is Captain W. H. Macy's *There She Blows!* (Boston, 1877), which describes a whaling voyage in 1841–44 over the same course as the *Emily Morgan's*.

5. Benson J. Lossing, *History of New York City* (N. Y., 1884), vol. ii, pp. 791–792.
6. *Loc. cit.*; Stimpson's *Boston Directory*, 1843–46; Adams' *New Directory of the City of Boston*, 1846–49; *The Boston Almanac*, 1842–49.
7. Marysville *Herald*, Aug. 6, 1850, p. 3.
8. *Ibid.*, Aug. 20, 1850, p. 3.
9. Earl Ramey, *The Beginnings of Marysville* (San Francisco, 1936), p. 59. Quoted by permission of California Historical Society.
10. The few details which can be assembled concerning Macy's venture in California have been drawn from the following sources: Jethro C. Brock, *A Correct List of Persons Now in California* (Nantucket, 1849), lent to me by Edouard A. Stackpole; advertisements in the Marysville *Herald* for Aug. and Sept., 1850, supplied through the courtesy of Earl Ramey of Marysville, Calif., and Mrs. Dolores Waldorf Bryant of San Francisco; S. J. Macy, *op. cit.*, p. 245; C. W. Haskins, *The Argonauts of California* (N. Y., 1890), pp. 463, 494; Ramey, *op. cit.*, pp. 55–59 and *passim*.
11. *Ibid.*, p. 57.
12. *Book of Deeds No. 1*, Yuba County, Calif., pp. 537–539, 616–617, supplied through the courtesy of Earl Ramey.
13. Lossing, *op. cit.*, p. 792.
14. S. J. Macy, *op. cit.*, pp. 371–372.
15. Ramey, *op. cit.*, *passim*.

CHAPTER II

1. In the absence of any original records relating to the business itself, the details of Macy's Haverhill business venture have been drawn from the Macy advertisements appearing in the Essex *Banner* and Haverhill *Gazette* for the years 1851–55, inclusive; Boston business directories for the years 1848–56; an advertising booklet published by R. H. Macy at the close of 1854; and an obituary of R. B. Macy published in the Nantucket *Inquirer* of Nov. 19, 1887.
2. Essex *Banner*, Apr. 5, 1851.
3. By this time, however, the dry goods trade was already departing from its time-honored spring and fall seasons. Hunt's *Merchants' Magazine and Commercial Review* (henceforth cited as *Merch. Mag.*), Aug., 1851, pp. 202–203; *United States Economist*, Nov. 6, 1852, p. 44.
4. Haverhill *Gazette*, June 14, 1851.
5. *Ibid.*
6. *Ibid.*, Dec. 27, 1851.
7. *Ibid.*, Jan. 17, 1852.
8. *Ibid.*, Apr. 3, 1852.
9. Chap. IV, page 89.
10. Haverhill *Gazette*, Nov. 20, 1852.
11. *Ibid.*, June 4, 1853.

12. One must recognize that "wholesaling" is an ambiguous term which was, and still is, applied to a variety of situations. Two types were common: (1) sale of merchandise to men and firms who, in turn, resold it to the public; (2) sale of merchandise to large users, such as restaurants, hotels, factories, and even individuals, who did not ordinarily resell it — at least, not in its original form. Many a farmer and workman with a large family bought his meat and groceries at wholesale. Firms in the wholesale trade handled one type or the other or both. Macy's "wholesale trade" may have consisted of a few sales to country storekeepers.

13. Advertising booklet, *Macy's New Year's Present, 1855*.

14. *Ibid.*

15. *Ibid.*

16. This is based upon the assumption that he hired the persons for whom he advertised on May 13 and June 17, 1854, in the Haverhill *Gazette*.

17. William Endicott, "Reminiscences of Seventy-five Years," *Proceedings of the Massachusetts Historical Society*, vol. xlvi (Nov., 1912), pp. 216–217.

18. There is a legend that the motto borne by the rooster was "While I live I'll crow" — see Edward Hungerford, *Romance of a Great Store* (N. Y., 1922), p. 22. Since none of the Macy advertisements show this, it must be dismissed along with many other details given in the source cited, as aprocryphal.

19. Haverhill *Gazette*, Apr. 15, 1854.

20. *Ibid.*, Oct. 24, 1854.

21. *Ibid.*, Nov. 20, 1852.

22. *Ibid.*, Jan. 21, 1854.

23. *Ibid.*, May 20, 1854.

24. *Ibid.*, Sept. 9, 1854.

25. *Ibid.*, Oct. 28, 1854.

26. *Ibid.*, Dec. 23, 1854.

27. *Ibid.*, July 16, 1853.

28. *Ibid.*, Jan. 6, 1853.

29. *Ibid.*, July 7, 1855.

30. I have obtained a considerable amount of information on Macy and his store from a set of private credit reports dating from 1858 to 1887. There can be no question about the authenticity of these reports; they constitute contemporary evidence of unusual interest and importance and they contain information which cannot be obtained from any other source. Unfortunately they cannot be made generally available for research at the present time, and their present owner feels, therefore, that the identity of the source should not be made public. Accordingly I am unable to give a complete citation.

The first entry, used at this point, is dated Nov. 1, 1858. This source will henceforth be cited as Cred. Rep.

31. *The Directory . . . of Haverhill and Bradford . . . for 1857* (Lawrence, Mass., 1857).

32. *Boston Almanac*, 1857.

33. Several pieces of evidence strongly indicate that Macy did not go to Wisconsin before the beginning of 1857: a poster advertising a "Firemen's Military and Civic Ball," to be given by Tiger Engine Co., No. 1, on Dec. 31, 1856, listed R. H. Macy as a member of the committee on arrangements; and his name also appears in *The Directory . . . of Haverhill and Bradford . . . for 1857*, which evidently was compiled in 1857. Macy was certainly in Massachusetts as late as May, 1856, for he was made a Knight Templar in Newburyport on May 23, 1856 (original certificate in the archives of R. H. Macy & Co., Inc.).

34. Lossing, *op. cit.*, p. 792; Superior (Wis.) *Times*, Jan. 3, 1874. I am indebted to John A. Bardon and Martha B. Merrell, librarian, of Superior, Wis., for help in unraveling Macy's Wisconsin venture.

CHAPTER III

1. There are countless volumes describing New York's life and history, but none of them yields the vivid cross-section which is to be obtained by perusing a few volumes of contemporary newspapers. In writing these paragraphs I have drawn mainly upon the N. Y. *Herald, Times,* and *Tribune* for 1858 and 1859.

2. Advt., N. Y. *Herald*, Feb. 10, 1859.

3. For fuller treatment of the concept of the secular trend in America see N. S. B. Gras, *Business and Capitalism* (N. Y., 1939), and N. S. B. Gras and Henrietta M. Larson, *Casebook in American Business History* (N. Y., 1939), pp. 661–744. On New York dry goods trade in 1858 see Chamber of Commerce of New York, *Annual Report*, 1858, pp. 35–37. No announcement of the opening has been discovered, but a credit report dated Nov. 1, 1858, stated that Macy "opened last Thursday," thus establishing beyond serious doubt the correct anniversary date.

In 1908 Macy's celebrated its fiftieth anniversary with a sale in February (advt., N. Y. *Herald*, Feb. 2, 1908), although in several previous years the birthday sale had taken place in the fall. Advisory Council minutes for Sept. 29, 1916, show that the anniversary sale was scheduled in February to stimulate business in a month the management had found to be characterized by poor volume. As a result the store now regularly anticipates its real birthday by eight months, a slight warping of historical fact which does no one any harm.

4. Advt., N. Y. *Herald*, Nov. 25, 1858, *et seq.*; letter from Cora A. Crossman to Abbie Golden, June 30, 1908. (Miss Crossman stated in an interview in 1931 that she began to work in Macy's in 1862.)

5. *Ibid.*; interviews with Lucy Clark, 1930 and 1939.

6. "New York," *Merch. Mag.*, vol. xxvii, no. 2 (Aug., 1852), p. 160; *Miller's New York As It Is* (N. Y., 1859), pp. 75–77. Contemporary advertisements and

directories show that various kinds of dry goods stores presented an almost continuous line along a section of Broadway. A few examples from the more prominent advertisers: Edward Lambert & Co. at 335 Broadway; S. B. Chittenden at 350; Strang, Adriance & Co. at 355; George Bulpin at 361; Lichtenstein's "Temple of Taste" at 387; Ubsdell, Pierson & Lake at 471; Beekman & Co. at 473; Charles Street & Co. at 475; G. M. Bodine & Co. at 481; and Genin's Bazaar at 513. Well above the rest but still below Macy's was James A. Hearn at 775, just above 9th Street.

7. Appleton's *Annual Cyclopaedia and Register* . . . *1861*, vol. i (N. Y., 1868), p. 526.

8. Cred. Rep., Nov. 1, 1858. According to the same source Macy told others that he was putting $10,000 into the business and that he had real estate in Wisconsin worth $15,000 above encumbrances. Of course all such statements must be treated with judicious skepticism.

9. Hunking's daughters said, in 1923, that their father had formed a deep friendship with Macy and had lent him the money. One must recognize the possibility that it might have been in connection with the Haverhill or Wisconsin venture rather than the store in New York. See an article on Macy's Haverhill store by Leonard Woodman Smith, curator of the Haverhill Historical Society, in the Haverhill *Evening Gazette*, July 24, 1923.

10. Hungerford, *op. cit.*, pp. 13, 27.

11. Cred. Rep., 1858–63; Cred. Rep. on Houghton and his wife, dated Sept. 3, 1863.

It is highly improbable that the credit investigators would not have discovered the partnership had one existed. Certainly Macy never advertised his business as a partnership until 1872 when it unquestionably became one, nor was any partnership registered in 1858 as would have been required by State law, nor did the various city directories list Houghton as a partner. We have learned from an indirect source that in 1863 Houghton had worked for Macy as a clerk after leaving Boston. It is difficult to see why either of the men should have concealed the fact if Houghton had actually been a partner.

12. Cf. *Documents Relative to the Manufactures in the United States, collected and transmitted to the House of Representatives . . . by the Secretary of the Treasury*, 2 vols., 22d Cong., 1st Sess., House Doc. 308 (Washington, 1833), *passim* (cited henceforth as *Docs. Rel. Mfs.*); *United States Economist*, June 4, 1853, p. 114; "Long Credit in Northern Cities," *Merch. Mag.*, vol. xxxiii, no. 2 (Aug., 1855); Endicott, *op. cit.*, p. 216.

One example of practice which was evidently typical is to be found in an advertisement of Bowen, McNamee & Co. (N. Y. *Tribune*, May 18, 1859), who did a wholesale as well as retail business in dry goods. They quoted prices on six months' credit, with 5% off for cash. A clever buyer would doubtless have got these terms liberalized.

13. Signed statement of J. Maidhof, dated Sept., 1896, now in the Macy

Archives. There are some unimportant errors of fact in the letter, such as an old man might make in recalling events nearly forty years old. Also, such details as the length of credit period may be inaccurate. But the firms mentioned actually appear in *Wilson's Business Directory of New York* for 1858, classified as Maidhof's letter indicates, and the main idea of the letter may be accepted as correct.

14. See pages 48–50.

15. Advts., N. Y. *Tribune*, Nov. 25, 1858, *et seq*. Details as to changes in Macy's merchandise are given in Chapter V.

16. For detailed description of the way in which imported goods were sold at these auctions, see N. S. Buck, *The Development of the Organization of Anglo-American Trade, 1800–1850* (New Haven, 1925); Fred M. Jones, *Middlemen in the Domestic Trade of the United States, 1800–1860*, Illinois Studies in the Social Sciences, vol. xxi, no. 3 (1937).

17. Cred. Rep., Dec. 31, 1859, Nov. 27, 1860, April 16, 1862; obituary of Robert B. Macy in the Nantucket *Inquirer and Mirror*, Nov. 19, 1887; *Trow's New York City Directory*, 1859–70.

18. Cred. Rep., Nov. 1, 1858, Feb. 9, 1860.

19. *Ibid.*; N. Y. *Tribune*, Nov. 10, 1858, p. 7.

20. N. Y. *Times*, Oct. 21, 1859, p. 5; Cred. Rep., Feb. 9, 1860. One might suspect that the fire was to be explained by excessive inventory or a tight financial situation, but the fact that it occurred at 6 o'clock in the afternoon, just at closing time, indicates that it was a genuine accident.

21. *Ibid.*, also Apr. 15 and Dec. 31, 1859.

22. *Trow's Directory*, 1859–63. Hungerford (*op. cit.*, p. 15) says that Macy first lived over his store, but the directories prove that he did not.

23. Cred. Rep., Nov. 1, 1858, to Mar. 10, 1863.

24. Interview with Mrs. Florence Macy Sutton, 1930.

25. Cred. Rep., Nov. 27, 1860, to Oct. 31, 1868.

26. *Ibid.*, Nov. 24, 1869.

27. Advts., N. Y. *Herald*, *Tribune*, and *Times*, 1858–70. The first specific mention appeared in the N. Y. *Tribune*, Jan. 22, 1859. A later advertisement in the *Tribune*, Oct. 24, 1870, attributes Macy's low prices to direct purchasing from manufacturers as well as to buying for cash.

28. Advt., N. Y. *Herald*, Dec. 21, 1858.

29. Advts., N. Y. *Commercial Advertiser*, Dec. 15, 1871; N. Y. *Herald*, Dec. 3, 1876. John Wanamaker's one-price policy did not prevent him from issuing "special privilege" cards to clergymen and others. As late as 1899 he gave ministers a 10% discount; dressmakers received 6%; customers who set themselves up as "purchasing agents" for out-of-town friends also received a discount at Wanamaker's. *Reports of the Industrial Commission on the relations and conditions of Capital and Labor employed in Manufactures and General Business* (Washington, 1901), vol. vii, p. 465 (hereafter this will be

referred to as *Rep. of Ind. Com.*); Herbert Adams Gibbons, *John Wanamaker* (N. Y., 1926), vol. i, p. 115.

30. Advts., N. Y. *Herald*, *Times*, and *Tribune*, July, 1858, to Dec., 1870.
31. Cred. Rep., Apr. 15, 1859, Sept. 3, 1861, and Mar. 10, 1863.
32. Advt., N. Y. *Herald*, Sept. 20, 1860.
33. *Ibid.*, Jan. 6, 1859. John Wanamaker claimed to have originated the clearance sale in 1877 (Gibbons, *op. cit.*, vol. i, p. 178). But in this, as in many other matters, Wanamaker was merely publicizing and claiming as his own a practice which had already been widely established. As indicated in the next chapter, other merchants had long anticipated Wanamaker's so-called innovations. I have yet to find a single instance in which a Wanamaker "first" can be substantiated for the period before 1900. His genius lay in dramatizing the commonplace.
34. Lossing, *op. cit.*, p. 792, shows that this legend goes back to 1884 at least, and he gives 1862 as the beginning of Macy's odd prices. Such odd prices as existed in 1862 are also to be found in advertisements for 1858 and 1859.
35. Charles H. Haswell, *Reminiscences of an Octogenarian* (N. Y., 1896), pp. 57–58.
36. Advts., N. Y. *Herald*, Feb. 1, 1859, *et seq.*
37. *Ibid.*, Oct. 24, 1875.
38. Any other conclusion on this point involves the highly improbable assumption that Macy hired a skilled copywriter as soon as he reached Haverhill, kept him until 1855, and was able to get him back in 1858, only to lose him as the New York business obtained abundant prosperity.
39. Advts., N. Y. *Tribune*, Nov. 25, 1858, *et seq.* Macy began in December to use the *Herald* also, and in 1859 he added the *Times*.
40. Frank Presbrey, *The History and Development of Advertising* (N. Y., 1929), pp. 206–210, 236–252.
41. Presbrey gives the credit to Macy and Lord & Taylor jointly (*op. cit.*, p. 248), but examination of the newspapers of 1865 proves definitely that Macy began to employ large, heavy type while Lord & Taylor still conformed to the established pattern. Indeed, the newspaper advertising which Presbrey reproduces (p. 249) clearly reveals the contrast between the two. It is fair to say, however, that Lord & Taylor took the lead in copy excellence a few years later.
42. Macy did not invent the idea of reiteration, nor did he carry it to the extreme of filling a whole page of repetitions as did the reputed originator, Robert Bonner, of the N. Y. *Ledger* (Presbrey, *op. cit.*, pp. 236–243). One can never be sure whether the layout of an advertisement of this period was determined by the advertiser or the printer. Comparison of Macy advertisements in different papers shows variation in the use of capitals but close similarity in layout, indicating that Macy himself planned the arrangement but left choice of type to the printer.
43. This paragraph and other generalizations in the present section are

based upon a careful examination of dry goods advertising from July, 1858, to 1900 and beyond. The time, labor, and eyestrain involved made an exhaustive study of all media out of the question. As a compromise, we followed Macy advertising from day to day in the *Herald*, shifting to other papers whenever Macy ceased to use that medium. We checked, in addition, the advertising of competitors in Dec. of every year, and in every tenth year we made spot checks in various other media to see which ones were being used. Most of the hard work of this task was performed by Alfred W. Swinyard while working on a Service Scholarship at the Harvard Business School.

44. N. Y. *Herald*, Jan. 5, 1859.
45. *Ibid.*, July 11, 1859.
46. N. Y. *Tribune*, Dec. 22, 1858.
47. N. Y. *Herald*, Nov. 3, 1861. It is quite possible that Macy got his idea of using the star for a trade-mark as a result of this effort. It is also possible that the verses were written by Margaret Getchell, described later in this chapter. Her diary shows that she often wrote verse, and it is highly unlikely that Macy himself could have done so without some assistance.
48. N. Y. *Tribune*, Dec. 23, 1858.
49. *Ibid.*, Jan. 22, 1859.
50. N. Y. *Herald*, Apr. 1, 1859.
51. *Ibid.*, Dec. 16, 1860.
52. N. Y. *Tribune*, Feb. 4, 1861.
53. N. Y. *Herald*, Dec. 22, 1860.
54. *Ibid.*, Dec. 3, 1858.
55. *Ibid.*, May 24, 1859.
56. N. Y. *Tribune*, Dec. 9, 1858.
57. N. Y. *Herald*, Dec. 31, 1858.
58. Cf. A. C. Cole, *The Irrepressible Conflict* (N. Y., 1934), pp. 344–352.
59. One obtains from old employees substantially the same account of Margaret Getchell that is related by Hungerford, *op. cit.*, pp. 16–19. I find no reference to her in New York directories before 1867 when she was living at 74 West 12th Street, which was also the Macys' residential address (*Trow's Directory*, 1867–68). Nor is her name subsequently listed. However, a certain amount of evidence concerning her whereabouts between 1857 and 1869 is to be found in records now in the possession of descendants, in particular an autograph book (with entries dating from 1859 to 1869), an incomplete diary, and an exercise book. Her children have understood that she was teaching school in Richmond, Virginia, at the outbreak of the Civil War, but signatures in her autograph book show that she was in New York City more or less continuously from May, 1860, to June, 1861, and the same source proves that she was acquainted with R. H. Macy as early as Jan. 23, 1861. I am indebted to Dr. Laurence La Forge and to Mrs. Rose La Forge Maxson for access to the few surviving papers left by their mother and for supplementary information about her.

CHAPTER IV

1. Two exceedingly useful historical studies may be noted here which recognize the importance of retailing: R. B. Westerfield, "Middlemen in English Business," *Transactions of the Connecticut Academy of Arts and Sciences*, vol. xix (May, 1915); and Jones, *op. cit*. Both treatments are necessarily brief, however, as a result of limitations of space (and, I suspect, lack of sufficient source material on the subject).

2. Leased departments exist in department stores, too, but they form a small proportion of the total number of departments and contribute an even smaller proportion of total sales (6.2% in 1930). See Stanley F. Teele, *Department Leasing in Department Stores*, Harvard Business Research Studies, no. 4 (Boston, 1933).

3. Cf. Paul H. Nystrom, "Retail Trade," in *Encyclopaedia of the Social Sciences* (N. Y., 1930–35), vol. xiii, pp. 346–354; Charles F. Phillips, *Marketing* (Boston, 1938), pp. 385–392; U. S. Department of Commerce, Bureau of the Census, *Census of Business. Retail Distribution: 1935*, vol. i.

4. Joseph Kulischer, "Fairs," *Encyc. Soc. Sci.*, vol. vi, pp. 58–63; Westerfield, *op. cit.*, pp. 329–340.

5. Paul Mantoux, *The Industrial Revolution in the Eighteenth Century* (N. Y., 1927), p. 114; J. H. Clapham, *The Economic Development of France and Germany* (Cambridge, England, 1921), pp. 118–119; Paul H. Nystrom, *Economics of Retailing* (N. Y., 1930), vol. i, pp. 53–59; L. F. Salzman, *English Trade in the Middle Ages* (Oxford, 1931), pp. 198–302.

6. *Ibid.*, pp. 100, 200–203; Mantoux, *loc. cit.*; Clapham, *loc. cit.*; Gabriel Cognacq, "Les Grands magasins," *Foreign Trade*, Sept., 1933, pp. 13–14.

7. Nystrom, *Econ. of Ret.*, vol. i, p. 61. For details of the arrangement in the Royal Exchange, see Westerfield, *op. cit.*, pp. 348–349; for the Halles, see Clapham, *op. cit.*, pp. 368–369. Cf. R. S. Lambert, *The Universal Provider* (London, 1938), pp. 52–55.

8. Westerfield, *op. cit.*, pp. 342–344.

9. Clapham, *op. cit.*, pp. 118–119; Mantoux, *loc. cit.*

10. Lambert, *op. cit.*, pp. 22–23.

11. Advertising booklet, London, 1839, in the collection of I. Warshaw of Albany, N. Y., to whom I am indebted for the information.

12. Lambert, *op. cit.*, pp. 62–63.

13. G. d'Avenel, *Le Mécanisme de la vie moderne* (Paris, 1902), p. 13; photostats of two original invoices, dated in 1838 and supplied to me through the courtesy of Joseph Mayer, formerly in charge of the Paris offices of R. H. Macy & Co., Inc. At the top of each of the invoices is a list, evidently complete, of the types of merchandise stocked by the Bon Marché. The only "hard goods" included are notions, sold in stores of this type for centuries before. Advertisements in the Paris *L'Illustration*, Nov. 4, 1843, p. 149, and Mar. 30,

1844, p. 79, plus an article on Paris stores in the issue of May 11, 1844, p. 173, clearly indicate that the *magasins de nouveautés* (not yet called *grands magasins*) were a recent innovation.

14. *Ibid.*, Nov. 4, 1843, p. 159, Mar. 30, 1844, p. 79, May 11, 1844, p. 173.

15. This theory of alternating swings towards and away from specialization in business is set forth in Gras, *Business and Capitalism*, in connection with the changing forms of capitalism. There may be disagreement among students of the subject as to the existence of wave-like alternating swings towards and away from specialization, but no one familiar with business history can question the fact that the three tendencies discussed have been at work, modifying the organization of business activities.

16. Edward Edelman, "Thomas Hancock, Colonial Merchant," *Journal of Economic and Business History*, Nov., 1928.

17. Gras, *Business and Capitalism*, chaps. iii, iv, and vi.

18. Edelman, *loc. cit.*

19. The combination of movements is discussed briefly but incisively in David A. Wells, *Recent Economic Changes* (N. Y., 1890), pp. 109–111.

20. Francis Ambière, *La Vie secrète des grands magasins* (Paris, 1938), pp. 231–232; Henri Vouters, *Le Petit commerce contre les grands magasins* . . . (Paris, 1910), pp. 43–84.

21. Nystrom, *Econ. of Ret.*, vol. i, pp. 73–82; Jones, *op. cit.*, pp. 44–47. Until recently very little attention was devoted to frontier retail trade as such, but it was mentioned in some way or other in countless narratives and biographies of the period. One good summary is contained in Solon J. Buck, "Frontier Economy in Southwestern Pennsylvania," *Western Pennsylvania Historical Magazine*, June, 1936; another is Howard C. Douds, "Merchants and Merchandising in Pittsburgh, 1759–1800," *ibid.*, June, 1937. Events farther westward after 1800 are described in Sister Marietta Jennings, *A Pioneer Merchant of St. Louis, 1810–1820* (N. Y., 1939), especially chaps. ii and iii.

22. The alleged advertisement by Temple was printed in the *Norfolk Repository* (Dedham, Mass.), vol. i, no. 8 (July 2, 1805), p. 64, under the heading "FOR THE MUSEUM" rather than among the advertisements of the issue. It was recently reprinted as if it were an authentic advertisement, in *A Calendar of Walter Baker & Company, Inc., and its Times, 1765–1940* (N. Y., 1940), pp. 20–21. The advertisement of Wheaton & Dixon, unquestionably genuine, first appeared in the *Norfolk Repository*, vol. i, no. 26 (May 6, 1806), p. 203, with the text as reproduced here, except for a few items which were added during the ensuing summer. The copy quoted has been taken verbatim from vol. i, no. 40 (Aug. 12, 1806).

23. One must make allowance for the distortion in the pattern caused by the fact that men setting up in business in America were bound to imitate, to a considerable degree, the structure of trade as they had learned it in England. As a result there was some specialization in American cities in the eighteenth

century which did not wholly belong there, being adapted rather to conditions in an extensive and well-developed market like London.

24. See, for example, Edelman, *op. cit.*, pp. 90–93; W. C. Ford, editor, "Henry Knox and the London Bookstore in Boston, 1771–1774," *Proc. of Mass. Hist. Soc.*, vol. lxi (1927–28), pp. 227–303; William T. Baxter, "Daniel Henchman, A Colonial Bookseller," *Essex Institute Historical Collections*, vol. lxx (1934).

The relative absence of specialization is plainly evident in the *New-York Mercantile and General Directory . . . 1805–6*, published by John F. Jones. Cf. Virginia D. Harrington, *The New York Merchant on the Eve of the Revolution* (N. Y., 1935), pp. 57–67.

25. For the early period this story is set forth in detail in Curtis Putnam Nettels, *The Money Supply of the American Colonies Before 1720* (Madison, Wis., 1934), esp. chap. viii; conditions at a later period are clearly evident in Harrington, *op. cit.*, especially pp. 64–65. Cf. Jennings, *op. cit.*, *passim*. Even more revealing is the extent to which money-barter was used as late as 1832, as shown in *Doc. Rel. Mfs.*

26. For a full statement of the forces behind nonspecialized business, see Gras, *Business and Capitalism*, chaps. iii and iv. Here again the concrete evidence is to be found chiefly in scattered sources. One study which pulls many facts together in useful fashion is Lewis E. Atherton, *The Pioneer Merchant in Mid-America*, University of Missouri Studies, vol. xiv, no. 2 (Apr., 1939). An illuminating account of one man's experience is given in Herbert Barber Howe, *Jedediah Barber, 1787–1876* (N. Y., 1939).

27. This paragraph is based upon an extensive examination of city directories, with special emphasis upon Boston, New York, Cincinnati, St. Louis, and New Orleans, during the period between 1800 and 1855, together with a study of advertisements of the same period. Cf. Jones, *op. cit.*, pp. 44–49; Nystrom, *Econ. of Ret.*, vol. i, pp. 70–84.

28. Like all simple generalizations this statement needs qualification before the special student of economic history can accept it. It is possible, even probable, that specialized stores occasionally emerged in places like London in the middle ages. At present we lack sufficient information to be certain one way or the other, and the present holocaust in Europe is probably depriving us of the means of finding out. I feel certain that any specialized stores (not shops) which came into existence were too isolated to invalidate my statement as to the dominant tendency.

29. "An Omnibus Store," quoted from the *Philadelphia Merchant* in *Merch. Mag.*, June, 1855, pp. 776–777.

For a good description of a typical New England general store of the 1840's see *Thirtieth Annual Report* of the Massachusetts Bureau of Statistics of Labor (Boston, 1900), pp. 58–64; henceforth cited as *Thirtieth Ann. Rep. of Mass. Bur. of Stat. of Labor*. Other sections of this valuable study show both the decline of the general store and the accompanying rise of the specialized retail store, followed by the emergence of department stores in metropolitan Boston.

30. *U. S. Economist*, May 28, 1853, p. 92.
31. Lossing, *op. cit.*, vol. ii, p. 606.
32. B. F. Foster, *The Merchant's Manual* (Boston, 1838), p. 36. Cf. Atherton, *op. cit.*, p. 81; Jones, *op. cit.*, pp. 9–10, 13–16.
33. Some of the main features have been discerned and briefly discussed by Professor Gras (*Business and Capitalism*, chap. v) in connection with the rise of industrial capitalism, but the treatment is avowedly tentative and incomplete, put forth with the hope of stimulating further research.
34. Harriet Martineau complained that she could find only six pieces of ribbon to choose from in Washington stores in 1835. *Society in America* (London, 1837), vol. ii, p. 25.
35. For an illuminating statement of the rise of the ready-made clothing industry, see Ch. of Com. of N. Y., *Ann. Rep., 1858*, pp. 38–39.
36. Endicott, *op. cit.*, pp. 212–213.
37. *Merch. Mag.*, vol. xviii (Apr., 1848), p. 452.
38. George Fox, *Journal* (Cambridge, England, 1911), p. 138. Cf. William Edmundson's *Journal* (London, 1774), p. 14, which describes the experience of a Quaker merchant in Ireland in 1654.
39. Cf. Oland D. Russell, *The House of Mitsui* (Boston, 1931), pp. 73–74.
40. Daniel Defoe, *Complete English Tradesman*, 2d ed. (London, 1727), pp. 227–228.
41. César de Saussure, *A Foreign View of England . . .* (London, 1912), p. 325, referring to events in 1729.
42. Ralph M. Hower, "The Wedgwoods — Ten Generations of Potters," *Journal of Economic and Business History*, Feb., 1932, pp. 303–304.
43. *L'Illustration*, Mar. 30, 1844, p. 79. Ambière (*op. cit.*, pp. 20–21) thinks that fixed prices, plainly marked, appeared in Paris before 1800.
44. Gibbons, *op. cit.*, vol. i, pp. 91–94.
45. Hower, "The Wedgwoods. . . ."
46. *L'Illustration*, Mar. 30, 1844, p. 79.
47. Photostats of 1838 invoices cited above, note 13.
48. Hower, "The Wedgwoods."
49. Advertising pamphlet, Warshaw Collection.
50. Clapham, *op. cit.*, p. 367; *L'Illustration*, Dec. 1, 1860, p. 375; d'Avenel, *op. cit.*, pp. 14, 34. Here again Ambière (*loc. cit.*) thinks the beginning in Paris was around 1800.
51. Defoe, *op. cit.*, p. 257.
52. Hower, "The Wedgwoods," p. 302.
53. Defoe, *op. cit.*, pp. 59–60, 340.
54. "Alexander Turney Stewart," *Dictionary of American Biography*, vol. xviii, pp. 3–5.

55. "Method in Trade Carried to Perfection," *Merch. Mag.*, Oct., 1847, pp. 441–442.

56. Edward Crapsey, "A Monument of Trade," *The Galaxy* (N. Y., Jan., 1870).

57. Lewis Tappan, *The Life of Arthur Tappan* (N. Y., 1870), pp. 59, 70–73.

58. Advt. reproduced in *The History of Lord & Taylor* (N. Y., 1926), p. 14.

59. Endicott, *loc. cit.*; advt. of Daniell & Co., in *Boston Almanac for 1845* (Boston, 1844), p. 163; Jones, *op. cit.*, pp. 54–55.

60. In his advertisement Foster indignantly denied the accusation of a competitor that he had failed to make good a pair of shoes returned as defective. *The Advertiser* (Manchester), Jan. 2, 1843.

61. Advt., Oswego *Palladium*, Apr. 27, 1855. The advertisement itself is dated Mar. 30, 1852, but the latter figure is doubtless a typographical error.

62. Advt., N. Y. *Tribune*, Feb. 5, 1859. I have not succeeded in finding a repetition of this announcement, which makes me suspect that the firm encountered difficulty in carrying out the policy. On the other hand, it is equally possible that the management regarded the guarantee as what one would expect from a reliable house, attached no particular importance to it, and felt no necessity of giving it great emphasis.

63. Crapsey, *loc. cit.*

64. Advts. dating from 1800 to 1850, Warshaw Collection, including one for Hastings & Taylor, of Lockport, 1843.

65. Advt. reproduced in *Dry Goods Economist*, Jan. 19, 1937, p. 24.

66. Farrell's Cash Ribbon House, for example, advertised regularly, "Try the Cash Style, and no ghostly dun shall worry your sleep" (N. Y. *Herald*, Apr. 16, 1859, *et seq.*). The U. S. Mantilla Store likewise asserted, "We sell for cash only. No credit. No Bad Debts" (*ibid.*, July 29, 1859).

67. Endicott, *op. cit.*; "The Long Credit of Northern Cities," *Merch. Mag.*, Aug., 1855; numerous account books in Baker Library, Harvard University, covering many concerns in the period before 1850. Cf. Howe, *op. cit.*, pp. 76–79.

68. *Ibid.*, pp. 78–80; advts. in Boston and New York newspapers between 1840 and 1860, plus scattered examples in the same period from other eastern towns. Cf. Jones, *op. cit.*, pp. 54–55.

69. *Merch. Mag.*, Apr., 1850, pp. 420–421. Cf. Ch. of Com. of N. Y., *Ann. Rep., 1859–1860*, p. 333.

CHAPTER V

1. Nystrom, *Econ. of Ret.*, mentions the origins of many leading department stores, and I have chanced upon others. Someone should make a study of this topic.

2. Advts., N. Y. *Tribune*, Nov. 11, Dec. 2, 4, 6, 9, 24, 27, 1858; N. Y. *Herald*, Dec. 14, 17, 1858.

3. Advts., N. Y. *Herald*, *Times*, and *Tribune*, Jan.–June, incl., 1859.
4. Advts., N. Y. *Tribune*, May 5, 1859; N. Y. *Herald*, Apr. 29, Sept. 15, 20, 1860.
5. *Ibid*., Sept. 20, 27, Dec. 16, 1860.
6. It is apparently impossible to obtain a precise contemporary definition of the terms "fancy goods" and "fancy dry goods." The classifications used in directories, trade papers, and classified advertising of the period vary widely. Fancy dry goods seem to have included lace, ribbons, gloves, hosiery, handkerchiefs, edgings, and the like, as distinct from heavy or staple dry goods (cf. Lambert, *op. cit*., pp. 30–31). Fancy goods included many of such items and, in addition, those known as "small wares" or Yankee notions: thread, yarn, needles, thimbles, scissors, hooks and eyes, buttons, beads, pins, hairpins, brushes, combs, fans, soaps and perfumes, belts, elastic goods, mirrors, pocketbooks, reticules, and parasols. (Cf. advt., Bowen, McNamee & Co., in N. Y. *Tribune*, Mar. 5, 1859; M. Attie Souder, *The Notion Department*, N. Y., 1917.) But one account goes so far as to include clothespins, augers, gimlets, and cut tacks (*Merch. Mag*., July, 1846).

French, German, and British fancy goods overlapped these categories so far as brushes, combs, buttons, scissors, and certain other items were concerned, but they went beyond to include all kinds of cutlery, leather goods, carved wooden articles, ornaments of various kinds, silverware, jewelry, and even watches (advt. of a New York wholesaler named Carter, who dealt in British, French, and German fancy goods, 1857, Warshaw Collection). Toys and dolls commonly came in this classification, as Macy's advertisements show, along with a limited line of china, picture frames, baskets, and small articles of furniture.

It is probably accurate to say that the word "notions" today refers only to goods used in dressmaking or connected with one's personal wardrobe in some way, thus excluding soaps and toiletries, parasols, cutlery (other than scissors), jewelry, silverware, and leather goods (cf. Souder, *op. cit*.). However, usage is still far from uniform: it is sometimes used interchangeably with "small wares," which may include everything sold on the first floor (John S. Wingate, *Manual of Retail Terms*, N. Y., 1931, p. 88).

7. Furs were first advertised in Dec., 1860 (N. Y. *Herald*, Dec. 16, 1860). The opening of the parasol department was regularly announced each succeeding spring, and the alternation is positively recorded in the oldest Macy record extant: Sales and Purchases book which opens with the week ending Sept. 4, 1869.
8. Advts., N. Y. *Herald*, Jan. 16, Mar. 17, Oct. 7, 20, 1861, and Mar. 9, 1862.
9. *Ibid*., Mar. 20, Nov. 28, 1864; N. Y. *Tribune*, Sept. 24, 1866, and Oct. 31, 1867.
10. *Ibid*., Dec. 7, 1868.
11. *Ibid*., Apr. 16, 19, and May 3, 1869.

NOTES TO CHAPTER V

12. *Ibid.*, Dec. 6, 1869.
13. *Ibid.*, Jan. 3, 1870.
14. Sales and Purchases, 1869–73.
15. *Ibid.*; also advts., 1870–72, incl.
16. N. Y. *Tribune*, Dec. 9, 23, 1872, and May 4, 1873; Sales and Purchases, 1873–81.
17. La Forge to Getchell, Apr. 5, 1873. A letter dated Mar. 19, 1873, after a reference to the plant department, stated: "R. H. [Macy] thinks your ideas are first rate and says to me quite often that if there is any money to be made this spring you will get it out of the biz."
18. The record of sales and purchases shows that the department terminated on Nov. 27, 1875. Lucy Clark, who began to work in the store in 1874, tells the story of Macy and the cash girl. The incident may well have occurred, but I find it impossible to believe that cash girls were subsequently allowed to help themselves. Doubtless pilfering would be more of a problem in the picnic department than elsewhere in the store. Sales for the entire period of operation (141 weeks) totaled $39,060, averaging less than $280 per week, against total purchases of $31,652. Hungerford asserts (*op. cit.*, p. 19) that the success of the department caused a leading firm of grocers to beg Macy to drop competition. In view of the small volume, this is obviously absurd; in any case is it unlikely that Macy would have been moved by any such plea.
19. Advt., N. Y. *Tribune*, Sept. 22, 1874.
20. The new departments were announced on Mar. 9 and opened to the public on Mar. 17 (N. Y. *Tribune*, Mar. 9 and 16, 1874). Details of the arrangement are given below, pages 183–189. For simplicity's sake I refer to the Straus departments as leased, but they were operated, technically, on a rather extreme consignment basis, as explained below. Rumors seem to have circulated in the trade that the departments were leased, but members of the Macy firm insisted, while refusing to give any details about the financial arrangements, that the firm owned the entire business. On at least one occasion they explicitly denied having any "leased counters;" while this was technically true, it was also a deceptive answer. (Cred. Rep., 1875, *et seq.*, esp. June 25, 1883.)
21. Advts., N. Y. *Tribune*, Feb. 8, Apr. 26, May 3, and June 7, 1875.
22. *Ibid.*, Apr. 26, 1875; Sales and Purchases, Aug. 2, 1873–Apr. 16, 1881. The lessee was a man named Bass.
23. *Ibid.*; advts., N. Y. *Tribune*, Feb. 28 and Sept. 18, 1876. Earlier advertisements had occasionally mentioned merinos, alpacas, and flannels, some of which were undoubtedly dress goods; but there was no dress goods department.
24. Compiled from Sales and Purchases, Aug. 2, 1873–Apr. 16, 1881. The use of "½" in a department number had no particular significance. Department 2½ split off from 2, while 8 and 8½ alternated with the seasons.
25. Advts., N. Y. *Evening Telegram*, June 5, 1872; *Hearth and Home*, Jan.

18, 1873; N. Y. *Herald*, Jan. 29, 1873, Apr. 4 and June 13, 1875; N. Y. *Daily Graphic*, Oct. 3, 1877; N. Y. *Tribune*, Sept. 22, 1874.

I have been unsuccessful in trying to discover when the term "department store" first came into general usage. An article by Samuel Hopkins Adams ("The Department Store," *Scribner's Magazine*, Jan., 1897) proves that it was current in 1897, but I suspect that it was not much used before 1895.

In the Macy files is an old photograph, often reproduced in recent Macy advertising, which is supposed to show the Macy store shortly after its founding. The four signs painted on the front of the building read: "R. H. Macy, / dealer in / dry goods, carpets, oil cloths, matting, &c. // importers and retailers of / shawls, cloaks, mantillas // silks, velvets, merinoes // laces, embroideries & hosiery." If authentic, this would prove that Macy had diversified his lines at a very early stage. But the picture as a whole is not authentic: the buildings shown are correct for the period before 1866, but the signs have been doctored, probably by superimposing signs taken from other photographs. Macy would not have used the plural form "importers and retailers" until he had a partner. In any case, it is unthinkable that Macy would have failed to advertise the carpets, silks, etc., if he had been carrying them. The evidence of Macy advertisements is supported by entries in contemporary business directories, the various recorded recollections of old employees, and the record of sales and purchases which begins in 1869. I suspect that the original bore no Macy sign at all.

26. Advts., N. Y. *Tribune*, June 13 and Sept. 24, 1866, Sept. 16, 1867, Sept. 8, 1868, Apr. 19, 1869; N. Y. *Evening Telegram*, Dec. 15, 1871, Apr. 4, 1872; Cred. Rep., Nov. 24 and 27, 1869; Cora Crossman to Abbie Golden, June 30, 1908; invitation to Capt. La Forge to attend a party on May 11, 1866; A. T. La Forge to his sister Susan La Forge, May 16, 1866.

27. Cred. Rep., Sept. 19, 1872; advt., N. Y. *Tribune*, Sept. 23, 1874, news item, Dec. 5, 1874, and advt., Sept. 25, 1876. Leases dated Apr. 29, 1874, and Apr. 20, 1875; La Forge's Diary, Oct. 2, 1871.

The exact dates of some of the additions are unknown, but surviving leases by which Macy subleased various pieces to R. H. Macy & Co. show that the firm in 1874 occupied Nos. 200 to 208 Sixth Avenue, 60 and 62 West 14th Street, and 67 West 13th; 65 West 13th was added in 1876 (Oct.). Leases by Louisa Macy to La Forge & Valentine show the addition of 194 Sixth Avenue in 1877 and the completion of the stretch along Sixth Avenue between 13th and 14th (Nos. 190 to 208) in Jan., 1878. It is apparent that Macy had acquired leases on a number of adjoining properties in anticipation of the store's need for additional space. Some of them were again sublet by the firm for short periods; thus Nos. 194 and 196 Sixth Avenue were sublet between May 1, 1878, and May 1, 1879. The rental at that time was $54,514.59 per annum.

28. *The Income Record . . . for the Year 1863* (N. Y., 1865), p. 58.

29. Cred. Rep., Feb. 29, 1864, Jan. 23, 1865, Nov. 24, 1869, Nov. 22 and Dec. 2, 1870.

30. The way in which Macy's failure in Haverhill dogged his steps in New York is remarkable. There was nothing particularly unusual about bankruptcy in this period, and the many failures which took place in 1857 should have, one would think, erased the bad marks earned before the panic. Yet the credit sources picked up trade comments as late as 1867, twelve years after Macy's failure and nine years after his new start in New York, suggesting that Macy would bear close watching. It was intimated that if he should become hard pressed financially, he might go through another bankruptcy and come out again with some money, as he had done in Haverhill. I strongly suspect that opinions of this sort came from rivals in the dry goods trade who hated Macy's low prices and diversification, envied his success, and sought to injure him by touching up, so to speak, the fading blot on his escutcheon.

31. Cred. Rep., July 11, 1873, Jan. 7, 1875, May 15 and Nov. 10, 1877, Jan. 24, 1880. *Income Record*, p. 123.

32. Advts., N. Y. *Herald*, Oct. 2, 9, 16, Nov. 7, 17, 1864, Mar. and Apr., 1865; N. Y. *Tribune*, Oct. 20, Nov. 10, 1873; G. F. Warren and F. A. Pearson, *Gold and Prices* (N. Y., 1935), pp. 13–20. The annual series calculated by Warren and Pearson shows that textile prices were slightly higher in 1865 than in 1864, but this is simply the result of averaging prices during the year. The monthly series shows that the turning point occurred in Nov., 1864. Contemporary newspaper advertisements indicate that the break began in October.

Difficulties with changes in the price of gold led Macy to make separate entries in the record of sales and purchases when goods were bought for gold. Apparently a gold account was kept in which gains and losses on exchange were recorded. The exact mechanism is not clear, but occasionally purchases were labeled "domestic gold" and "foreign gold," and the phrase "gold jobbing account" was sometimes used. In fact, the eventual segregation of items under the heading "jobbing account" refers not to sales at wholesale but rather to importations. This interpretation is supported by subsequent usage in the firm.

33. Advts., N. Y. *Herald*, Dec. 17, 1858; N. Y. *Tribune*, Dec. 24, 1858, *et seq.*; N. Y. *Herald*, Sept. 21, 1873; *Daily Graphic*, Mar. 15, 1874, Oct. 3, 1877; payroll, 1869–74; Sales and Purchases, 1873–81. None of the persons listed in the payroll appear to have had any connection with manufacturing until the summer of 1873, shortly before the millinery department was opened. Either the dressmaking was let out to subcontractors or the employees involved were listed on a separate payroll which is now lost.

34. Advts., N. Y. *Tribune*, Sept. 5, 1859, Dec. 31, 1866, Sept. 26 and Oct. 24, 1870, Oct. 27, 1873, Oct. 14, 1875; N. Y. *Herald*, Oct. 20, 1861, Dec. 7, 1862, Oct. 1, 1865; N. Y. *Commercial Advertiser*, Sept. 29, 1871; and others.

35. Advts., N. Y. *Tribune*, Sept. 26, 1870; N. Y. *Commercial Advertiser*, Sept. 29, 1871, *et seq.* In 1939 I was allowed to examine a package of letters in Macy's handwriting which had been offered for sale to R. H. Macy & Co. They were written from England in 1872 to Mrs. Macy and were not pur-

chased because they were entirely personal. They revealed, however, that Macy himself bought in Birmingham, Sheffield, Paris, St. Etienne, Nuremburg, Vienna, and Leipsic, and that other Macy buyers were in Europe at the same time. La Forge's Diary for 1873 tells of a three-month buying trip by Macy and La Forge over much the same itinerary.

36. Article, N. Y. *Tribune*, Dec. 5, 1874.

37. The first bid for wholesale trade was made in an advt. in the N. Y. *Herald*, Oct. 1, 1865; in Oct., 1873, a wholesale fancy goods department was announced (*Tribune*, Oct. 27), while wholesale business in china and glassware was occasionally solicited after 1874.

Entries in the record of sales and purchases were occasionally classified as "jobbing," but this refers to importations from Europe, segregated in the 1870's because of the fluctuations in gold prices and domestic prices. Cf. note 32 above.

Stewart's wholesale volume in 1870 was estimated at five-sixths of his total sales (Crapsey, *op. cit.*).

38. Advt., N. Y. *Herald*, Sept. 24, 1860.

39. Sworn testimony of old employees indicates that the star was first used on wrapping paper, stationery, delivery wagons, and so on, and that it was applied to certain items in the picnic department as early as 1873. Such testimony dates from 1880 through 1931 and has been collected in support of various trade-mark registrations and litigation. The red star appears on the oldest piece of stationery in the Macy Archives, a letter dated Dec. 27, 1869.

The first appearance of the star in newspaper advertising was in the N. Y. *Times*, Sept. 22, 1872, when it was used as a display piece — the earliest in Macy history. It was formed by arranging the letter "o" in the outline of a five-pointed star. Within a few days asterisks were substituted for the "o's." The same device was used in the *Herald* in 1872 and 1873.

40. One encounters the guide star legend in talking to all the old employees, and Hungerford gives the usual version (*op. cit.*, pp. 22–23). The letter by J. Maidhof, mentioned above, page 45, states that Macy had a red star tattooed on his arm which he showed to Maidhof as proof of his seafaring experience. Hungerford does not mention this, but says that Macy had tattoo marks on his hands which he usually tried to conceal. Of course, the exact origin, while of romantic interest, is of no particular historical importance. The use of the trade-mark, on the other hand, is very significant.

41. Letter from Cora A. Crossman to Abbie Golden, June 30, 1908.

42. The record of sales and purchases plainly shows the effort to segregate operating results by departments and the allocation of responsibility to department heads. At first the check on results was confined to figures on weekly sales and purchases, but by 1878 salaries were also allocated to departments. Presumably these included only the money paid to department heads and clerks directly connected with operations.

43. Payroll, 1869-74. This record does not list the superintendent and omits all buyers after 1871, from which I conclude that payments to certain high-salaried executives were posted in a special account in order to give additional privacy to the amounts paid. Entries indicate that anyone who received over $25 a week was listed in another record. This would mean that the staff as a whole was larger than the figures quoted by at least six or eight persons.

44. Sales and Purchases, 1869-73, 1873-81; interviews with employees. One soon learns from experience that human memory is a highly unreliable source, to be used with the utmost circumspection. It occasionally must serve when no other evidence can be found, but its main contribution is to open "leads" to evidence and to assist in interpretation of facts and events. Ordinarily I have made no direct use of interviews with old employees unless the "facts" obtained were confirmed by other interviews or supported by other types of evidence.

45. *Ibid.*; record of Sales and Purchases, 1869-73, 1873-81.

46. The centralization of these activities is largely evident in the payroll, 1869-74, which lists positions as well as names; and it is confirmed by interviews with old employees. Evidence on the disposition of advertising is incomplete, but the merchandise departments seem to have had very little to do with it in the 1870's.

47. The evidence on this point is not complete, but all the fragments I can find support the view presented. Old employees have repeatedly emphasized the tremendous authority and independence of buyers in the period before 1900, and it is clear that each took full responsibility for both buying and selling activities. There might have been an experiment in separating the two functions, but there is no evidence of it, and the prevailing managerial ideas make it highly unlikely.

48. Advt., N. Y. *Tribune*, Nov. 10, 1873; Cred. Rep., Jan. 31, 1874.

49. Because of the enormous difficulties involved it has been impracticable to make a complete check of all the publications which Macy might have used in this period. Examination of the chief New York dailies has revealed that, while the *Tribune* was apparently Macy's favorite medium throughout the years 1858-77, he inserted advertisements in others, including the *Commercial Advertiser, Evening Mail, Evening Post, Evening Telegram, Herald, Daily Graphic, Sun, Times,* and *World*. There was a certain amount of shifting from one medium to another (e.g., between 1865 and 1870 Macy made little use of the *Herald* because it refused to relax its restrictions on typography when other papers were allowing large type, display cuts, and broken columns; that is, an advertisement spreading across two or more columns in width). But there is clear evidence that both the amount of space and the number of papers used at any given time increased after 1865.

In addition, Macy used a number of magazines, among them *Harper's Weekly, Hearth and Home,* and *The Churchman*, in the 1870's. The first

NOTES TO CHAPTER V

mention of a catalog was in 1874 when mail orders began to be emphasized. The earliest chromo cards put out by Macy that I have seen were printed in 1875.

50. News item, N. Y. *Tribune*, Dec. 5, 1874; article, *Frank Leslie's Illustrated Newspaper*, Jan. 1, 1876.
51. Advt., N. Y. *Tribune*, Feb. 21, 1876.
52. Advts., N. Y. *Herald*, Nov. 18 and Dec. 26, 1875.
53. *Ibid.*, Nov. 15, 1863.
54. *Ibid.*, Jan. 21 and Nov. 7, 1861, Mar. 1, 23, Sept. 22, 1874, June 13, 1875. The first reference to a Macy catalog (Sept., 1874) may relate only to china and glassware, but that for 1875 seems to have covered all departments.
55. N. Y. *Herald*, Mar. 23, 1874.
56. *Ibid.*, Apr. 18, 1861, Jan. 8, 1862, Sept. 11 and Nov. 17, 1864, Mar. 19, 1865.
57. *Ibid.*, Oct. 1, 1865.
58. Advt., N. Y. *Tribune*, Oct. 24, 1870.
59. Advts., N. Y. *Herald*, Apr. 20, May 18, 1873; N. Y. *Sun*, Dec. 18, 1873.
60. Advts., N. Y. *Tribune*, May 11, 1874, Oct. 25, 1875.
61. *Ibid.*, Apr. 5, May 10, June 28, 1875; testimony of Samuel Walter Woodward before a Congressional investigating commission in 1900, as set forth in *Rep. of Ind. Com.*, vol. ii, p. 736.
62. Interviews with employees.
63. La Forge's Diary, 1865, 1866, 1871, 1873; letter from A. T. La Forge to Susan La Forge, Sept. 20, 1865. Probably Macy's conduct became more straight-laced after the Moody and Sankey revival meetings in 1875–76.
64. Obituary, Nantucket *Inquirer and Mirror*, Apr. 7, 1877; interview with Mrs. Florence Macy Sutton, 1930. The partnership agreement of 1874 reflects a concern for Macy's health in its careful provisions against the illness or death of the founder — provisions which are less in evidence in the agreement of 1872.
65. Cred. Rep. on Mary C. Houghton & Co. (Houghton set up the store in his wife's name), Sept. 3, 1863; interviews with Mrs. Florence Macy Sutton, 1930. Until 1863 the Macy and Houghton families continued to live together at 332 Sixth Avenue, after which they separated. Houghton dropped out of *Trow's Directory* after the issue of 1863–64.
66. Obituary notice, Nantucket *Inquirer and Mirror*, Nov. 19, 1887; interviews with old employees, 1930, 1939, 1940.
67. R. H. Macy's will, executed Feb. 8, 1877, on file in the N. Y. Municipal Hall of Records. Margaret Getchell La Forge's Diary records the fact that Rowland Macy, Jr., died suddenly in Boston, Mass., in Aug., 1878.
68. Entries in La Forge's Diary, 1864, 1865; La Forge to his sister Susan, Aug. 7, 1866; letter from the Adjutant General's Office to Mrs. A. C. Prentice (La Forge's daughter), Aug. 10, 1939; interviews with Dr. Laurence La Forge.

69. Letter from La Forge to General L. Thomas, June 12, 1865; entries in La Forge's Diary, 1865.
70. *Ibid.*, 1865, 1866; letter to Susan La Forge, Sept. 20, 1865.
71. *Ibid.*, May 16, 1866; La Forge's Diary, Dec. 24, 1867; interviews with Dr. Laurence La Forge.
72. Letters to Susan La Forge, Jan. 31, Feb. 15, and May 26, 1867, Feb. 25 and Mar. 16, 1869.
73. *Ibid.*, Mar. 16 and Apr. 26, 1869.
74. *Ibid.*, Aug. 29 and Oct. 24, 1869.
75. *Ibid.*, Dec. 11, 1870; partnership agreement for one year between R. H. Macy and A. T. La Forge, dated Jan. 1, 1871.
76. Partnership agreement, dated Jan. 31, 1872, effective as of Jan. 1, 1872; letter to Susan La Forge, Feb. 14, 1872.
77. La Forge's Diary, 1861, 1873; Margaret La Forge's Diary, 1871–78.
78. *Ibid.*; La Forge's Diary, 1871; memo from Margaret La Forge to her husband, undated but written late in 1874; memos of agreements between Macy and La Forge, July 1, 1875, and Jan. 6, 1877; letter from La Forge to his wife, May 8, 1873; La Forge's Ledger, 1871–77. I am indebted to Dorothy M. La Forge for access to those of her grandfather's papers which are in her possession.
79. Partnership agreement, dated Dec. 31, 1874, effective Jan. 1, 1875; S. J. Macy, *op. cit.*, p. 245; La Forge's Ledger, 1871–77. One old employee reported in 1930 that Valentine's father had served as night-watchman for the store and that his family lived over a part of it. The directories confirm the latter statement, but the payroll for 1869–74 does not contain any Valentines. Of course, the father may have been carried on a special payroll.
80. Cred. Rep., Nov. 29, 1869, Dec. 2, 1870.
81. Both the data published by the Harvard Bureau of Business Research and those supplied by the Controllers' Congress of the National Retail Dry Goods Association indicate that a good average stock-turn in recent years for stores with a volume of $1,000,000 is four times a year, approximately two-thirds the rate achieved by Macy in the 1870's.
82. I can find no evidence whatever to support the statement made by F. T. Hypps that department stores were operating on a gross margin of 15% in the 1860's ("The Department Store — A Problem of Elephantiasis," *An. of Amer. Acad. of Pol. & Soc. Sci.*, Sept., 1937, p. 72). It is worth noting that expenses in French *grands magasins* at this time averaged from 16 to 17% of sales and profits from 5½ to 6½%, which puts the gross margin well above 20% (cf. d'Avenel, *op. cit.*, pp. 41, 48).
83. La Forge's Ledger; La Forge's Diary, 1873; letters from La Forge to his wife, 1873.
84. Calculated from the payroll, Aug. 23, 1869, to Feb. 21, 1874. Macy and a few of his top executives were not included in the payroll, but I feel con-

fident that this fact does not cause an inflation of the sales per employee of more than 3 or 4% at the most. The increase in number of employees between 1869 and 1874 is revealed by the payroll and should certainly have resulted in better service.

85. Payroll, 1869–74.
86. La Forge's Diary, Dec. 23, 1871. See also news stories in the N. Y. *Sun*, *Tribune*, and *World*, Dec. 26–29, 1870, relating to the arrest of several "respectable" and well-to-do women for shoplifting in Macy's. In at least one of the cases the presiding judge insisted that the testimony of several Macy employees be disregarded because they must have been "mistaken." No information is available as to the outcome of the lawsuits which were instituted. Macy himself referred to the fact that "over 100 persons" had been arrested for stealing in his store, apparently between 1867 and 1870 (N. Y. *Tribune*, Dec. 27, 1870).

CHAPTER VI

1. See Appendix A for a discussion of the evidence concerning developments in retail trade in Paris for this period, together with citation of the evidence for the general statements presented here.
2. *L'Illustration*, Sept. 21, 1872, p. 189.
3. An excellent account of the history of Whiteley's store is to be found in Lambert's *The Universal Provider*, previously cited. The emergence of this enterprise as a department store is set forth on pp. 72–77.

During the 1850's and '60's English visitors in America were greatly impressed with the size and splendor of Stewart's and other New York stores. Isabella L. Bishop, *The Englishwoman in America* (London, 1856), pp. 340–341; W. H. Russell, *My Diary North and South* (Boston, 1863), p. 24.

Harrod's did not begin to expand beyond the original grocery line until 1868, the main diversification presumably coming some years later. J. Aubrey Rees, *The Grocery Trade* (London, 1910), vol. ii, pp. 240–241.

Lady M. Lejeune, "The Ethics of Shopping," *Fortnightly Review*, Jan., 1895, contrasts the English retail shops of the 1870's — small, highly specialized, and inferior to those in Continental cities — with the large, attractive, and diversified stores of the 1890's.

4. N. S. B. Gras, "An Old Store Still Young," *Bulletin of the Business Historical Society*, June, 1940; Jones, *op. cit.*, pp. 49–50.
5. *Ibid.*; advts., in N. Y. daily newspapers, particularly the *Herald* and *Tribune*, 1860–75; Crapsey, *op. cit.* The statement of Cole (*op. cit.*, p. 26) that Stewart had the first department store is an error; his assertion that "there was scarcely anything that its counters could not supply" is likewise untrue and is not supported by the sources he cites. Stewart's total volume in the 1870's was well over $50,000,000 per year. Judging by various statements of

average daily sales, number of employees, and total expense, the retail part of this total was over $8,000,000 and under $20,000,000.

6. Gibbons, *op. cit.*, vol. i, pp. 161-180; J. H. Appel, *The Business Biography of John Wanamaker* (N. Y., 1930), pp. 74-105.

7. Information supplied in a letter to me by the treasurer of the Jordan Marsh Co., 1938.

8. Newspaper advts. dated 1872 and 1879 reproduced in *Marshall Field & Company Exposition Number, 1852-1927* (Chicago, 1927), pp. 18-19, 44.

9. Nystrom, *Econ. of Ret.*, vol. i, p. 139.

10. Newspaper advts., N. Y. *Tribune*, 1865-75; Macy Sales and Purchases book, 1869-81.

11. *Rep. of Ind. Com.*, vol. vii, p. 454; cf. Henry Collins Brown, editor, *Valentine's Manual of Old New York*, No. 5, new series (N. Y., 1921), p. 106, in which an old New Yorker recalls Macy's as the first rather than Stewart's.

12. It is largely impossible to cite authorities for the generalizations set forth in this section. I have drawn upon many contemporary comments, the material used in the course in business history at the Harvard Business School, and Professor Gras' *Business and Capitalism*, especially chap. v. This whole development awaits careful study by some promising graduate student. For the present it is necessary to offer tentative conclusions based upon a few scraps of knowledge and a great deal of logical analysis. In general, however, the discussion set forth is supported by the testimony of many retailers before the Industrial Commission, as indicated below. Supporting evidence is also set forth in *Thirtieth Ann. Rep.* of Mass. Bur. of Stat. of Labor.

13. N. Y. Ch. of Com., *Ann. Rep., 1878/79*, p. xl.

14. Direct selling by manufacturers was unquestionably rare before 1850, but examples do exist even in the textile trade, and the movement, as evidenced by the increases in number of traveling salesmen, got well under way in the 1850's. (Cf. Jones, *op. cit.*, pp. 16-17, 52.) By 1858 the competition between hardware manufacturers and jobbers for sales to retailers had become so bitter as to receive adverse criticism in an annual review of the trade. N. Y. Ch. of Com., *Ann. Rep., 1858*, pp. 33-34.

15. *Rep. of Ind. Com.*, vol. ii, pp. 733-736, vol. vii, pp. 340-342, 699-700; cf. J. R. Doubman and J. R. Whitaker, *The Organization and Operation of Department Stores* (N. Y., 1927), pp. 12-15.

16. *Rep. of Ind. Com.*, vol. ii, p. 734.

17. The convenience of the department store was stressed in the testimony before the Industrial Commission in 1899 and 1900. The first mention I can find of it in Macy advertising is in 1878. After that time it is frequently emphasized in the firm's institutional advertising.

18. A good part of the savings was probably attributable to the fact that retail stores were able to buy direct without adding much to existing personnel and equipment. For the larger stores it is possible that the volume of purchases

from a single manufacturer might well exceed that of many wholesalers and that buyers were accordingly in a position to force prices to a lower level.

We know that in some instances no monetary savings at all were achieved in the process. However, the advantages of getting better service or merchandise better suited to the retailer's needs might be sufficient to justify the change. It certainly placed an additional burden on retail management and some firms were in no position to undertake new complications.

19. This opposition is clearly reflected in the testimony before the Industrial Commission. See especially the testimony of S. W. Roth, vol. ii, pp. 707, 711.

20. Of course, as already indicated above, Macy eschewed most of the foreign gilding. A. T. Stewart likewise resisted the French influence. He put up a handsome and expensive building, to be sure, but New Yorkers noted that there was no attempt at display on the interior. The floors were uncarpeted, the furnishings plain, and goods were piled up on shelves with no attempt to exhibit their beauty. Crapsey, *op. cit.*; A. T. Stewart Scrapbook.

21. In addition to the evidence collected in *Rep. of Ind. Com.*, vol. vii, and *Thirtieth Ann. Rep.* of Mass. Bur. of Stat. of Labor, one should also note a useful general statement on the rise of the department store, together with its advantages over the earlier institutions, in a pamphlet by William Cooke Daniels, *The Department Store System* (Denver, 1900).

22. Letter from Isidor to Nathan Straus, Nov. 16, 1894.

23. No attempt has been made to gather here the details of the opposition movement against department stores. The attitude of the small specialized retailer in France is admirably portrayed in Emile Zola's *Au Bonheur des dames*. A pamphlet which affords a good example of the literature of protest in Europe is Alexandre Weill, *Un Fléau national. Les grands magasins de Paris et les moyens de les combattre* (Paris, 1888). For a summary of the opposition in France, see Henri Garrigues, *Les Grands magasins et le petit commerce de détail* (Paris, 1898). Opposition to department stores in the United States often appears in the testimony printed in the *Rep. of Ind. Com.*, especially vol. vii, pp. 707, 711. For the effect of the rise of the department stores on the dry goods wholesalers, see *ibid.*, p. 736. Reference to restrictive legislation is made in *Thirtieth Ann. Rep.* of Mass. Bur. of Stat. of Labor, p. 3, and in Daniels, *op. cit.*, pp. 35–36.

CHAPTER VII

1. Partnership agreement, Dec. 31, 1874; Cred. Rep., July 12 and Oct. 10, 1877; "copy of points discussed by the representatives of R. H. Macy and R. H. Macy & Co.," undated but written in Apr., 1877; memo in La Forge's Ledger, July 9, 1877.

2. *Ibid.*; partnership agreement executed on June 21, 1877, effective as of Apr. 1, 1877; Cred. Rep., July 12 and Oct. 10, 1877.

3. La Forge's Diary, 1871, 1873; Margaret La Forge's Diary, 1871–78; obituary, N. Y. *Times*, Feb. 13, 1878; interviews with former Macy employees and with Dr. Laurence La Forge. The story of the La Forges' love, as revealed in letters and diaries, is one which hard-boiled moderns are likely to find very touching.

4. Agreement between Robert M. Valentine and Margaret La Forge, executrix, May 11, 1878.

5. Cred. Rep., Mar. 1, May 6 and 9, 1878.

6. *Ibid.*, July 24, 1878; interview with Webster's brother, Josiah L. Webster. The date of Webster's admission was July 8, 1878. Webster was listed as "salesman" in the firm of Josiah L. & C. A. Webster, dry goods, in Providence, R. I., in *The Providence Directory of . . . 1874* (Providence, 1874).

7. Cred. Rep., Feb. 18, Mar. 13, and May 23, 1879. Valentine died on Feb. 15, and Wheeler was admitted to partnership on May 1, 1879.

8. Personal interviews. For obvious reasons the identity of these informants must be kept confidential, but there is not the slightest doubt about the accuracy of their information.

9. *Ibid.*

10. Sales and Purchases, 1878–85; advts., N. Y. *Tribune*, Oct. 1 and 29, and Nov. 12, 1877, Oct. 28, 1878.

11. Sales and Purchases, 1878–85.

12. *Ibid.*; advt., N. Y. *Times*, June 10, 1878.

The Bon Marché had restaurant facilities in 1874 and probably some years earlier (*L'Illustration*, Oct. 10, 1874). It has been said that Wanamaker installed a restaurant in his store in 1876 (Appel, *op. cit.*, p. 101); John Wanamaker, *Golden Book of the Wanamaker Stores* (Philadelphia, 1911), vol. i, p. 18. There are a number of reasons for questioning this statement. Store restaurants were established, apparently invariably, for the convenience of women shoppers; Wanamaker did not begin to sell dry goods and women's clothing until 1877. Moreover, contemporary accounts of the 1877 opening describe a great many "innovations," but I have not found one that mentions a restaurant, a feature which would undoubtedly have attracted more attention than many of those which were described at some length. Nor does the list of Wanamaker departments which was published in 1877 mention a restaurant of any sort. I find no reference to lunchroom facilities in Wanamaker advertising until 1883 (Philadelphia *Weekly Press*, Sept. 27), and Gibbons, *op. cit.*, vol. i, p. 220, indicates without specific statement that the addition was made in 1882.

13. Macy catalog, 1879; memorandum book kept by Isidor Straus, hereafter referred to as I. S. Memo, which shows that serving of hot meat began in Sept. 1896; interview with Harry Bowyer (former employee), 1930. For a brief but accurate account of the construction of the Sixth Avenue "El," see William Fullerton Reeves, *The First Elevated Railroads in . . . New York* (N. Y., 1936).

14. Sales and Purchases, 1878–85; adv. circular, Macy book dept., 1880.
15. Sales and Purchases, 1878–85; semiannual balance, 1887.
16. Macy catalog for 1879, published late in 1878.
17. *Ibid.*, fall and winter seasons of 1882–83.
18. *Ibid.*, 1885; advts., N. Y. *World*, June 20, 1884, May 31, 1885. Men's suits, "manufactured in our own workrooms," were advertised as early as Mar. 2, 1884 (N. Y. *Herald*).
19. Advt., *ibid.*, Sept. 30, 1887.
20. News articles, N. Y. *World*, Sept. 28, 1880, Sept. 30, 1881; advts., Sept. and Mar., 1880, *et seq.*
21. Factory lease dated Aug. 28, 1879; catalogs, 1879, 1882–83, and 1885; adv. circular, 1885; advt., N. Y. *World*, April 25, 1886; semiannual statements, Dec., 1887, *et seq.*
22. Advts., N. Y. *Tribune*, Oct. 1, 1877; N. Y. *Times*, Jan. 13, 1878, N. Y. *World*, Mar. 28, 1886; N. Y. *Herald*, Mar. 16, 1884, and Oct. 10, 1887.
23. News article, N. Y. *World*, Dec. 19, 1886.
24. Scattered Macy advts., 1877 to 1888; article, N. Y. *World*, Apr. 4, 1886.
25. Advt., *ibid.*, Apr. 23, 1882.
26. Advts., N. Y. *Times*, May 5 and Dec. 15, 1878.
27. Advt., N. Y. *World*, Dec. 12, 1881.
28. Catalog for 1879.
29. Memo approving order for telephones, Nov. 22, 1877 (these must have been among the very first to be installed in New York City); advts., N. Y. *Times*, Nov. 30, 1879, and N. Y. *World*, Sept. 28, 1880.

R. T. Barrett, Historical Librarian of the American Telephone and Telegraph Co., informs me that the records of the Bell Telephone Co. show that the Macy lease was accepted on Dec. 1, 1877, but no information exists as to the date of installation. The bill for installation was paid on Dec. 5, 1877. The Macy firm name does not appear in two extant one-page lists of telephone subscribers published in 1878, but is in the first list in book form printed in 1879.

30. Advt., N. Y. *Times*, Sept. 26, 1880; article, N. Y. *World*, Sept. 28, 1880. The electric lights may have been installed in the store in 1879 when they were put into the show windows. The fact that the management chose arc lights supports this idea, for by 1880 Edison's lamps were being widely adopted.

Wanamaker had installed electric illumination late in 1878, apparently ahead of Macy's, but it is not true, as Gibbons (*op. cit.*, vol. i, pp. 217–219) attempts to prove, that Wanamaker put in Edison's new lamps at the outset; the first ones were Brush arc lights, probably the same as Macy's. Macy's, on the other hand, was two years ahead of Wanamaker in the installation of ventilation equipment. Cf. Appel, *op. cit.*, pp. 102–105. The Sales and Purchases record bears the notation "Awful hot" after each of the four weeks from Sept. 20 to Oct. 18, 1879.

31. Advt., *Century Magazine*, Oct., 1882.
32. For a brief but lucid exposition of this process see Henry Smith, *Retail Distribution* (Oxford, 1937), especially chaps. i, iv, and vi. This brilliant little analysis is one of the few outstanding contributions to our understanding of retail trade during the past decade or more and deserves careful attention.
33. On these points the contemporary evidence that I have found is not conclusive, but there is at least a strong probability that the generalizations given are correct. Here is an important problem which awaits detailed study.
34. Gleaned from contemporary advertisements and interviews with old Macy employees. At present no satisfactory account of New York's retail development is available, and it is therefore impossible to include in the Macy story more than a few fragments on the activities of competitors. Here is another excellent opportunity for some enterprising student.
35. R. H. Macy & Co. (Webster's handwriting) to J. J. Astor, Esq., Oct. 17, 1879.
36. Advt., N. Y. *World*, Nov. 25, 1883; article, Saratoga (N. Y.) *Eagle*, Dec. 22, 1883.
37. This generalization is based upon an admittedly incomplete but extensive examination of retail advertising in New York daily newspapers for the period. Macy's was apparently the only store to mention Easter in the *Times* during the spring of 1880, and this seems also to be true of the *World* in 1881. In 1882 and subsequent years other stores joined the effort to commercialize a religious festival.
38. *Ibid.*
39. Willard L. Thorp, *Business Annals* (N. Y. 1926), pp. 131–135.
40. Appel, *op. cit.*, pp. 104–108.
41. Of course, the addition of new lines of merchandise, by swelling total sales, would cause a decline in the ratio of sales in old departments to store total, even if all of them increased in volume at the same rate. This *apparent* lag must be allowed for in comparing the figures for 1887 with those of 1877.
42. For a good discussion of the significance of stock turnover, together with typical modern rates, see Paul D. Converse and Harvey W. Huegy, *The Elements of Marketing* (N. Y., 1940), pp. 610–618.
43. The explanation advanced here has been given to me by old employees and Percy S. Straus independently. It is supported by contemporary Macy advertising as well as by the operating figures.

I suspect that the extraordinarily high rate of stock-turn in owned departments was in part the result of reducing inventories to an abnormally low point just before stock-taking time.

CHAPTER VIII

1. All statements relating to the number and remuneration of Macy employees during the 1870's are based upon the sole surviving payroll ledger which started with the week ending Aug. 23, 1869, and terminated on Feb. 21, 1874. As indicated in an earlier footnote, the compensation of certain executives was not recorded in this book (after Feb. 18, 1871, buyers' salaries were transferred to another record), but this fact does not greatly impugn the accuracy of the remaining data. The total number of employees and executives was certainly not more than 5% greater than the figures given in the text.

2. Crapsey, *op. cit.*

3. James D. McCabe, Jr., *Great Fortunes and How They Were Made*, ... (Philadelphia, 1871), pp. 98–99.

4. *Merch. Mag.*, Aug., 1850, pp. 248–249, Dec., 1855, p. 766; Crapsey, *op. cit.*

5. I assume that Macy employed women in the Haverhill store from the fact that he advertised in 1854 that he wanted immediately "A First rate Sales-Woman." Haverhill *Gazette*, May 13, 1854.

6. Interviews with employees, 1920, 1930, and 1938; interview with Mrs. Florence Macy Sutton in 1930; payroll, 1869–74.

7. *Ibid.*; interviews with employees. The buying trip of Chase, an important Macy buyer, was as follows for 1880: Queenstown, Apr. 10; Belfast, Apr. 11–17; Glasgow and Scotland generally, Apr. 17–24; Manchester, London, and Nottingham, Apr. 24–May 1; Calais, May 1–3; Paris and vicinity, May 3–17; St. Gall, May 17–26; Paris on return, May 26–29; Nottingham, May 29–June 1; Belfast again, June 3–10; then back to New York (memo headed "Route for Spring 1880").

8. I. Straus to J. W. Hutchinson (a buyer), Mar. 9, 1889.

9. While it is impossible to obtain accurate information about department store wages in the 1870's to compare with Macy figures, later information indicates that low compensation was general in New York stores and that conditions in large stores were better than in the small ones. This was also true of Boston, Philadelphia, and other cities. Cf. "Our Shop Girls," N. Y. *Sun*, Oct. 14, 1888; S. H. Adams, *op. cit.*; J. L. Wright, J. S. Steele, and S. R. Kirkpatrick, "The Department Store in the East," *Arena*, Aug., 1899. See also testimony in *Rep. of Ind. Com.*, vol. vii, pp. 452–463, 695–700. Old Macy employees report that conditions and wages in Macy's were about the same as in other large stores.

10. *Merch. Mag.*, May, 1849, p. 570.

11. According to interviews with former employees the method of handling sales was as follows: After a clerk had sold merchandise, she listed the items in her sales book, totaled the amount of the sale, wrote down the sum of money handed to her by the customer, folded the money inside the book, and called "Cash!" The cash girl appeared and took the purchased articles and the

sales book in her basket to the cashier's desk for that particular division of the store. A parcel clerk wrapped the items and wrote on the outside of the package a list of the contents. The cashier checked the amounts listed on the sales book, stamped the sheet, and made change which the cash girl then took back to the clerk. The customer received no check, for the modern sales slip had not yet been invented. As a result of this arrangement the sales book contained a record of a clerk's transactions for the day, which in turn enabled the chief cashier to check the accuracy of the cashier's transactions. At the close of the day the sales book was turned in to the office and totaled. The amount of sales checked and stamped by a given cashier at once revealed the amount of cash which the cashier should have received during the day. To make the system work each clerk had two sales books, one of which was used on Monday, Wednesday, and Friday and the other on Tuesday, Thursday, and Saturday while the first was being checked.

If goods were to be delivered by the store, the clerk made out an address ticket which was placed with the merchandise and the purchases together with the address ticket were taken by the cash girl to the delivery department in the basement.

12. Payroll, 1869–74; interviews with employees.
13. *Ibid.*, payroll, 1869–74.
14. Interviews with employees.
15. *Ibid.*; payroll, 1869–74; interview with Macy, N. Y. *Sun*, Dec. 27, 1870.
16. S. H. Adams, *op. cit.*; interviews with employees, 1938–40.
17. *Ibid.*
18. La Forge's Diary, 1871; letter, La Forge to his sister, Sept. 12, 1872; Margaret La Forge's Diary, 1871–77.
19. Letter to Abbie Golden, June 30, 1908.
20. Written statement, made about 1920, by Miss Prunty, who had begun her employment in Macy's in Dec., 1877. Several unimportant corrections have been made in spelling and punctuation.

The existence of the lunchroom in 1872 is proved by payroll entries showing the employment of two lunchroom attendants in Sept., 1872. Their duties are unknown, but the firm began to serve tea and coffee free at an early date, and they probably were charged with making and distributing it.

21. Statement by Miss Prunty; interviews with old employees, 1938–40.
22. La Forge's Diary, July, 1871; advt. announcing early closing (at 1:00 P.M.) of Macy's, N. Y. *Tribune*, June 15, 1874; announcement of closing at 12 noon, *ibid.*, June 28, 1875; notices to the same effect in subsequent Junes; announcement of weekend closing, N. Y. *World*, July 1, 1882; article on early closing, *ibid.*, July 12, 1885, indicating collapse of widespread opposition on part of retail stores to the Saturday half-holidays in July and August.

Lord & Taylor advertised in the *Tribune* during July, 1871, that it would close at 3:00 P.M. on Saturdays during July and August. Arnold, Constable &

Co. advertised in the *Times*, during July, 1878, its decision to close at one o'clock. Other stores do not seem to have followed these examples. Wanamaker's began the practice in 1886, and the suggestion (*Golden Book*, vol. i, pp. 79–80) that it pioneered in this reform is simply one more Wanamaker claim which the known facts contradict.

That Boston stores were reluctant to grant half or whole holidays in the summer, even after 1900, is apparent from Mary La Dame, *The Filene Store* (N. Y., 1930), pp. 140–142.

23. Notations in the Black Book, 1870–1888. Wanamaker closed only half the day for Grant's funeral and apparently not at all for Garfield's (see Appel, *op. cit.*, pp. 105–107).

24. Newspaper advertisements reveal widely varying practice as to store hours in New York at this time. Stewart's hours are given in Crapsey, *op. cit.*, and descriptions of large stores in both eastern and western cities in 1899 show that hours were still generally long, longer in Chicago than in Macy's 20 years earlier (Wright *et al.*, *op. cit.*; W. M. Handy, E. C. Carlin, and E. Meredith, "The Department Store in the West," *Arena*, Sept., 1899). Boston stores commonly were open 16 hours a day in 1857 (*Merch. Mag.*, July, 1857, pp. 131–132), and were apparently still worse than New York after 1900 (La Dame, *op. cit.*, pp. 139–141). Conditions in the leading London stores in the 1880's are set forth in detail in Lambert, *op. cit.*, pp. 139–141, 148–151.

25. Interviews with employees, 1920, 1930, 1938–40.

26. Cora Crossman to Abbie Golden, June 30, 1908.

27. Memoir written about 1920. In the interest of clarity a few unimportant alterations have been made in the text, chiefly in spelling and punctuation.

28. *Ibid.*

29. Memoir written about the same time as Woods' and edited in the same way.

30. Statement written about 1920, slightly edited for punctuation, spelling, and clarity.

31. *Ibid.*

32. Statement of Miss Prunty.

33. Pamphlet containing constitution, bylaws, and reports for year ending Apr. 6, 1887. A study by my former colleague, Dr. J. Owen Stalson, *Marketing Life Insurance: Its History in America* (Cambridge, 1942), chaps. xix and xx, shows that mutual aid societies of one sort or another began to be numerous in the 1870's, and Macy's was not the first store to form one.

CHAPTER IX

1. Cred. Rep., Dec. 19 and 20, 1887; N. Y. *Herald*, Jan. 2, 1888.

2. Isidor Straus to Kleinwort, Sons & Co., Jan. 9, 1888.

3. The story of this episode comes indirectly from Isidor Straus, who cited it as the occasion of the admission of the Strauses to ownership in Macy's. Em-

bezzlements of this sort were not new among the prominent stores of New York. In 1884 Arnold, Constable & Co. discovered that two employees had robbed the firm of many thousands of dollars. News articles, N. Y. *World*, Sept. 26 and 27, 1884.

4. Interviews with former employees; Cred. Rep., Oct. 25, 1883, April 23 and Oct. 3, 1884, Feb. 19, 1885, Feb. 8, 1887.

Early in 1887 Wheeler told credit correspondents that his interests in Colorado were worth a million and a half dollars. While this was probably an exaggeration, all accounts agree that his western properties were valuable.

5. Confidential source known to be reliable. In matters of this sort the historian must rely on hearsay evidence, but the story given is the only one that explains a number of otherwise puzzling facts, including the embarrassed unwillingness of several women employees to tell what they knew about the cause of Wheeler's departure, together with the indignant refusal of surviving members of Webster's family to discuss the matter at all.

The firm let it be understood that Wheeler simply withdrew to give attention to western business, but it is difficult to see why he would willingly give up a partnership which yielded him at least $125,000 a year or why Webster flatly refused to have any further dealings with Wheeler, even going so far as to have Isidor Straus conclude the final details of settlement instead of writing to Wheeler himself. (Isidor Straus to J. B. Wheeler, Dec. 27, 1888.) A piece of evidence which practically clinches matters is a series of entries in Macy accounts showing that Webster later created a small trust fund for Martha Toye.

6. In this account of the Straus family I have drawn mainly upon a typescript autobiography, hereafter cited as Isidor's Autobiog., which Isidor Straus began in June, 1911, less than a year before his death. A great deal of it appears, almost verbatim, in the first chapter of Oscar S. Straus, *Under Four Administrations* (Boston, 1922). In addition I have used the obituary of Lazarus Straus published in the N. Y. *Times*, Jan. 15, 1898, and information obtained in conversations with Percy S. Straus.

7. Isidor's Autobiog., p. 12.
8. *Ibid.*, p. 26.
9. *Ibid.*, pp. 31–34.
10. *Ibid.*, p. 36.
11. *Ibid.*, pp. 37–42. This episode is confirmed in a letter from John Gibb of Mills & Gibb, N. Y., to Oscar Straus, Jan. 18, 1898, on the occasion of the death of Lazarus Straus. Bliss had related it to Gibb in 1873, before the Strauses had won fame and fortune.

The account given in Hungerford, *op. cit.*, pp. 54–55, is badly garbled, for Bliss could have sold only dry goods and the Strauses were dealing in chinaware. Lazarus went to him to pay a debt, not to get credit for the new business.

12. Isidor's Autobiog., p. 43.

13. *Ibid.*, p. 44; interviews with Percy S. Straus and Nathan's son, Hugh Grant Straus, 1938.

14. I have assumed that the agreement with Macy was similar to that made four years later with John Wanamaker. The fragmentary accounts extant for the 1870's support this assumption. In the Wanamaker agreement net cost for domestic goods was defined as invoice cost, including charges for packages, freight and cartage, all discounts deducted. For imported goods net cost meant invoice cost plus freight, port charges, banking and disbursement commissions, cash discounts on bankers' acceptances abroad, duty, customs fees, insurance, and 5% for breakage and buyers' expenses. These facts are briefly set forth in a letter from L. Straus & Sons to John Wanamaker, Sept. 20, 1878; and in greater detail in the published records relating to *L. Straus & Sons* v. *John Wanamaker* (34 Atlantic 648, 175 Pa. St. 213).

15. *Cf.* Teele, *op. cit.*, pp. 1–2.

16. Court records cited in note 14 above.

17. *Ibid.*; sales figures for the Straus china and silver departments in Wanamaker's are shown for the three years 1885 to 1887, inclusive. They totaled $378,289 for 1885, $437,922 for 1886, and $477,315 for 1887. For the fall season of 1887 they were $287,650 against $358,629 for the Straus departments in Macy's. Some of the difference is possibly accounted for by the fact that the departments in Macy's had a four-year head start over those in Wanamaker's, but by 1887 this factor must have been of little importance. The sales of Wanamaker's as a whole in the 1880's were apparently greater than those of Macy's, although no definite figures are available (see Appel, *op. cit.*, pp. 106–108).

18. The years 1875 and 1881 show a better ratio than those immediately preceding and following because the Straus sales were calculated to the Saturday nearest Dec. 31, resulting in 53 weeks of business for those years, compared with store sales for the calendar year of 52 weeks.

19. Advt., N. Y. *World*, May 1, 1884.

20. Statement of accounts for the half-year ending Dec. 31, 1887; entries in a private ledger account book kept by Isidor Straus, subsequently referred to as I. S. Private Accts.

21. Isidor Straus to J. B. Wheeler, Dec. 27, 1888.

22. I. S. Private Accts.; interviews with Percy S. Straus.

23. The first instance I have found is an advertisement in N. Y. *Tribune*, Apr. 5, 1875. Odd prices were not advertised in other departments until the summer of 1878.

24. Advt., N. Y. *Times*, Mar. 24, 1878.

25. Advt., N. Y. *World*, Mar. 21, 1886.

26. This impression (and it can be that only) is obtained from a careful perusal of the Macy advertising between 1877 and 1888 in various New York newspapers, together with a series of magazine advertisements in *Century*

Magazine during 1882–83. All the extant operating figures tend to confirm it.

27. The partnership agreements between Webster and the Strauses have apparently been destroyed, and I have had to rely upon the accounting details which Isidor Straus painstakingly noted in his private business ledger. The letters which Isidor Straus wrote to Webster between 1888 and 1895 contain many references to Webster's poor health. The formal announcement of the dissolution of the partnership stated that Webster retired because of illness, and this explanation is in accordance with the known facts.

28. I. S. Private Accts. The partners received 6% interest on their capital investment and on any sums of money left in the business as a loan. No interest was allowed on undivided profits.

29. *Ibid.*

30. Isidor Straus to Webster, Feb. 21, 1893.

31. *Ibid.*; also letters and cablegrams dated Jan. 30, 31, Feb. 1, 3, 16, and Mar. 3, 10, 17, 1893. I am indebted to Hugh Grant Straus of Abraham & Straus for an abstract of L. Straus & Sons' "Brooklyn" ledger, showing that Webster held a one-sixth interest in Abraham & Straus (i.e., one-third of one-half) from 1893 to August, 1902. After 1896 Isidor and Nathan Straus held their interest as trustees for L. Straus & Sons, but this made no difference to the relationship between the two stores.

32. Isidor Straus to Webster, Jan. 31, 1893, and to Nathan Straus, July 21, 1893; Isidor's Autobiog., pp. 39, 58.

33. *Ibid.*, pp. 39–41.

CHAPTER X

1. Cf. Warren and Pearson, *op. cit.*, pp. 17–42. Of course, no index can now be constructed for the prices of merchandise sold by Macy's at that time, but it is safe to assume that they moved closely with general commodity prices.

2. Cf. Thorp, *op. cit.*, pp. 135–139; Gras and Larson, *op. cit.*, pp. 706–725.

3. This list is based upon a careful examination of Macy advertisements which appeared between 1888 and 1902, principally in the N. Y. *Herald*, but occasionally supplemented by the *Evening Post*. The dates given are the earliest for which there is clear evidence of the introduction of the merchandise mentioned; doubtless a number of items were actually sold in the store before the year cited.

4. Advts., N. Y. *Herald*, Oct. 13, 1889, Oct. 20, 1895; semiannual balances, Dec., 1889, *et seq.*

5. Advts., N. Y. *Herald*, Mar. 17 and Oct. 10, 1892. The semiannual balances show that the grocery department had a separate existence from the spring of 1892.

6. Cf. above, pp. 103–104; Lambert, *op. cit.*, pp. 76–77. It is at least clear that none of the better-known stores in New York had grocery departments

NOTES TO CHAPTER X

at this date, and the same is true of Wanamaker's in Philadelphia, Jordan Marsh in Boston, and Marshall Field's in Chicago. Of course, there are many department stores today which do not sell groceries.

7. Semiannual balances, 1894 and 1895; notations, Oct. 6, 1894, and June 8, 1895, in I. S. Memo. According to a letter written by Isidor Straus on Feb. 28, 1893, the unexpected popularity of the department compelled a sudden increase in salesforce which resulted for a time in service below store standards.

8. Advts., N. Y. *Herald*, Sept. 13 and 14, 1896; interview with Percy S. Straus.

9. Advts., N. Y. *Herald*, Apr. 24, Oct. 19, and Nov. 27, 1898; letter to H. H. Pottle, Nov. 26, 1902; Gibbons, *op. cit.*, vol. ii, pp. 43–44.

10. Macy correspondence dated Oct. 9, 1901, Apr. 28, and Nov. 13, 1902, Mar. 9, 1903, Apr. 20, 1906; advt., N. Y. *Herald*, May 18, 1901. Cf. Lambert, *op. cit.*, pp. 114–115.

11. Except where otherwise indicated, this section is based principally on interviews with officers and employees of the firm. Precision as to dates and facts was unobtainable, but the main outline is probably correct.

12. Advts., N. Y. *Herald*, May 8 and July 24, 1892; N. Y. *World*, May 8, 1892.

13. The fact that Sloane's was selling agent for carpet manufacturers as well as retailers undoubtedly gave them a price advantage over Macy's, and I refer to them only because the firm's retail establishment is well known. Probably there were other rug retailers in New York in the 1890's whose trade far exceeded that of the Macy department.

14. For testimony on the amount of direct buying done by other department stores, see *Rep. of Ind. Com.*, vol. vii, pp. 458, 696, 736.

15. Macy's to William Foster, Aug. 2, 1892; Isidor Straus to C. B. Webster, July 5, 12, and Aug. 16, 1895.

16. *Ibid.*, Feb. 7, 1889.

17. Advts., N. Y. *Herald*, Apr. 24, 1892, Jan. 22 and Sept. 10, 1893.

18. *Ibid.*, Feb. 12, Oct. 22, 1893, Mar. 11, 1894, Aug. 16, 1896, Nov. 3, 1897.

19. Letter to Armour & Co., Sept. 29, 1896.

20. Isidor Straus to Thomas Wanamaker, Mar. 30, Apr. 3, 1888, July 7, 1892; to Henry Blun, May 10, 1892.

21. Isidor to Nathan Straus, June 2, 1893, Nov. 8, 1894; to Woodward & Lothrop, June 28, 1893; to Sigmund Maas, July 14, Oct. 19, 1893.

22. *Ibid.*, July 8, 1895.

23. *Ibid.*, Oct. 14, 1895.

24. *Ibid.*, Oct. 19, 1893; Isidor Straus to A. Abraham, June 26, 1894; interview in 1930 with Mr. Linnert, who was in the Macy foreign office from 1893 to 1925.

25. *American Cabinet Maker and Upholsterer*, Oct. 3, 1896, quoted in the N. Y. *Herald*, Nov. 18, 1896.

26. Advts., N. Y. *Herald*, Mar. 17, 1889, *et seq.*
27. Isidor Straus to Superintendent of Buildings, Mar. 19, 1889.
28. Advts., N. Y. *Herald*, Oct. 13, 1889, June 15, 1890, Sept. 20, 1891; news article, N. Y. *Herald*, Sept. 27, 1891; semiannual statements, 1889–91.
29. Advts., N. Y. *Herald*, Feb. 5, 12, 26, and July 2, 1893, Feb. 11, Apr. 15, and Nov. 11, 1894, May 12, 1895, Jan. 19, Sept. 14, 1896, Dec. 5, 1897; Isidor Straus to C. B. Webster, Aug. 9, 1895; semiannual statements, 1892–98.
30. The dates of the opening of these two factories are not known. A branch in Pennsylvania was being discussed in 1888 (Isidor Straus to M. H. Chase, June 12, 1888), but other evidence suggests that the Chester Branch actually began to operate about 1898. The Rutherford factory appears in the semiannual statements for the first time in the spring of 1902. By 1900 there was also a factory in Brooklyn, apparently replacing the one in Wallingford, Conn.
31. Advt., N. Y. *Herald*, Nov. 9, 1902.
32. Letter dated Nov. 16, 1894.
33. Letter dated Aug. 9, 1895.
34. Advt., N. Y. *Herald*, Sept. 26, 1898; interviews with Percy S. Straus.
35. Nathan Straus to G. M. Hull, Dec. 12, 1888.
36. *L'Illustration*, Mar. 31, 1872, p. 206; Lord & Taylor advts., N. Y. *Tribune*, 1874; Lambert, *op. cit.*, pp. 168–169; *Report of the Special Committee . . . of the Assembly . . . to Investigate Alleged Abuses in the Management of Railroads* (Albany, 1880), p. 62; *Dry Goods Econ.*, Mar. 17, 1900, p. 39, and Aug. 4, 1900, p. 68; article on the Claflin enterprise in N. Y. *Times*, June 26, 1914, p. 3; see also testimony of John Wanamaker in *Rep. of Ind. Com.*, vol. vii, pp. 454–457.
37. Report on Manufacturing Department, prepared by M. H. Chase, in Jan., 1900.
38. *Rep. of Ind. Com.*, vol. vii, pp. 456–457.
39. This statement is based upon the reorganizations reported by J. O. McKinsey in a 45-page pamphlet to the employees of Marshall Field & Co., published in Feb., 1936, together with information contained in the firm's annual reports for the years 1936 to 1938.
40. Trade-mark registrations, Nos. 24,255 and 24,256 (registered on Feb. 20, 1894); 24,290 and 24,304 (Mar. 6, 1894); 24,394 (Mar. 10, 1894); and 24,617 (May 1, 1894).
41. Advts., N. Y. *Herald*, 1888–1902. A hasty survey failed to uncover any mention of "Lily White" canned goods before 1896, but a letter to Havens & Beebe, Nov. 28, 1893, shows that Macy's had been using the name "Lily Bell," thereby unwittingly infringing upon an established trade-mark. Having to abandon it, the store presumably adopted "Lily White" as an acceptable modification. The Patent Office registration (No. 118,308), filed in 1916, declared that "Lily White" had been used since 1896, and this is supported by testi-

mony in *R. H. Macy* v. *Isador Habor*, Trade-Mark Opposition No. 7702, Mar., 1927.

42. Advt., N. Y. *Herald*, Mar. 17, 1889.

43. The theory of secular trends, propounded by N. D. Kondratieff, has been developed and applied to American business history with fairly satisfactory results. See Gras and Larson, *op. cit.*, pp. 661–744.

CHAPTER XI

1. Letter dated July 11, 1893.
2. Isidor Straus to Webster, July 19, 1895.
3. Except where otherwise noted, this section is based upon a careful examination of advertising in the N. Y. *Herald* for the period, accompanied by periodic checks in other New York papers designed to reveal the approximate amplitude of department store advertising.
4. Letter dated Dec. 14, 1894.
5. *Ibid.*, July 27, 1888.
6. R. H. Macy & Co. to Elizabeth Mayhon, Sept. 6, 1901; memo on advertising, undated, but apparently 1898–99.
7. R. H. Macy & Co. to William C. Alpers, Apr. 8, 1899; Wanamaker advt., N. Y. *Herald*, Apr. 3, 1899.
8. Isidor Straus to *Puck*, Oct. 3, 1888, and to P. W. Mason & Co., Oct. 18, 1888; memo referred to in note 6 above.
9. Advertising booklet, 1890; R. H. Macy & Co. to William J. McFarland, July 20, 1899, and to F. C. Townsend, Oct. 9, 1902; advt., N. Y. *Herald*, Apr. 25, 1897.
10. Isidor to Nathan Straus, May 5, 1893; photographs, undated but evidently taken about 1896.
11. Advts., N. Y. *Herald*, Mar. 19 and Apr. 23, 1893; semiannual statements for 1893 and 1894.
12. General catalog, 1891; Isidor Straus to Webster, Mar. 15, 1889, and to D. Lothrop Co., May 20, 1892; advt., N. Y. *Herald*, Jan. 9, 1894; grocery catalogs, July, Aug., and Oct., 1899, Mar. and Oct., 1900, Jan., May, Aug., and Nov., 1901; semiannual statements, 1888 to 1903.
13. Advts., N. Y. *Herald*, Mar. 17, 1889, and Nov. 23, 1890.
14. *Ibid.*, Nov. 20, 1898, Apr. 17, 1899, June 8 and 29, 1902.
15. *Ibid.*, Mar. 17, 1889.
16. *Ibid.*, Apr. 3, 1892.
17. *Ibid.*, Oct. 6, 1895.
18. *Ibid.*, Apr. 18, 1901. Similar statements appeared on Sept. 19, 1900, and May 22, 1901.
19. Two instances of misstatement may be cited, obviously not the only ones. In spite of repeated assertions that the store did not sell at low prices on

some articles and high on others, Macy's sometimes sold goods at cost in order to attract customers. A letter from Isidor Straus to Webster, July 19, 1895, reveals that bicycle lamps were being sold at the rate of 2,000 a month; he added, "It is true we make nothing on them, but they help all other articles." Again, an advertisement in the *Herald*, Sept. 16, 1900, asserted that sales volume for the month had "for the first time in 45 years" fallen below the figures for the year before. The store had not been in existence 45 years; moreover, such a decline had happened 75 times in the preceding 20 years! Of course, the usual fault was empty claims — the best quality, the lowest prices, half the cost of production, the largest crowd, and so on.

20. Advt., N. Y. *Sun*, Oct. 19, 1902.

21. Advt., N. Y. *Herald*, Sept. 19, 1900. Little information exists on the methods by which the store's advertising was handled. By 1901 there was an advertising office to which buyers sent copy, and this material was apparently worked into finished advertisements by special copywriters. Old buyers recall that they were given limits as to the amount which might be spent by each department, but the method of control is not clear, and considerable latitude was evidently permitted. A letter from Isidor Straus to Webster, Dec. 28, 1888, reports a new deal with Parmenter (an advertising agent) by which Parmenter passed on to Macy's all discounts allowed by publishers and received 2½% commission from the store on space used. Some space was purchased without recourse to an agent, but the precise arrangements are unknown.

22. Advertisements show that the exhibitions were opened during the last week in November. The store was willing to sell the displays after they had been used, but it had three old ones on hand early in 1889. Isidor Straus to Weinstock, Lubin & Co., Jan. 22, 1889.

23. Advt., N. Y. *Herald*, Oct. 4, 1900. A similar statement was published Mar. 31, 1901.

24. *Ibid.*, May 20, 1891.

25. News articles, N. Y. *Daily News*, Sept. 19, 1895, N. Y. *World*, Nov. 23, 1895, and Cleveland *Leader*, Nov. 29, 1895; advt., N. Y. *Herald*, Sept. 15, 1895; Isidor Straus to Lloyd Bryce, Oct. 28, 1895.

A letter to the president of the Englewood Improvement Association, Oct. 12, 1895, reveals that one of the cars was alleged to have driven through Englewood, N. J., "at a reckless speed, thus putting in jeopardy the lives and property of the citizens of the village."

26. Advts., N. Y. *Herald*, Feb. 27 and June 5, 1898.

27. *Ibid.*, Aug. 5, 1890, July 12, 1895, Aug. 8, 1897, July 23, 1899. Both the Macy and Wanamaker sales began with the week of Aug. 4, 1890. Cf. Appel, *op. cit.*, p. 109.

28. Advts., N. Y. *Herald*, Oct. 27, 1889, May 29, 1892, May 22, 1898, June 16, 1901.

29. *Ibid.*, Oct. 9, 1892, Mar. 13, 1898, Sept. 10 and 17, 1899.

30. Advts., N. Y. *Herald, Times,* and *World,* 1887 and 1888.

31. Advts., N. Y. *Herald,* July 19, 1896, and June 19, 1898; interview with William Breidinger, 1930. Breidinger began to work in the delivery department in 1879.

32. Advts., N. Y. *Herald,* Dec. 23, 1888, Dec. 23, 1892, Dec. 24, 1894, Dec. 23, 1897, Dec. 23, 1900; interviews with old employees.

33. Advt., N. Y. *Herald,* Dec. 15, 1897; letters to Alexander Rice, May 21, 1901, and Roger B. Pitman, Nov. 1, 1902; real estate accounts, 1888–1903; interviews with Percy S. Straus.

34. R. H. Macy & Co. to Mrs. J. M. Hobson, Jan. 30, 1901.

35. Advts., N. Y. *Herald,* Oct. 14, 1888, *et seq.*; letters to J. Stokes Walsh, Oct. 17, 1888; Mrs. E. N. Newell, Jan. 10, 1889; Mrs. William Pachman, Feb. 6, 1901; Mrs. C. H. Brown, Apr. 19, 1901; Isidor Straus to Webster, Feb. 1, 1889; returns data for 1891 and succeeding years supplied by the Controller's Office.

36. Advts., N. Y. *Herald,* Sept. 8 and 29, 1895; news article, N. Y. *Commercial Advertiser,* Sept. 14, 1895; semiannual statements, 1895–1900.

37. Advts., N. Y. *Herald,* Sept. 1, 1895, Dec. 8, 1897, Mar. 20, 1898, June 3 and 25, 1900.

38. Isidor Straus to Manhattan Electric Light Co., Sept. 22, 1888.

39. Isidor Straus to "Mr. Morse, Architect," Mar. 20, 1889; advt., *Frank Leslie's Illustrated Newspaper,* Oct. 26, 1889.

40. A description of the arrangement of Macy departments in 1890 ran as follows (from advertising booklet, 1890):

THE BASEMENT.

Our immense shipping department occupies a space of about 60 x 220 feet in the front. The remaining space, 120 x 220 feet, is devoted to China, Crockery, Glassware, Housefurnishing Goods, Wooden, Iron, and Tinware, and forms one grand salesroom, without doubt the largest of its kind in the world. The China, Crockery, and Glassware departments are liberally stocked with the products of the best French, German, English, and American makers. . . .

THE MAIN FLOOR,

with its spacious aisles, is always thronged with active buyers. It is a busy, bustling, place, its counters and shelves are laden with everything that is new and seasonable in the many departments, and certainly no other house in the city can boast of such perfect light and ventilation. There are two grand entrances on 14th Street, three on 6th Avenue, and one on 13th Street, and the immense number of ladies passing in and out indicates the life that is abounding through the store.

The various and large stocks next command our attention. At the left of the eastern 14th Street entrance is the Confectionery department, and facing it, what can be considered the largest Soda-water Fountain in the city. Adjoining the Confectionery department we find Toilet Articles, Patent Medicines, and Perfumery, and opposite, Stationery of every description; thence, stretching out over 200 feet of counters and shelving, and covering both sides of the aisle, the Dress Goods department, comprising a large variety of fabrics in every possible tint, shade and combination, and every desirable quality. From the Dress Goods department we reach our 13th Street annex, and here the visitor is attracted by what we believe to be the most complete stock of Furniture, Refrigerators, Ice-Boxes, Pictures, and Trunks in the country.

Returning to the main floor, we find on one side of our 13th Street entrance the Soap department, and on the other a long stretch of counter, devoted wholly to Notions, Fancy Goods in Metal, etc. Passing on, our grand display of Black and Colored Silks, Satins, Plushes, Velvets, etc., is attracting the attention of the visitor. These departments are leading features of our establishment, and are at all times fully stocked with the richest and latest novelties. Next, going towards 14th Street, we find an immense display of Umbrellas, Parasols, Canes, Books, Music, and Photographs on one side, and on the other, Notions, Cutlery, Fancy Plush and Optical Goods. We have now reached that part of our main floor fronting on 6th Avenue, and this magnificent space of 100 x 200 feet — unexcelled by any store in the city — is divided up in numerous sections with spacious aisles. Starting on the 14th Street side, the first section is given over to untrimmed Hats, the second to Flowers and Ribbons, where we show the most complete stock in the country, comprising a beautiful variety of shades and combinations in every desirable width and quality. The third section represents a beautiful exhibit of Jewelry, and numerous kinds of Fancy Goods in Plush, Leather, Metal, Wood and Ivory, Fans, etc., and facing this wondrous exhibit we show a large assortment of Shirts, Collars, and Cuffs, for gentlemen's wear. The fourth and fifth sections are occupied by Men's Furnishings and Men's Underwear, followed by section seven with Hosiery; section eight, Laces and Embroideries; section nine, Handkerchiefs and Ladies' Collars and Cuffs; section ten, Ladies' Gloves; section eleven, Laces, Curtains, etc.; section twelve, Linings; sections thirteen and fourteen, Table Linens, Napkins, Muslins, and Blankets; section fifteen, Buttons and Dress Trimmings; section sixteen, Rudolstadt Bisques and Artistic Pottery; section seventeen, Worsteds and Fancy Trimmings, and ending with our Ladies' and Children's Shoe department, a grand store by itself, and replete with the largest and most varied stock in the city.

THE SECOND FLOOR.

The ascent to our second floor can be made either by one of our handsome passenger elevators or by the two grand stairways. Going up the grand stairway near 14th Street, the visitor's attention is first attracted by our immense display of Ladies' Underwear, Corsets, and Children's Outfits. Thence, turning into our 14th Street annex, the magnificent Ladies' Cloak department presents itself, in which the best examples from world-renowned Parisian and Berlin houses are displayed side by side with the best of home production. Returning to the second floor, we find on the right the department of Trimmed Millinery, at all times aglow with the latest fashions; on the left, the Boys' and Youths' Clothing department, always fully stocked with the product of the most reliable makers, and on the right of the main aisle, a counter with samples of card engraving done on our premises. Our delightful Ladies' Restaurant is also situated on this floor with two entrances, one from our Boys' Clothing department and one from our Art Rooms.

The latter occupy the remainder of the second floor, a space of about 80 x 100 feet, and they are unsurpassed by any house. We show here the largest stock of rich deep-cut Glassware to be found in the country, together with a most superb collection of useful and artistic Pottery of the very highest grade, including all the novelties from the Rudolstadt, Royal Worcester, Royal Dresden, Carlsbad, and Daulton [*sic*] Potteries. We show also a magnificent line of Onyx, Bronze, and Marble Clocks, Mantel Sets, Bronze Groups, Statuettes, Busts, Silver, and Silver-plated Ware.

THE THIRD FLOOR,

reached either by our three new and handsome passenger elevators or by two grand stairways, presents a most beautiful aspect. Starting in the 14th Street annex, we have one show-room, 25 x 100 feet, devoted to artistic Furniture, fine Tapestries, etc., and another room of the same dimensions to Bedding, Beds, and Mattresses. Next we show what is conceded to be the largest Toy and Doll department in the city, and also a full line of Sporting Goods, Fishing Tackle, etc. Passing the Toy department we come to the three new departments added within the last year to our establishment: 60 x 150 feet are here devoted to the sale of Oriental Goods, Rugs, Upholstery, Saddlery and Harness. Our stock of Oriental Goods includes all the different grades, from the plainest and least expensive to the most elegant — everything marked at our popular prices. The same applies to our Upholstery Goods. Skilled buyers are commissioned to gather the best from wherever in the world the best can be found. In our Harness and Saddlery department we keep everything pertaining to a first-class Harness establishment, from the cheapest machine-made goods to the finest made in this or any other country. Our finer grades of Harness, Saddles, etc., are made on the premises, under the supervision of Mr. P. H. Comerford, whose reputation as one of the most renowned harness-makers requires no further commendation.

THE FOURTH FLOOR

contains our immense Millinery work-rooms, our Card Engraving and Printing establishment, and Reserve Stock. The manufacture of Ladies' and Children's Muslin Underwear, formerly carried on on this floor, was removed to our 13th Street annex, and the illustration shows but one of our large manufacturing rooms. The view on page 20 illustrates our Glass-cutting shop. . . .

CONVENIENCES.

For the accommodation of our lady patrons we have an elegantly appointed Parlor in our 13th Street annex; also, large Dressing Rooms for ladies, with lavatory and retiring rooms attached on our second floor, with entrance on the right of our Boys' Clothing department.

The "lost and found" desk is located in our 13th Street annex, adjoining Ladies' Parlor, and parcels, handbags, and the like, will be taken care of there, free of charge.

The Telegraph office (Western Union), with connection to every point, is near the centre door, 6th Avenue.

41. Advt., N. Y. *Herald*, Apr. 3, 1892; news article, *ibid.*, Mar. 26, 1893; semiannual statements, 1891–92. The Macy offices occupied the sixth floor of the new building.

42. *Ibid.* While Macy's never invested so heavily in paintings as Wanamaker (cf. Gibbons, *op. cit.*, vol. ii, pp. 72–81), it may well have imitated his efforts in establishing the artroom.

43. Advts., N. Y. *Herald*, Mar. 17 and Dec. 11, 1892, Nov. 12, 1893.

44. Advts., N. Y. *Herald*, May 26, 1895, Sept. 6, 12, and 26, 1896; Isidor Straus to Webster, Aug. 2, 1895; news articles, N. Y. *Commercial Advertiser*, Sept. 14, 1895, and *Mail & Express*, Oct. 31, 1895. The Strauses had bought the site of the annex in 1893, apparently in anticipation of further expansion, and presumably sold it to the syndicate to avoid a further heavy investment of capital (the building alone was estimated to cost $265,000). The Chisolms, who owned the corner property, were willing to put up a new building but refused to provide it with heating plant, elevators, and other necessary installations. The Boston syndicate installed all the required apparatus, receiving as rental $36,000 per year; Macy's paid the taxes and maintained the fire insurance at 80% of $265,000 (lease of Colonial Real Estate Association, dated Sept. 1, 1896).

45. Isidor Straus to Woodward & Lothrop, June 28, 1893; to Sigmund Maas, Jan. 2, 1896; advt., N. Y. *Herald*, Apr. 22, 1894.

46. *Ibid.*, June 7, 1899. Other advertisements after 1896 repeatedly emphasized the absence of crowding in Macy's.

47. June 26, 1894.

48. May 6, 1896.

49. Advt., N. Y. *Herald*, Oct. 8, 1898.

50. *Ibid.*, Oct. 7, 1900, Nov. 3, 1901; interviews with employees.

51. *Dry Goods Econ.*, Jan. 18, 1902.

52. That competitive price-cutting was not confined to New York was evident by the testimony in *Rep. of Ind. Com.*, vol. vii, pp. 460–461, 697.

53. Advt., N. Y. *Herald*, Dec. 13, 1899, *et seq.*

54. Letter to David L. Gluck, Oct. 31, 1901.

55. Advt., N. Y. *Herald*, Sept. 4, 1892.

56. *Ibid.*, Nov. 10, 1901.

57. *Ibid.*, Nov. 18, 1901. Copy published on Nov. 16 declared, "We are in the book business to stay, and we mean to have every book that is published."
58. This title actually was used, *ibid.*, Apr. 20, 1902.
59. *Ibid.*, Nov. 14, 21, 28, and Dec. 5, 1897.
60. Letter to Merritt Burial Co., Nov. 2, 1899. Other letters express the same policy, among them one to Maude B. Booth, May 9, 1892, and another to George A. Warburton, Nov. 4, 1899.
61. Advt., N. Y. *Herald*, Sept. 30, 1888.
62. *Ibid.*, Oct. 7 and Nov. 11, 1888.
63. *Ibid.*, Oct. 14, 1888.
64. *Ibid.*, Oct. 16, 1888.
65. *Ibid.*, Oct. 19, 1888.
66. *Ibid.*, Nov. 4, 1888.
67. The Hearn campaign began on Oct. 7, and the last advertisement referring to it appeared on Nov. 23, 1888. During the interval Hearn published 23 advertisements aimed at Macy's, 7 of them two columns in length and the remainder mostly one column long.
68. Advts., N. Y. *Herald*, Oct. 21, 1888, Mar. 18, 1894.
69. Isidor Straus to Kleinwort, Sons & Co., London, Jan. 9, 1888; to Oscar Straus, Jan. 7, 1888.
70. *Ibid.*, Jan. 14, 1888.
71. *Ibid.*, Feb. 25, 1888.
72. Isidor Straus to an unidentified correspondent, May 8, 1888. An accounting memo shows that the shoe department was purchased by Macy's on Mar. 3, 1888.

The letters written in 1888 and 1889 reveal Isidor gradually taking a hand in all branches of the business — advertising, supervision of buyers, inventory control, and so on, in addition to matters of accounting and finance.

73. Isidor to Nathan Straus, July 28 and Aug. 4, 1893.
74. Isidor to Webster, May 29, 1894, and subsequent cable and telegraph messages.
75. *Ibid.*, July 6, 1894.
76. Isidor to Nathan Straus, July 5, 1893.
77. Letter, Isidor Straus to Webster, July 24, 1894.
78. *Ibid.*, Feb. 9, 1889.
79. Isidor to Nathan Straus, July 5 and 14, 1893.
80. Letter to A. Abraham, Nov. 8, 1894.
81. This summary description of the Straus brothers is based upon numerous letters left by Isidor (Nathan left little correspondence), interviews with a great many employees, and the biographical material contained in the *Dict. of Amer. Biog.*
82. Isidor Straus to Webster, July 21 and Dec. 29, 1888, Feb. 2, 1889, Jan. 31, 1893; to J. W. Hutchinson, Mar. 9, 1889; to A. Abraham, Nov. 8 and 17, 1894;

I. S. Memo, 1895–98; interview with Nathan Straus reported in *Dry Goods Econ.*, June 1, 1901.

83. Semiannual statements, 1896–1903.

84. *Ibid.*; Isidor Straus to William G. Rice, Nov. 2, 1895, and to a Mr. Williams, Feb. 2, 1901.

85. Semiannual statements, 1888–1903; letter to American Institute of Social Service, Sept. 30, 1903; interviews with employees.

86. *Ibid.*; Isidor Straus to Nathan Straus, July 27, 1888; to Vernon Brown, Oct. 15, 1888; to H. H. Chandler, May 20, 1893; to Mrs. M. M. Smith, Sept. 28, 1895; and to Rev. J. P. Peters, Oct. 14, 1899. A payroll tabulation for the week ending Dec. 17, 1898, shows a total of 3,086 employees, 379 of them in manufacturing divisions. This figure would be close to the year's peak because of the season, but, on the other hand, the list does not include the special payrolls which contained a fairly large number of executives.

87. Interviews with employees; semiannual statements, 1896–1903.

88. News article, N. Y. *Sun*, Oct. 13, 1895; letter to Henry C. Bernheim, Oct. 1, 1902; card printed by Typographical Union No. 6 and Allied Printing Trades, 1899.

89. Advts., N. Y. *Herald*, Dec. 10, 1901, and Dec. 15, 1902; interviews with employees.

90. Memo book containing record of daily sales, 1888 to 1902.

CHAPTER XII

1. Entries in the Black Book; Isidor's letters, 1893; interviews with Percy S. Straus and Hugh Grant Straus.

2. *Ibid.*; the Black Book; Isidor's Autobiog.

3. The Black Book; conversations with Percy S. Straus.

4. *Ibid.*; I. S. Private Accts.; interviews with employees.

5. News articles, N. Y. *Evening Post*, Apr. 19 and 20, 1901.

6. Isidor Straus to John M. Bowers, June 11, 1894, to C. B. Webster, Aug. 2, 1895, and to George E. Chisolm, Aug. 30, 1899. However, the elevator accident which occurred in the store on June 18, 1902, injuring 14 persons, cannot be attributed to old equipment, for it took place in the newest part of the premises (N. Y. *Times*, June 19, 1902).

7. Sworn statement of Agnes Kane, May 10, 1901; written complaints of Mrs. Charles H. Simpson, Mar. 18, 1902, E. T. Maher, Mar. 28, 1902, and Mrs. Thomas Keyes, May 2, 1902; R. H. Macy & Co. to R. Smith & Co., May 11, 1901, and May 5, 1902.

8. Contemporary retail advertisements; article, N. Y. *Commercial Advertiser*, Nov. 7, 1902.

9. Correspondence between Isidor Straus and William Rhinelander Stewart, George E. Chisolm, and John M. Bowers (representing the Chisolm interests),

during the period from Nov. 13, 1899, to Jan. 5, 1901. The correspondence reveals the Chisolms as raising one obstacle after another, lowering their demands in one direction only to make new ones in another.

10. Interviews with Percy S. Straus; James Blaine Walker, *Fifty Years of Rapid Transit* (N. Y., 1918), chaps. xii and xiii; Merchants' Association of New York, *Passenger Transportation Service in the City of New York* (N. Y. 1903), p. 43; Reeves, *op. cit.*, pp. 46–47.

Contemporary newspaper accounts credit Nathan Straus with making the decision to move uptown, but Isidor's correspondence proves conclusively that the two senior partners would have been content to remain at 14th Street. According to Percy S. Straus, the idea of moving was first advanced by Jesse, and the two boys selected the site without any assistance from Isidor or Nathan.

Entries in the Real Estate Ledger, 1901–07, show that the first leases were acquired on Mar. 25, 1901.

11. N. Y. *Commercial Advertiser*, Nov. 7, 1902; H. W. Schotter, *The Growth and Development of the Pennsylvania Railroad Company* (Philadelphia, 1927), pp. 270–278, 313–318.

12. N. Y. *Evening Post*, Apr. 20, 1901.

13. Interviews with Percy S. Straus.

14. *Ibid.*; N. Y. *Times*, June 30, 1901.

15. N. Y. *Mail & Express*, June 6, 1901; interviews with Percy S. Straus; correspondence with Solwin W. Smith, son of Robert S. Smith, Dec., 1941.

The Smith explanation raises several points of difficulty. Siegel had leased the land at 14th Street and announced his intention to put up a new store fully two weeks *before* Smith negotiated the purchase from Pell, and Smith therefore knew that there would shortly be a large department store in operation beside his own store. Secondly, Smith would hardly have paid out $375,000 for a piece of land without first considering whether it was large enough for his requirements. At that price, Smith would have had to do a retail business of about $2,000,000 to cover his rent, a volume which would require the efforts of at least 200 employees working with the highest efficiency, to say nothing of the space required for merchandise and customers. It simply could not be done, and Smith must have known so at the time. Thirdly, Siegel unquestionably acquired title to the property within a very short time after Pell sold it, and it is difficult to see why he bought it unless he hoped to force the issue with the Strauses. The hypothesis that either Smith or Siegel bought the land as a speculative venture is ruled out by the fact that it was immediately offered to the Strauses at the purchase price. It should be added that the explanation given by Smith's son is a report of what the son remembers having heard many years ago and does not pretend to be a first-hand account.

16. N. Y. *Times*, June 30, 1901; interviews with Percy S. Straus; correspondence with Solwin W. Smith.

17. Lease to 65 West 13th Street, bearing cancellation agreement dated May 5, 1903.
18. Isidor Straus to Bowers & Sands, Mar. 19, 1903. This refusal was not directed at Siegel alone. They had already informed others that the store was to remain vacant for some months. Straus to David Blaustein, Nov. 21, 1902.
19. Article, N. Y. *Commercial Advertiser*, Nov. 7, 1902.
20. *Ibid.*, July 16, 1901; "Motion Pictures," *Dictionary of American History* (N. Y., 1940), vol. iv; Terry Ramsaye to J. G. Bashford, Oct. 27, 1938. In 1938 Macy's put up a bronze plaque on the side of the building to commemorate the event.
21. N. Y. *Mail & Express*, May 16, 1901.
22. *Ibid.*; N. Y. *Commercial Advertiser*, Nov. 7, 1902.
23. Contract dated Apr. 12, 1901; N. Y. *Mail & Express* and N. Y. *Herald*, May 16, 1901; the Black Book.
24. N. Y. *Herald*, Mar. 23, 1902.
25. *Ibid.*, June 10 and Sept. 27, 1901.
26. N. Y. *Sun*, Dec. 18, 1901.
27. *Dry Goods Econ.*, Nov. 15, 1902; N. Y. *Commercial Advertiser*, Nov. 7, 1902; N. Y. *Evening Journal*, Nov. 9, 1902. It is impossible to list the many letters which came to the store during 1902 and 1903 asking about the various innovations in equipment, but they indicate that Macy's had introduced on a large scale a number of devices — notably the belt conveyors, escalators, and vacuum cleaners — which were unfamiliar to other large stores, even some in New York City.
28. N. Y. *Times*, Jan. 16, 1902, quoting data taken from *The Electric World and Engineer*; details on fuel consumption are from Macy records, supplied to me by John J. Cogan, head of the Macy Maintenance Department.
29. N. Y. *Herald*, May 17, 1901; N. Y. *Commercial Advertiser*, Nov. 7, 1902; interviews with Percy S. Straus.
30. Real Estate Ledger, 1901–07; Isidor's Autobiog., pp. 57–58; interviews with Percy S. Straus.
Shortly before the completion of the building a dispute arose between the Strauses and the Fuller Co. over costs. The contract called for quality to match that of the Simpson, Crawford, Simpson building at a cost not to exceed 20 cents per cubic foot, plus 8% for the contracting company's overhead and profit. The cost exceeded the contract figure, and some of the equipment installations proved to be highly unsatisfactory, as a result of which the Strauses refused to pay the full amount demanded. The Fuller Co. sued for $1,181,048, and the matter was finally settled out of court (1909) for $545,000, in addition to which the Strauses had to pay $99,411 to complete work left undone by the Fuller Co., plus more than $107,000 in legal fees. Real Estate Ledger, 1901–07; memos and correspondence extending from 1902 to 1909.
The tax assessors appraised the property at $6,300,000, considerably above

the cash investment, but in 1908 the Strauses obtained a court decree assessing the value at $5,850,000 as of 1903, with increases in succeeding years bringing it up to $6,000,000 in 1906. It was raised to $6,500,000 in 1910 and $6,800,000 in 1911. Real Estate Ledgers, 1901–07, and 1908–11.

31. Interviews with Percy S. Straus; *Dry Goods Econ.*, Nov. 15, 1902; interviews with employees.

32. Macy newspaper advts., May through Dec., 1902; Mobile Rapid Transit Co. to Macy's, Dec. 12 and 13, 1902. Letters received by the store in 1903 show that a few people, especially those living on Staten Island, objected to going farther uptown to shop, but the main response was highly favorable.

33. Thorp, *op. cit.*, pp. 139–141; Warren and Pearson, *op. cit.*, pp. 14–31.

34. *Loc. cit.*; Thorp, *op. cit.*, p. 141.

35. Letter to R. Woodman Burbidge, Apr. 12, 1911.

36. Appel, *op. cit.*, pp. 126–131; Gibbons, *op. cit.*, vol. ii, pp. 103–112.

37. *Dry Goods Econ.*, Jan. 30, 1909, p. 24, and June 18, 1910, pp. 55, 69, 73; Macy advt., welcoming Gimbel's to Herald Square, Sept. 29, 1910.

38. History of Departments (a record maintained by the Controller's office); Stamford (Conn.) *Advocate*, Oct. 29, 1909; *Dry Goods Econ.*, Dec. 25, 1909; correspondence between Macy's and the *Matilda Ziegler Magazine for the Blind* between Nov., 1909, and Apr., 1912.

39. History of Departments.

40. Numerous letters dating from 1902 to 1913. The proposal from an astrologer, "Professor Astro," was acknowledged in a letter dated Dec. 2, 1910.

41. Macy's to Auburn Automobile Co., Feb. 13, 1903; to H. L. Jesperson, Feb. 16, 1903; Gibbons, *op. cit.*, vol. ii, pp. 92–97.

42. *Dry Goods Econ.*, May 28 and July 9, 1910; semiannual statements, 1910–13; interviews with Macy executives.

43. *Ibid.; Dry Goods Econ.*, Jan. 9, 1909, Feb. 17, 1912, Apr. 26, 1913; advts., N. Y. *Herald*, Feb. 17, 1912, *et seq.*

44. Semiannual statements, 1902–12; Macy catalogs, 1909–11; interviews with Macy executives.

45. *Ibid.*; semiannual statements.

46. Advts., N. Y. *Times*, Aug. 28, 1904, *et seq.*

47. *Ibid.*, Jan. 5, 1907.

48. Advts., N. Y. *World* and *Sun*, Dec., 1906; Macy's to *Collier's Weekly*, May 13, 1907; Macy's to P. Compton Miller, July 26, 1910.

49. *Dry Goods Econ.*, July 10, 1909, Jan. 8, Feb. 26, July 9, 1910; Real Estate Ledger, 1908–11.

50. *Dry Goods Econ.*, Feb. 22 and Apr. 26, 1913.

51. *Ibid.*, Sept. 23 and 30, 1911, Sept. 28, 1912, Mar. 15 and Sept. 27, 1913; letter, Percy S. Straus to his parents, Mar. 12, 1910.

52. *Dry Goods Econ.*, Dec. 11, 1909, Feb. 26, 1910, Mar. 25, May 20, June 17, July 1, Sept. 2, 1911. The numerous times which this trade publication

mentioned Macy displays and window decoration after 1909 may be the result of more effective publicity work on the part of the store, but the accompanying illustrations point unmistakably to improvement in Macy methods.

53. Letter to William Gaul, Nov. 29, 1909; also an examination of the advertising columns of the principal newspapers published in 1913 within commuting distance of New York City.

54. Advertising scrapbook, 1912–17.

55. These figures do not include C.O.D. purchases that were refused when delivery was attempted. Such transactions are common and entail a good deal of expense, but the firm does not include them in the sales figures because they are incomplete; the goods were never really sold.

56. *Dry Goods Econ.*, Apr. 26, 1913. Macy's refused to follow John Wanamaker's example when he began to give musical entertainment in his store. Macy's to J. L. Bauland, June 16, 1908.

57. Semiannual statements, 1902–13; Macy's to H. J. Heinz Co., Feb. 3, 1904; Percy S. Straus to his parents, Feb. 5 and Mar. 12, 1910; interviews with employees.

58. Delivery Dept. Ledger, 1902–17; letters from customers, 1902–14. In 1905 and for a number of years afterwards, Macy's held an annual parade of the store's delivery equipment. The horses were beautifully groomed, and the wagons and trucks shone in polished brass and bright red paint as if they had just left the factory. Macy's to N. Y. *Herald*, May 3, 1907; *Dry Goods Econ.*, May 15, 1909.

59. *Ibid.*, May 28, 1910; Delivery Dept. Ledger, 1902–17; Macy's to C. C. Stillman, July 28, 1910.

60. *Ibid.; Dry Goods Econ.*, May 28, 1910; Macy's to Taft & Pennoyer, Nov. 22, 1911; *Scientific American*, Oct. 26, 1912. The figures given in the last-named source failed to include recent Macy purchases of new equipment. The same source indicates that Wanamaker's delivery department was somewhat larger on the whole, having 150 wagons, 275 horses, 5 electric vehicles, and 70 gasoline trucks.

No reliable data are available on the comparative cost of using horses, gasoline, or electricity for motive power at the time. Macy repairs on gasoline trucks may have been rather expensive in the early years because this equipment was often used night and day for weeks on end, and the five-ton truck sometimes had to carry nine tons! Fisher Motor Vehicle Co. to Macy's, Jan. 12, 1903; Macy's to Fisher Motor Vehicle Co., Jan. 15, 1903; Macy's to Monham & Magor, Nov. 14, 1904.

61. *Wall Street Daily News*, Oct. 22, 1906.

62. *Dry Goods Econ.*, Jan. 5, 1910.

63. Macy advts., Oct., 1939; interviews with Percy S. Straus. See also Appel, *op. cit.*, pp. 68–69.

64. Advt., N. Y. *Evening Post*, Nov. 7, 1902; accounting records of R. H.

Macy & Co., Private Bankers. Macy's has occasionally publicized the No. 1 D/A identity card, bearing the date 1901. This card, issued to Mrs. Isidor Straus, was part of a preliminary experiment with the proposed D/A system, confined to members of the Straus family. The system was not opened for public use until November, 1902.

65. Advt., N. Y. *Herald*, Dec. 7, 1897; Macy's to Charles A. Fulle, Aug. 12, 1902, and to M. R. Hutchison, Sept. 22, 1902; Lambert, *op. cit.*, pp. 75–76. Credit for originating the deposit account business is attributed to Nathan Straus ("Nathan Straus," *Dict. of Amer. Biog.*), but Percy S. Straus assures me that his father, Isidor Straus, was the one who decided to introduce it into Macy's. Certainly Isidor's knowledge of banking would make him the more likely source. A letter from Macy's to F. Tennyson Neely Co., Nov. 4, 1901, explicitly states that Percy S. Straus was considering plans for the department, although Mr. Percy says now that his father was primarily responsible for the whole venture.

According to information given to me by one employee, the idea of having the D/A system was brought to Macy's by an English accountant, employed in the Macy bookkeeping department. He is said to have got the idea from the Army and Navy Co-operative Store in London. It is possible that Nathan, recognizing the possibilities of the plan, persuaded Isidor to adopt it. Beyond this possibility, I am firmly convinced that Nathan had nothing to do with planning or operating the D/A system.

66. Letters to Mrs. Julie Leerburger, Dec. 13, 1907, J. B. Stokes, Feb. 10, 1908, and to others between 1903 and 1909.

For many years before 1895 the Hager Store in Lancaster, Pa., accepted deposits from its customers, but the money was left for a year at a time for safe-keeping and interest, not in prepayment for purchases. Gras, "An Old Store Still Young," pp. 37–38.

67. Advts., N. Y. *Herald*, Nov. 30, 1906, May 21, 1907; semiannual statements, 1903–14.

68. No data are available for retail credit sales for the years 1902–14, but figures reported by department stores to the Harvard Bureau of Business Research show that department stores typically sell more than 50% of their volume for credit rather than for cash. Figures given in *Dry Goods Econ.*, Sept. 28, 1918, indicate that the proportion of cash business was somewhat higher 25 years ago.

69. Macy's to Clark Williams, Mar. 6, 1908, and to George C. Van Tuyl, Feb. 21, 1914; Jesse I. Straus to James A. Parker, Jan. 25, 1915.

70. Semiannual statements, 1902–14; the Black Book; interviews with officers and employees.

71. There have been a number of accounts of the *Titanic* disaster besides those which appeared in the New York papers in April, 1912, and the touching episode of the Strauses is substantially the same in all. Percy S. Straus told me

about the presence of Badenoch on the *Carpathia*. In a recent novel, Robert Prechtl's *Titanic* (N. Y., 1940), Isidor Straus is presented as an intensely orthodox Jew, but in fact he was not. In a letter written to Charles W. Eliot on Sept. 19, 1909, a few years before Isidor's death, he wrote: "While I was born in the Jewish faith, I have never belonged to any synagogue or temple; I have brought up a family of six children, all now having families of their own, none of whom have ever associated themselves with any religious organization. I have simply been unwilling to conform outwardly to ceremonies and creeds against which my inner soul rebelled, having always lived in the belief that to be honest with one's self is the first essential to enable a conscientious man to maintain his self-respect."

72. It is probably impossible to obtain a complete, objective account of the relations between Nathan Straus and his nephews. I have talked to Percy S. Straus about the matter at great length and have also discussed it with Hugh Grant Straus (Nathan's son). It is only fair to the latter to say that he does not agree with some of the views presented here. However, my account is supported by statements from a large number of Macy employees and executives who were personally acquainted with both Isidor and Nathan Straus; it it also supported by a number of letters among Percy Straus's personal papers which I have been permitted to see but which, for family reasons, cannot be quoted, with the single exception of the letter reproduced here in which Nathan Straus signified his willingness to sell on the terms set forth. There is no disagreement between the two branches of the family as to the main facts. It is natural that there should be a difference of opinion as to the sources of friction. My own view is that circumstances over which neither side had any control simply made the situation untenable.

73. Original letter in the files of Percy S. Straus, written without address or salutation but obviously intended for Jesse, Percy, and Herbert Straus, and signed by Nathan Straus. In view of this communication the fairness of the terms of sale cannot be questioned.

74. Data supplied through the courtesy of Hugh Grant Straus from his father's private account books.

CHAPTER XIII

1. Advt., N. Y. *Times*, Jan. 25, 1910.
2. For a general statement of the problem of resale price maintenance see E. R. A. Seligman and Robert A. Love, *Price Cutting and Price Maintenance* (N. Y., 1932), esp. pp. 19–44. Advocates of the Stevens bill explicitly stated that the fight was between department stores, chain stores, and mail-order houses, on the one hand, and small independent retail stores, on the other (*Jour. of Comm.*, Mar. 25, 1915).
3. In addition to the legal sources cited below, this section is based on inter-

views with Lillian Kinnear, formerly head of the Macy book department, and Percy S. Straus, together with contemporary correspondence, in the period from Apr. 15, 1901, through 1914, between various Macy executives, on the one hand, and, on the other, George S. Emory, manager of the American Publishers' Assoc., book-dealers, purchasing agents, and others.

4. Discussion of the suit of the Bobbs-Merrill Co. is based upon *Bobbs-Merrill Co.* v. *Isidor Straus & Nathan Straus*, 139 Fed. Rep. 155 (1905), 147 Fed. Rep. 15 (1906), and 210 U. S. 339 (1908). The Scribner's suit involved essentially the same legal points and court decisions; in fact, the Scribner's and Bobbs-Merrill cases were heard together by the Supreme Court because the same questions were involved. See *Charles Scribner & Arthur H. Scribner* v. *Isidor Straus & Nathan Straus* and *Charles Scribner's Sons, Inc.* v. *Isidor Straus & Nathan Straus*, 139 Fed. Rep. 193 (1905), 147 Fed. Rep. 28 (1906), 210 U. S. 339 (1908).

5. Statements concerning the Macy suit against the Publishers' Assoc. are based on *Isidor Straus & Nathan Straus* v. *American Publishers' Assoc.*, 85 App. Div. 446 (1903), 177 N. Y. 473 (1904), 127 App. Div. 935 (1908), 193 N. Y. 496 (1908), 199 N. Y. 548 (1910), 231 U. S. 222 (1913); also *Literary Digest*, Dec. 13, 1913, pp. 1158–1159.

6. The discussion of the Victor case is based upon *Victor Talking Machine Co.* v. *Jesse I. Straus, Percy S. Straus, & Herbert N. Straus, . . . trading as R. H. Macy & Co.*, 222 Fed. Rep. 524 (1915), 225 Fed. Rep. 535 (1915), 230 Fed. Rep. 449 (1916), 280 Fed. Rep. 717 (1916), 243 U. S. 490 (1917); *Straus* v. *Victor Talking Machine Co.*, 297 Fed. Rep. 791 (1924); *Jour. of Comm.*, Mar. 25, 1915; testimony of Edmond E. Wise in *Regulation of Prices, Hearings . . . on H. R. 13568* (Washington, 1917), pp. 4–25.

7. The merchandise sold by Macy's at prices fixed by the manufacturer in 1908 included Community Silver, E & W Collars, Arrow Collars, Bissell Carpet Sweepers, Thermos Bottles, Eastman Kodak equipment and supplies, Weed Tire Chains, Victor Phonographs and Records, Columbia Phonographs and Records, Gillette Razors, Star Razors, Autostrop Razors, and a long list of proprietary drugs and toiletries. In addition, the firm could not buy Singer Sewing Machines and Stetson Hats directly from the manufacturers but did manage to obtain them from other sources. The merchandise which Macy's refused to carry included E & W Shirts, Star Shirts, Sapolio, Fownes Gloves, Waterman Pens, Rajah Silks, Spaulding Tennis Rackets and Golf Balls, Whitall Wilton Rugs, and the Edison Phonograph and Records. Jesse Straus to E. E. Wise, May 6, 1908.

8. Correspondence between Macy's and L. C. Potter in 1901–02, especially letter of Jan. 14, 1902; interviews with Percy S. Straus and Lillian Kinnear.

9. J. E. Manix to Percy S. Straus, Jan. 6, 1912.

10. Macy's to Julian Ralph, Aug. 29, 1902; L. Marx to Macy's, Feb. 7, 1903.

11. Interviews with Percy S. Straus and Lillian Kinnear.

NOTES TO CHAPTER XIII

12. Refusal to make agreements is indicated in letters between Macy's and D. C. Hall & Co., Jan., 1903; H. J. Miller Cart Co., Feb., 1903; Nestor Gianarlis Co., Feb., 1906; N. Erlanger, Blumgart & Co., Oct., 1909–Jan., 1910. Dropping of price-fixed lines is indicated in Macy's to Kampfe Bros., Sept.–Oct., 1905, and to Edward Blum, May, 1908. Conclusion of agreements in letter of agreement with Columbia Graphophone Co., Jan. 16, 1907, and Nov. 26, 1909; Macy's to Howard P. Dennison, Apr. 2, 1907; Charles J. Liebman to Percy S. Straus, Dec. 15, 1914.

13. Letters between Macy's and Robert H. Ingersoll & Bro., Dec. 3–9, 1904; also correspondence between Macy's and Gillette Sales Co., May–Sept., 1905, and U. S. Post Office Inspector, May, 1906, revealing that Macy's had got hold of a shipment of razors which had been sold for export only. Violation of agreement was also alleged in Park & Tilford to Macy's, Mar. 28, 1902; Thermalite Co. to Macy's, Oct. 9, 1905.

14. Macy's to U. S. Dept. of Justice, Oct. 26, 1910. Partial success in obtaining Whitall rugs and Victor products revealed in letters from Harold Steinfeld to Percy S. Straus, Sept. 12, 1910, and H. E. Oliver to Jesse I. Straus, Apr. 8, 1916, as well as in the evidence produced in *Victor Talking Machine Co.* v. *Straus*, cited above.

15. Testimony of Percy S. Straus published in *Regulation of Prices. Hearings . . . on H. R. 13568*, pp. 114–159. Beyond the statements in the hearings it is impossible to verify the accuracy of the statement about the quality of Macy's private brands or the profits they yielded. Then, as now, the same manufacturer often produced the private brand which Macy's used in competition with a national brand and there is little doubt but that the quality was comparable. There can be no question about the existence of a substantial difference in price.

For additional discussion of the use of private brands, see Neil H. Borden, *The Economic Effects of Advertising* (Chicago, 1942), pp. 39–40, 589–606.

16. Perhaps the most comprehensive studies available are Seligman and Love, *op. cit.*, and Albert Haring, *Price Cutting and Its Control by Manufacturers* (N. Y., 1935). The first-mentioned contains a fairly complete bibliography. See also H. R. Tosdal, "Price Maintenance," *Amer. Econ. Rev.*, Mar., 1918, pp. 28–47.

17. F. W. Taussig, "Price Maintenance," *Proceedings* of the 27th annual meeting of the Amer. Econ. Assoc., Dec., 1915, p. 184.

18. Macy advts., 1902–15; letter from Macy's to the *Literary Digest*, undated but written in Dec., 1913; Macy's to Mrs. James M. Pereles, June 30, 1916; interviews with Percy S. Straus.

19. For a summary of the high-handed tactics used in obtaining the passage of the so-called "fair-trade laws," see *Final Report and Recommendations* of the Temporary National Economic Committee (Washington, 1941), pp. 232–249. This material should be read in conjunction with the particularly edifying

questions and arguments raised by Senator Tydings, joint author of the Miller-Tydings act. In the first 32 States in which "fair-trade laws" were passed, the proposed legislation was rushed through without any public hearings whatever.

20. See Julian Huxley, "Analogies: Dangerous and Otherwise," *Yale Review*, Spring, 1940, esp. pp. 544–555; see also his *Essays of a Biologist* (Penguin ed., 1939), esp. "Progress, Biological and Other" and "Biology and Sociology."

21. Cf. Ralph M. Hower, *The History of an Advertising Agency: N. W. Ayer & Son at Work, 1869–1939* (Cambridge, 1939), esp. pp. 488–500.

22. There is a shortage of Macy documentary material for the period from 1902 to 1914, and it is never easy, even when source material is plentiful, to trace administrative changes in a concrete way. The evolution involved is too subtle and intangible to leave much direct evidence. I have had to rely to a large extent upon the testimony of Macy executives who lived through the experience and helped to bring about reforms, especially Ernest Katz, Percy S. Straus, William Titon, the late William J. Wells, and Charles O. Winship.

23. The original letter was given back to the Macy firm within the past five years. Of course, the size of the business in 1874 permitted an executive to leave more to memory than would have been justifiable in 1900.

24. According to Percy S. Straus one buyer, receiving about $4,000 annually from Macy's, was discovered to be maintaining a fairly luxurious yacht!

25. Macy's to Jeroloman & Arrowsmith, Feb. 11, 1903, to Spiegelberg & Wise, Feb. 11, 1903, to C. W. Lyford & Son, Dec. 30, 1903, and to Rosenstein Bros., June 23, 1911. As late as 1915 the Macy management still found it necessary to remind buyers about having future orders signed by a member of the firm (minutes of the Advisory Council, May 28, 1914, and Sept. 24, 1915).

26. Advt., New Haven *Leader*, Nov. 15, 1902; interviews with Percy S. Straus.

27. Interviews with Messrs. Katz, Percy S. Straus, and Wells.

A letter from the Crane Co. to Macy's, Nov. 2, 1901, indicates that Macy's had made an attempt to hire college graduates as early as 1900, but the main emphasis upon such preparation came after 1912. Letters from Macy's to the Harvard Alumni Appointment Office, Apr. 13, 1912, Oct. 19 and 30, 1914.

28. Minutes of the Macy Managers' Assoc., 1908–19.

29. The exact date of the formation of the Board of Operations cannot be determined. The earliest bound volume of minutes starts in July, 1911, but scattered memos indicate that the board was functioning, perhaps informally, in 1908.

30. Statement announcing the organization of the Council, undated but apparently about Feb. 1, 1914. The minutes show that the first meeting took place Feb. 9, 1914.

31. Advisory Council Minutes, Jan. 11, 1918.

NOTES TO CHAPTER XIII

32. B. of O. Minutes, 1911–12; Macy's to Auerbach Co., Nov. 4, 1911; *Dry Goods Econ.*, Jan. 25, 1913, p. 81.
33. Advisory Council Minutes, 1914–19.
34. *Ibid.*; interviews with officers and employees.
35. Departmental Net Showings, 1905–19; interviews with Ernest Katz. An isolated accounting memo shows that an attempt was being made in 1901 to allocate rent to the various selling floors, but apparently nothing further was done until 1905.

In calculating the departmental results, certain constant expense ratios were applied to sales in all departments: executive salaries — 1.54%, expense — .31%, prepaid freight — .20%, repairs — .32%, stationery — .33%, heat, light, and power — .66%, catalogs and mail orders — .80%, loss on fixtures — .28%, sundry expense — .48%. The rate per season of delivery expense varied according to departments, from a minimum of 2.25% to 9% for furniture. Rent was charged on the basis of floor space used, the rate varying from $1.45 per square foot for main floor departments to $.253 on the fifth floor. Insurance and interest charges varied, apparently depending upon the value of the average inventory. The various percentage rates varied from year to year, of course, but no important changes were made in the method of calculation, with the exception that in 1912 delivery and packing expenses were allocated on the basis of the packages handled. The delivery charge per package for most departments was $.1259.

36. Semiannual statements, 1915–16; interviews with Ernest Katz.
37. Cf. National Retail Dry Goods Association, *Twenty-five Years of Retailing* (N. Y., 1936), pp. 36, 43.
38. Macy's to A. R. Pardington, May 25, 1906, to Elliott-Fisher Co., Sept. 20, 1906, to J. S. Bache & Co., Sept. 8, 1910, to M. C. Kiser Co., Nov. 10, 1910; B. of O. Minutes, Aug. 10 and 24, 1911, June 20, 1912, May 1 and Oct. 30, 1913, Jan. 18, Feb. 8, and May 17, 1917, Oct. 16 and 30, 1919; letter to D/A customers, Dec. 11, 1915.
39. A report of the study, *The Delivery System of R. H. Macy & Co. of New York* by H. F. Thompson, H. L. Manley, and A. L. Pashek, was published as Bulletin No. 6 (Sept., 1914) of the Research Division of the Electrical Engineering Dept., M. I. T. See also *Dry Goods Econ.*, Apr. 22, 1916, p. 79.
40. Advisory Council Minutes, 1914–19; B. of O. Minutes, 1912–19.
41. Minutes, Macy Mgrs.' Assoc., Mar. 1, 1910; Advisory Council Minutes, 1914–19; *Dry Goods Econ.*, Feb. 13, 1915, p. 39.
42. Report of Agnes Melville Brown, undated but written in 1917; *Dry Goods Econ.*, Dec. 14, 1918, p. 227.
43. Advisory Council Minutes, 1918; form used for reporting on vendors.
44. N. Y. *Times*, June 26, 1914; *Dry Goods Econ.*, June 27, 1914; *Jour. of Com.*, Jan. 2 and 3, 1914, Jan. 4, 1915, Jan. 4, 1916.
45. Letters, H. E. Oliver to Jesse I. Straus, Dec. 21, 1915, Mar. 31 and Apr.

8, 1916; Thorp, *op. cit.*, pp. 142–143; Warren and Pearson, *op. cit.*, pp. 20, 31–32.

46. Advisory Council Minutes, esp. Mar. 9 and 22, 1917, and Aug. 30, 1918.

47. *Ibid.*, Dec. 6, 1915, July 13 and 20, 1917; interviews with Otto Linnert, for many years in charge of Macy's foreign buying operations.

48. B. of O. Minutes, July 12, 1917, May 16, 24, and 31, 1918; advts., Oct., 1918; letter to employees, undated but late 1917.

49. Minutes, Macy Mgrs.' Assoc., Apr. 1, 1913, Sept. 2, 1915, Apr. 11, 1916; B. of O. Minutes, 1915–18; Advisory Council Minutes, 1915–18; *Dry Goods Econ.*, June 28, 1913, p. 17, Dec. 6, 1913, p. 29, Aug. 28, 1915, p. 11, Nov. 27, 1915, p. 55, Apr. 1, 1916, p. 151; *Sparks*, Oct., 1918; instructional booklets, 1916–19.

50. Advisory Council Minutes, Nov. 15 and Dec. 27, 1918, Jan. 3, 1919.

51. *Ibid.*, July 27 and Aug. 3, 1917; B. of O. Minutes, July 12, 1917, Aug. 23, 1918, June 13, 1918; *Dry Goods Econ.*, Aug. 24, 1918, p. 5.

52. B. of O. Minutes, 1918.

53. Advisory Council Minutes, Nov. 15, 1918; *Dry Goods Econ.*, Feb. 15, 1919, pp. 71, 73.

54. B. of O. Minutes, Sept. 19, 1918.

55. Telegram, Macy's to Roland Grangle, receiver, Feb. 18, 1904; advts., Feb. 10 and 12, 1907, June 14, 1910; letters, Macy's to Stern & Wolf, Jan. 9, 1910, and to A. A. Brager, June 10, 1912; interviews with Percy S. Straus.

56. Advisory Council Minutes, June 11, 1915; also 1914–18 *passim*.

57. *Ibid.*, July 2, 1915.

58. *Ibid.*, July 9, 1915.

59. *Ibid.*, Nov. 16, 1917; also 1916 and 1917 *passim*.

60. *Ibid.*, 1917 and 1918. Macy advertising at this time — circulars used in the store as well as the newspaper advertisements — reflect the growing interest in style.

61. National Civic Federation, *R. H. Macy & Co. . . . Report upon Condition of Employes . . .* (N. Y., 1915); *Dry Goods Econ.*, Jan. 25, 1913, p. 19.

62. Interviews with employees; employees' names appearing on various documents, 1900–19; Macy's to Miss K. F. Lawrence, July 15, 1907.

63. Percy S. Straus, quoted in *Dry Goods Econ.*, Jan. 16, 1915, p. 151; form letter to sales clerks, 1906; Macy's to Leslie Graff, May 27, 1913.

The quota was determined by a department's average selling expense for the preceding five years. If, for example, the average was 5% and a clerk's salary was $10 a week, his quota would be $200 (at which point his salary would equal the departmental selling cost) and he would receive a commission on all sales above that amount. In 1913 this commission was 1%.

64. Nat'l. Civic Fed. *Report*.

65. *Ibid.*

66. *Ibid.*; report of A. R. Dallmeyer, a student at the Harvard Business

School, setting forth his experiences while working at Macy's in the summer of 1915; *Red Star Rays*, Spring, 1916; Advisory Council Minutes, June 28, 1918.

67. *Ibid.*, Apr. 25 and May 16, 1919; *Dry Goods Econ.*, June 28, 1913, p. 36, and May 30, 1914, p. 60.

68. Macy's to M. B. Mabie, Aug. 11, 1910, and to B. J. Conroy, Jan. 4, 1911; Jesse I. Straus to Isaac N. Seligman, Jan. 16, 1911; handbills of the United Brotherhood of Carpenters and Joiners of America, local No. 247, Nov., 1910; stickers, cards, and calendars headed "Don't meet me at Macy's," Dec., 1910, and Jan. 1911; interviews with James Wood, Abbie Golden, and Miss Herring.

Information on the development of organized labor in Macy's is extremely scanty. It is clear, however, that the store management did not look upon labor unions with favor.

69. Memo, Isidor Straus to Pitt, June 19, 1903; Macy's to Miss E. C. Wheeler, Mar. 30, 1905; article in N. Y. *American*, Feb. 2, 1908; Nat'l. Civic Fed. *Report*; Advisory Council Minutes, Apr. 22, 1918.

70. Memo from Cowlishaw to Percy S. Straus, Oct. 23, 1909; *Dry Goods Econ.*, May 20, 1911, p. 57; Nat'l. Civic Fed. *Report*.

71. *Ibid.*; interviews with employees.

72. Committee of Fourteen in New York City, *Department Store Investigation* (N. Y., 1915); interview with Marjorie Sidney.

73. *Ibid.*; Exec. Memo, 1915-19; B. of O. Minutes, 1915-19.

It is difficult in this brief account to state clearly the personnel problem which arose in Macy's and to outline the solution required, but the reader will find an excellent discussion of comparable situations, in terms which the layman can understand, in F. J. Roethlisberger, *Management and Morale* (Cambridge, 1941).

In point of fact, Macy's had undertaken a certain amount of training some years earlier. Departmental managers, for example, frequently called their clerks together for lectures on merchandise as early as 1909, and in 1912 the firm arranged for Miss Kelly (known to the employees as "The Duchess") to give a series of talks on salesmanship (*Dry Goods Econ.*, Apr. 24, 1909); Nat'l. Civic Fed. *Report*; interviews with employees. One result of the firm's efforts to improve relations with employees was the publication (starting in 1918) of a monthly magazine for the staff. Christened *Sparks*, it has flourished ever since.

74. That Macy's had long been interested in obtaining employees of better education and offering them better opportunities is evident from a talk given by Sylvester Byrnes, general manager of Macy's in 1919 ("The Art of Selling," *Dry Goods Econ.*, Apr. 10, 1909, p. 51). For a good description of the average department store worker in the days before World War I, see M. R. Cranston, "Girl Behind the Counter," *World To-Day*, Mar., 1906.

75. The subject of the cost of distribution is far too complicated to be discussed here, and there is very little reliable evidence available for a satisfac-

tory discussion of the period before 1920. One recent study of value (though not without defects) is Paul W. Stewart and J. Frederic Dewhurst, *Does Distribution Cost Too Much?* (N. Y., 1939).

For the period since 1921 (together with scattered figures for a few years earlier) we have the valuable and comprehensive data compiled by Malcolm P. McNair, Stanley F. Teele, and Frances G. Mulhearn, *Distribution Costs: an International Digest* (Boston, 1941).

76. Remarks of Jesse I. Straus before the Nat'l. Ret. Dry Goods Assoc. quoted in *Dry Goods Econ.*, Feb. 5, 1919, pp. 71, 73.

INDEX

INDEX

Abraham & Straus, 156, 221, 228, 243–244, 247, 301, 312

Accounting, 92–93, 109, 172, 220, 224, 232, 265, 370–372, 417–422.
See also Operating figures; Profits

Adams Co., 267, 294

Additions,
buildings, 107, 284–286, 314–327, 330–331, 465, 468–469;
lines, 30, 163, 330, 439, 451.
See also Affiliated stores; Diversification; Expansion; Innovations; Service

Adjustments, *see* Return privileges

Administration, 18, 114, 157–190, 251, 282–283, 311–313, 330–348, 349, 353–408, 476.
See also Control; Management; Policy

Advertising, 48–65, 118;
allowances, 241, 268;
control of, 297, 300, 367–369, 403, 461;
cost of, 47, 132–133, 139, 177, 180–181, 258–259, 265, 275, 393–395;
institutional, 18–22, 51–52, 60–64, 164–168, 271–274, 335, 412;
magazine, 118, 164, 267–268, 443;
newspaper, 13, 17–30, 54–65, 78–80, 96, 113, 170, 182, 264–275, 432, 443;
seasonal, 57, 118, 169–170;
typography, 56–57, 431, 443.
See also Catalogs; Exhibitions; Trade-marks; Window displays

Advisory Council, 367–374, 377–382, 385, 476

Affiliated stores, 366, 404

Agreements, *see* Partnerships

Air-conditioning, 286, 400.
See also Ventilation

Albums, 106, 162, 421

Altman, B., & Co., 168–169, 286, 315, 372

American Booksellers' Association, 353

American Publishers' Association, 290, 353–356

Analysis of
D/A transactions, 343;
expenses, 257–259;
revenue, 256, 390;
sales transactions, 109, 171, 184, 254–257, 328;
of stock turnover, 186.
See also Operating figures

Annexes, 284–286.
See also Additions

Anniversary sales, 428

Arnold, Constable & Co., 43, 51, 54, 92, 142, 144, 168, 315, 453, 455

Art embroidery, 238, 303

Artists' supplies, 163, 238

Assets, 44, 133, 158, 224, 262, 396.
See also specific assets

Assortments, 188, 234, 373, 377, 381, 403.
See also Bargain lots; Diversification; Purchasing policy

Astor, John Jacob, II, 169

Athletic equipment, *see* Sporting goods

Auctions as source of supply, 11, 22, 28, 47, 241;
selling at, 14

Automobiles, 276, 331, 461.
  See also Delivery
Average
  expense per transaction, 376;
  inventory, 186;
  salary, 376;
  sales per employee, 47, 132, 192, 376

Badenoch, John A., 345, 365, 374, 473
Baking powder, 247
Bamberger, L., & Co., 366, 404
Banking functions, 344, 393.
  See also Deposit Account Department
Bankrupt stocks, 22.
  See also Auctions
Bargain counters, 225, 332
Bargain lots, 22, 51, 188, 241-242, 364, 381.
  See also Auctions; Purchasing policy
Bargaining, 89, 94.
  See also One-price policy
Barter, 81
Basement store, 104, 462
Bathing suits, 239
Bazaars, 3-4, 69, 71
Belfast, Ireland, 244, 271
Belle Jardinière, 91
Benefits to employees, 305, 384, 453.
  See also Macy Mutual Aid Association
Berlin (Germany), 242-243, 377
Bicycles and accessories, 235, 246, 248-249, 276, 283, 461
Blankets, 161, 239, 421
Bliss, George, 218, 229
Bloomingdale Bros., Inc., 267, 314
Blouses, 239, 246
Board of Operations, 367-369, 378-380, 476
Bobbs-Merrill Co., 354-355, 474
Bon Marché, 72, 90-91, 121, 142, 249, 413-415, 449

Bonuses and prizes, 304, 342, 373, 383
Bookkeepers, 43, 66, 114.
  See also Accounting
Books, 6-7, 74, 102, 106, 128, 136, 145, 161-162, 173-174, 238, 242, 289-290, 353-357, 474
Boston (Mass.), 11, 80, 82, 87, 94, 221, 436, 454
Boucicaut, Aristide, 73, 413-414
Bowen, McNamee & Co., 43, 94, 429
Bowyer, Marie, 194, 204
Boys' clothing and furnishings, 105-106, 162, 174, 239, 302, 421
Branch stores, 271, 404, 459.
  See also Affiliated stores
Brand policy, 112-113; 351.
  See also Private brands; Trademarks
Breakage, 137
Bribery, 364, 476
Bronzes, 175, 238
Brooklyn (N.Y.), 156, 221, 227, 312, 375
Buildings, 42-43, 98, 169, 231, 262-264, 284-286, 314-327, 399-400, 465, 468
  See also Additions; Equipment
Burdett, William, 206
Burglary, 47
Burkhalter, C., & Co., 241
Business conditions, 11, 40, 48, 352.
  See also Depressions; Panics
Business failures, 11-13, 441.
  See also Depressions
Business policy, 18-21.
  See also Credit; Distribution; Diversification; Guarantees; Price; Product; Purchasing; Return privileges
Bustles, 161-163, 175, 421
Buyers,
  duties of, 114-115, 194, 304, 443;
  European trips of, 194, 242, 452;

management of, 52, 116–117, 304, 363–365, 377–379;
salaries of, 125, 194, 304;
women as, 194
Buying, *see* Purchasing policy
Buying habits, consumer, 75, 146–148, 236, 427
Byrnes, Sylvester, 366–367, 374

Cable, transatlantic, 41
Cafeteria for employees, 325, 384
California, 12–15, 42
Callahan & Morrissey, 280
Candy, 106, 136, 162, 174, 237–238, 247, 421
Canes, 162, 239, 421
Canvas, 421
Capitalization, 17, 44, 128, 150, 155, 157–159, 223–230, 348
Car cards, 268
Carlsbad (Bohemia), 246, 271
Carpenters, 115, 235, 385
Carpets, 239, 458.
See also Rugs
Carriages, 235
Cash girls, 43, 93, 104, 115, 166, 193, 196, 200–201, 384, 439, 452
Cash policy,
in buying, 17, 20–21, 29, 49–50, 165, 243;
in selling, 13, 18, 20, 27, 46–49, 61, 91, 118, 165, 212, 282, 331, 341
Cash Ribbon House, 51
Cashiers, 43, 93, 115, 166, 193, 453
Cash-Time plan, 404–405
Catalogs, 118, 164, 269, 444;
cost of, 332
Centralization, 68–69, 71, 117, 198, 443
Ceramics, 165, 169
Chain stores, 69, 75, 156, 351, 399
Chamansky, Louis J., 374
Changes, 314–316.
See also Additions; Diversification; Economic changes; Expansion; Innovations; Service
Chapman, 70.
See also Pedlars
Charge accounts, *see* Cash-Time plan; Deposit Account Department
Charity, *see* Philanthropies
Chase, M. H., 452, 459
Checking of incoming merchandise, *see* Marking department
Chemnitz (Germany), 243
Chester (Pa.), 247, 459
Chicago, 202, 221, 241, 265, 324, 454.
See also Marshall Field & Co.
Children as employees, 383.
See also Cash girls
Children's clothing, 421–422
China and glassware, 90–91, 104, 106, 111, 118, 120, 133, 137, 145, 162, 175, 187, 238, 245–246, 255, 287, 422.
See also Leased departments; Straus, L., & Sons
Chocolat Menier, 241
Christmas season, 64, 118, 125, 169, 183–185, 192, 201, 275, 281, 306, 333, 383, 400–401
Cincinnati, 82
Civil War, 124, 216;
economic effects, 24, 48, 53, 194, 232
Claflin, H. B., Co., 125, 249, 375
Clearance sales, 52, 119, 326, 431;
advertising of, 18–19, 22.
See also Closing-out sales
Clerks, 194–196.
See also Employees; Salesforce; Salesmen; Saleswomen
Cloaks, 106, 161–162, 173–174, 239, 287.
See also Suits and cloaks
Clocks, 175, 238

Closing-out sales, 18–19, 22, 29–30, 58.
See also Clearance sales
Clothing, *see specific items*
Coffee, 246, 250
Collars and cuffs, 162, 422
C.O.D. sales, 380, 471
Combination, horizontal, 75
Commercial bribery, 364, 476
Commission sales, 331
Committee of Fourteen, 387–388
Comparison Department, 373, 402
Comparison of owned and leased departments, 109, 133–135, 171–175, 182–190, 220–226, 255, 456.
See also Ratio of leased to total sales
Compensation, *see* Bonuses; Salaries; Wages
Competition, 14, 18, 26–29, 41, 51, 77, 102, 151–153, 156, 169, 189, 242, 249, 257, 263–267, 274, 286–294, 335.
See also Price wars
Complaints, handling of, 282.
See also Return privileges
Consignment selling, 221, 439.
See also Leased departments
Constantinople, 243
Consumer demand,
changes in, 249, 252;
creation of, 91–92.
See also Advertising; Display; Sales promotion
Contests, 119, 169
Control
of stock, 134, 417–422, 451;
of quality, 248.
See also Accounting; Advertising; Buyers; Employees; Management; Management control; Sales control; Stock control
Controversy as to land site, 318–322, 468–469

Convenience of department stores, 165–166, 447, 465
Cooke, Jay, 32
Coöperative organization of employees, 385, 479.
See also Macy Mutual Aid Association; Unionization
Corsets, 64, 99, 105, 114, 161–162, 173, 175, 238, 246, 421
Cost of
distribution, 294, 479–480;
doing business, 47, 130–133, 257–260, 332, 477;
goods, 135–136, 139, 175–178, 186, 284, 456;
living, 195;
sales, 376, 478.
See also specific items
Credit, 13, 45, 91, 427–429, 437
Crossman, Cora, 194, 200
Curtains, 102, 105, 162, 238, 422
Cushman, Belle, 194–195
Cushman, E. F., 30
Customers,
classes of, 38–39, 316;
number of, 400;
privileged, 50, 430;
relations with, 188.
See also Return privileges

D/A, *see* Deposit Account Department
Damages, 356–357
Daniell, John, & Sons, 280, 315
Davison-Paxon Co., 404
Definitions, 67–70, 438
Delicatessen department, 330
Delivery, 90, 108, 114–115, 119, 180, 197–198, 279–280, 338–341, 372, 379, 400–401, 453, 471;
cost of, 132–133, 139, 177, 180–182, 258–260, 280–281, 339, 380, 394–395, 471, 477

Demand creation, *see* Advertising; Consumer demand; Sales promotion
Demonstrations, 277
Denning's, 168, 267, 280
Department stores, 3–4, 67–156;
definition, 67–70;
evolution, 4, 57–97, 411–416.
See also Europe
Departments,
dates of establishment, 238–239;
description of, 462–465;
list of, 161–162;
new, 30, 105–106, 160–162, 330–333, 439, 451;
rating, 421–422.
See also Operating figures; *specific departments; tables*
Deposit Account Department, 341–344, 366, 393, 472
Depreciation, 189, 262, 422
Depressions, 7, 11, 232–234, 264, 285, 296, 399.
See also Business conditions; Panics
Devotional merchandise, 235
Direct buying, 240, 255.
See also Middlemen, elimination of
Direct-mail advertising, 335.
See also Catalogs
Discounts, 50, 95, 130–131, 137, 173, 177, 180–184, 203, 255–256, 290–291, 354, 389–390, 430
Display, 91, 382;
technique of, 275–279, 334–335.
See also Exhibitions; Window displays
Dissolution, *see* Partnerships
Distribution,
cost of, 294, 479–480.
See also Marketing
Diversification, 70–88, 160–164;
of functions, 111;
of products, 23, 46, 68, 74, 98–106, 141–156, 234–237, 440.
See also Additions; Integration; Manufacturing by retailers; Wholesaling
Dolls, 100, 103, 106, 118, 136, 162, 173–174, 238, 421
Dress goods, 106, 160–162, 175, 238, 287–288, 421, 439.
See also Silks
Drugs, 161, 174, 239, 250.
See also Patent Medicines.
Drugstores, 83
Drunkenness, 200, 206
Dry goods, *see specific items*
Dull seasons, *see* Seasonal variations

Earnings, *see* Operating figures; Profits
Easter season, 170, 451
Economic changes, 10–11, 38–42, 45, 48, 146–156, 262–263, 337.
See also Civil War, economic effects
Ehrich Brothers, 266–267, 280, 294
Electrical equipment, 166, 262, 283, 400.
See also Illumination
Elevators, 262, 283, 324, 400
Embroideries, 12, 45–46, 55, 101–102, 105, 136, 161, 174, 238, 421
Emily Morgan, 7–10, 425
Employees,
benefits to, 305, 384, 386, 453;
nationality of, 383;
relations with, 104, 114–115, 193–194, 200–201, 366, 382–389;
training, 378–379, 388, 479.
See also Bonuses; Macy Mutual Aid Association; Number of employees; Salaries; Wages; Working conditions

England, 70, 434, 472.
See also London
Engraving department, 175, 239
Equipment, 96, 166, 262, 283–284, 384, 462–465, 469.
See also Buildings; Departments
Escalators, 324, 400
Ethics, 291, 350.
See also Competition
Europe,
 buying trips to, 103–104, 194, 242, 452;
 department stores in, 70–73, 88, 121, 141–143, 249, 411–416.
See also specific cities and countries
Exclusive agencies, 241
Executive Training Course, 379
Executives, *see* Administration; Employees; Management
Exhibitions, 118, 169, 225, 264, 325, 334, 461
Expansion, 22, 197, 234–237, 399–404.
See also Additions; Diversification
Expenses, *see* Cost; Operating figures

Factories of retailers, 246, 271, 459.
See also Manufacturing by retailers
Fair, The, 144
Fairs, mediaeval, 3–4, 69
Fancy dry goods, 17, 23, 46, 49, 103, 106, 136, 142, 145, 162, 173–174, 242, 414, 421, 442;
 definition, 438.
See also specific items
Fancy goods, definition, 438.
See also Fancy dry goods
Feathers, 101, 103, 106, 114, 136, 162, 174, 238, 421
Field, Leiter & Co., 144
Filene, Edward A., 301
Financing, 44–45, 326.
See also Accounting; Capitalization; Partnerships

Findings, 46.
See also Fancy dry goods; Notions; Trimmings
Fire extinguishers, 235
Firearms, 235
"Firsts," 142, 144–145, 160, 170, 413, 431, 446, 450
Fixed prices, *see* One-price policy
Fixtures, 262;
 depreciation of, 422.
See also Equipment
Flannels, 239
Floor coverings, 235.
See also Rugs
Floorwalkers, 115, 158, 194–195;
 women, 194.
See also Section managers
Flowers, 101, 103, 106, 114, 136, 162, 174, 238, 421
Fluctuations, *see* Business conditions; Cost of doing business; Volume of business
Food, *see* Groceries; Restaurant
Foreign offices, 163, 242–243, 271, 300, 377;
 services, 285–286.
See also Europe, buying trips; Imports
"Forty-Niners," 12–14
Foster, J. Sullivan, 94
Foster, Paul & Co., 241
Fox, George, 89, 436
France, 155, 241, 448–449.
See also Imports; Paris; *specific stores*
Fruit department, 330
Fuller, George A., Co., 322–323
Functions, *see* Diversification; Specialization
Furnishings, 103, 106.
See also Equipment; House furnishings; Men's furnishings

INDEX

Furniture, 103, 145, 234–235, 239, 241, 244, 261, 277, 285, 413–415; storage of, 283.
  See also House furnishings
Furs, 101, 103, 106, 136, 239, 421, 438; remodeling, 246, 250; storage, 235, 335–336

Garden supplies, 163
General manager, 366–367
General stores, 69, 78, 144
Georgia, 214–215, 242, 403
Germany, 214, 242–243, 377
Getchell, Margaret, *see* La Forge, Margaret Getchell
Gift merchandise, 183, 189; wrapping of, 333
Gilds, 71
Gimbel Bros., 92, 324, 329
Glassware, 106; manufacture of, 246.
  See also China and glassware; Straus, L., & Sons
Gloves, 43, 106, 111, 136, 162, 173–174, 238, 421; Foster, 164, 241, 277
Gold, as medium of exchange, 110, 119, 138, 441; importation of, 42; rush, 12–15
Goodwill, 226
Government regulation, 77, 156, 248, 349–360, 405–406, 473–475
Grading-up, 313, 381–382, 402.
  See also Product policy
Greenhut-Siegel, Cooper Co., 375.
  See also Siegel-Cooper Co.
Groceries, 103, 156, 235, 239, 241, 246, 333, 365, 403, 458
Gross margin, 136–137, 173–185, 256; definition of, 129, 173.
  See also Operating figures; Profits

Growth, 107–113.
  See also Additions; Expansion
Guarantees, 22, 29; money-back, 53–54.
  See also Return privileges

Haberdashery, 72
Hager Store, 144, 472
Hahne & Co., 375
Halles Centrales, 71
Hancock, Thomas, 74
Handicraft, 71
Handkerchiefs, 55, 162–163, 173, 175, 238, 244, 422
Harness, 235, 238, 246, 249
Harrod's, 68, 446
Haskins, David, 198
Hats, 103, 162, 174, 238–239, 421.
  See also Millinery
Haverhill (Mass.), 16–33, 46, 87, 194
Haverhill *Gazette*, 24–25, 29
Heard, Chas., & Co., 51
Hearn, James A., & Son, 168–169, 266, 288, 291–294
Heating facilities, 43, 262, 400
Hitchcock, W., & Co., 72, 90
Holidays, 202, 307.
  See also Christmas season; Vacations; Working conditions
Horizontal combination, 75
Horses, use of, 40, 108, 281, 339–340, 401.
  See also Delivery
Hosiery, 101, 103, 106, 114, 136, 161, 174, 238, 421
Houghton, George W., 11
Houghton, Louisa, *see* Macy, Mrs. Rowland Hussey
Houghton, Samuel S., 12, 44–45, 48, 123, 429, 444
Houghton & Dutton, 12
Hours of work, 200–202, 306, 378, 384–385, 453–454

House furnishings, 99, 103, 106, 137, 145, 162, 174, 234, 238, 413–415, 421.
See also specific items
House organs, 268, 479
Hovey, C. F., Co., 87
Hovey, Williams & Co., 87
Hunking, Caleb Dustin, 44, 429

Illumination, 166–167, 262, 283, 325, 400, 450
Immigrants, 86;
as customers, 286;
as employees, 196, 199
Imports, 11, 21, 28, 38, 47, 55, 87, 100, 111, 120, 130, 135, 163, 241, 246, 377–378, 403, 441–442
Improvements, 274, 283–286, 372.
See also Changes
Income from
jobbing, 130–131, 178–180;
taxes, 109–110.
See also Margins; Profits; Volume of business
Incorporation, 398, 407
Industrial Revolution, 85–86, 146, 149
Infants' goods, 102, 111, 162, 174, 235, 239
Ingersoll watches, 358
Innovations, 76, 235, 449, 469.
See also Additions; Changes
Installment sales, 405
Insurance, 139
Integration, 70–88, 92, 107–113, 141–156, 160–164, 249.
See also Manufacturing by retailers
Interdepartmental relations, 360–363
Interest, 127, 130, 177, 259;
on cash-time purchases, 405;
on D/A deposits, 341
Interviews
with applicants, 401;
with public, 373;
with vendors, 403
Inventory,
average, 186;
control, 134, 417–422, 451;
ratio to assets, 133–134, 261, 396;
value of, 129, 134.
See also Stock-turn
Ireland, 244, 271

Jaffrey's, 125
Japan, 89
Japanese tearoom, 333
Jewelry, 101, 103, 106, 162, 235, 238, 421;
repairing of, 235
Jewelry stores, 83
Jobbers, *see* Middlemen
Jobbing department,
income from, 130–131, 137, 178–180
Jordan Marsh Co., 32, 92, 144, 458

Katz, Ernest, 365, 374, 476–477
Kinnear, Lillian, 357, 474
Knit goods, 162–163, 175.
See also Hosiery; Underwear; Worsteds
Koster & Bial Music Hall, 322

Labor,
organization of, 306, 385, 479;
turnover in New York, 199.
See also Employees
Laces, 12, 45–46, 101–102, 105, 114, 125, 128, 135–136, 161, 163, 173–174, 238, 299, 302, 422
LaForge, Abiel T., 124–140, 157, 159, 181, 200–201, 212, 417–418
LaForge, Margaret Getchell, 65–66, 101, 103–104, 115, 125–140, 158, 194, 432
Lamps, 162
Land, 107, 440.
See also Buildings

Large-scale operations,
  disadvantages of, 151, 248;
  economies in, 150
Lasalle & Koch Co., 404
Lawsuits, 138, 221, 324, 474
Layout, *see* Advertising; Buildings; Departments
Leaders, 354, 461.
  See also Bargains
Leased departments, 104–105, 109, 133–139, 148, 161, 171–175, 182–190, 220–226, 233, 254–255, 258–259, 296, 328, 391, 433, 439, 456.
  See also China and glassware; Restaurant; Shoes; Silverware; Straus, L., & Sons
Leather goods, 162, 421
Le Boutellier Brothers, 168
Legislative action, *see* Government regulation
Lichtenstein, J., & Sons, 280
Lighting, *see* Illumination
Limitation of stocks, *see* Stock control
Limoges, 246, 271
Linens, 102, 105, 161, 238, 242, 244, 421.
  See also White goods
Lines, *see* Additions; Departments; *specific commodities*
Linings, 239
Liquor, 236, 239
Location,
  of Macy stores, 17, 42–43, 98, 440, 468;
  of retail district, 168–169, 264, 429.
  See also Branch stores
London,
  retailing in, 68, 88–91, 143, 202, 236, 435, 446, 454, 472
Long Island City, 400
Lord & Taylor, 43, 51, 54, 92, 94, 111, 142, 144–145, 156, 168–169, 201, 249, 315, 372, 375, 413, 431, 453

Louvre, 142, 415
Luggage, 162–163
Lunchroom, 160;
  employees', 200, 453.
  See also Restaurants
Luxury goods, 142.
  See also specific items

McCormick, Cyrus H., 32
McCracken, Dr. William, 208
McCreery, James, & Co., 92, 168, 315, 375

Macy & Co., 12–15
Macy, Andrew M., 6, 14–15
Macy Bureau of Standards, 403
Macy, Charles B., 6, 12–15
Macy, John, 6
Macy Journal, 268
Macy Managers' Association, 367
Macy Mutual Aid Association, 207–208, 305, 307, 385, 454
Macy, Robert B., 6, 16–19, 30, 47, 123
Macy, Rowland H.,
  administrative activities, 98–140;
  antecedents, 5–7;
  as business pioneer, 16, 33;
  as copywriter, 23, 25, 54–65;
  characteristics, 121–123;
  credit standing, 17, 19, 30–31, 109–110;
  death, 98, 123;
  early retailing experience, 11–33, 109–110;
  education, 6;
  European buying trips, 112, 127;
  failures, 441;
  in Boston, 87;
  in California, 12–15;
  in Haverhill, 16–33, 87, 100, 194, 441;
  in Wisconsin, 32–33, 44, 428;
  partnerships, 12–55, 123–128, 429;

personal appearance, 113, 116;
policies, 18, 48–54, 225;
real-estate activities, 32, 44, 429;
whaling experience, 7–11, 425;
wholesale activities, 13, 21
Macy, Mrs. Rowland Hussey, 11
Macy, Rowland Hussey, Jr., 12, 123–124, 212, 444
Macy, Sylvanus, 6
Macy, Thomas, 5, 425
Macyettes, 277
Macy's-Parkchester, 404
Magasin du Printemps, 142, 415
Magasins de nouveautés, 72, 143
Magasins du Coin de Rue, 91, 142, 414
Magazines,
advertising in, 118, 267–268, 443
Maidhof, J., 45, 442
Mail orders, 48, 119, 164, 177, 194, 269, 332–333, 444
Management, 52, 65, 114–117, 183–190, 249, 255, 264, 281–282, 287–289, 294–307, 363–364, 417–422, 461.
See also Administration; Centralization; Control; Management control
Management control, 93, 114, 151, 362–374, 402–403
Manuals, 379
Manufacturers, activities of, 351, 447.
See also Middlemen, elimination of
Manufacturing by retailers, 69, 87, 108, 111, 163, 175, 193, 244–251, 459, 467
Margins, 136–137, 173–185, 256;
definition, 129, 173.
See also Operating figures; Profits
Mark-downs, 188, 375–376, 418–420
Mark-ups, 17, 26, 91, 135–138, 418–420.
See also Price policy
Market analysis, 31, 38–44, 316, 373
Marketing, 74, 111, 148.
See also Diversification; Integration; Middlemen, elimination of
Marking department, 114, 123, 198
Marks, Edwin I., 399
Marshall Field & Co., 68, 144, 156, 250, 284, 324, 458–459
Marysville (Calif.), 12–15, 78, 87
Mattresses, 247–248
Mayer, Joseph, 374
Media, *see* Advertising
Mediaeval trading, 3–4, 69–72
Meeker & Maidhof, 45
Men's furnishings and clothing, 99, 136, 161–163, 174, 238–239, 285, 421
Merchandise bonds, 333
Merchandise councillors, 369
Merchandising, *see* Advertising; Brand policy; Diversification; Price policy; Product policy; Purchasing policy; Quality; Sales promotion; Specialization; Stock control
Metal goods, 175, 238–239
Middlemen,
elimination of, 21, 77, 87, 98, 112, 137, 149, 152–154, 164, 240, 248, 392, 447–448
Milliners, 115
Millinery, 101, 106, 111, 136, 161–162, 173, 239, 242, 244
Mills & Gibb, 125, 455
Miners' supplies, 12–15
Misses' clothing, 239
Mitchell, Charles B., 12
Mitsui firm, 89
Moby Dick, 8
Money-back guarantees, 29, 90, 94
Money-barter, 81, 95
Montgomery Ward Co., 119, 268
Motor equipment, *see* Automobiles; Delivery
Musical instruments, 235–236, 330–331

Nantucket (Mass.), 3–11, 64–66, 425
National capitalism, 407
Nationality,
  of customers, 38–39;
  of employees, 383
Neckwear, 239.
  See also Collars and cuffs
Negroes, 383
Net gain, 130, 133.
  See also Operating figures; Profits
Net worth, 47
New Bedford (Mass.), 9
New Hampshire, 94
New Haven (Conn.), 239, 246
New Jersey, 280, 366, 404
New Orleans, 82
New York City, 38–42, 80, 82, 87, 95, 146, 168–169, 199, 218, 239, 263–264, 274, 314, 317, 429, 452
New York (State), 94–95
New York Stock Exchange, 375
Newark (N. J.), 366, 404
Newspapers, *see* Advertising
Nonselling employees, 192, 385
Nonspecialization, 74, 154, 435.
  See also Diversification; Integration
Nontextile goods, 23, 98–106, 137, 173, 292.
  See also Furniture; *specific commodities*
Notions, 17, 23, 72, 100, 103, 105, 114, 136, 161–162, 174, 238, 421, 433;
  definition, 438
Number of
  customers, 400;
  employees, 23, 47, 114–115, 126, 134, 149, 191–193, 197, 281, 305, 383, 400–401, 404, 412, 443, 467;
  private brands, 402;
  sales transactions, 376, 400, 446.
  See also Assortments; Departments

Obsolescence, 185, 189.
  See also Depreciation
Odd lots, 101.
  See also Bargain lots
"Old Fashioned Macy's," 331–332
One-price policy, 6, 26–27, 29, 48, 50, 89–90, 94, 118, 412–413, 430
O'Neill, H., & Co., 168, 280
Opening of Macy's, 16, 42–48, 326–327
Operating figures, 109, 128–140, 171–190, 245, 253–263, 376, 389–397, 419
Optical goods, 162–163, 235, 239
Organization, 67–70, 92–93, 114–116, 149, 194–195, 242–243.
  See also Branch stores; Factories of retailers
Outdoor advertising, 164, 268
Overtime work, 306–307
Ownership, 157–160, 211–230, 311–313, 346–348, 398–399.
  See also Leased departments; Partnerships

Pacific Ocean, 7–9
Packing cost, 177, 258–259
Page, Abel, 27–29
Pages, *see* Cash girls
Paintings, 235, 284.
  See also Pictures
Panics, 32, 40, 45, 108, 110, 118, 241, 327, 441.
  See also Depressions
Parasols, 99, 106, 162, 421, 438
Parcel clerks, 197
Paris, 71–73, 88–91, 121, 142, 155, 160, 242–243, 249, 300, 412–416, 449
Partnerships, 157–160, 169–173, 211–213, 345–348, 429, 444, 457;
  dissolution of, 14, 213
Part-time employees, 376, 383
Patent medicines, 161–162, 421

Patents, 251, 459.
See also Trade-marks
Paterson (N. J.), 246
Pauvre Diable, 89
Payroll, 132, 139, 177, 180–181, 378.
See also Salaries; Wages
Pedlars, 70, 78
Pell, Alfred Duane, 319–321
Pennsylvania, 144;
Railroad, 317.
See also Philadelphia
Perfumery, 161–162, 421.
See also Toilet goods
Personnel, 114–116, 191–208.
See also Employees
Peters, John P., 387
Pets, supplies for, 163
Petty capitalists, 44, 406
Philadelphia, 80, 82–83, 92–93, 193, 202, 214, 218, 324, 372.
See also Wanamaker, John
Philanthropies, 119, 163, 178, 268, 297, 330.
See also Employees
Photographic supplies, 235, 239
Pianos, 236, 330–331
Picnic department, 103, 236, 439
"Pick-up booth," 331
Pictures, 235, 239;
frames and framing, 162, 247, 421
Pilfering, 439.
See also Theft
Pitt, William, 303, 366–367
Pittsburgh, 82
Policy, *see* Business policy
Politics, effect upon retailing, 39, 41, 328–329
Porters, 115
Portieres, 162, 421
Poughkeepsie (N. Y.), 244, 271
Premiums, 294
Prepayment,
of freight, 279–280.
See also Delivery
Price-cutting, *see* One-price policy; Price wars
Price-fixing, 289, 412.
See also Books; Price wars
Price levels, 108, 110, 132, 151–152, 195, 232–234, 327–328, 375, 399, 441, 457
Price maintenance, *see* Resale price maintenance
Price policy, 26–29, 48, 119, 137, 169, 369, 402–403, 412.
See also Competition; Mark-ups; One-price policy
Price wars, 21, 168, 288, 291–294, 349–360.
See also Competition
Prices,
advertising of, 28, 50–51, 64, 96, 165, 287–294;
quotation of, 23–24, 52–53, 120, 225.
See also Price policy
Pricing, 368, 417–422
Private brands, 112–113, 164, 251, 253, 359, 402, 459, 475.
See also Trade-marks
Prizes to employees, 373
Product policy, 188, 332; advertising of, 18, 22, 163.
See also Diversification; Expansion; Grading-up; Guarantees; Specialization
Profit policy, 91.
See also Mark-ups; Profits
Profit-sharing, 126
Profits, 14, 54, 111, 133, 233, 245, 256, 296, 380, 390–392, 405;
from manufacturing, 245.
See also Margins
Prunty, Miss, 204, 206
Publicity, 119, 275–279, 461, 471.
See also Advertising; Display; Sales promotion; Window displays

INDEX 495

Purchasing policy, 13, 17, 21, 26, 29, 49–52, 165, 237–244
Pygmalion, 89, 142

Quakers, 5, 7, 20, 89, 121, 436
Qualifications,
    of employees, 365
Quality, 381–382, 402.
    See also Comparison department; Product policy
Quotas, 383, 478
Quotation, *see* Prices, quotation of

Ratings, 417–422
Ratio
    of D/A to total sales, 343;
    of inventory to assets, 133–134, 261, 396;
    of leased to total sales, 109, 137, 139, 171, 174–178, 184, 222, 254;
    of returns to net sales, 261, 376, 396
Ready-to-wear, 163, 235, 436.
    See also specific commodities
Receiving department, 43, 108, 115, 123, 198, 312
Records, *see* Control; Management
Red star, 98, 112, 251–252, 432, 442
Refunds, 29.
    See also Guarantees; Return privileges
Religion, 5, 215, 425, 473.
    See also Quakers
Renard Frères, 241
Rent, 131, 180–181, 258–259, 393–394, 477
Resale price maintenance, 473–475
Restaurants,
    for employees, 325, 384;
    for public, 160, 162, 171, 175, 187, 238, 255, 325, 333, 422, 449
Restrictions, *see* Government regulation
Restrooms, 262, 283–284, 325, 465

Retailing,
    evolution of, 69–97;
    in California, 12–15.
    See also Chain stores; Department stores; Europe; New York City
Return privileges, 260–261, 282, 336, 368, 376, 379, 395–396, 412–413, 437
Revenue, *see* Operating figures; Profits
Ribbons, 46, 55, 101, 103, 105, 114, 136, 161, 174, 238, 421
Ridley's, 168–169, 280, 315
Risk-taking, 189
Rivals, study of methods of, 372–373.
    See also Competition
Rockefeller Center, 71
Royal Exchange, 71
Rubber goods, footwear, 163
Rudolstadt (Thuringia), 246, 271
Rugs, 234, 239–240, 243, 285
Ruml, Beardsley, 399
Rushmore, Cone & Co., 47
Rutherford (N. J.), 247

Saddlery, 238.
    See also Sporting goods
St. Louis, 82–83, 434
Saks & Co., 325, 329
Salaries, 125–126, 130, 181, 194, 258–259, 304, 376, 394, 443.
    See also Wages
Sales,
    annual, 169, 428;
    clearance, 18–19, 22, 52, 119, 326, 431;
    control, 92–93, 114;
    pre- and post-inventory, 169, 276.
    See also Volume of business
Salesforce,
    control of, 52–53, 93, 225
Salesmen, 193–196.
    See also Employees

Sales per employee, 47, 132, 192, 376, 400, 446
Sales promotion, 118–121, 164–170; in dull seasons, 57, 276, 428
See also Advertising; Catalogs; Clearance sales; Exhibitions; Window displays
Sales policy, 282; advertising of (*see* Advertising, institutional
See also Cash policy; Price policy; Return privileges
Sales quotas, 383, 478
Sales transactions, number per employee, 376, 400, 446; procedure, 452–453; size, 376
Saleswomen, 193–194.
See also Employees; Women
Salisbury (Mass.), 5
Satisfaction, guarantee of, *see* Return privileges
Scribner's, Charles, Sons, Inc., 355
Scrubwomen, 115
Seamstresses, 115
Sears, Roebuck & Co., 333
Seasonal merchandise, 99.
See also Seasonal variations
Seasonal variations, 99–100, 132, 136–137, 278, 426; in advertising, 57, 118, 169–170; leveling of, 277, 426.
See also Christmas season
"Seconds," 382
Section managers, 381.
See also Floorwalkers
Secular trends, 88, 151, 262–263.
See also Business conditions; Depressions
Sedentary merchants, 407
Seeligman & Macy, 47, 123
Seller's market, 352

Service, 54, 69, 88, 235, 260, 279–286, 333–337.
See also Delivery
Service manager, 381.
See also Floorwalkers
Sewing machines, 239
Sheet music, 238
Sherman Anti-Trust Act, 354, 356
Shillings in price quotations, 53
Shirts, men's, 163.
See also Men's furnishings
Shoes, 105–106, 120, 133–134, 137, 145, 162, 171, 175, 178, 186, 238–239, 254–255, 296, 403, 422, 466.
See also Leased departments
Shoplifting, 138, 446
Shopping districts, *see* Location; New York City
Shopping habits, *see* Buying habits, consumer
Shortages, 130, 138–139, 176–179, 283, 299, 304, 419
Show-windows, 334, 450.
See also Window displays
Sick benefits, 305.
See also Macy Mutual Benefit Association
Sidney, Marjorie, 388
Siegel-Cooper Co., 257, 265, 267, 274, 286, 296, 315, 319–321, 329, 375
Silk goods, 106, 136, 161–162, 164, 174–175, 238, 288, 421
Silverware, 104–105, 120, 133, 137, 145, 161, 175, 186–187, 238, 255, 421.
See also Leased departments; Straus, L., & Sons
Simpson, Crawford & Simpson, 168, 267, 286, 315, 375, 469
Single-price policy, *see* One-price policy

INDEX 497

Size, *see* Buildings; Number of employees; Volume of sales
Skirts, 239, 246–247.
  See also Women's wear
Sloan, T. L., Deverey & Co., 241
Sloane, W. & J., 240, 458
Slogans, 61, 270
Slow-selling merchandise, 261
Smallwares, 105, 136, 174, 421, 438.
  See also Fancy dry goods; Notions
Smith, R., & Co., 315, 319–320, 468
Smith & Strong, 94
Smokers' supplies, 236, 239, 246
Soda fountain, 103, 106, 136, 239, 421
Sources
  of general information, 373, 411;
  of employees, 196, 199, 366;
  of executives, 199, 212;
  of goods sold, 237–244, 403.
  See also Auctions; Bargain lots; Europe
Souvenir merchandise, 268, 277
Sparks, 479
Special-privilege customers, 50, 430
Specialization, 37, 46, 71–88, 151, 434–435
Specialty stores, 71, 75, 263
Speculation,
  real estate, 32, 44
Sport clothes, 163
Sporting goods, 103, 162, 234–235, 239, 285
Stables, 108, 133.
  See also Delivery
Staff, *see* Employees
Standard of living, 86, 304, 337;
  effect upon retailing, 168, 279
Standardization, 149
Stationery, 106, 136, 161–162, 173, 175, 234, 238, 246, 422
Statistics, *see* Accounting; Operating figures; Volume of business

Statuary, 162, 284
Steinschönau (Bohemia), 246, 271
Stern Brothers, 168, 315
Stewart, A. T., 43, 87, 92, 94, 96, 107, 110, 112, 121–122, 125, 141–142, 144, 168, 193–194, 202, 249–250, 266, 413–414, 416, 446, 448, 454
Stillman, James A., 326
Stock control, 22, 188, 299, 302–303, 365, 370, 381, 396–397, 417–422
Stock girls, 195
Stock-in-trade, 48.
  See also Inventory
Stockrooms, 108
Stock-taking, 137.
  See also Inventory
Stock-turn, 18, 49, 52, 129, 133–135, 185–186, 260–262, 395–397, 403, 445, 451
Storage,
  free, 283;
  fur, 235, 335–336.
  See also Warehouses
Stoves, 235;
  servicing of, 283
Strang, Adriance & Co., 51
Straus, Herbert, 313, 345, 393
Straus, Hugh Grant, 311, 345, 473
Straus, Isidor, 187, 211–230, 245, 247, 265–267, 287, 294–303, 311–313, 329, 345–347, 361–362, 466
Straus, Jack Isidor, 399
Straus, Jesse Isidor, 311–313, 316, 318, 328, 344–348, 361–366, 393, 399, 473
Straus, L., & Sons, 153, 206, 218–220, 228–229, 243, 245, 247, 294, 303, 326, 348, 358, 393, 457;
  relations with Macy's, 104, 183, 187–188.
  See also Leased departments
Straus, Lazarus, 214–215, 455.
  See also Straus, L., & Sons

Straus, Nathan, 187, 211–214, 219–220, 223–225, 245, 265, 268, 274, 276, 287, 294–303, 311–313, 384, 468, 473
Straus, Nathan, Jr., 311, 345
Straus, Oscar, 219
Straus, Percy Selden, 311–313, 316, 318, 344–348, 361–366, 387, 393, 399, 473
Straus, Sarah, 216
Strawbridge & Clothier, 372
Strikes, 306, 385
Style, emphasis upon, 153, 313, 381, 402.
  See also Grading-up
Style shows, 169, 334
Suburban stores, 404
Subway, 317–318
Suits and cloaks, 106, 136, 161–162, 173–174, 238, 287, 421
Summer
  deliveries, 280, 342;
  season, 99, 277–278
Superintendent, 115, 126, 194, 213, 303, 443
Superior City (Wis.), 32–33
Supermarkets, 69
Switzerland, 271
Syracuse branch, 404

Talking machines, 236, 356–357, 474–475
Tapis Rouge, 142–143, 415
Tappan, Arthur, 94
Tardiness, 385
Tea, 235
Telegraph and telephone facilities, 41, 166, 198, 400, 450, 465
Terms of sale, 45, 429.
  See also Credit; Deposit Account Department; Discounts
Theft, 47, 138, 446, 455, 476
Ties, ladies', 103, 106, 136, 421

Tires, 358
Titanic, 345–346, 472–473
Titon, William A., 365, 476
Tobacco, 239
Toilet goods, 101, 103, 106, 161–162, 173–174, 239, 246, 250, 421
Toledo (Ohio), 404
Tools, 235
Toye, Martha, 194, 197, 204–205, 213, 303
Toys, 63, 100, 103, 106, 136, 162, 173–174, 238, 421
Tracy, E. W., 14
Trade-marks, 24–25, 98, 112, 251, 459.
  See also Brand policy; Red star
Trading-posts, 78
Trading-up, 334
Training
  of employees, 378–379, 401, 479
Transportation, 40–42;
  improvements in, 86, 160, 164, 169, 281
Treu, Adam, 374
Trimmings, 45, 103, 136, 160–162, 175, 238, 421
Trucking, *see* Delivery
Tuberoom, 325, 383, 400
Typography, *see* Advertising

Uhler, Michael, 95
Umbrellas, 99, 106, 122, 162, 174, 239, 421
Underselling, 21, 28, 119, 225, 349–360.
  See also Books; Competition
Underwear, 102, 105, 111, 136, 161–163, 173–174, 238–239, 241, 244, 246, 421
Uniforms, 305–306
Unionization of employees, 306, 385, 479
Upholstery and upholstering, 161–162, 175, 238, 246, 250, 302, 422

INDEX 499

Urbanization, growth of, 146, 279, 284

Vacations, 200–202, 378
Valentine, Robert Macy, 128, 130, 157–159, 181, 200, 204, 417–418, 449
Vanderbilt, Cornelius, 32
Variety of merchandise, 413–416, 436.
See also Additions; Assortments; Departments; Expansion
Variety stores, 68
Velvet goods, 163–164
Ventilation, 167, 325, 450.
See also Air-conditioning
Victor Talking Machine Co., 356–357, 474–475
Vienna, 243
Ville de Paris, 73, 89–90, 412, 415
Visiting cards, 161–162, 239, 422
Volume of business, 47, 69, 73, 108–109, 125–126, 129–130, 135–136, 142, 158, 171, 174–178, 227, 245, 327–329, 375, 380, 399, 404, 412–414, 446, 456.
See also Leased departments; Operating figures

Wages, 132, 158, 192–199, 260, 383.
See also Bonuses; Payroll; Salaries
Waists, 239, 246
Waiting-rooms, 284.
See also Restrooms
Walker, Delos, 399
Walker, J. H., Co., 221
Wallingford (Conn.), 246
Wallpaper, 235, 239
Wanamaker, John, 59, 68, 90, 122, 141, 144–145, 168, 170, 221, 236, 242, 250, 257, 266–267, 271, 274, 276, 284, 286, 289, 315, 329, 340–341, 372, 430–431, 449–450, 454, 456, 458–459, 465, 471

War, effects of, 7, 65, 406.
See also Civil War; World War I
Warehouses, 400.
See also Delivery
Washington (D. C.), 221, 436
Watches, 234, 358;
  repairing of, 235
Watchmen, 115, 119, 445
Weather, effect of, upon business, 301
Webster, Charles B., 158–160, 169–173, 181–183, 186–188, 190, 203–204, 211–213, 225–228, 247–248, 264, 287, 292–297, 301, 304, 312, 449, 455, 457
Webster & Straus, 247
Wechsler & Abraham, 221, 227–228, 312.
See also Abraham & Straus
Wedgwood, Josiah, 89–91
Welfare, 384.
See also Macy Mutual Aid Association
Wells, William J., 366, 374, 476
Whaling industry, 6–11
Wheaton & Dixon, 78, 95
Wheeler, Jerome B., 159–160, 169–173, 181–183, 186–188, 211–213, 225, 264, 292, 449, 455
White, R. H., Co., 221
White goods, 102, 105, 135–136, 161, 174, 239, 421.
See also specific items
Whiteley's, 72, 143, 212, 236–237, 249, 342
Wholesaling, 13, 45, 70, 78, 85, 95, 125–126, 199, 249, 427;
  by retailers, 78, 92, 112, 241, 389, 442
Window displays, 55, 118, 166, 169, 264, 275–279, 382, 471
Wines, 235–236, 239, 241
Winship, Charles O., 204–206, 476
Wisconsin, 32–33, 44

Wise, Edmond E., 354
Women
  as employees, 191–208, 378, 383, 452;
  as executives, 65–66, 115, 306;
  compensation of, 195–197.
  See also La Forge, Margaret Getchell; Toye, Martha
Women's wear, 242, 247.
  See also specific commodities
Woods, Jimmie, 198, 203–204
Woodward & Lothrop, 221
Woolens, 377.
  See also Worsteds
Woolworth, F. W., Co., 70

Working conditions, 202–208, 303–307, 382–389.
  See also Employees, relations with; Hours of work; Vacations; Wages
World War I, effects of, 327, 349, 375–382, 389, 393, 395
Worsteds, 106, 136, 160–162, 173–175, 238, 421–422
Wrappers, 239
Wraps, 163

Youths' clothing, 106.
  See also Boys' clothing and furnishings.

RET'D NOV 7 1985
RET'D NOV 3 1986
NOV 7 1989

FEB 16 1993
APR 27 1993
MAY 11 1994
NOV 21 1994

DEC 22 **1995**